DOCUMENTS OF THE AFRICAN COMMISSION ON HUMAN AND PEOPLES' RIGHTS

Documents of the African Commission on Human and Peoples' Rights

Edited by

Rachel Murray

Queen's University Belfast

and

Malcolm Evans

University of Bristol

Produced in collaboration with the African Society of International and Comparative Law, Interights and the Centre for Human Rights, University of Pretoria

·HART·
PUBLISHING

OXFORD – PORTLAND OREGON

2001

Hart Publishing,
Oxford and Portland, Oregon

Published in North America (US and Canada) by
Hart Publishing
c/o International Specialized Book Services
5804 NE Hassalo Street
Portland, Oregon
97213-3644
USA

Distributed in Netherlands, Belgium and Luxembourg by
Intersentia, Churchillaan 108
B2900 Schoten
Antwerpen
Belgium

Hart Publishing is a specialist legal publisher based in Oxford, England. To order further copies of this book or to request a list of other publications please write to:

Hart Publishing, Salters Boatyard, Folly Bridge, Abingdon Rd, Oxford, OX1 4LB
Telephone: +44 (0) 1865 245533 Fax: +44 (0) 1865 794882
email: mail@hartpub.co.uk
WEBSITE: http//:www.hartpub.co.uk

British Library Cataloguing in Publication Data
Data Available

ISBN 1-84113-092-3

Typeset by Hope Services, Abingdon
Printed and bound in Great Britain by
Biddles Ltd, www.biddles.co.uk

CONTENTS

PART II

INTRODUCTION AND GUIDE TO USING THE DOCUMENTS

The African Charter on Human and Peoples' Rights establishes the African Commission on Human and Peoples' Rights as the regional human rights mechanism for the African continent. Regrettably, the work of the Commission is not as widely known as it deserves. This is at least partly due to the difficulty of gaining access to information about its functioning and to the documentation which it produces. This is as true in Africa itself as it is in the rest of the world. This collection attempts to address that problem and to promote both the Charter and the Commission by making the core and principal published documents more readily available. It is hoped that this will enable an expanded audience of scholars, academics, practitioners and those interested in international human rights to become familiar with the significant achievements of the Commission and, in consequence, to be better placed to understand and assess its contribution to the development of international human rights law in Africa and beyond. This volume contains the documents produced by the African Commission since its creation in 1987 up to and including its Twelfth Activity Report adopted in 1999. It is hoped that further supplementary volumes containing subsequent Reports and related material will be produced in the future.

Part One of the volume contains the basic constitutional documents of the Commission, including the African Charter itself, the Commission's Rules of Procedure as amended, and the Protocol on the establishment of an African Court (which as yet has not received the requisite number of ratifications to enter into force).

Part Two contains the other documents produced by the Commission over the course of its history. The Commission holds two sessions per year, usually in March/April and November/October. At the end of each session the Commission issues a Final Communiqué. It also produces an annual Activity Report, twelve of which are reproduced. Other documents produced by the Commission are inserted in the volume in date order. Thus Part Two provides a chronological account of the Commission's output.

Various tables of communications and resolutions are provided at pp.285–310 of this volume. They are inserted at this point since it was only in the subsequent Activity Reports that the Commission published Decisions on communications. It is hoped that these tables will assist the users in locating the Decisions which are published by the Commission as Annexes to the Annual Activity Reports. Communications and Resolutions are listed in numerical order, by Article number, and also by the state party involved.

The assiduous reader might note that some material appears to be missing—most notably, some of the Final Communiqués from the earlier sessions of the Commission. The reason is simple: it has not been possible to obtain copies of them. Other material may also appear to be rather *ad hoc*, with forms of output produced at one session not being reflected in the material reproduced from another. The reason for this is that the

Commission does not produce the same style of documents on a regular basis. Apart from the Final Communiqués and Annual Activity Reports, there is little consistency.

Above all else, it must be stressed that this is not an official publication of the African Commission on Human and Peoples' Rights. The material has been reproduced by the editors from copies made available to them from a number of sources, not all of which are uniform. We have, naturally, aimed to include those which we consider to be the most authentic, but this cannot be assured in every case. In addition, it must be recognised that in many of what we consider to be the most authentic version of the Commission's documents there are numerous presentational irregularities and grammatical infelicities. As editors, we concluded that it was inappropriate to amend the documents and decided to present them as they appear to have been adopted and disseminated by the Commission itself. We accept that between these two considerations, there is plenty of scope for editorial error and we accept the ultimate responsibility for those which remain.

The editors would like to thank the African Society of International and Comparative Law, Interights, and the Centre for Human Rights at the University of Pretoria in South Africa for their support, guidance and assistance in producing and disseminating this material. Finally, and most importantly, we would like to thank the African Commission on Human and Peoples' Rights and its Secretariat for allowing attendance at its sessions and making available its material. It is our hope that this publication will be of some assistance to the Commission in its work in addressing the human rights needs of the peoples of Africa.

Rachel Murray
Malcolm D Evans

May Day, 2001.

PART I

BASIC DOCUMENTS

African Charter on Human and Peoples' Rights

Adopted by the 18th Assembly of the Heads of State and Government of the Organization of African Unity, Nairobi, Kenya, 26 June 1981; entered into force on 21 October 1986

PREAMBLE

The African States members of the Organisation of African Unity, parties to the present convention entitled "African Charter on Human and Peoples Rights";

Recalling Decision 115 (XVI) of the Assembly of Heads of State and Government at its Sixteenth Ordinary Session held in Monrovia, Liberia from 17 to 20 July 1979 on the preparation of "a preliminary draft on an African Charter on Human and Peoples' Rights providing *inter alia* for the establishment of bodies to promote and protect human and peoples' rights";

Considering the Charter of the Organisation of African Unity, which stipulates that "freedom, equality, justice and dignity are essential objectives for the achievement of the legitimate aspirations of the African peoples";

Reaffirming the pledge they solemnly made in Article 2 of the said Charter to eradicate all forms of colonialism from Africa, to coordinate and intensify their cooperation and efforts to achieve a better life for the peoples' of Africa and to promote international cooperation having due regard to the Charter of the United Nations and the Universal Declaration of Human Rights;

Taking into consideration the virtues of their historical tradition and the values of African civilisation which should inspire and characterise their reflection on the concept of human and peoples' rights;

Recognising on the one hand, that fundamental human rights stem from the attributes of human beings, which justifies their international protection and on the other hand that the reality and respect of peoples' rights should necessarily guarantee human rights;

Considering that the enjoyment of rights and freedoms also implies the performance of duties on the part of everyone;

Convinced that it is henceforth essential to pay a particular attention to the right to development and that civil and political rights cannot be dissociated from economic, social and cultural rights in their conception as well as universality and that the satisfaction of economic, social and cultural rights is a guarantee for the enjoyment of civil and political rights;

Conscious of their duty to achieve the total liberation of Africa, the peoples of which are still struggling for their dignity and genuine independence, and undertaking to eliminate colonialism, neo-colonialism, apartheid, zionism and to dismantle aggressive foreign military bases and all forms of discrimination [notably those based on race, ethnic group, colour, sex,] language, religion of political opinion;

Reaffirming their adherence to the principles of human and peoples' rights and freedoms contained in the declarations, conventions and other instruments adopted by the Organisation of African Unity, the Movement of Non-Aligned Countries and the United Nations;

Firmly convinced of their **duty** to promote and protect human and peoples' rights and freedoms taking into account the importance traditionally attached to these rights and freedoms in Africa;

HAVE AGREED AS FOLLOWS:

PART I: RIGHTS AND DUTIES

Chapter I – Human and Peoples' Rights

Article 1

The Member States of the Organisation of African Unity parties to the present Charter shall recognise the rights, duties and freedoms enshrined in this Charter and shall undertake to adopt legislative or other measures to give effect to them.

Article 2

Every individual shall be entitled to the enjoyment of the rights and freedoms recognised and guaranteed in the present Charter without distinction of any kind such as race, ethnic group, colour, sex, language, religion, political or any other opinion, national or social origin, fortune, birth or other status.

Article 3

1. Every individual shall be equal before the law.
2. Every individual shall be entitled to equal protection of the law.

Article 4

Human beings are inviolable. Every human being shall be entitled to respect for his life and the integrity of his person. No one may be arbitrarily deprived of this right.

Article 5

Every individual shall have the right to the respect of the dignity inherent in a human being and to the recognition of his legal status. All forms of exploitation and degradation of man particularly slavery, slave trade, torture, cruel, inhuman or degrading punishment and treatment shall be prohibited.

Article 6

Every individual shall have the right to liberty and to the security of his person. No one may be deprived of his freedom except for reasons and conditions previously laid down by law. In particular, no one may be arbitrarily arrested or detained.

Article 7

1. Every individual shall have the right to have his cause heard. This comprises:
(a) The right to an appeal to competent national organs against acts violating his fundamental rights as recognised and guaranteed by conventions, laws, regulations and customs in force;
(b) the right to be presumed innocent until proven guilty by a competent court or tribunal;
(c) the right to defence, including the right to be defended by counsel of his choice;
(d) the right to be tried within a reasonable time by an impartial court or tribunal.

2. No one may be condemned for an act or omission which did not constitute a legally punishable offence at the time it was committed. No penalty may be inflicted for an offence for which no provision was made at the time it was committed. Punishment is personal and can be imposed only on the offender.

Article 8

Freedom on conscience, the profession and free practice of religion shall be guaranteed. No one may, subject to law and order, be submitted to measures restricting the exercise of these freedoms.

Article 9

1. Every individual shall have the right to receive information.
2. Every individual shall have the right to express and disseminate his opinions within the law.

Article 10

1. Every individual shall have the right to free association provided that he abides by the law.
2. Subject to the obligation of solidarity provided for in Article 29 no one may be compelled to join an association.

Article 11

Every individual shall have the right to assemble freely with others. The exercise of this right shall be subject only to necessary restrictions provided for by law in particular those enacted in the interest of national security, the safety [of others], health, ethics and rights and freedoms of others.

Article 12

1. Every individual shall have the right to freedom of movement and residence within the borders of a State provided he abides by the law
2. Every individual shall have the right to leave any country including his own, and to return to his country. This right may only be subject to restrictions, provided for by law for the protection of national security, law and order, public health of morality.
3. Every individual shall have the right, when persecuted, to seek and obtain asylum in other countries in accordance with the law of those countries and international conventions.
4. A non-national legally admitted in a territory of a State Party to the present Charter, may only be expelled from it by virtue of a decision taken in accordance with the law.
5. The mass expulsion of non-nationals shall be prohibited. Mass expulsion shall be that which is aimed at national, racial, ethnic or religious groups.

Article 13

1. Every citizen shall have the right to participate freely in the government of his country, either directly or through freely chosen representatives in accordance with the provisions of the law.
2. Every citizen shall have the right of equal access to the public service of his country.
3. Every individual shall have the right of access to public property and services in strict equality of all persons before the law.

Article 14

The right to property shall be guaranteed. It may only be encroached upon in the interest of public need and in accordance with the provisions of appropriate laws.

Article 15

Every individual shall have the right to work under equitable and satisfactory conditions, and shall receive equal pay for equal work.

Article 16

1. Every individual shall have the right to enjoy the best attainable state of physical and mental health.

2. States Parties to the present Charter shall take the necessary measures to protect the health of their people and to ensure that they receive medical attention when they are sick.

Article 17

1. Every individual shall have the right to education.

2. Every individual may freely take part in the cultural life if his community.

3. The promotion and protection of morals and traditional values recognised by the community shall be the duty of the State.

Article 18

1. The family shall be the natural unit and basis of society. It shall be protected by the State which shall take care of its physical health and moral.

2. The State shall have the duty to assist the family which is the custodian of morals and traditional values recognised by the community.

3. The State shall ensure the elimination of every discrimination against women and also ensure the protection of the rights of the women and the child as stipulated in international declarations and conventions.

4. The aged and the disabled shall also have the right to special measures of protection in keeping with their physical or moral needs.

Article 19

All peoples shall be equal; they shall enjoy the same respect and shall have the same rights. Nothing shall justify the domination of a people by another.

Article 20

1. All peoples shall have the right to existence. They shall have the unquestionable and inalienable right to self-determination. They shall freely determine their political status and shall pursue their economic and social development according to the policy they have freely chosen.

2. Colonised or oppressed peoples shall have the right to free themselves from the bonds of domination by resorting to any means recognised by the international community.

3. All peoples shall have the right to the assistance of the States Parties to the present Charter in their liberation struggle against foreign domination, be it political, economic or cultural.

Article 21

1. All peoples shall freely dispose of their wealth and natural resources. This right shall be exercised in the exclusive interest of the people. In no case shall a people be deprived of it.

2. In case of spoliation the dispossessed people shall have the right to the lawful recovery of its property as well as to an adequate compensation.

3. The free disposal of wealth and natural resources shall be exercised without prejudice to the obligation of promoting international economic cooperation based on mutual respect, equitable exchange and the principles of international law.

4. States Parties to the present Charter shall individually and collectively exercise the right to free disposal of their wealth and natural resources with a view to strengthening African unity and solidarity.

5. States Parties to the present Charter shall undertake to eliminate all forms of foreign exploitation particularly that practised by international monopolies as to enable their peoples to fully benefit from the advantages derived from their national resources.

Article 22

1. All peoples shall have the right to their economic, social and cultural development with due regard to their freedom and identity and in the equal enjoyment of the common heritage of mankind.

2. States shall have the duty, individually or collectively, to ensure the exercise of the right to development.

Article 23

1. All peoples shall have the right to national and international peace and security. The principles of solidarity and friendly relations implicitly affirmed by the Charter of the United Nations and reaffirmed by that of the Organisation of African Unity shall govern relations between States.

2. For the purpose of strengthening peace, solidarity and friendly relations, States Parties to the present Charter shall ensure that:

(a) any individual enjoying the right to asylum under Article 12 of the present Charter shall not engage in subversive activities against his country of origin or any other State Party to the present Charter;

(b) their territories shall not be used as bases for subversive or terrorist activities against the people of any other State Party to the present Charter.

Article 24

All peoples shall have the right to a general satisfactory environment favourable to their development.

Article 25

States Parties to the present Charter shall have the duty to promote and ensure through teaching, education and publication, the respect of the rights and freedoms contained in the present Charter and to see to it that these freedoms and rights as well as the corresponding duties are understood.

Article 26

States Parties to the present Charter shall have the duty to guarantee the independence of the courts and shall allow the establishment and improvement of appropriate national institutions entrusted with the promotion and protection of the rights and freedoms guaranteed by the present Charter.

Chapter II – Duties

Article 27

1. Every individual shall have duties towards his family and society, the State and other legally recognised communities and the international community.

2. The rights and the freedoms of each individual shall be exercised with due regard to the rights of others, collective security, morality and common interest.

Article 28

Every individual shall have the duty to respect and consider his fellow beings without discrimination, safeguarding and reinforcing mutual respect and tolerance.

Article 29

The individual shall also have the duty:

1. To preserve the harmonious development of the family and to work for the cohesion and respect of the family; to respect his parents at all times, to maintain them in case of need;

2. To serve his national community by placing his physical and intellectual abilities at its service;

3. Not to compromise the security of the State whose national or resident he is;

4. To preserve and strengthen social and national solidarity, particularly when the latter is threatened;

5. To preserve and strengthen the national independence and the territorial integrity of his country and to contribute to his [its] defence in according with the law;

6. To work to the best of his abilities and competences, and to pay taxes imposed by the law in the interest of the society;

7. To preserve and strengthen positive African cultural values in his relations with other members of the society, in the spirit of tolerance, dialogue and consultation and, in general, to contribute to the promotion of the moral well being of society;

8. To contribute to the best of his abilities, at all times and at all levels, to the promotion and achievement of African unity

PART II: MEASURES OF SAFEGUARD

Chapter I – Establishment and Organisation of the African Commission on Human and Peoples' Rights

Article 30

An African Commission on Human and Peoples' Rights, hereinafter called "the Commission", shall be established within the Organisation of African Unity to promote human and peoples' rights and ensure their protection in Africa.

Article 31

1. The Commission shall consist of eleven members chosen from amongst African personalities of the highest reputation, known for their high morality, integrity, impartiality and competence in matters of human and peoples' rights; particular consideration being given to persons having legal experience.

2. The members of the Commission shall serve in their personal capacity.

Article 32

The Commission shall not include more than one national of the same State.

Article 33

The members of the Commission shall be elected by secret ballot by the Assembly of Heads of State and Government, from a list of persons nominated by the States Parties to the present Charter.

Article 34

Each State Party to the present Charter may not nominate more than two candidates. The candidates must have the nationality of one of the States Parties to the present Charter. When two candidates are nominated by a State, one of them may not be a national of that State.

Article 35

1. The Secretary General of the Organisation of African Unity shall invite States Parties to the present Charter at least four months before the elections to nominate candidates;

2. The Secretary General of the Organisation of African Unity shall make an alphabetical list of the persons thus nominated and communicate it to the Heads of State and Government at least on month before the elections.

Article 36

The members of the Commission shall be elected for a six year period and shall be eligible for re-election. However, the term of office of four of the members elected at the first election shall terminate after two years and the term of office of three others, at the end of four years.

Article 37

Immediately after the first election, the Chairman of the Assembly of Heads of State and Government of the Organisation of African Unity shall draw lots to decide the names of those members referred to in Article 36.

Article 38

After their election, the members of the Commission shall make a solemn declaration to discharge their duties impartially and faithfully.

Article 39

1. In the case of death or resignation of a member of the Commission the Chairman of the Commission shall immediately inform the Secretary General of the Organisation of African Unity, who shall declare the seat vacant from the date of death or from the date on which the resignation takes effect.

2. If, in the opinion of other members of the Commission, a member has stopped discharging his duties for any reason other than temporary absence, the Chairman of the Commission shall inform the Secretary General of the Organisation of African Unity, who shall then declare the seat vacant.

3. In each of the cases anticipated above, the Assembly of Heads of State and Government shall replace the member whose seat became vacant for the remaining period of his term unless the period is less than six months.

Article 40

Every member of the Commission shall be in office until the date his successor assumes office.

Article 41

The Secretary General of the Organisation of African Unity shall appoint the Secretary of the Commission. He shall provide the staff and services necessary for the effective discharge of the duties of the Commission. The Organisation of African Unity shall bear cost of the staff and services.

Article 42

1. The Commission shall elect its Chairman and Vice Chairman for a two-year period. They shall be eligible for re-election.
2. The Commission shall lay down its rules of procedure.
3. Seven members shall form the quorum.
4. In case of an equality of votes, the Chairman shall have the casting vote.
5. The Secretary General may attend the meetings of the Commission. He shall neither participate in the deliberations nor shall he be entitled to vote. The Chairman of the Commission may, however, invite him to speak.

Article 43

In discharging their duties, members of the Commission shall enjoy diplomatic immunities provided for in the General Convention on the Privileges and Communities of the Organisation of African Unity.

Article 44

Provision shall be made for the emoluments and allowances of the members of the Commission in the Regular Budget of the Organisation of African Unity.

Chapter II – Mandate of the Commission

Article 45

The functions of the Commission shall be:

1. To promote Human and Peoples' Rights and in particular:
   (a) to collect documents, undertake studies and researches in African problems in the field of human and peoples' rights, organise seminars, symposia and conferences, disseminate information, encourage national and local institutions concerned with human and peoples' rights and, should the case arise, give its views or make recommendations to Governments.
   (b) to formulate and lay down, principles and rules aimed at solving legal problems related to human and peoples' rights and fundamental freedoms upon which African Governments may base their legislation.
   (c) co-operate with other African and international institutions concerned with the promotion and protection of human and peoples' rights.

2. Ensure the protection of human and peoples' rights under the conditions laid down by the present Charter.

3. Interpret all the provisions of the present Charter at the request of a State Party, an institution of the OAU or an African Organisation recognised by the OAU.

4. Perform any other tasks which may be entrusted to it by the Assembly of Heads of State and Government.

Chapter III – Procedure of the Commission

Article 46

The Commission may resort to any appropriate method of investigation; it may hear from the Secretary General of the Organisation of African Unity or any other person capable of enlightening it.

Communication from States

Article 47

If a State Party to the present Charter has good reasons to believe that another State Party to this Charter has violated the provisions of the Charter, it may draw, by written communication, the attention of that State to the matter. The communication shall also be addressed to the Secretary General of the OAU and to the Chairman of the Commission. Within three months of the receipt of the communication, the State to which the communication is addressed shall give the enquiring State written explanation or statement elucidating the matter. This should include as much as possible, relevant information relating to the laws and rules of procedure applied and applicable and the redress already given or course of action available.

Article 48

If within three months from the date on which the original communication is received by the State to which it was addressed, the issue is not settled to the satisfaction of the two States involved through bilateral negotiation or by any other peaceful procedure, either State shall have the right to submit the matter to the Commission through the Chairman and shall notify the other States involved.

Article 49

Notwithstanding the provisions of Article 47, if a State Party to the present Charter considers that another State Party has violated the provisions of the Charter, it may refer the matter directly to the Commission by addressing a communication to the Chairman, to the Secretary General of the Organisation of African Unity and the State concerned.

Article 50

The Commission can only deal with a matter submitted to it after making sure that all local remedies, if they exist, have been exhausted, unless it is obvious to the Commission that the procedure of achieving these remedies would be unduly prolonged.

Article 51

1. The Commission may ask the States concerned to provide it with all relevant information.
2. When the Commission is considering the matter, States concerned may be represented before it and submit written or oral representation.

Article 52

After having obtained from the States concerned and from other sources all the information it deems necessary and after having tried all appropriate means to reach an amicable solution based on the respect of Human and Peoples' Rights, the Commission shall prepare, within a reasonable period of time from the notification referred to in Article 48, a report to the States concerned and communicated to the Assembly of Heads of State and Government.

Article 53

While transmitting its report, the Commission may make to the Assembly of Heads of State and Government such recommendations as it deems useful.

Article 54

The Commission shall submit to each ordinary Session of the Assembly of Heads of State and Government a report of its activities.

Other Communications

Article 55

1. Before each session, the Secretary of the Commission shall make a list of the Communications other than those of States Parties to the present Charter and transmit them to the Members of the Commission, who shall indicate which communications should be considered by the Commission.
2. A communication shall be considered by the Commission if a simple majority of its members so decide.

Article 56

Communication relating to Human and Peoples' Rights referred to in Article 55 received by the Commission, shall be considered if they:

1. Indicate their authors even if the latter request anonymity,

2. Are compatible with the Charter of the Organisation of African Unity or with the present Charter.

3. Are not written in disparaging or insulting language directed against the State concerned and its institutions or to the Organisation of African Unity.

4. Are not based exclusively on news disseminated through the mass media,

5. Are sent after exhausting local remedies, if any unless it is obvious that this procedure is unduly prolonged,

6. Are submitted within a reasonable period from the time local remedies are exhausted, or form the date the Commission is seized with the matter, and

7. Do not deal with cases which have been settled by these states involved in accordance with the principles of the Charter of the United Nations, or the Charter of the Organisation of African Unity or the provisions of the present Charter.

Article 57

Prior to any substantive consideration, all communications shall be brought to the knowledge of the State concerned by the Chairman of the Commission.

Article 58

1. When it appears after deliberations of the Commission that one or more communications apparently relate to special cases which reveal the existence of a series of serious or massive violations of Human and Peoples' Rights, the Commission shall draw the attention of the Assembly of Heads of State and Government to these special cases.

2. The Assembly of Heads of State and Government may then request the Commission to undertake an in-depth study of these cases and make a factual report, accompanied by its finding and recommendations.

3. A case of emergency duly noticed by the Commission shall be submitted by the latter to the Chairman of the Assembly of Heads of State and Government who may request an in-depth study.

Article 59

1. All measures taken within the provisions of the present Charter shall remain confidential until such a time as the Assembly of Heads of State and Government shall otherwise decide.

2. However, the report shall be published by the Chairman of the Commission upon the decision of the Assembly of Heads of State and Government.

Chapter IV – Applicable Principles

Article 60

The Commission shall draw inspiration from international law on Human and Peoples' Rights, particularly from the provisions of various African instruments on Human and Peoples' Rights, the Charter of the United Nations, the Charter of the Organisation of African Unity, the Universal Declaration of Human Rights, other instruments adopted by the United Nations and by African countries in the field of Human and Peoples' Rights as well as from the provisions of various instruments adopted within the Specialised Agencies of the United Nations of which the parties to the present Charter are members.

Article 61

The Commission shall also take into consideration, as subsidiary measures to determine the principles of law, other general or special international conventions, laying down rules expressly recognised by member states of the Organisation of African Unity, African practices consistent with international norms of Human and Peoples' Rights, customs generally accepted as law, general principles of law recognised by African states as well as legal precedents and doctrine.

Article 62

Each State Party shall undertake to submit every two years, form the date the present Charter comes into force, a report on the legislative or other measures taken with a view to giving effect to the rights and freedoms recognised and guaranteed by the present Charter

Article 63

1. The present Charter shall be open to signature, ratification or adherence of the member states of the Organisation of African Unity.

2. The instruments of ratification or adherence to the present Charter shall be deposited with the Secretary General of the Organisation of African Unity.

3. The present Charter shall come into force three months after the reception by the Secretary General of the instruments of ratification or adherence of a simple majority of member states of the Organisation of African Unity.

PART III: GENERAL PROVISIONS

Article 64

1. After the coming into force of the present Charter, members of the Commission shall be elected in accordance with the relevant Articles of the present Charter.
2. The Secretary General of the Organisation of African Unity shall convene the first meeting of the Commission at the Headquarters of the Organisation within three months of the constitution of the Commission. Thereafter, the Commission shall be convened by its Chairman whenever necessary but at least once a year.

Article 65

For each of the States that will ratify or adhere to the present Charter after its coming into force, the Charter shall take effect three months after the date of the deposit of by that State of its instruments of ratification or adherence

Article 66

Special protocols may, if necessary, supplement the provisions of the present Charter.

Article 67

The Secretary General of the Organisation of African Unity shall inform member states of the Organisation of the deposit of each instrument of ratification or adherence.

Article 68

The present Charter may be amended if a State Party makes a written request to that effect to the Secretary General of the Organisation of African Unity. The Assembly of Heads of State and Government may only consider the draft amendment after all the States Parties have been duly informed of it and the Commission has given its opinion on it at the request of the sponsoring State. The amendment shall be approved by a simple majority of the States Parties. It shall come into force for each state which has accepted it in accordance with its constitutional procedure three months after the Secretary General has received notice of the acceptance.

Reservations and Declarations to the African Charter

EGYPT

In the name of the people
Mehamed Husni Mubarak
President of the Arab Republic of Egypt

Having considered the African Charter on Human and Peoples' Rights the Arab Republic of Egypt signed the said charter on 16/11/1981, and attached hereto is the following instrument of ratification:

Having accepted all the provisions of the African Charter on Human and Peoples' Rights with the approval of the people's Assembly and with the reservation that article 8 and paragraph 3 of article 8 and paragraph 3 of article 18 be implemented in accordance with the Islamic Law and that, as far as the Arab Republic of Egypt is concerned, the provision of the first paragraph of article 9 should be confirmed to such information as could be obtained within the limits of the Egyptian Laws and regulations;

We hereby declare sub acceptance and ratification of the said charter.

In witness thereof, we have signed this instrument and directed that it be sealed with the official stamp of the Republic.

Signed

Cairo: 1984

By order of the President of
the Arab Republic of Egypt

Deputy Prime Minister and
Minister of Foreign Affairs
Kamal Hassan Ali

REPUBLIC OF ZAMBIA

Instrument of Ratification

WHEREAS the African Charter on Human and people's Rights was adopted by the Assembly of Heads of State and Government of the Member States of the

Organisation of African Unity held at Nairobi in June, 1981;

AND WHEREAS the Government of the Republic of Zambia signed the Charter on 17th January, 1983;

AND WHEREAS the Charter provides that the Charter is subject to ratification by the States Parties which are signatories to the Charter;

AND WHEREAS the Republic of Zambia is a State Party to the Charter on whose behalf the Charter has been signed;

NOW THEREFORE the Government of Zambia is a State Party to the Charter on whose behalf the Charter has been signed;

NOW THEREFORE the Government of the Republic of Zambia having considered the aforesaid Charter hereby CONFIRMS AND RATIFIES the same on behalf of the Republic of Zambia and undertakes faithfully to observe the provisions and carry out all the stipulations therein contained subject to the following amendments and reservations:

(i) Article 13 paragraph 3 should read:–
"Every individual shall have the right of access to any place, services or public property intended for use by the general public."

(*Explanation*:– the purpose of this reservation is to exclude any claim for the right to use by all citizens of *all* public property other than as fairly established.)

(ii) Article 37 should read:–
"Immediately after the first election the Chairman of the Assembly of Heads of State of the Organisation of African Unity shall announce the names of those members referred to in Article 36."

(*Explanation*:– This is to avoid calling on the Chairman, who is after all a Head of State, carrying out the rather menial exercise of drawing lots. It being understood that the Secretary-General of the Organisation of African Unity would draw such lots.)

(iii) There should be an extra article which should read:–
"After the establishment of the Commission all members of the O.A.U. not ratifying or adhering to the Charter shall submit reports to the Commission, at appropriate intervals, on the position of their laws and practices in regard to the matters dealt with in the Charter, and showing the extent to which effort has been given, or is proposed to be given, to any of the provisions of the Charter by legislation or administrative action and stating the difficulties which prevent or delay ratification or adherence to the Charter."

(*Explanation*:– In the interest of early universal ratification of the Charter by the Organisation of African Unity Countries and also since all Heads of State of the O.A.U. will together tackle the problems of administering or enforcing the Charter including, where necessary, criticising fellow Heads of State who are proved to have violated the Charter, all members of the O.A.U. should carry some responsibility, under the Charter, for the state of Human and People's rights in their respective countries.)

IN WITNESS WHEREOF I, IAMECK KAZEMBE HAZA GOMA, Minister of Foreign Affairs of the Republic of Zambia have signed this instrument.

DONE at Lusaka this 10th day of January, One thousand Nine hundred and eighty-four.

SOUTH AFRICA

While acceding to the African Charter on Human and Peoples' Rights it is the view of the Republic of South Africa that there should be consultation between States parties to the Charter, *inter alia*, to:

(i) consider possible measures to strengthen the enforcement mechanisms of the Charter;
(ii) clarify the criteria for the restrictions of rights and freedoms recognised and guaranteed in the Charter; and
(iii) bring the Charter into line with the United Nations' resolutions regarding the characterisation of Zionism.

Rules of Procedure of the African Commission on Human and Peoples' Rights

Deliberated and adopted on 6 October 1995 by the Commission at its 18th Session held in Praia, Cape Verde[1]
ACHPR/RP/XIX

The African Commission on Human and Peoples' Rights,

Having Considered the African Charter on Human and Peoples' Rights,

Acting in accordance with Article 42.2 of the Charter,

HAS ADOPTED the present revised Rules of Procedure:

PART ONE
GENERAL PROVISIONS
ORGANISATION OF THE COMMISSION

Chapter I – Sessions

Rule 1 – Number of Sessions

The African Commission on Human and Peoples' Rights (hereinafter referred to as "the Commission") shall hold the sessions which may be necessary to enable it to carry out satisfactorily its functions in conformity with the African Charter on Human and Peoples' Rights (hereinafter referred to as "The Charter").

Rule 2 – Opening Date

1. The Commission shall normally hold two ordinary sessions a year each lasting for about two weeks.
2. The ordinary sessions of the Commission shall be convened on a date fixed by the Commission on the proposal of its Chairman and in consultation with the Secretary General of the Organisation of African Unity (OAU) (hereinafter referred to as "The Secretary General").
3. The Secretary General may change under exceptional circumstances, the opening date of a session, in consultation with the Chairman of the Commission.

(03) Rules of Procedure

[1] These Rules replace those found in the First Activity Report, Annex V, which are reproduced below at p. 136.

Rule 3 – Extraordinary Session

1. The Commission may decide to hold extraordinary sessions, When the Commission is not in session, the Chairman may convene extraordinary sessions in consultation with the members of the Commission.

The Chairman of the Commission shall also convene extraordinary sessions:

(a) At the request of the majority of the members of the Commission; or
(b) At the request of the current Chairman of the Organisation of African Unity.

2. Extraordinary sessions shall be convened as soon as possible on a date fixed by the Chairman, in consultation with the Secretary General and the other members of the Commission.

Rule 4 – Place of Meetings

The sessions shall normally be held at the Headquarters of the Commission. The Commission, in consideration with the Secretary General decide to hold a Session elsewhere.

Rule 5 – Notifications of the Opening Date of the Sessions

The Secretary of the Commission (hereinafter referred to as the Secretary) shall inform members of the Commission of the date and venue of the first meeting of each session. This notification shall be sent, in the case of an Ordinary Session, at least eight eight (8) weeks and, in the case of an Extraordinary Session, at least three (3) weeks, if possible, before the Session.

Chapter II – Agenda

Rule 6 – Drawing up the Provisional Agenda

1. The Provisional Agenda for each Ordinary Session shall be drawn up by the Secretary in consultation with the Chairman of the Commission in accordance with the provisions of the Charter and these Rules.

2. The Provisional Agenda shall include if necessary, items on: "Communications from States", and "Other Communications" in conformity with the provisions of Article 55 of the Charter. It should not contain any information relating to such communications.

3. Except as specified above on the communications, the Provisional Agenda shall include all the items listed by the present Rules of Procedure as well as the items proposed by:

(a) The Commission at a previous Session;
(b) The Chairman of the Commission or another member of the Commission;

(c) A State party to the Charter;
(d) The Assembly of Heads of State and Government or the Council of Ministers of the Organisation of African Unity;
(e) The Secretary General of the Organisation of African Unity on any issue relating to the functions assigned to him by the Charter;
(f) A national liberation movement recognized by the Organisation of African Unity or by a non-governmental organisation;
(g) A specialized institution of which the State parties to the Charter are members.

4. The items to be included in the provisional agenda under sub paragraphs (b), (c), (f) and (g) of paragraph 3 must be communicated to the Secretary, accompanied by essential documents, not later than eight (8) weeks before the Opening of the Session.

5.

(a) All national liberation movements, specialised institutions, intergovernmental or non-governmental organisations wishing to propose the inclusion of an item in the Provisional Agenda must inform the Secretary at least ten (10) weeks before the opening of the meeting. Before formally proposing the inclusion of an item in the Provisional Agenda, the observations likely to be made by the Secretary must duly be taken into account;
(b) All proposals made under the provisions of the present paragraph shall be included only in the Provisional Agenda of the Commission, if at least two thirds (2/3) of the members present and voting so decide.

6. The Provisional Agenda of the Extraordinary Session of the Commission shall include only the item proposed to be considered at that Extraordinary Session.

Rule 7 – Transmission and Distribution of the Provisional Agenda

1. The Provisional Agenda and the essential documents relating to each item shall be distributed to the members of the Commission by the Secretary who shall endeavour to transmit them tot members at least six (6) weeks before the opening of the Session.

2. The Secretary shall communicate the Provisional Agenda of that session and have the essential documents relating to each Agenda item distributed at least six weeks before the opening of the Session of the Commission to the members of the Commission, member States parties to the Charter, to the current Chairman of the Organisation of African Unity and observers.

3. The draft agenda shall also be sent to the specialised agencies, to non-governmental organisations and to the national liberation movements concerned with the agenda.

4. In exceptional cases the Secretary may, while giving his reasons in writing, have the essential documents relating to some items of the Provisional Agenda distributed at least four (4) weeks prior to the opening of the Session.

Rule 8 – Adoption of the Agenda

At the beginning of each session, the Commission shall if necessary, after the election of officers in conformity with rule 17, adopt the agenda of the Session on the basis of the Provisional Agenda referred to in Rule 6.

Rule 9 – Revision of the Agenda

The Commission may, during the Session, revise the Agenda if need be, adjourn, cancel or amend items. During the Session, only urgent and important issues may be added to the Agenda.

Rule 10 – Draft Provisional Agenda for Next Session

The Secretary shall, at each session of the Commission, submit a Draft Provisional Agenda for the next session of the Commission, indicating with respect to each item, the documents to be submitted on that item and the decisions of the deliberative organ which authorized their preparation so as to enable the Commission to consider these documents as regards the contribution they make to its proceedings, as well as their urgency and relevance to the prevailing situation.

Chapter III – Members of the Commission

Rule 11 – Composition of the Commission

The Commission shall be composed of eleven (11) members elected by the Assembly of Heads of State and Government hereinafter referred to as "the Assembly", in conformity with the relevant provisions of the Charter.

Rule 12 – Status of the Member

1. The members of the Commission shall be eleven (11) personalities appointed in conformity with the provisions of Article 31 of the Charter.
2. Each member of the Commission shall sit on the Commission in a personal capacity. No member may be represented by another person.

Rule 13 – Term of Office of the Members

1. The term of office of the members of the Commission elected on 29 July 1987 shall begin from that date. The term of office of the members of the Commission elected at subsequent elections shall take effect the day following the expiry date of the term of office of the members of the Commission they shall replace.
2. However, if a member is re-elected at the expiry of his or her term of office, or elected to replace a member whose term of office has expired or will expire, the term of office shall begin from that expiry date.

3. In conformity with Article 39(3) of the Charter, the member elected to replace a member whose term has not expired, shall complete the term of office of his or her predecessor, unless the remaining term of office is less than six (6) months. In the latter case, there shall be no replacement.

Rule 14 – Cessation of Functions

1. If in the unanimous opinion of the other members of the Commission, a member has stopped discharging his duties for any reason other than a temporary absence, the Chairman of the Commission shall inform the Secretary General of the Organisation of African Unity, who shall then declare the seat vacant.

2. In case of the death or resignation of a member of the Commission, the Chairman shall immediately inform the Secretary General who shall declare the seat vacant from the date of the death or from that on which the resignation took effect. The member of the Commission who resigns shall address a written notification of his or her resignation directly to the Chairman or to the Secretary General and steps to declare his or her seat vacant shall only be taken after receiving the said notification. The resignation shall make the seat vacant.

Rule 15 – Vacant Seat

Every seat declared vacant in conformity with Rule 14 of the present Rules of Procedure shall be filled on the basis of Article 39 of the Charter.

Rule 16 – Oath

Before coming into office, every member of the Commission shall make the following solemn commitment at a public sitting. "I swear to carry out my duties well and faithfully in all impartiality."

Chapter IV – Officers

Rule 17 – Election of Officers

1. The Commission shall elect among its members a Chairman and Vice Chairman.

2. The elections referred to in the present Rule shall be held by secret ballot. Only the members present shall vote, the member who shall obtain the two-thirds majority of the votes of the members present and voting shall be elected.

3. If no member obtains this two-thirds majority in a second, third and fourth ballot, the member having the highest number of votes at the fifth ballot shall be elected.

4. The officers of the Commission shall be elected for a period of two (2) years. They shall be eligible for re-election. None of them, may, however, exercise his or her functions if he or she ceases to be a member of the Commission.

Rule 18 – Power of the Chairman

The Chairman shall carry out the functions assigned to him by the Charter, the Rules of Procedure and the decisions of the Commission. In the exercise of his functions the Chairman shall be under the authority of the Commission.

Rule 19 – Absence of the Chairman

1. The Vice Chairman shall replace the Chairman during a session if the latter is unable to attend a whole or part of a sitting of a session.

2. In the absence of both the Chairman and Vice Chairman, members shall elect an acting Chairman.

Rule 20 – Functions of the Vice Chairman

The Vice Chairman, acting in the capacity of the Chairman, shall have the same rights and the same duties as the Chairman.

Rule 21 – Cessation of the Functions of an Officer

If any of the officers ceases to carry out his or her functions or declares that he or she is no longer able to serve as an officer or exercise the functions of a member of the Commission, a new officer shall be elected for the remaining term of office of his or her predecessor.

Chapter V – Secretariat

Rule 22 – Function of the Secretary General

1. The Secretary General or his representative may attend the meeting of the Commission. He shall neither participate in the deliberations, nor in the voting. He may, however, be called upon by the Chairman of the Commission to make written or oral statements at the sittings of the Commission.

2. He shall appoint, in consultation with the Chairman of the Commission, a Secretary of the Commission.

3. He shall, in consultation with the Chairman, provide the Commission with the necessary staff, means and services for it to carry out effectively the functions and missions assigned to it under the Charter.

4. The Secretary General acting through the Secretary shall take all the necessary steps for the meetings of the Commission.

Rule 23 – Functions of the Secretary to the Commission

The Secretary of the Commission shall be responsible for the activities of the Secretariat under the general supervision of the Chairman, and particularly:

(a) He/she shall assist the Commission and its members in the exercise of their functions;
(b) He/she shall serve as an intermediary for all the communications concerning the Commission;
(c) He/she shall be the custodian of the archives of the Commission;
(d) The Secretary shall bring immediately to the knowledge of the members of the Commission all the issues that will be submitted to him/her.

Rule 24 – Estimates

Before the Commission approves a proposal entailing expenses, the Secretary shall prepare and distribute, as soon as possible, to the members of the Commission, the financial implications to the proposal. It is incumbent on the Chairman to draw the attention of the members to those implications so that they discuss them when the proposal is considered by the Commission.

Rule 25 – Financial Rules

The Financial Rules adopted pursuant to the provisions of Articles 41 and 44 of the Charter, shall be appended to the present Rules of Procedure.

Rule 26 – Financial Responsibility

The Organisation of African Unity shall bear the expenses of the staff and the facilities and services placed at the disposal of the Commission to carry out its functions.

Rule 27 – Records of Cases

A special record, with a reference number and initialled, in which shall be entered the date of registration of each petition and communication and that of the closure of the procedure relating to them before the Commission, shall be kept at the Secretariat.

Chapter VI – Subsidiary Bodies

Rule 28 – Establishment of Committees and Working Groups

1. The Commission may during a session, taking into account the provisions of the Charter, establish, if it deems it necessary for the exercise of its functions, committees or working groups, composed of the members of the Commission and send them any agenda item for consideration and report.

2. These committees or working groups may, in consultation with the Secretary General, be authorized to sit when the Commission is not in session.

3. The members of the committees or working groups shall be appointed by the Chairman subject to the approval of the absolute majority of the other members of the Commission.

Rule 29 – Establishment of Sub Commissions

1. The Commission may establish Sub Commissions of experts after the prior approval of the Assemble.

2. Unless the Assembly decides otherwise, the Commission shall determine the functions and composition of each Sub Commission.

Rule 30 – Offices of the Subsidiary bodies

Unless the Commission decides otherwise, the subsidiary bodies of the Commission shall elect their own officers.

Rule 31 – Rules of Procedure

The Rules of Procedure of the Commission shall apply, as far as possible to the proceedings of its subsidiary bodies.

Chapter VII – Public Sessions and Private Sessions

Rule 32 – General Principle

The sittings of the Commission and of its subsidiary bodies shall be held in public unless the Commission decides otherwise or it appears from the relevant provisions of the Charter that the meeting shall be held in private.

Rule 33 – Publication of Proceedings

At the end of each private or public sitting, the Commission or its subsidiary bodies may issue a communiqué.

Chapter VIII – Languages

Rule 34 – Working Languages

The working languages of the Commission and of all its institutions shall be those of the Organisation of African Unity.

Rule 35 – Interpretation

1. The address delivered in one of the working languages shall be interpreted in the other working languages.

2. Any person addressing the Commission in a language other than one of the working languages, shall, in principle, ensure the interpretation in one of the working languages. The interpreters of the Secretariat may take the interpretation of the original language as source language for their interpretation in the other working languages.

Rule 36 – Languages to be Used for Minutes of Proceedings

The summary minutes of the sittings of the Commission shall be drafted in the working languages.

Rule 37 – Languages to be Used for Resolutions and Other Official Decisions

All the official decisions and documents of the Commission will be rendered in the working languages.

Rule 38 – Tape Recordings of the Session

The Secretariat shall record and preserve the tapes of the sessions of the Commission. It may also record and conserve the tapes of the sessions of the committees, working groups and sub commissions if the Commission so decides.

Rule 39 – Summary Minutes of the Sessions

The Secretariat shall draft the summary minutes of the public and private sessions of the Commission and of its subsidiary bodies. It shall distribute them as soon as possible in a draft form to the members of the Commission and to all other participants in the session. All those participants may, in the thirty (30) days following the receipt of the draft minutes of the session, submit corrections to the Secretariat. The Chairman may, under special circumstances, in consultation with the Secretary-General, extend the time for the submission of the corrections.

In case the corrections are contested, the Chairman of the Commission or the Chairman of the subsidiary body whose minutes they are, shall resolve the disagreement after having listened to, if necessary, the tape recordings of the discussions. If the disagreement persists, the Commission or the subsidiary body shall decide. The corrections shall be published in a distinct volume after the closure of the session.

Rule 40 – Distribution of the Minutes of the Private Sessions and Public Sessions

1. The final summary minutes of the public and private sessions shall be the document intended for general distribution, unless the Commission decides otherwise.

2. The minutes of the private sessions of the Commission shall be distributed forthwith to all members of the Commission.

Rule 41 – Reports to be Submitted After Each Session

The Commission shall submit to the current Chairman of the Organisation of African Unity, a report on the deliberations of each session. This report shall contain a brief summary of the recommendations and statements on issues to which the Commission would like to draw the attention of the current Chairman and member States of the Organisation of African Unity.

Rule 42 – Submission of Official Decisions and Reports

The text of the decisions and reports officially adopted by the Commission shall be distributed to all members of the Commission as soon as possible.

Chapter X – Conduct of the Debates

Rule 43 – Quorum

The quorum shall be constituted by seven (7) members of the Commission, as specified in Article 42(3) of the Charter.

Rule 44 – Additional Powers of the Chairman

1. In addition to the powers entrusted to him/her under other provisions of the present Rules of Procedure, the Chairman shall have the responsibility to open and close each session; he/she shall direct the debates, ensure the application of the present Rules of Procedure, grant the use of floor, submit to a vote matters under discussion and announce the result of the vote taken.

2. Subject to the provisions of the present Rules of Procedure, the Chairman shall direct the discussions of the Commission and ensure order during meeting. The Chairman may during the discussion of an agenda item, propose to the Commission to limit the time allotted to speakers, as well as the number of interventions of each speaker on the same issue and close the list of speakers.

3. He/she shall rule on the points of order. He/she shall also have the power to propose the adjournment and the closure of debates as well as the adjournment and suspension of a sitting. The debates shall deal solely with the issues submitted to the Commission and the Chairman may call a speaker, whose remarks are irrelevant to the matter under discussion, to order.

Rule 45 – Points of Order

1. During the debate of any matter a member may, at any time, raise a point of order and the point of order shall be immediately decided by the Chairman, in

accordance with the Rules of Procedure. If a member appeals against the decision, the appeal shall immediately be put to the vote and if the Chairman's ruling is not overruled by the majority of the members present, it shall be maintained.

2. A member raising a point of order cannot, in his or her comments, deal with the substance of the matter under discussion.

Rule 46 – Adjournment of Debates

During the discussion on any matter, a member may move the adjournment of the debate on the matter under discussion. In addition to the proposer of the motion one member may speak in favour of and one against the motion after which the motion shall be immediately put to the vote.

Rule 47 – Limit the Time Accorded to Speakers

The Commission may limit the time accorded to each speaker on any matter, when the time allotted for debates is limited and a speaker spends more time than the time accorded, the Chairman shall immediately call him to order.

Rule 48 – Closing the List of Speakers

The Chairman may, during a debate, read out the list of speakers and with the approval of the Commission, declare the list closed. Where there are no more speakers, the Chairman shall, with the approval of the Commission, declare the debate closed.

Rule 49 – Closure of Debate

A member may, at any time, move for the closure of the debate on the matter under discussion, even if the other members or representatives expressed the desire to take the floor. The authorisation to take the floor on the closure of the debate shall be given only to two speakers before the closure, after which the motion shall immediately be put to the vote.

Rule 50 – Suspension or Adjournment of the Meeting

During the discussion of any matter, a member may move for the suspension or adjournment of the meeting. No discussion on any such motion shall be permitted and it shall be immediately put to the vote.

Rule 51 – Order of the Motions

Subject to the provisions of Rule 45 of the present Rule of Procedure the following motions shall have precedence in the following order over all the other proposals or motions before the meeting:

(a) To suspend the meeting;
(b) To adjourn the meeting;
(c) To adjourn the debate on the item under discussion;
(d) For the closure of the debate of the item under discussion.

Rule 52 – Submission of Proposals and Amendment of Substance.

Unless the Commission decides otherwise the proposals, amendments or motions of substance made by members shall be submitted in writing to the Secretariat; they shall be considered at the first sitting following their submission.

Rule 53 – Decisions on Competence

Subject to the provisions of Rule 45 of the Procedure, any motion tabled by a member for a decision on the competence of the Commission to adopt a proposal submitted to it shall immediately be put to the vote.

Rule 54 – Withdrawal of a Proposal or a Motion

The sponsor of a motion or a proposal may still withdraw it before it is put to the vote, provided that it has not been amended. A motion or a proposal thus withdrawn may be submitted again by another member.

Rule 55 – New Consideration of a Motion

When a proposal is adopted or rejected, it shall not be considered again at the same session, unless the Commission decides otherwise. When a member moves for the new consideration of a proposal, only one member may speak in favour of and one against the motion, after which it shall immediately be put to the vote.

Rule 56 – Interventions

1. No member may take the floor at a meeting of the Commission without prior authorisation on the Chairman. Subject to Rules 45, 48, 49 and 50 the Chairman shall grant the use of the floor to the speakers in the order in which it has been requested.

2. The debates shall deal solely with the matter submitted to the Commission and the Chairman may call to order a speaker whose remarks are irrelevant to the matter under discussion.

3. The Chairman may limit the time accorded to speakers and the number of the interventions which each member may make on the same issue, in accordance with Rule 44 of the present Rules.

4. Only two members in favour and two against the motion of fixing such time limits shall be granted the use of the floor after which the motion shall immediately be put to the vote. For questions of procedure the time allotted to each speaker shall not

exceed five minutes, unless the Chairman decides otherwise. When the time allotted discussions is limited and a speaker exceeds the time accorded the Chairman shall immediately call him to order.

Rule 57 – Right to Reply

The right of reply shall be granted by the Chairman to any member requesting it. The member must, while exercising this right, be as brief as possible and take the floor preferably at the end of the sitting at which this right has been requested.

Rule 58 – Congratulations

The congratulations addressed to the newly elected members to the Commission shall only be presented by the Chairman or a member designated by the latter. Those addressed to the newly elected officers shall only be presented by the outgoing Chairman or a member designated by him.

Rule 59 – Condolences

Condolences shall be exclusively presented by the Chairman on behalf of all the members. The Chairman may, with the consent of the Commission, send a message of condolence.

Chapter XI – Vote and Elections

Rule 60 – Right to Vote

Each member of the Commission shall have one vote. In the case of equal number of votes the Chairman shall have a casting vote.

Rule 61 – Asking for a Vote

A proposal or a motion submitted for the decision of the Commission shall be put to the vote if a member so requests. If no member asks for a vote, the Commission may adopt a proposal or a motion without a vote.

Rule 62 – Required Majority

1. Except as otherwise provided by the Charter or other Rules of the present Rules of Procedure, decisions of the Commission shall be taken by a simple majority of the members present and voting.

2. For the purpose of the present Rules of Procedure, the expression "members present and voting" shall mean members voting for or against or blank. The members who shall abstain from voting shall be considered as non-voting members.

3. Decisions may be taken by consensus, failing which, Commission shall resort to voting.

Rule 63 – Method of Voting

1. Subject to the provisions of Rule 68, the Commission, unless it otherwise decides, shall normally vote by show of hands, but any member may request the roll-call vote, which shall be taken in the alphabetical order of the names of the members of the Commission beginning with the member whose name is drawn by lot by the Chairman. In all the votes by roll-call each member shall reply "yes", "no" or "abstention". The Commission may decide to hold a secret ballot.

2. In case of vote by roll-call, the vote of each member participating in the ballot shall be recorded in the minutes.

Rule 64 – Explanation of Vote

Members may make brief statements for the only purpose of explaining their vote, before the beginning of the vote or once the vote has been taken. The member who is the sponsor of a proposal or a motion cannot explain his vote on that proposal or notion except if it has been amended.

Rule 65 – Rules to be Observed while Voting

A ballot shall not be interrupted except if a member raises a point of order relating to manner in which the ballot is held. The Chairman may allow members to intervene briefly, whether before the ballot beginning or when it is closed, but solely to explain their vote.

Rule 66 – Division of Proposals and Amendments

Proposals and amendments may be separated if requested. The parts of the proposals or of the amendments which have been adopted shall later be put to the vote as a whole; if all the operative parts of a proposal have been rejected, the proposal shall be considered to have been rejected as a whole.

Rule 67 – Amendment

An amendment to a proposal is an addition to, deletion from or revision of part of that proposal.

Rule 68 – Order of Vote on Amendments

When an amendment is moved to a proposal, the amendment shall be voted on first.

When two or more amendments are moved to a proposal, the Commission shall first vote on the amendment furthest removed in substance from the original proposal and then on the amendment next furthest removed therefrom and so on until all the amendments have been put to the vote. Nevertheless, when the adoption of an amendment implies the rejection of another amendment, the latter shall not be put to the vote. If one or several amendments are adopted, the amended proposal shall then be put to the vote.

Rule 69 – Order of Vote on the Proposals

1. If two or more proposals are made on the same matter, the Commission, unless it decides otherwise, shall vote on these proposals in the order in which they were submitted.

2. After each vote the Commission may decide whether it shall put the next proposal to the vote.

3. However, the motions which are not on the substance of the proposals shall be voted upon before the said proposals.

Rule 70 – Elections

Elections shall be held by secret ballot unless the election is for a post for which only one candidate has been proposed and that candidate has been agreed upon by the members of the Commission.

Chapter XII – Participation of Non-Members of the Commission

Rule 71 – Participation of States in the Deliberations

1. The Commission or its subsidiary bodies may invite any State to participate in the discussion of any issue that shall be of particular interest to that State.

2. A State thus invited shall have no voting right, but may submit proposals which may be put to the vote at the request of any member of the Commission or of the subsidiary body concerned.

Rule 72 – Participation of other Persons or Organisations

The Commission may invite any organisation or persons capable of enlightening it to participate in its deliberations without voting rights.

Rule 73 – Participation of Specialised Institutions and Consultation with the Latter

1. Pursuant to the agreements concluded between the Organisation of African Unity and the specialised institutions, the latter shall have the right to:

(a) Be represented in the public sessions of the Commission and its subsidiary bodies;

(b) Participate, without voting rights, through their representatives in deliberations on issues which shall be of interest to them and to submit, on these issues, proposals which may be put to vote at the request of any member of the Commission or the interested subsidiary body.

2. Before placing on the provisional agenda an issue submitted by a specialised institution, the Secretary General should initiate such preliminary consultations as may be necessary, with this institution.

3. When an issue proposed for inclusion in the provisional agenda of a session, or which has been added to the agenda of a session pursuant to Rule 5 of the present Rules of Procedure, contains a proposal requesting the Organisation of African Unity to undertake additional activities relating to issues concerning directly one or more specialised institutions, the Secretary General should enter in to consultation with the institutions concerned and inform the Commission of the ways and means of ensuring coordinated utilisation of the resources of the various institutions.

4. When at a meeting of the Commission, a proposal calling upon the Organisation of African Unity to undertake additional activities relating to issues directly concerning one or several specialised institutions, the Secretary General, after consulting as far as possible the representatives of the interested institutions, should draw the attention of the Commission to the effects of that proposal.

5. Before taking a decision on the proposals mentioned above, the Commission shall make sure that the institutions concerned have been duly consulted.

Rule 74 – Participation of other Inter-Governmental Organisations

1. The Secretary shall inform, not later that 4 weeks before a session, non-governmental organisations with observer status of the days and agenda of a forthcoming session.

2. Representatives of inter-governmental organisations to which the Organisation of African Unity has granted permanent observer status and other organisations recognised by the Commission, may participate, without voting rights, in the deliberations of the Commission on issues falling within the framework of the activities of these organisations.

Chapter XIII – Relations with and Representation of Non-Governmental Organisations

Rule 75 – Representation

Non-governmental organisations, granted observer status by the Commission, may appoint authorised observers to participate in the public sessions of the Commission and of its subsidiary bodies.

Rule 76 – Consultation

The Commission may consult the non-governmental organisations either directly or through one or several committees set up for this purpose. These consultations may be held at the invitation of the Commission or at the request of the organisation.

Chapter XIV – Publication and Distribution of the Reports and Other Official Documents of the Commission

Rule 77 – Report of the Commission

Within the framework of the procedure of communication among States parties to the Charter, referred to in Articles 47 and 49 of the Charter, the Commission shall submit to the Assembly a report containing, where possible, recommendations it shall deem necessary.

The report shall be confidential. However, it shall be published by the Chairman of the Commission after reporting unless the Assembly directs otherwise.

Rule 78 – Periodical Reports of Member States

Periodical reports and other information submitted by States parties to the Charter as requested under Article 62 of the Charter, shall be documents for general distribution. The same thing shall apply to other information supplied by a State party to the Charter, unless the Commission decides otherwise.

Rule 79 – Reports on the Activities of the Commission

1. As stipulated in Article 54 of the Charter, the Commission shall each year submit to the Assembly, a report on its deliberations, in which it shall include a summary of the activities.

2. The report shall be published by the Chairman after the Assembly has considered it.

Rule 80 – Translation of Reports and Other Documents

The Secretary shall endeavour to translate all reports and other documents of the Commission into the working languages.

PART TWO
PROVISIONS RELATING TO THE FUNCTIONS OF THE COMMISSION

Chapter XV – Promotional Activities
Reports Submitted by States Parties to the Charter under Article 62 of the Charter

Rule 81 – Contents of Reports

1. States parties to the Charter shall submit reports in the form required by the Commission on measures they have taken to give effect to the rights recognised by the Charter and on the progress made with regard to the enjoyment of these rights. The reports should indicate, where possible, the factors and difficulties impeding the implementation of the provisions of the Charter.
2. If a State party fails to comply with Article 62 of the Charter, the Commission shall fix the date for the submission of that State party's report.
3. The Commission may, through the Secretary General, inform State parties to the Charter of its wishes regarding the form and contents of the reports to be submitted under Article 62 of the Charter.

Rule 82 – Transmission of the Reports

1. The Secretary may, after consultation with the Commission, communicate to the specialised institutions concerned, copies of all parts of the reports which may relate to their areas of competence, produced by member States of these institutions.
2. The Commission may invite the specialised institutions to which the Secretary has communicated parts of the report, to submit observations relating to these parts within a time limit that it may specify.

Rule 83 – Submission of Reports

The Commission shall inform, as early as possible, member States parties to the Charter, through the Secretary, of the opening date, duration and venue of the Session at which their respective reports shall be considered.

Representatives of the States parties to the Charter may participate in the sessions of the Commission at which their reports shall be considered. The Commission may also inform a State party to the Charter from which it wanted complementary information, that it may authorise its representative to participate in a specific session. This representative should be able to reply to questions put to him/her by the Commission and make statements on reports already submitted by this State. He may also furnish additional information from his State.

Rule 84 – Non-Submission of Reports

1. The Secretary shall, at each session, inform the Commission of all cases of non-submission of reports or of additional information requested pursuant to Rules 81 and 85 of the Rules of Procedure. In such cases, the Commission may send, through the Secretary, to the State party to the Charter concerned, a report or reminder relating to the submission of the report or additional information.

2. If, after the reminder referred to in paragraph 1 of this Rule, a State party to the Charter does not submit the report or the additional information requested pursuant to Rules 81 and 85 of the Rules of Procedure, the Commission shall point it out in its yearly report to the Assembly.

Rule 85 – Examination of Information Contained in Reports

1. When considering a report submitted by a State party to the Charter under Article 62 of the Charter, the Commission should first make sure that the report provides all the necessary information including relevant legislation pursuant to the provisions of Rule 81 of the Rules of Procedure.

2. If, in the opinion of the Commission, a report submitted by a State party to the Charter does not contain adequate information, the Commission may request this State to furnish the additional information required, by indicating the date on which the information needed should be submitted.

3. If, following the consideration of the reports, and the information submitted by a State party to the Charter, the Commission decides that the State has not discharged some of its obligations under the Charter, it may address all general observations to the State concerned as it may deem necessary.

Rule 86 – Adjournment and Transmission of the Reports

1. The Commission shall, through the Secretary, communicate to States parties to the Charter for comments, its general observations made following the consideration of the reports and the information submitted by States parties to the Charter. The Commission may, when necessary, fix a time limit for the submission of the comments by the States parties to the Charter.

2. The Commission may also transmit to the Assembly, the observations mentioned in paragraph 1 of this Rule, accompanied by copies of the reports it has received from the States parties to the Charter as well as the comments supplied by the latter if possible.

Rule 87 – Promotional Activities

1. The Commission shall adopt and carry out a programme of action which gives effect to its obligations under the Charter, particularly Article 45(1).

2. The Commission shall carry out other promotional activities in member States and elsewhere on a continuing basis.

3. Each member of the Commission shall file a written report on his/her activities at each session including countries visited and organisations contacted.

Chapter XVI – Protection Activities Communications from the States Parties to the Charter

Section I – Procedure for the Consideration of Communications Received in Conformity with Article 47 of the Charter: Procedure for Communications-Negotiations

Rule 88 – Procedure

1. A communication under Article 47 of the Charter should be submitted to the Secretary General, the Chairman of the Commission and the State party concerned.
2. The communication referred to above should be in writing and contain a detailed and comprehensive statement on the actions denounced as well as the provisions of the Charter alleged to have been violated.
3. The notification of the communication to the State party to the Charter, the Secretary General and the Chairman of the Commission shall be done through the most practicable and reliable means.

Rule 89 – Register of Communications

The Secretary shall keep a permanent register for all communications received under Article 47 of the Charter.

Rule 90 – Reply and Time Limit

1. The reply of the State party to the Charter to which a communication is addressed should reach the requesting State party to the Charter within three (3) months following the receipt of the notification of the communication.
2. It shall be accompanied particularly by:

(a) Written explanations, declarations or statements relating to the issues raised;
(b) Possible indications and measures taken to end the situation denounced;
(c) Indications on the law and rules of procedure applicable or applied;
(d) Indications on the local procedures for appeal already used, in process or still open.

Rule 91 – Non-Settlement of the Issue

1. If within three (3) months from the date the notification of the original communication is received by the addressee State, the issue has not been settled to the satisfaction of the two interested parties, through the selected channel of negotiation or

through any other peaceful procedure selected by common consent of the parties, the issue shall be referred to the Commission, in accordance with the provisions of Article 48 of the Charter.

2. The issue shall also be referred to the Commission if the addressee State party to the Charter fails to react to the request made under Article 47 of the Charter, within the same 3 months' period of time.

Rule 92 – Seizing of the Commission

At the expiration of the 3 months time limit referred to in Article 47 of the Charter, and in the absence of a satisfactory reply or in case the addressee State party may submit the communication to the Commission through a notification addressed to its Chairman, the other interested State party and the Secretary General.

Section II – Procedure for the Consideration of the Communications Received in Conformity with Articles 48 and 49 of the Charter: Procedure for Communication-Complaint

Rule 93 – Seizing of the Commission

1. Any communication submitted under Articles 48 and 49 of the Charter may be submitted to the Commission by any one of the interested States parties through notification addressed to the Chairman of the Commission, the Secretary General and the State party concerned.

2. The notification referred to in paragraph 1 of the present Rule shall contain information on the following elements or accompanied particularly by:

(a) Measures taken to try to resolve the issue pursuant to Article 47 of the Charter including the text of the initial communications and any future written explanation from the interested States parties to the Charter relating to the issue;
(b) Measures taken to exhaust local procedure for appeal;
(c) Any other procedure for the international investigation or international settlement to which the interested States parties have resorted.

Rule 94 – Permanent Register of Communications

The Secretary shall keep a permanent register for all communications received by the Commission under Articles 48 and 49 of the Charter.

Rule 95 – Seizing of the Members of the Commission

The Secretary shall immediately inform the members of the Commission of any notification received pursuant to Rule 91 of the Rules of Procedure and shall send to them, as early as possible, a copy of the notification as well as the relevant information.

Rule 96 – Private Session and Press Release

1. The Commission shall consider the communications referred to in Articles 48 and 49 of the Charter in closed session.

2. After consulting the interested States parties to the Charter, the Commission may issue through the Secretary, release on its private sessions for the attention of the media and the public.

Rule 97 – Consideration of the Communication

The Commission shall consider a communication only when:

(a) The procedure offered to the States parties by Article 47 of the Charter has been exhausted;
(b) The time limit set in Article 48 of the Charter has expired;
(c) The Commission is certain that all the available local remedies have been utilised and exhausted, in accordance with the generally recognized principles of international law, or that the application of these remedies is unreasonably prolonged or that there are no effective remedies.

Rule 98 Amicable Settlement

Except the provisions of Rule 96 of the present Rules of Procedure, the Commission shall place its good offices at the disposal of the interested States parties to the Charter so as to reach an amicable solution on the issue based on the respect of human rights and fundamental liberties, as recognized by the Charter.

Rule 99 – Additional Information

The Commission may through the Secretary, request the States parties or one of them to communicate additional information or observations orally or in writing. The Commission shall fix a time limit for the submission of the written information or observations.

Rule 100 – Representation of States Parties

1. The States parties to the Charter concerned shall have the right to be represented during the consideration of the issue by the Commission and to submit observations orally and in writing or in either form.

2. The Commission shall notify, as soon as possible, the States parties concerned, through the Secretary, of the opening day, the duration and the venue of the session at which the issue will be examined.

3. The procedure to be followed for the presentation of oral or written observations shall be determined by the Commission.

Rule 101 – Report of the Commission

1. The Commission shall adopt a report pursuant to Article 52 of the Charter within 12 months, following the notification referred to in Article 48 of the Charter and Rule 90 of the present Rules of Procedure.
2. The provisions of paragraph 1 of Rule 99 of these Rules of Procedure shall not apply to the deliberations of the Commission relating to the adoption of the report.
3. The report referred to above shall concern the decisions and conclusions that the Commission will reach.
4. The report of the Commission shall be communicated to the States parties concerned through the Secretary.
5. The report of the Commission shall be sent to the Assembly through the Secretary General, together with the recommendations that it shall deem useful.

Chapter XVII – Other Communications
Procedure for the Consideration of the Communications Received in Conformity with Article 55 of the Charter

Section I – Transmission of Communications to the Commission

Rule 102 – Seizing of the Commission

1. Pursuant to these Rules of Procedure, the Secretary shall transmit to the Commission the communications submitted to him for consideration by the Commission in accordance with the Charter.
2. No communications concerning a State which is not a party to the Charter shall be received by the Commission or placed in a list under Rule 103 of the present Rules.

Rule 103 – List of Communications

1. The Secretary of the Commission shall prepare lists of communications submitted to the Commission pursuant to Rule 101 above, to which he/she shall attach a brief summary to their contents and regularly cause the lists to be distributed to members of the Commission. Besides, the Secretary shall keep a permanent register of all these communications which shall be made public.
2. The full text of each communication referred to the Commission shall be communicated to each member of the Commission on request.

Rule 104 – Request for Clarifications

1. The Commission, through the Secretary, may request the author of a communication to furnish clarifications on the applicability of the Charter to his/her communication, and to specify in particular:

(a) His name, address, age and profession by justifying his very identity, if ever he/she is requesting the Commission to be kept anonymous;
(b) Name of the State party referred to in the communication;
(c) Purpose of the communication;
(d) Provision(s) of the Charter allegedly violated;
(e) The facts of the claim;
(f) Measures taken by the author to exhaust local remedies, or explanation why local remedies will be futile;
(g) The extent to which the same issue has been settled by another international investigation or settlement body.

2. When asking for clarification or information, the Commission shall fix an appropriate time limit for the author to submit the communication so as to avoid undue delay in the procedure provided for by the Charter.

3. The Commission may adopt a questionnaire for the use by the author of the communication in providing the above-mentioned information.

4. The request for clarification referred to in paragraph 1 of this rule shall not prevent the inclusion of the communication on the lists mentioned in paragraph 1 of Rule 102 above.

Rule 105 – Distribution of Communications

For each communication recorded, the Secretary shall prepare as soon as possible, a summary of the relevant information received, which shall be distributed to the members of the Commission.

Section II – General Provisions Governing the Consideration of the Communications by the Commission or its Subsidiary Bodies

Rule 106 – Private Session

The sessions of the Commission or its subsidiary bodies during which the communications are examined as provided for in the Charter shall be private.

Rule 107 – Public Sessions

The sessions during which the Commission may consider other general issues, such as the application procedure of the Charter, shall be public.

Rule 108 – Press Releases

The Commission may issue, through the Secretary and for the attention of the media and the public, releases on the activities of the Commission in its private session.

Rule 109 – Incompatibilities

1. No member shall take part in the consideration of a communication by the Commission

(a) If he/she has any personal interest in the case; or
(b) If he /she has participated, in any capacity, in the adoption of any decision relating to the case which is the subject of the communication.

2. Any issue relating to the application of paragraph 1 above shall be resolved by the Commission.

Rule 110 – Withdrawal of a Member

If, for any reason, a member considers that he/she should not take part or continue to take part in the consideration of a communication, he/she shall inform the Chairman of his/her decision to withdrawal.

Rules 111 – Provisional Measures

1. Before making its final views know to the Assembly on the communication, the Commission may inform the State party concerned of its views on the appropriateness of taking provisional measures to avoid irreparable damage being caused to the victim of the alleged violation. In so doing, the Commission shall inform the State party that the expression on its views on the adoption of those provisional measures does not imply a decision on the substance of the communication.

2. The Commission, or when it is not in session, the Chairman, in consultation with other members of the Commission, may indicate to the parties any interim measure, the adoption of which seems desirable in the interest of the parties or the proper conduct of the proceedings before it.

3. In case urgency when the Commission is not in session, the Chairman in consultation with other members of the Commission, may take any necessary action on behalf of the Commission. As soon as the Commission is again in session, the Chairman shall report to it on any action taken.

Rule 112 – Information to the State Party to the Charter

Prior to any substantive consideration, every communication should be made known to the State concerned through the Chairman of the Commission, pursuant to Article 57 of the Charter.

Section III – Procedures to Determine Admissibility

Rule 113 – Time Limits for Consideration of the Admissibility

The Commission shall decide, as early as possible and pursuant to the following provisions, whether or not the communication shall be admissible under the Charter.

Rule 114 – Order of Consideration of the Communication

1. Unless otherwise decided, the Commission shall consider the communications in the order they have been received by the Secretariat.
2. The Commission may decide, if it deems it good, to consider jointly two or more communications.

Rule 115 – Working Groups

The Commission may set up one or more working groups, each composed of three of its members at most, to submit recommendations on admissibility as stipulated in Article 56 of the Charter.

Rule 116 – Admissibility of the Communications

The Commission shall determine questions of admissibility pursuant to Article 56 of the Charter.

Rule 117 – Additional Information

1. The Commission or a working group set up under Rule 113, request the State party concerned or the author of the communication to submit in writing additional information or observations relating to the issue of admissibility of the communication. The Commission or the working group shall fix a time limit for the submission of the information or observations to avoid the issue dragging on too long.
2. A communication may be declared admissible if the State party concerned has been given the opportunity to submit the information and observations pursuant to paragraph 1 of this Rule.
3. A request under paragraph 1 of this Rule should indicate clearly that the request does not mean any decision whatsoever has been taken on the issue of admissibility.
4. However, the Commission shall decide in the issue of admissibility if the State party fails to send a written response within three (3) months from the date of notification of the text of the communication.

Rule 118 – Decision of the Commission on Admissibility

1. If the Commission decides that a communication is inadmissible under the Charter, it shall make its decision known as early as possible, through the Secretary to the author of the communication and, if the communication has been transmitted to a State party concerned, to that State.

2. If the Commission has declared a communication inadmissible under the Charter, it may reconsider this decision at a later date if it receives a request for reconsideration.

Section IV – Procedures for the Consideration of Communications

Rule 119 – Proceedings

1. If the Commission decides that a communication is admissible under the Charter, its decision and text of the relevant documents shall as soon as possible, be submitted to the State party concerned, through the Secretary. The author of the communication shall also be informed of the Commission's decision through the Secretary.

2. The State party to the Charter concerned shall, within the three (3) ensuing months, submit in writing to the Commission, explanations or statements elucidating the issue under consideration and indicating, if possible, measures it was able to take to remedy the situation.

3. All explanations or statements submitted by a State party pursuant to the present Rule shall be communicated, through the Secretary, to the author of the communication who may submit in writing additional information and observations within a time limit fixed by the Commission.

4. States parties from whom explanations or statements are sought within specified times shall be informed that if they fail to comply within those times the Commission will act on the evidence before it.

Rule 120 – Final Decision of the Communication

1. If the communication is admissible, the Commission shall consider it in the light of all the information that the individual and the State party concerned has submitted in writing; it shall make known its observations on this issue. To this end, the Commission may refer the communication to a working group, composed of three (3) of its members at most, which shall submit recommendations to it.

2. The observations of the Commission shall be communicated to the Assembly through the Secretary General and to the State party concerned.

3. The Assembly or its Chairman may request the Commission to conduct an in-depth study on these cases and to submit a factual report accompanied by its findings and recommendations, in accordance with the provisions of the Charter. The Commission may entrust this function to a Special Rapporteur or a working group.

Final Chapter – Amendment and Suspension of the Rules of Procedure

Rule 121 – Method of Amendment

Only the Commission may modify the present Rules of Procedure.

Rule 122 – Method of Suspension

The Commission may suspend temporarily, the application of any Rule of the present Rules of Procedure, on condition that such a suspension shall not be incompatible with any applicable decision of the Commission or the Assembly or with any relevant provision of the Charter and that the proposal shall have been submitted 24 hours in advance. This condition may be set aside if no member opposes it. Such a suspension may take place only with a specific and precise object in view and should be limited to the duration necessary to achieve that aim.

Deliberated and adopted by the Commission at its 18th Session held in Praia, Cape Verde.

Guidelines for National Periodic Reports

INTRODUCTION

1. It is directed by Article 62 of the African Charter on Human and Peoples' Rights (1981) that States Parties shall undertake to submit every two years reports on the legislative and other measures they have taken with a view to giving effect to the rights and freedoms recognized and guaranteed by the Charter. This direction was found necessary because, as we know, elaboration and acceptance of human rights legal instruments like the Universal Declaration of Human Rights and the African Charter on Human and Peoples' Rights, important as they are, are by themselves a mere beginning in the essential exercise of promotion, protection and restoration of human and peoples' rights; implementation of those instruments, by word and deed, is of parallel significance and is equally needed. One recalls the words of His Excellency Sir Dauda Jawara, referring to the African Charter, that the instrument should not be allowed merely to collect dust on our shelves while we sat back and did nothing about it. This message of His Excellency the President of the Gambia should establish the spirit in which these reports are to be compiled. In that the reports should show not only the achievements made on the statute book but should also lucidly reveal the extent of implementation in terms of how far the rights and fundamental freedoms of the Charter are being fulfilled and how far the duties are being successfully carried out.

2. The urgent desire of the Commission is that this system of periodic reports would create a channel for constructive dialogue between the States and itself on human and peoples' rights. The States being invited to report on the measures they have adopted and the progress made in achieving the objectives of the Charter, as well as indicating any factors and difficulties affecting the degree of fulfilment. The Commission, on the other hand, furnishing suggestions, advice and other assistance on satisfying the requirements of the Charter.

3. As a basic approach to the subject of reporting, it is suggested that the States begin with an initial general report, which would subsequently be followed by detailed periodic reports on the previous initial general report. Of course. a country with adequate resources and extensive satisfaction of all the requirements of the Charter might decide to make a voluminous, initial report showing comprehensive treatment of all the matters. The benefit from this approach is that subsequent reports may be thereby reduced in volume.

4. However, it is recommended that the initial report is, as it were, the foundation report on which the subsequent ones will be based, or it will constitute the background. In the first report the Governments would describe the basic conditions prevailing in their countries as well as the basic programmes and institutions relevant to the rights and duties covered in the Charter. For example, in nearly all the main

topics of the Charter such as the Civil and Political Rights; Economic and Social Rights; Elimination of all Forms of Discrimination Against Women; Elimination of all Forms of Racial Discrimination, etc; the initial report would begin by describing the Constitutional and other statutory provisions respecting those matters, the programmes and other measures intended to meet the concerns of the Charter. In the following periodic reports, the Governments would indicate the measures taken (if these were already reported on close reference to those previous reports would suffice), the progress made in achieving the observance of the rights and duties of the Charter, and spell out the difficulties limiting success which they encountered in their efforts. A report on the new measures such as new legislation, new administrative decisions or judicial judgements passed to uphold these rights since the submission of the initial report would also be added. This means that the subsequent periodic reports will follow the topics as discussed in the initial reports.

5. In submitting the reports, it will facilitate their consideration if copies of the principal laws. regulations, collective agreements and judicial decisions mentioned in them are also forwarded.

6. Finally, in preparing these guidelines provisions of Articles 50 and 61 of the Charter have been the lighthouse directing the course followed and determining the substance included in this document. In this regard heavy reliance has been placed on international law of human and peoples' rights, the Charter of the United Nation, and that of the Organization of African Unity, the Universal Declaration of Human Rights and other instruments of the United Nations and its Agencies accepted by African States. Purely African instruments and other written materials, which could be obtained, African practices, not all variance with international norms on human rights and other sources envisaged by the Charter have also been tapped in the preparation of this paper.

I. GENERAL GUIDELINES REGARDING THE FORM AND CONTENTS OF REPORTS FROM STATES ON CIVIL AND POLITICAL RIGHTS

1. Reporting obligations of States Parties on the rights. duties and freedoms enshrined in the Charter regarding the legislative and other measures they have adopted to give effect to them, as expressed in Article 62 of the Charter, call for preparation of periodic reports every two years from the effective date of the Charter. It is suggested that these reports be divided in A, Initial Reports; B, Periodic Reports.

Initial Reports

2. The purpose of these guidelines is to ensure that the reports are made in a uniform manner, reduce the need for the Commission requesting additional information and for it to obtain a clearer picture of the situation in each State regarding the implementation of the rights, fundamental freedoms and duties of the Charter.

3. Civil and political rights include the following: right to life; prohibition of torture and ill-treatment; prohibition of arbitrary arrest or detention; arrested or detained persons to be treated with humanity; equality before the law and entitlement to equal protection before the law; freedom from slavery, servitude and forced labour: right to a fair trial; freedom of conscience, expression and assembly; right to receive and impart information; freedom of movement and residence; right to free participation in government of the country, and to equal access to public service; no imprisonment for breach of mere contractual obligation; right to privacy; no conviction for crime which was not a crime at the time of commission and right to nondiscrimination on the basis of race, ethnic group, colour, sex, language, religion, political or any other opinion, national or social origin, fortune, birth or other status. And all the other rights and duties recognized in Articles 2 to 13 of the Charter.

4. The report should be in two parts.

(a) Part One: General

A brief description of the general legal framework within which civil and political rights are protected in the reporting State. The report should indicate:

(i) Whether the rights, fundamental freedoms and duties in paragraph 3 (Articles 2–13 of the Charter) are protected by the Constitution of the country or by a "Bill of Rights" and whether there are provisions for derogations and in what circumstances;
(ii) Whether the provisions of the Charter can be invoked before the courts, other tribunals or administrative authorities for direct enforcement or whether they have to be transformed into internal laws or regulations before they are enforceable by the authorities;
(iii) What judicial, administrative or other authorities have jurisdiction affecting human rights;
(iv) What remedies are available to an individual whose rights are violated;
(v) What other measures have been taken to implement the provisions of the Charter.

(b) Part Two

Information in relation to each of the rights, duties and fundamental freedoms mentioned in paragraph 3, Articles 2–13. Here the report should give a description of the basis of applicable Articles of the Charter:

(i) The legislative, administrative or other measures in force with regard to the rights, duties or fundamental freedoms;
(ii) Any restrictions or limitation imposed thereon;
(iii) Any factors or difficulties affecting Satisfaction thereof;
(iv) Any other information on the progress made on them.

5. Reports should be accompanied by copies of the principal legislative and other texts referred to in them. Where this is not possible the report should contain enough information to be understood in the absence of the text.

6. The intention is to develop a constructive dialogue between States and the Commission in regard to the implementation and thereby contribute to mutual understanding, friendly and peaceful relations between States.

Periodic Reports

7. The aim of these reports is to complete the information required concerning each of these rights, duties and fundamental freedoms. These reports would also be in two parts:

(a) Part One

Information concerning the general framework within which the Civil and Political rights recognized by the Charter are protected in the reporting State.

(b) Part Two

Information on each of these rights, duties and fundamental freedoms in relation to appropriate individual articles of the Charter.

8. The contents of the report should bring out the following:

(a) Completion of the information before the Commission as to the measures adopted, taking account of questions raised in the Commission on the examination of any previous report including in particular additional information as to questions not previously answered or not fully answered;
(b) Information taking into account general comments which the Commission has made and transmitted to the reporting State, which general comments may also have been sent to the Assembly of Heads of State together with copies of the reports received from States Parties;
(c) Information on changes made or proposed to be made in the laws and practices relevant to the Charter;
(d) Information on action taken as a result of experience gained in cooperation with the Commission;
(e) Information on factors affecting and difficulties experienced in the implementation of the Charter;
(f) Information on progress made since the last report of fulfilment of the Charter.

9. The aim of the exercise is to show the degree of actual satisfaction of the rights, duties, and freedoms of the Charter; the reporting obligation therefore extends to the practices of the courts and administrative organs of the State Party, and other relevant facts.

10. The report is to be sent with copies of principal legislative and other texts mentioned in it.

II. GENERAL GUIDELINES REGARDING THE FORM AND CONTENTS OF REPORTS ON ECONOMIC AND SOCIAL RIGHTS

1. As under civil and political rights it is suggested that the reports under economic and social rights should be of two types: Initial Reports and Subsequent Periodic Reports. The rights. duties and fundamental freedoms to be reported on should include the following: – the right to work, just and favourable conditions of work; right to form and belong to free and independent trade unions, right to social security and social insurance, right to protection of family; right to highest attainable standard of physical and mental health, right to education; right to compulsory primary education; right to economic development, right to equal pay for equal work; etc.

Initial Reports

2. Government should describe the basic conditions prevailing in their countries as well as the basic programmes and institutions relevant to the right dealt with. Especially in the subject of economic development, the programmes directed at economic advancement should be stressed with regard to conditions and institutions envisaged or already developed.

The Right to Work – Article 15

3. *Principal laws*, administrative regulations, collective agreements and court decisions designed to promote and safeguard the right the work.

4. *Employment*
Provide information on:

(a) The right of everyone to gain his living by work he freely chooses, with freedom from compulsion in the choice of employment and absence of discrimination in access to work;
(b) Policies and techniques to achieve steady economic and social development and full productive employment while safeguarding fundamental political and economic freedom of individuals;
(c) Measures ensuring the best possible organisation of employment market with reference to manpower planning procedures, collection and analysis of employment statistics and the organization of an employment service;
(d) Technical and vocational guidance and training programmes;
(e) Protection against arbitrary termination of employment;
(f) Protection against unemployment.

5. *Statistical and other available information*
On the level of employment and extent of unemployment and underemployment in the country; difficulties affecting the degree of realization of the right to work and progress achieved.

Right to Just and Favourable Conditions of Work – Article 15

6. *Remuneration*

(a) Principal laws, administrative regulations, collective agreements and court decisions designed to promote and safeguard the right to fair remuneration;
(b) Principal methods used for fixing wages (minimum wagefixing machinery, collective bargaining, statutory regulations, etc.) in the various sectors, and numbers of workers involved, information on the categories and numbers of workers for whom wages are not set by such methods;
(c) Information on components of workers' remuneration other than wages, such as bonuses, temporary cost of living differentials, etc.;
(d) Statistical data showing the evaluation of the levels of remuneration (covering minimum wages and average earnings in a representative sample of occupations);
(e) Provisions and methods devised to ensure respect for the right to equal pay for work of equal value, and to ensure women are guaranteed conditions of work not inferior to those of men. with equal pay for work of equal value.

7. *Safe and healthy working conditions*

(a) Principal laws, administrative regulations, collective agreements and court decisions designed to promote and safeguard the right to safe and healthy working conditions generally and in particular occupations;
(b) Principal arrangements and procedures to ensure that these provisions are effectively respected in work places, such as inspection services, at national, industrial local levels entrusted with promotion or supervision of health and safety at work;
(c) Information on any categories of workers for which these measures have not yet been fully implemented, and any progress made there;
(d) Information on the number, nature and frequency of occupational accidents and cases of occupational disease.

8. *Equal opportunity for promotion*

(a) Principal laws, administrative regulations, collective agreements and court decisions designed to further and safeguard equality of opportunity for promotion in employment;
(b) Principal arrangements and procedures to implement this right in the public and private sectors, including training programmes, placement policies, promotion procedures, career planning and the extent of the participation of the workers' representatives in such arrangements;

(c) Factors and difficulties affecting the degree of realization of this right and progress achieved.

9. *Rest, leisure, limitation of working hours, and holiday with pay*

(a) Principal laws, administrative regulations. collective agreements and court decisions designed to promote and safeguard the rights to rest, leisure, reasonable limitation of working hours, and periodic holidays with pay;
(b) Information on the position, in law and practice. in the various sectors of activity as regards:

(i) weekly rest;
(ii) normal hours of work and overtime;
(iii) holidays with pay;
(iv) remuneration for public holidays;

(c) Principal arrangements and procedures to implement these rights in the various sectors including industries and services where work is organized on a continuous basis. such as health care, the police. etc.;
(d) Factors and difficulties affecting the degree of realization of these rights and progress achieved.

Trade Union Rights

10. *Principal laws*, administrative regulations, collective agreements and court decisions designed to promote, safeguard or regulate trade union rights in their various aspects as defined in this Article.

11. *Right to form and join trade unions*

(a) An indication of the legal or other provisions governing the right to join and form the trade union of one's choice. If formal provisions exist, a description of how the right is ensured in practice;
(b) Any restrictions which are placed upon the exercise of this right, with precise details of the legal provisions prescribing such restrictions.

12. *Rights of trade unions to federate*
Legal or other provisions governing the right of trade unions to join national federations and confederations and the right of the latter to form and join international trade union organizations; if no formal provisions exist, description of how this right is ensured in practice.

13. *Right of trade unions to function freely*

(a) Conditions under which trade unions may exercise their right to function freely;
(b) Any limitations to which this right may be subject.

14. *Right to strike*
Legal or other provisions governing or affecting the exercise of the right to strike. if no formal provisions exist, description of the position in practice in regard to this right.

15. Any special restrictions imposed upon the exercise of the trade union rights mentioned above by members of the armed forces. the police or the administration of the State.

16. Factors and difficulties affecting the degree of realisation of trade union rights in their various aspects, and progress achieved in this field.

Article 16.2 – Right to Social Security

17. Principal laws, administrative regulations, collective agreements, court decisions and other types of arrangements relating to the social security system, including social insurance schemes.

18. *Main features of the schemes in force* for each of the branches of social security listed below, indicating in particular, for each branch, the percentage of the population covered, the nature and level of benefits, and the method of financing the scheme:

(a) Medical;
(b) Cash sickness benefits;
(c) Maternity benefits;
(d) Invalidity benefits;
(e) Old-age benefits;
(f) Survivors' benefits;
(g) Employment injury, benefits;
(h) Unemployment benefits;
(i) Family benefits.

19. *Factors and difficulties* affecting the degree of realization of the right to social security; progress achieved as regards, in particular. the covering of new fields of social security; the extension of existing schemes to further groups of the population and improvements in the nature or level of benefits.

Periodic Reports

20. States Parties are invited to report on the measures that they have adopted and the progress made in achieving the observance of the rights recognized and to indicate any factors and difficulties affecting the degree of fulfilment of their obligations under these Articles.

21. In the preparation of their second periodic report. States Parties are invited, in particular, to follow the same order of headings suggested in the general guidelines for the preparation of their initial report. However, information provided under each of those headings should concentrate especially on the following:

(a) Any new legislative or other measures adopted since the submission of the initial report to give effect to the rights recognized; developments regarding basic programmes and institutions which have taken place;
(h) Any changes made or proposed with regard to laws, regulations and practices affecting the exercise of the rights recognized;
(c) The extent to which effective progress has been made during the reporting period in achieving the observance of the recognized rights as a result of the enactment or modification of legislation, or as a result of collective agreements and court decisions;
(d) Factors and difficulties affecting the degree of realization of the rights recognized;
(e) Replies to questions raised and observations made in the Commission or the Assembly of Heads of State and Government;
(f) Action taken as a result of the cooperation and dialogue with the Commission on the initial report.

22. Where relevant information has previously been submitted in the initial report, it will not be necessary to reproduce this information, but a precise reference to the information so furnished, preferably with indications of the relevant documents, will suffice.

23. It will be appreciated if copies of the principal laws, regulations, collective agreements and court decisions mentioned in the second periodic report are also forwarded.

A. GUIDELINES FOR REPORTING ON ALL THE FAMILY; ADEQUATE STANDARD OF LIFE AND TO THE HIGHEST ATTAINABLE LEVEL OF HEALTH – ARTICLES 16 AND 18

Initial Reports

24. Governments are invited to report on "the measures that they have adopted and the progress made in achieving the observance of the rights recognized" in those Articles, and to indicate any "factors and difficulties affecting the degree of fulfilment of their obligations under these Articles".

25. It is suggested that, in this second series of reports, Governments should describe the basic conditions prevailing in their countries as well as the basic programmes and institutions relevant to the rights dealt with, and that they should stress the developments regarding these conditions, programmes and institutions which have taken place since the entry into force of the Charter, June 1981.

26. Where relevant information has previously been furnished, it will not be necessary to reproduce this information; a precise reference to the information so furnished, preferably with indications of the relevant documents, will suffice.

27. It will be appreciated if copies of the principal laws, regulations, collective agreements and court decisions mentioned in the reports are attached.

Protection of the Family, Mothers and Children

28. It is suggested that information concerning the protection of the family should include:

(a) The principal laws, administrative regulations and collective agreements designed to promote the protection of the family, and relevant court decisions, if any;
(b) Guarantees of the right of men and women to enter into marriage with their full and free consent and to establish a family, and measures taken to abolish such customs. ancient laws and practices as may affect the freedom of choice of a spouse;
(c) Measures to facilitate the establishment of a family, such as subsidies or installation grants, the provision of housing and other benefits;
(d) Measures aimed at maintaining, strengthening and protecting the family, such as family allowances, tax-exemption facilities, child-care institutions, etc.

29. Information on measures for maternity protection could include:

(a) The principal laws, administrative regulations and collective agreements governing the various aspects of maternity protection, and relevant court decisions, if any;
(b) Pre-natal and post-natal protection and assistance, including appropriate medical and health care and maternity and other benefits, irrespective of marital status;
(c) Special protection and assistance accorded to working mothers, including paid leave or leave with social security benefits and guarantees against dismissal during a reasonable period before and after childbirth;
(d) Specific measures, if any, in favour of working mothers who are self-employed or participating in a family enterprise, especially in agriculture or in small crafts and trades, including adequate guarantees against loss of income;
(e) Specific measures designed to help mothers to maintain their children in the case of their husband's death or absence;
(f) Special measures devised to help the aged and the disabled to protect them in keeping with their moral and physical needs.

30. Information on measures for the protection of children and young persons could include:

(a) The principal laws, administrative regulations and other measures, including collective agreements and court decisions, if any, aimed at protecting and assisting all children and young persons, in order to give them opportunities and facilities for their healthy physical and psychological development without distinction or discrimination on account of birth, parentage, social origin or other conditions;

(b) Special measures for the care and education of children separated from their mothers or deprived of a family; physically, mentally, or socially handicapped children; and delinquent minors;
(c) Measures to protect children and young persons against economic, social and all other forms of exploitation, neglect or cruelty and from being subject to trafficking;
(d) Provisions governing work by children and young persons, including minimum age for paid or unpaid employment, regulation of hours of work and rest. prohibition or restriction of night work and penalties imposed for violations of such provisions;
(e) Measures taken to prevent the employment of children and young persons in any work which would be dangerous to them. harmful to their moral or health or likely to hamper their normal physical and psychosocial development. and penalties imposed for violations of such measures;
(f) Statistical and other available data showing the number of children and young persons in the various age groups who are in fact working, and the sectors or type of work in which they are employed.

The Right to an Adequate Standard of Living

31. States are asked to provide information on general and specific measures taken to achieve an adequate standard of living and a continuous improvement of living conditions of people.

32. Information on measures concerning the right to adequate food could include:

(a) The principal laws, administrative regulations and collective agreements designed to promote the right of everyone to adequate food, and relevant court decisions, if any;
(b) Measures taken to develop or reform existing agrarian systems, in order to achieve the most efficient development and utilization of natural resources;
(c) Measures taken to improve methods of production and the quantity and quality of food produced, and to increase the yield per unit of cultivated land and to improve methods of animal husbandry, including animal health, by making full use of technical and scientific knowledge, in particular:

    (i) The promotion of agricultural research, introduction and use of appropriate material, equipment and techniques;
    (ii) Measures to disseminate knowledge on the use of such material, equipment and techniques;

(d) Measures taken to improve and disseminate knowledge regarding methods of food conservation, in particular to reduce crop and post-harvest losses and waste (e.g., through pest control and adequate food storage facilities) and to prevent degradation of resources through soil conservation and water management);

(e) Measures taken to improve food distribution. such as the improvement of communications between areas of production and food-marketing centres, the facilitation of access to markets, the introduction of price support and stabilization measures. the control of abusive practices, and the assurance of minimum supplies to needy groups;
(f) Measures taken to improve food consumption levels and nutrition, with particular reference to the most vulnerable groups of the population;
(g) Measures taken (including the adoption of food standards) to reduce food adulteration and contamination and to improve the quality and safety of food, at market and storage levels, as well as food hygiene at all levels;
(h) Measures taken to disseminate knowledge of the principles of nutrition;
(i) Participation in international cooperation efforts and projects aimed at ensuring the right of everyone to be free from hunger, in particular through an equitable distribution of world food supplies in relation to need, account being taken of the related problems of both food-importing and food-exporting countries;
(j) Statistical and other available data on the realization of the right to adequate food.

33. Information concerning the right to adequate clothing could include:

(a) The principal laws, administrative regulations and collective agreements designed to promote the right to adequate clothing;
(b) Measures taken, including specific programmes, to improve the methods of production and distribution of articles of clothing;
(c) Scientific and technical methods used to achieve an adequate supply of articles of clothing;
(d) The extent of participation in international cooperation contributing to the promotion of the right to adequate clothing.

34. Information concerning the right to housing could include:

(a) The principal laws, administrative regulations and collective agreements designed to promote the right to housing, and relevant court decisions, if any;
(b) Measures taken, including specific programmes, subsidies and tax incentives, to expand housing construction to meet the needs of all categories of the population, particularly low-income families;
(c) Information on the use of scientific and technical knowledge and of international cooperation for developing and improving housing construction, including safety measures against earthquakes, floods and other natural hazards;
(d) Measures taken or envisaged to solve the special problems of housing, water supply and sanitary conditions in rural areas;
(e) Measures taken for the protection of tenants, such as rent control and legal guarantees;
(f) Statistical and other available data on the realization of the right to housing.

The Right to Physical and Mental Health

35. It would be appreciated if information could be provided on the principal laws, administrative regulations, collective agreements and other types of arrangements designed to promote and safeguard the right of everyone to the enjoyment of the highest attainable standard of physical and mental health, and relevant court decisions, if any, should be described.

36. Information should be provided on:

(a) Measures taken to reduce the still-birth rate and infant mortality;
(b) Measures taken for the healthy development of children;
(c) Measures taken to protect and improve all aspects of environmental and industrial hygiene, to prevent air, land and water pollution, to overcome the adverse effects of urban development and industrialization, etc.;
(d) Comprehensive schemes and specific measures, including vaccination programmes to prevent, treat and control epidemic, endemic, occupational and other diseases and accidents in urban and rural areas;
(e) Comprehensive plans and specific measures to assure to all age groups and all other categories of the population, including in particular in rural areas, adequate health services including adequate medical attention in the event of sickness or accident;
(f) The main features of existing arrangements for the provision of medical care and methods of financing them.

37. Statistical and other available data are requested on the realization of the right to health, in particular, statistics on infant mortality, number of doctors per inhabitant, number of hospitals and hospital beds, etc.

Periodic Report

38. States Parties are invited to report on the *measures* that they have adopted and the progress made in achieving the observance of the rights recognized and to indicate any *factors* and *difficulties* affecting the degree of fulfilment of their obligations under these articles.

39. In the preparation of their second periodic report, States Parties are invited, in particular, to follow the same order of headings suggested in the general guidelines for the preparation of their initial reports on the implementation. However, information provided under each of those headings should concentrate especially on the following

(a) Any new legislative or other measures adopted since the submission of the initial report to give effect to the rights recognized, in particular, developments regarding basic programmes and institutions which have taken place during the present reporting period;
(b) Any changes made which had been proposed with regard to laws, regulations and practices affecting the exercise of the recognized rights;

(c) The extent to which effective progress has been made during the reporting period in achieving the observance of the recognized rights as a result of the enactment or modification of legislation, or as a result of collective agreements and court decisions;
(d) Factors and difficulties affecting the degree of realization of the rights;
(e) Replies to questions raised and observations made by the Commission;
(f) Comments on matters arising out of the consideration of reports;
(g) Action taken as a result of the cooperation and dialogue with the Commission.

40. Where relevant information has previously been submitted in the initial report or has been furnished – it will not be necessary to reproduce this information, but a precise reference to the information so furnished, preferably with indications of the relevant documents, will suffice.

41. It will be appreciated if copies of the principal laws, regulations, collective agreements and court decisions mentioned in the second periodic report are attached.

B. GUIDELINES FOR REPORTING ON ALL THE RIGHTS TO EDUCATION; TO COMPULSORY PRIMARY EDUCATION

Initial Reports

42. Governments are invited to report on the measures which they have adopted and the progress made in achieving the observance of the recognized rights and to indicate any factors and difficulties affecting the degree of fulfilment of obligations.

43. It is suggested that in this third series of reports, Governments should describe the basic conditions prevailing in their countries as well as the basic programmes and institutions relevant to the rights dealt with, and that they should stress the developments regarding these conditions, programmes and institutions which have taken place since the entry into force of the Charter in June 1981.

44. It will not be necessary to reproduce this information, but a precise reference to the information so furnished, preferably with indications of the relevant documents, will suffice.

45. It will be appreciated if copies of the principal laws, regulations, collective agreements and court decisions mentioned in the reports are attached.

Article 17.1 – Right to Education

46. Principal laws, administrative regulations, collective agreements, and other arrangements, court decisions and other arrangements relevant to the right of everyone to education in its various aspects.

47. Measures taken to promote the full realization of the right of everyone to education with a view of achieving:

(a) The full development of the human personality and the sense of its dignity;
(b) The strengthening of respect for human rights and fundamental freedoms;
(c) The development of human rights teaching;
(d) The effective participation of all persons in a free society;
(e) The promotion of understanding, tolerance and friendship among all nations and all racial, ethnic or religious groups.

48. *Right to primary education*

(a) Measures taken to achieve the full realization of the right of everyone to receive compulsory and free primary education, including special provisions relating to specific groups such as young girls, children of low-income groups, children in rural areas, children who are physically or mentally disabled, children of immigrants and of migrant workers, children belonging to linguistic, racial, religious or other minorities, and children belonging to indigenous sectors of the population, where applicable;
(b) Percentage of children covered by primary education;
(c) Extent to which primary education is free;
(d) Factors and difficulties affecting the degree of realization of this right and progress achieved.

49. *Right to secondary education*

(a) Measures aimed at making secondary education in its different forms generally available and accessible to everyone;
(b) Measures aimed at making technical and vocational secondary education generally available and accessible to everyone;
(c) Plans and legal provisions adopted or proposed in order to achieve the progressive introduction of free secondary education for all with reference to problems encountered therein;
(d) Factors and difficulties affecting the degree of realization of this right.

50. *Right to higher education*

(a) General and specific measures taken to make higher education equally accessible to all, on the basis of capacity;
(b) Practical steps taken to provide financial and other assistance to students in higher education, introduction of free higher education;
(c) Factors and difficulties related to making higher education equally accessible to all, including, in particular, problems of discrimination.

51. *Right to fundamental education*

(a) General and specific measures taken to encourage and intensify fundamental education for persons who have not received or completed the whole period of their primary education – for example, details of adult literacy programmes;
(b) Factors and difficulties affecting the implementation of this right, including information on specific and disadvantaged groups, particularly in rural areas, for which appropriate measures have not yet been fully implemented;

(c) Statistical data showing the evolution in the realization of the right to fundamental education.

52. *Development of a system of schools*

(a) Principal laws, administrative regulations and collective agreements designed to promote the development of a system of schools at all levels;
(b) Comprehensive schemes and practical measures taken to develop a system of schools, such as the provision of finance, the building of schools and the provision of educational material;
(c) Statistical and other comparative data relating to the development of a system of schools at all levels;
(d) Factors involved and difficulties encountered.

53. *Establishment of an adequate fellowship system*

(a) Principal laws, administrative regulations and collective agreements designed to establish an adequate fellowship system for all types of education;
(b) Measures taken or proposed. including reference to programmes of affirmative action designed to overcome obstacles such as all forms of discrimination or poverty;
(c) Factors involved and difficulties encountered.

54. *Improvement of the material conditions of teaching staff*

(a) Principal laws, administrative regulations and collective agreements and other types of arrangements designed to continuously improve the material conditions of teaching staff;
(b) Measures adopted in the public and private sectors, including those relating to working conditions, salaries, social security, career possibilities and continuing education for teaching staff;
(c) Extent to which teachers and their organizations are able to participate in the formulation of educational plans, both national and in the educational establishment in which they are employed, and preparation of curricula and teaching materials;
(d) Factors and difficulties affecting improvement of the material conditions of teaching staff.

55. *Right to choice of school*

(a) Principal laws, administrative regulations, collective agreements and court decisions relating to the promotion of the right of parents and legal guardians to choose for their children schools other than those established by the public authorities;
(b) Measures taken or proposed in order to promote the right of parents to ensure the religious and moral education of their children in conformity with their own convictions;

(c) Measures taken or proposed in order to promote respect for this right, including the opportunity to attend a school where teaching is in the native language;
(d) Factors and difficulties affecting the degree of realization of this right.

56. *Liberty to establish and direct educational institutions*

(a) Principal laws, administrative regulations and collective agreements designed to prevent interference with the liberty of individuals and bodies to establish and direct educational institutions;
(b) Practical measures designed to prevent interference with this liberty.

Principle of Compulsory Education, Free of Charge for All

57. Principal laws, administrative regulations and other decisions designed to secure in the territories under the jurisdiction of the reporting State, the principle of compulsory primary education, free of charge for all.

58. Details of the plan of action, general and specific measures and stages adopted for the progressive implementation of the principle of compulsory education free of charge for all.

59. Factors and difficulties affecting the promotion of this principle.

III. GENERAL GUIDELINES REGARDING THE FORM AND CONTENTS OF REPORTS TO BE SUBMITTED ON THE PEOPLES' RIGHTS ARTICLES 19 TO 24 OF THE CHARTER

1. Reporting on these rights should have the same form as that on economic and social rights or that on civil and political rights.

Article 19 – All Peoples shall be Equal

Initial Reports

2. To state the constitutional and statutory framework which seek to protect the different sections of national community. Any administrative regulations with the same intention as well as judicial decisions intended to establish the same rights.

Precautions taken to proscribe any tendencies of some people dominating another as feared by the Article.

Periodic Reports

3. Information on the progress made since the submission of the initial report and further development on legislative and other measures undertaken in continuing the improvements initiated in the earlier report.

Article 20 – Right to Self-Determination

Initial Report

4. Information on legislative and administrative machinery that exists to give effect to the provisions of the Article namely that:

(i) All communities are allowed full participation in political activities and are allowed equal opportunities in the economic activities of the country both of which should be according to the choices they have made independently;
(ii) Provide information on any form of assistance rendered to dominated people, in their liberation struggle against foreign domination be it political, economic or cultural;
(iii) Information on assistance in any form given to colonized or oppressed peoples to help them free themselves.

Periodic Reports

5. Information on the development in the efforts envisaged in the Article.

Articles 21 and 22 – All Peoples shall Freely Dispose of their Wealth or National Resources – Rights to Development

6. These rights consist in ensuring that the material wealth of the countries are not exploited by aliens to no or little benefit to the African countries. Establishment of machinery which would monitor the exploitation of natural resources by foreign companies and strictly contrasted to the economic and material benefit accruing to the country. Cooperation with the Organization of African Unity and the appropriate United Nations Agencies on the viability and profitability of ventures for exploitation of natural resources proposed by foreign companies. Insistence on adequate taxation on all income derived by foreign companies in the reporting State. Adherence to compensatory ideas like payment of mineral royalty, etc., in addition to taxation. Cooperation with other African States in removing economic exploitation of African countries by international monopolies. Measures taken to encourage national entrepreneurship, either in the private or public sector, including such matters as provision of facilities for loan capital for industrial utilization of local natural resources and wealth.

Initial Report

7. Report on the basic legal framework to safeguard the country against international exploitation.

Periodic Reports

8. Progress report on the development since the initial report.

Article 23 – Peoples' Right to National and International Peace and Security

9. To work for international and national peace and security in accordance with the principles of solidarity and friendly relations affirmed by the organization of African Unity Charter and that of the United Nations.

10. Information on statutory and administrative measures designed to restrain refugees allowed into the country under Article 12 from engaging in subversive activities against their country of origin or any other State Party to this Charter. Prohibition of subversive or terrorist activities against other States Parties to this Charter being organized or launched from their territories.

Article 24 – Peoples' Right to Satisfactory Environment

11. The main purpose here is to protect the environment and keep it favourable for development. Establish a system to monitor effective disposal of waste in order to prevent pollution. As a nation and in cooperation with other African States to prohibit and penalise disposal of waste on the African soil by any company.

Initial Report

12. The principal legislation and other measures taken to fulfil the intentions of the Article regarding prohibition of pollution and efforts to prevent international dumping of toxic wastes or other wastes from industrialized countries. Scientific and efficient methods utilized for effective disposal of locally produced wastes.

Periodic Report

13. Continuation of development to curb wastes and removal of pollution on land, in water and in the air.

Article 17.2 – Right to Take Part in Cultural Life and to Enjoy the Benefits of Scientific Progress and the Protection of the Interests of Authors

14. Right to take part in cultural life.

(a) Principal laws, administrative regulations, collective agreements and court decisions relating to the right of everyone to take part in cultural life, including those aimed at the conservation, development and diffusion of culture;

(b) Practical measures for realization of this right, including:

(i) Information on the availability of funds for the promotion of cultural development and popular participation in cultural life. including information on public support for private initiative;
(ii) A description of the institutional infrastructure established for the implementation of policies to promote popular participation in culture, such as cultural centres. museums. libraries, theatres and cinemas;
(iii) Overall policy and specific measures aimed at the promotion of cultural identity as a factor of mutual appreciation among individuals, groups, nations and regions;
(iv) An indication of measures and programmes aimed at promoting awareness and enjoyment of the cultural heritage of national ethnic groups and minorities and of indigenous sectors of the population;
(v) A description of the role of mass media and communications media in promoting participation in cultural life;
(vi) Overall policy and specific measures aimed at the preservation and presentation of mankind's cultural heritage;
(vii) Legislation protecting the freedom of artistic creation and performance, including the freedom to disseminate the results of such activities, as well as an indication of any restrictions or limitations imposed on this freedom;
(viii) Information on professional education in the field of culture and art;
(ix) Any other measures taken for the conservation, development and diffusion of culture.

(c) Factors involved and difficulties encountered.

15. *Right to enjoy the benefits of scientific progress and its applications*

(a) Principal laws, administrative regulations, collective agreements and court decisions relevant to the promotion of the right of everyone to enjoy the benefits of scientific progress and its applications, including those aimed at the conservation, development and diffusion of science;
(b) Measures taken to ensure the application of scientific progress for the benefit of everyone, including measures to promote a healthy and pure environment and information on the institutional infrastructures established for that purpose;
(c) An indication of measures taken to promote the diffusion of information on scientific progress;
(d) Measures taken to prevent the use of scientific and technical progress for purposes which are contrary to the enjoyment of all human rights, including the rights to life, health, personal freedom, privacy and the like;
(e) Any restrictions which are placed upon the exercise of this right, with details of the legal provisions prescribing such restrictions.

16. *Protection of moral and material interests of authors*

(a) Principal laws, administrative regulations, collective and other agreements and court decisions relevant to the right of everyone to benefit from the protection of moral and material interests resulting from any scientific, literary, or artistic work of which he or she is the author;
(b) Information on the practical measures aimed at the full implementation of this right, including provision of the necessary conditions for scientific, literary and artistic activities, and the protection of intellectual property rights resulting from such activities;
(c) Difficulties affecting the degree of realization of this right.

17. *Steps taken for the conservation, development and diffusion of science and culture*

(a) Principal laws, administrative regulations, collective agreements and court decisions designed to conserve, develop and diffuse science and culture at the constitutional level, within the national educational system and by means of the communications media;
(b) Information on all other practical steps taken to promote such conservation, development and diffusion.

18. *Right to the freedom of scientific research and creative activity*

(a) Principal laws, administrative regulations, collective agreements and other types of arrangements designed to promote the right of everyone to the freedom indispensable for scientific research and creative activity;
(b) Information on measures designed to promote enjoyment of this right including promotion of all necessary conditions and facilities for scientific research and creative activity;
(c) Measures taken to guarantee the free exchange of scientific, technical and cultural information, views and experience between scientists, writers, creative workers, artists and other creative activists;
(d) Factors involved and difficulties encountered.

19. *Encouragement and development of international contacts and cooperation in the scientific and cultural fields*

(a) Principal laws, administrative regulations and collective agreements designed to encourage and develop international contacts and cooperation in the scientific and cultural fields;
(b) Information on measures taken for:

   (i) The fullest utilization, by all the States concerned, of the facilities afforded by their adherence to regional and international conventions, agreements and other instruments in the scientific and cultural fields;
   (ii) Participation by scientists. writers, artists and others involved in scientific research or creative activity, in international scientific and cultural conferences, seminars. symposiums. etc.;

(c) Factors and difficulties affecting the development of international cooperation in the scientific and cultural fields.

IV. GENERAL GUIDELINES REGARDING THE FORM AND CONTENTS OF REPORTS TO BE SUBMITTED ON SPECIFIC DUTIES UNDER THE CHARTER

1. These reports are to be submitted on the specific duties expressed in the Charter. These duties are either for States Parties or for individual persons in these countries. The format of these reports should be the same as on rights, namely they should consist of Initial Reports and Periodic Reports.

Specific Duties on States

Article 25 – Duty to Promote Awareness of the Charter

2. This Article requires the States to take measures which will bring awareness of the provisions of the Charter to their people. It envisages organization of seminars and studies on the activities of the Organization of African Unity in the area of human and peoples' rights; promotion and encouragement of observance of the rights and duties recognized in the Charter; report on what steps your country has taken in this area.

Article 26 – Duty to Guarantee the Independence of the Courts

3. The Article requires the States to take steps to guarantee the independence of the judiciary with regard to the following:

(a) Establishment of a legal educational system designed to protect human and peoples' rights and respect for the rule of law;
(b) A legal educational system directed at training independently-minded lawyers;
(c) Appointment of judges to be based purely on merit and qualifications;
(d) Judges to be assured tenure of office and not to be lightly removed save for misconduct after a recommendation by a special commission appointed for the purpose of investigating the misconduct;
(e) Encourage formation of institutions charged with the responsibility to promote and protect rights guaranteed by the Charter.

Specific Duties for Everyone

Article 27

4. Every individual shall have duties towards other people, society, family and the international community. The personal rights shall be enjoyed subject to the rights and fundamental freedoms of others. Personal and private rights shall not be selfishly

insisted upon at the expense of family, society, state, other legally recognized communities' and international community's interests. Individual rights are to be enjoyed with due regard to the rights of others, collective security, morality and common interest. Activities in curbing personal and private interests for the benefit of the interests protected by the Article.

Article 28

5. Everyone shall abstain from discrimination against fellow human beings and shall maintain relations conducive to promoting, safeguarding and reinforcing mutual respect and tolerance.

Article 29

6. Every individual shall observe the duties enunciated in the Article. A full report on each of the duties should be provided.

Initial Report

7. On each of these duties the reporting State should furnish the principal statutes and administrative regulations and, where applicable, courts' decisions establishing the atmosphere for enforcement and effectuation of these duties.

Periodic Reports

8. Some of these valuable traditional duties might have been treated lightly in some African countries because of the overwhelming Western influence in the past colonial days; it might therefore become necessary to establish programmes for carrying out these duties. The Commission would expect periodic reports on the progress on these programmes.

V. GENERAL GUIDELINES CONCERNING THE FORM AND CONTENTS OF REPORTS BY STATES PARTIES ON THE ELIMINATION OF ALL FORMS OF RACIAL DISCRIMINATION

1. Although there is no specific or direct prohibition of racial discrimination, as such, in the Charter except as mentioned in Articles 2, 19 and generally elsewhere in the Charter, the general tone of the Charter abhors racial discrimination. Further, Africa, for so long the victim of racial discrimination, would expect the Commission and the States Parties to the Charter to work for elimination of all forms of racial discrimination. It was therefore decided that the subject of racial discrimination should be included as a subject for periodic reports in full recognition of the Charter of the Organization of African Unity commitment to elimination of racial discrimination.

2. The same basic approach to the subject in preparing reports on other topics is equally applicable to the one on racial discrimination; the International Convention on the Elimination of All Forms of Racial Discrimination is here used as the basis for preparing these guidelines.

3. In selecting information for inclusion in their reports, States Parties should bear in mind the definition of the term "racial discrimination" as reflected in Article 1, paragraph 1, of the Convention, as well as the provisions of Article 1, paragraphs 2, 3 and 4, which refer to situations not considered as racial discrimination.

4. The report should also reflect in all its parts the actual situation as regards the practical implementation of the provisions of the Convention and the progress achieved.

5. The report should be presented in two parts. as follows:

A. Part One – General

6. This part should:

(a) Describe briefly the policy of eliminating racial discrimination in all its forms and the general legal framework within which racial discrimination as defined in Article 1, paragraph 1, of the Convention is prohibited and eliminated in the reporting State, and the recognition, enjoyment of exercise, on an equal footing, of human rights and fundamental freedoms in the political, economic, social, cultural or any other field of public life are promoted and protected;

(b) Indicate whether the provisions of the Convention can be invoked before, and directly enforced by, the courts, other tribunals or administrative authorities or whether they have to be implemented by way of internal laws or administrative regulations in order to be enforced by the authorities concerned.

B. Part Two – Information in Relation to Articles 2 to 7 of the Convention

7. This part should provide specific information in relation to Articles 2 to 7, in accordance with the sequence of those articles and their respective provisions.

8. The Commission requests States Parties to incorporate in this part, under the appropriate headings, the texts of the relevant laws, judicial decisions and regulations referred to therein as well as all other elements which they consider essential for the Commission's consideration of their reports.

9. The information should be arranged as follows:

Article 2

(a) Information on the legislative, judicial, administrative or other measures which give effect to the provisions of Article 2, paragraph 1, of the Convention, in particular:

(i) Measures taken to give effect to the undertaking to engage in no act or practice of racial discrimination against persons, groups of persons or institutions and to ensure that all public authorities and public institutions, national and local, shall act in conformity with this obligation;

(ii) Measures taken to give effect to the undertaking not to sponsor, defend or support racial discrimination by any persons or organizations.

10. The States Parties should provide information on which of the suggested steps they have taken, such as:

(i) To declare illegal and prohibit organizations. and also organized and all other propaganda activities, which promote and incite racial discrimination, and to recognize participation in such organizations or activities as an offence punishable by law;

(ii) Not to permit public authorities or public institutions, national or local, to promote or incite racial discrimination;

(b) Information on appropriate measures taken to give effect to General Recommendation that the States Parties whose legislation was deficient in respect of the implementation of Article 4 should consider, in accordance with their national legislative procedures, the question of supplementing their legislation with provisions conforming to the requirement of Article 4(a) and (b) of the Convention;

(c) States are requested:

(i) To indicate what specific penal internal legislation designed to implement the provisions of Article 4(a) and (b) has been enacted in their respective countries and to transmit to the Commission in one of the official languages the texts concerned, as well as such provisions of general penal law as must be taken into account when applying such specific legislation specific

(ii) Where no such legislation has been enacted, to inform the Commission of the manner and the extent to which the provisions of the existing penal laws, as applied by the courts, effectively implement their obligations under Article 4(a) and (b), and to transmit to it in one of the official languages the texts of those provisions.

Article 5

11. Information on the legislative, judicial, administrative or other measures which give effect to the provisions of Article 5 of the Convention; in particular, measures taken to prohibit racial discrimination in all its forms and to guarantee the right of everyone, without distinction as to race, colour, or national or ethnic origin, to equality before the law notably in the enjoyment of:

(i) The right to equal treatment before tribunals and all other organs administering justice;

(ii) The right to security of person and protection by the State against violence or bodily harm, whether inflicted by government officials or by any individual, group or institution;

(iii) Political rights, in particular the right to participate in elections – to vote and to stand for election – on the basis of universal and equal suffrage, to take part in the Government as well as in the conduct of public affairs at any level and to have equal access to public service;

(iv) Other civil rights, in particular those enumerated under Article 5(d)(i) to (ix), of the Convention;

(v) Economic, social and cultural rights, in particular those enumerated under Article 5(r)(i) to (vi) of the Convention;

(vi) The right of access to any place or service intended for use by the general public, such as transport, hotels, restaurants, cafes, theatres and parks;

(a) Information on the legislative, judicial, administrative or other measures which give effect to to the provisions of Article 6 of the Convention, in particular, measures taken to assure to everyone within the jurisdiction of the reporting State effective protection and remedies, through the competent national tribunals and other State institutions, against any acts of racial discrimination which violate his human rights and fundamental freedoms;

(b) Measures taken to assure to everyone the right to seek from such tribunals just and adequate reparation or satisfaction for any damage as a result of such discrimination;

(c) Information on the practice and decisions of the courts and other judicial and administrative organs relating to cases of racial discrimination as defined under Article I of the Convention.

Article 7

12. Information on the legislative, judicial, administrative or other measures which give effect to the provisions of Article 7 of the Convention.

13. In particular, the reports should provide as much information as possible on each of the main subjects mentioned in Article 7 under the following separate headings:

Education and teaching,

Culture, *Information*;

within these broad parameters, the information provided should reflect the measures taken by the States Parties:

(i) to combat prejudices which lead to racial discrimination:

(ii) to promote understanding, tolerance and friendship among nations and ethnic groups.

Education and teaching

14. This part should describe legislative and administrative measures, including some general information on the educational system, taken in the field of education and teaching to combat racial prejudices which lead to racial discrimination.

15. It should indicate whether any steps have been taken to include in school curricula and in the training of teachers and other professionals, programmes and subjects to help promote human rights issues which would lead to better understanding, tolerance and friendship among nations and racial or ethnic groups.

16. It should also provide information on whether the purposes and principles of the Charter of the United Nations and that of the Organization of African Unity, the Universal Declaration of Human Rights, the United Nations Declaration on the Elimination of All Forms of Racial Discrimination and International Convention on the Elimination of All Forms of Racial Discrimination are included in education and teaching.

Culture

17. Information should be provided in this part of the report on the role of institutions or associations working to develop national culture and traditions, to combat racial prejudices and to promote intranational and intracultural understanding, tolerance and friendship among nations and racial or ethnic groups,

18. Information should also be included on the work of solidarity committees or United Nations Associations and the Organization of African Unity activities to combat racism and racial discrimination, and on the observance by States Parties of Human Rights Days or Campaigns against racism and Apartheid.

Information

19. This part should provide information:

(a) On the role of State media in the dissemination of information to combat racial prejudices which lead to racial discrimination. and to inculcate better understanding of the purposes and principles of the above-mentioned instruments;
(b) On the role of the mass information media, i.e. the press, radio and television, in the publicizing of human rights and disseminating of information on the purposes and principles of the above-mentioned human rights instruments.

20. If needed, the reports should be accompanied by sufficient copies in one of the working languages (English, French, Arabic or Portuguese) of all other supplementary documentation which the reporting States may wish to have distributed to all members of the Commission in connection with their reports.

VI. GENERAL GUIDELINES REGARDING THE FORM AND CONTENTS OF REPORTS TO BE SUBMITTED BY STATES PARTIES ON THE SUPPRESSION AND PUNISHMENT OF THE CRIME OF APARTHEID

1. Under Article VII of the International Convention on the Suppression and Punishment of the Crime of Apartheid, the States Parties to the Convention undertake "to submit periodic reports to the Group established under Article IX on the legislative, judicial, administrative or other measures that they have adopted and that give effect to the provisions of the Convention". The system of Apartheid is such an obnoxious institution to Africa that the Commission decided that it would welcome periodic reports on the efforts to eliminate the system.

2. The Commission suggests that reports be submitted on these lines:

(a) Information on the legislative, judicial, administrative or other measures that have been adopted and that give effect to the following provisions of the Convention:

(i) That Apartheid is a crime against humanity and that inhuman acts resulting from the policies and practices of Apartheid and similar policies and practices of racial segregation and discrimination as in Article II of the Convention, are crimes violating the principles of international law, in particular the purposes and principles of the Charters of the United Nations and the Organization of African Unity, and constituting a serious threat to international peace and security;

(ii) That organizations, institutions and individuals committing the crime of Apartheid are considered criminal;

(b) Information on the legislative, judicial, administrative or other measures that have been adopted and give effect to the following provisions of the Convention:

(i) The undertaking as required under Article IV(b) of the Convention, to adopt legislative, judicial and administrative measures to prosecute, bring to trial and punish in accordance with their jurisdiction persons responsible for, or accused of, the acts defined in Article II of the Convention, whether or not such persons reside in the territory of the State in which the acts are committed or are nationals of that State or of some other State or are stateless persons;

(ii) Article III of the Convention, that international criminal responsibility shall be applied, irrespective of the motive involved, to individuals, members of organizations and institutions and representatives of the State, whether residing in the territory of the State in which acts are perpetrated or in some other State, whenever they (1) commit, participate in, directly incite or conspire in the commission of the acts mentioned in Article II of the Convention; (2) directly abet, encourage or co-operate in the commission of the crime of Apartheid;

(iii) The undertaking, as provided for under Article XI of the Convention, to grant extradition in accordance with their legislation and with the treaties in force, in cases enumerated in Article II of the Convention;

(c) Information on the legislative, judicial, administrative or other measures that have been adopted:

(i) To undertake, as required under Article IV(a) of the Convention, to adopt any legislative or other measures necessary to suppress as well as to prevent any encouragement of the crime of Apartheid and similar segregationist and discriminatory policies or their manifestations and to punish persons guilty of that crime;

(ii) To acquaint the public as widely as possible with the evils of Apartheid and the text of the Convention using all the information and other media at their disposal;

(d) Information on the legislative, judicial, administrative or other measures that have been adopted and that give effect to the undertaking, as required under Article VI of the Convention. to accept and carry out in accordance with the Charter of the United Nations the decisions taken by the Security Council aimed at the prevention, suppression and punishment of the crime of Apartheid, and to co-operate in the implementation of decisions adopted by other competent organs of the United Nations with a view to achieving the purposes of the Convention, similarly to likewise carry out the decisions of the Assembly of Heads of State on the painful subject of Apartheid;

(e) States Parties should endeavour where possible to identify in their periodic reports individuals, organizations, institutions and representatives of States which are alleged to be responsible for the crimes enumerated in Article II of the Convention, as well as those against whom legal proceedings have been undertaken by the State Party to the Convention;

(f) The reports should contain, as appropriate, decisions of the courts or the competent tribunal of the State party relating to cases falling within the scope of Article 11 of the Convention, as provided for under Article V of the Convention. as well as information relating to cases of extradition in accordance with Article XI of the Convention.

VII. GENERAL GUIDELINES REGARDING THE FORM AND CONTENTS OF REPORTS RECEIVED FROM STATES PARTIES ON THE ELIMINATION OF ALL FORMS OF DISCRIMINATION AGAINST WOMEN

1. Under Article 18 of the Convention on the Elimination of All Forms of Discrimination against Women, each State Party has undertaken to submit a report on the legislative, judicial, administrative or other measures which it has adopted to give effect to the provisions of the Convention and on the progress made in this respect within one year after the entry into force of the Convention for the reporting State and thereafter at least every four years and further whenever the Committee on the Elimination of Discrimination against Women established under the Convention so requests.

2. Discrimination against women in Africa is of such widespread occurrence that the Commission would also like to receive reports on measures to eliminate this anachronism.

3. The report should be in two parts. Part One should describe:

(a) As concisely as possible the actual, general, social, economic, political and legal framework within which a State Party approaches the elimination of discrimination against women in all its forms, as defined in the Convention;
(b) Any legal and other measures adopted to implement the Convention or their absence as well as any effects which ratification of the Convention has had on the State Party's actual, general, social, economic, political and legal framework since entry into force of the Convention for the reporting State;
(c) Whether there are any institutions or authorities which have as their task to ensure that the principle of equality between men and women is complied with in practice, and what remedies are available to women who have suffered discrimination;
(d) The means used to promote and ensure the full development and advancement of women for the purpose of guaranteeing them the exercise and enjoyment of human rights and fundamental freedoms in all fields on a basis of equality with men;
(e) Whether the provisions of the Convention can be invoked before, and directly enforced by, the courts, other tribunals or administrative authorities or whether the provisions of the Convention have to be implemented by way of internal laws or administrative regulations in order to be enforced by the authorities concerned.

4. Part Two should provide specific information in relation to each provision of the Convention:

(a) The constitutional, legislative and administrative provisions or other measures in force;
(b) The developments that have taken place and the programmes and institutions that have been established since the entry into force of the Convention;
(c) Any restrictions or limitations, even of a temporary nature, imposed by law or practice or in any other manner on the enjoyment of each right;
(d) Any other factors or difficulties affecting the exercise and enjoyment of each right;
(e) Any other information on progress made in the fulfilment of each right.

5. It is recommended that the reports should not be confined to mere lists of legal instruments adopted in the country concerned in recent years but should also include information indicating how these legal instruments are reflected in the actual, economic, political and social realities and general conditions existing in their countries. Data concerning these realities and conditions should also be supplied with a breakdown of the statistics on the category of sex.

6. States Parties are invited to submit copies of the principal legislative, judicial, administrative and other texts referred to in the report so that these can be made available to the Commission. It is desirable therefore that. when a text is not actually quoted in or annexed to the report itself, the report should contain sufficient information to be understood without the actual reference.

7. The reports should reveal obstacles to the participation of women on an equal basis with men in the political, social, economic and cultural life of their countries, and give information on types and frequencies of cases of non-compliance with the principle of equal rights.

8. The reports should also pay due attention to the role of women and their full participation in the solution of problems and issues which are referred to in the preamble and which are not covered by the Articles of the Convention.

9. The reports and the supplementary documentation should be submitted in one of the working languages of the Commission (Arabic, English, French, Portuguese) in as concise a form as possible.

Amendment of the General Guidelines for the Preparation of Periodic Reports by States Parties

Twenty-third Ordinary Session
Banjul, The Gambia, 20–29 April 1998
DOC/OS/27 (XXIII)

GUIDELINES TO PERIODIC REPORTING UNDER ARTICLE 62 OF THE AFRICAN CHARTER ON HUMAN AND PEOPLES' RIGHTS BY U. O. UMOZURIKE

It was realized that the present guidelines to periodic reporting are too lengthy and probably serve as a disincentive to the object – encouraging states to report on their human rights conditions.

Two seminars were organised to discuss the guidelines – one in English organised in Harare and the other in French organised in Tunis. The Summary given below takes account of the conclusions of the two Seminars.

1. An initial report (the first report) should contain a brief history of the state, its form of government, the legal system and the relationship between the arms of government.

2. The initial report should also include the basic documents – the constitution, the criminal code and procedure and landmark decisions on human rights.

3. The major human rights instruments to which the state is a party and the steps taken to internalize them.

4. How is the party implementing the following rights protected by the charter:

(a) Civil and political rights;
(b) Economic, social and cultural rights;
(c) Group rights?

5. What is the state doing to improve the condition of the following groups mentioned in the Charter:

(a) Women
(b) Children
(c) Disabled?

6. What steps are being taken to protect the family and encourage its cohesion?

7. What is being done to ensure that individual duties are observed?

8. What are the problems encountered in implementing the Charter having regard to the political, economic or social circumstances of the state?

9. How is the state carrying out its obligations under Article 25 of the Charter – on human rights education?

10. How is the state, as an interested party, using the Charter in its international relations, particularly in ensuring respect for it?

11. Any other information relevant to the implementation and promotion of the Charter.

Protocol to the African Charter on Human and Peoples' Rights on the Establishment of an African Court on Human and Peoples' Rights

OAU/LEG/MIN/AFCHPR/PROT (I) Rev. 2
Adopted June 1998

The Member States of the Organization of African Unity hereinafter referred to as the "OAU", States Parties to the African Charter on Human and Peoples' Rights,

Considering that the Charter of the Organization of African Unity recognizes that freedom, equality, justice, peace and dignity are essential objectives for the achievement of the legitimate aspirations of the African peoples,

Noting that the African Charter on Human and Peoples' Rights reaffirms adherence to the principles of human and peoples' rights, freedoms and duties contained in the declarations, conventions and other instruments adopted by the Organization of African Unity, and other international organizations,

Recognizing that the twofold objective of the African Charter on Human and Peoples' Rights is to ensure on the one hand promotion and on the other protection of human and peoples' rights, freedoms and duties,

Recognizing further, the efforts of the African Commission on Human and Peoples' Rights in the promotion and protection of human and peoples' rights since its inception in 1987,

Recalling Resolution AHG/Res. 230 (XXX) adopted by the Assembly of Heads of State and Government in June 1994 in Tunis, Tunisia, requesting the Secretary-General to convene a Government experts' meeting to ponder, in conjunction with the African Commission, over the means to enhance the efficiency of the African Commission and to consider in particular the establishment of an African Court on Human and Peoples' Rights,

Noting the first and second Government legal experts' meetings held respectively in Cape Town, South Africa (September 1995) and Nouakchott, Mauritania (April 1997), and the third Government legal experts' meeting held in Addis Ababa, Ethiopia (December 1997), which was enlarged to include diplomats,

Firmly convinced that the attainment of the objectives of the African Charter on Human and Peoples' Rights requires the establishment of an African Court on Human and Peoples' Rights to complement and reinforce the functions of the African Commission on Human and Peoples' Rights,

HAVE AGREED AS FOLLOWS:

Article 1 – Establishment of the Court

There shall be established within the Organization of African Unity an African Court on Human and Peoples' Rights hereinafter referred to as "the Court", the organization, jurisdiction and functioning of which shall be governed by the present Protocol.

Article 2 – Relationship between the Court and the Commission

The Court shall, bearing in mind the provisions of this Protocol, complement the protective mandate of the African Commission on Human and Peoples' Rights hereinafter referred to as "the Commission", conferred upon it by the African Charter on Human and Peoples' Rights, hereinafter referred to as "the Charter".

Article 3 – Jurisdiction

1. The jurisdiction of the Court shall extend to all cases and disputes submitted to it concerning the interpretation and application of the Charter, this Protocol and any other relevant human rights instrument ratified by the States concerned.

2. In the event of a dispute as to whether the Court has jurisdiction, the Court shall decide.

Article 4 – Advisory Opinions

1. At the request of a Member State of the OAU, the OAU, any of its organs, or any African organization recognized by the OAU, the Court may provide an opinion on any legal matter relating to the Charter or any other relevant human rights instruments, provided that the subject matter of the opinion is not related to a matter being examined by the Commission.

2. The Court shall give reasons for its advisory opinions provided that every judge shall be entitled to deliver a separate or dissenting opinion.

Article 5 – Access to the Court

1. The following are entitled to submit cases to the Court

(a) The Commission;
(b) The State Party which has lodged a complaint to the Commission;
(c) The State Party against which the complaint has been lodged at the Commission;
(d) The State Party whose citizen is a victim of human rights violation;
(e) African Intergovernmental Organization.

2. When a State Party has an interest in a case, it may submit a request to the Court to be permitted to join.

3. The Court may entitle relevant Non-Governmental Organizations (NGOs) with observer status before the Commission, and individuals to institute cases directly before it, in accordance with Article 34(6) of this Protocol.

Article 6 – Admissibility of Cases

1. The Court, when deciding on the admissibility of a case instituted under Article 5(3) of this Protocol, may request the opinion of the Commission which shall give it as soon as possible.
2. The Court shall rule on the admissibility of cases taking into account the provisions of Article 56 of the Charter.
3. The Court may consider cases or transfer them to the Commission.

Article 7 – Sources of Law

The Court shall apply the provisions of the Charter and any other relevant human rights instruments ratified by the States concerned.

Article 8 – Consideration of Cases

The Rules of Procedure of the Court shall lay down the detailed conditions under which the Court shall consider cases brought before it, bearing in mind the complementarity between the Commission and the Court.

Article 9 – Amicable Settlement

The Court may try to reach an amicable settlement in a case pending before it in accordance with the provisions of the Charter.

Article 10 – Hearings and Representation

1. The Court shall conduct its proceedings in public. The Court may, however, conduct proceedings in camera as may be provided for in the Rules of Procedure.
2. Any party to a case shall be entitled to be represented by a legal representative of the party's choice. Free legal representation may be provided where the interests of justice so require.
3. Any person, witness or representative of the parties, who appears before the Court, shall enjoy protection and all facilities, in accordance with international law, necessary for the discharging of their functions, tasks and duties in relation to the Court.

Article 11 – Composition

1. The Court shall consist of eleven judges, nationals of Member States of the OAU, elected in an individual capacity from among jurists of high moral character

and of recognized practical, judicial or academic competence and experience in the field of human and peoples' rights.

2. No two judges shall be nationals of the same State.

Article 12 – Nominations

1. States Parties to the Protocol may each propose up to three candidates, at least two of whom shall be nationals of that State.

2. Due consideration shall be given to adequate gender representation in the nomination process.

Article 13 – List of Candidates

1. Upon entry into force of this Protocol, the Secretary-General of the OAU shall request each State Party to the Protocol to present, within ninety (90) days of such a request, its nominees for the office of judge of the Court.

2. The Secretary-General of the OAU shall prepare a list in alphabetical order of the candidates nominated and transmit it to the Member States of the OAU at least thirty days prior to the next session of the Assembly of Heads of State and Government of the OAU hereinafter referred to as "the Assembly".

Article 14 – Elections

1. The judges of the Court shall be elected by secret ballot by the Assembly from the list referred to in Article 13(2) of the present Protocol.

2. The Assembly shall ensure that in the Court as a whole there is representation of the main regions of Africa and of their principal legal traditions.

3. In the election of the judges, the Assembly shall ensure that there is adequate gender representation.

Article 15 – Term of Office

1. The judges of the Court shall be elected for a period of six years and may be re-elected only once. The terms of four judges elected at the first election shall expire at the end of the two years, and the terms of four more judges shall expire at the end of four years.

2. The judges whose terms are to expire at the end of the initial periods of two and four years shall be chosen by lot to be drawn by the Secretary-General of the OAU immediately after the first election has been completed.

3. A judge elected to replace a judge whose term of office has not expired shall hold office for the remainder of the predecessor's term.

4. All judges except the President shall perform their functions on a part-time basis. However, the Assembly may change this arrangement as it deems appropriate.

Article 16 – Oath of Office

After their election, the judges of the Court shall make a solemn declaration to discharge their duties impartially and faithfully.

Article 17 – Independence

1. The independence of the judges shall be fully ensured in accordance with international law.
2. No judge may hear any case in which the same judge has previously taken part as agent, counsel or advocate for one of the parties or as a member of a national or international court or a commission of enquiry or in any other capacity. Any doubt on this point shall be settled by decision of the Court.
3. The judges of the Court shall enjoy, from the moment of their election and throughout their term of office, the immunities extended to diplomatic agents in accordance with international law.
4. At no time shall the judges of the Court be held liable for any decision or opinion issued in the exercise of their functions.

Article 18 – Incompatibility

The position of judge of the Court is incompatible with any activity that might interfere with the independence or impartiality of such a judge or the demands of the office, as determined in the Rules of Procedure of the Court.

Article 19 – Cessation of Office

1. A judge shall not be suspended or removed from office unless, by the unanimous decision of the other judges of the Court, the judge concerned has been found to be no longer fulfilling the required conditions to be a judge of the Court.
2. Such a decision of the Court shall become final unless it is set aside by the Assembly as its next session.

Article 20 – Vacancies

1. In case of death or resignation of a judge of the Court, the President of the Court shall immediately inform the Secretary General of the Organization of African Unity, who shall declare the seat vacant from the date of death or from the date on which the resignation takes effect.
2. The Assembly shall replace the judge whose office became vacant unless the remaining period of the term is less than one hundred and eighty (180) days.
3. The same procedure and considerations as set out in Articles 12, 13 and 14 shall be followed for the filling of vacancies.

Article 21 – Presidency of the Court

1. The Court shall elect its President and one Vice-President for a period of two years. They may be re-elected only once.
2. The President shall perform judicial functions on a full-time basis and shall reside at the seat of the Court.
3. The functions of the President and the Vice-President shall be set out in the Rules of Procedure of the Court.

Article 22 – Exclusion

If a judge is a national of any State which is a party to a case submitted to the Court, that judge shall not hear the case.

Article 23 – Quorum

The Court shall examine cases brought before it, if it has a quorum of at least seven judges.

Article 24 – Registry of the Court

1. The Court shall appoint its own Registrar and other staff of the registry from among nationals of Member States of the OAU according to the Rules of Procedure.
2. The office and residence of the Registrar shall be at the place where the Court has its seat.

Article 25 – Seat of the Court

1. The Court shall have its seat at the place determined by the Assembly from among States parties to this Protocol. However, it may convene in the territory of any Member State of the OAU when the majority of the Court considers it desirable, and with the prior consent of the State concerned.
2. The seat of the Court may be changed by the Assembly after due consultation with the Court.

Article 26 – Evidence

1. The Court shall hear submissions by all parties and if deemed necessary, hold an enquiry. The States concerned shall assist by providing relevant facilities for the efficient handling of the case.
2. The Court may receive written and oral evidence including expert testimony and shall make its decision on the basis of such evidence.

Article 27 – Findings

1. If the Court finds that there has been violation of a human or peoples' right, it shall make appropriate orders to remedy the violation, including the payment of fair compensation or reparation.

2. In cases of extreme gravity and urgency, and when necessary to avoid irreparable harm to persons, the Court shall adopt such provisional measures as it deems necessary.

Article 28 – Judgment

1. The Court shall render its judgment within ninety (90) days of having completed its deliberations.

2. The judgment of the Court decided by majority shall be final and not subject to appeal.

3. Without prejudice to sub-article (2) above, the Court may review its decision in the light of new evidence under conditions to be set out in the Rules of Procedure.

4. The Court may interpret its own decision.

5. The judgment of the Court shall be read in open court, due notice having been given to the parties.

6. Reasons shall be given for the judgment of the Court.

7. If the judgment of the Court does not represent, in whole or in part, the unanimous decision of the judges, any judge shall be entitled to deliver a separate or dissenting opinion.

Article 29 – Notification of Judgment

1. The parties to the case shall be notified of the judgment of the Court and it shall be transmitted to the Member States of the OAU and the Commission.

2. The Council of Ministers shall also be notified of the judgment and shall monitor its execution on behalf of the Assembly.

Article 30 – Execution of Judgment

The States parties to the present Protocol undertake to comply with the judgment in any case to which they are parties within the time stipulated by the Court and to guarantee its execution.

Article 31 – Report

The Court shall submit to each regular session of the Assembly, a report on its work during the previous year. The report shall specify, in particular, the cases in which a State has not complied with the Court's judgment.

Article 32 – Budget

Expenses of the Court, emoluments and allowances for judges and the budget of its registry, shall be determined and borne by the OAU, in accordance with criteria laid down by the OAU in consultation with the Court.

Article 33 – Rules of Procedure

The Court shall draw up its Rules and determine its own procedures. The Court shall consult the Commission as appropriate.

Article 34 – Ratification

1. This Protocol shall be open for signature and ratification or accession by any State Party to the Charter.
2. The instrument of ratification or accession to the present Protocol shall be deposited with the Secretary-General of the OAU.
3. The Protocol shall come into force thirty days after fifteen instruments of ratification or accession have been deposited.
4. For any State Party ratifying or acceding subsequently, the present Protocol shall come into force in respect of that State on the date of the deposit of its instrument of ratification or accession.
5. The Secretary-General of the OAU shall inform all Member States of the entry into force of the present Protocol.
6. At the time of the ratification of this Protocol or any time thereafter, the State shall make a declaration accepting the competence of the Court to receive cases under Article 5(3) of this Protocol. The Court shall not receive any petition under Article 5(3) involving a State Party which has not made such a declaration.
7. Declarations made under sub-article (6) above shall be deposited with the Secretary-General, who shall transmit copies thereof to the State Parties.

Article 35 – Amendments

1. The present Protocol may be amended if a State Party to the Protocol makes a written request to that effect to the Secretary-General of the OAU. The Assembly may adopt, by simple majority, the draft amendment after all the States Parties to the present Protocol have been duly informed of it and the Court has given its opinion on the amendment.
2. The Court shall also be entitled to propose such amendments to the present Protocol as it may deem necessary, through the Secretary General of the OAU.
3. The amendment shall come into force for each State Party which has accepted it thirty days after the Secretary General of the OAU has received notice of the acceptance.

List of NGOs Granted Observer Status with the African Commission on Human and Peoples' Rights

20th Ordinary Session
Grand Bay, Mauritius, 21–31 October 1996
ACHPR/NGOS/XX

No.	*Name and Address of Organization*	*Date Granted Observer Status*	*Session of the Commission*
1.	**Amnesty International** International Secretariat 1 Easton St London WCIX 8DJ United Kingdom Tel: (44) 2074135500 Fax: 9561157 Telex: 28502	28 April 1988	**3rd Session** Libreville, Gabon
2.	**International Commission of Jurists (Commission Internationale des Juristes)** PO Box 160 26 Chemin de Joinville CH-1216 Cointrin Geneva Suisse Tel: (4122) 7884747 Fax: (4122) 7884880 Fax: (4122) 7884725 Telex: 418 531 ICJ CH	28 April 1988	**3rd Session** Libreville, Gabon
3.	**African Association of International Law (Association Africaine de Droit International)** University of Nairobi PO Box 30197 Nairobi Kenya	28 April 1988	**3rd Session** Libreville, Gabon

4.	**International Training Centre on Human Rights and Peace Teaching (Centre International de Formation a l'Enseignement des Droits de l'Homme et de la Paix)** c/o EIP, 5 Rue du Simplon CH-1207 Geneve Suisse Tel: (022) 7352422 Fax: (022) 7364863 Telex: 423 118 TXC CH	18 October 1988	4th Session Cairo, Egypt
5.	**The Arab Lawyers Union (Union des Avocats Arabes)** 13 Ittehad El-Mouhameen El Arab Street Garden City Cairo Egypt Tel: 3557132/3552486 Fax: (022) 7364863 Telex: 22266 ALU – UN	18 October 1988	4th Session Cairo, Egypt
6.	**Egyptian United Nations Association (Nations-Unies)** 28 Talaat Harb Street Flat 710 Cairo Egypt Tel: 746217	18 October 1988	4th Session Cairo, Egypt
7.	**The African Journalists Union (Union des Journalistes Africains)** 1 Talaat Harb Street PO Box 71 Bab El Louk Cairo Egypt Tel: 740175/750242	22 October 1988	4th Session Cairo, Egypt

8.	**The African Society (La Societe Africaine)** 5 Ahmed Hishmat Street Zamalik Cairo Egypt Tel: 807658	22 October 1988	4th Session Cairo, Egypt
9.	**Association Senegalaise d'Etudes et de Recherches Juridiques (ASERJ)** Palais de Justice BP 9003 Dakar Senegal	12 April 1989	5th Session Benghazi, Libya
10.	**Association de Consultants Internationaux en Droits de l'Homme (CID) (Association of International Consultants on Human Rights)** Case Postale 529 CH-1211 Geneve Suisse Tel: (4422) 364452	12 April 1989	5th Session Benghazi, Libya
11.	**Human Rights Internet** PO Box 20147 Ottawa Ontario KIN 9P4 Canada Tel: (1613) 5643492 Fax: (1613) 7302320 Telex: 0533338	4 November 1989	6th Session Banjul, The Gambia
12	**Le Mouvement Burkinabe des Droits de l'Homme et des Peuples (MBDHP) (The Burkinabe Movement on Human and Peoples' Rights)** 01 BP 2055 Ouagadougou 01/Burkina Faso	4 November 1989	6th Session Banjul, The Gambia

13.	**The Lawyers Committee for Human Rights** 330 Seventh Avenue 10th Floor N New York, NY 10001 USA Tel: (212) 6296170 Fax: (212) 9670916 Telex: 5106005783 (LCHRNYC)	4 November 1989	6th Session Banjul, The Gambia
14.	**The African Centre for Democracy and Human Rights Studies** Kairaba Avenue Banjul The Gambia Tel: 94525, 94961 Fax: 94962	4 November 1989	6th Session, Banjul, The Gambia
15.	**Arab Organization for Human Rights** 17 Midan Aswan-Mohandessin Giza – Postal Code 12311 Cairo Egypt Tel: 3466582 Fax: 3448166 **Geneva Office:** PO Box 82 CH-1211 Geneva 28 Suisse Tel: 7916182 Fax: 7910361 Telex: 415730 OIK CH	4 November 1989	6th Session, Banjul, The Gambia
16.	**Observatiore de l'Information** 17 rue abbé-de-l'Epée 34000 Montpellier France Tel: 67798182 Fax: 67696080 Telex: 485816	4 November 1989	6th Session, Banjul, The Gambia

17.	**Human Rights Watch/Africa** 2nd Floor 33 Islington High Street London Nl 9LH United Kingdom Tel: (44) 207131995 Fax: (44) 207131800	4 November 1989	6th Session, Banjul, The Gambia
18.	**The Catholic Commisson for Justice and Peace in Zimbabwe** PO Box 8493 Causeway Harare, Zimbabwe Tel: 792380 Telex: 2390	28 April 1990	7th Session, Banjul, The Gambia
19.	**The International Organization for the Elimination of all Forms of Racial Discrimination (EAFORD)** 2025 Eye Street, NW Suite 1120 Washington DC 20006 USA Tel: (202) 2232324 Fax: (202) 4670557	28 April 1990	7th Session, Banjul, The Gambia
20.	**Association Internationale des Jeunes Avocats (AIJA)** 26 Cours Albert 1er F-75008 Paris France Tel: (331) 40756130 Fax: (331) 42563765 Telex: 290261	12 October 1990	8th Session, Banjul, The Gambia

21.	**The African Society of International and Comparative Law** Private Bag 520 Kairaba Avenue KSMD Banjul The Gambia Tel: (220) 224968 Fax: (220) 224969	12 October 1990	8th Session, Banjul, The Gambia
22.	**Federation Internationale des Droits de l'Homme** 27 RUE Jean-Dolent 75014 Paris France Tel: (331) 43319495	12 October 1990	8th Session, Banjul, The Gambia
23.	**Commonwealth Secretariat** Marlborough House Pall Mall London SW1Y 5HX United Kingdom Tel: (44) 2078393411 Fax: (44) 2079300827 Telex: 27678	12 October 1990	8th Session, Banjul, The Gambia
24.	**The Fund for Peace** 823 United Nations Plaza New York, NY 10017 USA Tel: (212) 6615900 Fax: (212) 6615904	12 October 1990	8th Session, Banjul, The Gambia
25.	**Civil Liberties Organization (CLO)** 24 Mbonu Ojike Street Alhaji Masha Road Surulere Lagos, Nigeria Tel: (01) 840288	12 October 1990	8th Session, Banjul, The Gambia

26.	**Interights (The International Centre for the Legal Protection of Human Rights)** Lancaster House 33 Islington High Street London Nl 9LH United Kingdom Tel: (44) 202783230 Fax: (071) 22784334	12 October 1990	8th Session, Banjul, The Gambia
27.	**Institut International des Droits de l'Homme** 1 Quai Lezay-Marnesia 67000 Strasbourg France Tel: (33) 88350550 Fax:: (33) 88363855	12 October 1990	8th Session, Banjul, The Gambia
28.	**Union Interafricanie des Avocats** 12 Rue de Prince My Abdellah Casablanca (01) Maroc Tel: (02) 271017/275210 Fax: (02) 204686 Telex: 22853	12 October 1990	8th Session, Banjul, The Gambia
29.	**Institut Arabe des Droits de l'Homme** 10 Rue Ibn Massoud (Par la rue El Moez) 1004 El Menzah, Tunis Tunisie Tel: (2161) 767003/767889 Fax: (2161) 750911	12 October 1990	8th Session, Banjul, The Gambia
30.	**Ligue Burkinabe des Droits de l'Homme** et des Peuples Case Postale 2540 CH-1211 Geneve 2 Suisse	12 October 1990	9th Session, Lagos, Nigeria

31.	**Commission Africaine des Promoteurs de la Sante et des Droits de l'Homme** BP 250 Conakry Ré6publique de Guinée Tel: (224) 441105	20 March 1991	9th Session, Lagos, Nigeria
32.	**Human Rights Africa** 34 Aje Street PO Box 2959 Sabo, Yaba Lagos Nigeria Tel: 860 37 **New York Office:** 12 East 33rd 7th Floor New York 10016 Tel: (212) 6794120 Fax: (212) 6792570	20 March 1991	9th Session, Lagos, Nigeria
33.	**Lawyers' Committee for Civil Rights Under Law** Suite 400 1450 G Street, NW Washington DC 20005 USA Tel: (202) 6628342 Fax: (202) 7830857/7830951	20 March 1991	9th Session, Lagos, Nigeria
34.	**International Human Rights Association of American Minorities** Suite 253 919C Albert, Regina SK S4R 2P6 Canada Fax: 3065698649 Telex: 6503571727	20 March 1991	9th Session, Lagos, Nigeria

35.	**Constitutional Rights Project** 18 Awoyemi Close Off Ayinde Giwa Street Surulere, Lagos, Nigeria PO Box 4447 Surulere, Lagos, Nigeria Tel: (2341) 843041/848498 Fax: (2341) 848571	20 March 1991	9th Session, Lagos, Nigeria
36.	**Ligue Tunisienne pour la Defense des Droits de l'Homme** 23 Rue du Yemen Tunis 1002 Tunisie Tel:/Fax: 793874	20 March 1991	9th Session, Lagos, Nigeria
37.	**Committee for the Defence of Human Rights** 8 Imaria Street Anthony Village PO Box 7274 Lagos Nigeria Tel: 960363/966555 Fax: 960363	20 March 1991	9th Session, Lagos, Nigeria
38.	**International Human Rights Law Group** 1601 Connecticut Ave. NW Suite 700 Washington DC 20009 USA Tel: (202) 2328500 Fax: (202) 2326731	9 October 1991	10th Session, Banjul, The Gambia
39.	**Minnesota Advocates for Human Rights** 400 Second Avenue South Suite 1050 Minneapolis MN 55401 USA Tel: (612) 3413302 Fax: (612) 3412971	9 October 1991	10th Session, Banjul, The Gambia

40.	**Federation Internationale de l'Action des Chretiens pour l'Abolition de la Torture (FIACAT)** 27 rue de Maubeuge 75009 Paris France Tel: (1) 42800160 Fax: (1) 42802089 Telex: 20661	9 October 1991	10th Session, Banjul, The Gambia
41.	**Union Interafricaine des Avocats (African Union of Lawyers)** 41 Kasr El-Nil St Cairo Egypt Tel: 3910067 Fax: 3552194	9 October 1991	10th Session, Banjul, The Gambia
42.	**Groupe d'Etude et de Recherche sur la Democratie et le Developpement Economique et Social en Afrique** BP 1258 Cotonou Benin Fax: 315623 Telex: 5050	9 October 1991	10th Session, Banjul, The Gambia
43.	**Anti-Slavery International for the Protection of Human Rights** Unit 4 Stableyard Broomgrove Road London SW9 9TL United Kingdom Tel: (44) 2079249555 Fax: (44) 2077384110	9 October 1991	10th Session, Banjul, The Gambia
44.	**Congressional Human Rights Foundation** 901 31 Street, NW Washington DC 20007-3838 USA	9 October 1991	10th Session, Banjul, The Gambia

45,	**L'Association des Juristes Africains (AJA)** 8 Rue Abdou Karim Bourgi BP 9053 Dakar Senegal Tel: 211948 Fax: 217557	9 October 1991	10th Session, Banjul, The Gambia
46.	**La Ligue Ivorienne des Droits de l'Homme (LIDHO)** BP V 179 Abidjan Côte d'Ivoire	9 October 1991	10th Session, Banjul, The Gambia
47.	**L'Association pour la Promotion de l'Etat de Droit (APED)** 17 Avenue du 24 Janvier BP 7827 Lome-Togo Tel: (228) 217685 Fax: (228) 216884 Telex: 5074	9 October 1991	10th Session, Banjul, The Gambia
48.	**Rencontre Africaine pour la Defense des Droits de l'Homme** 9/E Immeuble Pasteur Dakar Senegal Tel: 218327/350157	9 October 1991	10th Session Banjul, The Gambia
49.	**The Decade of Human Rights Education, Inc (DHRE)** 526 West 111th St Suite 3B New York, NY 100025 USA Tel: (212) 7493156 Fax: (518) 8517338	9 October 1991	10th Session Banjul, The Gambia

50.	**Marangopoulos Foundation for Human Rights (MFHR)** 1 Lycavittou Street 106 72 Athens Greece Tel: 3637455/3626111 Fax: 3622454	9 October 1991	10th Session, Banjul, The Gambia
51.	**Legal Research and Resource Development Centre** 9 Huges Avenue Yaba PO Box 73180 Victoria Island Lagos Nigeria Tel: (01) 865679	9 October 1991	10th Session, Banjul, The Gambia
52.	**Organization Mondiale Contre la Torture** Case Postale 119 CH-1211 Geneve 20 CIC Suisse Tel: (4122) 7333140, Fax: (4122) 7331051 Telex: 412127 CIL CH	9 October 1991	10th Session, Banjul, The Gambia
53.	**International Service for Human Rights** 1 rue de Varembe POB 16 CH-1211 Geneva 20 Suisse Tel: (4122) 7335123 Fax: 7330826	9 October 1991	10th Session, Banjul, The Gambia
54.	**International League for Human Rights** 432 Park Avenue South 11th Floor New York, NY 10016 USA Tel: (212) 6841221	9 October 1991	10th Session, Banjul, The Gambia

55.	**Association Nationale des Droits de l'Homme** BP 4347 Libreville Gabon	9 October 1991	10th Session, Banjul, The Gambia
56.	**African Bar Association** c/o Assistant Secretary General (Eric S. Ng'maryo Esq) PO Box 1856 KNCU Building Kibo Road Moshi Tanzania	9 October 1991	10th Session, Banjul, The Gambia
57.	**Ligue Centrafricaine des Droits de l'Homme (LCDH)** BP 2094 Bangui RCA Tel: (236) 612571	9 October 1991	10th Session, Banjul, The Gambia,
58.	**Egyptian Organization for Human Rights** 8/10 Mathaf El Manial Street Manial Elroda Cairo Egypt Tel : (202) 3636811 Fax : (202) 3621613 Telex: (202) 3620467	9 October 1991	10th Session, Banjul, The Gambia
59.	**Institut des Droits de l'Homme de l'Universite Catholique de Lyon** 10–12 Rue Fochier 69002 Lyon Tel: 72325050	2–9 March 1992	11th Session, Tunis, Tunisia
60.	**Ligue Bissao-Guineene des Droits de l'Homme** BP 599 - Bissau R Guinee-Bissao Tel: 211368	2–9 March 1992	11th Session, Tunis, Tunisia

61.	**International Society for Human Rights** The Gambia Group PMB 457 Serrekunda The Gambia	2–9 March 1992	11th Session, Tunis, Tunisia
62.	**Syndicat National de la Presse Marocaine** 27 Avenue Prince Aoulay Abdellah Rabat Morrocco Tel: 703077	2–9 March 1992	11th Session, Tunis, Tunisia
63.	**Lawyers for Human Rights** 3rd Floor Cnr Von Wielligh & Commissioner Sts PO Box 5156 Johannesburg 2000 South Africa Tel: (011) 3313465/66 Fax: (011) 3316860	2–9 March 1992	11th Session, Tunis, Tunisia
64.	**Observatoire Panafricain de la Democratie (OPAD)** 17 Avenue du 24 Janvier Boite Postale 7827 Lome, Togo Tel: (228) 217685 Fax (228) 216884 Telex: 5300	2–9 March 1992	11th Session, Tunis, Tunisia
65.	**Comité International de la Croix Rouge** 19 Avenue de la Paix CH-1202 Genève Suisse Tel: (4122) 7346001 Fax: (4122) 7332057 Telex: 414226	2–9 March 1992	11th Session, Tunis, Tunisia

66.	**"Article 19" International Centre Against Censorship** 90 Borough High Street London SE1 1LL United Kingdom Tel: (44) 2074034822 Fax: (44) 2074031943	2–9 March 1992	11th Session, Tunis, Tunisia
67.	**Comité National des Droits de l'Homme (CONADHO)** BP 900 Brazzaville Republique Populaire du Congo Tel: 831986	2–9 March 1992	11th Session, Tunis, Tunisia
68.	**Commission Beninoise des Droits de l'Homme** BP 03-2686 Cotonou Republique du Benin Tel: 314334 Fax: (229) 315931 Telex: 5208	2–9 March 1992	11th Session, Tunis, Tunisia
69.	**Arab Libyan Commission for Human Rights** PO Box 91211 Tripoli Libya Tel: (0021821) 39307 Fax: (0021821) 39307 Telex: 22030	2–9 March 1992	11th Session, Tunis, Tunisia
70*	**Federation des Juristes Africaines** 01 BP 5866 Abidjan 01 Côte d'Ivoire	2–9 March 1992	11th Session, Tunis, Tunisia

71.	**International Centre for Human Rights and Democratic Development** Head Office 63 Rue de Bresoles Montreal H2Y 1V7 Canada Tel: (514) 2836073 Fax: (514) 2833792	2–9 March 1992	11th Session, Tunis, Tunisia
72.	**Federation Nationale des Unions de Jeunes Avocats** s/c Roger-Vincent Calatayud Délégué National 20 Rue Brauhauban Résidence la Lorraine 65000 Tarbes France Tel: 62341083 Fax: 62513909	13 October 1992	12th Session, Banjul, The Gambia
73.	**Association Tchadienne pour la Promotion et la Defense des Droits de l'Homme (ATPDH)** BP 4082 N'Djaména Tchad	13 October 1992	12th Session, Banjul, The Gambia
74	**Union Interafricaine des Droits de l'Homme (Interafrican Union for Human Rights)** 01 BP 1346 Ouagadougou 01 Ouagadougou Burkina Faso Tel.: 316145 Fax: 316144	13 October 1992	12th Session, Banjul, The Gambia
75.	**Swaziland Association of Human Rights (HUMARAS)** PO Box A 411 Swazi Plaza Mbabane Swaziland	13 October 1992	12th Session, Banjul, The Gambia

76.	**Women in Law and Development in Africa (WILDAF)** PO Box UA 171 Union Avenue Harare Zimbabwe Tel: (2634) 729151 Fax: (2634) 731901/2	13 October 1992	12th Session, Banjul, The Gambia
77.	**Southern African Research and Documentation Centre (SARDC)** PO Box 5690 Harare Zimbabwe Tel: (2634) 738695 Fax: (2634) 738693 Telex: 26035 ZPH ZW	13 October 1992	12th Session, Banjul, The Gambia
78.	**Network of Activists and Researchers on Integrated Human Rights in Africa (NARIHRA)** Rue Base Ntchinga 361 Haputo Mozambique Tel. (2581) 416062	13 October 1992	12th Session, Banjul, The Gambia
79.	**African Studies Association** Emory University Credit Union Building Atlanta Georgia 30322 USA Tel: (404) 3296410	13 October 1992	12th Session, Banjul, The Gambia
80.	**Association Malienne des Droits de l'Homme** BP 3129 Bamako Mali Tel: 228524/223462 Fax: 223462/220804	13 October 1992	12th Session, Banjul, The Gambia

81.	**Sudan Human Rights Organisation** London BM Box 8238 London WC1N 3XX United Kingdom Fax: (44) 2073788029	13 October 1992	12th Session, Banjul, The Gambia
82.	**Zimbabwean Human Rights Association (ZIMMRIGHTS)** 55 Herbert Chitepo Ave PO Box 3951 Harare Zimbabwe Tel: (2634) 738609 Fax: (2634) 796589	13 October 1992	12th Session, Banjul, The Gambia
83.	**Association pour le Developpement des Initiatives Villeageoises (ASSODIV)** BP 06733 Cotonou Bénin Tel: (229) 321522	13 October 1992	12th Session, Banjul, The Gambia
84.	**International PEN** 9/10 Chater House Buildings Goswell Road London EC1M 7AT United Kingdom Tel: (44) 2072534308 Fax: (44) 2072535711	13 October 1992	12th Session, Banjul, The Gambia
85.	**World University Service** 5 Chemin des Iris 1216 Geneva (Cointrin) Suisse Tel: 7988711/12 Fax: 7980829 Telex: 415537 WUS CH	13 October 1992	12th Session, Banjul, The Gambia

86.	**Ligue Burundaise pour la Defense et la Promotion des Droits de l'Homme "SONERA"** BP 600 Avenue de France Bujumbura Burundi Tel: 221732	13 October 1992	12th Session, Banjul, The Gambia
87.	**Ligue Camerounaise des Droits de l'Homme pour la Defense des Libertes Fondamentales et du Pluralisme** 85 Bd Saint-Michel 75005 Paris France Tel: 43258050	13 October 1992	12th Session, Banjul, The Gambia
88.	**Organization Marocaine des Droits de l'Homme** 24 Avenue de France-Agdal Rabat Maroc Tel: (07) 770060	14 October 1992	12th Session, Banjul, The Gambia
89.	**MULEIDE – Woman, Law and Development** Rua Base Ntchinga No. 361 CP 2998 Maputo Mozambique Tel: 490164	14 October 1992	12th Session, Banjul, The Gambia
90.	**Ghana Committee on Human and Peoples' Rights** PO Box 207 Accra Ghana Tel: (23321) 229875 Fax: (23321) 774338	14 October 1992	12th Session, Banjul, The Gambia

91.	**Organization Guineenne de Defense des Droits de l'Homme et du Citoyen** BP 615 Bis Conakry République de Guinée	29 March 1993	13th Session, Banjul, The Gambia
92.	**Association des Journalistes Tunisiens** 15 Rue Ali Bach-Hamba Tunis Tel: 258374	29 March 1993	13th Session, Banjul, The Gambia
93.	**The Danish Centre for Human Rights** Grundtvigs Hus Studiestraede 38 DK-1455 Copenhagen K Denmark Tel: (45) 33911299 Fax: (45) 33910299	29 March 1993	13th Session, Banjul, The Gambia
94.	**African Human Rights and Justice Protection Network** PO Box 6400 708 Capital Centre Levison Arcade Windhoek, Namibia Tel: (061) 228251 Fax: (061) 228207	29 March 1993	13th Session, Banjul, The Gambia
95.	**Agir Ensemble pour les Droits de l'Homme** 31 Cours Emile Zola 69100 Villeurbanne, France Tel: 72442499 Fax: 78895866	29 March 1993	13th Session, Banjul, The Gambia
96.	**Association Rwandaise pour la Defense des Droits de la Personne et des Libertes Publiques** BP 1932 Kigali, Rwanda Tel: 77564 Fax: 77737	29 March 1993	13th Session, Banjul, The Gambia

97.	**Centre Beninois pour le Developpement des Initiatives à la Base** BP 256 Bohicon République de Bénin Tel: (229) 510485 Fax: (229) 510295	30 March 1993	13th Session, Banjul, The Gambia
98.	**CUSO West Africa Office** PO Box 9060 House No. F49 15 Klottey Walk North Labone Accra, Ghana Tel: 773596 Fax: (00) 23321772948	30 March 1993	13th Session, Banjul, The Gambia
99.	**National Society for Human Rights of Namibia** PO Box 23592 Windhoek 9000 Republic of Namibia Tel: (26461) 36183 Fax: (26461) 225628	30 march 1993	13th Session, Banjul, The Gambia
100.	**Association Chretienne pour l'Abolition des Tortures et pour le Respect des Droits de l'Homme** 20 BP 1377 Abidjan 20 République de Côte d'Ivoire	30 March 1993	13th Session, Banjul, The Gambia
101.	**The African Institute for Human Rights and Peace Research** PO Box 430 Banjul The Gambia	30 March 1993	13th Session, Banjul, The Gambia
102.	**International Association of Lawyers for Human Rights Studies** 59 Buckle Street Banjul, The Gambia	30 March 1993	13th Session, Banjul, The Gambia

103.	**Universal Defenders of Democracy** Top Floor 49 Ogunlana Drive PO Box 6811 Surulere Lagos Nigeria Tel: (01) 845848/846919	30 March 1993	13th Session, Banjul, The Gambia
104.	**Women Concerned** 64 Adeniran Ogunsanya Street Surulere Lagos Nigeria Tel: (01) 832378	30 March 1993	13th Session, Banjul, The Gambia
105.	**Association Egyptienne des Supporters des Droits de l'Homme** 1 Avenue Osiris Garden City Le Caire Egypt	30 March 1993	13th Session, Banjul, The Gambia
106.	**Comité International pour le Respect et l'Application de la Charte Africaine (CIRAC)** Genève Case PO Box 82 1211 Geneve 20 CCP 12-21954-4 Geneve Suisse	30 March 1993	13th Session, Banjul, The Gambia
107.	**Centre de Promotion des Droits de l'Homme** BP 2588 Bujumbura République du Burundi Tel: (257) 232910 Fax: (257) 233139	30 March 1993	13th Session, Banjul, The Gambia

108.	**Ligue Cap-Verdienne des Droits de l'Homme et des Peuples** CP 586 Praia Cap Verde Tel: 613539/614081 Fax: 611173/616466	30 March 1993	13th Session, Banjul, The Gambia
109.	**Legal Research and Resource Center for Human Rights** 7 Al Higaz Street Heliopolis Cairo Egypt Tel:/Fax: 20 22596622	30 March 1993	13th Session, Banjul, The Gambia
110.	**Ligue Tchadienne des Droits de l'Homme** BP 2037 Ndjamena Chad Tel: 516135 Fax: 516109	30 March 1993	13th Session, Banjul, The Gambia
111.	**International Federation of Women Lawyers (FIDA)** Kenya Chapter No. 1 Addalyn Flats Ngong Road PO Box 46324 Nairobi, Kenya Tel: 717169 Fax: 716840	2 December 1993	14th Session, Addis Ababa, Ethiopia
112.	**Organisation Nationale des Droits de l'Homme du Senegal Membre de la FIDH** 180 Bd de la République 7ème Etage Dakar Senegal Tel: 222800	2 December 1993	14th Session, Addis Ababa, Ethiopia

113.	**National Justice and Peace Commission, Catholic Mission** PO Box 165 Banjul	2 December 1993	14th Session, Addis Ababa, Ethiopia
114.	**Collectif des Ligues et Association de Defense des Droits de l'Homme au (CLADHO)** BP 1868 Kigali Rwanda	2 December 1993	14th Session, Addis Ababa, Ethiopia
115.	**International Work for Indigenous Affairs** Fiolstraede 10 DK-1171 Copenhagen K Denmark	2 December 1993	14th Session, Addis Ababa, Ethiopia
116.	**The Centre for Human Rights** Faculty of Law University of Pretoria 0002 Pretoria South Africa Tel: 27 (12) 4203034 Fax: 27 (12) 434021	2 December 1993	14th Session, Addis Ababa, Ethiopia
117.	**Ligue des Droits de la Personne dans la Region des Grands Lacs (LDGL)** BP 1782 Kigali, Rwanda Tel: (250) 85878/77564 Fax: (250) 77737	2 December 1993	14th Session, Addis Ababa, Ethiopia
118.	**International Commission of Jurists (Kenya Section)** City Hall Annexe 14th Floor Muindi Mbingu St PO Box 59743 Nairobi, Kenya Tel: (2542) 212762 Fax: (2542) 330306/335438	2 December 1993	14th Session, Addis Ababa, Ethiopia

119.	**Foundation for Human Rights Initiative** PO Box 11027 Kampala Uganda Tel: 530095	2 December 1993	14th Session, Addis Ababa, Ethiopia
120.	**Media Rights Agenda** 42 Falolu Street Surulere Lagos Nigeria Tel: 831852 Fax: 833606	2 December 1993	14th Session, Addis Ababa, Ethiopia
121.	**Inter African Network for Human Rights** PO Box 32565 Lusaka Zambia	2 December 1993	14th Session, Addis Ababa, Ethiopia
122.	**International Alert** 1 Glyn Street London SE11 5HT United Kingdom Tel: (44) 2077938383 Fax: (44) 2077937975	2 December 1993	14th Session, Addis Ababa, Ethiopia
123.	**University of Namibia** Private Bag 13301 Windhoek Namibia Tel: (06) 3072000	2 December 1993	14th Session, Addis Ababa, Ethiopia
124.	**Ligue Camerounaise des Droits de la Personne** BP 1514 Yaounde Cameroun Tel: (237) 317018	2 December 1993	14th Session, Addis Ababa, Ethiopia

125.	**Ethiopian Human Rights Council** PO Box 2432 Addis Ababa Ethiopia Tel: (2511) 514539/514489 Fax: (2511) 514539	2 December 1993	14th Session, Addis Ababa, Ethiopia
126.	**L'Association pour la Defense des Droits de l'Homme et des Libertes (Djibouti)** BP 2410 Djibouti	2 December 1993	14th Session, Addis Ababa, Ethiopia
127.	**Penal Reform International** 169 Clapham Road London SW9 0PU United Kingdom Tel: (44) 2075826500 Fax: (44) 2077354666	2 December 1993	14th Session, Addis Ababa, Ethiopia
128.	**Association Zairoise de Defense de Droits de l'Homme (AZADHO)** BP 16737 Kinshasa 1, Zaire Tel: 20906/21174	2 December 1993	14th Session, Addis Ababa, Ethiopia
129.	**Association de Journalistes du Cap Vert** CP 144-C Praia Republica de Cabo Verde	2 December 1993	14th Session, Addis Ababa, Ethiopia
130.	**Community Legal Resource and Advice Centre** 2nd Floor Speedy Shopping Complex PO Box 0383 Maseru West 105 Lesotho Tel: 323976 Fax: 310361	19 April 1994	15th Session, Banjul, The Gambia

131.	**The Botswana Centre for Human Rights** Private Bag 00416 Gaborone Botswana Tel: (267) 306998/373742 Fax: (267) 307778	19 April 1994	15th Session, Banjul, The Gambia
132.	**African Network for the Prevention and Protection Against Child Abuse and Neglect** PO Box 71420 Nairobi Kenya Tel: 717549/726794 Fax: 718605	25 October 1994	16th Session, Banjul, The Gambia
133.	**Centre for Applied Legal Studies University of the Witwatersrand** Private Bag 3, Wits 2050 South Africa Tel: (2711) 4036918 Fax: (2711) 4032341 Telex: 427125 SA	25 October 1994	16th Session, Banjul, The Gambia
134.	**Mouvement de Protestation Civique** Mairie 43400 Chambon-Sur-Lignon France Tel: (33) 71658987 Fax: (33) 71592505	25 October 1994	16th Session, Banjul, The Gambia
135.	**International Society for Human Rights** Zaire Section PO Box 5774 Kinshasha/Gombe Zaire	25 October 1994	16th Session, Banjul, The Gambia

136.	**Organisation Senegalaise d'Appui au Developpement et aux Droits de l'Homme (OSAD/DH)** Sénégal, Siège Social Zone B, No. 22 BP 540, Dakar Séné6gal Tel: (221) 225104 Fax: (221) 225039	25 October 1994	16th Session, Banjul, The Gambia
137.	**All African Conference of Churches** PO Box 14205 Nairobi Kenya	25 October 1994	16th Session, Banjul, The Gambia
138.	**Centre for Justice and International Law (CEJIL)** 1522 K Street, NW Suite 800 Washington DC 20005-1202 USA Tel: (1202) 3716592 Fax: (1202) 3718032	25 October 1994	16th Session, Banjul, The Gambia
139.	**The English International Association of Lund** PO Box 722 22007 Lund Sweden Tel: (46) 157368 Fax: (46) 142238	25 October 1994	16th Session, Banjul, The Gambia
140.	**Swedish NGO Foundation for Human Rights** Droffininggatan 101 S-113 60 Stockholm Sweden Tel: (468) 303150 Fax: (468) 303031	25 October 1994	16th Session, Banjul, The Gambia

141.	**Association Angolaise des Droits de l'Homme** Rua Const Julio Vilhena No. 249 Andar Apt 19 Luanda Angola Tel: 391943 Fax: 392289	13 March 1995	17th Session, Lomé, Togo
142.	**Human Rights Information and Documentation Systems (HURIDOCS)** Huridocs Secretariat 2 rue Jean-Jaquet CH-1201 Geneva Suisse Tel: (4122) 7411767 Fax: (4122) 7411768	13 March 1995	17th Session, Lomé, Togo
143.	**Women Justice Program** 15A Moloney Street PO Box 73586 Victoria Island Lagos, Nigeria Tel: 2632999	13 March 1995	17th Session, Lomé, Togo
144.	**Association Mondiale pour les Orphelins et Enfants Abandonnes** 45 Rue du Séminaire BP 80242 Lomé, Togo Tel: (228) 214113 Fax: (228) 222681 Telex: s/c UNICEF LOME 5197	13 March 1995	17th Session, Lomé, Togo
145.	**Comité Africain pour le Droit et Developpement** 8 Boulevard du Sud Point E BO 15.107 Dakar-Fann Senegal Tel: (221) 244101 Fax: (221) 247102	13 March 1995	17th Session, Lomé, Togo

146.	**Association Mauritanienne des Droits de l'Homme** BP 522 Nouakchott Mauritanie Tel: (2222) 51502 Fax: (2222) 52894	13 March 1995	17th Session, Lomé, Togo
147.	**Mouvement des Refugies Mauritaniens au Senegal pour la Defense des Droits de l;Homme (MRMSDDH)** BP 10346 Dakar, Senegal Tel: 266508	13 March 1995	17th Session, Lomé, Togo
148.	**SOS Esclaves (Mauritanie)** BP 4302 Nouakchott Mauritanie	13 March 1995	17th Session, Lomé, Togo
149.	**Groupe d'Etudes et de Recherches sur la Democratie et le Developpement Economique et Social en Mauritanie (GERDDES)** BP 522 Nouakchott Mauritanie Tel: (2222) 51502 Fax: (2222) 52894	13 March 1995	17th Session, Lomé, Togo
150.	**Tchad Non-Violence** BP 1266 N'Djamena Tchad	13 March 1995	17th Session, Lomé, Togo
151.	**Human Rights Society of The Gambia (HRSG)** 31 OAU Boulevard PO Box 698 Banjul, The Gambia Fax: (220) 224839	13 March 1995	17th Session, Lomé, Togo

152.	**The Ugandan Association of Women Lawyers (FIDA-UGANDA)** PO Box 2157 Kampala Uganda Tel: 530848	13 March 1995	17th Session, Lomé, Togo
153.	**Liberia Human Rights Chapter** PO Box 3095 Tubman Blvd 9th Street Sinkor Monrovia Liberia	13 March 1995	17th Session, Lomé, Togo
154.	**Institut Africain pour la Democratie** 3 Bd Djily Mbaye Immmeuble Fahd BP 1780 Dakar, Senegal Tel: 235720 Fax: 235721	13 March 1995	17th Session, Lomé, Togo
155.	**Comité Algerien des Droits de l'Homme et des Peuples** Cite des Annassers 4 Coopemad Sud BT 64 No. 1 Kouba, Algerie Tel: (02) 661180 Fax: (02) 661195	2 October 1995	18th Session, Praia, Cape Verde
156.	**Observatoire International des Prisons (OIP)** 16 Avenue Berthelot BP 7083, 69301 Lyon Cedex 07 France Tel: (33) 72718383 Fax: (33) 78587211	2 October 1995	18th Session, Praia, Cape Verde

157.	**Association Nationale pour l'Alphabetisation et la Formation des Adultes (ANAFA)** s/c Congad Villa 3089 BIS - Amitie 1 BP 4109 Dakar Senegal Tel: 244116 Fax: 244413	2 October 1995	18th Session, Praia, Cape Verde
158.	**Association pour le Progres de la Femme et de l'Enfant** Republique du Burundi ASBL – IGAA D/S 150 Bujumbura Tel: 224167	2 October 1995	18th Session, Praia, Cape Verde
159.	**Liberia Watch for Human Rights Inc.** Vai Town PO Box 5480 Monrovia, Liberia Tel: 221900	2 October 1995	18th Session, Praia, Cape Verde
160.	**Ligue Togolaise des Droits de la Femme (LTDF)** BP 30694 Lomé, Togo Tel: 269155	2 October 1995	18th Session, Praia, Cape Verde
161.	**Foundation for Research on Women's Health,** Productivity and the **Environment (BAFROW)** 214 Tafsir Demba Mbye Road Tobacco Road Estate Banjul PO Box 2854 Serrekunda The Gambia Tel: (220) 225270	2 October 1995	18th Session, Praia, Cape Verde

162.	**Synergies Africa** 5 Route des Morillons CH-1218 Grand-Saconnex Tel: (4122) 7888586 Fax: (4122) 7888590	2 October 1995	18th Session, Praia, Cape Verde
163.	**Association des Refugies Mauritaniens au Senegal (ARMS)** BP 1730 Dakar, Senegal Tel:/Fax: 210082	2 October 1995	18th Session, Praia, Cape Verde
164.	**Centre Nord-Sud** Avenida de Liberdade, 229-4° P-1200 Lisbonne Portugal Tel: (3511) 3522903 Fax: (3511) 3531329	2 October 1995	18th Session Praia, Cape Verde
165.	**Association pour la Prevention de la Torture (APT)** Case Postale 2267 CH-1211 Geneve 2, Suisse Tel: (4122) 7342088 Fax: (4122) 7345649	2 October 1995	18th Session, Praia, Cape Verde
166.	**The Association of Female Lawyers of Liberia** Law Library Ashmun Street PO Box 20-4248 Liberia 1000 Monrovia 20 Fax: (231) 226171	2 October 1995	18th Session, Praia, Cape Verde
167.	**Association Internationale pour la Democratie en Afrique (AID-AFRIQUE)** BP 803 Abidjan 08 RCIV Côte d'Ivoire Tel: (225) 221863 Fax: (225) 224857	2 October 1995	18th Session, Praia, Cape Verde

168.	**Liga Mocainbicana Dos Direitos Humanos (LDH)** Avenue 24 de Julho No. 776 R/C Maputo Mozambique Tel: 423185/430705 Fax: 430706	26 March 1996	19th Session, Ouagadougou, Burkina Faso
169.	**Forum Das ONG Dos Direitos Do Homen E** Da Crianca Dos PALOP CP No. 599 Bissau Guinee-Bissau Tel: 213777 Fax: 201766	26 March 1996	19th Session, Ouagadougou, Burkina Faso
170.	**Association des Juristes Maliennes** Rue 422 x 499 Niarela BPE 1094 Villa N' 537 Bamako Mali Tel:/Fax: 232383	26 March 1996	19th Session, Ouagadougou, Burkina Faso
171.	**Pan African Congress** Plot 3 Parliament Avenue PO Box 7168 Kampala, Uganda Tel: (256) 41267075/266012/3 Fax: (256) 41267664	26 March 1996	19th Session, Ouagadougou, Burkina Faso
172.	**Conseil pour le Developpement de la Recherche Economique et Sociale en Afrique (CODESRIA)** BP 3304 Dakar Sebegal Tel: (221) 259822/23 Fax: (221) 241289 Telex: 61339 Codes SG	26 March 1996	19th Session, Ouagadougou, Burkina Faso

173.	**Shelter Rights Initiative** Bank Charnbers Anamba House 27/29 Martins Street (3rd Floor) Lagos Nigeria Tel:/Fax: 2661947	26 March 1996	19th Session, Ouagadougou, Burkina Faso
174.	**Mouvement International pour le Development en Afrique (MIDA)** BP 10403 Rue 3 x Q Derkle Dakar Senegal Tel: 247835	26 March 1996	19th Session, Ouagadougou, Burkina Faso
175.	**Association Tchadienne des Juristes (ATJ)** BP 2046 N'Djamena Tchad	26 March 1996	19th Session, Ouagadougou, Burkina Faso
176.	**Foundation Idole "Foni"** BP 2216 Messa Yaounde Cameroun Tel: (237) 317239 Fax: (237) 317239	26 March 1996	19th Session, Ouagadougou, Burkina Faso
177.	**SOS Orphelins** BP 6941 Djibouti – RDD	26 March 1996	19th Session, Ouagadougou, Burkina Faso
178.	**African Centre for Democracy Human Rights and the Protection of Prisoners** BP 20395 Lomé Togo Tel: (228) 225352 Fax: (228) 221440/222723	26 March 1996	19th Session, Ouagadougou, Burkina Faso

179.	**Avocats Sans Frontieres** Rue de la Loi 23 B-1040 Bruxelles Belgique Tel: 02/287,2000 Fax: 02/231,1661	26 March 1996	19th Session, Ouagadougou, Burkina Faso
180.	**Rassembllement Democratique des Femmes du Niger** BP 11933 Nianey Niger Tel: 73 24 65	26 March 1996	19th Session, Ouagadougou, Burkina Faso
181.	**Association de Sauvegarde de l'Enfance en Danger** 09 BP 311 Ouaga 09 Tel: (226) 362523	26 March 1996	19th Session, Ouagadougou, Burkina Faso
182.	**Association Ivoirienne pour la Promotion des Droits de l'Homme** 04 BP 1023 Abidjan 04 Abidjan Côte d'Ivoire Fax: (220) 390764	26 March 1996	19th Session, Ouagadougou, Burkina Faso

PART II

ACTIVITY REPORTS AND RELATED MATERIALS

First Activity Report of the African Commission on Human and Peoples' Rights

Adopted on 28 April 1988
Covering the period from November 1987 through April 1988
(1st to 3rd Session)

I. ORGANIZATION OF WORK AND ANY OTHER BUSINESS

A. Status of Ratifications

1. As at 28 April 1988, date of the closing of the Third Session of the African Commission on Human and Peoples' Rights, there were 35 States Parties to the African Charter on Human and Peoples' Rights, the instrument adopted by the 18th Assembly of Heads of State and Government held in Nairobi from 24–27 June 1981, and opened immediately for signature and for ratification or adhesion.

2. The African Charter on Human and Peoples' Rights entered into force on 21 October 1986 in accordance with the provisions of Article 63(3).

3. The list of States parties to the African Charter on Human and Peoples' Rights is contained in Annex I of the present report.

B. Sessions and Agenda

4. Since the solemn ceremony of 2 November 1987 in Addis Ababa, Ethiopia, the African Commission on Human and Peoples' Rights has held three (3) Sessions:

- the First Session took place in Addis Ababa, Ethiopia, on 2 November 1987;
- the Second Session was held in Dakar, Senegal, from 8–13 February 1988;
- the Third Session was held in Libreville, Gabon, from 18–28 April 1977.

5. The agenda of each of these Sessions is contained in Annex III.

C. Composition and Participation

6. The eleven members of the African Commission on Human and Peoples' Rights were elected during the 23rd Ordinary Session of the Assembly of Heads of State and Government held in Addis Ababa, Ethiopia, pursuant to Article 33 of the Charter. The election was held in accordance with Articles 36 and 37 of the Charter. The list of the members of the Commission is contained in Annex II. All the members of the Commission attended the three Sessions, except however that:

- Mr. Mabanga-Chipoya was absent at the First Session with apology,
- Mr. Grace Ibingira was absent at the Second Session with apology,
- Mr. Grace Ibingira was absent at the Third session.

D. Solemn Declaration

7. At the First session convened by the Secretary General of the OAU, pursuant to the provisions of Article 64(2) of the Charter, the elected members of the Commission made solemn declarations before taking office pursuant to Article 38 of the Charter.

8. The text of the solemn declaration is contained in Annex IV.

E. Election of the Chairman and the Vice-Chairman

9. At its First Session on 2 November 1987, the Commission elected a Chairman and a Vice-Chairman in conformity with the provisions of Article 42 of the Charter:

Chairman:	Mr. Isaac NGUEMA
Vice Chairman:	Mr. Ibrahim Ali Badawi El SHEIKH

10. In accordance with the provisions of Article 41 of the Charter, the OAU Secretary-General appointed Mrs Esther Tchouta-Moussa, OAU Legal Adviser, Secretary to the Commission.

11. The Secretary-General of the OAU, who attended all the sittings of the First Session, also provided the Commission with all the information it needed in order to carry out its mission. He encouraged it and expressed his readiness to assist. The Commission extended its congratulations and gratitude to him.

F. Any Other Business

12. At each of its three sessions held since its establishment, the Commission considered various issues concerning its functioning, methods of work and programme of action. The general information given by the Chairman of the Commission at the Second and Third Sessions were noted and discussed by members of the Commission. The reports of the three Sessions dealt with all the other issues raised.

G. Adoption of the Activity Report

13. At its 26th sitting on 27 April 1988, the Commission considered the draft of its first activity report on the deliberations of the First, Second and Third Sessions held in 1987 and 1988 successively in Addis Ababa, Ethiopia, Dakar, Senegal and Libreville, Gabon. The report as amended during the discussion was unanimously adopted.

II. GENERAL OBSERVATIONS OF THE COMMISSION

14. At each of the three Sessions, the Commission discussed at length the various tasks assigned to it by the Charter and the ways and means of executing them in order to attain the objectives set.

15. It felt that the magnitude and complex nature of the tasks it had to carry out demanded that it should stand on a solid foundation so as to make slow but sure lasting progress.

A. Rules of Procedure

16. At its Second Ordinary Session held in Dakar, Senegal, the Commission drew up, discussed and adopted a Rules of Procedure which is attached to this report as Annex V.

17. As a first step to the implementation of the Charter, that 120 Rules legal instrument was intended to make the Commission a rational and functional effective organization. It also defined its Rules of Procedure.

18. Two issues especially engaged the attention of the Commission during the preparation of the Rules of Procedure: the choice of Headquarters and the Financial Rules and Regulations of the Commission.

(a) Choice of Headquarters

19. The Commission noted that the African Charter on Human and Peoples' Rights had not formally dealt with its Headquarters. There was no provision in the OAU Charter which dealt with this issue either.

20. At its Third Session held in Libreville, Gabon, it made a recommendation requesting the Twenty-fourth Ordinary Session of the Assembly of Heads of State and Government to take a decision on the issue. The recommendation appears in Annex VI of this report.

(b) Financial Rules and Regulations Governing Functioning of the Commission

21. The Commission analysed Articles 41 and 44 of the Charter dealing with the material and human resources, on the one hand, and the emoluments and allowances of members of the Commission, on the other.

22. Pursuant to Rule 24 of its Rules of Procedure, the Commission recommended to the Assembly of Heads of State and Government to take a decision on the proposals it had made. The text of the recommendation is contained in Annex VII of this report.

B. Promotional Activities

22. The Commission attached particular importance to this essential mission entrusted to it by the Charter. Right from its Second Session held in Dakar, Senegal, it drew up a comprehensive Programme of Action aimed at promoting human and peoples' rights in Africa.

23. Specific proposals were included in the Commission's 1989–1990 draft budget on the financing of a selected part of the Programme of Action, to be implemented in successive stages.

25. The Programme of Action is attached as Annex VIII of this report.

C. Protection Activities

26. The Commission noted with interest this aspect of its mandate. As from its First Session held in Addis Ababa, Ethiopia, it took cognizance of communications which had already been received at the OAU General Secretariat well before the installation of the Commission. During its Third Session, the Commission evolved a methodology for receiving and considering communications. The documents are analysed in Part IV of this report.

D. Other Activities

27. The Commission had not yet received any tasks or actions for execution from a State party, an institution of the OAU or the Assembly of Heads of State and Government.

28. It received offers of collaboration from three non-governmental organizations during its Third Session held in Libreville. Pursuant to its Rules of Procedure, it accepted to cooperate with those organizations.

III. CONSIDERATION OF PERIODIC REPORTS SUBMITTED BY MEMBER STATES PURSUANT TO ARTICLE 62 OF THE CHARTER

29. The Commission discussed this important issue which was of double significance, namely, promotion and protection. It analyzed the relevant provisions of the Charter.

30. After having concluded that the Charter did not specifically entrust it with the task of considering the periodic reports on the human and peoples' rights of State parties, the Commission recommended to the Assembly of Heads of State and Government to specifically assign it with the mandate to enable it to consider and indicate the general orientation as regards the form and substance of the said reports.

31. The recommendation which also suggested that the OAU Secretary-General be empowered by the Assembly of Heads of State and Government to receive and forward the said documents to the Commission appears in Annex IX of the present report.

IV. CONSIDERATION OF COMMUNICATIONS

32. Since its Second Session, the Commission had considered the various aspects of that mission. It prepared a document especially meant to guide the Secretariat in receiving communications from States Parties and other communications and following up the procedure stages.

33. The Commission also drew up and adopted model reports aimed at facilitating the consideration of the communications and model decisions to enable the quick processing of communications already received.

34. After having briefly studied them, the Commission decided to allot them to the various members who would submit reports at the Fourth Session.

V. NEXT SESSIONS

35. Responding favourably to the invitations of the Governments of the Arab Republic of Egypt and the Libyan Arab Jamahiriya, the Commission decided to hold its Fourth Session in Cairo, Egypt, in October 1988 and its Fifth Session in Benghazi, Libya. The respective Governments of these two countries would discuss the modalities for the organization of the two meetings with the OAU Secretary-General.

ANNEX I

African Charter on Human and Peoples' Rights
List of Countries which have Signed, Ratified or Adhered to the Charter

No.	Country	Date of Signature	Date of Ratification/ Adhesion	Date Deposited
1.	Algeria	10/04/86	01/03/87	20/03/87
2.	Angola			
3.	Benin		20/01/86	25/02/86
4.	Botswana		17/07/86	22/07/86
5.	Burundi			
6.	Burkina Faso	05/03/84	06/07/84	21/09/74
7.	Cameroon	23/07/87		
8.	Cape Verde	31/03/86	02/06/87	06/08/87
9.	Central African Republic		26/04/86	27/07/86

No.	Country	Date of Signature	Date of Ratification/ Adhesion	Date Deposited
10.	Chad	29/05/86	09/10/86	11/11/86
11.	Comoros		01/06/86	18/07/86
12.	Congo	27/11/81	09/12/82	17/01/83
13.	Djibouti			
14.	Egypt	16/11/81	20/03/84	03/04/84
15.	Equatorial Guinea	18/08/86	07/04/86	18/08/86
16.	Ethiopia			
17.	Gabon	26/02/82	20/02/86	26/06/86
18.	Gambia	11/02/83	08/06/83	13/03/83
19.	Ghana			
20.	Guinea	09/12/81	16/02/82	13/05/82
21.	Guinea-Bissau		04/12/85	06/03/86
22.	Ivory Coast			
23.	Kenya			
24.	Lesotho	07/03/84		
25.	Liberia	31/01/83	04/08/82	29/12/82
26.	Libya	30/05/85	19/07/86	26/03/87
27.	Madagascar			
28.	Malawi			
29.	Mali	13/11/81	21/12/81	22/01/82
30.	Mauritania	25/02/82	14/06/86	26/06/86
31.	Mauritius			
32.	Mozambique			
33.	Niger	09/07/86	15/07/86	21/07/86
34.	Nigeria	31/08/82	22/06/83	22/07/83
35.	Rwanda	11/11/81	15/07/83	22/07/83
36.	Saharawi Arab Dem. Rep.	10/04/86	02/05/86	23/05/86
37.	Sao Tome & Principe		23/05/86	28/07/86
38.	Senegal	23/09/81	13/08/82	25/10/82
39.	Seychelles			
40.	Sierra Leone	27/08/81	21/09/83	27/01/84
41.	Somalia	26/02/82	31/07/85	20/03/86
42.	Sudan	03/09/82	18/02/86	11/03/86
43.	Swaziland			
44.	Tanzania	31/05/82	18/02/84	09/03/84
45.	Togo	26/02/82	05/11/82	22/11/82
46.	Tunisia		16/03/83	22/04/83
47.	Uganda	18/08/86	10/05/86	27/05/86
48.	Zaire	23/07/87	20/07/87	28/07/87
49.	Zambia	17/01/83	19/01/84	02/02/84
50.	Zimbabwe	20/02/86	30/05/86	12/06/86

ANNEX II

Members of the African Commission on Human and Peoples' Rights

No.	Name	Country of Origin	Duration of Term
1.	Mr. Alioune BLONDIN BEYE	Mali	2 years
2.	Mr. Ali Mahmoud BUHEDMA	Libya	6 years
3.	Dr. Ibrahim Ali Badawi EL SHEIKH	Egypt	2 years
4.	Mr. Alexis GABOU	Congo	6 years
5.	Mr. Grace S. IBINGIRA	Uganda	4 years
6.	Mr. Sourahata B. SEMEGA	Gambia	2 years
7.	Mr. Habesh Robert KISANGA	Tanzania	4 years
8.	Mr. M. B. MOKAMA	Botswana	6 years
9.	Mr. C. L. C. MUBANGA-CHIPOYA	Zambia	4 years
10.	Mr. Youssoupha NDIAYE	Senegal	6 years
11.	Mr. Isaac NGUEMA	Gabon	2 years

ANNEX III

Agendas of the Three Sessions

I. Agenda of the Addis Ababa Meeting (2 November 1987)

A. Opening of the Meeting
B. Election of a Provisional Bureau of the Meeting
C. Adoption of Agenda
D. Election of the Bureau of the Commission
E. Organization of the Future Work of the Commission
F. Date and Venue of the Next Session of the Commission
G. Any Other Business
H. Adoption of the Report of the First Session of the Commission

III. Agenda of the Dakar Meeting (8–13 February 1988)

A. Opening of the Meeting
B. Organization of Work
C. Adoption of the Report of the First Session
D. Brief Information on the Inter-Session
E. Consideration of the Draft Rules of Procedure of the Commission
F. Future Programme of Activities of the Commission
G. Adoption of the Final Communique
H. Date and Venue of the Next Session
I. Any Other Business
J. Closing Session

III. Agenda of the Libreville Meeting (18–28 April 1988)

A. Opening Ceremony
B. Organization of Work
C. Adoption of the Report of the Second Ordinary Session
D. Information on the Inter-Session
E. Procedure for the Consideration of Complaints (methodology)
F. Consideration of Guidelines for Form and Content of Periodic Reports
G. Consideration of the Financial Rules and Regulations
H. Consideration of Complaints Received
I. Headquarters of the Commission
J. Date and Venue of the Fourth Ordinary Session
K. Any Other Business
L. Adoption of the Report of the Third Session
M. Report to be Submitted to the Assembly of Heads of State and Government
N. Final Communiqué
O. Closing Session

ANNEX IV

Solemn Declaration

I solemnly declare to discharge my duties impartially and faithfully.

ANNEX V

Rules of Procedure of the African Commission on Human and Peoples' Rights[1]

Adopted on 13 February 1988

Part One: *General Provisions (Rules 1–80)*
Sessions (1–5), Agenda (6–12), Members of the Commission (13–17), Officers (18–22), Secretariat (23–28), Subsidiary Bodies (28–31), Public Sessions and Private Sessions (32–33), Languages (34–37), Minutes and Reports (38–42), Conduct of the Debates (43–59), Vote and Elections (60–71), Participation of Non-Members of the Commission (72–75), Consultations with NGOs and Representation of NGOs (76–77), Publication and Distribution of Reports and Other Official Documents of the Commission (78–80)

[1] The Rules have been replaced. The current Rules are reproduced above at p. 21.

PART ONE
GENERAL PROVISIONS
ORGANIZATION OF THE COMMISSION

Chapter I – Sessions

Rule 1 – Number of Session

The African Commission on Human and Peoples' Rights hereinafter referred to as "The Commission" shall hold the sessions which may be necessary to enable it to carry out satisfactorily its functions in conformity with the African Charter on Human and Peoples' Rights (hereinafter referred to as "The Charter").

Rule 2 – Opening Date

The Commission shall normally hold two ordinary sessions a year each lasting two weeks.

The ordinary sessions of the Commission shall be convened on a date fixed by the Commission on the proposal of its Chairman and in consultation with the Secretary-General of the Organization of African Unity (OAU) (hereinafter referred to as "The Secretary-General").

The Secretary-General may change, under exceptional circumstances, the opening date of a session, in consultation with the Chairman of the Commission.

Rule 3 – Extraordinary Sessions

1. Extraordinary sessions shall be convened on decisions of the Commission. When the Commission is not in session, the Chairman may convene extraordinary sessions

in consultation with the members of the Commission. The Chairman of the Commission shall also convene extraordinary sessions:

(a) at the request of the majority of the members of the Commission;
(b) at the request of the Current Chairman of the Organization of African Unity (OAU).

2. Extraordinary sessions shall be convened as soon as possible on a date fixed by the Chairman, in consultation with the Secretary-General and the other members of the Commission.

Rule 4 – Place of Meetings

The sessions shall normally be held at the Headquarters of the Commission. The Commission may, in consultation with the Sectary-General, decide to hold a session in another place.

Rule 5 – Notification of the Opening Date of the Sessions

The Secretary-General shall inform members of the Commission of the date of the first sitting of each session and its venue. This notification shall be sent, in the case of an Ordinary session, at least eight (8) weeks and, in the case of an Extraordinary session, at least three (3) weeks, if possible before the session.

Chapter III – Agenda

Rule 6 – Drawing up the Provisional Agenda

The Provisional Agenda for each Ordinary session shall be drawn up by the Secretary-General, in consultation with the Chairman of the Commission in accordance with the provisions of the Charter and these Rules.

The Provisional Agenda shall include if necessary, items on: "Communications from States", and "Other Communications" in conformity with the provisions of Article 55 of the Charter. It should not contain any information relating to such communications.

Except what has been specified above on the communications, the Provisional Agenda shall include all the items listed by the present Rules of Procedure as well as the Items proposed:

(a) by the Commission at a previous session;
(b) by the Chairman of the Commission or another member of the Commission;
(c) by a State party to the Charter,
(d) by the Assembly of Heads of State and Government (or the Council of Ministers of the Organization of African Unity),
(e) by the Secretary-General of the Organization of African Unity for every issue relating to the functions assigned to him by the Charter,
(f) by a national liberation movement recognized by the OAU or by a non-governmental Organization,

(g) by a specialized institution of which the States Parties to the Charter are members.

The items to be included in the provisional agenda under sub-paragraphs b, c, f and g of paragraph 3 must be communicated to the Secretary-General, accompanied by essential documents, not later than eight (8) weeks before the first sitting of each Session.

5. (a) All national liberation movements or non-governmental Organizations wishing to propose the inclusion of an item in the Provisional Agenda must inform the Secretary-General at least ten (10) weeks before the opening of the meeting. Before formally proposing the inclusion of an item in the Provisional Agenda, the observations likely to be made by the Secretary-General must duly be taken into account.

(b) The proposal, accompanied by essential documents, must formally be submitted not later than eight (8) weeks before the opening of the session.

All proposals made under the provisions of the present paragraph shall be included in the Provisional Agenda of the Commission, if at least two-thirds (2/3) of the members present and voting so decide.

6. The Provisional Agenda of the Extraordinary session of the Commission shall include only the item proposed to be considered at that Extraordinary session.

Rule 7 – Transmission and Distribution of the Provisional Agenda

1. The Provisional Agenda and the essential documents relating to each item shall be distributed to the members of the Commission by the Secretary-General who shall endeavour to transmit them to members at least six (6) weeks before the opening of the session.

2. The Secretary-General shall communicate the Provisional Agenda of that session and have the essential documents relating to each Agenda item distributed at least six weeks before the opening of the session of the Commission to the members of the Commission, member States parties to the Charter, to the Current Chairman of the OAU.

3. The Draft Agenda shall also be sent to the specialized agencies, to non-governmental Organizations and to the national liberation movements concerned with the agenda.

4. In exceptional cases, the Secretary-General may, while giving his reasons in writing, have the essential documents relating to some items of the Provisional Agenda distributed at least four (4) weeks prior to the opening of the session.

Rule 8 – Adoption of the Agenda

At the beginning of each session, the Commission shall if necessary, after the election of officers in conformity with Rule 18, adopt the agenda of the session on the basis of the Provisional Agenda referred to in Rule 6.

Rule 9 – Revision of the Agenda

The Commission may, during the session, revise the Agenda if need be, adjourn, cancel or amend items. During the session, only urgent and important issues may be added to the Agenda.

Rule 10 – Draft Provisional Agenda for the Next Session

The Secretary-General shall, at each session of the Commission, submit a Draft Provisional Agenda for the text session of the Commission, indicating, with respect to each item, the documents to be submitted on that item and the decision of the deliberative organ which authorized their preparation, so as to enable the Commission to consider these documents as regards the contribution they make to its proceedings, as well as their urgency and relevance to the prevailing situation.

Chapter III – Members of the Commission

Rule 11 – Composition of the Commission

The Commission shall be composed of eleven (11) members elected by the Assembly of Heads of State and Government hereinafter referred to as "the Assembly", in conformity with the relevant provisions of the Charter.

Rule 12 – Status of the member

1. The members of the Commission shall be the eleven (11) personalities appointed in conformity with the provisions of Article 31 of the Charter.
2. Each member of the Commission shall sit on the Commission in a personal capacity. No member may be represented by another person.

Rule 13 – Term of Office of the Members

1. The term of office of the members of the Commission elected on July 1987 shall begin from that date. The term of office of the members of the Commission elected at subsequent elections shall take effect the day following the expiry date of the term of office of the members of the Commission they shall replace.
2. However if a member is re-elected at the expiry of his or her term of office, or elected to replace a member whose term of office expired or will expire, the term of office shall begin from that expiry date.
3. In conformity with Article 39(3) of the Charter, the member elected to replace a member whose term of office has not expired, shall complete the term of office of his or her predecessor, unless the remaining term of office is less than six (6) months. In the latter case, there shall be no replacement.

Rule 14 – Cessation of Functions

1. If in the unanimous opinion of the other members of the Commission, a member has stopped discharging his duties for any reason other than a temporary absence, the Chairman of the Commission shall inform the Secretary-General of the Organization of African Unity, who shall then declare the seat vacant.

2. In case of the demise or resignation of a member of the Commission, the Chairman shall immediately inform the Secretary-General who shall declare the seat vacant from the date of the demise or from that on which the resignation took effect. The member of the Commission who resigns shall address a written notification of his or her resignation directly to the Chairman or to the Secretary-General and steps to declare his or her seat vacant shall only be taken after receiving the said notification. The resignation shall make the seat vacant.

Rule 15 – Vacant Seat

Every seat declared vacant in conformity with Rule 15 of the present Rules of Procedure shall be filled on the basis of Article 39 of the Charter.

Rule 16 – Oath

Before coming into office, every member of the Commission shall make the following solemn commitment at a public sitting:

"I swear to carry out my duties well and faithfully in all impartiality."

Chapter IV – Officers

Rule 17 – Election of Officers

1. The Commission shall elect among its members a Chairman and a Vice-Chairman.

2. The elections referred to in the present Rule shall be held by secret ballot. Only the members present shall vote, the member who shall obtain the two-thirds majority of the votes of the members present and voting shall be elected.

3. If no member obtains this two-thirds majority, a second and third and fourth ballot shall be held. The member having the largest number of votes at the fifth ballot shall be elected.

4. The officers of the Commission shall be elected for a period of two (2) years. They shall be re-eligible. None of them, may, however, exercise his or her functions if he or she ceases to be a member of the Commission.

Rule 18 – Powers of the Chairman

The Chairman shall carry out the functions assigned to him by the Charter, the Rules of Procedure and the decisions of the Commission. In the exercise of his functions the Chairman shall be under the authority of the Commission.

Rule 19 – Absence of the Chairman

The Vice-Chairman shall replace the Chairman during a session if the latter is unable to attend a whole or part of a sitting of a session.

Rule 20 – Functions of the Vice-Chairman

The Vice-Chairman, acting in the capacity of the Chairman, shall have the same rights and the same duties as the Chairman.

Rule 21 – Cessation of the Functions of an Officer

If any of the officers ceases to carry out his or her functions or declares that he or she is no longer able to exercise the functions of a member of the Commission or is no longer in a position for one reason or another, to serve as an officer, a new officer shall be elected for the remaining term of office of his or her predecessor.

Chapter V – Secretariat

Rule 22 – Function of the Secretary-General

1. The Secretary-General or his representative may attend the meetings of the Commission. He shall participate neither in the deliberations, nor in the voting. He may, however, be called upon by the Chairman of the Commission to address the meeting. He may make written or oral statements at the sittings of the Commission.
2. He shall appoint, in consultation with the Chairman of the Commission, the Secretary of the Commission.
3. He shall, in consultation with the Chairman provide the Commission with the necessary staff, material means and services for it to actually carry out effectively the functions and missions assigned to it under the Charter.
4. The Secretary-General shall take all the necessary steps for the meetings of the Commission.
5. The Secretary-General shall bring immediately to the knowledge of the members of the Commission all the issues that would be submitted to them for consideration.

Rule 23 – Estimates

Before the Commission shall approve a proposal entailing expenses, the Secretary-General shall prepare and distribute, as soon as possible, to the members of the Commission the financial implications of the proposal. It shall be incumbent on the Chairman to draw the attention of the members to those implications so that they discuss them when the proposal shall be considered by the Commission.

Rule 24 – Financial Rules

The Financial Rules adopted pursuant to the provisions of Article 41 and 44 of the Charter, shall be appended to the present rules of Procedure.

Rule 25 – Powers of the Secretary of the Commission

The Secretary of the Commission hereinafter referred to as "Secretary" shall be responsible for the activities of the Secretariat under the general supervision of the Chairman, and, particularly:

(a) He/she shall assist the Commission and its members in the exercise of their functions.
(b) He/she shall serve as an intermediary for all the communications concerning the Commission.
(c) He/she shall be the custodian of the archives of the Commission.

Rule 26 – Records of Cases

A special record, with a reference number and initialled, in which shall be entered the date of the registration of each petition and communication and that of the closure of the procedure relating to them before the Commission shall be kept at the Secretariat.

Rule 27 – Financial Responsibility

The Organization of African Unity shall bear the expenses of the staff and the means and services placed at the disposal of the Commission to carry out its functions.

Chapter VI – Subsidiary Bodies

Rule 28– Establishment of Committees and Working Groups

1. The Commission may during a session, taking into account the provisions of the Charter and in consultation with the Secretary-General, establish, if it deems it necessary for the exercise of its functions, Committees or Working Groups, composed of the members of the Commission and send them any Agenda item for consideration and report.

2. These Committees or Working Groups may with the prior consent of the Secretary-General, be authorized to sit when the Committee is not in session.

3. The members of the Committees or Working Groups shall be appointed by the Chairman, subject to the approval of the absolute majority of the other members of the Commission.

Rule 29 – Establishment of Sub-Commissions

1. The Commission may establish sub-Commissions of experts after the prior approval of the Assembly.

2. Unless the Assembly decides otherwise, the Commission shall determine and functions and composition of each sub-Commission.

Rule 30 – Officers of the Subsidiary Bodies

Unless the Commission decides otherwise, the subsidiary bodies of the Commission shall elect their own officers.

Rule 31: Rules of Procedure

The Rules of Procedure of the Commission shall apply, as far as possible, to the proceedings of its subsidiary bodies.

Chapter VII – Public Sessions and Private Sessions

Rule 32 – General Principle

The sittings of the Commission and of its subsidiary bodies shall be private and shall be held "in camera".

Rule 33 – Publication of Proceedings

At the end of each private sitting, the Commission or its subsidiary bodies may issue a communique through the Secretary-General.

Chapter VIII – Languages

Rule 34 – Working Languages

The working languages of the Commission and of all its institutions shall be those of the Organization of African Unity (OAU).

Rule 35 – Interpretation

1. The address delivered in one of the working languages shall be interpreted in the other working languages.
2. Any person addressing the Commission in a language other than one of the working languages, shall, in principle, ensure the interpretation in one of the working languages. The interpreters of the Secretariat may take the interpretation of the original language as source language for their interpretation in the other working languages.

Rule 36 – Languages to be Used for Minutes of Proceedings

The summary minutes of the sittings of the Commission shall be drafted in the working languages.

Rule 37 – Languages to be used for Resolutions and other Official Decisions

All the official decisions of the Commission shall be communicated in the working languages, that shall also apply to the other official documents of the Commission.

Chapter IX – Minutes and Reports

Rule 38 – Tape Recording of the Sessions

The Secretariat shall record and conserve the tapes of the sessions of the Commission. It may also record and conserve the tapes of the sessions of the Committees, Working Groups and sub-commissions if the Commission so decides.

Rule 39 – Summary Minutes of the Sessions

The Secretariat shall draft the summary minutes of the private and public sessions of the Commission and of its subsidiary bodies. It shall distribute them as soon as possible in a draft form to the members of the Commission and to all other participants in the session. All those participants may, in the seven (7) working days following the receipt of the draft minutes of thee session, submit corrections to the Secretariat. The Chairman may, under special circumstances, in consultation with the Secretary-General, extend the time for the submission of the corrections.

In case the corrections are contested, the Chairman of the Commission or the Chairman of the subsidiary body whose minutes they are, shall resolve the disagreement after having listened to, if necessary, the tape recording of the discussions. If the disagreement persists, the Commission or the subsidiary body shall decide. The corrections shall be published in a distinct volume after the closure of the session.

Rule 40 – Distribution of the Minutes of the Private Sessions and Public Sessions

1. The final summary minutes of the public and private sessions shall be documents intended for general distribution unless, under exceptional circumstances, the Commission decides otherwise.

2. The minutes of the private sessions of the Commission shall be distributed forthwith to all members of the Commission and to any other participants in the sessions.

Rule 41 – Reports to be Submitted After Each Session

The Commission shall submit to the Current Chairman of the OAU, a report on the deliberations of each session. This report shall contain a brief summary of the recommendations and statements on issue to which the Commission would like to draw the attention of the Current Chairman and member States of the OAU.

Rule 42 – Submission of Official Decisions and Reports

The text of the decisions and reports officially adopted by the Commission shall be distributed to all the members of the Commission as soon as possible.

Chapter X – Conduct of the Debates

Rule 43 – Quorum

The quorum shall be constituted by seven (7) members of the Commission, as specified in Article 42(3) of the Charter.

Rule 44 – General Powers of the Chairman

In addition to the powers entrusted to him under other provisions of the present Rules of Procedure, the Chairman shall have the responsibility to declare each session of the Commission opened and closed; he shall direct the debates, ensure the application of the present Rules of Procedure, grant the use of the floor, submit to a vote matters under discussion and announce the result of the vote taken. Subject to the provisions of the Present Rules of Procedure, grant the use of the floor, submit to a vote matters under discussion and announce the result of the vote taken. Subject to the provisions of the Present rules of Procedure, the Chairman shall direct the discussions of the Commission and ensure order during meetings. The Chairman may during the discussion of an agenda item, propose to the Commission to limit the time accorded to speakers, as well as the number of interventions of each speaker on the same issue and close the list of speakers. He shall rule on the points of order. He shall also have the power to propose the adjournment and the closure of debates as well as the adjournment and suspension of a sitting. The debates shall deal solely with the issue submitted to the Commission and the Chairman may call a speaker whose remarks are irrelevant to the matter under discussion to order.

Rule 45 – Points of Order

1. During the debate of any matter a member may, at any time, raise a point of order and the point of order shall be immediately decided by the Chairman, in accordance with the Rules of Procedure. If a member appeals against the decision, the appeal shall immediately be put to the vote and if the Chairman's ruling is not cancelled by the simple majority of the members present, it shall be maintained.
2. A member raising a point of order cannot. in his or her comments, deal with the substance of the matter under discussion.

Rule 46 – Adjournment of Debates

During the discussion on any matter, a member may move the adjournment of the debate on the matter under discussion. In addition to the proposer of the motion one member may speak in favour of and one against the motion after which the motion shall be immediately put to the vote.

Rule 47 – Limit of the Time Accorded to Speakers

The Commission may limit the time accorded to each speaker on any matter, when the time allotted for debates is limited and a speaker spends more than one time accorded, the Chairman shall immediately call him to order.

Rule 48 – Closing of the List of Speakers

The Chairman may, during a debate, read out the list of speakers and with the approval of the Commission, declare the list closed. Where there are no more speakers, the Chairman shall, with the approval of the Commission, declare the debate closed. This closure shall have the same effect as the one decided by the Commission.

Rule 49 – Closure of Debate

A member may, at any time, move the closure of the debate on the matter under discussion, even if other members or representatives expressed the desire to take the floor. The authorization to take the floor on the closure of the debate shall be given only to two speakers against the closure, after which the motion shall immediately be put to the vote.

Rule 50 – Suspension or Adjournment of the Meeting

During the discussion of any matter, a member may move the suspension or adjournment of the meeting. No discussion on any such motion shall be permitted and it shall immediately be put to the vote.

Rule 51 – Order of the Motions

Subject to the provisions of Rule 45 of the present Rules of Procedure. the following motions shall have precedence In the following order over all the other proposals or motions before the meeting:

(a) to suspend the meeting;
(b) to adjourn the meeting;
(c) to adjourn the debate on the tells under discussion;
(d) for the closure of the debate on the item tinder discussion.

Rule 52 – Submission of Proposals and Amendments of Substance

Unless the Commission decides otherwise the proposals, amendments or motions of substance made by members shall be submitted in writing to the Secretariat; if a member makes the request, they shall be considered at the first sitting following their submission.

Rule 53 – Decisions on Competence

Subject to the provisions of Rule 45 of the present Rules of Procedure, any motion tabled by a member for a decision on the competence of the Commission to adopt a proposal submitted to it shall immediately be put to the vote before the said proposal is put to the vote.

Rule 54 – Withdrawal of a Proposal or a Motion

The sponsor of a motion or a proposal may still withdraw it before it is put to the vote, on condition that it has not been amended. A motion or a proposal thus withdrawn may be submitted again by another member.

Rule 55 – New Consideration of Proposals

When a proposal is adopted or rejected, it shall not be considered again at the same session, unless the Commission decides otherwise. When a member moves the new consideration of a proposal, only one member may speak in favour of and one against the motion, after which it shall immediately be put to the vote.

Rule 56 – Interventions

1. No member may take the floor at a meeting of the Commission without prior authorization of the Chairman. Subject to Rules 50, 49, 45 and 48 the Chairman shall grant the use of the floor to the speakers in the order in which it has been requested.

2. The debates shall deal solely with the matter submitted to the Commission and the Chairman may call to order a speaker whose remarks are irrelevant to the matter under discussion.

3. The Chairman may limit the time 'accorded to speakers and the number of interventions which each member may make on the same issue, in accordance with Rule 44 of the present Rules.

Only two members in favour of motion and two against the motion of fixing such time limits shall be granted the use of the floor after which the motion shall immediately be put to the vote. For question of procedure the time accorded to each speaker shall not exceed five minutes, unless the Chairman decides otherwise. When the time allotted for discussions is limited and a speaker exceeds the time accorded the Chairman shall immediately call him to order.

Rule 57 – Right of Reply

The right of reply shall be granted by the Chairman to any member requesting it. The member must try, while exercising this right, to be as brief as possible and to take the floor preferably at the end of the sitting at which this right has been requested.

Rule 58 – Congratulations

The congratulations addressed to the newly elected members to the Commission shall only be presented by the Chairman or a member designated by the latter. Those addressed to the newly elected officers shall only be presented by the outgoing Chairman or a member designated by him.

Rule 59 – Condolences

Condolences shall be exclusively presented by the Chairman on behalf of all the members; the Chairman may, with the consent of the Commission, send a message on behalf of all the members of the Commission,

Chapter XI – Vote and Elections

Rule 60 – Right to Vote

Each member of the Commission shall have one vote. In the case of equal number of votes the Chairman shall have the casting vote.

Rule 61 – Asking for a Vote

A proposal or a motion submitted to the decision of the Commission shall be put to the vote if a member so requests. If no member asks for a vote, the Commission may adopt a proposal or a motion without a vote.

Rule 62 – Required Majority

1. Except in the cases the Charter or other Rules of the Present Rules of Procedure otherwise provide, decisions of the Commission shall be taken by the simple majority of the members present and voting.

2. For the purpose of the present Rules of Procedure, the expression "members present and voting" shall mean members voting for or against. The members who shall abstain from voting shall be considered as non-voting members.

3. Nevertheless decisions may be taken by consensus before resorting to voting, subject to compliance with the provisions of the Charter and the Rules of Procedure, and that the process for reaching that consensus shall not delay unduly the proceedings of the Commission.

Rule 63 – Method.of Voting

1. Subject to the provisions of Rule 68, the Commission unless it otherwise decides shall normally vote by show of hands, but any member may request the roll-call vote, which shall be taken in the alphabetical order of the names of the members of the

Commission beginning by the member whose name is drawn by lot by the Chairman. In all the votes by roll-call each member shall reply "yes", "no", or "abstention". The Commission may decide to hold a secret ballot.

2. In case of vote by roll-call, the vote of each member participating in ballot shall be recorded in the Minutes.

Rule 64 – Explanation of Vote

Members may make brief statements for the only purpose of explaining their vote, before the beginning of the vote or once the vote has been taken. The member who is the sponsor of a proposal or a motion cannot explain his vote on that proposal or motion except if it has been amended.

Rule 65 – Rules to be Observed while Voting

When the ballot shall begin, it may not be interrupted except if a member raises a point of order relating to the manner in which the ballot is held. The Chairman may allow members to intervene briefly, whether before the ballot beginning or when it is closed, but solely to explain their vote.

Rule 66 – Division of Proposals and Amendments

The division of proposals and amendments shall be done if so requested. The parts of the proposals or of the amendments which have been adopted shall later be put to the vote as whole; if all the operative parts of a proposal have been rejected, the proposal shall be considered to have been rejected as a whole.

Rule 67 – Amendment

An amendment shall simply comprise an addition to or a deletion of another proposal of a change in a part of the said proposal.

Rule 68 – Order of Vote on Amendments

When an amendment is moved to a proposal, the amendment shall be voted on first. When two or more amendments are moved to a proposal, the Commission shall first vote on the amendment furthest removed in substance from the original proposal and then on the amendment next furthest removed therefrom and so on until all the amendments have been put to the vote. Nevertheless when the adoption of an amendment shall necessarily imply the rejection of another amendment, the latter shall not be put to the vote. If one or several amendments are adopted, the amended proposal shall then be put to the vote.

Rule 69 – Order of Vote on the Proposals

1. If two or more proposals are made on the same matter, the Commission, unless it decides otherwise, shall vote on these proposals in the order in which they have been submitted.

2. After each vote the Commission may decide whether it shall put the next proposal to the vote.

3. However, the motions which do not require the opinion of the Commission on the substance of the proposals shall be considered as previous issues and put to the vote before the said proposals.

Rule 70 – Elections

The elections shall be held by secret ballot, unless the Commission otherwise decides when the election concerns one post for which only one candidate has been proposed and that the candidate or the list of candidates has been agreed upon.

Rule 71 – Majority Required to be Elected

When one post must be filled by election the candidate who shall obtain in the first ballot the majority of the votes cast and the largest number of votes shall be elected.

Chapter XII – Participation of Non-Members of the Commission

Rule 72 – Participation of States in the Deliberations

1. The Commission ma invite any State to participate in the discussion of any issue that shall be of particular interest to that State.

2. A subsidiary body of the Commission may invite any State to participate in the discussion of any issue that shall be of particular interest to the State.

3. A State thus invited shall have the voting right, but may submit proposals which may be put to the vote at the request of any member of the Commission or of the subsidiary be concerned.

Rule 73 – Participation of National Liberation Movements

The Commission may invite any National Liberation Movement recognized by the OAU or by virtue resolutions adopted by the Assembly to participate, without voting rights, in the discussion of any issue which shall be of particular interest to this Movement.

Rule 74 – Participation of Specialized Institutions and Consultations with the Latter

1. Pursuant to the agreement concluded between the OAU and the Specialized Institutions, the latter shall have the right to:

(a) be represented in the public sessions of the Commission and of subsidiary bodies,
(b) participate, without voting rights through their representatives in deliberations on issues which shall be of interest to them and to submit, on these issues, proposals which may be put to the vote at the request of any member of the Commission or interested subsidiary body.

Before placing in the Provisional Agenda an issue submitted by a Specialized Institution, the Secretary-General should initiate such preliminary consultations as may be necessary, with this institution.

3. When an issue proposed for inclusion in the Provisional Agenda of a session, or which has been added to the Agenda of a session pursuant to Rule 5 of the present Rules of Procedure, contains a proposal requesting the Organization of African Unity to undertake additional activities relating to issues concerning directly one or several Specialized Institutions. the Secretary-General should enter into consultation with the Institutions concerned and inform the Commission of the ways and means of ensuring co-ordinated utilization of the resources of the various Institutions.

4. When at a meeting of the Commission, a proposal calling upon the Organization of African Unity to undertake additional activities relate to issues directly concerning one or several Specialized Institutions, the Secretary-General, after consulting as far as possible the representatives of the interested Institutions, should draw the attention of the Commission to the effects of that proposal.

5. Before taking a decision on the proposals mentioned above, the Commission shall make sure that the Institutions concerned have been duly consulted.

Rule 75 – Participation of Other Inter-governmental Organizations

Representatives of Intergovernmental Organizations to which OAU has granted permanent observer status and other Inter-governmental Organizations permanently designated by the OAU or invited by the Commission, may participate, without voting rights, in the deliberations of the Commission on issues falling within the framework of the activities of these organizations.

Chapter XIII – Consultations with Non-governmental Organizations and Representation of these Organizations

Rule 76 – Representation

Non-governmental Organizations may appoint authorized observers to participate in the public sessions of the Commission and of its subsidiary bodies. The Non-governmental Organizations on the list as established by the Commission may sent observers to these sessions where issues falling within their area of activity are being considered.

Rule 77 – Consultation

1. The Commission may consult the Non-governmental Organizations either directly or through one or several Committees set up for this purpose. In any case, these consultations may be held at the invitation of the Commission or at the request of the organization.

2. Upon recommendation of the Secretary-General and at the request of the Commission, organizations on the above-mentioned list may also be heard by the Commission.

Chapter XIV – Publication and Distribution of the Reports and Other Official Documents of the Commission

Rule 78 – Report of the Commission

Within the framework of the procedure of communication among States parties to the Charter referred to in Articles 47 & 49 of the Charter, the Commission shall submit to the Assembly a report containing, where possible, recommendations it shall deem necessary. The report shall be confidential. However, it shall be published by the Chairman of the Commission if the Assembly so decides.

Rule 79 – Periodical Reports of Member States

Periodical reports and other information submitted by States parties to the Charter as requested under Article 62 of the Charter, shall be documents for general distribution. The same shall apply to other information supplied by a State party to the Charter, unless this State shall request otherwise.

Rule 80 – Reports on the Activities of the Commission

1. As stipulated in Article 54 of the Charter, the Commission shall each year submit to the Assembly, a report on its deliberations, in which it shall include a summary of its activities.

2. The report shall be published by the Chairman after the Assembly shall have considered it.

PART TWO
PROVISIONS RELATING TO THE FUNCTIONS OF THE COMMISSION

Chapter XV – Promotional Activities

Reports submitted by States Parties to the Charter under Article 62 of the Charter

Rule 81: Contents of Reports

1. States parties to the Charter shall submit reports on measures they would have taken to give effect to the rights recognized by the Charter and on the progress made with regard to the enjoyment of these rights. The reports should indicate, where possible, the factors and difficulties impeding the implementation of the provisions of the Charter.

2. Whenever the Commission shall request States parties to the Charter to submit reports as provided for by Article 62 of the Charter, it shall fix the date for the presentation of these reports.

3. The Commission may, through the Secretary-General, inform States parties to the Charter of its wishes regarding the form and the contents of the reports to be submitted under Article 62 of the Charter.

Rule 82 – Transmission of the Reports

1. The Secretary-General may, after consultation with the Commission, communicate to the Specialized Institutions concerned, copies of all parts of the reports which may relate to their areas of competence, produced by member States of these Institutions.

2. The Commission may invite the Specialized Institutions to which the Secretary-General has communicated parts of the reports, to submit observations relating to these parts within a time limit that it may specify.

Rule 83 – Submission of Reports

The Commission shall inform, as early as possible, member States parties to the Charter, through the Secretary-General, of the opening date, duration and venue of the Session at which their respective reports shall be considered. Representatives of the States parties to the Charter may participate in the sessions of the Commission at which their reports shall be considered. The Commission may also inform a State party to the Charter from which it wanted complementary information, that it may authorize its representative to participate in a specific session. This representative should be able to reply to questions to be put to him by the Commission and make statements on reports already submitted by this State. He may also furnish additional information from his State.

Rule 84 – Non-submission of Reports

1. The Secretary-General shall, at each session, inform the Commission of all cases of non-submission of reports or of additional information requested pursuant to Rules 81 and 85 of the Rules of Procedure. In such cases, the Commission may send, through the Secretary-General, to the State party to the Charter concerned, a report relating to the submission of the report or additional information.

2. If, after the reminder referred to in paragraph I of this rule, a State party to the Charter does not submit the report or the additional information requested pursuant to Rules 81 and 85 of the Rules of Procedure, the Commission shall point it out in its yearly report to the Assembly.

Rule 85 – Examination of Information Contained in Reports

1. When considering a report submitted by a State party to the Charter under Article 62 of the Charter, the commission should first make sure that the report provides all the necessary information pursuant to Rule 61 of the Rules of Procedure.

2. If, in the opinion of Commission, a report submitted by a State party to the Charter, does not contain adequate information, the Commission may request this State to furnish the additional information required, by indicating the date on which the information needed should submitted.

3. If, following the consideration of the reports, and the information submitted by a State party to the Charter, the commission decides that the State not discharged its obligations under the Charter, it may address all general observations to the State concerned as it may deem necessary.

Rule 86 – Adjournment and Transmission of the Reports

1. The Commission shall, through the Secretary-General, communicate to States parties to the Charter for comments, its general observations made following the consideration of the reports and the information submitted by States parties to the Charter. The Commission may, where necessary, fix a time limit for the submission of the comments by the States parties to the Charter.

2. The Commission may also transmit to the Assembly, the observations mentioned in paragraph 1 of this Rule, accompanied by copies of the reports it has received from the States parties to the Charter as well as the comments supplied by the latter, if possible.

Chapter XVI – Protection Activities Communications from the States Parties to the Charter

Section I – Procedure for the Consideration of Communications Received in Conformity with Article 47[2] of the Charter: "Procedure for Communications – Negotiations"

Rule 87 – Procedure

1. Any Communication submitted under Article 47 of the Charter should be submitted to the Secretary-General and the Chairman of the Commission.
2. The communication referred to above should be in writing and contain a detailed and comprehensive statement on the actions denounced as well as the provisions of the Charter alleged to have been violated.
3. The notification of the communication to the State party to the Charter, the Secretary-General and the Chairman of the Commission shall be done through a registered letter accompanied by an acknowledgement receipt form or through any known technical means.

Rule 88 – Register of Communications

The Secretary-General shall keep a permanent register for all communications received under Article 47 of the Charter.

Rule 89 – Reply and Time Limit

1. The reply of the State party to the Charter seized of a written communication should reach the requesting State party to the Charter within 3 months following the receipt of the notification of the Communication.
2. It shall he accompanied particularly by:
(a) written explanations, declarations or statements relating to the issues raised;
(b) possible indications and measures taken to end the situation denounced;
(c) indications on the law and rules of procedure applicable or applied;
(d) indications on the local procedures for appeal already used, in process or still open.

[2] Article 47 reads:
"If a State party to the present Charter has good reasons to believe that another State party to this Charter has violated the provisions of the Charter, it may draw, by written communication, the attention of the State to the matter. This communication shall also be addressed to the Secretary General of the OAU and to the Chairman of the Commission. Within three months of the receipt of the communication, the State to which the communication is addressed shall give the enquiring State, written explanation or statement elucidating the matter. This should include as much as possible relevant information relating to the laws and rules of procedure applied and applicable, and the redress already given or course of action available."

Rule 90 – Non-settlement of the Issue

1. If within three (3) months from the date the notification of the original communication is received by the addressee State, the issue has not been settled to the satisfaction of the two interested parties, through the selected channel of negotiation or through any other peaceful procedure selected by common consent of the parties, the issue shall be referred to the Commission, in accordance with the provisions of Article 47 of the Charter.

2. The issue shall also be referred to the Commission if the addressee State party to the Charter fails to react to the request made under Article 47 of the Charter, within the same 3 months' period of time.

Rule 91 – Seisin of the Commission

At the expiration of the 3 months' time limit referred to in Article 47 of the Charter, and in the absence of a satisfactory reply or in case the Addressee State party to the Charter fails to react to the request, each State party may submit the **communication** to the Commission through a **notification** addressed to **its Chairman**, to the other **interested** State party and to the Secretary-General.

Section II – Procedure for the Consideration of the Communications Received in Conformity with Articles 48 and 49 of the Charter: "Procedure for Communication – Complaint"

Rule 92 – Seisin of the Commission

1. Any communication submitted under Articles 48 and 49 of the Charter may be submitted to the Commission by any one of the interested States parties through notification addressed to the Chairman of the Commission, the Secretary-General and the State party concerned.

The notification referred to in paragraph 1 of the present Rule shall contain information on the following elements or be accompanied particularly by:

(a) measures taken to try to resolve the issue pursuant to Article 47 of the Charter including the text of the initial communication and any future written explanation from the interested States parties to the Charter relating to the issue;
(b) measures taken to exhaust local procedures for appeal;
(c) any other procedure for international investigation or international settlement to which the interested States parties have resorted.

Rule 93 – Permanent Register of Communications

The Secretary-General shall keep a permanent register for all communications received by the Commission under Articles 48 and 49 of the Charter.

Rule 94 – Seisin of the Members of the Commission

The Secretary-General shall immediately inform members of the Commission of any notification received pursuant to Rule 91 of these Rules of Procedure and shall send to them, as early as possible, a copy of the notification as well as the relevant information.

Rule 95 – Private Session and Press Releases

1. The Commission shall consider the communications referred to in Article 48 and 49 of the Charter in closed session.
2. After consulting the interested States parties to the Charter, the Commission may issue through the Secretary-General, releases on its activities for the attention of the media and the public at a closed session.

Rule 96 – Consideration of the Communication

The Commission shall consider communication only when:

(a) the procedure offered to the States parties by Article 47 of the Charter has been exhausted;
(b) the time limit set in Article 48 of the Charter has expired;
(c) the Commission is certain that all the available local remedies have been utilized and exhausted, pursuant the generally recognized principles of international law, or that the process of achieving these remedies extends beyond reasonable time limit or has been unduly prolonged.

Rule 97 – Amicable Settlement

Except for the provisions of Rule 96 of the present Rules of Procedure, the Commission shall place its good offices at the disposal of the interested States parties to the Charter so as to reach an amicable solution on the issue based on the respect of human rights and fundamental liberties, as recognised the Charter.

Rule 98 – Additional Information

The Commission may, through the Secretary-General, request the States parties concerned or one of them communicate to additional information or observations orally or in writing. The Commission shall fix a time limit for submission of the written information or observations.

Rule 99 – Representation of States Parties to Charter

1. The States parties to the Charter concerned shall have the right to be represented during the consideration of the issue by the Commission and to submit observations orally and in writing or in either form.

2. The Commission shall notify as soon as possible, the States parties concerned, through the Secretary-General, of the opening date, the duration and the venue of the session at which the issue will be examined.

3. The procedure to be followed for the presentation of oral or written observations shall be determined by the Commission.

Rule 100 – Report of the Commission

1. The Commission shall adopt a report pursuant to Article 52 of the Charter within a reasonable time limit which should not exceed 12 months, following the notification referred to in Article 48 of the Charter and Rule 90 of the present Rules of Procedure.

2. The provisions of paragraph 1 of Rule 99 of these Rules of Procedure shall not apply to the deliberations of the Commission, relating to the adoption of the report.

3. The report referred to above shall concern the decisions and conclusions that the Commission will reach.

4. The report of the Commission shall be communicated to the States parties concerned through the Secretary-General.

5. The report of the Commission shall be sent to the Assembly through the Secretary-General, together with the recommendations it shall deem useful.

Chapter XVII – Other Communications
Procedure for the Consideration of the Communications Received in Conformity with Article 55[3] of the Charter

Section I – Transmission of Communications to the Commission

Rule 101 – Session of the Commission

1. Pursuant to these Rules of Procedure, the Secretary-General shall transmit to the Commission the communications submitted to him for consideration by the Commission in accordance with the Charter.

Rule 102 – List of Communications

1. The Secretary of the Commission shall prepare lists of communications submitted to the Commission pursuant to Rule 101 above, to which he shall attach a brief

[3] Article 55 reads:

"1. Before each Session, the Secretary of the Commission shall make a list of the communications other than those of States parties to the present Charter and transmit them to the members of the Commission, who shall indicate which communications should be considered by the Commission.

2. A communication shall be considered by the Commission if a simple majority of its members so decide."

summary of their contents and regularly cause these lists to be distributed to members of the Commission. Besides, the Secretary shall keep a permanent register of all these communications.

2. The full text of each communication referred to the Commission shall be communicated to each member of the Commission on request.

Rule 103 – Request for Clarifications

1. The Commission, through the Secretary-General, may request the author of a communication to furnish clarifications on the applicability of the Charter to his communication, and to specify in particular:

(a) his name, address, age and profession by justifying his very identity, if ever he is requesting the Commission to be kept anonymous;
(b) name of the State party referred to in the communication;
(c) purpose of the communication;
(d) provision(s) of the Charter allegedly violated;
(e) "De facto" means of law;
(f) measures taken by the author to exhaust local remedies;
(g) the extent to which the same issue is already being considered by another international investigating or settlement body.

2. When asking for clarification or information, the Secretary-General shall fix an appropriate time limit for the author to submit the communication so as to avoid undue delay in the procedure provided for by the Charter.

3. The Commission may adopt a questionnaire for use by the author of the communication in providing the above mentioned information.

4. The request for clarification referred to in paragraph 1 of this Rule shall not prevent the inclusion of the communication on the lists mentioned in paragraph 1 of Rule 102 above.

Rule 104 – Distribution of Communications

For each communication recorded, the Secretary-General shall prepare as soon as possible, a summary of the relevant information received, which it shall distribute to the members of the Commission.

Section II – General Provisions Governing the Consideration of the Communications by the Commission or its Subsidiary Bodies

Rule 105 – Private Session

The sessions of the Commission or of its subsidiary bodies during which the communications provided for in the Charter are examined shall be considered private. The sessions during which the Commission may consider general issues, such as the application procedure of the Charter, may be public, if the Commission so desires.

Rule 106 – Press Releases

The Commission may issue, through the Secretary-General and for the attention of the media and the public, releases on the activities of the Commission in its private session.

Rule 107 – Incompatibilities

1. No member shall take part in the consideration of a communication by the Commission:

(a) if he has any personal interest in the case; or
(b) if he has participated, in any capacity, in the adoption of any decision relating to the case which is the subject of the communication.

2. Any issue relating to the application of paragraph 1 above shall be resolved by the Commission.

Rule 108 – Withdrawal of a Member

If, for any reason, a member considers that he should not take part or continue to take part in the consideration of a communication, he shall inform the Chairman of his decision to withdraw.

Rule 109 – Provisional Measures

Before making its final views on the communication known to the Assembly, the Commission may inform the State party concerned of its views on the appropriateness of taking provisional measures to avoid irreparable prejudice being caused to the victim of the alleged violation. In so doing, the Commission shall inform the State party that the expression of its views on the adoption of those provisional measures does not imply a decision on the substance of communication.

Rule 110 – Information to the State Party to the Charter

Prior to any substantive consideration, every communication should be made known to the State concerned through the Chairman of the Commission pursuant to Article 57 of the Charter.

Section III – Procedures to Determine Admissibility

Rule 111 – Time Limits for Consideration of the Admissibility

The Commission shall decide, as early as possible and pursuant to the following provisions, whether or not the communication shall be admissible under the Charter.

Rule 112 – Order of the Consideration of the Communications

1. Unless otherwise decided, the Commission shall consider communications in the order they have been received by the Secretariat.
2. The Commission may decide, if it deems it good, to consider jointly two several communications.

Rule 113 – Working Groups

1. The Commission may set up one of several Working Groups, composed of its members at most, to submit recommendations on the conditions of admissibility stipulated In Article 56 the Charter.

Rule 114 – Admissibility of the Communication

1. Communications may be submitted to the Commission by:

(a) an alleged victim of a violation by a State party to the Charter of one of the rights enunciated in the Charter or, in his name, when it appears that the latter is unable to submit the communication himself;
(b) an individual or an organisation alleging, with proofs in support, serious or massive cases of violation of human and peoples' rights.

2. The Commission may accept such communications from any individual or organisation irrespective of where they shall be.
3. In order to decide on the admissibility of communication, pursuant to the provisions of the Charter, the Commission shall ensure:

(a) that the communication indicates the identity of the author even if he requests the Commission to be anonymous, in which case the Commission shall not disclose his name;
(b) that the author alleges to be a victim of a violation, by a State party, of any one of the rights enunciated in the Charter and. if necessary, that the communication is submitted in the name of an individual who is a victim (or individuals who are victims) who would be unable to submit a communication or to authorize it to be done;
(c) that the communication does not constitute an abuse of the right to submit a communication under the Charter;
(d) that the communication is not incompatible with the provisions of the Charter;
(e) that the communication is not limited solely to information published or disseminated through the mass communication media;
(f) that the same issue is not already being considered by another international investigating or settlement body;
(g) that the alleged victim has exhausted all the available local remedies or that the processes of such remedies are unduly taking a long time;

(h) that the communication has been submitted within a reasonable time limit from the time the local remedies have been exhausted or from a period decided by the Commission.

Rule 115 – Additional Information

1. The Commission or a Working Group set up under Rule 113, may, through the Secretary-General, request the State party concerned or the author of the communication to submit in writing additional information or observations relating to the issue of admissibility of the communication. The Commission or the Working Group shall fix a time limit for the submission of the information or observations to avoid the issue dragging too long.

2. A communication may be declared admissible only on condition that the State party concerned has received the text of the communication and that it has been given the opportunity to submit the information and observations pursuant to paragraph 1 of this Rule.

3. A request made under paragraph 1 of this Rule should indicate clearly that the request does not mean that any decision whatsoever has been taken on the issue of admissibility.

Rule 116 – Decision of the Commission on Admissibility

1. If the Commission decides that a communication is inadmissible under the Charter, it shall make its decision known as early as possible, through the Secretary-General, to the author of the communication and, if the communication has been transmitted to a State party concerned, to that State.

2. If the Commission has declared a communication inadmissible under the Charter, it may re-consider this decision at a later date if it is seized by the interested individual or on his behalf, of a written request containing the information to the effect that the grounds for the inadmissibility have ceased to exist.

Section IV – Procedures for the Consideration of Communications

Rule 117 – Proceedings

1. If the Commission decides that a communication is admissible under the Charter, its decision and the text of the relevant documents shall as soon as possible, be submitted to the State party concerned, through the Secretary-General. The author of the communication shall also he informed of the Commission's decision through the Secretary-General.

2. The State party to the Charter concerned shall, within the 4 ensuing months, submit in writing to the Commission explanations or statements elucidating the issue under consideration and indicating, if possible, measures it was able to take to remedy the situation.

3. All explanations or statements submitted by a State party pursuant to the present Rule shall be communicated, through the Secretary-General, to the author of the communication who may submit in writing additional information and observations within a time limit fixed by the Commission.

4. The Commission may review the decision by which it has declared a communication admissible, in the light of the explanations and statements submitted by the State party under the present Rule.

Rule 118 – Final Decision of the Commission

1. If the communication is admissible, the Commission shall consider it in the light of all the information that the individual and the State party concerned has submitted in writing; it shall make known its observations on this issue. To this end, the Commission may refer the communication to a Working Group, composed of 3 of its members at most, which shall submit recommendations to it.

2. The observations of the Commission shall be communicated to the Assembly through the Secretary-General.

3. The Assembly or its Chairman may request the Commission to conduct an indepth study on these cases and to submit a factual report accompanied by its findings and recommendations, in accordance with the provisions of Article 58 subparagraph 2 of the Charter.

Final Chapter – Amendment and Suspension of the Rules of Procedure

Rule 119 – Method of Amendment

Only the Commission may modify the present Rules of Procedure.

Rule 120 – Method of Suspension

The Commission may suspend temporarily, the application of any Rule of the present Rules of Procedure, on condition that such a suspension shall not be incompatible with any applicable decision of the Commission or the Assembly or with any relevant provision of the Charter and that the proposal shall have been submitted 24 hours in advance. This condition may be set aside if no member oppose it. Such a suspension may take place only with a specific and precise object in view and should be limited to the duration necessary to achieve that aim.

Deliberated and adopted by the Commission at its second session held in Dakar, Senegal, on 1 February 1988.

ANNEX VI

Recommendation on the Headquarters of the African Commission on Human and Peoples' Rights

The African Commission on Human and Peoples' Rights, meeting in its Third Ordinary Session in Libreville, Gabon, from 18 to 28 April 1988,

Recalling that the African Charter on Human and Peoples' Rights which entered into force on 21 October 1986, established a Commission whose members were elected on 29 July 1987 by the OAU Assembly of Heads of State and Government and which held its First Session in Addis Ababa,

Noting that the Charter does not contain any formal provision indicating that the Headquarters of the Commission is established at the Headquarters of the OAU,

Noting indeed that Article 30 of the Charter specifies only that an African Commission on Human and Peoples' Rights is established within the OAU, charged with promoting human and peoples' rights and ensuring their protection in Africa,

Noting also that Article 64 of the Charter stipulates that the OAU Secretary-General will convene the first meeting of the Commission at the Headquarters of the Organization and that subsequently the Commission will be convened whenever necessary and at least once every year by its Chairman.

Bearing in mind the quasi-legislative nature of the Commission and its need for a full-time Secretariat, it is not desirable to have the Headquarters of the Commission where the political and administrative organs of the OAU are located,

Convinced that the Headquarters of the Commission can only be hosted by a State which has ratified the Charter and which offers to the Commission substantial material and human resource facilities for its establishment, work and researches,

1. RECOMMENDS to the OAU Assembly of Heads of State and Government to establish the Headquarters of the African Commission on Human and Peoples' Rights in a country other than the one hosting the political and administrative organs of the OAU;-

2. RECOMMENDS ALSO to the Assembly of Heads of State and Government to choose, in order to establish the Headquarters of the Commission, a country which has ratified the African Charter on Human and Peoples' Rights and which offers to the Commission substantial material and human resource facilities for its establishment, work and researches.

ANNEX VII

Recommendation on the Financial Rules and Regulations Governing the Functioning of the African Commission on Human and Peoples' Rights

The African Commission on Human and Peoples' Rights, meeting in its Third Ordinary Session in Libreville, Gabon, from 18 to 28 April 1988,

Considering that the African Charter on Human and Peoples' Rights adopted in Nairobi on 28 June 1981, entered into force on 21 October 1986, and that members of the African Commission on Human and Peoples' Rights set up to apply it, were elected on 29 July 1987, and installed on 2 November 1987,

Reaffirming their duty to ensure the promotion and protection of human and peoples' rights and freedoms, duly taking into account, the primordial importance traditionally attached to these rights and freedoms in Africa,

Conscious of the fundamental role of the African Commission on Human and Peoples' Rights to assist States Parties to the African Charter on Human and Peoples' Rights in the promotion and protection of human and peoples' rights and freedoms,

HAS AGREED THAT:

1. The Financial Rules and Regulations of the OAU dated 4 March 1979, apply to the African Commission on Human and Peoples' Rights, without prejudice to the following rules:

2. The Organization of African Unity shall bear the financial cost of the Commission, pursuant to the relevant provisions of the OAU Charter and the African Charter on Human and Peoples' Rights. Article 41 of which stipulates

> "The Secretary-General of the Organization of African Unity shall appoint a Secretary of the Commission. He shall provide the staff and services necessary for the effective discharge of the duties of the Commission. The Organization of African Unity shall bear the cost of the staff and services"

and Article 44 of which stipulates:

> "Provision shall be made for the emoluments and allowances of the members of the Commission in the Regular Budget of the Organization of African Unity."

3. The Commission's budget shall form part of the Regular Budget of the Organization of African Unity, but this budget shall be distinct and managed separately.

The Secretary-General of the OAU shall be the Accounting Officer and, in this capacity, shall be responsible for its management. He may however delegate any part of his powers to the Chairman of the Commission for application of financial rules and regulations of the OAU and the relevant provisions for Rules of Procedure of the Commission.

The Accountant of the OAU shall be responsible for keeping the accounts and shall be responsible for receiving financial resources and making relevant payments. He may, following the exigencies of the service, delegate all or part of his powers to a staff member of the Secretariat of the Commission, in consultation with the Commission.

4. The Secretary-General of the OAU shall prepare and submit for consideration to the Advisory Committee on Administrative, Budgetary and Financial Matters, the OAU Programme of Action which shall include the programme of action of the Commission and the budgetary appropriation including those of the Commission.

5. The following are expenditure codes necessary for the effective execution of the

tasks assigned to the Commission pursuant to the provisions of Article 2 on the Financial Rules and Regulations of the OAU, to cover:

- the emoluments and allowances for the members of the Commission, as provided for in Article 44 of the Charter;
- staff costs of the Secretariat of the Commission.
- cost of facilities and activities of the Commission.

6. As regards additional resources to the financial contribution of the OAU or the Commission, the latter may accept in consultation with the OAU Secretary-General, grants, bequests and other donations compatible with the objectives of the African Charter of Human and Peoples' Rights.

7. If the budgetary appropriations of the Commission have not been approved or are inadequate or if new expenses are to be incurred as a result of financial implications of approved decisions after the Regular Budget of the OAU has been adopted, the Secretary-General of the OAU shall, in consultation with Commission, submit to the Advisory Committee or sub-Advisory Committee a rectified additional programme and budget for consideration. He shall subsequently submit the same to the Council of Ministers for approval. This would enable the Commission to carry out its task effectively.

The Secretary-General may also identify new financial sources by drawing from the overall balances available under some codes after the normal closing of the financial year.

8. If the budgetary estimates of the Commission are not adopted before 1 July one-twelfth of the previous budget shall be released in accordance with Article 00 of the OAU Financial Rules and Regulations.

ANNEX VIII

Programme of Action of the African Commission On Human and Peoples' Rights

A. Research and Information Activities

1. Establishment of African Library and a Documentation Centre on Human Rights;
2. Printing and dissemination of the African Charter on Human and Peoples' Rights including its Rules of Procedures;
3. Publication of an African Review on Human and Peoples' Rights;
4. Periodical radio broadcasts and television programmes on Human Rights in Africa;
5. Integration of Teaching of Human Rights on the Syllabi of secondary education;
6. Proclamation of a Human Rights Day;
7. Participation in the bicentenary activities of the Declaration on the Rights of Man and of the Citizen 1789;

8. Institution of a prize for and a competition on Human Rights;
9. Recommendation on the Establishment of National Human Rights Committees;
10. Recommendation on the Establishment of Human Rights Institutes.
11. Symposia or Seminars on Apartheid.

B. Quasi-Legislative Activities

1. Charter ratification campaign within countries which have not yet ratified it;
2. Ratification of Human Rights Treaties prepared by international organizations (United Nations, ILO, etc.);
3. Introduction of the provisions of the Charter in the constitutions of States.

C. Co-operation Activities

1. Co-operation with international inter-state or non-governmental organizations: European Commission, American Commission, United Nation Commission, International Commission of Jurists, International Academy of Human Rights, Amnesty International;
2. Co-operation with African organizations: Inter-African Union of Lawyers, Association of African Jurists, Association of African International Law;
3. Periodic Reports of States.

ANNEX IX

Recommendation on Periodic Reports

The African Commission on Human and Peoples' Rights, meeting in its Third Ordinary Session in Libreville, Gabon, from 18 to 28 April 1988,

Having carefully examined the African Charter on Human and Peoples' Rights and, particularly, its Article 62 which stipulates:

> "Each State Party shall undertake to submit every two years, from the date the present Charter comes into force, a report on the legislative or other measures taken with a view to giving effect to the rights and freedoms recognized and guaranteed by the present Charter",

Considering that this provision of the Charter contains only the obligation which is that of a State Party to submit the report,

Considering that the Charter does not stipulate to which authority or body the periodic report should be directed,

Considering that the Charter has not specifically entrusted to the Commission, the responsibility to consider the periodic reports on Human Rights,

Considering further that it is difficult to see which other organ of the OAU could accomplish this work,

Considering that the African Commission on Human and Peoples' Rights is the only appropriate organ of the OAU capable not only of studying the said periodic reports, but also of making pertinent observations to States Parties, and providing them with general guidelines on the form and contents of the reports which they should submit, pursuant to Article 62 referred to above,

RECOMMENDS that the Assembly of Heads of State and Government:

1. Mandate the General Secretariat of the OAU to receive the said reports and communicate them to the Commission without delay;

2. Specifically entrust it with the task of examining the periodic reports submitted by the States Parties pursuant to Article 62 and other relevant provisions of the African Charter on Human and Peoples' Rights;

3. Authorize it to give the States Parties general guidelines on the form and contents of the said periodic reports.

ANNEX X

Communications: Procedures (Register Forms)

Register No. 1: Page 1
Communication from a State Party against another State Party:
Article 47 Procedure for Communications

1	Applicant State
2	Respondent State
3	Date Communication Written (Date on Communication)
4	Subject of the Communication: Provisions Violated
5	Date Communication Received by State Concerned
6	Date of Notification of the OAU Secretary General
7	Date of Notification of the Chairman of the Commission (Article 47)
8	Date of Expiry of Three Month Period (Article 48)
9	Settlement of the Dispute
10	Date of Notification of the Commission (Article 48)
11	Date of Notification of the Secretary General (Article 48)
12	Date of notification of Other State (Article 48)

Register No. 1: Page 2
Communication from a State Party against another State Party:
Procedure for Direct Seisin

1 Applicant State
2 Respondent State
3 Date of Communication
4 Subject of the Communication: Provisions Violated
5 Date of Reception of the Communication by State Concerned
6 Date of Seisin of OAU Secretary General
7 Date of Seisin of the Chairman of the Commission
8 Exhaustion of Local Remedies
9 Information Requested
10 Attempt at Conciliation
11 Report of the Commission (Article 52)
12 Recommendations made to the Assembly of Heads of State and Government
13 Date Report sent to the State Concerned
14 Date Report sent to the Assembly of Heads of State and Government

Register No. 2: Page 1
Procedure for Investigation of the Communication – Article 55

1 Serial Number
2 Date of Communication
3 Date Received
4 Notification of State Concerned
5 Rapporteur Appointed
6 Date of Appointment
7 Work to be Carried Out
8 Date Report Deposited
9 Decision of the Commission
10 Decision of the Assembly of Heads of State and Government

Register No. 2: Page 2
Communication – Complaint: – Article 55
Information Relative to the Author of the Communication

1	Family name and first names of the author
2	Address
3	Age
4	Profession
5	State concerned (Party or not)
6	Subject of the Communication
7	Date of Communication (Date of Communication)
8	Provisions violated
9	Means of fact (summary of facts)
10	Measures taken by the author to exhaust local remedies
11	Examination before another international body of enquiry or settlement

Second Activity Report of the African Commission on Human and Peoples' Rights

Adopted on 14 June 1989
Covering the 4th and 5th Ordinary Sessions (October 1988 and April 1989) and the Extraordinary Session in Banjul in June 1989 as well as intersession activities

I. ORGANIZATION OF WORK AND ANY OTHER BUSINESS

A. Period Covered by the Report

1. The First Activity Report of the African Commission on Human and Peoples' Rights was adopted by the Commission on 28 April 198 in Libreville. It covered the activities of the Commission from 2 November, 1987 the date of its inception to that date. This report, the second one, relates to the period 29 April 1988 to 14 June 1989.

B. Status of Ratification

2. Ghana has become the 36th State Party. It ratified the Charter on 24 January 1989 and deposited its instrument of ratification on 1 March 1989.
3. The list of States that have ratified or adhered to the African Charter on Human and Peoples' Rights is attached to this Report as Annex I.
4. The Chairman has on behalf of the Commission written to all non States Parties urging them to ratify the African Charter on Human and Peoples' Rights. The letter of the Chairman is annexed hereto as Annex II.

C. Sessions and Agenda

5. The Commission has held two ordinary sessions and one extra-ordinary session since its First Activity Report was adopted.

- the Fourth Ordinary Session was held in Cairo, Egypt from 17–26 October 1988;
- the Fifth Ordinary Session was held in Benghazi, Peoples' Socialist Libyan Arab Jamahiriya, from 3–14 April 1989;
- the Extraordinary Session, which was the very First Extraordinary Session held by the Commission, took place in Banjul, The Gambia, from 13–14 June 1989.

6. The Agenda of all these sessions is attached to this Report as Annex III.

D. Composition and Participation

7. The composition of the African Commission on Human and Peoples' Rights has changed since Mr. Grace S. Ibingira resigned from the Commission on 25 April 1989 and his seat was declared vacant as at 29 May 1989. The remaining ten founder members still constitute the Commission. The list of members of the Commission is attached to this Report as Annex IV.

8. Attendance at sessions has been very good:

- at the Fourth Ordinary Session, Mr. Alioune Blondin Beye was absent with apology,
- at the Fifth Ordinary Session, Mr. Grace Ibingira was absent,
- at the First Extraordinary Session, Mr. Moleleki D. Mokama and Mr. Alioune Blondin Beye were absent with apology.

E. Chairman, Vice-Chairman and Secretary

9. The mandate of the Chairman, Isaac Nguema and Vice-Chairman, Dr. Ibrahim Ali Badawi has not expired.

10. On 10 February 1989, Mr. Jean Ngabishema Mutsinzli, the Secretary of the Commission, took office in place of Mrs. Esther Tchouta-Moussa. The members expressed their gratitude to Mrs. Tchouta-Moussa for the satisfactory service she rendered to the Commission during her term of office.

F. Any Other Business

(a) Matters relating to Burundi

11. At its Fourth Session, upon the request of the Republic of Burundi which has not ratified the Charter, the Commission heard statements from a Burundi Government envoy on the tragic events which took place in that country in August 1988. The Chairman was instructed by the Commission to meet the Current Chairman of the OAU in Bamako:

- to consider in cooperation with the Government of Burundi sending a delegation of the Commission to Burundi to conduct an in-depth study off the human rights situation in Burundi;
- to urge the Government of Burundi to take steps to ratify the Charter.

The Chairman of the Commission was granted audience by the Current Chairman of the OAU on 10 February 1989.

12. However, no information has yet been received as to the follow-up to the Commission's request.

(b) Information

Inauguration of Commission's Headquarters

13. The Headquarters of the Commission was inaugurated on Monday, 12 June 1989. The inaugural ceremony took place opposite the Headquarters' grounds in Fajara, Greater Banjul.

14. Present at the ceremony were The Gambia President, His Excellency Sir Dawda Kairaba Jawara, the Commissioners, Gambian dignitaries and other guests who included the Secretary General of the OAU, Mr. Ide Oumarou, the Under Secretary General for Human Rights of the United Nations, Mr. Jan Martenson, the President of the Inter-American Commission of Human Rights, Mr. Oliver Jackman, and a representative from the European Commission of Human Rights, Sir Basil Hall.

15. After the delivery of speeches by His Excellency Sir Dawda Kairaba Jawara, Mr. Ide Oumarou, Mr. Martenson and Mr. Nguema, the Commission's Chairman, the Gambian President formally handed over the keys of the Headquarters' building to the Secretary General of the OAU.

G. Adoption of the Activity Report

16. On 14 June 1989, at its Extraordinary Session. the Commission considered the draft of this Second Activity Report. After discussions resulting in amendments, the Activity Report, covering a period during which two ordinary sessions and one extraordinary session were held successively in Cairo, Benghazi and Banjul, was adopted by the Commission.

II. GENERAL REMARKS OF THE COMMISSION

A. Promotional Activities

(a) Seminars

17. In keeping with the Programme of Action members of the Commission attended seminars which are listed in Annex V.

(b) Publications

18. The Chairman of the Commission, in the absence of funds being available to the Commission, has asked the Secretary General of the OAU to print and disseminate its First Activity Report in the working languages. As at 14 June 1989, the Activity Report has not been published.

19. The Commission decided to publish a Review on Human and Peoples' Rights and expressed satisfaction at the fact that UNESCO had granted it a subvention for that purpose.

(c) Notable Anniversaries

20. The Commission decided to associate itself with the various celebrations of the Fortieth Anniversary of the Universal Declaration of Human Rights. On that occasion the Chairman of the Commission called a press conference in Libreville, Gabon. In addition he sent to the Heads of State a solemn declaration attached hereto as Annex VI.

21. The Commission passed a resolution at its Fourth Session recommending that all member States of the Organization of African Unity adopt 21 October of each year for celebrating the African Day on Human and Peoples' Rights. The resolution is attached to this Report as Annex VII.

22. On the occasion of the celebrations, the Chairman requested the OAU General Secretariat in compliance with instructions given by the Commission to publish a booklet including the Charter and Rules of Procedure on the one hand and a review of the activities of the Commission on the other hand. To date the booklet has not been published.

(d) Human Rights Committee

23. At its Fourth Session the Commission adopted a resolution recommending the setting up by States Parties of committees on Human and Peoples' Rights at national and regional levels. The resolution is attached to this report as Annex VIII.

(e) Educational Measures

24. The Commission is fully aware of the promotional value of education and information in the field of Human and Peoples' Rights. Therefore, at its Fifth Session it made recommendations to the States Parties:

- for the teaching of Human and Peoples' Rights in schools at all levels in all systems of education;
- the broadcast of human rights programmes on radio and television;
- the establishment of national and regional human rights institutes devoted to study and research and the dissemination of knowledge on the subject matter of human and peoples' rights and the duties of citizens.

25. The recommendation solution concerned is attached to this report as Annex IX.

(f) Observers

26. In pursuance of Rules 76 and 77 of its Rules of Procedure, the Commission has granted certain non-governmental organizations observer status and has in fact granted audience to some of their representatives. The criteria for admitting observers are clear and flexible and serious non-governmental organizations concerned with human rights are welcome especially if they submit with their applications a resumé of their activities and supporting documentation to the Commission's Secretariat.

27. The NGOs which have so far been granted observer status are in the list attached to this report as Annex X.

B. Protective Activities

28. In order to harmonize the legal systems of States Parties, the Commission recommended the introduction of Articles 1–29 of the Charter into the Constitutions and laws of States Parties where the latter have not yet done so or do not have equivalent legal provisions. The Recommendation is attached to this Report as Annex XI.

C. Measures Adopted by the Twenty-fourth Session of the Assembly of Heads of State and Government of the OAU following the Activity Report Presented by the Commission

29. The Twenty-fourth Session of the Assembly of Heads of State and Government decided by Resolution AHG/Dec. I (XXIV) that Banjul, capital of the Gambia, be the Headquarters of the Secretariat of the African Commission on Human and Peoples' Rights.

30. On the other hand, by Resolution AHG/Res. 176 (XXIV) the Assembly adopted the Activity Report of the Commission, approved its Rules of Procedure and the Financial Rules and Regulations governing its functioning and adopted the Recommendation on the National Periodic Reports.

III. PERIODIC REPORTS

31. At their Twenty-fourth Ordinary Session the Heads of State and Government, on the Commission's recommendation, entrusted the Commission with the task of examining periodic reports submitted by States Parties pursuant to Article 62 of the Charter and also authorized the Commission to prepare and deliver general guidelines on the form and contents of the periodic reports.

32. At its Fourth Ordinary Session [October 1988] the Commission adopted the general guidelines relating to the form and contents of the periodic reports that States Parties are committed to submit pursuant to Article 62 of the Charter. The "Guidelines for National Periodic Reports" is attached to this Report as Annex XII.

33. It was decided by the Commission that the Guidelines will be progressively delivered to States Parties in order to attract prompt, clear and precise responses.

34. The Chairman has on the direction of the Commission despatched letters to States Parties requesting the submission of their initial respective periodic reports within a specified time. The Chairman has in addition sent reminders to States Parties on the same subject. The letters are annexed hereto as Annex XIII and the reminder as Annex XIV.

IV. CONSIDERATION OF COMMUNICATIONS

Since its establishment, the Commission has received 38 communications, some of which arrived at the OAU General Secretariat well in advance of the election of members. Action on these communications is still in progress.

Out of the communications received:

- 24 cases decided on with regard to their admissibility;
- 3 cases declared inadmissible;
- 6 cases dealt with a decision taken or a communication by the Commission;
- 5 cases will be considered at future sessions.

35. At its Fourth Ordinary Session, the Commission settled ten cases. The decisions, for the time being, remain confidential in conformity with Article 59 of the African Charter on Human and Peoples' Rights.

36. It is worth mentioning here, that a communication that is not levelled against a State Party to the Charter is not admissible and will not be considered by the Commission on the merits.

37. At its Fifth Session [April 1989] the Commission appointed five Rapporteurs from among its members to deal with certain communications received by the Secretariat, which should in the near future translate the communications in the working languages and despatch them to the Rapporteurs concerned for action.

38. In the same Session the Commission considered five pending cases and took preliminary or other decisions on each of them.

V. NEXT SESSIONS

39. Dates and venues of the next sessions will be determined in consultation with the OAU General Secretariat.

ANNEX I

African Charter on Human and Peoples' Rights
List of Countries which have Signed, Ratified or Adhered to the Charter

Corresponding to the first list of ratifications there have been 35 ratifications. The list delivered within this 2nd Report indicates 36 (Ghana having ratified on 24 January 1989). Up to the 3rd Report an additional four countries (Burundi, Cameroun, Malawi and Mozambique) have ratified.

ANNEX II

Letter by the Chairman of the African Commission on Human and Peoples' Rights

Addis Ababa, 21 February 1989

Honourable Minister,

I have learnt from reliable sources that your country is about to ratify the African Charter on Human and Peoples' Rights.

If this information is correct, I would request Your Excellency to confirm it and communicate the instrument of ratification to the OAU General Secretariat in conformity with Article 63 of the said Charter.

Please accept, Your Excellency, the assurance of my highest consideration.

Isaac NGUEMA
Chairman of the African Commission on
Human and Peoples' Rights

To His Excellency
Minister for Foreign/External Affairs

ANNEX III

Agenda of the Two Ordinary Sessions and One Extraordinary Session (Cairo, Benghazi and Banjul)

I. Agenda of the Fourth Ordinary Session (Cairo, 17–26 October 1988)

1. Opening Session
2. Adoption of the Agenda
3. Organization of Work
4. The Question of Observers and the Participation of States not Parties to the Charter
5. Implementation of Decisions and Resolutions of the 24th Ordinary Session of the Assembly of Heads of State and Government on the Commission

   (a) General Directives on the Preparation and Presentation of Periodic Reports
   (b) Consideration of the Draft Agreement on the Headquarters of the Commission's Permanent Secretariat
   (c) Implementation of the Resolution on the Amendment of the OAU Financial Rules and Regulations
   (d) Publication of the activity report

6. Brief Report Covering the Inter-session Period
7. Consideration of the Communications
8. Consideration of the Report on the OAU General Convention on Privileges and Immunities
9. Any Other Business
10. Date and Venue of the Next Session
11. Adoption of the:

    (a) Report of the 4th Session
    (b) Final Communiqué

12. Closing of the 4th Session

II. Agenda of the Fifth Ordinary Session (Benghazi, 3–14 April 1989)

1. Opening of the Session
2. Adoption of the Agenda
3. Organization of Work
4. Matters Relating to Observers
5. Implementation of Decisions and Resolutions of the Twenty-fourth Ordinary Session of the Assembly of Heads of State and Government Relating to the Commission

    (a) Guidelines Concerning the Preparation of Periodic Reports
    (b) Consideration of the Draft Headquarters Agreement of the Permanent Secretariat of the Commission and Inauguration of the Headquarters of the Commission
    (c) Implementation of the Resolution Relating to the Amendment of the Financial Rules and Regulations of the OAU
    (d) Publication of the Activity Report

6. Follow up of the Recommendation Adopted by the Fourth Session
7. Activity Report of the Chairman and the Members of the Commission During the Intersession
8. Consideration of Communications
9. Consideration of the Report on the General Convention of the OAU on Privileges Immunities
10. Promotional Activities
11. Any Other Business
12. Date and Venue and Agenda of the Next Session
13. Adoption of the:

    (a) Report of the Fifth Ordinary Session
    (b) Final Communiqué

14. Closing Session

First Extraordinary Session (Banjul, 13–14 June 1989)

1. Opening of the Session
2. Adoption of the Agenda
3. Organization of Work
4. Matters Relating to the Organization of the Session
5. Preparation of the Second Activity Report of the Commission
6. Any Other Business

ANNEX IV

Members of the African Commission on Human and Peoples' Rights

No.	Name	Country	Term of Office
1.	M. Alioune Blondin Beye	Mali	2 years
2.	M. Ali Mahmoud Buhedma	Libya	6 years
3.	Dr. Ibrahim Ali Badawi El Sheikh	Egypt	2 years
4.	M. Alexis Gabou	Congo	6 years
5.	M. Sourahata B. Semega Janneh	Gambia	2 years
6.	M. Habesh Robert Kisanga	Tanzania	4 years
7.	M. M. D. Mokama	Botswana	6 years
8.	M. C. L. C. Mubanga-Chipoya	Zambia	4 years
9.	M. Youssoupha Ndiaye	Senegal	6 years
10.	M. Isaac Nguema	Gabon	2 years

N.B.: Mr. Grace Stuart Ibingira, a national of Uganda, resigned for personal reasons.

ANNEX V

List of Seminars in which Members of the Commission have Participated

As regards participation in international meetings, the Commission involved in the: on the Universal Declaration on Human Rights, I.n Lorn6,

1. Seminar organised on the Universal Declaration on Human Rights, in Lomé, from 5–7 April 1988, by the Government of Togo the Togolese Commission on Human Rights, the United Nations Centre for Human Rights, and the UN Regional Centre for Peace and Disarmament in Africa, thanks to the contribution of Mr. Isaac Nguema

2. Training course organised in Lomé, from 8–15 April 1988, by the United Nations Centre for Human Rights, thanks to the contribution of Mr. Isaac Nguema.

3. Training programme organised from 22 August to 2 September 1988 by the Regional Centre for Peace and Disarmament in Africa in collaboration with the Economic Community of West African States (ECOWAS): participation guaranteed thanks to the contribution of Mr. Isaac Nguema.

4. Seminar on Human Rights and Social and Economic Progress, organised by the Friedrich Naumann Foundation, National University of Benin and the Economic Community of West African States, in Cotonou, from 30 May to 4 June 1988, thanks to the contribution of Mr. Alioune Blondin Beye.

5. International Symposium of Peoples' Rights as condition for Human Rights organised in Brussels. from 7–8 May 1988, by the International Association of Democratic Lawyers, thanks to the contribution of Mr. Isaac Nguema and Mrs. Tchouta-Moussa.

6. Symposium organised in Libya from 9–11 June 1988 on the drafting of the Green Charter and Peace, thanks to the participation and contribution of Mrs. Tchotita-Moussa and Mr. Isaac Nguema.

7. Training Seminar organised by UNITAR and the Centre for Human Rights in Kigali, from 6–17 June 1988, thanks to the contribution of Mr. Isaac Nguema.

8. Debate Conference organised in Kinshasa, by the Association of Young Zairean Lawyers, on 30 August 1988, thanks to the contribution of Mr. Isaac Nguema.

9. Training Course on the teaching of Human Rights organised from 22–24 August 1988 in Conakry by the Ecole Instrument de Paix: participation guaranteed by Mr. Youssoupha Ndiave.

10. Symposium organised from 25 September–2 October 1988, by the United Nations Centre for Human Rights, in Tunis, on Justice in Arab Countries, thanks to the contribution of Mr. Isaac Nguema.

11. 20th Anniversary of the Zairean Bar organised from 28–30 October 1988 thanks to the contribution of Mr. Alexis Gabou.

12. Symposium organised in Strasbourg, from 8–14 November 1988, by the Friedrich Naumann Foundation, the Pan-African Institute of International Relations and the Council of Europe, thanks to the contribution of Mr. Isaac Nguema.

13. International Symposium organised in Paris by UNESCO, from 5–14 December 1988, within the framework of activities commemorating the Universal Declaration on Human Rights, thanks to the contribution of Mr. Isaac Nguema.

14. International Seminar of "Human Dignity and ACP/EEC Conventions" organised in Brussels, from 8–10 December 1988, by the Foundation for ACP/EEC Cultural Cooperation, with the assistance of the European Communities Commission, thanks to the contribution of Mr. Isaac Nguema and Mr. Youssoupha Ndiaye.

15. Seminar organised in Geneva, from 5–9 December 1988, by the United Nations Centre for Human Rights on the Education of Human Rights. thanks to the participation of Mr. Isaac Nguema.

16. Twentieth Congress organised in Paris, from 7–12 January 1988 by the "Institut International de Droit d'Expression française" on Human Rights in the Work Place, thanks to the contribution of Mr. Isaac Nguema.

17. International Symposium organised in Paris, by the International Association of Democratic Lawyers, from 9–11 March 1989, on Currency Universality and Prospects for the Declaration on Human Rights and Citizens of 1789, thanks to the contribution of Mr. Isaac Nguema.

18. Symposium organised in Kigali from 13–17 March 1989 by the Rwanda Government and the American Embassy in Rwanda, on the application of Human Rights in Africa, thanks to the contribution of Mr. Grace Stuart Ibingira and Mr. Isaac Nguema.

19. International Symposium organised in Strasbourg, from 17–19 April 1989, on the universality of Human Rights in a pluralistic world,[1] by the Council of Europe thanks to the contribution and the participation of Mr. Isaac Nguema and Mr. Ali Ibrahim Badawi El Sheikh.

20. Training course organised in Banjul, from 24–30 April 1989, by the Centre for Human Rights, the African Commission on Human and Peoples' Rights and the Gambian Government, thanks to the contribution of the Chairman and some of the members of the Commission.

21. Seminar organised in Harare from 22 May–8 June 1989, by the Catholic Commission for Peace and Justice in Zimbabwe, on Human Rights in Africa.

ANNEX VI

Statement by the Chairman of the African Commission on Human and Peoples' Rights on the Occasion of the Celebration of the 40th Anniversary of the Universal Declaration of Human Rights

To the Heads of State and Government of the OAU.

This year, the entire world is celebrating the Fortieth Anniversary of the Universal Declaration of Human Rights proclaimed by the United Nations General Assembly on 10 December 1948. This solemn declaration to which the entire international community attaches the greatest importance, is significant to Africa from at least three points of view.

For the first time in its history, the international community has come to discover and acknowledge the fact that all men are born free and have equal rights, irrespective of race, colour, sex, language, religion, nationality, social status, fortune, political opinion, etc. . . .

The Universal Declaration of Human Rights also expresses the determination to make the principles thus proclaimed an everyday reality, which should enable Africa to free itself from the yoke of colonialism and slavery of which it has been a victim.

This Universal Declaration of Human Rights which serves as a point of reference for the majority of the constitutions of African States, even though its principles are not directly incorporated in them, reflects the aspirations and fundamental values

[1] The Proceedings of the Colloquy have been published in summer 1990 as a coedition of the Council of Europe and N. P. Engel, Publisher. The volume contains the three reports, the nine exposés by members of the two panels, summaries of the 43 interventions during the four speeches given during the discussions, the two written communications, the four speeches given during the opening session, the final report and the list of participants.

which form the very basis of the Charter of the Organization of African Unity, and which stand for Liberty, Equality, Dignity and Justice.

For this reason, the African Commission on Human and Peoples' Rights which met in Cairo from 17–26 October 1988 and whose main task is to promote and protect Human and Peoples' Rights in Africa, decided to participate fully in the celebrations.

I therefore have the honour to invite the Heads of State and Government of OAU Member States to organize public commemorative activities lending a particular brilliance to the celebration of the fortieth anniversary of the Universal Declaration of Human Rights, conceived not only as a common ideal to be achieved by all peoples and all nations, but also as a fundamental source of inspiration for efforts aimed at promoting the development of Africa in particular.

I avail myself of this opportunity to launch a solemn appeal to those States which have not yet done so, to ratify the African Charter on Human and Peoples' Rights, whose principles are based on the Universal Declaration of Human Rights

Isaac NGUEMA

ANNEX VII

Resolution on the Celebration of an African Day of Human Rights

The Commission

Recalling that the African Charter on Human and Peoples' Rights, adopted by the 18th Assembly of Heads of State and Government, in June 1981, in Nairobi (Kenya), entered into force on 21 October 1986, in accordance with the provisions of its Article 63,

Recalling that, as a safeguard measure, the Charter established an African Commission on Human and Peoples' Rights, under the provisions of its Article 64, which was seated on 2 November 1987, after the election of its members, in July 1982,

Considering that the UNO which has always endeavoured to conclude regional arrangements for the promotion and protection of Human Rights, has welcomed the adoption of the Charter and its entry into force,

Considering that the UNO has always encouraged the celebration of anniversaries in the field of Human Rights,

Conscious of the fact that these celebrations make it possible to widely disseminate the regional or international instruments, and the Human Rights and fundamental liberties they proclaim, and revive interest in these rights and liberties liberties as well as promote a better awareness thereof,

Convinced that the celebration of the anniversary of the coming into force of the African Charter on Human and Peoples' Rights would involve the peoples of the world in general and the African peoples in particular in the activities of the African Commission on Human and Peoples' Rights in the field of Human and Peoples' Rights and promote, as well, at the level of the African community in particular, the actual exercise and enjoyment of human and peoples' rights and of the basic freedoms:

INVITES the OAU Member States and all organizations concerned to adopt the 21 October of every year as an African Day of Human Rights:

- to celebrate on that Day the coming into force of the African Charter on Human and Peoples' Rights;
- to intensify their efforts to enable Africa to achieve new progress in that field.

ANNEX VIII

Resolution on the Establishment of Committees on Human Rights or Other Similar Organs at National, Regional or Sub-regional Level

The Commission

Considering that the establishment of a Committee on Human Rights or other similar organs at the national, regional or sub-regional level, as a means whereby to ensure an effective respect for and as wide a promotion as possible of Human Rights has always been of interest to the various organs of the United Nations since the setting up of the Organization,

Considering in particular Resolution 33/46 of 14 December 1978, adopted by the UN General Assembly, and Resolution 24 (XXXV) of 14 March 1979, adopted by the Human Rights Commission, which approved the guiding principles advocated by the Seminar, held in Geneva on 18 and 19 September 1978, as regards national or local institutions for the promotion and protection of Human Rights,

Considering that it is desirable that the mission aimed at promoting human and peoples' rights sent by the African Commission on Human and Peoples' Rights, by virtue of its Charter, under Article 45, would be carried out through the assistance and support of national or regional committees established for that purpose, and composed of eminent personalities, which should also help governments solve their national or local problems relevant to human rights, thus promoting a better awareness of issues related to human rights:

1. INVITES all the States, parties to the Charter, where no national institutions as yet exist for the promotion and protection of human rights, to take appropriate measures to establish such institutions;

2. CALLS ON THE STATES, parties to the Charter. to take due account, when establishing national institutions, of those guiding principles, in planning their structure and functioning, born of the Seminar on national and local institutions for the promotion and protection of human rights, held in Geneva from 18–29 September 1978.

3. REQUESTS the OAU Secretary General to submit a detailed report on existing national institutions.

ANNEX IX

Recommendation on Some Modalities for Promoting Human and Peoples' Rights

The African Commission on Human and Peoples' Rights meeting in its Fifth Ordinary Session, in Benghazi, Libya, from 3–14 April 1989,

Taking into account Resolution AHG/Res. 176 (XXIV) adopted by the Twenty-fourth Ordinary Session of the Assembly of Heads of State and Government held in Addis Ababa, Ethiopia, in May 1988, approving the Activity Report of the Commission, its programme and the attached recommendations:

RECOMMENDS that the Assembly of Heads of State and Government of the OAU adopt the following recommendations:

"The Assembly of Heads of State and Government of the OAU meeting . . .

Recalling that African States 'firmly convinced of their duty to ensure the promotion and protection of human and peoples' rights and freedoms, duly taking into account the primary importance traditionally attached to these rights and freedoms in Africa' adopted in Nairobi on 28 June 1981, the African Charter on Human and Peoples' Rights which came into force on 21 October 1986,

Taking into account Resolution AHG/Res. 176 (XXIV) adopted by the 24th Ordinary Session of the Assembly of Heads of State and Government held in Addis Ababa. Ethiopia, in May 1988, approving the Activity Report of the Commission, its programmes and the attached recommendations,

Aware of the fact that ignorance is the main obstacle to the respect for human and peoples' rights and that consequently it is necessary to promote the knowledge and the science of these rights and freedoms in the interest of the African public pursuant to Article 45 paragraph 1(a) of the African Charter on Human and Peoples' Rights:

RECOMMENDS that African States, parties to the African Charter on Human and Peoples' Rights:

(i) introduce the teaching of human and peoples' rights at all levels of their educational systems (higher, secondary, primary, general, technical, professional, etc.);

(ii) periodically broadcast, with the help of the African Commission on Human and Peoples' Rights, radio and television programmes on human rights in Africa;

(iii) establish national or regional institutes of human and peoples' rights responsible for conducting studies and researches in cooperation with the African Commission on Human and Peoples' Rights, and for disseminating the knowledge and information on human and peoples' rights."

ANNEX X

List of NGOs Granted Observer Status

During the period covered by this 2nd Activity Report seven Nongovernmental Organizations were admitted, nine others following up to the 3rd Activity Report. For the complete chronological list, see below at . . .[2]

ANNEX XI

Resolution on the Integration of the Provisions of the African Charter on Human and Peoples' Rights into National Laws of States

The African Commission on Human and Peoples' Rights meeting in its Fifth Ordinary Session, in Benghazi, Libya from 3 to 14 April 1989,

Considering that its mission to promote Human and Peoples' Rights includes the promotion and formulation of principles and rules which will enable African States to solve their legal problems relating to the enjoyment of Human and Peoples' Rights and fundamental freedoms in conformity with Article 45, paragraph 1, sub-paragraph (b) of the African Charter on Human and Peoples' Rights,

Bearing in mind the fact that the reception of international law is not uniform in all States Parties,

REQUESTS the Assembly of Heads of State and Government to adopt the following recommendation:

> "The Assembly of Heads of State and Government, meeting . . .
>
> *Recalling* that African States solemnly declared in the OAU Charter, their duty to unite by harmonizing their general policies and ensuring the well-being of their peoples, by furthering their legitimate aspirations to freedom, equality, justice and dignity,
>
> *Bearing in mind* Resolution AHG/Res. 176 (XXIV) adopted by the Assembly of Heads of State and Government of the OAU at its Twenty-fourth Ordinary Session in Addis Ababa, Ethiopia, in May 1988 approving the Commission's Activity Report, its programme and recommendations appended,
>
> RECOMMENDS that Member States of the OAU, parties to the African Charter on Human and Peoples' Rights;
>
> INTRODUCES the provisions of Articles 1 to 29 of the African Charter on Human and Peoples' Rights in their Constitutions, laws, rules and regulations and other acts relating to Human and Peoples' Rights."

[2] This list is omitted. The most up-to-date list is reproduced above at p. 90.

ANNEX XII

Guidelines for National Periodic Reports[3]

ANNEX XIII

Letter by Mr. Isaac Nguema

Your Excellency,

As we begin a session of the African Commission on Human and Peoples' Rights which was set up under the African Charter on Human and Peoples' Rights and which was convened for the first time, on 2 November 1987, in Addis Ababa, by the OAU Secretary General in accordance with the provisions of Article 64.2 of the said Charter, I have the honour and the pleasure to respectfully call your attention to a question to which the Commission attaches the greatest importance.

As you are no doubt aware, and in conformity with the provisions of Article 62 of the Charter, each State Party to the Charter had pledged to present within a period of two years, starting from the entry into force of the Charter, a report on the measures it had taken to implement those decisions.

The Charter entered into force on 21 October 1986. Thus States Parties were to present their initial reports to the Commission from 21 October 1989.

Some general directives were prepared to that effect and were discussed at length by the Commission at its Fourth Session held in Cairo from 17 to 26 October 1988.

However, in view of the fact that the Commission wished to adopt an original approach to this question owing to the specific nature of the problems facing our countries, the presentation of the initial reports was postponed.

The Commission decided to resort to one method which is found in the extract from the report of the Fourth Session which you will find attached hereto.

The Commission hopes that the constructive dialogue it would like to establish with States Parties in the field of Human and Peoples' Rights will be well received.

I should be grateful if you could kindly inform me of the position of your government on this matter.

Please accept, Your Excellency, the assurances of my highest consideration.

ISAAC NGUEMA
Chairman of the African Commission
on Human and Peoples' Rights

[3] These are reproduced above at p. 49.

ANNEX XIV

Letter of Reminder by the Chairman of the Commission Sent to States Parties

AFRICAN COMMISSION ON HUMAN AND PEOPLES' RIGHTS
B.P. 962, Libreville, Gabon

Benghazi, 11 April 1989

Your Excellency,

I had the honour, on behalf of the African Commission on Human and Peoples' Rights, to send you a letter dated 2 December 1988, respectfully drawing your attention to an issue to which the Commission attaches to the greatest importance; an issue relating to the periodic reports which each State Party to the African Charter on Human and Peoples' Rights undertook to send in two years' time after the entry into force of the Charter in accordance with the Provisions of Article 2 of the latter.

Anxious to keep up the constructive dialogue initiated by the Commission and which the latter hopes to maintain with the States Parties in matters relating to Human and Peoples' Rights, I have the honour to send you, as a reminder, a copy of that letter as well as a copy of the extract from the report of the Fourth Session of the Commission which was attached to it, particularly drawing your attention to the fact that States should submit their initial reports to the Commission not as from 21 October 1989 as erroneously stated in the letter of 2 December 1988, but from 21 October 1988.

1 would be very grateful if you could let me know the stand of your Government on the issue at your earliest convenience.

Accept, Sir, the assurance of my highest consideration.

ISAAC NGUEMA
Chairman of the African Commission
on Human and Peoples' Rights

Honourable Minister of
Foreign/External Affairs

ANNEX XV

Recommendation of the Commission

The African Commission on Human and Peoples' Rights, meeting in its First Extraordinary Session in Banjul, the Gambia, on 13 and 14 June 1989,

Considering that by its Resolution AHG/Res. 176 (XXIV), the Twenty-fourth Ordinary Session of the Assembly of Heads of State and Government reaffirmed its determination to ensure the promotion and protection of Human and Peoples' Rights in Africa.

Recalling the autonomous nature and the specific role which the Assembly of Heads of State and Government meeting in its Twenty-fourth Ordinary Session had conferred on the African Commission on Human and Peoples' Rights by adopting the specific financial rules and regulations of the Commission,

Considering that the appropriations voted for the Commission under the 1989/90 budget are inadequate for the realisation of the task assigned to the Commission by the African Charter on Human and Peoples' Rights,

Considering that the components of the emoluments approved for the members of the Commission are not commensurate with their actual responsibilities,

Considering that the Commission has no administrative staff to carry out human rights promotion and protection tasks as assigned to it by the Charter and that, pending the next financial year's allocations, it is urgent to provide the Commission with:

- a legal officer responsible for matters relating to human rights promotion;
- a legal officer responsible for human rights protection;
- a documentalist;
- a French/English translator,

1. REAFFIRMS the commitment of the Members of the Commission to do everything possible to carry out missions assigned to them by the Charter;

2. PROPOSES that the emoluments of the Members of the Commission now fixed at US $250 for each day of meeting be raised to US $300;

3. REQUESTS the Assembly of Heads of State and Government to grant the Commission an additional budget, until the next financial year, to enable it to carry out successfully its human rights promotion activities and to appoint the staff needed for the realization of the above-mentioned promotion and protection task.

Final Communiqué of the Fourth Ordinary Session of the African Commission on Human and Peoples' Rights

Cairo, 26 October 1988

1. The African Commission on Human and Peoples' Rights held its 4th Ordinary Session in Cairo (Egypt) from 17–16 October 1988 under the chairmanship of Mr. Isaac NGUEMA.

2. The following members have participated in the session: Dr. Ibrahim Ali Badawi El-Sheikh, Mr. Ali Mahmoud Buhedma, Mr. Alexis Gabou, Mr. Grace Stuart Ibingira, Mr. Sourahata B. Semega Janneh, Mr. Habesh Robert Kisanga, Mr. Moleleki D. Mokama, Mr. C. L. C. Mubanga-Chipoya, Mr. Youssoupha Ndiaye, Mr. Isaac Nguema.

3. The session was opened under the chairmanship of his Excellency Dr. Boutros Boutros Ghali, Minister of State for Foreign Affairs, representing His Excellency Mr. Hosni Mubarak, President of the Arab Republic of Egypt.

4. The following took the floor:

- The Chairman of the Commission, Mr. Isaac Nguema, who welcomed, on behalf of his colleagues, the participants in this opening ceremony, which was also attended by members of the Government and of African diplomatic missions;
- H.E. Dr. Sylvestre Nsanzimana, Assistant Secretary-General, representing the Secretary-General of the Organization of African Unity;
- H.E. Mr. Gabriel G. Farngalo, Dean of the African Diplomatic Corps, and Ambassador of Liberia in Egypt;
- H.E. Dr. Boutros Boutros Ghali, Minister of State for Foreign Affairs of the Arab Republic of Egypt.

5. After the opening ceremony, the Commission, resuming its work, considered and adopted a 12-item agenda comprising the following:

- The question of observers and participation of States non party to the Charter;
- The implementation of decision and resolution adopted by the 24th Session of the Assembly of Heads of State and Government on the Commission;
- General directives regarding the preparation and presentation of periodic reports;
- Consideration of the draft Headquarters Agreement;
- Publication of the Progress Report;
- Consideration of communications-complaints;
- Activities during the intersession.

6. For the first time, the Commission heard representatives of certain non-governmental organizations with observer status within the Commission. Thus did:

- Amnesty International;
- the Arab Lawyers Union;
- the Egyptian United Nations Association;

express their wish to establish sound, multiform and lasting cooperation with the Commission.

7. The Commission expressed great satisfaction in this collaboration which would enable it to widen and further the scope of its action for promotion and protection.

8. Moreover, the Commission accorded observer status to other non-governmental organizations.

9. At the request of Burundi, the Commission heard an exposé made by the Representative of that country on the events that occurred since the month of August 1988.

10. The Commission took cognizance with satisfaction of the decision and resolution of the Twenty-Fourth Session of the Conference of Heads of State and Government that especially called for establishing the permanent seat of the Commission in Banjul (The Gambia).

11. The Commission studied and adopted the general directives concerning the drafting and submission of periodic reports by the States, parties to the Charter. These directives are characterized by their simplicity.

12. The Commission examined, according to a procedure sanctioned by all members, a certain number of complaints submitted to it by physical and moral persons, in accordance with the provisions of Article 55 of the Charter. Some decisions were taken in respect of about thirty of them.

13. The Commission heard the exposé on the activities pertaining to promotion which the Chairman and some members carried out during the intersession. It took cognizance of the short-term programmes that were submitted and which it would endeavour to achieve.

14. The Commission, after examining the requests made by some States that were not parties to the Charter, to the effect that they wished to participate in its activities, avails itself of this opportunity to launch a solemn appeal to all Member States of the OAU which have as yet not ratified the Charter, to do so.

15. A vote of thanks was addressed to the Egyptian Government.

16. The Commission decided to hold its next meeting in Benghazi (Libya) at a date that will be fixed later on.

17. The closing ceremony was performed by H.E. Dr. Boutros Boutros Ghali, Minister of State for Foreign Affairs of the Arab Republic of Egypt.

Third Activity Report of the African Commission on Human and Peoples' Rights

Adopted on 28 April 1990
Covering the 6th and 7th Ordinary Sessions in Banjul
(October/November 1989 and April 1990) as well as intersession activities

I. ORGANIZATION OF WORK AND ANY OTHER BUSINESS

A. Period Covered by the Report

1. The Second Activity Report of the African Commission on Human and Peoples' Rights was adopted by the Commission on 14 June 1989 in Banjul. It covered two ordinary sessions (Cairo 17–26 October 1988 – Benghazi 3–14 April 1989) and one extraordinary session (13–14 June 1989, Banjul). The Second Report was adopted by the Twenty-fifth Session of the Assembly of Heads of State and Government of the OAU by its Resolution AHG/188 (XXV).

This Report, the Third one, relates to the Sixth and Seventh Ordinary Sessions (Banjul), 23 October to 4 November 1989 and 18–28 April 1990.

B. Status of Ratification

2. Mozambique has become the 40th State Party. It acceded to the Charter on 22 February 1989 and deposited its instrument of accession on 7 March 1990.

3. The list of States that have ratified or adhered to the African Charter on Human and Peoples' Rights is attached to this Report as Annex I.

4. The Chairman has on behalf of the Commission re-written to all non States Parties urging them to ratify the African Charter on Human and peoples' Rights. (The letter dated 21 February 1990 is contained in Annex II.)

C. Session and Agenda

5. The Commission has held two Ordinary Sessions since its Second Activity Report was adopted:

- the Sixth Ordinary Session was held in Banjul, The Gambia from 23 October to 4 November 1989;
- the Seventh Ordinary Session was held in Banjul, The Gambia from 18–28 April 1990.

The Agenda of all these sessions is attached to this Report as Annexes III and IV.

D. Composition and Participation

6. The composition of the African Commission on Human and Peoples' Rights has changed. Mr. Umozurike was elected in July 1989 to fill the remaining period of Mr. Ibingira who had resigned. The list of members of the Commission is attached to this Report as Annex V.

7. Attendance at sessions has been as follows:

- all Commissioners attended the Sixth Session,
- at the Seventh Ordinary Session, Messrs Alioune Blondin Beye, Alexis Gabou and M. D. Mokama were absent with apology.

E. Chairman, Vice-Chairman and Secretary of the Commission

8. The mandate of the Chairman, Mr. Isaac Nguema and Vice-Chairman, Dr. Ibrahim Ali Badawi expired.

9. At its Sixth Session, the Commission went ahead with the election of its office bearers on the 24 October, the results of which are as follows:

- Prof. U. O. Umozurike, was duly elected Chairman of the Commission in accordance with Article 17 of the Rules of Procedure of the Commission,
- Mr. A. Gabou was duly elected as Vice-Chairman.

10. Taking the chair, Professor Umozurike thanked the members for electing him and Mr. Gabou as Chairman and Vice-Chairman respectively, and pledged to work hard in order to rise to the expectations of members. He paid tribute to Mr. Nguema for his total devotion and commitment in conducting the affairs of the Commission during its formative days, a task which was obviously very delicate and most demanding. He promised to carry on from where Mr. Nguema had stopped, and counted on the members for the necessary support in trying to achieve the set objectives of the Commission.

11. Mr. Ngabishema Mutsinzi continues to be the Secretary of the Commission.

F. Other Business

Matters Relating to Situation of Human Rights in Africa

12. In the course of the general discussions, the African Commission on Human and Peoples' Rights dwelt on the situation of human rights and freedoms in certain African countries. It expressed its heartfelt satisfaction at the release of Nelson Mandela and the Independence of Namibia which has become the 51st Member State of the OAU since 10 April 1990.

13. It approved the messages of support and solidarity issued on these occasions by the Chairman of the Commission.

14. It expressed the hope that the people of South Africa will continue the struggle in unity and solidarity until apartheid is totally dismantled and a democratic and non-racial society emerges.

15. During the in-depth and serious discussions, members of the Commission unanimously expressed their grave concern about the situation of human and peoples' rights in Africa. All African countries should take this concern into account with a view to ensuring the rule of law in each State. This was the solemn pledge made by African countries when they instituted and adopted a Charter which guarantees, inter alia, the right to life, the inviolability of the human being, the security of the person, the right to be tried within a reasonable period by an impartial court or tribunal and the right of each citizen to participate freely in the government of his country.

16. However, mass media reports have proved that certain African countries had deliberately violated this solemn pledge.

17. The African Commission issued a solemn and strong appeal to these countries to immediately take all necessary measures to put an end to that.

18. It gave mandate to its Chairman to approach these countries and the authorities of the OAU on that matter with a view to verifying these informations and reporting to the Commission at its next session.

G. Adoption of the Activity Report

19. On 28 April 1990, the Commission considered the draft of this third Activity Report. After discussions resulting in amendments, the Activity Report was adopted by the Commission.

II. GENERAL REMARKS OF THE COMMISSION

Promotional Activities

(a) Seminars

20. In keeping with the Programme of Action members of the Commission attended seminars which are listed in Annex VI.

(b) Publications

- On the issue of publications, the Commission noted with concern that the General Secretariat has not published the first and second reports of activity of the Commission apparently because of lack of funds. For making up for that situation, the Commission sought the help of the United Nations Centre for Human Rights in Geneva whereby the Centre had promised to help the Commission with the publication of 2000 copies of the first and second reports of the activities of the Commission.

- The Centre has graciously agreed also to publish and circulate, as UN documents, some of the documents containing information on the Commission notably the text of the African Charter and the Rules of Procedure of the Commission.
- At present, the Commission prepares to launch the first edition of its own publication "The African Review on Human and Peoples' Rights", using contributions provided by the UNESCO and the Commission of the European Community.

(c) Observers

21. In pursuance of Rules 76 and 77 of its Rules of Procedure, the Commission has granted certain non-governmental organizations observer status.

22. The NGOs which have so far been granted observer status are in the list attached to this report as Annex VII.

III. PERIODIC REPORTS

23. The Great Socialist Peoples' Libyan Arab Jamahiriya was the first State Party to submit a periodic report in accordance with Article 62 of the Charter. This report will be examined at a next session.

IV. CONSIDERATION OF COMMUNICATIONS

Protection Activities

24. Since its beginning, the Commission received and considered 105 communications of which 16 are directed against States Parties to the Charter.

25. With a view to continuous improving the handling of the communications, the Commission instructed its Secretary as to ways and means which should be followed in processing complaints.

V. NEXT SESSIONS

26. Dates and venues of the next sessions will be determined in consultation with the OAU General Secretariat.

ANNEX I

African Charter on Human and Peoples' Rights
List of Countries which have Signed, Ratified or Adhered to the Charter

No.	Country	Date of Signature	Date of Ratification/ Adhesion	Date Deposited
1.	Algeria	10/04/86	01/03/87	20/03/87
2.	Angola			
3.	Benin		20/01/86	25/02/86
4.	Botswana		17/07/86	22/07/86
5.	Burundi		28/07/80	30/08/89
6.	Burkina Faso	05/03/84	06/07/84	21/09/84
7.	Cameroon	23/07/87	20/06/89	18/09/89
8.	Cape Verde	31/03/86	02/06/87	06/08/87
9.	Central African Republic		26/04/86	27/07/86
10.	Chad	29/05/86	09/10/86	11/11/86
11.	Comoros		01/06/86	18/07/86
12.	Congo	27/11/81	09/12/82	17/01/83
13.	Djibouti			
14.	Egypt	16/11/81	20/03/84	03/04/84
15.	Equatorial Guinea	18/08/86	07/04/86	18/08/86
16.	Ethiopia			
17.	Gabon	26/02/82	20/02/86	26/06/86
18.	Gambia	11/02/83	08/06/83	13/06/83
19.	Ghana		24/01/89	01/03/89
20.	Guinea	09/12/81	16/02/82	13/05/82
21.	Guinea-Bissau		04/12/85	06/03/86
22.	Côte d'Ivoire			
23.	Kenya			
24.	Lesotho	07/03/84		
25.	Liberia	31/01/83	04/08/82	29/12/82
26.	Libya	30/05/85	19/07/86	26/03/87
27.	Madagascar			
28.	Malawi		17/02/89	23/02/90
29.	Mali	13/11/81	21/12/81	22/01/82
30.	Mauritania	25/02/82	14/06/86	26/06/86
31.	Mauritius			
32.	Mozambique		22/02/89	07/03/90
33.	Namibia			
34.	Niger	09/07/86	15/07/86	21/07/86
35.	Nigeria	31/08/82	22/06/83	27/07/83
36.	Rwanda	11/11/81	15/07/83	22/07/83
37.	Saharawi Arab Dem. Rep.	10/04/86	02/05/86	23/05/86
38.	Sao Tome & Principe		23/05/86	28/07/86
39.	Senegal	23/09/81	13/08/82	25/10/82
40.	Seychelles			

No.	Country	Date of Signature	Date of Ratification/ Adhesion	Date Deposited
41.	Sierra Leone	27/08/81	21/09/83	27/01/84
42.	Somalia	26/02/82	31/07/85	20/03/86
43.	Sudan	03/09/82	18/02/86	11/03/86
44.	Swaziland			
45.	Togo	26/02/82	05/11/82	22/11/82
46.	Tunisia		16/03/83	22/04/83
47.	Uganda	18/08/86	10/05/86	27/05/86
48.	Tanzania	31/05/82	18/02/84	09/03/84
49.	Zaire	23/07/87	20/07/87	28/07/87
50.	Zambia	17/01/83	10/01/84	02/02/84
51.	Zimbabwe	20/02/86	20/05/86	12/06/86

ANNEX II

Ratification of the African Charter on Human and Peoples' Rights

His Excellency
President of the People's Republic
of

African Commission
Human and Peoples' Rights
P.O. Box 673, Banjul,
The Gambia

21 February 1990

May I recall, Your Excellency, that the African Charter on Human and Peoples' Rights was adopted by the Assembly of African Heads of State in Nairobi in 1981 and came into force on 21 october 1986. The Commission of the African Charter on Human and Peoples' Rights was inaugurated on 2 November 1987 and has been doing its best to carry out the responsibilities vested on it by the Charter.

As we go through the latest list of ratifications, we notice that your Excellency's State is not yet included. This does not imply that you are not concerned with the activities of the Commission. Your Excellency's State helps to fund the Commission through its contributions to the OAU; it considers the annual reports and through the Assembly and Secretariat generally exercises control over the Commission. What remains therefore is to formally recognize your interest, obligations and responsibilities under the Charter.

The Charter is considered to reflect the hopes of African people for a fuller and better life in which their States accept to observe certain minimum standards of treatment for their citizens. The Charter incorporates authentic African philosophy on human and peoples' rights which are regarded as unique in the doctrine of human rights. I am convinced, Your Excellency, that it will be in furtherance of Your Excellency's State's role in Africa to ratify the Charter and give formal recognition to the activities you are already performing in furthering the promotion and protection of human rights in Africa. This hope is well-founded and I crave for Your Excellency's personal intervention in the matter.

I have the honour to be.

Yours faithfully,
Prof. U. O. UMOZURIKE,
Chairman, African Commission
on Human and Peoples' Rights

ANNEX III

Agenda of the Sixth Ordinary Session (23 October–4 November 1989)

1. Opening Session
2. Election of Bureau
3. Adoption of Agenda
4. Organisation of Work
   - (a) 10 hrs–13 hrs; 16 hrs–18.30 hrs
     – Friday, 27 October Afternoon – Free; Saturday, 28 October Afternoon – Free; 1 November – Working Session; 3 November – Working Session
   - (b) Appointment of Rapporteur
5. Action by the 25th Session of the Assembly of Heads of State and Government on the 2nd Activity Report of the Commission
6. Report of the Activities of the President and members of the Commission during the Intersession period
7. Consideration of Communications
8. Promotional Activities; Publications and Distribution
9. Question of Observers
10. Questions Relating to the Headquarters
11. Relations Between the Commission and the African Centre for Democracy and Human Rights Studies
12. Consideration of the Report on Privileges and Immunities of Commissioners
13. Any Other Business
14. Date, Venue and Draft Agenda of the 7th Session
15. Adoption of the Report of the Session
16. Final Communiqué

ANNEX IV

Agenda of the Seventh Ordinary Session (18–28 April 1990)

1. Opening Session
2. Adoption of Agenda
3. Organization of Work
4. Appointment of Rapporteur
5. Matters Arising from the Last Meeting
6. Consideration of National Periodic Reports
7. Reports of Activities of the Chairman, Members and Secretary of the Commission During the Intersession:

   (a) Report of the Chairman
   (b) Report of Members
   (c) Report of the Secretary

8. OAU Convention on Privileges and Immunities:
   Privileges and Immunities of Members of the Commission
9. Organization of the Activities of the Commission:

   (a) Protective Activities
   (b) Promotional Activities

10. Consideration of the Rules of Procedure
11. Report on the Activities of the OAU Relevant to the Commission
12. Annual Activity Report
13. Observers
14. Draft Budget of the Commission
15. Any Other Business
16. Date, Venue and Draft Agenda of the 8th Session
17. Adoption of the Report of the Session
18. Final Communique

ANNEX V

List of Members of the Commission

1. Prof. U. Oji Umozurike, Chairman
2. Alexis Gabou, Vice-Chairman
3. Alioune Blondin Beye, Member
4. Ali Mahmoud Buhedma, Member
5. Dr. Ibrahim Ali Badawi El Sheikh, Member
6. Sourahata Baboucar Semega Janneh, Member

7. Justice Robert Habesh Kisanga, Member
8. Moleleki D. Mokama, Member
9. C. L. C. Mubanga-Chipoya, Member
10. Youssoupha Ndiaye, Member
11. Isaac Nguema, Member

Secretary to the Commission: Ngabishema Mutsinzi

ANNEX VI

Seventh Session of the African Commission on Human and Peoples' Rights
Intersession Activity Report of the Chairman of the African Commission on Human and Peoples' Rights
November 1989–April 1990

1. Three members of the Commission – Mr. R. H. Kisanga, Mr. I. Nguema, and Prof. U. O. Umozurike – attended a symposium on the Judiciary and Human Rights organized in Banjul by the African Society of International Law in collaboration with the African Commission on Human and Peoples' Rights and the African Centre for Democracy and Human Rights Studies. Prof. Umozurike delivered a paper on Autochthony in the African Charter.

2. The Chairman addressed staff and students of the University of Lagos on the African Commission on 5 December 1989.

3. The Chairman issued a statement on the 10 December 1989 to mark the 41st Anniversary of the Universal Declaration on Human Rights.

4. On 5 January 1990, the Chairman issued a call to Nigerian non-governmental organisations to seek observer status with the African Commission on Human and Peoples' Rights.

5. Six members of the Commission – Mr. R. H. Kisanga, Mr. Y. Ndiaye, Dr. A. Gabou, Mr. I. Nguema, Mr. S. Semega-Janneh and Prof. U. O. Umozurike – attended a Seminar organised jointly in Costa Rica by the Inter-American Institute of Human Rights, Inter-American Court of Human Rights and Inter-American Commission on Human Rights on 8–12 January 1990. All the Members participated in discussions on the Inter-American Commission and African Commission.

6. On 16 January 1990, the Chairman paid a courtesy call on the Nigerian President, General Ibrahim Babangida.

7. The Chairman attended the Ministerial Council of African Foreign Ministers held in Addis Ababa 19–24 February 1990 and delivered an address. He and the Secretary held discussions with the Secretary-General of the OAU and observed the deposit of instruments of ratification of the African Charter by the Republic of Malawi and addressed letters to Heads of State that have not yet ratified the Charter.

8. The Chairman attended the Meeting of the UN Commission on Human Rights held in Geneva and delivered an address on 9 March 1990. He held discussions with the officials of the Commission on the requirements of the African Commission.

9. Four Members of the Commission – Mr. B. Beye,Mr. R. H. Kisanga, Dr. A. Gabou and Prof. U. O. Umozurike – attended the Afro-European Conference on Human Rights organized in Strasbourg by the Friedrich Naumann Foundation on 26–30 March. The Chairman delivered a paper on the working of the African Commission on Human and Peoples' Rights. The Commissioners discussed cooperation between (the European and) African Commission with their European counterparts.

10. The Chairman addressed a letter to President Nujoma on the occasion of Namibia's Independence.

11. The Chairman received an application by the Catholic Commission for Justice and Peace in Zimbabwe for observer status dated 13 March 1990.

12. The Chairman received a complaint from International Pen Writers in Prison Committee against Malawi, dated 12 March 1990.

13. The Chairman is convinced of the need to carry on promotion activities in all member states through lectures and seminars and urges the Commission to address itself seriously to them.

U. O. Umozurike
Chairman, African Commission on
Human and Peoples' Rights

Banjul 20 April 1990

ANNEX VII

List of NGOs Granted Observer Status[1]

PRESENTATION OF THE 3RD ACTIVITY REPORT

by the Chairman of the Commission, Professor U. O. Umozurike to the 26th Session of the Assembly of Heads of State and Government of the Organization of African Unity (9–11 July 1990)

Your Excellencies,
I have the honour to present to you the third activity report of the African Commission on Human and Peoples' Rights. May I seize this opportunity to thank Your Excellencies for considering me worthy enough to be a member of the African Commission. On my election as the Chairman of the Commission by my colleagues in October 1989, I promised to carry on from where my illustrious predecessor,

[1] This list is omitted. The most up-to-date list is reproduced above at p. 90.

Mr. Isaac Nguema, stopped and urged for their cooperation and dedication. I am pleased to report that the Commission has been doing its best in setting out its procedures and in acquiring the necessary tools for its work.

Our responsibilities are broadly two-fold: protective and promotional. We commenced the procedure in respect of the 16 complaints made against Member States and in some respects our mere intervention was enough to secure the human rights of the persons affected. We also dealt with communications relating to our work generally.

Our promotional responsibilities are very wide but we have not the resources for them. Our facilities in some respects are still rudimentary. We have no library yet. We are therefore seeking help in acquiring the facilities, to enable us to perform effectively.

Presently, 40 States have acceded to or ratified the Charter. May I respectfully urge members that have not yet done so, to give serious consideration to the matter in order to make the Charter a truly african document. May I remind you that such members already contribute to maintain the African Commission through their regular contributions to the OAU; they join in electing the Commissioners and in discussing the reports; they join in exercising general supervision of the Commission which is now an organ of the OAU. All that is left is for the members to assure their own citizens the benefits of the Charter. All States in the international community are already bound by the international customary law principle of respect for human rights. The Charter is a commitment to sister African States that those rights and obligations will be respected in every state in the spirit of African brotherhood.

We have made several recommendations to Member States which I crave your indulgence to let me recount here:

(a) To incorporate the Charter in national legal systems as required by Article 1 of the Charter;
(b) To promote the Charter through incorporating it at all levels of the educational systems;
(c) To form or encourage national or regional bodies interested in human rights;
(d) To conduct regular broadcasts on the Charter;
(e) To observe 21 October as African Day on Human and Peoples' Rights. The Charter came into force on 21 October 1986;
(f) To render reports every two years on the steps members are taking to implement the Charter.

The African Charter is more ambitious than the European and American Charters that preceded it, even though it does not incorporate the court system. The implementation of the first generation of rights, e.g. the right to free movement, assembly, thought, the right to life, etc. mainly requires governments to refrain from interfering with the dignity and liberty of individuals and may be readily observed in a democratic set-up no matter its peculiarities. However, the implementation of the second generation of rights, such as the right to work, to education, to free medical treatment, etc., all of which are embodied in the Charter, may be difficult to achieve in the present hostile economic circumstances. Our Charter requires that all of these rights and more should be implemented now. It is for every Member State to organise seminars and symposia on the impact of the Charter on its domestic laws. This will task the energy of policy makers and the thinkers in Member States. One solution is to pass laws that provide for programmatic implementation. A second solution is to include the expensive rights in that part of the Constitution that deals with fundamental objectives and directive principles of State policy. It is a task that must be carried out by every ratifying State.

It has been repeated by honourable speakers on this floor that human rights can only flourish in conditions of peace, progress and good government. The second generation of rights, in particular can only flourish if our citizens work hard and if the maximum use is made of our human and material resources.

Despite some setbacks, we are convinced that the stage has been reached where the human rights of all Africans have become the concern of all other Africans. The process is irreversible. No more can human rights breaches be swept under the carpet as internal affairs, for the protection and promotion of these rights are indeed the fundamental purpose of all governments. The light of democracy has been rekindled in several parts of the world including our own continent and this should result in an enhanced integrity of the African personality.

May I express the thanks of the Commission for the support that your Excellencies have given us. The Secretariat has been ever willing within its resources to enable us to stand on our feet. May I acknowledge before you the support and cooperation of the U.N. Commission on Human Rights, UNESCO, EEC and the European and American Human Rights Commissions who have been of help and enabled us to gain familiarity with other human rights protection systems. Our host, the Gambia, has always been cooperative.

I wish to thank the governments that have hosted our sessions. The occasion of our meetings offers a great opportunity to promote knowledge of the Charter and of the Commission. We wish to be invited to as many States as possible.

We expect shortly to produce concrete results for our publications will be out in a matter of months. The confidentiality of our procedures in fact keeps some of our activities from the public. We crave for your continued support even though all Africa is passing through difficult times. I have the honour to submit the Third Annual Report of the African Commission on Human and Peoples' Rights.

Your Excellencies, I thank you.

Fourth Annual Activity Report of the African Commission on Human and Peoples' Rights 1990–1991

Adopted on 25 March 1991
Covering the 8th and 9th Ordinary Sessions in Banjul (October 1990) and Lagos (March 1991)

I. ORGANIZATION OF WORK

A. Period Covered by the Report

1. The Third Activity Report was adopted by the Twenty-sixth Session of the Assembly of Heads of State and Government of the OAU by its resolution AHG/198 (XXVI). This report, the Fourth one, relates to the Eighth and Ninth Ordinary Sessions (Banjul) 8–21 October 1990 and Lagos 18–25 March 1991.

B. Status of Ratifications

2. The list of States that have ratified or adhered to the African Charter on Human and Peoples' Rights is attached to this Report as Annex I.

C. Sessions and Agenda

3. The Commission has held two Ordinary Sessions since its Third Activity Report was adopted.

- The Eighth Ordinary Session was held in Banjul, The Gambia, from 8–21 October 1990.
- The Ninth Ordinary Session was held in Lagos, Nigeria, from 18–25 March 1991

The Agendas of both these sessions are attached to this Report as Annexes II and III.

D. Composition and Participation

4. The composition of the African Commission on Human and Peoples' Rights has not changed. The list of members of the Commission is attached to this Report as Annex IV.

5. Attendance at Sessions has been as follows:

– At the Eighth Ordinary Session, nine Commissioners attended:
Messrs Alioune Blondin Beye,
Ali M. Buhedma,
Alexis Gabou,
Ibrahim Badawi El Sheikh,
Robert H. Kisanga,
C. L. C. Mubanga-Chipoya,
Moleleki D. Mokama,
Youssoupha Ndiaye,
U. O. Umozurike.

Two Commissioners were absent with apology: Messrs Sourahata B. Semega Janneh and Isaac Nguema.

– At the Ninth Ordinary Session, six Commissioners attended:
Messrs Ibrahim Badawi El Sheikh,
Robert H. Kisanga,
Sourahata B. Semega Janneh,
C. L. C. Mubanga-Chipoya,
Isaac Nguema,
U. O. Umozurike.

Five Commissioners were absent with apology: Messrs Alioune Blondin Beye, Ali M. Buhedma, Alexis Gabou, Moleleki D. Mokama, Youssoupha Nidaye.

E. Chairman, Vice-Chairman of the Commission

6. Messrs U. O. Umozurike and Alexis Gabou continue to be, respectively, Chairman and Vice-Chairman.

F. Consideration of the Annual Activity

7. On 25 March 1991, the Commission considered this Fourth Activity Report.

II. ACTIVITIES OF THE COMMISSION IN GENERAL

Promotional Activities

(a) Seminars

8. In keeping with the Programme of Action, members of the Commission attended seminars in Africa and Europe.

(b) Publications

9. At present, the Commission prepares to launch the first edition of its own publication, "The African Review on Human and Peoples' Rights".

(c) Observers

10. In pursuance of Rules 76 and 77 of its Rules of Procedure, the Commission has granted certain non-governmental organizations observer status.

11. The NGOs which have so far been granted observer status are in the list attached to this Report as Annex V.

III. PERIODIC REPORTS

12. The Commission considered at its Ninth Ordinary Session the Periodic Reports of the following countries: The Great Socialist Peoples' Libyan Arab Jamahiriya, Tunisia and Rwanda. These documents are public documents and are available at the Secretariat of the Commission.

IV. CONSIDERATION OF COMMUNICATIONS

Protective Activities

13. At its Eighth and Ninth Sessions, the Commission considered 16 communications directed against States Parties to the Charter of which 6 were new.

V. NEXT SESSION

14. The Commission decided to convene its Tenth Session from 7–14 October 1991. At the same time, the Commission requested the Chairman to explore the possibility of convening the 10th Session in the southern part of Africa.

ANNEX I

African Charter on Human and Peoples' Rights
List of Countries which have Signed, Ratified or Adhered to the Charter

No.	Country	Date of Signature	Date of Ratification/ Adhesion	Date Deposited
1.	Algeria	10/04/86	01/03/87	20/03/87
2.	Angola			
3.	Benin		20/01/86	25/02/86
4.	Botswana		17/07/86	22/07/86
5.	Burundi		28/07/80	30/08/89
6.	Burkina Faso	05/03/84	06/07/84	21/09/84
7.	Cameroon	23/07/87	20/06/89	18/09/89
8.	Cape Verde	31/03/86	02/06/87	06/08/87
9.	Central African Republic		26/04/86	27/07/86
10.	Chad	29/05/86	09/10/86	11/11/86
11.	Comoros		01/06/86	18/07/86
12.	Congo	27/11/81	09/12/82	17/01/83
13.	Djibouti			
14.	Egypt	16/11/81	20/03/84	03/04/84
15.	Equatorial Guinea	18/08/86	07/04/86	18/08/86
16.	Ethiopia			
17.	Gabon	26/02/82	20/02/86	26/06/86
18.	Gambia	11/02/83	08/06/83	13/03/83
19.	Ghana		24/01/89	01/03/89
20.	Guinea	09/12/81	16/02/82	13/05/82
21.	Guinea-Bissau		04/12/85	06/03/86
22.	Ivory Coast			
23.	Kenya			
24.	Lesotho	07/03/84		
25.	Liberia	31/01/83	04/08/82	29/12/82
26.	Libya	30/05/85	19/07/86	26/03/87
27.	Madagascar			
28.	Malawi	23/02/90	17/02/89	23/02/90
29.	Mali	13/11/81	21/12/81	22/01/82
30.	Mauritania	25/02/82	14/06/86	26/06/86
31.	Mauritius			
32.	Mozambique		22/02/89	07/03/90
33.	Namibia			
34.	Niger	09/07/86	15/07/86	21/07/86
35.	Nigeria	31/08/82	22/06/83	27/07/83
36.	Rwanda	11/11/81	15/07/83	22/07/83
37.	Saharawi Arab Dem. Rep.	10/04/86	02/05/86	23/05/86
38.	Sao Tome & Principe		23/05/86	28/07/86
39.	Senegal	23/09/81	13/08/82	25/10/82
40.	Seychelles			

No.	Country	Date of Signature	Date of Ratification/ Adhesion	Date Deposited
41.	Sierra Leone	27/08/81	21/09/83	27/01/84
42.	Somalia	26/02/82	31/07/85	20/03/86
43.	Sudan	03/09/82	18/02/86	11/03/86
44.	Swaziland			
45.	Tanzania	31/05/82	18/02/84	09/03/84
46.	Togo	20/02/82	05/11/82	22/11/82
47.	Tunisia		16/03/83	22/04/83
48.	Uganda	18/08/86	10/05/86	27/05/86
49.	Zaire	23/07/87	20/07/87	28/07/87
50.	Zambia	17/01/83	19/01/84	02/02/84
51.	Zimbabwe	20/02/86	30/05/86	12/06/86

ANNEX II

Agenda of the Eighth Ordinary Session (Banjul, The Gambia, 8–21 October 1990)

1. Opening of Session
2. Adoption of Agenda
3. Organization of Work

   (a) Appointment of Rapporteur
   (b) Working hours: Morning 10.00 am to 13.00 hrs
   Afternoon 16.00 hrs to 19.00 hrs

4. Measures Taken for the Implementation of Recommendations and Decisions of the 7th Session

   (a) Report of the Chairman
   (b) Report of the Secretary

5. Consideration of the Annual Report of the Commission by the Assembly of Heads of State and Government
6. Report of the Activities of the OAU Relevant to the Commission

   (a) Refugees
   (b) Cultural Activities
   (c) Economic Activities

7. Intersession Activity Reports of members of the Commission
8. Consideration of Periodic Reports
9. Activities of the Commission

   (a) Protective Activities
   (b) Promotional Activities
   (c) Report of Consultants on Programme of Activities

10. OAU Convention on Privilege and Immunities: Privileges and Immunities of the Members of the Commission
11. Observers
12. Consideration of Rules of Procedure
13. Any Other Business
14. Date, Venue and Agenda of the 9th Session
15. Adoption of the Report
16. Final Communiqué
17. Closing Ceremony

ANNEX III

Agenda of the Ninth Session (Lagos, Nigeria, 18–25 March 1991)

1. Opening Ceremony.
2. Adoption of Agenda
3. Organization of Work
4. (a) Appointment of Rapporteur
   (b) Working Hours
5. Adoption of the Report of the 8th Session
6. Matters Arising from Last Session
   (a) Report of the Chairman
   (b) Report of the Secretary
   (c) Reports of Members of the Commission
7. Report of the Activities of the OAU Relevant to the Commission
8. Observers
9. Draft Annual Budget
10. Consideration of Rules of procedure
11. Activities of the Commission
    (a) Protective Activities
    (b) Promotional Activities
12. Consideration of National Periodic Reports
13. Report of Consultants on the Programme of Activities
14. Any Other Business
15. Date, Venue and Agenda of the 10th Session
16. Adoption of the Report of the Proceedings
17. Adoption of the Annual Report
18. Final Communiqué
19. Closing Ceremony

ANNEX IV

List of Members of the Commission

1. Prof. U. Oji Umozurike, Chairman
2. Alexis Gabou, Vice-Chairman
3. Alioune Blondin Beye, Member
4. Ali Mahmoud Buhedma, Member
5. Dr. Ibrahim Ali Badawi El Sheikh, Member
6. Sourahata Baboucar Semega Janneh, Member
7. Justice Robert Habesh Kisanga, Member
8. Moleleki D. Mokama, Member
9. C. L. C. Mubanga-Chipoya, Member
10. Youssoupha Ndiaye, Member
11. Isaac Nguema, Member

Secretary to the Commission: Ngabishema Mutsinzi

ANNEX V

List of NGOs Granted Observer Status[1]

[1] This list is omitted. The most up-to-date list is reproduced above at p. 90.

Final Communiqué of the Eighth Ordinary Session of the African Commission on Human and Peoples' Rights

Banjul, 8–21 October 1990

1. The African Commission on Human and Peoples' Rights held its 8th Ordinary Session in Banjul from 8–21 October 1990, under the Chairmanship of Professor U. O. Umozurike.

2. The following members were present at the Session:

Prof. U. O. Umozurike;
Dr. Ibrahim Ali Badawi El Sheikh;
MM. Ali M. Buhedma;
Robert Habesh Kisanga;
C. L. C. Mubanga-Chipoya;
Youssoupha Ndiaye;
Alioune Blondin Beye;
Moleleki D. Mokama;
Alexis Gabou.

3. The opening session was attended by the Assistant Secretary-General of the OAU, Mr. Ahmed Haggag, Representatives of the African Centre for Democracy and Human Rights Studies, the Lawyers Committee for Human Rights, Amnesty International and Human Rights Internet.

4. After the welcome address by Prof. Umozurike, speeches were made by the following:

(i) Mr. Ahmed Haggag, Assistant Secretary General of OAU;
(ii) Mr. Tiebile Drame of Amnesty International;
(iii) Miss Sarah Norman of Human Rights Internet;
(iv) Ms. Yolande Diallo, Representative of United Nations Centre for Human Rights;
(v) Mr. Abdourahmane Boly of Burkinabe Movement on Human and Peoples' Rights.

5. The Commission dealt with, *inter alia*, the following items:

- matters arising from the last session;
- consideration of periodic reports;
- activity reports of members of the Commission during the intersession;
- consideration of six new communications against States;
- consideration of Rules of Procedure;
- observers.

6. The Commission considered six new communications against States Parties to the Charter.

7. The Commission admitted 9 Non-Governmental Organisations to observer status as follows:

(i) International Association of Young Lawyers
(ii) African Society of International and Comparative Law, London;
(iii) International Federation of Human Rights;
(iv) Fund for Peace;
(v) Civil Liberties Organisation;
(vi) Interights, London;
(vii) International Institute of Human Rights, Strasbourg;
(viii) Inter-African Union of Lawyers
(ix) Arab Institute for Human Rights;

as well as the Commonwealth Secretariat, London.

8. The Commission considered a report on the Privileges and Immunities of members of the Commission.

9. The Commission mandated the eleven Commissioners to carry out promotional activities in OAU Member States as follows:

(i) Dr. Ibrahim Ali Badawi El-Sheikh: Comoros, Seychelles, Ile Maurice, Egypt, Sudan, Tunisia;
(ii) Mr. Alioune Blondin Beye: Benin, Burkina Faso, Côte d'Ivoire, Mali, Togo;
(iii) Mr. Ali Mahmoud Buhedma: Algeria, Libya, Mauritania, Djibouti, Saharawi Republic;
(iv) Mr. Alexis Gabou: Cameroon, Central African Republic, Chad, Congo, Sao Tome;
(v) Mr. Sourahata Baboucarr Semega Janneh: The Gambia, Liberia, Sierra Leone;
(vi) Mr. Robert Habesh Kisanga: Ethiopia, Kenya, Somalia, Uganda, Tanzania;
(vii) Mr. Moleleki D. Mokama: Botswana, Lesotho, Malawi, Swaziland;
(viii) Mr. C. L. C. Mubanga-Chipoya: Angola, Mozambique, Zambia, Zimbabwe, Namibia;
(ix) Mr. Youssoupha Ndiaye: Cape Verde, Niger, Senegal, Guinea, Guinea-Bissau.

Fifth Annual Activity Report of the African Commission on Human and Peoples' Rights 1991–1992

Adopted on 9 March 1992
Covering the 10th and 11th Ordinary Sessions in Banjul (8–15 October) and Tunis (2–9 March)

I. ORGANIZATION OF WORK

A. Period Covered by the Report

1. The Fourth Activity Report was adopted by the Twenty-seventh Ordinary Session of the Heads of State and Government of the OAU by its resolution AHG/Res. 202 (XXVII). This Fifth Report covers the Tenth and Eleventh Ordinary Sessions which were held in Banjul 8–15 October 1991, and Tunis, 2–9 March respectively.

B. Status of Ratification

2. As at the date of the 11th ordinary Session of the Commission, 43 Member States had ratified the Charter. The list of those states which have ratified the Charter is attached hereto as Annex I.

C. Sessions and Agenda

3. The Commission has held two ordinary sessions since its Fourth Annual Activity Report was adopted:

- the Tenth Ordinary Session was held in Banjul, The Gambia, 8–15 October 1991;
- the Eleventh Ordinary Session was held in Tunis, Tunisia, 2–9 March 1992.

The Agenda of both sessions are attached hereto as Annexes II and III respectively.

D. Composition and Participation

4. The following members of the Commission were reelected by the 27th Ordinary Session of the Assembly of Heads of State and Government after their term of office had expired:

- Mr. Robert H. Kisanga,
- Mr. C. L. C. Mubanga-Chipoya,
- Professor U. O. Umozurike.

5. The composition of the Commission has changed following the death of Commissioner Mubanga-Chipoya in December 1991. The Chairman of the Commission has duly notified the Secretary General of the OAU of the vacancy created by the death of the late Commissioner Mubanga-Chipoya.

The list of the remaining members of the Commission is attached hereto as Annex IV.

6. The attendance at sessions has been as follows:

At the Tenth Ordinary Session, nine Commissioners attended:

Mr. Ibrahim A. Badawi El-Sheikh,
Mr. Alioune Blondin Bèye,
Mr. Ali Mahmoud Buhedma,
Mr. Robert Habesh Kisanga,
Mr. C. L. C. Mubanga-Chipoya,
Mr. Moleleki D. Mokama,
Mr. U. O. Umozurike,
Mr. Sourahata B. S. Janneh,
Mr. Isaac Nguema.

Mr. Youssoupha Ndiaye was absent with apology
Mr. Alexis Gabou did not attend.

7. At the Eleventh Ordinary Session, nine Commissioners attended:

Dr. Ibrahim A. Badawi El-Sheikh,
Mr. Alioune Blondin Bèye,
Mr. Ali Mahmoud Buhedma,
Mr. Robert H. Kisanga,
Mr. Moleleki D. Mokama,
Mr. Youssoupha Ndiaye,
Mr. Sourahata B. S. Janneh,
Mr. Isaac Nguema,
Prof. U. O. Umozurike.

Mr. Alexis Gabou did not attend.

E. Chairman and Vice-Chairman of the Commission

8. The mandate of the Chairman Commissioner Umozurike and Vice-Chairman Commissioner Alexis Gabou expired.

9. At its Tenth Ordinary Session in October 1991 the Commission proceeded to elect its office bearers, the results of which were as follows:

Dr. Ibrahim A. Badawi El-Sheikh was duly elected Chairman of the Commission in accordance with Article 17 of the Rules of Procedure of the Commission.

Mr. C. L. C. Mubanga-Chipoya was duly elected Vice-Chairman but, as already stated, Commissioner Mubanga-Chipoya passed away in December 1991.

At its 11th Session Commissioner Sourahata B. S. Janneh was elected Vice-Chairman.

F. Adoption of Annual Activity Report

10. On 9 March 1992 the Commission considered and adopted this Fifth Activity Report.

II. ACTIVITIES OF THE COMMISSION

A. Examination of Reports.

11. At its Eleventh Ordinary Session, the Commission considered the initial reports submitted by Egypt and Tanzania under Article 62 of the Charter. The Commission expressed its appreciation to both Governments for submitting their reports and sending representatives to have a dialogue with the Commission. In the Commission's view, the conduct of Egypt and Tanzania reflected the will of both Governments to co-operate with the Commission in the implementation of the Charter.

The representatives of both Governments promised to research further into the questions put by the Commissioners and to give their answers when presenting their second periodic reports.

As at the Eleventh Session of the Commission, only eight States submitted their first periodic reports, namely, the Jamahiriya of the Libya, Zimbabwe, Egypt, Nigeria, Tunisia, Tanzania, Rwanda and Togo. Accordingly, the Commission recommended to the Assembly of the Heads of State and Government the adoption of Draft Resolution on overdue reports (see Annex IX).

B. Promotional Activities

(i) Activities of the Commissioners

12. Commissioners undertook promotional activities in a number of African States. Such activities were undertaken with the co-operation of the competent authorities of the States visited by the Commissioners. The object of the activities was to publicize the African Charter and explain the work of the Commission.

In this context, Commissioners gave lectures, attended seminars, and initiated contacts in Africa and elsewhere.

(ii) Seminars

13. At its Tenth Session, the Commission decided to organize a number of Seminars. These included:

(1) Implementation of the African Charter in the internal legal systems;
(2) Status of women under the Charter in relation to specific socio-economic problems;
(3) The Right to a Fair Trial with special reference to legal assistance;
(4) The situation of Refugees and displaced persons in Africa;
(5) The Role of the African Media in the promotion and protection of human rights; and
(6) Post-Apartheid South Africa.

14. The Commission, at its eleventh Session decided to organize a Seminar on popular participation and non-formal education. In addition, the Commission adopted a Programme of Activities which includes several other seminars.

(iii) Publications

15. The Commission published the first edition of its publication, "The African Review on Human and Peoples' Rights" in October 1991. The Commission will publish subsequent editions in accordance with its Programme of Activities.

16. In addition to the Review, the Commission is preparing to publish a Brochure on the African Charter as well as a Bulletin on the activities of the African Commission.

17. The Commission decided to embark on a project for the purposes of distributing widely its public documents such as the Rules of Procedure and annual Reports. Furthermore, the Commission decided to establish a Documentation and Information Center at its Secretariat in Banjul, the objectives of which include, research on human rights problems in Africa.

(iv) International Co-operation

18. The Commission conducted a number of activities which were supported financially by the UN Centre for Human Rights, the European Community, the Swedish and the Danish Governments.

(v) Observers

19. In pursuance of Rule 76 of its Rules of Procedure, The Commission granted observer status to a number of non-governmental organizations. The NGOs which have so far been granted observer status are shown in the list attached hereto as Annex V.

20. At its Eleventh Session the Commission reaffirmed its wish for the continued co-operation with the NGOs in the performance of its functions but emphasized the need to observe the limits within which that co-operation is to be rendered, bearing in mind the independence of the Commission and its nature as a Commission of experts operating within the context of the African Charter.

21. The Commission has always taken the view that the NGOs which have been granted observer status with the Commission should from time to time inform the Commission of their activities in the field of human rights to assist the Commission in its work. In line with this view, the Commission, at its Eleventh Session, reiterated that such NGOs should, at least every two years, report to the Commission of their activities which are relevant to the work of the Commission.

C. Consideration of Substantive Rights

22. In accordance with its policy to deepen the understanding of substantive rights guaranteed by the Charter, the Commission at its Eleventh Session considered:

(1) The Right to Recourse Procedure and Fair Trial (Art. 7); and
(2) The Right to Freedom of Association (Art. 10) and adopted resolutions in respect thereof. The two resolutions are attached hereto as Annexes VI and VII, respectively.

D. Protective Activities

(i) Consideration of Communications

23. At its Tenth and Eleventh Sessions, the Commission received a total of 16 new communications. With regard to these communications, the Commission took preliminary and provisional measures in accordance with the provisions of the African Charter and the Commission's Rules of Procedure. The Commission made a follow-up on the old communications as relevant. The communications were examined in closed meetings.

(ii) Establishment of Inter-sessional Working Group

24. Considering that the Commission usually meets only twice a year, at its Eleventh Session, the Commission established an inter-sessional working group for the purpose of expediting its work.

E. Programme of Activities

25. At its Tenth and Eleventh Sessions, the Commission adopted a programme of activities which has a number of components including the establishment of a documentation and information center, organizing seminars and workshops, and training courses.

F. Observer Mission to Mali

26. At its Eleventh Session the Commission received a request from the Government of Mali for the Commission to send observers during the Presidential Election in that country which is scheduled for 12 and 26 April 1992. The Commission acceded to the request and appointed Commissioner Youssoupha Nidaye as Leader of its Mission to Mali, and entrusted him with the responsibility of working out the modalities for the carrying out of this exercise.

G. Conclusions and Recommendations

Conclusions

27. The Commission has been functioning for only five years. During this short period and despite its financial constraints, the Commission has successfully carried out a number of promotional and protective activities. However, the Commission realizes that it has a lot more to accomplish.

To this end, the Commission has adopted a programme of activities, and has underlined the need that the OAU Budget caters for the requirements of the Commission.

28. The Commission reaffirms its commitment to the protection of human rights in Africa and will continue to rely on the co-operation with States, inter-governmental and non-governmental organizations.

Recommendations

(i) Draft Resolutions to the OAU Assembly

29. The Commission recommends the following draft resolutions for consideration and adoption by the Assembly of Heads of State and Government:

(1) Draft Resolution on Ratification of the African Charter on Human and Peoples' Rights (Annex VIII);
(2) Draft Resolution on overdue reports (Annex IX);
(3) Draft Resolution on Promotional Activities (Annex X).

(ii) Resolutions Adopted by the Commission

30. The Commission at its Eleventh Session adopted the following resolutions:

(1) Resolution on the Right to Recourse Procedure and Fair Trial – Annex VI;
(2) Resolution on the Right to Freedom of Association – Annex VII.

ANNEX I

African Charter on Human and Peoples' Rights
List of Countries which have Signed, Ratified or Adhered to the Charter

No.	Country	Date of Signature	Date of Ratification/ Adhesion	Date Deposited
1.	Algeria	10/04/86	01/03/87	20/03/87
2.	Angola		02/03/90	09/10/90
3.	Benin		20/01/86	25/02/86
4.	Botswana		17/07/86	22/07/86
5.	Burundi		28/07/80	30/08/89
6.	Burkina Faso	05/03/84	06/07/84	21/09/84
7.	Cameroon	23/07/87	20/06/89	18/09/89
8.	Cape Verde	31/03/86	02/06/87	06/08/87
9.	Central African Republic		26/04/86	27/07/86
10.	Chad	29/05/86	09/10/86	11/11/86
11.	Comoros		01/06/86	18/07/86
12.	Congo	27/11/81	09/12/82	17/01/83
13.	Djibouti		11/11/91	20/12/91
14.	Egypt	16/11/81	20/03/84	03/04/84
15.	Equatorial Guinea	18/08/86	07/04/86	18/08/86
16.	Ethiopia			
17.	Gabon	26/02/82	20/02/86	26/06/86
18.	Gambia	11/02/83	08/06/83	13/03/83
19.	Ghana		24/01/89	01/03/89
20.	Guinée	09/12/81	16/02/82	13/05/82
21.	Guinée-Bissau		04/12/85	06/03/86
22.	Côte d'Ivoire		06/01/92	31/03/92
23.	Kenya		23/01/92	10/02/92
24.	Lesotho	07/03/84	10/02/92	27/02/92
25.	Liberia	31/01/83	04/08/82	29/12/82
26.	Libya	30/05/85	19/07/86	26/03/87
27.	Madagascar		09/03/92	19/03/92
28.	Malawi	23/02/90	17/11/89	23/02/90
29.	Mali	13/11/81	21/12/81	22/01/82
30.	Mauritanie	25/02/82	14/06/86	26/06/86
31.	Mauritius			
32.	Mozambique		22/02/89	07/03/90
33.	Namibia			
34.	Niger	09/07/86	15/07/86	21/07/86
35.	Nigeria	31/08/82	22/06/83	27/07/83
36.	République Rwandaise	11/11/81	15/07/83	22/07/83
37.	Saharawi Arab Dem. Rep.	10/04/86	02/05/86	23/05/86
38.	Sao Tome & Principe		23/05/86	28/07/86
39.	Senegal	23/09/81	13/08/82	25/10/82
40.	Seychelles		13/04/92	30/04/92
41.	Sierra Leone	27/08/81	21/09/83	27/01/84

No.	Country	Date of Signature	Date of Ratification/ Adhesion	Date Deposited
42.	Somalia	26/02/82	31/07/85	20/03/86
43.	Sudan	03/09/82	18/02/86	11/03/86
44.	Swaziland			
45.	Togo	20/02/82	05/11/82	22/11/82
46.	Tunisia		16/03/83	22/04/83
47.	Uganda	18/08/86	10/05/86	27/05/86
48.	Tanzania	31/05/82	18/02/84	09/03/84
49.	Zaire	23/07/87	20/07/87	28/07/87
50.	Zambia	17/01/83	19/01/84	02/02/84
51.	Zimbabwe	20/02/86	30/05/86	12/06/86

ADOPTED: by the 18th Assembly of Heads of State and Government, on 27 June 1981
REQUIRES: ratification or adherence of a simple majority of OAU Member States to come into force
ENTERED INTO FORCE: 21st day of October 1986
REGISTERED: with the United Nations on ___________ day of 19__

ANNEX II

Agenda of the Tenth Ordinary Session

1. Opening Ceremony
2. Oath by the New Elected Members of the Commission
3. Election of the Chairman and the Vice-Chairman of the Commission
4. Adoption of Agenda
5. Organisation of Work:

   (a) Appointment of Rapporteur
   (b) Working Hours

6. Observers

   (a) Requests for Observer Status
   (b) Consideration of the Conclusions of the Workshop on NGO Participation in the Work of the African Commission

7. Matters Arising from Preceding Session:

   (a) Report of the Chairman
   (b) Report of the Members of the Commission
   (c) Report of the Secretary

8. Activities of the Commission:

    (a) Protective Activities
    (b) Promotional Activities

9. Consideration of Periodic Reports
10. Report of the Consultants on the Programme of Activities
11. Consideration of Rules of Procedure
12. Report of the Activities of the OAU Relevant to the Commission
13. Any Other Business
14. Date, Venue and Agenda of the 11th Session
15. Adoption of the Report of the 10th Session
16. Final Communique
17. Closing Ceremony

ANNEX III

Agenda of the Eleventh Ordinary Session (Tunis, 2–9 March 1992)

1. Opening Ceremony
2. Adoption of Agenda
3. Election of the Vice-Chairman
4. Organization of Work:

    (a) Appointment of Rapporteur
    (b) Working Hours

5. Observers
6. Consideration of Periodic Reports
7. Promotional Activities
8. Protective Activities
9. The Right to Free Association (Articles 10 and 11 of the African Charter)
10. The Right to Recourse Procedure and Fair Trial (Article 7 of the African Charter)
11. Administrative and Financial Matters
12. Methods of Work of the Commission Including Rules of procedure
13. Report of the Activities of the OAU Relevant to the Commission
14. Date, Venue and Draft Agenda of the 12th Session
15. Any Other Business
16. Adoption of the Report of the 11th Session
17. Adoption of the Fifth Annual Report
18. Adoption of the Annual Report
19. Final Communique and Closing Ceremony

ANNEX IV

List of Addresses of Commissioners of the African Commission on Human and Peoples' Rights

1. Dr. Ibrahim Ali BADAWI EL SHEIKH — Chairman
Embassy of Egypt
7 Aberdeen Road
Avondale
A 433 AVONDALE
HARARE/ZIMBABWE
Tel Office: (2634) 303445/303447
Telex: 24653 BOUSTA ZW
Fax: (2634) 303115

2. Mr. Sourahata Baboucar Semega JANNEH — Vice-Chairman
15 Hagan Street
PO Box 212
BANJUL/THE GAMBIA
Tel Office: (220) 28174
Tel Res: (220) 95117
Telex: 2216 GV (NOVOTEL)

3. Mr. Alioune Blondin BEYE — Member
BP 487 Cedex 1
ABIDJAN/COTE D'IVOIRE
Tel Office: (225) 332833
Tel Res: (225) 415891
Fax: (225) 217471

4. Mr. Ali Mahmoud BUHEDMA — Member
No 7 Elmagroun Street
14 Fueihat
PO Box 889
BENGHAZI/LIBYA
Tel: (21861) 21215
Telex: 40341 HILAL LY (BENGHAZI)

5. Mr. Alexis GABOU — Member
Conseil Constitutionnel au MIN. AE
PO Box 811
BRAZZAVILLE/CONGO
Tel Office: (24312) 813311
Telex: 5210 PRECONGO KG

6. Mr. Robert Habesh KISANGA — Member
Court of Appeal
PO Box 9004
DAR-ES-SALAAM/TANZANIA
Tel Office: (25551) 27843/26011

7. Mr. Moleleki D. MOKAMA — Member
Private Bag 1 LOBATSE
GABORONE/BOTSWANA
Tel Office: (26731) 330644
Tel Res: (26731) 353378
Telex: 2758 COURT BD
Fax: (26731) 332317

8. Mr. Youssoupha NDIAYE — Member
c/o Cour d'Appel
Palais de Justice
DAKAR/SENEGAL
Tel Office: (01) 220367/217966
Tel Res: 217257

9. Mr. Isaac NGUEMA — Member
BP 963
LIBREVILLE/GABON
Tel Office: (241) 732420
Tel Res: (241) 732027
Telex: 5255 GO
Fax: (241) 760993

10. Prof. U. Oji UMOZURIKE — Member
Faculty of Law
University of Calabar
CALABAR/NIGERIA
Tel Office: (234) 87224748/49 Ext. 9
Tel Res: (234) 87220543
Telex: 65103 UNICAL, NG
Fax: (234) 87220111/87220543
or
c/o Liaison Officer
University of Calabar
LAGOS/NIGERIA
Tel: (2341) 835615

Secretary to the Commission
Mr. Ngabishema MUTSINZI
PO Box 673
BANJUL/THE GAMBIA
Tel: (220) 92964/92962
Telex: (996) 2346 OAU BJL GV
Fax: (220) 90764

ANNEX V

List of NGOs Granted Observer Status[1]

ANNEX VI

Resolution on the Right to Recourse Procedure and Fair Trial

Conscious of the fact that the African Charter on Human and Peoples' Rights is designed to promote and protect human rights in accordance with the provisions contained in the Charter and recognized international human rights standards.

Recognizing that the right to a fair trial is essential for the protection of fundamental human rights and freedoms.

Bearing in mind Article 7 of the African Charter on Human and Peoples' Rights,

1. CONSIDERS THAT every person whose rights or freedoms are violated is entitled to have an effective remedy.

2. CONSIDERS FURTHER THAT the right to fair trial includes, among other things, the following.

A. All persons shall have the right to have their cause heard and shall be equal before the courts and tribunals in the determination of their rights and obligations.

B. Persons who are arrested shall be informed, at the time of arrest, in a language which they understand of the reasons for their arrest and shall be informed promptly of any charges against them.

C. Persons arrested or detained shall be brought promptly before a judge or other officer authorized by law to exercise judicial power and shall be entitled to trial within a reasonable time or be released.

D. Persons charged with a criminal offence shall be presumed innocent until proved guilty by a competent court.

E. In the determination of charges against individuals, the individuals shall be entitled in particular to:

[1] This list is omitted. The most up-to-date list is reproduced below at p. 90.

(1) Have adequate time and facilities for the preparation of their defence and to communicate in confidence with the counsel of their choice.
(2) Be tried within a reasonable time.
(3) Examine, or have examined, the witnesses against them and to obtain the attendance and examination of witnesses on their behalf under the same conditions as witnesses against them.
(4) Have the free assistance of an interpreter if they cannot speak the language used in court.

3. Persons convicted of an offence shall have a right of appeal to a higher court.

4. RECOMMENDS to States Parties to the African Charter on Human and Peoples' Rights to create awareness of the accessibility of the recourse procedures and to provide needy with legal aid.

5. DECIDES TO continue to be seized with the right to recourse procedures and fair trial with the view of elaborating further principles concerning this right.

ANNEX VII

Resolution on the Right to Freedom of Association

The African Commission on Human and Peoples' Rights:

Taking into consideration **all rights** stipulated in the Universal Declaration of Human Rights, with special reference to Articles 20, 23 guaranteeing the right to freedom of peaceful assembly and association,

Recalling Article of the international Covenant on Civil and Political Rights, and Article 8 of the International Covenant on Economic, Social and Cultural Rights assuring that everyone shall have the right to freedom of association with others,

Highly evaluating the UN Sub-Commission on the Prevention of Discrimination, Resolution No 13 (XXXIII) on 11 September 1980 which adopted the right to freedom of association,

Taking into consideration the provisions of the African Charter for Human and Peoples' Rights, in particular Article 10(1), guaranteeing every individual the right to free association provided that he abides by the law.

CONSIDERS THAT:

1. The competent authorities should not override constitutional provisions or undermine fundamental rights guaranteed by the Constitution and international human rights standards.

2. In regulating the use of this right, the component authorities should not enact provisions which would limit the exercise of this freedom.

3. The regulation of the exercise of the right to freedom of association should be consistent with States' obligations under the African Charter for Human and Peoples' Rights.

ANNEX VIII

Draft Resolution on Ratification of the African Charter

The Assembly of Heads of State and Government of the Organization of African Unity, recalling the 10th Anniversary of the adoption of the African Charter on Human and Peoples' Rights in June 1981 and the fifth anniversary of its entry into force on 21 October 1991,

Noting that the members of the African Commission on Human and Peoples' Rights are elected by the Organization of African Unity,

Further recalling that all the Member States of the Organization of African Unity have pledged in the Preamble of the Charter of the Organization of African Unity "to promote international co-operation, having due regard to the Charter of the United Nations and the Universal Declaration of Human Rights",

Remembering that the Assembly of Heads of State and Government of the Organization of African Unity at its 24th Ordinary Session in May 1988 "strongly" urged Member States which had not yet ratified the African Charter "to do so as soon as possible",

Emphasizing the importance of adherence to the African Charter on Human and Peoples' Rights by all Member States of the Organization of African Unity,

Expressing deep gratitude to the 27 Member States of the Organization of African Unity which have become States Parties to the African Charter on Human and Peoples' Rights,

1. STRONGLY URGES those Member States which have not yet ratified the African Charter on Human and Peoples' Rights to do so as soon as possible;
2. DIRECTS the Secretary General of the OAU to transmit this Resolution to each Member State of the Organization of African Unity which has not yet ratified or acceded to the African Charter on Human and Peoples' Rights;
3. REQUESTS the African Commission on Human and Peoples' Rights to report on the implementation of this resolution.

ANNEX IX

Draft Resolution on Overdue Reports for Adoption

The Assembly of Heads of State and Government of the OAU,

Noting with concern that as of 9 March 1992 only eight States parties to the African Charter on Human and Peoples' Rights have submitted their initial periodic reports in accordance with Article 62 "on the legislative or other measures taken with a view to giving effect to the rights and freedoms recognized and guaranteed by the (African) Charter" to the African Commission on Human and Peoples' Rights,

Realizing the importance of the reporting procedure in helping the African Commission on Human and Peoples' Rights to assist States Parties to ensure that the rights and freedoms recognized by the African Charter on Human and Peoples' Rights are given effect in national law and practice,

Expressing its deep appreciation to the States parties which have submitted their initial periodic reports, Egypt, Libyan Arab Jamahiriya, Nigeria, Rwanda, Tanzania, Togo, Tunisia, Zimbabwe, Senegal, Cape Verde and Gambia,

Taking note of the benefits of the dialogue the African Commission on Human and Peoples' Rights and States parties which occurs during examination of periodic reports for the implementation of human and peoples' rights,

1. URGES the States Parties to the African Charter on Human and Peoples' Rights which have not yet submitted their initial reports to submit them as soon as possible;

2. REQUESTS that the States should report not only on legislative measures, but also on other measures taken to give effect to each of the rights and freedoms recognized and guaranteed by the African Charter on Human and Peoples' Rights and on the problems encountered in giving effect to these rights and freedoms;

3. ENCOURAGES States Parties which encounter difficulties in preparing and submitting their periodic reports to seek help as soon as possible from the African Commission on Human and Peoples' Rights which will arrange for assistance in this task through its own or other resources.

ANNEX X

Draft Resolution on Promotional Activities

The Assembly of the Heads of State and Government of the Organization of African Unity Recalling at its 27th Ordinary Session held at Abuja, Federal Republic of Nigeria, from 3 to 5 June 1991 recommend in Resolution AHG/Res. 202 (XXVII) that Member States celebrate the anniversary of the entry into force of the African Charter on Human and Peoples' Rights on 21 October of every year "by organizing activities aimed at promoting Human and Peoples' Rights".

Further recalling and reaffirming its own resolutions to the effect that Member States should observe this anniversary each year on 21 October, and that all States Parties should incorporate the rights and freedoms recognized in their internal legal systems and guaranteed in the African Charter on Human and Peoples' Rights, that States Parties should establish and support national institutions with responsibility for promoting and protecting human and peoples' rights, and that human and peoples' rights should be included in the curriculum at all levels of education and that the press should be encouraged to promote human and peoples' rights,

1. URGES all States Parties to the African Charter on Human and Peoples' Rights to reflect the rights and freedoms recognized and guaranteed by the African Charter in their law and practice;

2. REQUESTS that all States Parties should implement Article 26 of the African Charter on Human and Peoples' Rights by establishing national institutions with responsibility for promoting and protecting human and peoples' rights where they do not exist and strengthening all such institutions;

3. FURTHER REQUESTS that all Member States should implement Article 25 of the African Charter on Human and Peoples' Rights by ensuring, inter alia, that human rights are included in the curriculum at all levels of public and private education and in the training of all law enforcement officials;

4. INVITES States Parties to ensure that the right of individuals to receive information and to freedom of expression recognized and guaranteed by Article 9 of the African Charter on Human and Peoples' Rights in fully respected;

5. CALLS upon all States Parties to report on these questions in their periodic reports to the African Commission on Human and Peoples' Rights;

6. REQUESTS the African Commission on Human and Peoples' Rights to report on the implementation of this resolution.

Final Communiqué of the Tenth Ordinary Session of the African Commission on Human and Peoples' Rights

Banjul, 8–15 October 1991

1. The African Commission on Human and Peoples' Rights held its 10th Ordinary Session in Banjul, The Gambia, from 8–15 October 1991 under the Chairmanship of Dr. Ibrahim Ali Badawi El Sheikh.

2. The Session coincided with the 10th Anniversary of the African Charter on Human and Peoples' Rights adoption, in Nairobi, in June 1981, by the Assembly of the Heads of State and Government of the OAU and with the 4th Anniversary of the installation of the African Commission on Human and Peoples' Rights on 2 November 1987.

3. The session was attended by the following members:

(i) Dr. Ibrahim Ali Badawi El Sheikh;
(ii) Mr. Alioune Blondin Bèye;
(iii) Mr. Ali Mahmoud Buhedma;
(iv) Mr. Robert Habesh Kisanga;
(v) Mr. Moleleki D. Mokama;
(vi) Mr. Sourahata B. Semega Janneh;
(vii) Mr. Chama L.C. Mubanga-Chipoya;
(viii) Prof. Isaac Nguema;
(ix) Prof. U. O. Umozurike.

4. The opening was presided over by Prof. Umozurike, the outgoing Chairman of the Commission and His Excellency, the President of the Republic of The Gambia was represented by the Honourable Hassan B. Jallow, Attorney General and Minister of Justice.

5. After the welcome address by Professor Umozurike other speeches were made by:

- The Honourable Hassan B. Jallow, Attorney-General and Minister of Justice representing the President of the Republic of The Gambia;
- Mr. Robinson, Chairman of the Inter-American Commission on Human Rights;
- Mr. Falk, representing the United Nations Under-Secretary-General for Human Rights;
- Mr. Adama Dieng, Secretary-General of the ICJ; and
- Mr. N. Mutsinzi, the Secretary to the African Commission on Human and Peoples' Rights representing the Secretary-General of the OAU.

6. In his Statement the Honourable Hassan B. Jallow assured the Commission of the enduring commitment of the Gambian government to the facilitation of the work

of the Commission by providing the necessary assistance to enable it achieve its objectives.

7. On commencement of their formal deliberations, the recently reelected members of the Commission, at the 27th Ordinary Session of the Assembly of Heads of State and Government, took their oath of office. The newly re-elected members are:

- Mr. Robert Hababesh Kisanga;
- Mr. Chama L.C. Mubanga-Chipoya;
- Prof. U. O. Umozurike.

8. Following the expiry of the two year term of office for Umozurike and Gabou elected on 24 November 1989 as Chairman and Vice-Chairman, respectively, the Commission in conformity with Rule 17 of the Rules of Procedure elected as Chairman: Dr. Ibrahim Ali El-Sheikh and as Vice-Chairman: Mr. Chama L. C. Mubanga-Chipoya.

9. The Commission deliberated, in particular, on the following topics:

(i) Observers:

(a) requests for observer status;
(b) consideration of the conclusions of the workshop organized by the ICJ and the African Centre for Democracy and Human Rights on NGO participation in the work of the African Commission.

(ii) Matters arising from the preceding session:

(a) report of the Chairman;
(b) reports of the members of the Commission;
(c) report of the Secretary.

(iii) Activities of the Commission:

(a) protective activities;
(b) promotional activities.

(iv) Consideration of Periodic Reports.
(v) Report of the consultants on the Programme of Activities.
(vi) Consideration of the Rules of Procedure.
(vii) Report of the activities of the OAU relevant to the Commission
(viii) Date, venue and agenda of the 11th Session.
(ix) Adoption of the report of the 10th Session.
(x) Final Communiqué.

10. Following consideration of their requests the Commission granted observer status to the following NGOs:

(i) International Human Rights Law Group;
(ii) Minnesota Lawyers International Human Rights Committee;
(iii) Fédération internationale de l'action des chrétiens pour l'abolition de la torture (FIACAT);

(iv) African Union of Lawyers;
(v) Groupe d'étude et de recherche sur la démocratie et le développement économique et social;
(vi) Anti-Slavery International for the Protection of Human Rights;
(vii) Congressional Human Rights Foundation;
(viii) La Ligue ivoirienne des droits de l'homme;
(ix) L'Association des juristes africains (AJA);
(x) L'Association pour la promotion de l'Etat de droit (APED);
(xi) Rencontre africaine pour la défense des droits de l'homme (RADHO);
(xii) The Decade of Human Rights Education , INC (DHRE);
(xiii) Marangopoulos Foundation for Human Rights (MFHR);
(xiv) Legal Research and Resource Development Centre;
(xv) Organization mondiale contre la torture;
(xvi) International Service for Human Rights;
(xvii) International League for Human Rights;
(xviii) L'Association nationale des droits de l'homme (Gabon).

The following were given observer status subject to their presentation of their basic documents:

- African Bar Association
- Ligue centrafricaine des droits de l'homme

11. On obtaining observer status the NGOs expressed gratitude to the Commission and reaffirmed their respective commitment to the promotion and protection of human rights in Africa.

12. The Commission learned from the Statement of the Chairman of the Inter-American Commission who cited examples of measures which the African Commission could utilize to enhance its own performance. Measures such as, inter alia, possibility of carrying out investigations in States Parties; the possibility of undertaking actions and adopting interim measures in order to avoid irreparable prejudice to victims of human rights violations; measures to be taken to counter delaying tactics used by some member States to impede settlement of cases presented to the Commission; and, the possibility of visiting prisons, preparing special reports on human rights situations in a given country and exempting indigent complaints from stipulations governing the exhaustion of local procedures.

13. On the role of the Commission and the NGOs in the discharge of their protective and promotional functions the NGOs emphasized:

- the need for members of the Commission to enjoy full diplomatic immunity while engaged in these activities even in their own countries;
- the need to simplify the rules of procedure resulting in the reduction of delays in settling communications thereby enabling the Commission to intervene with greater efficiency in emergency situations;
- the need for the Commission to act with greater audacity in carrying out its assigned functions;

- the need for NGOs working hand in hand with the members of the Commission in order to address the difficulties which might arise from the execution of these functions;
- the need to improve the effectiveness of the Secretariat of the Commission by developing dynamic methods in discharging its functions and making maximum use of the efforts of the members of the Commission.

14. The newly elected Chairman, Dr. Badawi El Sheikh, the Commissioners and the Secretary-General submitted their reports on their respective activities in the inter session period. The fruitful discussions on these reports led to various observations and suggestions.

15. The Commissioners agreed to a reorganization of the list of countries for each member for the purpose of their direct promotion and protection activities in these countries; an exercise first enunciated at the 8th Ordinary Session.

16. The continuing decline of the resources allocated to the Commission by the OAU, brought about by the difficulties encountered by the OAU in recovering the total amount of budget contributions, remains a source of great worry to the Commission. In this regard the Commission received with gratitude grants from Organizations such as:

- UN Centre for Human Rights;
- UNESCO;
- EC;
- DANIDA;
- The Raoul Wallemberg Institute of Human Rights and Humanitarian Law.

17. The Commission appointed a Commissioner to work out ways of systematic utilization of the funds made available to it and to establish an appropriate and reliable machinery for hiring personnel to help it acquire equipment for use at its headquarters and whenever it might hold its sessions. Another Commissioner was requested to indicate additional ways in which the DANIDA Fund could be put towards the efficient fulfilment of its promotional activities.

18. Among other seminars and discussions the members of the Commission may hold or attend in their promotional activities, the Commission decided to send a representative to the seminar to be held from 29 November to 2 December 1991 in Tunis organized by the Arab Institute for Human Rights and the Tunisian League for Defence of Human Rights on Criminal Law and Penal Reform, who are to provide lodging and boarding free of charge.

19. With regard to the protective activities, the Commission considered complaints other than those of States Parties, namely:

- cases already declared admissible;
- new cases.

20. Concerning the new cases presented to the Commission for consideration, in accordance with Article 55 of the Charter, the Commission considered 18 new communications and made the following decisions:

For 15 of these cases, the communications must be brought to the knowledge of the State concerned and its author should be requested to indicate whether all local remedies have been exhausted. For 2 cases, the Commission should refer the matter to the current Chairman of the OAU, in conformity with Article 58 paragraph 3 of the Charter. For one of the cases the Commission decided to request the State concerned for a temporary suspension of the measures envisaged.

21. Regarding cases already declared admissible, the Commission considered 7 communications which have been settled in a satisfactory manner, and closed the dossiers.

22. The subject of revising the Rules of Procedure was also tackled and a Commissioner appointed to consolidate the amendments have been made for a full debate on the matter at the coming 11th Session.

23. Mindful of the need to monitor the human and peoples' rights situation in the States Parties and to establish a dialogue with them, the Commission vigorously tackled the matter of periodic reports from States. The Commission formally directed a number of questions to the States concerned in an effort to lay out a foundation on which to build this work according to Guidelines already prepared. It has also been indicated to the States concerned on which dates their reports would be considered at the next session.

24. Ever mindful of the situation of apartheid in South Africa, and since the Commission has received reports of the continuing violence in that country, and noting with sadness from these reports that much of the violence appears to be sponsored, encouraged or supported by certain elements of the Government. And following the recent signing of the National Peace Accord by Organizations including the African National Congress, the Inkhata Freedom Party and the South African government, intended to end this violence.

THE COMMISSION:

(a) Condemns the use of violence in South Africa to settle disputes by anybody in South Africa and in particular the recent massacre of 18 people in Thokoza near Johannesburg.

(b) Appeals to the government to fully comply with its undertakings under the National Peace Accord.

(c) Calls on the government to accede to the demands of the majority of South Africans for the establishment of an interim government and a constituent assembly.

(d) In keeping with the preamble of the Charter of the Organization of African Unity requiring total commitment to the elimination of apartheid, calls upon the Heads of State of the OAU to consider carefully the human rights conditions prevailing in South Africa.

25. The Commission decided to hold its 11th Session from 2–9 March 1992 in a venue which will be announced and that, in future, ordinary sessions will be held during the first half of March and the second half of October each year.

26. The Commission decided on the agenda of the 11th Session copy of which is attached.

Done in Banjul, 15 October 1991

Press Release

15 October 1991

MESSAGE OF THE AFRICAN COMMISSION ON HUMAN AND PEOPLES' RIGHTS ON THE OCCASION OF THE TENTH ANNIVERSARY OF THE ADOPTION OF THE AFRICAN CHARTER ON HUMAN AND PEOPLES' RIGHTS

I. Approved by the Assembly of Heads of State and Government in Nairobi, Kenya, in June 1981, the African Charter on Human and Peoples' Rights entered into force on 21 october 1986.

Since then, this important date in the promotion of human rights in Africa is commemorated every year as African Human and Peoples' Rights Day.

For the commemoration of this anniversary the Commission indicated:

- that the event be given all due solemnity and significance with a view to sensitizing African Public Opinion on the need to promote and defend the basic freedoms and rights of the human being;

The Commission believes that the situation which prevailed in Africa in 1981, during the adoption of the Charter has changed considerably. The present situation is characterized by a strong demand for the rights to peace, freedom, democracy and development.

II. The African Commission on Human and Peoples' Rights seizes this opportunity to make a solemn and pressing appeal to States, NGOs, peoples and individuals, and to the International Community.

It therefore calls on States which have yet to ratify the Charter to do so as soon as possible, and on all OAU Member States to take concrete steps to abide by the provisions of the Charter.

The Commission draws attention to the resolution relating to human and peoples' rights which, inter alia:

Reaffirms its position declared during the 25th Ordinary Session held in July 1989 stating that the promotion and protection of human and peoples' rights are essential factors for the progress of African citizens and *constitutes* a significantly contribution to the attainment of their aspirations for development;

Calls on Member States, parties to the Charter to submit regularly, periodic reports on legislative or other measures taken with a view to giving effect to the rights and freedoms recognized and guaranteed by the present Charter, in accordance with Article 62;

Recommends that Member States of the OAU celebrate the anniversary of the entry into force of the Charter on 21 October of every year by organizing activities aimed at promoting human and peoples' rights.

The Commission appeals to NGOs to play a more active role in the areas of promotion and protection of human rights and cooperate more closely among themselves and with the Commission with a view to executing their mission as effectively as possible.

Done in Banjul, 15 October 1991

The Chairman of The African Commission for Human Rights

Final Communiqué of the Eleventh Ordinary Session of the African Commission on Human and Peoples' Rights

Tunis, 9 March 1992
ACHPR/COMM/FIN(XI) Rev. 1

1. The African Commission on Human and Peoples' Rights held its 11th Ordinary Session from 2–9 March 1992 in Tunis, at the invitation of the Tunisian government, and chaired by Dr. Ibrahim A. Badawi El Sheikh.

2. This session held just before the African Preparatory Conference on Human Rights organised by the United Nations and planned for November 1992 in Tunis, was preceded by the meeting of a workshop organised in the Tunisian capital from 29 February to 1 March 1992 by the International Commission of Jurists (ICJ) on NGO support for the Commission's work in cooperation with the African Commission.

3. At a time when Africa is proud to see one of its renowned sons, Dr. Boutros Ghali, at the head of the UN General Secretariat, at a time when the wind of democracy is blowing through the whole Continent and when Africa has just started on the process of dismantling the apartheid system in force in its southern part, the Commission has adopted a detailed programme of action and reaffirmed its determination to ensure the promotion and the protection of human and peoples' rights in Africa.

4. The following Commissioners took part in this session:

Dr. Ibrahim A. Badawi El Sheikh (Chairman);
Mr. Alioune B. Bèye;
Mr. Ali Mahmoud Buhedma;
Mr. Robert H. Kisanga;
Mr. Sourahata B. Semega Janneh (Vice-Chairman);
Mr. Molefeki D. Mokama;
Mr. Youssoupha Ndiaye;
Mr. Isaac Nguema;
Prof. U. O. Umozurike.

5. The Commission paid tribute to the last Commissioner C. L. C. Mubanga-Chipoya and observed a minute of silence.

6. The opening session took place in the presence of His Excellency Mr. Hamed Kaouri, Prime Minister, representing the President of the Republic, Zine El Abidine Ben Ali.

- Members of the Government and dignitaries of the host country;
- Ambassadors and Heads of Diplomatic Missions;

- Commission Members;
- Mr. Ahmed Haggag, the OAU's Assistant Secretary General;
- International and African NGO representatives;
- Representatives from the International Press and guests.

7. In his welcoming speech, Dr. Badawi El Sheikh, after praising Tunisia for her sustained policy on human rights, pointed at the importance of this meeting, whose agendas covered notably both the examining of Egypt's Togo's, Tanzania's and Nigeria's periodic reports and the studying of the right to freedom of association and the right of recourse. In his opening speech to the work of the 11th Session, Prime Minister Mr. Hamed Karoui stressed both the new era's commitment to human rights and to African aspirations and just causes and the need to set up a new international economic order, based on justice, equality of peoples and many-sided mutual help among African countries, finishing with a mention of how very much the Tunisian government had done to promote and protect human rights.

8. The Commission elected a new Vice-Chairman Mr. Sourahata B. Janneh in replacement of the late Commissioner C. L. C. Mubanga-Chipoya.

9. The Commission's work was particularly focused on the four main questions that follow:

(i) adopting a promotion programme;
(ii) examining the periodic reports;
(iii) examining complaints;
(iv) studying Article 10 of the Charter on the right to free association and the right of recourse.

10. Before starting its deliberations, the Commission recorded a certain number of Statements and also the conclusions reached by the workshop organised by the NGOs' Forum.

11. In their speeches, the representatives of the governmental and non-governmental organisations stressed their organisations' willingness to give support and aid to the functioning of the Commission for the Promotion and Protection of Human Rights in Africa. Such was the sense and significance of the speeches made in particular by:

- Mr. Falk, representing the United Nations Deputy Secretary-General for Human Rights;
- Miss Catherine Cisse, on behalf of the Commission of the European Communities;
- The representative of the Swedish government;
- Mr. Nasr S. N. Ramadan, representing the Tunisian government;
- Mr. Farouk Abu Eissa, Chairman of the Union of Arab Lawyers;
- Dr. Philip Amoah, representing the International Commission of Jurists;
- Mr. Christopher Hall, representing Amnesty International;
- Mr. Fayek, Secretary-General of the Arab Organisation for Human Rights;
- Mr. Zouhir Chelli, Tunisia's honorary delegate at United Nations High Commissariat for Refugees.

12. Presenting the report of the workshop organised by the International Commission of Lawyers, Mrs. Mona Abdallah Rishmawi first repeated the conclusions and recommendations made by the workshop, held from 5–7 October 1992 in Banjul on the organisation and functioning of the African Commission on Human and Peoples' Rights, before making recommendations on the contents of the right to freedom of association and of the right of recourse, provided for in Articles 10 and 7 of the African Charter on Human Rights. According to Mrs. Rishmawi, the workshop examined the provisions of the African Charter on Human and Peoples' Rights and particularly those of the above-mentioned articles concerning the right to freedom of association and the right of recourse, so that the content of these rights conform to other international legal tools.

13. Taking up the question of the programme of action and working methods, the Commission drew up a timetable of seminars and symposia which it intends to organise, either in cooperation with other international organisations or alone. In this way, the Commission reiterated its intention of organising:

(i) A seminar on integration and the implementing of the African Charter in African legal systems (Banjul 1992);
(ii) A seminar on refugees and displaced persons, jointly with the UNHCR;
(iii) A seminar on the role of women in development;
(iv) A seminar on popular participation and informal education (in cooperation with UNESCO and the Economic Commission for Africa);
(v) A seminar on post-apartheid South Africa (in cooperation with UNESCO).

As regard working methods, the Commission decided:

- to set up an Information and Documentation Centre within the Secretariat;
- to adopt an organigram for the Secretariat's departments, and the need for recruiting the corresponding staff;
- to publish a press bulletin concerning the activities of the Commission and concerning human rights in Africa;
- to continue with publishing the African Commission on Human and Peoples' Rights Review;
- to publish annual reports and other Commission's documents including periodic reports.

14. During the deliberations, the Commission had the task of examining the reports made by the Arab Republic of Egypt and the Republic of Tanzania. Examination of these reports aimed at examining the legislative or other measures taken by the States to give effect to the rights and freedoms recognised and guaranteed by the African Charter on Human and Peoples' Rights.

15. Nonetheless, the Commission hailed the usefulness and the appropriateness of the constructive dialogue which had developed between the Commission and the States concerned, and thanked the Governments of the Arab Republic of Egypt and of Tanzania for their reports and for their willingness to cooperate with the Commission.

16. It appealed to the States which had not yet submitted their reports to do so as quickly as possible.

17. On the subject of complaints the allegation that human rights were being violated in some African countries, the Commission recorded five new communications, and 22 communications are still pending as the session meets. The Commission, after taking the appropriate decision in each case, regretted the administrative delay which in many cases holds up the affairs of investigations procedure.

18. As regards promotion activities, besides those which appear in the programme of action adopted by the Commission, the Commission will submit to the Conference of OAU Heads of State and Government to be held in Dakar in June–July 1992 a certain number of draft resolutions particularly concerning the ratifying of the Charter, promotional activities and the States' reports. Moreover, the Commission passed two resolutions, one on the right to freedom of association and one on the right of recourse. As far as right of recourse is concerned, the Commission is appealing to the States to give effect to the exercise of this right, which includes:

(i) the right to refer to the competent national courts any acts that violate the basic rights which are recognised and guaranteed to one by the conventions, laws, regulations and customs in force;
(ii) the right to be presumed innocent until one's guilt is established by a competent court;
(iii) the right to be defended, including that of being helped by counsel of one's choice;
(iv) the right of being tried within a reasonable period of time by an impartial court.

19. During this session, the Commission granted Observer Status to the following non-governmental organisations:

(i) Human Rights Institute at the Catholic University of Lyon;
(ii) Guinea-Bissau Human Rights League;
(iii) International Society for Human Rights – the Gambia Group;
(iv) National Union of the Moroccan Press;
(v) Lawyers for Human Rights;
(vi) Observatoire Panafricain de la Démocratie (OPAD);
(vii) International Centre against Censorship;
(viii) National Human Rights Committee;
(ix) Libyan Arab Human Rights Commission;
(x) Benin Human Rights Commission;
(xi) African Lawyers' Federation;
(xii) International Centre for Human Rights and Democratic Development.

20. It also granted Observer Status to the International Committee of the Red Cross.

21. Finally before ending the examination of its agenda, the Commission adopted its report of the 5th annual report, which will be submitted to the next session of the Conference of OAU Heads of State and Government.

22. The Commission noted with satisfaction the request made by the Malian government to the Commission to send a mission to observe the Presidential Elections to be held on 12 April and 26 April 1992.

23. The Commission expressed its sincere thanks to his Excellency President Zine El Abidine Ben Ali, President of the Republic of Tunisia, and to the Tunisian Government and People, for their warm welcome and hospitality. The Commission stated that the Tunisian Government had supported the work of the Commission. In the Commission's view the support of the Government of Tunisia made the former's work successful.

24. The next session is scheduled to be held from 12 to 21 October 1992.

Done in Tunis, 9 March 1992

Sixth Annual Activity Report of the African Commission on Human and Peoples' Rights 1992–1993

Adopted on 7 April 1993
Covering the 12th and 13th Ordinary Sessions in Banjul (12–21 October 1992 and 29 March to 7 April 1993)

I. ORGANIZATION OF WORK

A. Period Covered by the Report

1. The Fifth Report was adopted by the Twenty-fifth Session of the Heads of State and Government of the OAU by its resolution AHG/207 (XXXVIII). The present Report, which is the Sixth, covers the Twelfth and Thirteenth Ordinary Sessions held in Banjul, The Gambia, from 12–21 October 1992 and from 29 March to 7 April 1993 respectively.

B. Status of Ratification

2. At the 13th Session of the Commission, 48 African States had ratified the African Charter on Human and Peoples' Rights. The list of those States which have ratified the Charter or which have adhered thereto is contained in Annex I.

C. Sessions and Agenda

3. The Commission has held two ordinary sessions since the adoption of the Fifth Activity Report:

- the Twelfth Ordinary Session was held in Banjul, The Gambia, from 12–21 October 1992;
- the Thirteenth Ordinary Session was held in Banjul, The Gambia, from 29 March to 7 April 1993.

The Agenda of each of these sessions is contained in Annexes II and III.

D. Composition and Participation

4. The composition of the African Charter on Human and Peoples' Rights has changed since the last report. Mr. Mohammed Hatem Ben Salem was elected by the

28th Session of the Assembly of the Heads of State and Government, on 1 July 1992, following the vacancy created by the death of the Commissioner C. L. C. Mubanga-Chipoya. The list of Members of the Commission is contained in Annex IV.

5. The attendance at sessions has been as follows:

The following Commissioners attended the Twelfth Session:

(1) Dr. Ibrahim A. Badawei El-Sheikh,
(2) Mr. Sourahata B. S. Janneh,
(3) Mr. Alioune B. Beye,
(4) Mr. Ali Mahmud Buhedma,
(5) Justice Robert H. Kisanga,
(6) Justice Youssoupha Ndiaye,
(7) Mr. Isaac Nguema,
(8) Dr. Mohammed H. Ben Salem,
(9) Professor U. O. Umozurike.

(Justice Moleleki D. Mokama was absent with apology, Mr. Alexis Gabou was absent.)

The following Commissioners attended the Thirteenth Session:

(1) Dr. Ibrahim A. Badawei El-Sheikh,
(2) Mr. Sourahata B. S. Janneh,
(3) Mr. Alioune B. Beye,
(4) Mr. Ali Mahmud Buhedma,
(5) Mr. Alexis Gabou,
(6) Justice Robert H. Kisanga,
(7) Justice Moleleki D. Mokama,
(8) Dr. Mohammed H. Ben Salem,
(9) Mr. Isaac Nguema,
(10) Professor U. O. Umozurike.

(Justice Youssoupha Ndiaye was absent with apology.)

E. Chairman, Vice-Chairman of the Commission

6. Dr. Ibrahim A. Badawi El-Sheikh and Mr. Sourahata B. S. Janneh are respectively Chairman and Vice-Chairman of the Commission.

F. Adoption of the Sixth Annual Report

7. On 7 April 1993, the Commission considered and adopted its Sixth Annual Report.

II. ACTIVITIES OF THE COMMISSION

A. Examination of Periodic Reports

8. At its Twelfth and Thirteenth Ordinary Sessions, the Commission considered the initial reports submitted by The Gambia, Zimbabwe, Togo and Nigeria and the initial and second reports from Senegal. The Commission expressed its appreciation to the said Governments for submitting their reports and sending representatives to have a dialogue with the Commission. In the Commission's view, this reflected the will of the Governments to cooperate with the Commission in the implementation of the Charter.

9. The Commissioners made comments and asked a number of questions on the reports submitted, and the representatives of the Governments concerned responded verbally at the session. They further indicated that they would later provide the Commission with additional information.

10. It is to be noted that according to Article 62 each State shall undertake to submit every two years, from the date the Charter comes into force, a report on legislative or other measures taken with a view to giving effect to the rights and freedoms recognized and guaranteed by the Charter. In this regard as at the start of the Thirteenth Ordinary Session of the Commission only 14 States had submitted periodic reports, namely: Libya, Rwanda, Tunisia (9. session), Egypt, Tanzania (11. session), The Gambia, Senegal, Zimbabwe (12. session), Togo, Nigeria (13. session), Benin, Ghana, Cape Verde, Mozambique (remain to be examined). This means that 37 states still have to submit their reports (see Annex V).

11. The Assembly of Heads of State and Government of the OAU, adopted the Resolution AHG/207 (XXVIII), in which the Assembly, among other things, urged the States party to the African Charter on Human and Peoples' Rights which have not yet submitted their initial report to submit them as soon as possible. It requested that the States should report not only on legislative matters, but also on other measures taken to give effect to each of the rights and freedoms recognized and guaranteed by the African Charter and on the problems encountered in giving effect to these rights and freedoms. The Assembly also encouraged State parties which encounter difficulties in preparing and submitting their periodic reports to seek help as soon as possible from the African Commission which will arrange for assistance in this task through its own or other resources.

B. Promotional Activities

(i) Activities of the Commissioners

12. The Chairman of the Commission met on 20 October 1992, with His Excellency President Abdou Diouf, President of the Republic of Senegal and the Chairman of the OAU to brief His Excellency the President on the activities of the

Commission. The Chairman met also, on several occasions, with His Excellency Dr. Salim A. Salim, Secretary General of the OAU and discussed with His Excellency issues relevant to the Commission.

13. The Chairman and commissioners undertook promotional activities in a number of African States. Such activities were undertaken with the co-operation of the competent authorities of the States visited by the Commissioners. The object of the activities was to publicize the African Charter and explain the work of the Commission. (See Annex VI, which contains the list of distribution of countries for promotional work.)

14. In addition some commissioners gave lectures, and attended seminars, and initiated contacts in Africa and elsewhere.

(ii) Programme of Activities

15. It is to be recalled that at its Tenth and Eleventh sessions, the Commission adopted a programme of activities which has a number of components including the establishment of a documentation and information centre, organizing seminars and workshops and training courses (see Annex VII). The following paragraphs point out to seminar activities during the period covered by this report.

(a) The Commission organized, in collaboration with the Raoul Wallenberg Institute of Sweden, a seminar on the National Implementation of the African Charter on Human and Peoples' Rights in the Internal Legal Systems in Africa, held in Banjul, 26–30 October 1992. (See Annex VIII, containing the conclusions and recommendations of the seminar.)

(b) The Commission organized in co-operation with the Union of African Journalists, the Tunisian Association of Journalists and others, a seminar on the role of the African media in the promotion and the protection of Human Rights, held in Tunis, 31 October to 1 November 1992. (See Annex IX which contains the report of the seminar.)

(c) The Commission will be convening in Harare, Zimbabwe from 12–16 July 1993, a seminar on African Refugees and internal displaced persons.

(d) At its 13th session the Commission decided to organize in collaboration with the Arab Lawyers Union and some other Non Governmental Organizations a seminar on the right to a fair trial with special reference to legal assistance.

(e) The Commission also decided to organize in cooperation with the Raoul Wallenberg Institute of Sweden two seminars on the implementation of the African Charter with a special reference to the reporting procedure.

(f) Furthermore the Commission decided to initiate contacts for the preparation and organization of a seminar on the role of the African media in the promotion and protection of Human Rights and a seminar on the role of women under the African Charter.

(iii) Right to Development

16. The Commission examined at its 12th and 13th Sessions the right to development in the light of the provisions of the African Charter.

(iv) Regional and International Co-operation

17. The Commission has participated in a number of regional and international Human Rights related activities, notably:

(a) the African preparatory conference in Tunis from 2–6 November 1992 on the World Conference on Human Rights,
(b) the world congress concerning education on Human Rights and democracy from 8–12 March 1993, organized by UNESCO in Montréal, Canada.
(c) Furthermore the Commission will be participating in the World Conference on Human Rights which will be convened in Vienna, June 1993. In this regard the Commission has communicated to the Secretariat of the Conference the conclusions and recommendations of its seminar on the National Implementation of the African Charter in the Internal legal systems in Africa, held in Banjul. In addition the Commission entrusted its Chairman to submit a report to the Conference on the major activities of the Commission as a contribution to the World Conference.

(v) Publications

18. The Commission published a booklet in French and English on the African Commission. This booklet contains a brief summary of the organization and functions of the Commission as well as of its procedure concerning communications. Hopefully this publication will come out soon also in Arabic.

C. Administrative and Financial Problems.

19. The Commission, at its 13th Session, decided to draw the kind attention of the Assembly of the Heads of State and Government to the very alarming situation of the Commission in terms of logistics as follows:

20. Since the entry into force of the African Charter on Human and Peoples' Rights and the establishment of the Commission, the latter has suffered from a chronic lack of staff, resources and services necessary for the effective discharge of its functions. No funds are allocated in the Commission's budget for promotional activities.

21. The considerable delay registered in the processing and management of communications could be attributed to the fact that the Commission deals mainly with legal matters and that it was only recently that it was provided with the service of a legal officer.

22. The Secretariat has only a skeleton staff and is not endowed with the basic facilities for the execution of certain basic functions such as producing documents on time.

23. In spite of serious administrative and financial shortcomings and the repeated requests of the Commission, no substantial measure has been taken to resolve this situation. Furthermore drastic cuts are being made on the operational budget with a total reduction of about 25% for the year 1993/94 alone.

24 In the light of all these alarming developments and conscious of the dire financial situation of the OAU and the efforts of the Secretary General of the OAU to support the Commission, the Commission expresses the hope that the Assembly of Heads of State and Government will ensure the necessary support for the execution of the noble assignment it has entrusted the Commission with and under its direct authority.

25. Meanwhile the Commission notes with gratitude the voluntary contributions which it had received from the United Nations Centre for Human Rights, the European Community, the Swedish, Danish, and Austrian Governments.

D. Observers

26. In accordance with the provisions of Rules 76 and 77 of its Rules of Procedure, the Commission granted observer status to a certain number of NGOs. The organizations which enjoy observer status are indicated in Annex X.

27. At its 12th and 13th Sessions, the Commission listened in public meetings to a number of NGOs observers under relevant agenda items.

E. Protective Activities

28. At its 12th and 13th Sessions the Commission received 14 communications under Article 55 of the African Charter, that is communications from sources other than States. With regard to these communications the Commission took measures in accordance with the provisions of the African Charter and the Commission's Rules of Procedure. The Commission also followed up on 41 old communications. The communications were examined in closed meetings.

29. In accordance with Article 59 of the African Charter, the details of the above mentioned communications are contained in a confidential annex.

III. CONCLUSIONS AND RECOMMENDATIONS

A. Conclusions

30. The African Commission, basing itself on the political will of Africa as manifested basically in the African Charter on Human and Peoples' Rights, has been pursuing its mission of promoting and ensuring Human and Peoples' Rights in the spirit of understanding, co-operation and dialogue with States, Inter-Governmental and Non-Governmental organizations.

31. The Commission has been heartened by the Declaration adopted on 11 July 1990 by the Assembly of Heads of State and Government of the Organization of African Unity on the political and socio-economic situation in Africa and the fundamental changes taking place in the world which, among other things, linked the process of socio-economic transformation and integration with the need to promote popular participation and political environment which guarantees human rights and observance of the rule of law.

32. The African Commission, in spite of the encountered financial and administrative problems, will continue to strive to realize its mission in accordance with the provisions of the African Charter and for the sake of the cause of human and peoples' rights in Africa which is the cause of justice, peace, stability and development.

B. Recommendation

33. The Commission recommends for consideration and adoption by the Assembly of Heads of State and Government the following draft resolution:

RESOLUTION ON THE AFRICAN COMMISSION ON HUMAN AND PEOPLES' RIGHTS

The Assembly of Heads of State and Government of the Organization of African Unity, meeting in its Twenty-ninth Ordinary Session in Cairo, Egypt, from 28–30 June 1993,

Considering the Sixth Annual Activity Report of the African Commission on Human and Peoples' Rights, submitted by the Chairman Dr. Ibrahim A. Badawi El Sheikh in conformity with Article 54 of the African Charter on Human and Peoples' Rights,

Recalling that the Charter of the Organization of African Unity declares that freedom, equality, justice and dignity are essential objectives for the achievement of the legitimate aspirations by the African peoples,

Recalling also the entry into force of the African Charter on Human and peoples' Rights on 21 October 1986 and the Declaration on the Political and Socio-Economic Situation in Africa and the On-going Changes in the World, adopted by the Twenty-sixth Ordinary Session of the Assembly of Heads of State and Government in July 1990,

Convinced of the need to provide the African Commission on Human and Peoples' Rights in Africa with all possible human and material resources it needs to carry out its work,

Considering that pursuant to Article 1 of the African Charter, State Parties to it shall recognize the rights, duties and freedoms enshrined in this Charter and shall undertake to adopt legislative or other measures to give effect to them,

Noting with satisfaction that the African Charter is the first treaty that sanctions the right to development as a human right.

A. The Activities of the Commission

1. UNDERLINES THE IMPORTANCE of ensuring respect for human and peoples' rights with the view of enhancing peace, stability and development in Africa;
2. REAFFIRMS that the right to development is an alienable human right by virtue of which every human person is entitled to participate in, contribute to and enjoy the economic, social, cultural and political development of the society;
3. STRONGLY SUPPORTS AND ENCOURAGES the activities of the African Commission on Human and Peoples' Rights to promote and protect human and peoples' rights in Africa, particularly in its efforts aimed to encourage States Parties to ensure strict implementation of their obligations under the African Charter on Human and Peoples' Rights to promote and protect the rights recognized and guaranteed in the African Charter;
4. RECOMMENDS that States Parties to the African Charter designate high ranking officials to act as focal points in the relation between the Commission and the States as such focal points would facilitate the follow-up on the Commission's recommendations and contact between states and the Commission;
5. REQUESTS the Secretary General of the Organization of African Unity to consider possible ways and means to respond as a matter of urgency, to the requirements of the African Commission to enable it to fulfil its mission.

B. Overdue Periodic Reports

1. EXPRESSES ITS DEEP APPRECIATION to the States Parties which have submitted their initial and periodic report: Benin, Cape Verde, The Gambia, Ghana, Egypt, Libyan Arab Jamahiriya, Mozambique, Nigeria, Rwanda, Senegal, Tanzania, Togo, Tunisia and Zimbabwe;
2. URGES the States Parties to the African Charter on Human and Peoples' Rights which have not yet submitted their reports to submit them as soon as possible;
3. REQUESTS that the States should report not only on legislative measures, but also on other measures taken to give effect to each of the rights and freedoms recognized and guaranteed by the African Charter on Human and Peoples' Rights and on the problems encountered in giving effect to these rights and freedoms;
4. RECOMMENDS that the States in their periodic reports give information on the implementation of the right to development;
5. ENCOURAGES States Parties which encounter difficulties in preparing and submitting their periodic reports to seek help as soon as possible from the African Commission on Human and Peoples' Rights which will arrange for assistance in this task through its own or other resources.

C. Promotional Activities

1. URGES all States Parties to the African Charter on Human and Peoples' Rights to reflect the rights and freedoms recognized and guaranteed by the African Charter in their law and practice, and to ensure availability of appropriate recourse procedure in case of abuse of the said rights;

2. REQUESTS that all States Parties should implement Article 26 of the African Charter on Human and Peoples' Rights by establishing national institutions with responsibility for promoting and protecting human and peoples' rights where they do not exist and strengthening all such institutions;

3. FURTHER REQUESTS that all States should ensure among other things:

(a) that human rights is included in the curriculum at all levels of public and private education and in the training of all law enforcement officials; and
(b) that education for human rights and democracy should involve every organ of the society as well as the media.

D. Publication of the Sixth Annual Activity Report

TAKES NOTE WITH APPRECIATION of the Sixth Annual Report on the Activities of the African Commission on Human and Peoples' Rights and authorizes its publication.

ANNEX I

African Charter on Human and Peoples' Rights List of Countries which have Signed, Ratified or Adhered to the Charter

No.	Country	Date of Signature	Date of Ratification/ Adhesion	Date Deposited
1.	Algeria	10/04/86	01/03/87	20/03/87
2.	Angola		02/03/90	09/10/90
3.	Benin		20/01/86	25/02/86
4.	Botswana		17/07/86	22/07/86
5.	Burundi		28/07/80	30/08/89
6.	Burkina Faso	05/03/84	06/07/84	21/09/84
7.	Cameroon	23/07/87	20/06/89	18/09/89
8.	Cape Verde	31/03/86	02/06/87	06/08/87
9.	Central African Republic		26/04/86	27/07/86
10.	Chad	29/05/86	09/10/86	11/11/86
11.	Comoros		01/06/86	18/07/86

No.	Country	Date of Signature	Date of Ratification/ Adhesion	Date Deposited
12.	Congo	27/11/81	09/12/82	17/01/83
13.	Côte d'Ivoire		06/01/92	31/03/92
14.	Djibouti		11/11/91	20/12/91
15.	Egypt	16/11/81	20/03/84	03/04/84
16.	Equatorial Guinea	18/08/86	07/04/86	18/08/86
17.	Ethiopia			
18.	Gabon	26/02/82	20/02/86	26/06/86
19.	Gambia	11/02/83	08/06/83	13/03/83
20.	Ghana		24/01/89	01/03/89
21.	Guinée	09/12/81	16/02/82	13/05/82
22.	Guinée-Bissau		04/12/85	06/03/86
23.	Kenya		23/01/92	10/02/92
24.	Lesotho	07/03/84	10/02/92	27/02/92
25.	Liberia	31/01/83	04/08/82	29/12/82
26.	Libya	30/05/85	19/07/86	26/03/87
27.	Madagascar		09/03/92	19/03/92
28.	Malawi	23/02/90	17/11/89	23/02/90
29.	Mali	13/11/81	21/12/81	22/01/82
30.	Mauritanie	25/02/82	14/06/86	26/06/86
31.	Mauritius	27/02/92	19/06/92	07/07/92
32.	Mozambique		22/02/89	07/03/90
33.	Namibia		30/07/92	16/09/92
34.	Niger	09/07/86	15/07/86	21/07/86
35.	Nigeria	31/08/82	22/06/83	27/07/83
36.	République Rwandaise	11/11/81	15/07/83	22/07/83
37.	Sahrawi Arab Dem. Rep.	10/04/86	02/05/86	23/05/86
38.	Sao Tome & Principe		23/05/86	28/07/86
39.	Senegal	23/09/81	13/08/82	25/10/82
40.	Seychelles		13/04/92	30/04/92
41.	Sierra Leone	27/08/81	21/09/83	27/01/84
42.	Somalia	26/02/82	31/07/85	20/03/86
43.	Sudan	03/09/82	18/02/86	11/03/86
44.	Swaziland			
45.	Togo	20/02/82	05/11/82	22/11/82
46.	Tunisia		16/03/83	22/04/83
47.	Uganda	18/08/86	10/05/86	27/05/86
48.	Tanzania	31/05/82	18/02/84	09/03/84
49.	Zaire	23/07/87	20/07/87	28/07/87
50.	Zambia	17/01/83	19/01/84	02/02/84
51.	Zimbabwe	20/02/86	30/05/86	12/06/86

ADOPTED: by the 18th Session of the Assembly of Heads of State and Government, June 1981

REQUIRES: ratification or adherence of a simple majority of Member States to come into force

ENTERED INTO FORCE: 21st day of October 1986

REGISTERED: with the United Nations on 10 September 1991, No. 26363

ANNEX II

Agenda of the Twelfth Ordinary Session

1. Opening Ceremony
2. Oath of Office by the New Commissioner
3. Adoption of Agenda
4. Organisation of Work:
    - (a) Appointment of Rapporteur
    - (b) Working Hours
    - (c) Organization of Work
5. Observers
    - (a) Consideration of Applications for Observer Status
    - (b) Relationship with Observers
6. Consideration of Periodic Reports
7. Protective Activities
8. Promotional Activities
9. Administrative and Financial Matters
    - (a) Commission's Annual Activity Report to the OAU Summit
    - (b) Report of the Secretary to the Commission
10. Work Methods of the Commission Including the Rules of Procedure
11. Report on the Activities of the OAU Relevant to the Commission
12. Examination of the Right to Development
13. Date, Venue and Agenda of the 13th Session
14. Any Other Business
15. Adoption of the Report of the 12th Session
16. Final Communique and Closing Ceremony

ANNEX III

Agenda of the Thirteenth Ordinary Session

1. Opening Ceremony
2. Adoption of Agenda
3. Organisation of Work:
    - (a) Appointment of Rapporteur
    - (b) Working Hours
    - (c) Organization of Work

4. Observers
   (a) Consideration of Application for Observer Status
   (b) Relationship with Non-Governmental Organizations
5. Consideration of Periodic Reports
6. Promotional Activities
7. Administrative and Financial Matters
   (a) Report of the Chairman
   (b) Report of the Secretary to the Commission
   (c) Implementation of the Recommendations of the Previous Sessions
   (d) Budget Proposals 1994–1995
8. Protective Activities
9. Work Methods of the Commission:
   Consideration of Amendments to the Rules of Procedure Postponed to the Next Session
10. Examination of the Right to Development
11. Report on the Activities of the OAU Relevant to the Commission
12. World Conference on Human Rights
13. Date, Venue and Draft Agenda of the 14th Session
14. Any Other Business
15. Adoption of the Report of the 12th Session
16. Adoption of the Report of the 13th Session
17. Adoption of the 6th Annual Activity Report of the Commission
18. Final Communique and Closing Ceremony

ANNEX IV

List of Addresses of Commissioners of the African Commission on Human and Peoples' Rights

1. Dr. Ibrahim Ali BADAWI EL SHEIKH — Chairman
   11 Khalil Ben Kalawoon Street
   El-Nozham, Heliopolis
   CAIRO/EGYPT
   Tel Res: (202) 2425387
   Fax: (202) 725571

2. Mr. Sourahata Baboucar Semega JANNEH — Vice-Chairman
   15 Hagan Street
   PO Box 212
   BANJUL/THE GAMBIA
   Tel Office: (220) 28174
   Tel Res: (220) 95117
   Telex: 2216 GV (NOVOTEL)

3. Mr. Atsu-Koffi AMEGA — Member
BP 1262
LOME/TOGO
Tel: (228) 213396
Telex: 5239
Fax: (228) 213974

4. Mr. Alioune Blondin BEYE — Member
BP 487 Cedex 1
ABIDJAN/CÔTE D'IVOIRE
Tel Office: (225) 222833
Tel Res: (225) 443286
Telex: (983) 22203/23263/23717
Fax: (225) 204949/221317

5. Mr. Emmanuel Victor O. DANKWA — Member
Faculty of Law/University of Ghana
PO Box 70
LEGON/GHANA
FAX: (23321) 222621

6. Mr. Robert Habesh KISANGA — Member
Court of Appeal
PO Box 9004
DAR-ES-SALAAM/TANZANIA
Tel Office: (25551) 27843/26011
Telex: (989) 41848 RAC TZ

7. Mrs Vera DUARTE MARTINS — Member
CP 117
PRAIA/CAP VERT
Tel Res: (238) 612137
Tel Office: (238) 615809
Fax: (238) 614519 MJ (PT)

8. Mr. Youssoupha NDIAYE — Member
Premier Président de la Cour de Cassation
Ancien Musée Dynamique
DAKAR/SENEGAL
Tel Office: (01) 223738/221816
Tel Res: 217257
Telex: (906) 21776 MINAFET SG

9. Mr. Isaac NGUEMA — Member
BP 962
LIBREVILLE/GABON
Tel Office: (241) 732420
Tel Res: (241) 732027
Telex: 5255 GO
Fax: (241) 760993

10. Mr. Mohammed H. Ben SALEM — Member
1 Rue de Naplouse
LAMANOUBA/TUNISIE
Tel Office: (2611) 520270
Tel Res: (2611) 750911
Fax (Tunis): (2166) 750911
Fax (Paris): (331) 43806771

11. Prof. U. Oji UMOZURIKE — Member
Faculty of Law
University of Calabar
CALABAR/NIGERIA
Tel Office: (234) 87224748/49 Ext. 9
Tel Res: (234) 87220543
Telex: 65103 UNICAL, NG
Fax: (234) 87220111/87220543
or
c/o Liaison Officer
University of Calabar
LAGOS/NIGERIA
Tel: (2341) 835615

Secretary to the Commission
Mr. Ngabishema MUTSINZI
PO Box 673
BANJUL/THE GAMBIA
Tel: (220) 392962
Telex: (996) 2346 OAU BJL GV
Fax: (220) 390764

ANNEX V

List of Countries which have Submitted their Periodic Report

1. Benin
2. Cape Verde

3. Egypt
4. The Gambia
5. Ghana
6. Libya
7. Mozambique
8. Nigeria
9. Rwanda
10. Senegal
11. Tanzania
12. Togo
13. Tunisia
14. Zimbabwe

ANNEX VI

Distribution of Countries by Members of the Commission for Promotional Work as at 4 April 1993

1. **Dr. Ibrahim A. Badawi El-Sheikh**
   Comores
   Seychelles
   Ile Maurice
   Madagascar
   Egypt

2. **Mr Alioune Blondin Bèye**
   Benin
   Equatorial Guinea
   Sao-Tome & Principe
   Togo

3. **Mr. Ali Mahmoud Buhedma**
   Algerie
   Libye
   Mauritanie
   Djibouti
   Republique Arabe Sahraouie Democratique

4. **Mr. Sourahata B. Semega-Janneh**
   Gambia
   Liberia
   Sierra Leone

5. **Mr. Robert H. Kisanga**
   Ethiopia
   Kenya
   Somalia
   Uganda
   Tanzania
   Mozambique
   Zambia

6. **Mr. Moleleki D. Mokama**
   Botswana
   Lesotho
   Malawi
   Swaziland
   Zimbabwe
   Namibia
   Angola

7. **Mr. Youssoupha Ndiaye**
   Cap Vert
   Niger
   Senegal
   Republique de Guinée
   Guinea-Bissau

8. **Mr. Isaac Nguema**
   Zaïre
   Burkina Faso
   Congo
   Rwanda

9. **Prof. U. O. Umozurike**
   Nigeria
   Ghana
   Cameroon

10. **Mr Alexis Gabou**
    Central African Republic
    Burundi
    Tchad
    Gabon

11. **Mr. M. Ben Salem**
    Côte d'Ivoire
    Sudan
    Mali
    Tunisia

ANNEX VII

African Commission on Human and Peoples' Rights
Programme of Activities 1992–1996

INTRODUCTION

Mandate of the Commission

1. The African Commission on Human and Peoples' Rights has a permanent mission defined in Article 45 of the African Charter on Human and Peoples' Rights, as follows:

A. To promote Human and Peoples' Rights and in particular:

(1) To collect documents, undertake studies and research on African problems in the field of human and peoples' rights, organize seminars, symposia and conferences, disseminate information, encourage national and local institutions concerned with human and peoples' rights, and should the case arise, give its view or make recommendations to Governments.
(2) To formulate and lay down, principles and rules aimed at solving legal problems relating to human and peoples' rights and fundamental freedoms upon which African Governments may base their legislation.
(3) Co-operate with other international institutions concerned with the promotion and protection of human and peoples' rights.

B. Ensure the protection of human and peoples' rights under conditions laid down by the present Charter.

C. Interpret all the provisions of the present Charter at the request of a State Party, an institution of the OAU or an African Organization recognized by the OAU.

D. Perform any other tasks which may be entrusted to it by the Assembly of Heads of State and Government.

Preliminary Programme of Action

2. At its Second Session (Dakar, Senegal, 8–13 February 1988), the Commission adopted a preliminary Programme of Action (see Annex I of the Programme of Activities for the years 1992–1996).

Adoption of Programme of Activities (1992–1996)

3. At its Sixth Session (Banjul, The Gambia, 23 October to 3 November 1989), and on the proposal of Commissioner Dr. Ibrahim Badawi, the Commission decided to elaborate a concrete Programme of Activities.

Dr. Badawi was entrusted to prepare Terms of Reference for Consultants to submit a Report on the subject with the view to facilitating the task of the Commission in elaborating and adopting the said Programme.

4. At its Seventh Session (Banjul, The Gambia, 18–28 April 1990), the Commission adopted the Terms of Reference referred to above (see Annex II of the Programme of Activities). It also entrusted Mr. Adama Dieng and Wolfgang Benedek to prepare as Consultants, the Report mentioned in paragraph 3 on the basis of the said Terms of Reference.

5. The Consultants submitted their final Report to the Tenth Ordinary Session (Banjul, 8–17 October 1991).

6. The Commission, taking into consideration the said Report, and on the basis of elaborate discussions, adopted at its 9th meeting on 6 March 1992, at its Eleventh Session (Tunis, 2–9 March 1992) its Programme of Activities for the years 1992–1996.

The Components of the Programme of Activities

7. In adopting its Programme of Activities the Commission underlined the following:

A. The execution of the said programme of activities is of capital importance for fulfilling the Commission's tasks.

B. The financing of the programme is the primary responsibility of the OAU. However, given the present financial crisis of the OAU, it is hoped that international co-operation would be forthcoming in support of this programme.

8. The programme as adopted by the Commission contains the following main components:

A. Establishment of Information and Documentation Centre.

B. Convening Seminars, Workshops and Training Courses.

C. Promotional Activities by Commissioners.

D. Translation and Distribution of Public documents of the Commission including States' Reports and relevant Summary records.

E. Publication of Annual Reports of the Commission, the Revue, Bulletin, Brochure and other publications.

F. Convening inter-sessional working groups.

G. Recruiting Personnel urgently needed starting with one Jurist, one Documentalist, one Administrative officer, and one Translator.

Major Steps in Implementing the Programme

Establishment of Information and Documentation Centre

9. Commissioners Ndiaye and Janneh were entrusted to assist the Secretary of the Commission in setting out the qualifications and the conditions of service of the personnel to be recruited for the Centre. The Secretary would then, as a matter of urgency, proceed to recruit one Jurist, one Documentalist, one Administrative officer and one Translator.

10. Commissioners Ndiaye and Janneh were also requested to monitor the process of establishing the Centre and to advise the Secretary as relevant to speed up the establishment of the Centre.

Decisions to Convene Seminars

11. At its 10th and 11th Sessions, the Commission decided to convene the following Seminars:

A. How the African Charter on Human and Peoples' Rights has been received, in the Legal Systems of States Party to the African Charter;

B. African Refugees and internally displaced persons;

C. Popular Participation and non-formal education;

D. The role of women under the African Charter, in relation to specific socio-economic problems;

E. The Right to Fair Trial and Legal Assistance;

F. Post-Apartheid South Africa;

G. The Role of the African Media in the Promotion and Protection of Human Rights.

Internal Co-operation

12. While adopting its Programme of Activities, the Commission noted with gratitude that several international and regional organizations as well as Governments were willing to support in principle its programme.

Conclusion

13. Since its inception in 1987, the Commission has tried to effect a number of activities to fulfil its mandate despite a lack of resources. The adoption of the

programme of activities (1992–1996) would help, on one hand, the Commission to plan and execute its activities and, on the other hand, donors to appreciate and support these activities.

14. The Programme of Activities would be executed in a flexible manner so as to adjust to the needs and priorities of Africans in the field of Human Rights.

I. Information and Documentation Centre (IDOC)

The Information and Documentation Centre (IDOC) will provide the necessary infrastructure for the African Commission to pursue its activities in the field of promotion of human and peoples' rights in Africa. The IDOC will be an integral part of the Secretariat, but will have the autonomy necessary to carry out the following tasks:

A. Documentation

1. Documentation of the African Commission

The documents of the African Commission and all other pertinent OAU documents will be catalogued and made available in sufficient number to meet the needs of the African Commission, observers and the public. To facilitate retrieval of these documents, they will be catalogued, classified and indexed on a computer database.

2. Documents Essential to the Work of the Commission

The IDOC will collect basic documents essential to the work of the Commission: on human rights law, international law, African constitutions, and relevant African legislation and jurisprudence; and major African and international journals dealing with human rights. The IDOC will also be responsible for the acquisition of relevant documents and publications of intergovernmental and non-governmental organizations.

3. Academic and Research Literature

The IDOC will collect academic and research literature, while bearing in mind the competent and complimentary activities of institutions such as the African Centre for Democracy and Human Rights Studies.

B. Information Activities of the African Commission

The IDOC will be responsible for disseminating information for the African Commission and in particular:

(1) The African Charter, in various African languages;
(2) Public documents of the African Commission;
(3) Publications of the African Commission as noted in C below.

C. Publications of the African Commission

The IDOC will be responsible for the publications of the African Commission, including:

(1) The Annual Report of the Commission;
(2) The **Bulletin** of the Commission, at least twice a year;
(3) The **Review** of the African Commission on Human and Peoples' Rights, twice a year;
(4) The Summary records of the Commission;
(5) Reports of seminars, workshops, and other activities of the Commission;
(6) Reference works on the African Charter and the Work of the Commission;
(7) Research studies of, or undertaken on behalf of, the African Commission; and
(8) Educational materials produced by, or on behalf of, the African Commission.

D. Translation and Distribution of Documents

The IDOC will be responsible for the translation and distribution of documents for the African Commission including the translation and distribution of:

(1) The Annual Report of the Commission;
(2) Reports of States parties to the African Charter;
(3) Summary records of sessions of the African Commission, specially the summary records relating to the public examination of states' reports.

E. Research Programme of the Commission

The IDOC will undertake research for the African Commission on issues relating to the African Charter, especially on the substantive content of the rights and duties in the Charter, and on human rights in Africa and outside the continent, such as comparative studies of the rules and practices of other human rights instruments and bodies to elucidate the possible impact of the "applicable principles" in Articles 60 and 61 of the Charter; customary law and human rights in Africa; ongoing human rights research in Africa and on Africa; the role and problems of African human rights NGOs; and African cultures and human and peoples' rights as well as other topics related to the priorities and needs of human rights in Africa.

F. The Structure of IDOC

The IDOC will be structured and equipped in such a way as to make possible the efficient performance of the above-mentioned tasks, and any other tasks that might be entrusted to it by the Commission. This (Budget and Structure) would be basically as follows:

(1) **Staff**
- Information Officer
- Documentalist
- Legal Officer
- Administrative Officer
- Translator
- Typist
- Intern

(2) **Equipment**
- Details are being worked out

(3) **Acquisition of Documents**	
– Initial purchase	$50,000
– Annual supplement	$30,000
(4) **Publications** (Printing)	
– African Charter	$10,000
– Bulletin 2/YR	$7,000
– Review 2/YR	$19,000
– Annual Reports	$6,000
– Special Reports	$6,000
(5) **Translation**	$30,000
(6) **Research**	$50,000
(7) **Mailing**	
– Bulletin: 1,500 copies	$3,000
– Review: 2,000 copies	$4,000
(8) **Xeroxing, Supplies, etc.**	$5,000

II. Human Rights Conferences and Workshops

A. Human Rights Education

The African Commission will assist in the development of:

(1) Curricula in human rights education for primary and secondary education;
(2) Courses for adult education;
(3) Courses for non-formal education; and
(4) Training courses for Government officials working in different fields such as ministries of Justice, Interior, Defence, Education, Information and Social Affairs, persons with direct responsibility for ensuring human rights protection, such as police, prison wardens, or other officers, different professional groups, such as judges, lawyers and journalists, and human rights activists (see C below).

B. Promotional Workshops and Seminars

The Commission will organize a series of workshops and seminars on topics of importance to the protection and promotion of human rights in Africa. Some, identified as priorities for the African Commission itself, will be organized by the Commission, with the Commission accepting the sole or prime responsibility for the meetings. Other workshops and seminars will be organized in collaboration with African or other human rights organizations.

The following list is intended to be illustrative of the topics which the Commission considers to be high priority subjects, recognizing, however, that topics may be redefined in the light of new developments or changing circumstances.

C. Topics Already Agreed Upon by the Commission

(a) How the African Charter has been received in the Internal Legal Systems of States Parties;
(b) African Refugees and Internally displaced persons;
(c) Popular Participation and non-formal education;
(d) The Role of Women under the African Charter, in relation to specific socio-economic problems;
(e) The Rights to Fair Trial and Legal Assistance;
(f) Human Rights in Post-Apartheid South Africa;
(g) The Role of the African Media in the promotion and protection of Human Rights.

D. Other Topics which could be Selected for Seminars, Workshops or Studies

The Systems of protection in the African Charter in comparison with other Regional Systems:

(a) Freedom of Expression, of Association and of Assembly in contemporary Africa;
(b) Economic, Social and Cultural Rights and the Right to Development;
(c) Combating torture in a global and a regional perspective;
(d) Human Rights of Children under the African Charter;
(e) The African Charter and the Independence of Judiciary;
(f) African Culture and Human and Peoples' Rights;
(g) Freedom of Movement and Rights to Asylum in Africa;
(h) The African Commission and National Structures for the promotion and protection of human and peoples' rights;
(i) The Role of National Institutions (Ombudsmen, Mediators, Parliamentary Commission, etc.) responsible for the protection and promotion of human rights and the African Charter;

(j) State reporting in a comparative perspective;
(k) Protection of NGOs in the field of Human Rights;
(l) Structural Adjustment policies and their impact on human rights;
(m) Role of African Commission in relation to Democracy, Nation Building and creation of culture of Human Rights;
(n) The peaceful resolution of ethnic and social conflicts from a Human Rights Perspective.

E. Training Courses

Training Courses as discussed in A(4) above, such as:

(1) Training courses on Reporting Obligations under the African Charter (Article 62);
(2) Training courses for Officials of Police and other Professional groups;
(3) Training courses on Human Rights Documentation in co-operation with such organizations as the African Centre for Democracy and Human Rights Studies, Human Rights Internet, and Huridocs.

F. Cost of Seminars and Training Courses

Preliminary estimated costs of Seminars and Training courses are as follows:

(1) **Cost per Workshop**

– Travel cost of 20 participants of which 15 from sub-regional at US $800 on average	$16,000
– Per diem for 20 participants for 5 days at US $100 on average	$10,000
– 5 Resource Persons at US $1,800	$9,000
– Facilities	$1,000
– Xerox, Documents, Communication, etc.	$2,000
– Staff from Banjul, Administration	$2,000
– Contingency at 10%	$3,350
	$43,350
2 seminars per year 1992–1996	$86,700

(2) **Cost per Seminar**

– Air Fares of 20 Participants at US $1,400	$28,000
– 2 Consultants at US $1,000	$2,000
– Per diem for 20 participants for 5 days at US $120	$14,000
– Facilities	$1,500
– Xerox, Documents, Communication, etc.	$2,500
– Staff and Administration	$2,000
– Contingency at 10%	$5,000
	$54,350
2 courses per year 1992–1996	$108,800

III. Promotional Activities by Commissioners

Commissioners are entrusted to promote Human Rights in africa. The promotional Activities include, among other things, contacts with officials, media and local NGOs as well as giving public lectures and attending relevant Seminars and workshops.

Commissioners will basically conduct such activities in countries assigned to them according to the following list:

1. **Dr. Ibrahim A. Badawi El-Sheikh**
   Comores
   Seychelles
   Ile Maurice
   Egypt
   Sudan
   Tunisia
   Madagascar

2. **Mr. Alioune Blondin Bèye**
   Benin
   Burkina Faso
   Côte d'Ivoire
   Mali
   Togo
   Gabon

3. **Mr. Ali Mahmoud Buhedma**
   Algerie
   Libye
   Mauritanie
   Djibouti
   Republique Arabe Sahraouie Democratique

4. **Mr. Sourahata B. Semega-Janneh**
   Gambia
   Liberia
   Sierra Leone
   Tchad

5. **Mr. Robert H. Kisanga**
   Ethiopia
   Kenya
   Somalia
   Uganda
   Tanzania
   Mozambique
   Zambia

6. **Mr. Moleleki D. Mokama**
   Botswana
   Lesotho
   Malawi
   Swaziland
   Zimbabwe
   Namibia
   Angola

7. **Mr. Youssoupha Ndiaye**
   Cap-Vert
   Niger
   Senegal
   Republique de Guinée
   Guinea-Bissau

8. **Mr. Isaac Nguema**
   Zaïre
   Guinée Equatoriale
   Sao Tome et Principe
   Congo
   République Centrafricain
   Rwanda
   Burundi

9. **Prof U. O. Umozurike**
   Nigeria
   Ghana
   Cameroon

The preliminary cost of such activities could be about US $6,000 for each Commissioner per year × 11 = $66,000.

Inter-Sessional Working Group

- An Inter-Sessional Working Group composed of five Commissioners would meet for five working days a year.
- Preliminary estimated costs of such meeting is as follows:

(1) Air Fares (5 × 2,000)	$10,000
(2) Per diem of Commissioners (5 × 5 × 130)	$3,250
(3) Hiring of Conference Hall & Facilities	$2,000
(4) Interpreters	
(a) Honorarium 5 × 300 × 6	$9,000
(b) Per diem 5 × 130 × 6	$3,900

(5) Translators	
(a) Honorarium 5 × 151,9 × 3	$2,278,5
(b) Per diem 5 × 130 × 3	$1,950
(6) Bilingual Secretary 5 × 60	$ 300
(7) Hiring of Interpretation Equipment	$1,500
	$34,178,5
+ Contingencies 5%	$1,708
Total	$35,886,5

PRELIMINARY PROGRAMME OF ACTION ADOPTED AT THE SECOND SESSION (DAKAR, 8–13 FEBRUARY 1988)

A. Promotional Projects

(a) Research and Information Activities

(1) Establishment of an African Library and a Documentation Centre on Human Rights;
(2) Printing and Dissemination of the African Charter on Human and Peoples' Rights;
(3) Publication of an African Review on Human and Peoples' Rights;
(4) Periodical radio broadcasts and television programmes on human rights in Africa;
(5) Integration of the teaching of human rights in the syllabi of secondary education;
(6) Proclamation of a Human Rights Day;
(7) Participation in the Bicentennial activities of the Declaration on the Rights of Man and the Citizen, 1789;
(8) Institution of a Prize for and a competition on Human Rights;
(9) Recommendation on the establishment of national human rights committee;
(10) Recommendation on the establishment of human rights institutes;
(11) Symposium or Seminars especially on apartheid;
(12) Charter ratification campaign within countries which have not yet ratified it;
(13) Ratification of human rights treaties prepared by international organizations (United Nations, ILO, etc.);
(14) Introduction of the provisions of the Charter in the Constitution of States;
(15) Periodical Reports of States.

(b) Co-operation Activities

(1) Co-operation with international, inter-State or non-governmental organizations;
(2) Co-operation with African Organizations.

Terms of Reference for Consultant with the view to preparing a Report for consideration by the Commission.

Background Information

During its Second Ordinary Session, held in Dakar (Senegal) from 8–13 February 1988, the African Commission on Human and Peoples' Rights (hereinafter called the Commission) adopted a draft programme of action for carrying out its mission of promoting Human and Peoples' Rights (Annex I).

The Commission decided that this programme will be implemented in successive stages and that emphasis will be placed on:

- Large scale popularization of the Charter and the Rules of Procedure;
- Promotion through education, teaching, communication and exchanges;
- Preparation of samples of States Parties' periodic reports and of the annual report of the Commission;
- Creation of appropriate reception facilities;
- Constant dialogue with all organizations capable of relating and supporting the activities of the Commission.

During its Sixth Ordinary Session, held in Banjul (Gambia) from 23 October to 3 November 1989, the Commission mandated one of its members, Dr. Ibrahim A. Badawei El-Sheikh, to prepare a draft terms of reference for a consultancy mission relating to the programme of action of the Commission and submit it to the earliest session of the Commission (Annex II).

Objectives

The main objective of the envisaged consultancy mission is to translate into concrete and realistic project the key ideas contained in the draft programme of action.

There is need however, to take into account achievements already made within the framework of the United Nations or other Institutions pursuing the same objectives as far as the promotion of human and peoples' rights in Africa is concerned.

The planning of projects should be spread over a five-year period and should reflect a geographic and thematic distribution which takes into account the specific need of the African continent.

The objective is to also evaluate the cost of project and explore the human and logistic resources for their implementation.

Scope of Consultancy

The tasks to be undertaken by the consultant, without being necessarily restrictive, are:

(a) To identify priorities in the field of human and peoples' rights on the basis of the programme and directives of the Commission;
(b) To formulate topics for seminars, symposia, workshops, training programmes and roundtables which are integrated into and incorporate adequate African national programmes on the promotion of human and peoples' rights;
(c) To undertake, on the basis of the results of paragraph (b), a geographical distribution of meetings to be organized, at three levels: continental, subregional and national;
(d) To identify, on the basis of proposals ensuing from paragraph (b) and (c), target groups capable of serving as agents for popularizing promotional activities;
(e) Make an inventory of and assess current United Nations' programme for Africa, relating to consultancy services and the worldwide campaign for human rights, so as to avoid not only duplication of topics and targets, but also to benefit from the results obtained;
(f) To draw up a list, at the level of the OAU, of all relevant texts pertaining to human and peoples' rights, as well as of the activities undertaken by the organization which have some bearing on human and peoples' rights, in order to better attain the common objectives of the Commission and other organs of the OAU;
(g) To draw up an inventory of all the national and international institutions with which the Commission could establish co-operation ties in the promotion of human and peoples' rights;
(h) To outline the main areas of possible co-operation between the Commission and other organizations, such as the African Centre for Democracy and Human Rights Studies in order to maximize the available resources at the Secretariat of the Commission. In the same vein, to define the nature of the relations which the Commission should maintain with organizations pursuing the same objectives;
(i) To evaluate the human and technical resources which the Secretariat of the Commission needs to implement the Commission's programme of action;
(j) To prepare a draft budget for each project and identify possible sources of funding (for example: OAU's Ordinary Budget, voluntary contributions from States Parties to the Charter, etc.);
(k) To define any other mode of funding, particularly, the setting up of a special fund to be run autonomously by the Commission;
(l) Apart from reports of seminars, symposia and other meetings which will be published (with cost estimates for each project), to evolve a policy for the publication of reference and popular works and to evaluate their cost;

(m) Taking into account the high rate of illiteracy in Africa, to spell out the main points of a policy of co-operation with States Parties for the production of radio and television programmes in national languages;
(n) To visit the headquarters of the OAU, of the Commission, the United Nations Centre for Human Rights and of the European Commission on Human Rights in order to collect maximum documents;
(o) To formulate topics for studies which should be published by the Commission.

Profile of the Consultant

The person who will be charged by the Commission with undertaking the envisaged consultancy should be a national of a Member State of the OAU. He should have wide experience in the area of human rights in Africa, in activities relating to human rights within the United Nations and Regional organizations concerned with human rights as well as in non-governmental organizations.

The consultant should be capable of writing in the two working languages of the OAU and shall undertake to submit his consultancy report within a maximum period of six months as from the date of signature of the contract.

In the event where the Commission does not have the necessary resources to recruit a consultant, it could solicit the good offices of the United Nations Centre for Human Rights.

ANNEX VIII

Conclusions and Recommendations of the Seminar on the National Implementation of the African Charter on Human and Peoples' Rights in the Internal Legal Systems in Africa 26–30 October 1992, Banjul, The Gambia

The Seminar on the National Implementation of the African Charter on Human and Peoples' Rights held in Banjul, the Gambia from 26–30 October 1992 adopted the following conclusions and recommendations:

1. The Seminar notes the following in relation to the status of the Charter;

(a) States party to the African Charter shall accord the Charter a definitive legal status in their national legal systems.
(b) In the event of a conflict involving a provision of the Charter and national legislation the Charter provision shall prevail.
(c) The African Charter is a treaty within the definition of the Vienna convention on the Law of Treaties. It enshrines the fundamental principle pacta sunt servanda and an obligation is imposed on parties thereto not to invoke their municipal laws as an excuse for failure to perform an obligation imposed by the Charter.

(d) The provisions of the African Charter as are in force shall not be repealed, amended or suspended save in accordance with general principles of international law.

The Seminar considers that:

2. The following points should be observed in relation to the incorporation of the African Charter in internal legal systems:

(a) The automatic incorporation of the African Charter into the internal legal system of the parties thereto could be advantageous to the States Parties to the Charter in the sense of sparing them the difficulties of reviewing their present legislation so as to conform to the African charter.
(b) Whatever means a State party to the African Charter may choose in order to make the Charter applicable in its internal legal system, the provisions of the Charter are nevertheless to be fully observed in accordance with the requirements of international law.

3. The Seminar believes that human rights must primarily be secured within the national legal system of each State Party to the Charter. In this regard it is vital that:

(a) The Rule of Law is strictly respected in all activities of the State and all branches of public administration.
(b) The judiciary is guaranteed full independence. In this regard States party to the Charter are requested to facilitate the establishment and improvement of appropriate national institutions for the promotion and protection of the rights and freedoms guaranteed by the Charter in accordance with Article 26 of the Charter.
(c) Access to Courts of law is secured to all individuals regardless of their financial means.

4. The Seminar is of the view that:

(a) The African Charter should be interpreted in the light of the impressive body of jurisprudence which has developed on similar provisions in other universal and regional instruments on human rights and related matters. Such instruments could be of practical relevance and value to judges and counsel and should as often as possible be referred to.
(b) It is within the proper nature of the judicial process and well established judicial functions for national courts to have regard to international obligations which a country undertakes whether or not they have been incorporated into domestic law – for the purpose of removing ambiguity or uncertainty from national constitutions and laws written or unwritten.
(c) Judges and Lawyers have a special contribution to make in administration of justice in fostering universal respect for fundamental rights and freedoms.
(d) It is particularly important to ensure that all persons including judges, lawyers, litigants and others are made aware of applicable human rights norms wherever

they may be stated and particularly those in the Charter. In this respect the Seminar underlines the importance of Article 25 of the African Charter which obligates states party to the charter to promote and ensure through teaching, education and publication, respect for the rights and freedoms expressed in the Charter.

5. The Seminar welcomes the fact that 47 African States have ratified the Charter. It is hoped that such ratification is followed by compliance by the states of their obligation to submit reports under Article 62 of the Charter on the measures taken with a view to implementing the African Charter.

6. The Seminar notes with interest the activities undertaken so far by the African Commission on Human and Peoples' Rights and expresses the views that:

(a) It is important that a State's report submitted to the African Commission should indicate:

(i) Whether the rights, fundamental freedoms and duties expressed in the Charter are protected by the Constitution of that State or by a "Bill of Rights" and whether there are provisions for derogations and in what circumstances;
(ii) Whether the provisions of the Charter can be invoked before the courts, other tribunals or administrative authorities for direct implementation or application or whether they have to be incorporated into internal laws or regulations before they are enforceable by the authorities;
(iii) What judicial, administrative or other authorities have jurisdiction affecting human rights;
(iv) What remedies are available to an individual whose rights are violated;
(v) Non-legislative measures adopted to implement the Charter;
(vi) Difficulties encountered in the process of implementing the Charter.

(b) It would facilitate the work of the Commission and that of the OAU Member States if the States designate high ranking officials to act as focal points in the relations between the Commission and the States. Such focal points would facilitate the follow-up on the Commission's recommendations and contact between states and the Commission.

(c) It is noted that the lack of legal aid services in Africa precludes the majority of the African population from asserting their human rights. It is recommended that the question of legal aid and recourse procedures should be accorded greater attention in the work of the African Commission and that States and NGOs should take the initiative to promote the establishment of legal aid services.

(d) The commission should find ways to provide advisory services upon request to states, in relation to the incorporation of the African Charter in their internal legal systems, preparation of their reports and other matters relating to the implementation of the Charter.

(e) The resources and time allocated for the work of the Commission are inadequate. In this regard the Assembly of Heads of State and Government of the OAU are requested to provide the Commission with full political, financial and administrative support with a view to enabling the Commission to properly carry out its mandate in accordance with the Charter which is vital for ensuring promotion of respect for and protection of the rights expressed in the Charter and thus securing peace, stability and development in Africa.

7. The Seminar considers it advisable that the OAU takes initiatives to revise the Charter including the possibility of creating an African Human Rights Court. Such revision should be carried out by the adoption of additional protocols under Article 66 of the Charter. The seminar looks upon such a revision as a move towards strengthening the work of the Commission as well as a response to developments occurring since the adoption of the Charter.

8. The Seminar presumes that after adopting the African Charter and creating an independent Commission the Assembly of the Heads of State and Government of the OAU shall see to it that the Commission's recommendations are responded to, that they are published and that just satisfaction is afforded to injured parties.

9. The Seminar underlines the importance of the African Commission taking advantage as it shall consider appropriate, or relevant universal and regional mechanisms established to promote and protect human rights.

10. The Seminar, aware of the links existing between human rights and international humanitarian law, wishes to underscore the need to disseminate and implement the provisions of international humanitarian law applicable in time of armed conflicts.

11. The Seminar calls upon all Contracting Parties to instruments relating to international humanitarian law to adopt adequate measures at the national level to ensure the implementation of the provisions of international humanitarian law. Such measures are necessary for the protection of the human being in time of armed conflicts.

ANNEX IX

Final Report of the African Conference on "The Journalist and Human Rights in Africa" 31 October to 1 November 1992, Tunis

An African conference on the Theme "The Journalist and Human Rights in africa" was organized in Tunis from 31 October to 1 November 1992 by the Association of Tunisian Journalists in collaboration with the International Organization of Journalists, the African Commission on Human and Peoples' Rights and the United nations Centre for Human Rights within the framework of the African regional preparatory meeting for the World Conference on Human Rights.

The agenda of the Conference dealt with 4 (four) items:

- The state of the press in Africa and the problems encountered by journalists in the discharge of their professional duties.
- The role of the African journalist in the World human rights programme and the African Charter on Human and Peoples' Rights.

The opening session was attended by Messrs. Fathi Houidi, Secretary of State at the Prime Minister's Office responsible for information within the Government, John Pace, representative of the United Nations organization, Gerard Gatinot, Secretary General of the International Organization of Journalists, Lee Woodyer, Human Rights Officer at the International Federation of Journalists, Ibrahim Bawadi, Chairman of the African Commission on Human and Peoples' Rights, Ambassador Fouad Badaoui, representative of the Union of African Journalists and Mohamed Ben Salah, President of the Association of Tunisian Journalists.

The proceedings were attended by the representatives of several organizations of journalists in African countries as well as many Tunisian journalists and correspondents of international press organizations.

A group of Tunisian and African experts presented papers during this Conference.

During the discussion of item 1 (state of the press and problems encountered by journalists in the discharge of their professional duties), the participants noted that the press in Africa suffers from many handicaps especially the lack of freedom of expression and impartial and objective information as is the case in most third world countries.

The speakers emphasized the following points:

- Need to respect the right of the citizen to impartial information, provide the journalist with the appropriate working conditions and enable him/her to freely exercise his/her profession so as to be able to meet the expectations of the public.
- Appeal to Governments to lift the constraints on the freedom of the press and abstain from any pressure or monopoly by the State on the media.
- Put an end to the international monopolisation of the media which violates the principles enshrined in the universal declaration of human rights.
- Ensure the independence of African press agencies and national radio-television bodies and, their autonomy of action in the area of information as public bodies whilst strengthening them to enable them to ensure coverage of current events in the continent instead of relying exclusively on foreign agencies.
- Promulgate national legislation and adopt international resolutions capable of halting the expansionism of multinationals and preventing them from monopolizing the media and appropriating national information organs.
- Facilitate the task of journalists and enable them to get access to sources of information and do their work professionally, free from interventions and pressures and within the framework of freedom and objectivity provide them, simultaneously, with the requisite protection to carry out their mission of informing in the manner expected of them by the African citizen and as dictated by their duty as journalists.

In this spirit the participants expressed their solidarity with imprisoned or persecuted journalists and called for their release and the full restoration of their rights.

- Guarantee the right of journalists to form their own trade unions at the level of each country.
- Calls upon all competent local and international parties to facilitate this task and envisage setting up regional unions of journalists with the aim of protecting the press and journalists and safeguarding the right to impartial information, freedom of expression, communication and association.
- Guarantee the Rights of the female journalist as well as actual equality between the latter and her other colleagues, and offer her better prospects in terms of professional training and promotion in the career.

The participants also considered item II (development and human rights). They laid particular emphasis on the following points:

- Development should be perceived as an integral part of human rights from which it could not be dissociated and as such development and human rights should therefore be guaranteed concomitantly and similarly.
- Need to apprehend human rights in their global dimension including the rights of the individual and the rights of communities; from this viewpoint it is imperative to guarantee the rights of the human being as an individual within a single community and guarantee, simultaneously the rights of communities at the international level.
- Ensure access to technology by all peoples as a key element for the dissemination of human rights.
- Consider development as not being exclusively aimed at economic enrichment but also the promotion of the human being at all levels, thus making it necessary to recognize the right of the individual to development and happiness within the same community as well as the right of each community to development and prosperity within the international community.
- Consider that man is the key element in the creation of wealth. Promulgate national legislation and adopt international resolutions for preserving human resources and guaranteeing these rights at both the local and international levels.
- Ensure that the system of visas does not constitute an obstacle to the free movement of persons as enshrined in the universal declaration of human rights.

The participants then went on to consider item III (the media and the serious problems encountered by the African such as the question of women, epidemics, illiteracy and refugees).

In this respect they emphasized the following points:

- Need for governments, international organizations and the OAU to treat problems with all the requisite interest, and devise comprehensive strategies to resolve them whilst insisting on the overriding need for scientific research and a collective effort to address medically, socially and psychologically the problem of AIDS as well as other serious diseases.

- Urge the UN and subsidiary organs and specialized agencies (WHO, UNDP, UNESCO, UNWR) as well as the OAU to devise an effective information strategy for dealing with these problems and involve the media and journalists in the preparation and implementation of this strategy.

The participants ended their proceedings by discussing item IV (role of journalists in the World human rights programme and the implementation of the African Charter on Human and Peoples' Rights).

Their interventions centred on the following points:

- Adoption of international human rights concept as defined concretely in the universal declaration of human rights.
- Support the African Commission on Human and Peoples' Rights through the OAU and UN so as to provide it with the means to devise and implement a durable and large scale information strategy allowing African media to publicize the African Charter on Human and Peoples' Rights.
- Appeal to journalists and the media to monitor international action in the area of human rights and ensure that these rights are respected and that the regimes in place comply with them as pledged in ratifying the relevant international conventions and the African Charter.
- Celebrate AFRICAN HUMAN RIGHTS DAY on 21 October of every year as an occasion to disseminate human rights principles and evaluate the degree of compliance with these principles.
- Ensure freedom of the press and expression and allow journalists to discharge their duties of promoting human rights whilst affording these journalists protection whilst carrying out this mission which is fraught with risks.
- Institute an African Journalist and Press Freedom Day to be celebrated throughout the continent.
- Put in place national mechanisms for monitoring compliance with human rights at the regional level within the African continent, forge links between the different mechanisms, journalists' organizations and the media to enable them to play their rightful role in the promotion and protection of the rights of the African.
- Cooperate with international journalists' organizations and those dealing with the protection of human rights so as to ensure strict application of the World Programmes on Human and Peoples' Rights.

The participants expressed their thanks to the experts who were kind enough to introduce the various topics of discussion on the agenda, as well as to all those who contributed to the organization and success of the conference.

ANNEX X

List of NGOs Granted Observer Status[1]

[1] This list has been omitted. The most up-to-date list is reproduced above at p. 90.

Final Communiqué of the Twelfth Ordinary Session of the African Commission on Human and Peoples' Rights

Banjul, 12–21 October 1992

1. The African Commission on Human and Peoples' Rights held its 12th Ordinary Session from 12–21 October 1992 in Banjul, The Gambia.

2. This Session was preceded by the meeting of a workshop jointly organized in The Gambia from 9–11 October 1992 by the International Commission of Jurists and the African Centre for Democracy and Human Rights Studies on the following themes:

(i) The need to revise the rules of procedure of the Commission;
(ii) The need to formulate guidelines on the exhaustion of national remedies;
(iii) The right to development;
(iv) The rights of women especially the appointment of women commissioners.

3. This Session was attended by the following Commissioners:

- Dr. Ibrahim A. Badawi El-Sheikh, Chairman;
- Mr. Sourahata B. S. Janneh, Vice Chairman;
- Mr. Ali Mahmoud Buhedma;
- Justice Robert Habesh Kisanga;
- Mr. Youssoupha Ndiaye;
- Mr. Isaac Nguema;
- Professor U. O. Umozuriki;
- Dr. Mohammed H. Ben Salem.

4. The Commission observed a minute of silence in memory of the victims of the civil war, internal conflicts, drought and famine raging in Ethiopia and many other parts of Africa and the martyrs of acts of violence in South Africa. During its third sitting, the members of the Commission and NGO representatives also observed a minute's silence in memory of the victims of the earthquake which struck Egypt the previous day.

5. The opening Session was held on 12 October 1992 at 10 a.m. at the Kombo Beach Hotel Novotel in the presence of His Excellency the Honourable Hassan Jallow, Minister of Justice of the Gambia and the following dignitaries:

- Ambassadors and Heads of Diplomatic Missions;
- Representatives of International and African NGOs;
- Representatives of the press and other invitees.

6. In his introductory speech, Dr. Badawi El-Sheikh Stated that the Commission is confronted with the task of addressing the serious human rights situation in Africa. Furthermore, the Chairman Stated that the OAU has demonstrated its willingness to promote and protect rights by its Resolution on the African Commission adopted at its 28th Ordinary Session held in Dakar, Senegal. In his speech, Dr. Badawi noted that the Commission is facing a certain number of constraints such as an inadequate secretariat and limited financial resources. The Commission has, however, managed to attain some of its objectives.

The Honourable Hassan Jallow paid tribute to the Commission for its achievements. He Stated that in spite of the difficulties encountered, the Commission has managed to accomplish some of its objectives. He underscored the commitment of His Excellency Sir Dawda Kairaba Jawara to support the Commission both at the national level and at the level of the OAU. In this regard, the Minister informed the Commission that the Gambia government was in the process of establishing contacts with other friendly countries to initiate amendments to the Charter.

7. The proceedings of the Commission mainly focused on five major issues, viz:

(i) adoption of a programme;
(ii) consideration of periodic reports;
(iii) consideration of complaints;
(iv) administrative and financial matters;
(v) consideration of the right to development.

8. At the beginning of its proceedings, the Commission heard, on the one hand, a certain number of Statements and, on the other hand, the conclusions of the workshop organized by the forum of NGOs before the session.

9. In their interventions, the representatives of Governmental and Non-Governmental Organizations underscored the resolve of their Organizations to help and assist in the functioning of the Commission to enhance the promotion and protection of human rights in Africa. These were the essence and thrust of the Statements made notably by:

- Mr. Christopher Hall of Amnesty International;
- Mr. Salim A. Salim of the Libyan Arab League;
- Mrs. Iris Almeida, of the International Centre for Human Rights and the Development of Democracy;
- Dr. Amin M. Medani of the Sudan Human Rights Organization;
- Salem Mezhoud of Anti-Slavery International;
- Dr. Tunji Abayoumi of Human Rights Africa;
- Dr. S. Gutto of Network on Integrated Human Rights in Africa (NARIHRA).

10. In presenting the report of the workshop organized by the International Commission of Jurists and the African Centre for Democracy and Human Rights Studies, Mrs. Mona Rishmawi and Dr. Philip Amoah of the ICJ thanked the Commission for accepting its offer to explore ways of initiating a preliminary study on the question of women's rights. For her part, Mrs. Mona Rishmawi Stated that

NARIHRA will consult women's organizations and NGOs with observer status with the Commission in carrying out the exercise. The Commission was also requested to look into the problem of structural adjustment and to organize a seminar on the subject. The meeting was also informed that the ICJ will conduct a preliminary investigations on the subject and make proposals to the Commission. The representative of Amnesty International reported on the measures adopted by his organization to assist the Commission in the discharge of its functions.

11. Dealing with its programme of action and New Methods of Work, the Commission drew up a calendar of seminars and symposia it intends to organize either on its own or jointly with other international organizations. In this regard, the Commission, reiterated its will to organize:

(i) A seminar on "How the African Charter on Human and Peoples' Rights has been received in the Legal Systems of States Parties to the African Charter" (Banjul from 26–30 October 1992);
(ii) A seminar on the role of the African media in the promotion and protection of human rights (Tunis from 31 October to 1 January 1992);
(iii) A seminar on African refugees and internally displaced persons;
(iv) A seminar on popular participation and informal education;
(v) A seminar on post-apartheid South Africa (early January 1993);
(vi) A seminar on the right to fair trial;
(vii) A seminar on the role of women under the African Charter;
(viii) A meeting of the inter-sessional working group of the African Commission on Human and Peoples' Rights (Banjul, mid-January 1993).

Regarding its methods of work, the Commission decided as follows:

- adoption of an organizational chart for the Secretariat and the need to recruit the necessary staff;
- the publication of the fifth annual activity report of the Commission and the second edition of the Review of the Commission;
- the publication of annual reports and other documents of the Commission including the periodic report.

12. During its deliberations, the Commission examined the periodic reports submitted by the Republic of Senegal (initial report and report no 1), the Republic of Zimbabwe (initial report) and the Republic of The Gambia (initial report).

13. The Commission expressed satisfaction at the usefulness and relevance of the constructive dialogue established between the Commission and States concerned and thanked the Government of the Republic of Senegal, the Republic of Zimbabwe and the Republic of The Gambia for their reports and their willingness to cooperate with the Commission.

14. It appealed to States who have not yet submitted their reports to do so as soon as possible.

15. Regarding complaints pertaining to allegations of human rights violations in some African countries, examined 34 old communications and 20 new communications.

After taking the appropriate decisions in each case the Commission deplored the administrative delays encountered in the consideration of complaints.

16. Under promotional activities, the Commission received the report of Commissioner Ndiaye on the mission sent to Mali to monitor the presidential elections. This mission was a success and the elections were free and fair.

17. The Chairman also informed the Commission that its annual report was well received by the Assembly of Heads of State and Government of the OAU. In this regard, the Assembly adopted a resolution requesting that the Commission be provided with the requisite resources for the implementation of its programme of activities (AHG/Res. 207 (XXXVII)).

18. The Commission learnt with consternation of the death of Mr. Orton Chirwa whilst in detention together with his wife for their political beliefs.

The Commission recalls that this regrettable incident occurred whilst it had been seized with this case and one of its members was carrying out on-the-spot investigations.

The Commission expresses to the family of the deceased its most profound sympathy and reiterates its grave concern about the fate of the spouse who is still in detention.

19. On the last day of its session the Commission noted with dismay the recent mass expulsion of Nigerian nationals living in Gabon. The Commission reminds States Parties to the Charter on Human and Peoples' Rights that these measures coming in the wake of others taken recently constitute a flagrant violation of the relevant provisions of Article 12 paragraph 5 which expressly stipulates as follows:

> "The mass expulsion of non-nationals shall be prohibited. Mass expulsion shall be that which is aimed at national, racial, ethnic or religious groups."

20. As regards the venue of the 13th Session, the Commission agreed to wait until the end of December for the response of the Government of Botswana. Otherwise the 13th Session will be held in Banjul during the first fortnight of April 1993.

Done in Banjul, 21 October 1992.

Final Communiqué of the Thirteenth Ordinary Session of the African Commission on Human and Peoples' Rights

Banjul, 27 March to 7 April 1993

1. The African Commission on Human and Peoples' Rights held its 13th Ordinary Session at its headquarters in Banjul, The Gambia from 29 March to 7 April 1993.

2. This Session was preceded by the fourth Workshop on NGO participation in the work of the African Commission jointly organized in The Gambian capital from 26–28 April 1993 by the International Commission of Jurists and the African Centre for Democracy and Human Rights Studies.

3. The 13th Session was attended by the following Commissioners:

- Dr. Ibrahim A. Badawi El-Sheikh, Chairman;
- Mr. Sourahata B. S. Janneh, Vice Chairman;
- Mr. Alioune B. Beye;
- Mr. Ali Mahmoud Buhedma;
- Justice Robert Habesh Kisanga;
- Mr. Youssoupha Ndiaye;
- Prof. Isaac Nguema;
- Professor U. O. Umozurike;
- Dr. Mohammed H. Ben Salem;
- Mr. Alexis Gabou;
- Mr. Moleleki D. Mokama;

4. The opening ceremony took place on 29 March 1993 at 10 a.m. at the Kairaba Beach Hotel in the presence of His Excellency the Honourable Hassan Jallow, Attorney General and Minister of Justice of the Gambia and H.E. Ambassador Abdullahi Said Osman, Assistant Secretary-General of the Organization of African Unity and the following dignitaries:

- Ambassadors and Heads of Diplomatic Missions;
- Representatives of International And African NGOs;
- Members of the press and other invitees.

5. In his introductory Statement the Vice-Chairman Mr. Sourahata B.S. Janneh underscored the Actions deployed by the African Commission towards the promotion of human and peoples' rights in Africa.

6. H.E. Ambassador Abdullahi Saod Osman, expressed his delight in participating and deputizing for the Secretary-General of the OAU, H.E. Dr. Salim Ahmed Salim.

He also reaffirmed the readiness of the General Secretariat of the OAU to do its utmost to support the Commission in the efficient and successful discharge of its functions.

7. In his opening address, the Honourable Hassan Jallow welcomed all the participants and urged that greater priority be accorded to Africa during the forthcoming World Conference on Human Rights so that it would enjoy the solidarity of the international community in its untiring development efforts.

8. The proceedings of the Commission dealt mainly with the following major issues:

(i) consideration of applications for Observer Status;
(ii) consideration of periodic reports;
(iii) consideration of communications – complaints;
(iv) administrative and financial matters;
(v) consideration of the right to development.

9. Observer Status was granted to the following 18 Organizations:

(i) Organization guineenne de défense des droits de l'homme et du citoyen;
(ii) Association des journalistes tunisiens;
(iii) Danish Centre for Human Rights;
(iv) African Rights and Justice Protection Network;
(v) Agir ensemble pour les droits de l'homme;
(vi) Association rwandaise pour la défense des droits de la personne et des libertés publiques;
(vii) Centre beninois pour le dévelopement des initiatives à la base;
(viii) CUSO, The Gambia;
(ix) National Society for Human Rights of Namibia;
(x) Association chretienne pour l'abolition des tortures et pour le respect des droits de l'homme;
(xi) African Institute for Human Rights and Peace Research;
(xii) International Association of Lawyers for Human Rights Studies;
(xiii) Universal Defenders of Democracy;
(xiv) Women Concerned;
(xv) Egyptian Association of Supporters of Human Rights;
(xvi) Comité international pour le respect et l'application de la charte africaine (CIRAC);
(xvii) Centre de promotion des droits de l'homme du burundi;
(xviii) Comissão Nacional des Direitos Humanos de Cabo Verde.

10. These 18 Organizations join the 90 already granted Observer Status by the African Commission.

11. At the beginning of its proceedings, the Commission was addressed by a number of NGO representatives including the representatives of the International Commission of Jurists (ICJ) who presented the conclusions and recommendations of the Dakar symposium of January 1993 and the 4th NGO Workshop which preceded the Session of the African Commission.

12. During its proceedings, the Commission considered the initial periodic reports submitted by the Republic of Togo and the Federal Republic of Nigeria.

13. The consideration of these reports is geared towards assessing the legislative or other measures, taken by States with a view to giving effect to the rights and freedoms enshrined in the African Charter on Human and Peoples' Rights.

14. The Commission thanks the Government of Togo and the Government of Nigeria for presenting their report before the Commission. The Commission, nevertheless, urged the two States concerned to reply in writing to the questions which were not answered or for which the response was unsatisfactory.

15. The Commission appealed to the States which have not yet submitted their reports to do so as soon as possible.

16. As regards protective activities, the Commission considered 55 communications, from sources other than States Parties including 14 new ones. For some of them, the Commission noted that they relate to special cases which appear to reveal the existence of a series of serious and massive violations of human and peoples' rights.

17. In the face of such situations in certain African countries the Commission decided to apply the relevant provisions of the Charter especially paragraphs 1 and 3 of Article 58.

18. Moreover, in dealing with certain communications, the Commission resorted to the provisions of Article 46 of the Charter.

19. As regards promotional activities the Commission intends to organize with the assistance of the Raoul Wallenberg Institute training courses on the obligations contained in the African Charter in Harare and Tunis during the course of 1993. Moreover, a seminar on refugees and displaced persons will be organized in Harare from 12–16 July 1993, with the assistance of the Centre for Documentation and Research of Southern Africa.

20. The Commission will hold its 14th Session during the last ten days of November in Banjul, The Gambia.

Done in Banjul, 7 April 1993

PART II

Tables of Communications and Resolutions

TABLE I: COMMUNICATIONS IN NUMERICAL ORDER

Communications marked with * were initially assigned registration numbers by the Commission but subsequently not treated as communications. Other communications missing from the list have not yet been reported upon by the Commission.

TABLE II: RESOLUTIONS IN DATE ORDER

TABLE III: COMMUNICATIONS AND RESOLUTIONS BY ARTICLE

Article 1

(A) Communications

74/92 Commission Nationale des Droits de l'Homme et des Libertés v Chad
102/93 Constitutional Rights Project and Civil Liberties Organisation v Nigeria
129/94 Civil Liberties Organization v Nigeria
136/94 William Courson v Zimbabwe
137/94, 139/94, 154/96, 161/97 International PEN, Constitutional Rights Project, Interights (on behalf of Ken Saro-Wiwa Jr), Civil Liberties Organisation v Nigeria

(B) Resolutions

Resolution on the African Commission on Human and Peoples' Rights (1994, 15th Session)

Article 2

(A) Communications

27/89, 46/ 91, 49/91, 99/93 Organisation Mondiale Contre la Torture and Association Internationale des Juristes Democrates, Commission Internationale des Juristes, Union Interafricaine des Droits de l'Homme v Rwanda
65/92 Ligue Camerounaise des Droits de l'Homme v Cameroon
71/92 Rencontre Africaine pour la Defense des Droits de l'Hommes v Zambia
102/93 Constitutional Rights Project and Civil Liberties Organisation v Nigeria
136/94 William Courson v Zimbabwe
144/95 William A Courson v Equatorial Guinea

159/96 Union Interafricaine des Droits de l'Homme, Federation Internationale des Ligues des Droits de l'Homme, Rencontre Africaine des Droits de l'Homme, Organisation Nationale des Droits de l'Homme au Sénégal and Association Malienne des Droits de l'Homme v Angola
162/97 Mouvement des Réfugiés Mauritaniens au Sénégal v Senegal
198/97 SOS Esclaves v Mauritania
212/98 Amnesty International v Zambia

(B) Resolutions

Resolution on Nigeria (1995, 17th Session)

Article 3

(A) Communications

136/94 William Courson v Zimbabwe
198/97 SOS Esclaves v Mauritania

(B) Resolutions

. . .

Article 4 (Right to Life)

(A) Communications

16/88, 17/88, 18/88 Comité Culturel pour la Démocratie au Benin, Badjoume Hilaire, El Hadj Boubacar Diawara v Benin
21/88 Centre Haitien des Liberté Publiques v Ethiopia
25/89, 47/40, 56/91, 100/93 Free Legal Assistance Group, Lawyers' Committee for Human Rights, Union Interafricaine des droits de l'homme, Les Temoins de Jehovah v Zaire
27/89, 46/91, 49/91, 99/93 Organisation Mondiale Contre la Torture and Association Internationale des Juristes Democrates, Commission Internationale des Juristes, Union Interafricaine des Droits de l'Homme v Rwanda
29/89 Commission Française Justice et Paix v Ethiopia
42/90 International PEN v Malawi
43/90 Union des Scholaires Nigeriens, Union Generale des Etudients Nigeriens au Benin v Nigeria
60/91 Constitutional Rights Project (in respect of Wahab Akamu, G Adega and others) v Nigeria
64/92, 68/92, 78/92 Krishna Achuthan (on behalf of Aleke Banda), Amnesty International (on behalf of Orton and Vera Chirwa), Amnesty International (on behalf of Orton and Vera Chirwa) v Malawi

65/92 Ligue Camerounaise des Droits de l'Homme v Cameroon
74/92 Commission Nationale des Droits de l'Homme et des Libertés v Chad
83/92, 88/93, 91/93 Jean Y Degli (on behalf of N Bikagni), Union Interafricaine des droits de l'homme, Commission Internationale des Juristes v Togo
87/93 Constitutional Rights Project (in respect of Zamani Lakwot and six others) v Nigeria
104/94, 109–126/94 Centre for Independence of Judges and Lawyers v Algeria and Others
136/94 William Courson v Zimbabwe
137/94, 139/94, 154/96, 161/97 International PEN, Constitutional Rights Project, Interights (on behalf of Ken Saro-Wiwa Jr), Civil Liberties Organisation v Nigeria
198/97 SOS Esclaves v Mauritania
212/98 Amnesty International v Zambia
221/98 Alfred B Cudjoe v Ghana

(B) Resolutions

Resolution on the Situation in Rwanda (1994, 15th Session)
Resolution on Rwanda (1994, 16th Session)
Resolution on Sudan (1995, 17th Session)
Resolution on Anti-Personnel Mines (1995, 17th Session)
Resolution on Burundi (1996, 19th Session)
Resolution on the Ratification of the Convention on Anti-Personnel Mines (1998, 24th Session)

Article 5 (Torture/Inhuman Treatment)

(A) Communications

2/88 Iheanyichukwu A Ihebereme v USA
7/88 Committee for the Defence of Political Prisoners v Bahrain
8/88 Nziwa Buyingo v Uganda
9/88 International Lawyers Committee for Family Reunification v Ethiopia
16/88, 17/88, 18/88 Comité Culturel pour la Démocratie au Benin, Badjoume Hilaire, El Hadj Boubacar Diawara v Benin
25/89, 47/40, 56/91, 100/93 Free Legal Assistance Group, Lawyers' Committee for Human Rights, Union Interafricaine des droits de l'homme, Les Temoins de Jehovah v Zaire
26/89 Austrian Committee Against Torture v Burundi
27/89, 46/ 91, 49/91, 99/93 Organisation Mondiale Contre la Torture and Association Internationale des Juristes Democrates, Commission Internationale des Juristes, Union Interafricaine des Droits de l'Homme v Rwanda

37/90 Georges Eugene v USA and Haiti
47/90 Lawyers' Committee for Human Rights v Zaire
62/92 Amnesty International v Tunisia
64/92, 68/92, 78/92 Krishna Achuthan (on behalf of Aleke Banda), Amnesty International (on behalf of Orton and Vera Chirwa), Amnesty International (on behalf of Orton and Vera Chirwa) v Malawi
65/92 Ligue Camerounaise des Droits de l'Homme v Cameroon
70/92 Ibrahima Dioumessi, Sekou Kande, Ousmane Kaba v Guinea
74/92 Commission Nationale des Droits de l'Homme et des Libertés v Chad
83/92, 88/93, 91/93 Jean Y Degli (on behalf of N Bikagni), Union Interafricaine des droits de l'homme, Commission Internationale des Juristes v Togo
97/93 John K Modise v Botswana
104/94, 109–126/94 Centre for Independence of Judges and Lawyers v Algeria and Others
136/94 William Courson v Zimbabwe
137/94, 139/94, 154/96, 161/97 International PEN, Constitutional Rights Project, Interights (on behalf of Ken Saro-Wiwa Jr), Civil Liberties Organisation v Nigeria
142/94 Muthuthirin Njoka v Kenya
159/96 Union Interafricaine des Droits de l'Homme, Federation Internationale des Ligues des Droits de l'Homme, Rencontre Africaine des Droits de l'Homme, Organisation Nationale des Droits de l'Homme au Sénégal and Association Malienne des Droits de l'Homme v Angola
162/97 Mouvement des Réfugiés Mauritaniens au Sénégal v Senega
198/97 SOS Esclaves v Mauritania
212/98 Amnesty International v Zambia

(B) Resolutions

Resolution on Contemporary Forms of Slavery (1994, 16th Session)
Resolution on the Gambia (1994, 16th Session)
Resolution on Prisons in Africa (1995, 17th Session)
Resolution on Sudan (1995, 17th Session)

Article 6 (Arbitrary Detention)

(A) Communications

2/88 Iheanyichukwu A Ihebereme v USA
4/88 Coordinating Secretary of the Free Citizens Convention v Ghana
6/88 Dr Kodj Kofi v Ghana
7/88 Committee for the Defence of Political Prisoners v Bahrain

8/88 Nziwa Buyingo v Uganda
9/88 International Lawyers Committee for Family Reunification v Ethiopia
10/88 Getachew Abebe v Ethiopia
11/88 Henry Kalenga v Zambia
14/88 Dr Abd Eldayem AE Sanussi v Ethiopia
15/88 Mpaka-Nsusu Andre Alphonse v Zaire
16/88, 17/88, 18/88 Comité Culturel pour la Démocratie au Benin, Badjoume Hilaire, El Hadj Boubacar Diawara v Benin
19/88 International PEN v Malawi, Ethiopia, Cameroon, Kenya
20/88 Austrian Committee Against Torture v Morocco
22/88 International PEN v Burkina Faso
25/89, 47/40, 56/91, 100/93 Free Legal Assistance Group, Lawyers' Committee for Human Rights, Union Interafricaine des droits de l'homme, Les Temoins de Jehovah v Zaire
26/89 Austrian Committee Against Torture v Burundi
17/89, 46/ 91, 49/91, 99/93 Organisation Mondiale Contre la Torture and Association Internationale des Juristes Democrates, Commission Internationale des Juristes, Union Interafricaine des Droits de l'Homme v Rwanda
28/89 Association Internationale des Juristes Democrates v Ethiopia
31/89 Maria Baes v Zaire
39/90 Annette Pagnoulle (on behalf of Abdoulaye Mazou) v Cameroon
41/90 Andre Houver v Morocco
47/90 Lawyers' Committee for Human Rights v Zaire
55/91 International PEN v Chad
59/91 Embga Mekongo Louis v Cameroon
60/91 Constitutional Rights Project (in respect of Wahab Akamu, G Adega and others) v Nigeria
62/91 Committee for the Defence of Human Rights (in respect of Ms Jennifer Madike) v Nigeria
62/92 Amnesty International v Tunisia
64/92, 68/92, 78/92 Krishna Achuthan (on behalf of Aleke Banda), Amnesty International (on behalf of Orton and Vera Chirwa), Amnesty International (on behalf of Orton and Vera Chirwa) v Malawi
65/92 Ligue Camerounaise des Droits de l'Homme v Cameroon
66/92 Lawyers Committee for Human Rights v Tanzania
67/92 Civil Liberties Organization v Nigeria
70/92 Ibrahim Dioumessi, Sekou Kande, Ousmane Kaba v Guinea
71/92 Rencontre Africaine pour la Defense des Droits de l'Hommes v Zambia
74/92 Commission Nationale des Droits de l'Homme et des Libertés v Chad
83/92, 88/93, 91/93 Jean Y Degli (on behalf of N Bikagni), Union Interafricaine des droits de l'homme, Commission Internationale des Juristes v Togo
87/93 Constitutional Rights Project (in respect of Zamani Lakwot and six others) v Nigeria
92/93 International PEN (in respect of Kemal al-Jazouli) v Sudan

101/93 Civil Liberties Organization (in respect of the Nigeria Bar Association) v Nigeria
102/93 Constitutional Rights Project and Civil Liberties Organisation v Nigeria
103/93 Alhassan Abubakar v Ghana
105/93, 128/94, 130/94, 152/96 Media Rights Agenda, Constitutional Rights Project, Media Rights Agenda and Constitutional Rights Project v Nigeria
108/93 Monja Joana v Madagascar
136/94 William Courson v Zimbabwe
131/94 Ousman Manjang v Gambia
137/94, 139/94, 154/96, 161/97 International PEN, Constitutional Rights Project, Interights (on behalf of Ken Saro-Wiwa Jr), Civil Liberties Organisation v Nigeria
138/94 International PEN (on behalf of Senn and Sangare) v Côte d'Ivoire
142/94 Muthuthirin Njoka v Kenya
162/97 Mouvement des Réfugiés Mauritaniens au Sénégal v Senegal
198/97 SOS Esclaves v Mauritania

(B) Resolutions

Resolution on the Right to Recourse Procedure and Fair Trial (1992, 11th Session)
Resolution on Nigeria (1994, 16th Session)
Resolution on the Gambia (1994, 16th Session)
Resolution on Sudan (1995, 17th Session)
Resolution on Nigeria (1995, 17th Session)
Resolution on Nigeria's Return to Democratic System (1998, 24th Session)
Resolution on the Extension of the Mandate of the Special Rapporteur on Prisons and Conditions of Detention in Africa (1999, 25th Session)

Article 7 (Fair Trial)

(A) Communications

6/88 Dr Kodj Kofi v Ghana
13/88 Hadjali Mohamed v Algeria
16/88, 17/88, 18/88 Comité Culturel pour la Démocratie au Benin, Badjoume Hilaire, El Hadj Boubacar Diawara v Benin
25/89, 47/40, 56/91, 100/93 Free Legal Assistance Group, Lawyers' Committee for Human Rights, Union Interafricaine des droits de l'homme, Les Temoins de Jehovah v Zaire
27/89, 46/ 91, 49/91, 99/93 Organisation Mondiale Contre la Torture and Association Internationale des Juristes Democrates, Commission Internationale des Juristes, Union Interafricaine des Droits de l'Homme v Rwanda
31/89 Maria Baes v Zaire
39/90 Annette Pagnoulle (on behalf of Abdoulaye Mazou) v Cameroon
40/90 Bob Ngozi Njoku v Egypt

53/91 Alberto Capitao v Tanzania
59/91 Embga Mekongo Louis v Cameroon
60/91 Constitutional Rights Project (in respect of Wahab Akamu, G Adega and others) v Nigeria
64/92, 68/92, 78/92 Krishna Achuthan (on behalf of Aleke Banda), Amnesty International (on behalf of Orton and Vera Chirwa), Amnesty International (on behalf of Orton and Vera Chirwa) v Malawi
65/92 Ligue Camerounaise des Droits de l'Homme v Cameroon
70/92 Ibrahima Dioumessi, Sekou Kande, Ousmane Kaba v Guinea
71/92 Rencontre Africaine pour la Defense des Droits de l'Hommes v Zambia
74/92 Commission Nationale des Droits de l'Homme et des Libertés v Chad
87/93 Constitutional Rights Project (in respect of Zamani Lakwot and six others) v Nigeria
90/93 Paul S Haye v the Gambia
92/93 International PEN (in respect of Kemal al-Jazouli) v Sudan
97/93 John K Modise v Botswana
101/93 Civil Liberties Organization (in respect of the Nigeria Bar Association) v Nigeria
103/93 Alhassan Abubakar v Ghana
104/94, 109–126/94 Centre for Independence of Judges and Lawyers v Algeria and Others
105/93, 128/94, 130/94, 152/96 Media Rights Agenda, Constitutional Rights Project, Media Rights Agenda and Constitutional Rights Project v Nigeria
129/94 Civil Liberties Organization v Nigeria
137/94, 139/94, 154/96, 161/97 International PEN, Constitutional Rights Project, Interights (on behalf of Ken Saro-Wiwa Jr), Civil Liberties Organisation v Nigeria
138/94 International PEN (on behalf of Senn and Sangare) v Côte d'Ivoire
144/95 William A Courson v Equatorial Guinea
159/96 Union Interafricaine des Droits de l'Homme, Federation Internationale des Ligues des Droits de l'Homme, Rencontre Africaine des Droits de l'Homme, Organisation Nationale des Droits de l'Homme au Sénégal and Association Malienne des Droits de l'Homme v Angola
198/97 SOS Esclaves v Mauritania
212/98 Amnesty International v Zambia
221/98 Alfred B Cudjoe v Ghana

(B) Resolutions

Resolution on the Right to Recourse Procedure and Fair Trial (1992, 11th Session)
Resolution on Nigeria (1994, 16th Session)
Resolution on the Gambia (1994, 16th Session)
Resolution on Nigeria (1995, 17th Session)
Resolution on Burundi (1996, 19th Session)

Article 8

(A) Communications

25/89, 47/40, 56/91, 100/93 Free Legal Assistance Group, Lawyers' Committee for Human Rights, Union Interafricaine des droits de l'homme, Les Temoins de Jehovah v Zaire
136/94 William Courson v Zimbabwe
212/98 Amnesty International v Zambia

(B) Resolutions

Resolution on Nigeria (1995, 17th Session)

Article 9 (Freedom of Expression)

(A) Communications

25/89, 47/40, 56/91, 100/93 Free Legal Assistance Group, Lawyers' Committee for Human Rights, Union Interafricaine des droits de l'homme, Les Temoins de Jehovah v Zaire
64/92, 68/92, 78/92 Krishna Achuthan (on behalf of Aleke Banda), Amnesty International (on behalf of Orton and Vera Chirwa), Amnesty International (on behalf of Orton and Vera Chirwa) v Malawi
65/92 Ligue Camerounaise des Droits de l'Homme v Cameroon
83/92, 88/93, 91/93 Jean Y Degli (on behalf of N Bikagni), Union Interafricaine des droits de l'homme, Commission Internationale des Juristes v Togo
86/93 M S Cessay v The Gambia
93/93 International PEN v Ghana
102/93 Constitutional Rights Project and Civil Liberties Organisation v Nigeria
105/93, 128/94, 130/94, 152/96 Media Rights Agenda, Constitutional Rights Project, Media Rights Agenda and Constitutional Rights Project v Nigeria
136/94 William Courson v Zimbabwe
137/94, 139/94, 154/96, 161/97 International PEN, Constitutional Rights Project, Interights (on behalf of Ken Saro-Wiwa Jr), Civil Liberties Organisation v Nigeria
144/95 William A Courson v Equatorial Guinea
198/97 SOS Esclaves v Mauritania
212/98 Amnesty International v Zambia

(B) Resolutions

Resolution on Nigeria (1994, 16th Session))
Resolution on the Human Rights Situation in Africa (1994, 16th Session)

Resolution on Nigeria (1995, 17th Session)
Resolution on the Gambia (1995, 17th Session)

Article 10

(A) Communications

25/89, 47/40, 56/91, 100/93 Free Legal Assistance Group, Lawyers' Committee for Human Rights, Union Interafricaine des droits de l'homme, Les Temoins de Jehovah v Zaire
64/92, 68/92, 78/92 Krishna Achuthan (on behalf of Aleke Banda), Amnesty International (on behalf of Orton and Vera Chirwa), Amnesty International (on behalf of Orton and Vera Chirwa) v Malawi
74/92 Commission Nationale des Droits de l'Homme et des Libertés v Chad
101/93 Civil Liberties Organization (in respect of the Nigeria Bar Association) v Nigeria
135/94 Kenya Human Rights Commission v Kenya
136/94 William Courson v Zimbabwe
137/94, 139/94, 154/96, 161/97 International PEN, Constitutional Rights Project, Interights (on behalf of Ken Saro-Wiwa Jr), Civil Liberties Organisation v Nigeria
144/95 William A Courson v Equatorial Guinea
212/98 Amnesty International v Zambia

(B) Resolutions

Resolution on the Right to Freedom of Association (1992, 11th Session)
Resolution on Nigeria (1995, 17th Session)
Resolution on the Gambia (1995, 17th Session)

Article 11

(A) Communications

136/94 William Courson v Zimbabwe
25/89, 47/40, 56/91, 100/93 Free Legal Assistance Group, Lawyers' Committee for Human Rights, Union Interafricaine des droits de l'homme, Les Temoins de Jehovah v Zaire
137/94, 139/94, 154/96, 161/97 International PEN, Constitutional Rights Project, Interights (on behalf of Ken Saro-Wiwa Jr), Civil Liberties Organisation v Nigeria
198/97 SOS Esclaves v Mauritania

(B) Resolutions

Resolution on the Gambia (1995, 17th Session)

Article 12

(A) Communications

8/88 Nziwa Buyingo v Uganda

25/89, 47/40, 56/91, 100/93 Free Legal Assistance Group, Lawyers' Committee for Human Rights, Union Interafricaine des droits de l'homme, Les Temoins de Jehovah v Zaire

27/89, 46/ 91, 49/91, 99/93 Organisation Mondiale Contre la Torture and Association Internationale des Juristes Democrates, Commission Internationale des Juristes, Union Interafricaine des Droits de l'Homme v Rwanda

33/89 Simon B Ntaka v Lesotho

71/92 Rencontre Africaine pour la Defense des Droits de l'Hommes v Zambia

73/92 Mohamed L Diakite v Gabon

103/93 Alhassan Abubakar v Ghana

159/96 Union Interafricaine des Droits de l'Homme, Federation Internationale des Ligues des Droits de l'Homme, Rencontre Africaine des Droits de l'Homme, Organisation Nationale des Droits de l'Homme au Sénégal and Association Malienne des Droits de l'Homme v Angola

162/97 Mouvement des Réfugiés Mauritaniens au Sénégal v Senegal

212/98 Amnesty International v Zambia

(B) Resolutions

Resolution on the Human Rights Situation in Africa (1994, 16th Session)

Resolution on Sudan (1995, 17th Session)

Resolution on Nigeria (1995, 17th Session)

Resolution on Burundi (1996, 19th Session)

Resolution on Zaire (1997, 21st Session)

Article 13

(A) Communications

44/90 Peoples' Democratic Organization for Independence and Socialism v The Gambia

75/92 Katangese Peoples' Congress v Zaire

83/92, 88/93, 91/93 Jean Y Degli (on behalf of N Bikagni), Union Interafricaine des Droits de l'Homme, Commission Internationale des Juristes v Togo

97/93 John K Modise v Botswana

102/93 Constitutional Rights Project and Civil Liberties Organisation v Nigeria
144/95 William A Courson v Equatorial Guinea
212/98 Amnesty International v Zambia

(B) Resolutions

Resolution on South Africa (1994, 15th Session)
Resolution on the Gambia (1994, 16th Session)
Resolution on the Military (1994, 16th Session)
Resolution on Nigeria (1994, 16th Session)
Resolution on the Human Rights Situation in Africa (1994, 16th Session)
Resolution on Nigeria (1995, 17th Session)
Resolution on the Gambia (1995, 17th Session)
Resolution on Liberia (1996, 19th Session)
Resolution on Electoral Process and Participatory Governance (1996, 19th Session)
Resolution on Nigeria's Return to Democratic System (1998, 24th Session)
Resolution on the Situation in Comoros (1999, 25th Session)
Resolution on the Situation in Niger (1999, 25th Session)

Article 14 (Right to Property)

(A) Communications

8/88 Nziwa Buyingo v Uganda
10/88 Getachew Abebe v Ethiopia
25/89, 47/40, 56/91, 100/93 Free Legal Assistance Group, Lawyers' Committee for Human Rights, Union Interafricaine des droits de l'homme, Les Temoins de Jehovah v Zaire
28/89 Association Internationale des Juristes Democrates v Ethiopia
71/92 Rencontre Africaine pour la Defense des Droits de l'Hommes v Zambia
73/92 Mohamed L Diakite v Gabon
105/93, 128/94, 130/94, 152/96 Media Rights Agenda, Constitutional Rights Project, Media Rights Agenda and Constitutional Rights Project v Nigeria
142/94 Muthuthirin Njoka v Kenya
159/96 Union Interafricaine des Droits de l'Homme, Federation Internationale des Ligues des Droits de l'Homme, Rencontre Africaine des Droits de l'Homme, Organisation Nationale des Droits de l'Homme au Sénégal and Association Malienne des Droits de l'Homme v Angola

(B) Resolutions

. . .

Article 15 (Right to Work)

(A) Communications

3/88 Centre for the Independence of Judges and Lawyers v Yugoslavia
12/88 Mohamed El-Nekheily v OAU
39/90 Annette Pagnoulle (on behalf of Abdoulaye Mazou) v Cameroon
127/94 Sana Dumbuya v The Gambia
159/96 Union Interafricaine des Droits de l'Homme, Federation Internationale des Ligues des Droits de l'Homme, Rencontre Africaine des Droits de l'Homme, Organisation Nationale des Droits de l'Homme au Sénégal and Association Malienne des Droits de l'Homme v Angola
162/97 Mouvement des Réfugiés Mauritaniens au Sénégal v Senegal
198/97 SOS Esclaves v Mauritania
221/98 Alfred B Cudjoe v Ghana

(B) Resolutions

. . .

Article 16

(A) Communications

25/89, 47/40, 56/91, 100/93 Free Legal Assistance Group, Lawyers' Committee for Human Rights, Union Interafricaine des droits de l'homme, Les Temoins de Jehovah v Zaire
105/93, 128/94, 130/94, 152/96 Media Rights Agenda, Constitutional Rights Project, Media Rights Agenda and Constitutional Rights Project v Nigeria
136/94 William Courson v Zimbabwe
137/94, 139/94, 154/96, 161/97 International PEN, Constitutional Rights Project, Interights (on behalf of Ken Saro-Wiwa Jr), Civil Liberties Organisation v Nigeria

(B) Resolutions

. . .

Article 17

(A) Communications

25/89, 47/40, 56/91, 100/93 Free Legal Assistance Group, Lawyers' Committee for Human Rights, Union Interafricaine des droits de l'homme, Les Temoins de Jehovah v Zaire

72/92 Bamidele Aturu v Nigeria
159/96 Union Interafricaine des Droits de l'Homme, Federation Internationale des Ligues des Droits de l'Homme, Rencontre Africaine des Droits de l'Homme, Organisation Nationale des Droits de l'Homme au Sénégal and Association Malienne des Droits de l'Homme v Angola

(B) Resolutions

Resolution on Human and Peoples' Rights Education (1993, 14th Session)

Article 18

(A) Communications

71/92 Rencontre Africaine pour la Defense des Droits de l'Hommes v Zambia
108/93 Monja Joana v Madagascar
142/94 Muthuthirin Njoka v Kenya
159/96 Union Interafricaine des Droits de l'Homme, Federation Internationale des Ligues des Droits de l'Homme, Rencontre Africaine des Droits de l'Homme, Organisation Nationale des Droits de l'Homme au Sénégal and Association Malienne des Droits de l'Homme v Angola
212/98 Amnesty International v Zambia

(B) Resolutions

Resolution on the Human Rights Situation in Africa (1994, 16th Session)
Resolution on the Ratification of the Convention on Anti-Personnel Mines (1998, 24th Session)
Resolution on the Ratification of the African Charter on the Rights and Welfare of the Child (1999, 25th Session)
Resolution on the Designation of a Special Rapporteur on the Rights of Women in Africa (1999, 25th Session)

Article 19

(A) Communications

. . .

(B) Resolutions

. . .

Article 20

(A) Communications

24/89 Union Nationale de Liberation de Cabinda v Angola
75/92 Katangese Peoples' Congress v Zaire
102/93 Constitutional Rights Project and Civil Liberties Organisation v Nigeria
136/94 William Courson v Zimbabwe
144/95 William A Courson v Equatorial Guinea

(B) Resolutions

Resolution on the Military (1994, 16th Session)
Resolution on Nigeria (1994, 16th Session)
Resolution on the Gambia (1994, 16th Session)
Resolution on the Human Rights Situation in Africa (1994, 16th Session)
Resolution on Nigeria (1995, 17th Session)
Resolution on the Gambia (1995, 17th Session)
Resolution on Liberia (1996, 19th Session)
Resolution on Electoral Process and Participatory Governance (1996, 19th Session)
Resolution on Nigeria's Return to Democratic System (1998, 24th Session)
Resolution on the Situation in Comoros (1999, 25th Session)
Resolution on the Situation in Niger (1999, 25th Session)

Article 21

(A) Communications

. . .

(B) Resolutions

. . .

Article 22

(A) Communications

136/94 William Courson v Zimbabwe

(B) Resolutions

Resolution on the African Commission on Human and Peoples' Rights (1994, 15th Session)
Resolution on the Human Rights Situation in Africa (1994, 16th Session)

Article 23

(A) Communications

. . .

(B) Resolutions

. . .

Article 24

(A) Communications

136/94 William Courson v Zimbabwe

(B) Resolutions

. . .

Article 25

(A) Communications

. . .

(B) Resolutions

Resolution on Human and Peoples' Rights Education (1993, 14th Session)

Article 26

(A) Communications

129/94 Civil Liberties Organization v Nigeria

137/94, 139/94, 154/96, 161/97 International PEN, Constitutional Rights Project, Interights (on behalf of Ken Saro-Wiwa Jr), Civil Liberties Organisation v Nigeria

(B) Resolutions

Resolution on the Establishment of Committees on Human Rights or other Similar Organs at National, Regional or Sub-Regional Level (1988, 4th Session)

Resolution on the Gambia (1995, 17th Session)

Resolution on Liberia (1996, 19th Session)

Resolution on the Respect and the Strengthening of the Independence of the Judiciary (1996, 19th Session)

Resolution on the Role of Lawyers and Judges in Integration of the Charter and Enhancement of the Commission's Work in National and Sub-Regional Systems (1996, 19th Session)
Resolution on Burundi (1996, 19th Session)
Resolution on National Human Rights Institutions (1998, 24th Session)
Resolution on the Situation in Comoros (1999, 25th Session)
Resolution on the Situation in Niger (1999, 25th Session)

Article 27

(A) Communications

105/93, 128/94, 130/94, 152/96 Media Rights Agenda, Constitutional Rights Project, Media Rights Agenda and Constitutional Rights Project v Nigeria

(B) Resolutions

. . .

Article 28

(A) Communications

. . .

(B) Resolutions

. . .

Article 29

(A) Communications

. . .

(B) Resolutions

. . .

TABLE IV: COMMUNICATIONS AND RESOLUTIONS BY STATE PARTY

Algeria

13/88 Hadjali Mohamad v Algeria
104/94, 109–126/94 Centre for Independence of Judges and Lawyers v Algeria and Others

Angola

24/89 Union Nationale de Liberation de Cabinda v Angola
159/96 Union Interafricaine des Droits de l'Homme, Federation Internationale des Ligues des Droits de l'Homme, Rencontre Africaine des Droits de l'Homme, Organisation Nationale des Droits de l'Homme au Sénégal and Association Malienne des Droits de l'Homme v Angola

Benin

16/88, 17/88, 18/88 Comité Culturel pour la Démocratie au Benin, Badjoume Hilaire, El Hadj Boubacar Diawara v Benin

Resolution on Electoral Process and Participatory Governance (1996, 19th Session)

Botswana

97/93 John K Modise v Botswana

Burkina Faso

22/88 International PEN v Burkina Faso

Burundi

26/89 Austrian Committee Against Torture v Burundi

Resolution on Burundi (1996, 19th Session)

Cameroon

39/90 Annette Pagnoulle (on behalf of Abdoulaye Mazou) v Cameroon
59/91 Embga Mekongo Louis v Cameroon
65/92 Ligue Camerounaise des Droits de l'Homme v Cameroon
106/93 Amuh Joseph Vitine v Cameroon

Chad

55/91 International PEN v Chad
74/92 Commission Nationale des Droits de l'Homme et des Libertés v Chad

Comoros

Resolution on Electoral Process and Participatory Governance (1996, 19th Session)
Resolution on the Situation in Comoros (1999, 25th Session)

Côte d'Ivoire

138/94 International PEN (on behalf of Senn and Sangare) v Côte d'Ivoire

Egypt

40/90 Bob Ngozi Njoku v Egypt

Equatorial Guinea

144/95 William A Courson v Equatorial Guinea

Ethiopia

9/88 International Lawyers Committee for Family Reunification v Ethiopia
10/88 Getachew Abebe v Ethiopia
14/88 Dr Abd Eldayem A E Sanussi v Ethiopia
21/88 Centre Haitien des Liberté Publiques v Ethiopia
28/89 Association Internationale des Juristes Democrates v Ethiopia
29/89 Commission Française Justice et Paix v Ethiopia

Gabon

73/92 Mohamed L Diakite v Gabon

Gambia

44/90 Peoples' Democratic Organization for Independence and Socialism v The Gambia
86/93 M S Cessay v The Gambia
90/93 Paul S Haye v the Gambia
127/94 Sana Dumbuya v The Gambia
131/94 Ousman Manjang v Gambia

Resolution on The Gambia (1994, 16th Session)
Resolution on The Gambia (1995, 17th Session)

Ghana

4/88 Coordinating Secretary of the Free Citizens Convention v Ghana
6/88 Dr Kodj Kofi v Ghana
93/93 International PEN v Ghana
103/93 Alhassan Abubakar v Ghana
221/98 Alfred B Cudjoe v Ghana

Guinea

70/92 Ibrahim Dioumessi, Sekou Kande, Ousmane Kaba v Guinea

Guinea-Bissau

Resolution on the Peace Process in Guinea Bissau (1998, 24th Session)

Kenya

19/88 International PEN v Malawi, Ethiopia, Cameroon, Kenya
135/94 Kenya Human Rights Commission v Kenya
142/94 Muthuthirin Njoka v Kenya

Lesotho

33/89 Simon B Ntaka v Lesotho

Liberia

1/88 Frederick Korvah v Liberia

Resolution on Liberia (1996, 19th Session)

Madagascar

108/93 Monja Joana v Madagascar

Malawi

42/90 International PEN v Malawi
63/92 Congress for the Second Republic of Malawi v Malawi
64/92, 68/92, 78/92 Krishna Achuthan (on behalf of Aleke Banda), Amnesty International (on behalf of Orton and Vera Chirwa), Amnesty International (on behalf of Orton and Vera Chirwa) v Malawi

Mauritania

198/97 SOS Esclaves v Mauritania

Morocco

20/88 Austrian Committee Against Torture v Morocco
41/90 Andre Houver v Morocco

Niger

Resolution on the Situation in Niger (1999, 25th Session)

Nigeria

43/90 Union des Scholaires Nigeriens, Union Generale des Etudients Nigeriens au Benin v Nigeria
45/90 Civil Liberties Organisation v Nigeria

57/91 Tanko Bariga v Nigeria
60/91 Constitutional Rights Project (in respect of Wahab Akamu, G Adega and others) v Nigeria
62/91 Committee for the Defence of Human Rights (in respect of Ms Jennifer Madike) v Nigeria
67/91 Civil Liberties Organization v Nigeria
72/92 Bamidele Aturu v Nigeria
87/93 Constitutional Rights Project (in respect of Zamani Lakwot and six others) v Nigeria
101/93 Civil Liberties Organization (in respect of the Nigeria Bar Association) v Nigeria
102/93 Constitutional Rights Project and Civil Liberties Organisation v Nigeria
105/93, 128/94, 130/94, 152/96 Media Rights Agenda, Constitutional Rights Project, Media Rights Agenda and Constitutional Rights Project v Nigeria
107/93 Academic Staff of Nigerian Universities v Nigeria
129/94 Civil Liberties Organization v Nigeria
137/94, 139/94, 154/96, 161/97 International PEN, Constitutional Rights Project, Interights (on behalf of Ken Saro-Wiwa Jr), Civil Liberties Organisation v Nigeria

Resolution on Nigeria (1994, 16th Session)
Resolution on Nigeria, (1995, 17th Session)
Resolution on Nigeria's Return to a Democratic System (1998, 24th Session)

Rwanda

27/89, 46/ 91, 49/91, 99/93 Organisation Mondiale Contre la Torture and Association Internationale des Juristes Democrates, Commission Internationale des Juristes, Union Interafricaine des Droits de l'Homme v Rwanda

Resolution on the Situation in Rwanda (1994, 15th Session)
Resolution on Rwanda (1994, 16th Session)

Senegal

162/97 Mouvement des Réfugiés Mauritaniens au Sénégal v Senegal

Seychelles

Resolution Concerning the Republic of Seychelles Refusal to Present its Initial Report (1999, 25th Session)

Sierra Leone

Resolution on Electoral Process and Participatory Governance (1996, 19th Session)

South Africa

Resolution on South Africa (1994, 15th Session)

Sudan

92/93 International PEN (in respect of Kemal al-Jazouli) v Sudan

Resolution on Sudan (1995, 17th Session)

Tanzania

53/91 Alberto Capitao v Tanzania
66/92 Lawyers Committee for Human Rights v Tanzania

Togo

35/89 Seyoum Ayele v Togo
83/92, 88/93, 91/93 Jean Y Degli (on behalf of N Bikagni), Union Interafricaine des droits de l'homme, Commission Internationale des Juristes v Togo

Tunisia

69/92 Amnesty International v Tunisia

Uganda

8/88 Nziwa Buyingo v Uganda

Zambia

11/88 Henry Kalenga v Zambia
71/92 Rencontre Africaine pour la Defense des Droits de l'Hommes v Zambia
212/98 Amnesty International v Zambia

Zaire

15/88 Mpaka-Nsusu Andre Alphonse v Zaire
25/89, 47/40, 56/91, 100/93 Free Legal Assistance Group, Lawyers' Committee for Human Rights, Union Interafricaine des droits de l'homme, Les Temoins de Jehovah v Zaire
31/89 Maria Baes v Zaire
75/92 Katangese Peoples' Congress v Zaire

Resolution on Zaire (1997, 21st Session)

Zimbabwe

136/94 William Courson v Zimbabwe

Seventh Annual Activity Report of the African Commission on Human and Peoples' Rights 1993–1994

Adopted on 27 April 1994
Covering the 14th and 15th Ordinary Sessions in Addis Ababa (1–10 December 1993 and Banjul (18–27 April 1994)
AHG/198 (XXX) REV. 2

I. ORGANISATION OF WORK

A. Period Covered by the Report

1. The Sixth Annual Activity Report of the African Commission on Human and Peoples' Rights was adopted by the Twenty-ninth Session of the Assembly of Heads of State and Government of the OAU in its Resolution AHG/Res. 227 (XXIX) Rev. 1. The present Report, the Seventh, covers the Fourteenth and Fifteenth Ordinary Sessions held in Addis Ababa, Ethiopia, from 1–10 December 1993 and in Banjul, The Gambia, from 18–27 April 1994 respectively.

B. Status of Ratification

2. By the 15th Session of the Commission all the members of the OAU, with the exception of Ethiopia, Swaziland and Eritrea, had ratified or acceded to the African Charter on Human and Peoples' Rights. The list of States and the dates of signature, ratification/adhesion and deposit of documents is attached as Annex I.

C. Sessions and Agenda

3. The Commission held two ordinary sessions since the adoption of its Sixth Annual Activity Report.

- the 14th Ordinary Session held in Addis Ababa, Ethiopia, 1–10 December, 1993;
- the 15th Ordinary Session held in Banjul, The Gambia, 18–27 April, 1994.

The Agenda for each of the two Sessions is contained respectively in Annexes II and III of this Report. The items on extra-judicial executions, human rights education and the Fourth World Conference on Women (Beijing 1995) were respectively proposed by the following NGOs: Amnesty International; The Decade for Human Rights Education and the Centre for the Development of Legal Resources and

Research, in accordance with Article 6(5)(a) of the Rules of Procedure of the Commission.

D. Composition and Participation

4. The terms of three Commissioners (Mr. Ali Mahmud Buhedma, Justice Moleleki D. Mokama and Mr. Alexis Gabou) expired and three new Commissioners, including a lady, were elected (Mrs. Vera Valentina Duarte Martins, Mr. Atsu Koffi Amega and Dr. Emmanuel Victor Dankwa) during the same 29th Ordinary Session of the Assembly of Heads of State and Government (Cairo, Egypt, 28–30 June 1993). The list of members of the Commission as from June 1993 is contained in Annex IV.

5. The following Commissioners attended the 14th Session:

(1) Prof. Isaac Nguema – Chairman,
(2) Prof. Mohamed Hatem Ben Salem – Vice-Chairman,
(3) Mr Sourahata B. S. Janneh,
(4) Justice Robert H. Kisanga,
(5) Dr. Ibrahim A. Badawi El-Sheikh,
(6) Prof. O. U. Umozurike,
(7) Mr. Youssoupha Ndiaye,
(8) Dr. Emmanuel V. O. Dankwa,
(9) Mrs. Vera Valentina D. M. Duarte Martins,
(10) Mr. Atsu Koffi Amega.
(Mr Alioune Blondin Beye was absent, with apology, on account of a mission for the UN.)

The following Commissioners attended the 15th Session:

(1) Prof. Isaac Nguema – Chairman,
(2) Prof. Mohamed Hatem Ben Salem – Vice-Chairman,
(3) Mr. Sourahata B. S. Janneh,
(4) Justice Robert H. Kisanga,
(5) Dr. Ibrahim A. Badawi El-Sheikh,
(6) Prof. O. U. Umozurike,
(7) Mr. Youssoupha Ndiaye,
(8) Dr. Emmanuel V. O. Dankwa,
(9) Mrs. Vera Valentina D. M. Duarte Martins.
(Messrs. Alioune Blondin Beye and Atsu Koffi Amega were absent with apologies.)

NGO participation was quite active and massive. That of Intergovernmental Organisations, although not quite as massive, was quite remarkable. Representatives of States Parties also attended the session.

E. Chairman and Vice-Chairman of the Commission

6. Professor Isaac Nguema and Professor Mohammed Hatem Ben Salem were elected Chairman and Vice-Chairman respectively at the 14th Session for a period of two years.

F. Adoption of the 7th Annual Activity Report

On 27 April 1994, the Commission considered and adopted its 7th Annual Activity Report.

II. ACTIVITIES OF THE COMMISSION

A. Consideration of Periodic Reports

8. Under Article 62, each State undertakes to submit a report every two years, on the legislative or other measures it is taking to give effect to the rights and freedoms guaranteed by the Charter. No State submitted a report at the 15th Session.

9. At its 14th Ordinary Session, the Commission considered the initial report submitted by Ghana under Article 62 of the Charter. It expressed its appreciation for the report and the presence of the representative of Ghana sent to present it and to undertake discussions with the Commission. The Commission acknowledge Ghana's preparedness to cooperate with the Commission in the application of the Charter.

10. Following the presentation, members of the Commission raised several questions which were answered by the representative who promised to provide more detailed information about some of the questions.

By the 15th Session, the following States had submitted their preliminary reports: Libya, Rwanda, Tunisia (9th Session), Egypt and Tanzania (11th Session), The Gambia, Senegal, Zimbabwe (12th Session), Togo, Nigeria (13th Session), Benin, Ghana, Cape Verde and Mozambique (14th Session). It follows that 38 States were yet to submit their preliminary reports (Annex V).

B. Promotional Activities

(i) Report of the Chairman

11. During the session, the Chairman informed the Commission of the response of the President of the Republic of Côte d'Ivoire to the message of condolence sent to him following the passing away of His Excellency Houphouet Boigny, First President of the Republic of Côte d'Ivoire.

12. As part of the activities undertaken from April to November 1993, the Chairman participated in the following symposia, seminars, workshops and conferences:

(1) The conference organized in Lisbon from 5–7 April 1993 on "the role of women in an interdependent world", by the North-South Centre of the Council of Europe and the Organization of African Unity.
(2) A lecturing visit on the anthropological bases of human rights in Africa, within the framework of a (DEA) doctoral thesis at the University of Paris I (Pantheon, Sorbonne) from 20 April to 24 May 1993.
(3) The meeting of the Permanent Consultative Committee on Security in Central Africa, held in Libreville from 30 August to 3 September 1993 under the auspices of the United Nations as a lecturer on the theme: "Democratisation, Human Rights and Stability in Central Africa".
(4) Lecture given within the framework of a (DEA) doctoral thesis on "Comparative French and French inspired Law and the Development of Law" on 13 May 1993 at the University of Paris V (René Descartes) on the theme: "African Human Rights".
(5) The Human Rights trainers workshop held Darda (Chad) from 22–27 November 1993 by the International Federation of Human Rights Leagues in co-operation with the Chadian Human Rights League, as a resource person.
(6) The fifth workshop organized by the International Commission of Jurists (ICJ), from 28–30 November 1993, in Addis Ababa, on the participation of NGOs in the work of the African Commission on Human and Peoples' Rights.

13. As regards research and publication, the Chairman published an article on the "African Commission on Human and Peoples' Rights (organization, mission, procedures and activities)" in the Review "Parlements et francophonie", issue No. 88–89 published in Paris.

14. During the period from 10 December 1993 to 17 April 1994, the Chairman participated in the following conferences, symposia, seminars and workshops:

(1) The seminar on the training of human rights trainers organized from 7–11 February 1994 by the Zairean Human Rights League and the International Human Rights Federation in Kinshasa.
(2) The meeting of experts on UNESCO/Commandant Cousteau's team organized by the Tri-Continental Institute for Parliamentary Democracy of La Laguna University at Santa Cruz de Tenerife from 25–26 February 1994 on the human rights of future generations. The meeting gave rise to the Universal Declaration of the Human Rights of Future Generations.
(3) The conference on Electoral Freedom and the international monitoring of elections, organized from 28 February to 2 March 1994 by the Tri Continental Institute for Parliamentary Democracy and Human Rights of La Laguna University and the National Assembly of Portugal. The conference resulted in the drafting of the Jorge Capinos International Convention on Electoral Freedom and the international monitoring of elections.
(4) The Action Forum colloquium organized by the North-South Centre of the Council of Europe, from 11–12 March 1994 in Lisbon (Portugal), on strategies

to be implemented in the area of human rights within the framework of North-South relations.

(5) The Sixth Workshop on the Participation of NGOs in the work of the African Commission on Human and Peoples' Rights organised by the International Commission of Jurists and the African Centre for Democracy and Human Rights Studies in Banjul from 15–17 April 1994.

15. During this same period the Chairman communicated information to students and researchers at the Universities of Montreal, Brussels and Portugal on the African Charter on Human and Peoples' Rights as well as on the studies he had just published on human rights and democracy in Africa.

16. With regard to publications, the Chairman undertook the following work:

(a) he ensured the supervision of the publication of the second edition of the Review of the African Commission on Human and Peoples' Rights which came out in April 1994;

(b) he sent in a presentation on the African Commission on Human and Peoples' Rights to the Preparatory Committee of the World Conference on Human Rights held in Vienna in June 1993. That paper was circulated under reference: A/CONF 157/PC/62/ADD.2 of 23 March 1993.

17. He briefed members of the Commission on the amount received as subvention from the Raoul Wallenberg Institute and how it was to be used in conformity with the 2-year agreement signed on 12 April 1993 between the Secretary to the Commission and the Raoul Wallenberg Institute. Members of the Commission were also informed of how the fax machines donated by the Raoul Wallenberg Institute to facilitate communication between them, on the one hand and between the latter and the Secretariat of the Commission as well as the other institutions concerned, on the other, during the inter-session, were to be acquired. Following the discussions held during the 15th Session, the representative of the Raoul Wallenberg Institute intimated that the Institute could bear part of the running costs of the fax machines on conditions that the latter be predetermined. The Chairman then informed members of the Commission of the expenses already incurred from the subvention granted by the Raoul Wallenberg Institute.

18. The Chairman reported on the progress of the discussions with Interights of London which had already received the sum of 75,000 ECUS from the Commission of the European Communities for assistance to the Commission, among other things. Interights had been requested to account for the use of that amount before offering any other services to the Commission.

19. The Chairman recalled the guidelines that members of the Commission could use in preparing periodic reports. He recommended that NGOs be involved in such an exercise by submitting an alternative, if need be, with particular emphasis on:

(1) the factors and difficulties impeding the implementation of the African Charter on Human and Peoples' Rights;

(2) the positive aspects of the reports;

(3) the main areas of concern;
(4) suggestions and recommendations.

20. To ensure a certain degree of transparency in the Commission's management, the Chairman requested members to copy correspondence dealing with Commission-related issues to the Secretary and Chairman respectively.

21. The Chairman finally informed the Commission of his contacts with officials of UNESCO and the E.C.A with a view to strengthening co-operation between the United Nations Agencies and the Commission.

22. He also pointed out that he was envisaging the establishment of relations of cooperation between the African Commission on Human and Peoples' Rights and the Tri-Continental Institute for Parliamentary Democracy and Human Rights of the La Laguna University (Santa Cruz Tenerife).

(ii) Activities of other Members of the Commission

23. The allocation of countries to respective Commissioners for the purpose of promotional activities is as shown in Annex VI of this Report.

During the inter-session, members of the Commission visited and/or carried out promotional activities in the following countries: Egypt (Dr. Ibrahim A. Badawi El-Sheikh), Tunisia (Prof. H. Ben Salem), Togo (Mr. Atsu K. Amega), Senegal (Mr. Youssoupha Ndiaye), Ghana (Dr. E. V. O. Dankwa), Cape Verde (Mrs. Vera V. D. M. Duarte-Martins), Nigeria (Prof. U. O. Umozurike), Tanzania (Mr. R. Kisanga), Guinea-Bissau (Mrs Vera V. D. M. Duarte-Martins), Uganda (Mr. R. Kisanga), Gabon (Prof. I. Nguema), The Gambia (Mr. S. B. Semega-Janneh), Zaire (Prof. I. Nguema), Chad (Prof. I. Nguema), Zimbabwe (Dr. Ibrahim A. Badawi El-Sheikh), Swaziland (Prof. U. O. Umozurike) and Lesotho (Prof. U. O. Umozurike).

(iii) Conference and Symposia Organized

24. During the two inter-sessions, the following seminars were organized and held:

(1) Seminar on State Reporting for the English Speaking Countries. The Seminar was organized in collaboration with the Raoul Wallenberg Institute and held in Harare, Zimbabwe, from 23–27 August 1993 with the participation of Dr. Ibrahim A. Badawi El-Sheikh.
(2) Seminar on Refugees and Internally Displaced Persons in Africa. The Seminar was organized in collaboration with the Southern Africa Centre for Research and Documentation and held in Harare, Zimbabwe, from 16–18 February 1994 with the participation of the following members of the Commission: Dr. Ibrahim A. Badawi El-Sheikh and Prof. H. Ben Salem. The conclusions of that seminar are hereto attached as Annex VII.
(3) The Fifth Workshop on NGO participation in the work of the African Commission. The workshop held in Addis Ababa, Ethiopia, from 28–30 November 1993 was organized by the International Commission of Jurists in

collaboration with the African Commission on Human and Peoples' Rights. The following one held in Banjul, The Gambia, from 15–17 April 1994, was also organized by the International Commission of Jurists with the collaboration of the African Commission and the African Centre for Democracy and Human Rights Studies. It was attended by the following members of the Commission: Prof. I. Nguema, Prof. Hatem Ben Salem, Mrs. Vera Duarte-Martins, Dr. E. V. O. Dankwa, Prof. U. O. Umozurike, Mr. S. B. Semega-Janneh, Mr. R. Kisanga and Mr. A. K. Amega.

(4) Seminar on State Reporting for Francophone, Arabophone and Lusophone countries held in Tunis, Tunisia, from 24–27 May 1994 with the participation of Prof. Ben Salem and the collaboration of the Raoul Wallenberg Institute.

(iv) Programme of Action

25. The Commission agreed to organize and hold the following seminars:

(1) Seminar on Fair Trial to be organized in collaboration with the Arab Lawyers Union and which will be held in Cairo at a date to be determined.
(2) Seminar on Human rights Education in South Africa to be organized in collaboration with the South African Lawyers Committee for Human Rights and which will be held in South Africa at a date to be determined.
(3) Seminar on the Africa Charter and the Status of Women to be held in Banjul, The Gambia, at a date to be determined.
(4) Seminar on Non-Formal Education and Popular Participation.

26. Furthermore, the Commission appointed its Vice-Chairman, Prof. Mohamed H. Ben Salem, as Special Rapporteur on Extra-judicial Executions in Africa. For the time being, he was mainly to focus attention on the situation in Rwanda.

(v) Regional and International Co-operation

(a) World Conference on Human Rights

27. As a contribution to the proceedings of the Fourth Session of the preparatory Committee of the World Conference on Human Rights Held in Geneva, from 19–30 April 1993, Professor Nguema sent in a paper on the organization and functioning of the Commission, its promotional and protective activities in the area of human and peoples' rights, its role of interpreting the African Charter on Human and Peoples' Rights as well as on the follow-up procedure applicable before the Commission.

The contribution was highly appreciated by the Preparatory Committee.

The outgoing Chairman of the Commission Dr. Ibrahim A. Badawi El-Sheik represented the Commission in the said Conference (Vienna, Austria, June 1993).

He presented a paper on the African Commission as requested by the Commission. He made several statements before the said Conference. He briefed the 14th Session of the Commission on the outcome of the said Conference, in particular about the Final Declaration and Programme of Action of the Vienna Conference. He underlined the importance of the follow-up of the matters considered by the Vienna Conference and referred also to several activities undertaken in relation to the World Conference on Human Rights.

(b) Visit of H.E. Mr. Ibrahima Fall, United Nations Under-Secretary General for Human Rights to the African Commission on Human and peoples' Rights (21–25 April 1994)

(a) During the 15th Ordinary Session held in Banjul, The Gambia, the Commission played host to His Excellency Mr. Ibrahima Fall, United Nations Under-Secretary General for Human Rights.

During his working visit, H.E. Mr. Ibrahima Fall held lengthy discussions with members of the Commission on the state of cooperation between the Human Rights Centre and the Commission since the latter's establishment.

(b) After considering the functioning and essential needs of the Commission, the parties exchanged views on ways and means of improving the latter's performance in the discharge of its human rights promotional and protective activities. In that regard, the parties jointly identified the areas in which the Human Rights Centre could assist the Commission with financial or other resources. practical ways and means were determined to that effect. The two parties agreed to spare no efforts in enhancing cooperation between their respective institutions and expressed gratification about the positive outcome of their meeting.

(c) The UN Centre for Human Rights organized a Regional Seminar on the Drafting and Preparation of Periodic Reports in Abidjan, Côte d'Ivoire from 20–24 June 1994. The African Commission which was invited was represented at the seminar by Prof. Ben Salem.

(d) The Commission decided to strengthen cooperation with national human rights NGOs especially through the regular exchange of information on the promotion and protection of human rights within States Parties in which such NGOs operate. That would enable the Commission to benefit from the assistance of NGOs for certain field investigations in areas it cannot itself visit.

(vi) Publications

28. The second edition of the Review of the African Commission on Human and Peoples' Rights came out on 15 April 1994 thanks to the assistance of the African Society for International and Comparative Law and the diligence of the drafting committee and its Chairman. The members of the Commission were urged to make available to the Chairman of the Drafting Committee, articles and other contributions for the following edition of the Review which was to be published in October 1994.

29. As regards the proposed publication of a quarterly newsletter and brochure of the Commission, it was to be done in English, French and Arabic. Prof. Ben Salem was entrusted with exploring its feasibility and ensuring its supervision in Tunis (Tunisia).

C. Administrative and Financial Matters

(i) The OAU Budget

30. The budget allocated by the OAU to the Commission for the 1993/1994 financial year is as follows:

Code	Description	Appropriations 1992/1993	Actual Expenditure 1991/1992	Appropriations 1993/94	Increase (Decrease)
100	Established Posts	85,614	69,336	101,771	32,435
101	Post Adjustment	23,942	12,397	21,182	8,785
102	Temporary Assistant	1,000	1,023	1,500	477
103	Overtime Payments	250	276	250	−26
104	Commissioners Honorarium	55,000	34,000	33,000	−1,000
204–212	Common Staff Costs	117,375	43,777	79,098	35,321
300	Official Missions	20,000	18,599	20,000	1,401
401–406	Maintenance Costs	19,000	13,700	16,500	2,800
501–504	Communication Costs	7,000	6,465	6,500	35
600–610	Supplies and Services	12,700	44,596	16,000	−28,596
800	Meetings	160,000	188,438	135,000	−53,438
	TOTAL	501,881	432,607	430,801	−1,806

(ii) Subventions from the United Nations Centre for Human Rights

31. The Secretariat of the Commission, as at the date of 7 December 1993, received an initial transfer of 35,000 dollars as part of the subvention of 71,300 dollars granted by letter of 22 July 1993 and earmarked for the following:

(a)	*Strengthening of the Documentation Centre*	
	1 – Library	$7,500
	2 – Printing of the Charter	$7,500
(b)	*Thematic Seminar* (20%)	$14,000
(c)	*Regional Seminar* (20%)	$18,000
(d)	*Freelance Support Staff*	$24,000
	Total	$71,300

The participation of 4 members of the Commission in the Seminar on Refugees and Displaced Persons held in February 1994 at Harare was financed by this Project. Moreover, the Secretariat of the Commission has already secured the services of a Documentalist and a Programme Officer within the framework of the Project for a period of eleven months.

32. Anticipated Subvention of 214,285 Dollars: Contacts are still under way with the United Nations Centre for the release of that subsidy which should be used for the computerisation of the secretariat and the enhancement of promotional and protective activities.

(iii) Assistance from the Raoul Wallenberg Institute

33. The details relating to the financial assistance from Raoul Wallenberg Institute as per the agreement of 28 May 1993 are as follows:

(1) Promotional activities carried out by members of the Commission:	SEK 250,000
– World Conference on Human Rights	SEK 38,000
– Umozurike (Swaziland and Lesotho)	SEK 46,000
– Umozurike (Nigeria and Cameroun)	SEK 40,000
Total	SEK 124,000
Balance	SEK 126,000
(2) Printing of the Review of the African Commission on Human and Peoples' Rights:	SEK 100,000
Printing of the Review of the African Society of International and Comparative Law:	SEK 100,000
Balance 000,000.	
(3) Faxes for the members of the Commission	SEK 65,000

Ben Salem	SEK 25,000
Janneh	SEK 7,000
Badawi	SEK 25,000
Total	SEK 57,000
Balance	SEK 8,000

(4) Emergency Missions: SEK 185,000
Balance SEK 185,000
Used Amount in Total SEK 281,000
Balance in Total SEK 319,000 (Eqv. USD 39,000).

(iv) Commission of the European Communities

34. The Secretariat of the Commission received in two instalments, dated 6 February 1990 and 31 December 1992 respectively, a subvention of US$ 54,811.57 (46,851.05 dollars + 7,960.52 dollars) from the Commission of the European Communities. The subvention was earmarked to cover the publication costs for the review, the annual activity reports of the Commission, as well as provide for the media coverage of the sessions of the Commission.

D. Observers

35. In accordance with the provisions of Rules 76 and 77 of its Rules of Procedure, the Commission granted observer status to two NGOs, i.e. the Community Legal Resource and Advice Centre, Lesotho and the Botswana Centre for Human Rights.

The Organizations which enjoy observer status are indicated in Annex VIII of this report.

E. Protective Activities

36. At its 14th and 15th Sessions, the Commission received 33 communications under Article 55 of the African Charter. That brought the total number of communications received by the Commission to 136. Those were communications from sources other than States. With regard to those communications, the Commission took measures in accordance with the provisions of the African Charter and the Commission's Rules of Procedure. The Commission also followed up on old communications. The communications were examined in closed meetings. It should be noted that the Commission completed the consideration of 78 communications including two which were submitted to the Assembly of heads of State and Government. 58 communications are still pending.

37. In accordance with Article 59 of the African Charter, the details of the above-mentioned communications are contained in Annex IX.

F. Resolutions of the 14th and 15th Sessions and Press Communique

38. During the 14th Session, the Commission adopted two resolutions respectively, on:

(a) Human Rights Education.
(b) Promotion and Respect of International Humanitarian Law and Human and Peoples' Rights.

The text of these two resolutions is attached to this report (Annexes X and XI).

During its 15th session, the Commission adopted a resolution on the situation in Rwanda (Annex XII) and issued a press communique (Annex XIII). The Commission also adopted a resolution on South Africa which is hereto attached as Annex XIV.

G. Adoption of the Report by the Assembly of Heads of State and Government

39. Following the consideration of this Report, the Assembly of Heads of State and Government adopted a resolution by which it took note of it and authorized its publication; the Assembly also decided to set up an intergovernmental committee of experts to consider the possibility of creating an African Court on Human and Peoples' Rights. The text of this resolution is appended to this report as Annex XV.

ANNEX I

African Charter on Human and Peoples' Rights
List of Countries which have Signed, Ratified or Acceded to the Charter

No.	Country	Date of Signature	Date of Ratification/ Adhesion	Date Deposited
1.	Algeria	10/04/86	01/03/87	20/03/87
2.	Angola		02/03/90	09/10/90
3.	Benin		20/01/86	25/02/86
4.	Botswana		17/07/86	22/07/86
5.	Burundi		28/07/80	30/08/89
6.	Burkina Faso	05/03/84	06/07/84	21/09/84
7.	Cameroon	23/07/87	20/06/89	18/09/89
8.	Cape Verde	31/03/86	02/06/87	06/08/87
9.	Central African Republic		26/04/86	27/07/86
10.	Chad	29/05/86	09/10/86	11/11/86
11.	Comoros		01/06/86	18/07/86
12.	Congo	27/11/81	09/12/82	17/01/83
13.	Côte d'Ivoire		06/01/92	31/03/92
14.	Djibouti	20/12/91	11/11/91	20/12/91
15.	Egypt	16/11/81	20/03/84	03/04/84
16.	Equatorial Guinea	18/08/86	07/04/86	18/08/86
17.	Eritrea			
18.	Ethiopia			
19.	Gabon	26/02/82	20/02/86	26/06/86
20.	Gambia	11/02/83	08/06/83	13/03/83
21.	Ghana		24/01/89	01/03/89
22.	Guinea	09/12/81	16/02/82	13/05/82
23.	Guinea-Bissau		04/12/85	06/03/86
24.	Kenya		23/01/92	10/02/92
25.	Lesotho	07/03/84	10/02/92	27/02/92
26.	Liberia	31/01/83	04/08/82	29/12/82
27.	Libya	30/05/85	19/07/86	26/03/87
28.	Madagascar		09/03/92	19/03/92
29.	Malawi	23/02/90	17/11/89	23/02/90
30.	Mali	13/11/81	21/12/81	22/01/82
31.	Mauritania	25/02/82	14/06/86	26/06/86
32.	Mauritius	27/02/92	19/06/92	07/07/92
33.	Mozambique		22/02/89	07/03/90
34.	Namibia		30/07/92	16/09/92
35.	Niger	09/07/86	15/07/86	21/07/86
36.	Nigeria	31/08/82	22/06/83	27/07/83
37.	Rwanda	11/11/81	15/07/83	22/07/83
38.	Sahrawi Arab Dem. Rep.	10/04/86	02/05/86	23/05/86
39.	Sao Tome & Principe		23/05/86	28/07/86
40.	Senegal	23/09/81	13/08/82	25/10/82
41.	Seychelles		13/04/92	30/04/92

No.	Country	Date of Signature	Date of Ratification/ Adhesion	Date Deposited
42.	Sierra Leone	27/08/81	21/09/83	27/01/84
43.	Somalia	26/02/82	31/07/85	20/03/86
44.	Sudan	03/09/82	18/02/86	11/03/86
45.	Swaziland			
46.	Togo	20/02/82	05/11/82	22/11/82
47.	Tunisia		16/03/83	22/04/83
48.	Uganda	18/08/86	10/05/86	27/05/86
49.	Tanzania	31/05/82	18/02/84	09/03/84
50.	Zaire	23/07/87	20/07/87	28/07/87
51.	Zambia	17/01/83	19/01/84	02/02/84
52.	Zimbabwe	20/02/86	30/05/86	12/06/86

ADOPTED: by the 18th Session of the Assembly of Heads of State and Government, June 1981
REQUIRES: ratification or accession by a simple majority of Member States, to come into force
ENTERED INTO FORCE: 21st day of October 1986
DEPOSITED: with the United Nations on 10 September 1991, No. 26363

ANNEX II

Agenda of the Fourteenth Ordinary Session

1. Opening Ceremony
2. Swearing-in of the the Newly Elected Members of the Commission
3. Election of the Chairman and the Vice-Chairman of the Commission
4. Adoption of the Agenda
5. Organisation of Work:
   (a) Appointment of the Rapporteur
   (b) Working Hours
   (c) Programme of Work
6. Observers:
   (a) Consideration of Applications for Observer Status
   (b) Relationship with Observers
7. Consideration of Periodic Reports
8. Promotional Activities

9. Administrative and Financial Matters:
   (a) Report of the Chairman
   (b) Report of the Secretary to the Commission
   (c) Implementation of the Recommendations of the Preceding Sessions
10. Protective Activities
11. Working Procedures of the Commission:
    (a) Consideration of Amendments to the Rules of Procedure
    (b) Consideration of Article 58 of the Charter
12. Report on OAU Activities Relevant to the Commission
13. Date, Venue and Agenda of the Fifteenth Session
14. Any Other Business
15. Adoption of the Report of the Fourteenth Session
16. Final Communiqué and Closing Ceremony

ANNEX III

Agenda of the Fifteenth Ordinary Session

1. Opening Ceremony
2. Adoption of the Agenda
3. Organization of Work
   (a) Appointment of the Rapporteur of the Session
   (b) Appointment of the Rapporteur to Prepare the Seventh Annual Activity Report
   (c) Working Hours
   (d) Programme of Work
4. Observers
   (a) Consideration of Applications for Observer Status.
   (b) Relationship with Observers
5. Consideration of the Initial Report Submitted by Mozambique
6. Promotional activities
   (a) Report of Activities by Members of the Commission
   (b) Consideration of Extra-judicial Executions
   (c) Creation of an African Court of Human and Peoples' Rights
   (d) Fourth World Conference on Women (1995) and Setting-up of a Working Group to Prepare the Commission's Declaration
   (e) The Organization of Forthcoming Seminars and Conferences
   (f) The Regional Seminar on the Drafting and Preparation of Periodic Reports

(g) Publication of the Commission's Review and Newsletter
(h) Funding of the Publication of Minutes and Periodic Reports
(i) Report of the Seminar on the Protection of Refugees and Internally Displaced Persons in Africa

7. Protective Activities
8. Administrative and Financial Matters

(a) Report of the Chairman
(b) Report of the Secretary to the Commission
(c) Implementation of the Recommendation of the Previous Sessions
(d) Draft Rules on Contracts of Consultants

9. Working Procedures of the Commission

(a) Consideration of Amendments to the Rules of Procedure
(b) Examination of Article 58 of the Charter

10. Report on the Activities of OAU Relevant to the Commission
11. Dates, Venue and Draft Agenda of the Sixteenth Session
12. Preparation of:

(a) Sessional Report
(b) Annual Activity Report
(c) Final Communiqué

13. Adoption of the Report
14. Adoption of the Seventh Annual Activity Report
15. Final Communiqué and Closing Ceremony

ANNEX IV

List of Addresses of Members of the African Commission on Human and Peoples' Rights

1. Mr. Isaac NGUEMA — Chairman
BP 962
LIBREVILLE/GABON
Tel Office: (241) 732420
Tel Res: (241) 732027
Telex: 5255 GO
Fax: (241) 760993

2. Mr. Mohammed Hatem Ben SALEM — Vice-Chairman
1 Rue de Naplouse
BP 219, Lamanouba 2010
TUNIS/TUNISIE
Tel Office: (2161) 520270
Fax: (2166) 520270

3. Mr. Atsu-Koffi AMEGA — Member
BP 1262
LOME/TOGO
Tel: (228) 213396
Fax: (228) 213974
Telex: 5239

4. Mr. Alioune Blondin BEYE — Member
UNAVEM II
Vila Espa
PO Box 5185, Central Post Office
LUANDA/ANGOLA
Tel: (2442) 341882/341824 (Ext. 201/342)
(1212) 9633011 (Ext. 201/342)
Fax: (2442) 341882/341824 (Ext. 309
(1212) 9631951
Fax (Lusaka): (2601) 260766 (Direct)
(2601) 294415 (Centre de Conférence)

5. Mr. Emmanuel Victor Oware DANKWA — Member
Faculty of Law
University of Ghana
PO Box 70
LEGON/GHANA
FAX: (233) 21222621 [*or*] (23321) 774338

6. Mr. Sourahata Baboucar Semega JANNEH — Member
15 Hagan Street
PO Box 212
BANJUL/THE GAMBIA
Tel Office: (220) 228174
Tel Res: (220) 495117
Telex: (996) 2216 GV (NOVOTEL)

7. Mr. Robert Habesh KISANGA — Member
Court of Appeal
PO Box 9004
DAR-ES-SALAAM/TANZANIA
Tel Office: (25551) 27843/26011
Telex: (989) 41848 RAC TZ

8. Mrs Vera DUARTE MARTINS — Member
Supremo Tribunal de Justiça
CP 117
PRAIA/CAP VERT
Tel Res: (23861) 2137
Tel Office: (23861) 5809
Fax: (23861) 4519 MJ (PT)

9. Mr. Youssoupha NDIAYE — Member
Président du Conseil Constitutionnel
Ancien Musée Dynamique
DAKAR/SENEGAL
Tel Office: (01) 224450
Tel Res: (01) 227257
Telex: (906) 21776 MINAFET SG
Fax: (01) 228187

10. Dr. Ibrahim Ali BADAWI EL SHEIKH — Member
Embassy of Egypt
Borweg 1.
THE HAGUE/NETHERLANDS
Tel Office: (2597) 3542000/3554066
Tel Res: (2597) 3607791
Fax: (00) (31) (70) 3543304

11. Prof. U. Oji UMOZURIKE — Member
Faculty of Law
University of Calabar
CALABAR/NIGERIA
Tel Office: (234) 87224748/49 Ext. 9
Tel Res: (234) 87220543
Telex: 65103 UNICAL, NG
Fax/Tel: (234) 87220111/87220543
[*or*]
c/o Liaison Officer
University of Calabar
LAGOS/NIGERIA
Tel: (2341) 835615

Secretary to the Commission
Mr. Germain BARICAKO
PO Box 673
BANJUL/THE GAMBIA
Tel: (220) 392962
Telex: (996) 2346 – OAU BJL GV
Fax: (220) 390764

ANNEX V

In accordance with Article 62 of the Charter reports are due from States Parties on the following dates:

No.	State Party	First Report	Second Report	Third Report
1.	Algeria	20/06/89	1993	1991
2.	Angola	09/01/92	1994	1996
3.*	Benin	21/10/88	1990	1992
4.	Botswana	21/10/88	1990	1992
5.	Burundi	30/11/91	1993	1995
6.	Burkina Faso	21/10/88	1990	1992
7.	Cameroon	18/12/91	1993	1995
8.*	Cape Verde	06/11/89	1991	1993
9.	Central African Republic	21/10/88	1990	1992
10.	Chad	11/02/89	1991	1993
11.	Comoros	21/10/88	1990	1992
12.	Congo	21/10/88	1990	1992
13.	Côte d'Ivoire	01/07/94	1996	1998
14.	Djibouti	20/03/93	1995	1997
15.	Egypt	21/10/88	1990	1992
16.	Equatorial Guinea	18/11/88	1990	1992
17.	Ethiopia	–	–	–
18.	Eritrea	–	–	–
19.	Gabon	21/10/88	1990	1992
20.	Gambia	21/10/88	1990	1992
21.	Ghana	01/06/91	1993	1995
22.	Guinea	21/10/88	1990	1992
23.	Guinea Bissau	21/10/88	1990	1992
24.	Kenya	10/05/94	1996	1998
25.	Lesotho	27/05/94	1996	1998
26.	Liberia	21/10/88	1990	1992
27.*	Libya	26/06/89	1991	1993
28.	Madagascar	19/06/94	1996	1998
29.	Malawi	23/05/92	1994	1996
30.	Mali	21/10/88	1990	1992
31.	Mauritania	21/10/88	1990	1992
32.	Mauritius	07/10/92	1994	1996
33.	Mozambique	07/06/92	1994	1996
34.	Namibia	16/12/94	1996	1998
35.	Niger	21/10/88	1990	1992
36.*	Nigeria	21/10/88	1990	1992
37.	Rwanda	21/10/88	1990	1992
38.	SADR	21/10/88	1990	1992
39.	Sao Tome & Principe	21/10/88	1990	1992
40.†	Senegal	21/10/88	1990	1992
41.	Seychelles	30/07/94	1996	1998
42.	Sierra Leone	21/10/88	1990	1992
43.	Somalia	21/10/88	1990	1992
44.	Sudan	21/10/88	1990	1992

No.	State Party	First Report	Second Report	Third Report
45.	Swaziland	21/10/88	1990	1992
46.*	Tanzania	21/10/88	1990	1992
47.*	Togo	21/10/88	1990	1992
48.†	Tunisia	21/10/88	1990	1992
49.	Uganda	21/10/88	1990	1992
50.	Zaire	28/10/89	1991	1993
51.	Zambia	21/10/88	1990	1992
52.	Zimbabwe	21/10/88	1990	1992

* has presented its preliminary report
† has presented its preliminary report and periodic report

ANNEX VI

Distribution of Countries by Members of the Commission for Promotional Work as at 10 December 1993

1. **Mr. Atsu-Koffi Amega**
   Togo
   Central African Republic
   Burundi
   Tchad
   Gabon
   Djibouti

2. **Dr. Ibrahim A. Badawi El-Sheikh**
   Comoros
   Seychelles
   Mauritius
   Madagascar
   Egypt

3. **Mr. Alioune Blondin Beye**
   Benin
   Equatorial Guinea
   Côte d'Ivoire
   Mauritania

4. **Mr. Emmanuel Victor Oware Dankwa**
   Ghana
   Zimbabwe
   Malawi

5. **Mr. Sourahata Baboucar Semega Janneh**
   Gambia
   Liberia
   Sierra Leone
   Botswana
   Namibia

6. **Mr. Robert Habesh Kisanga**
   Ethiopia
   Kenya
   Somalia
   Uganda
   Tanzania
   Zambia

7. **Mrs. Vera V. D. M. Duarte Martins**
   Cape Verde
   Mozambique
   Angola
   Guinea Bissau
   Sao Tome & Principe

8. **Mr. Youssoupha Ndiaye**
   Mali
   Niger
   Senegal
   Republic of Guinea

9. **Prof. Isaac Nguema**
   Zaire
   Burkina Faso
   Congo
   Rwanda

10. **Prof. Mohammed H. Ben Salem**
   Tunisia
   Algeria
   Libya
   Sahrawi Arab Democratic Republic
   Sudan
   Eritrea

11. **Prof. U. Oji Umozurike**
   Nigeria
   Cameroon
   Lesotho
   Swaziland

ANNEX VII

Conclusions of the Seminar on Protection of African Refugees and Internally Displaced Persons Harare, 16–18 February 1994

The African Commission on Human and Peoples' Rights, within the context of its programme of activities, to promote and ensure respect for human rights in Africa, convened a seminar on "The Protection of African Refugees and Internally Displaced Persons" In Harare from 16–18 February 1994.

The seminar was officially opened by the Honourable John Nkomo, Minister of the Public Service, Labour and Social Welfare, Government of Zimbabwe.

The seminar debated the following main issues:

A. Reviewing the general picture of national, regional and international, governmental or non-governmental action, in favour of African refugees and internally displaced persons.

B. Problems of African refugees and internally displaced persons in the context of promotion and ensuring respect for human rights with the view of consolidating action in their favour, with special reference to the needs of children and women.

The seminar came to the following general conclusions:

The plight of African refugees and internally displaced persons is a flagrant violation of human dignity and basic human rights. This plight also constitutes a permanent threat to orderly and peaceful development in African countries.

The tragedy of African refugees and internally displaced persons is rooted in causes such as violation of human rights, civil strife, internal disturbances, political conflicts, armed conflicts, ethnic violence, religious intolerance and mass poverty.

The participants noted in particular the African Charter on Human and Peoples' Rights, international human rights instruments, namely the UN Convention on Refugees of 1951 and its protocol of 1967, the OAU Conventions of 1969, the Geneva Conventions of 1949 and the two additional protocols of 1977.

The participants, having noted the above-mentioned instruments, were of the opinion that the basic documents provide essential legal ground for protecting African refugees and internally displaced persons provided that African states adhere strictly to them and ensure their implementation in law and practice.

The solving of the problems of African refugees and internally displaced persons, though the primary responsibility of African states, requires whole-hearted solidarity on the part of the international community to enable Africa to address the root causes and effects and to find durable solutions to the problems of refugees and internally displaced persons.

The seminar noted the efforts of African governments, inter-governmental agencies such as the United nations High Commissioner for Refugees (UNHCR) and international organizations such as the International Committee of the Red Cross (ICRC) and the NGOs vis-à-vis the problems of African refugees and internally displaced persons. However, the problems of their protection continue to exist.

The seminar considered the reports of the following three working groups constituted by the seminar:

Group A which was entrusted with elaborating the conclusions on: Reviewing the general picture of national, regional, and international, governmental or non-governmental action, in favour of African refugees and internally displaced persons.

Group B which was entrusted with elaborating the conclusions on: Problems of African refugees and internally displaced persons in the context of promotion of, and ensuring respect for, human rights.

Group C which was entrusted with elaborating the conclusions: The specific needs of children and women.

The seminar adopted the conclusions of the said working groups which are reproduced in the following text:

Group A presented the following conclusions:

1. A disaster preparedness and early warning system should be established.

2. States should be encouraged to respect human rights and to observe existing binding instruments namely the UN Convention on Refugees, OAU Convention on Refugees, International Humanitarian Law, African Charter on Human and Peoples' Rights, and also the UN Convention on Mines.

3. Procedures should be created to penalise states which violate these conventions, and an African Court of Human Rights should be established.

4. NGOs should increase their efforts in promoting the rights of refugees and internally displaced persons, and assist them in redressing violations of these rights.

5. Action should be taken to promote and assist refugees and internally displaced persons to participate in the planning and implementation of their own repatriation and resettlement.

6. Programmes should be promoted that endorse the fact that the best protectors of human rights are those with the greatest vested interests in their protection, i.e. the people themselves, and not support agencies, and that education for self protection needs to be based on their own methods and their own ideas for improvement.

7. In spite of the negative image of refugees and internally displaced persons often portrayed by the media and which weakens the position of the former, the media has an important role in promoting the empowerment of people to protect and exercise their rights as well as expose violations thereof.

Group B presented the following conclusions:

Problem of Displacement

1. The seminar urges African governmental international organizations, NGOs at national and international level and all other parties concerned with the situation of violence to recommit themselves to address root causes of displacement, to prevent refugee flows and to create conditions which would allow refugees and internally displaced persons to return to their normal places of habitual residence in safety and dignity.

2. The seminar calls upon governments to continue to observe and implement the applicable international principles and norms for the protection of refugees, particularly the principle of non-refoulement and treatment of refugees and asylum-seekers in accordance with principles and norms of international law and recognized humanitarian standards.

3. The seminar calls upon governments who have not done so to promulgate national refugee legislation to give expression to international refugee standards, and establish procedures and mechanisms for dealing with all aspects of refugee protection.

4. The seminar calls upon governments to ensure that the detention, expulsion or deportation of refugees and asylum-seekers be subject to legal and judicial safeguards.

5. The seminar encourages governments to respect and promote the human rights of refugees over and beyond the enjoyment of asylum and protection against refoulement.

6. The seminar calls upon the relevant national, regional and international NGOs to continue providing the necessary support towards the protection and assistance of refugees.

7. Governments should take all necessary measures to ensure adequate and effective security in refugee hosting areas and, in particular, to protect the refugees against all forms of personal violence, particularly rape. All perpetrators of such violence should be expeditiously punished according to applicable penal law.

8. In view of the phenomenal political, social and economic developments that have taken place regionally and globally, the traditional solutions to refugee problems, i.e.

resettlement, local integration and voluntary repatriation need to be seriously reviewed. In particular, it should be examined whether under the changed circumstances, these continue to offer a durable solution in reality and whether, in the case of voluntary repatriation, it is always the best solution.

9. Refugees should always be consulted and involved in the planning and implementation of their voluntary repatriation. In planning such voluntary repatriation, the concerns of refugees, particularly regarding safety, education, social and economic facilities, and access to settlement on and use of land, should be given the highest priority.

10. While in exile, refugees should be provided with civic education so that the period in refuge contributes to the solution of their situation and to rebuilding a new and better society after their return home.

Internally Displaced Persons

The Seminar,

1. Calls upon states and relevant organisations and institutions to respect and adhere to the relevant principles and the norms of humanitarian law in order to ensure the dignity and integrity of the civilians, and allow for the effective response to such protection and assistance problems as and when they arise.

2. Urges governments and all concerned parties to recognize the right of humanitarian assistance to victims of war and displaced persons, and to allow humanitarian organisations access to all these populations in particular by respecting the impartiality and neutrality of humanitarian aid and allowing its delivery in safety.

3. Calls upon states to accede to all relevant treaties, enforce them in their domestic law and practice, disseminate knowledge of these laws, and ensure effective functioning of the international and regional mechanisms of implementation and control.

4. Calls upon the international community to review and further develop the international protection and assistance framework with particular reference to cases of internal displacement not adequately covered by existing humanitarian and human rights law as well as strengthening assistance to host communities.

5. Calls for the provision of legal aid and assistance to refugees and internally displaced persons to enable them to exercise their right of access to the African Commission on Human and Peoples' Rights in order to seek redress to violations of their human rights.

6. Recognizes that whereas under certain specific circumstances, so-called "safety zones" might be established to protect and assist displaced victims of armed conflict, such mechanisms should not be used to prevent refugees from seeking and being granted asylum outside their countries of origin.

Information and Dissemination

1. The seminar noted the need for information to be provided to refugees, returnees and internally displaced persons concerning the relevant principles of protection and international law to enable them to invoke their rights themselves.

2. The seminar calls upon governments, inter-governmental agencies and NGOs to create or consolidate mechanisms for dissemination of information about the rights of internally displaced, refugees and returnees to ensure their active participation in the protection of their rights.

3. Taking into account the world plan of action on education for human rights and democracy adopted in March 1993 by the international congress on education for human rights and democracy, the seminar calls upon states and NGOs to develop specific programmes and strategies for ensuring the widest human rights education possible, with particular reference to the needs of the African refugees and internally displaced persons, notably, women and children.

Landmines

1. The seminar calls upon African governments to ratify the 1980 Convention, supports the review of the Convention which has been initiated by the General Assembly, and hopes that this review will lead to a total ban on the production, stockpiling, trade in and use of landmines.

2. The seminar calls upon African governments, Inter-governmental Agencies, NGOs and the public at large to gather and disseminate detailed information on the social, medical, economic and ecological consequences of landmines so as to promote efforts for the control or ban of the production, trade, stockpiling and use of landmines.

3. The seminar calls upon African governments and the international community at large to provide all the necessary resources and assistance to support effective and long-term initiatives for mine clearance and mine awareness in all the mine-infested areas in Africa.

Role of National, Regional and International NGOs

1. The seminar calls upon national, regional and international NGOs to coordinate and collaborate in their efforts to assist refugees and internally displaced persons in securing protection according to international human rights principles and norms, and to support national NGO initiatives and encourage community participation, particularly where refugees and internally displaced persons are themselves directly involved.

2. The seminar encourages relevant NGOs to consider including in their mandates, the monitoring of the human rights.

3. The seminar urges African governments to support and allow NGOs to carry out their humanitarian work on behalf of refugees and internally displaced persons at all times and according to the principles of neutrality and impartiality. In particular, no political or other considerations should be allowed to prevent NGOs from carrying out humanitarian activities for the benefit of refugees and internally displaced persons, especially where life-threatening situations exist.

4. The seminar calls upon African governments in particular and other relevant organizations to support and strengthen the relevant regional institutions, especially

the African Commission on Human and Peoples' Rights, the Conflict Resolution mechanisms, and the Bureau for Refugees and Internally Displaced Persons so as to enable them to better and more effectively carry out their respective mandates.

5. In order to improve the system of human rights enforcement in Africa, the seminar calls for the establishment of an African Charter of Human Rights and the pre-requisite goodwill of governments necessary to make such a court or any other such structure effective. Additionally, it should be examined how the mandate of the recently appointed United Nations High Commissioner for Human Rights could improve the enforcement of human rights in Africa in generally and of internally displaced persons in particular.

6. The mandate and work of the relevant organs of the OAU, particularly the Commission of 15 on Refugees should be reviewed so as to enable the question of internally displaced persons to be considered and dealt with specifically and in its own right.

Group C presented the following conclusions:

1. In view of the fact that over 50 percent of refugees and internally displaced persons are women, the staffing of institutions, and the setting and implementing of policies, as well as the allocation of funds and other resources, should accurately reflect the gender balance of these populations.

2. Donors, agencies, host governments, and the media should make an effort to become better informed about the special protection and assistance needs of refugee and internally displaced women beyond their basic requirements of food, clothing, shelter and health services.

3. The African Commission on Human and Peoples' Rights should review the African Charter on the Rights and Welfare of the Child with the aim of implementing its provisions.

4. The African Commission on Human and Peoples' Rights should take cognizance of the special needs of repatriated refugees and internally displaced persons.

5. Efforts should be made by the international community and the African Commission on Human and Peoples' Rights to inform refugees and internally displaced persons of their human rights.

6. With regard to the African Charter on Human and Peoples' Rights, it is recommended that the following articles be reflected upon for further clarity and operational pragmatism in the light of the protection of women and the protection of children:

- *Article 13, paragraph 2* – equal access to public service: the question is how does the commission ensure that this takes place and what measures are in place to ensure such success?
- *Article 16, paragraph 1* – the psycho-social needs (including education), for refugees and internally displaced persons need to be identified as essential components of equal importance to material assistance.
- *Article 17, paragraph 3* – what power has the Commission in cases of failure by states to promote and protect common morals?

- *Article 18, paragraph 3* – the state shall ensure the elimination of every discrimination against women and also ensure the protection of the rights of the woman and the child as stipulated in international declarations and conventions; how does this fit with national legislation?
- *Articles 25 and 26* – the duty to ensure the respect of rights and freedoms and the duty to guarantee the independence of the courts.
- *Chapter II, Article 31* – how valid is the necessity for legal experience given the mandate of the commission, as stated in Chapter II, article 45, paragraphs 1(a) and 2. By stating a preference for legal experience, women are automatically excluded, because this is a traditionally male-dominated field. Commission members should include a variety of skills including psycho-social sciences.
- *Chapter III, Articles 56 and 58* – when massive violation of human and peoples' rights takes place the commission is to do an in-depth study and write a report. how can this help the victims of such violations?

7. Noting that the African Charter on Human and Peoples' Rights obligates States to afford "every individual" basic human rights without discrimination, such as, the rights to equality before the law, fair trial, economic, social and cultural rights; noting also that the Charter refers to the right to asylum and prohibits mass expulsion of nationals, it is thus binding upon African states to observe fully the Charter and reflect its provisions related to refugees and displaced persons in the reports submitted to the African Commission under Article 67 of the Charter. It is incumbent on the African Commission to pay special attention to the issue of displaced persons and make its own contributions in this regard.

Final Conclusions

1. The participants called upon the international community to intensify its efforts in favour of African refugees and internally displaced persons, especially women and children.

2. The participants indicated that the conclusions of the seminar should be annexed to the annual reports of the African Commission to be submitted to the OAU summit and other participants, with the view of acting on these conclusions. The hope was also expressed that the African Commission on Human and Peoples' Rights will act on these conclusions.

3. The participants expressed their warm gratitude and thanks to the government of Zimbabwe for having graciously accepted the convening of the seminar in Harare and in designating the Honourable Minister of Public Services, Labour and Social Welfare, John Nkomo, to officially open the seminar.

Harare, Zimbabwe, 18 February 1994

ANNEX VIII

List of NGOs Granted Observer Status[1]

ANNEX IX

Decisions/Recommendations on Communications

1. 1/88 Frederick Korvah v Liberia

Communication on the situation in Liberia including corruption, immorality, etc. dated 26 July 1987.

Final Decision:

"The African Commission on Human and Peoples' Rights, established under Article 30 of the African Charter on Human and Peoples' Rights;

Meeting at its Fourth Ordinary Session held from 17–26 October 1988;

Considering that the communication is not addressed to the Commission but to the Liberian Government;

Considering further that the five matters described in this communication do not amount to violations of human rights under the provisions of the Charter;

DECLARES the communication inadmissible." (Article 114 of the Rules of Procedure; Article 56 of the Charter.)

2. 2/88 Iheanyichukwu a. Ihebereme v USA

Communication on false imprisonment, police brutality, etc. dated 13 July 1987.

Final Decision:

"The African Commission on Human and Peoples' Rights, established under Article 30 of the African Charter on Human and Peoples' Rights;

Meeting at its Fourth Ordinary Session held from 17–26 October 1988;

Considering that the communication is directed against a State non-party to the African Commission on Human and Peoples' Rights;

DECLARES the communication inadmissible." (Article 101 of the Rules of Procedure.)

3. 3/88 Centre for the Independence of Judges and Lawyers v Yugoslavia

Communication on alleged deprivation of right to practice a profession dated 26 January 1986.

[1] This list is omitted. The most up-to-date list is reproduced above at p. 90.

Final Decision:

"The African Commission on Human and Peoples' Rights, established under Article 30 of the African Charter on Human and Peoples' Rights;

Meeting at its Fourth Ordinary session held from 17–26 October 1988;

Considering that the communication is directed against a state non-party to the African Charter on Human and Peoples' Rights;

DECLARES the communication inadmissible." (Article 101 of the Rules of Procedure.)

4. 4/88 Coordinating Secretary of the Free Citizens Convention v Ghana

Communication about arrest and detention of persons dated 25 June 1987.

Final Decision:

"The African Commission on Human and Peoples' Rights, established under Article 30 of the African Charter on Human and Peoples' Rights;

Meeting at its Fourth Ordinary Session held from 17–26 October 1988;

Considering that the communication is directed against a State non-party to the African Charter on Human and Peoples' Rights;

DECLARES the communication inadmissible." (Article 101 of the Rules of Procedure.)

5. 5/88 Prince J. N. Makoge v USA

Communication on the activities of USA in Africa dated 29 August 1986.

Final Decision:

"The African Commission on Human and Peoples' Rights, established under Article 30 of the African Charter on Human and Peoples' Rights;

Meeting at its Fourth Ordinary session held from 17–26 October 1988;

Considering that the communication is directed against a State non-party to the African Charter on Human and Peoples' Rights;

DECLARES the communication inadmissible." (Article 101 of the Rules of Procedure.)

6. 6/88 Dr. Kodji Kofi v Ghana

Communication on arrest and detention without trial dated 11 April 1988.

"The African Commission on Human and Peoples' Rights, established under Article 30 of the African Charter on Human and Peoples' Rights;

Meeting at its Fourth Ordinary Session held from 17–26 October 1988;

Considering that the communication is directed against a State non-party to the African Charter on Human and Peoples' Rights;

DECLARES the communication inadmissible." (Decision of 26 October 1988; Article 101 of the Rules of Procedure.)

7. 7/88 Committee for the defence of Political Prisoners v Bahrain

Communication on alleged, false imprisonment of persons and torture dated 26 February 1988.

"The African Commission on Human and Peoples' Rights, established under Article 30 of the African Charter on Human and Peoples' Rights;

Meeting at its Fourth Ordinary Session held from 17–26 October 1988;

Considering that the communication is directed against a State non-party to the African Charter on Human and Peoples' Rights,

DECLARES the communication inadmissible." (Article 101 of the Rules of Procedure.)

8. 9/88 International Lawyers Committee for Family Reunification v Ethiopia

Communication on alleged false imprisonment of persons and torture dated 14 April 1988.

"The African Commission on Human and peoples' Rights, established under Article 30 of the African Charter on Human and Peoples Rights;

Meeting at its Fourth Ordinary Session held from 17–26 October 1988;

Considering that the communication is directed against a State non-party to the African Charter on Human and Peoples' Rights;

DECLARES the communication inadmissible." (Article 101 of the Rules of Procedure.)

9. 10/88 Getachew Abebe v Ethiopia

Communication on false imprisonment and deprivation of property dated 1 June 1988.

"The African Commission on Human and peoples Rights, established under Article 30 of the African charter on Human and Peoples' Rights;

Meeting at its Fourth Ordinary Session held from 17–26 October 1988;

Considering that the communication is directed against a state non-party to the African Charter on Human and Peoples' Rights;

DECLARES the communication inadmissible." (Article 101 of the Rules of Procedure.)

10. 11/88 Henry Kalenga v Zambia

A communication on false imprisonment, 2 August 1988. The author was released after a member of the African Commission on Human and Peoples' Rights effected an amicable settlement. This file is closed. (Article 97 of the Rules of Procedure; Article 56, 1 of the Charter.)

11. 12/88 Mohamed El-Nekheily v OAU

Communication about wrongful dismissal, non-payment of salaries, etc. dated 28 May 1988.

"The African Commission on Human and Peoples' Rights established under Article 30 of the African Charter on Human and Peoples' Rights;

Meeting at its Fourth Ordinary Session held from 17–26 October 1988;

Considering that the communication is directed against a non-party to the African Charter on Human and Peoples' Rights;

DECLARES the communication inadmissible." (Article 101 of the Rules of Procedure.)

12. 13/88 Hadjali Mohamad v Algeria

Communication about slow judicial process but no specific breaches dated 29 August 1988.

"The African Commission on Human and Peoples' Rights, established under Article 30 of the African Charter on Human and Peoples' Rights;

Considering that the communication does not state the complaints directed against the State concerned or/the human rights violations suffered by the author of the communication or the procedures engendered by these violations;

DECLARES the communication inadmissible." (Article 114 of the Rules of Procedure; Article 56 of the Charter.)

13. 14/88 Dr. Abd Eldayem A. E. Sanussi v Ethiopia

Communication about arbitrary detention dated 29 February 1988.

"The African Commission on Human and Peoples' Rights, established under Article 30 of the African Charter on Human and Peoples' Rights;

Meeting at its Fourth Ordinary Session held from 17–26 October 1988;

Considering that the communication is directed against a state non-party to the African Charter on Human and Peoples' Rights;

DECLARES the communication Inadmissible." (Article 101 of the Rules of Procedure; Article 56 of the Charter.)

14. 15/88 Mpaka-Nsusu Andre Alphonse v Zaire

Communication on false imprisonment dated 12 September 1988.

"The African Commission on Human and Peoples' Rights;

Considering that the communication had already been referred for consideration to the Human Rights Committee established under the International Covenant on Civil and Political Rights;

DECLARES the communication inadmissible." (Article 114 of the Rules of Procedure; Article 56/7 of the Charter.)

15. 16/88 Comite Cultural pour la Democratie au Benin v Benin dated 3 August 1988

17/88 Badjogoume Hilaire v Benin dated 10 October 1988

18/88 El Hadj Boubacar Diaware v Benin dated 15 July 1988

Communications about false imprisonments.

"The African Commission on Human and Peoples' Rights established under Article 30 of the African Charter on Human and Peoples' Rights;

Meeting at its Fifteenth Ordinary Session held in Banjul, The Gambia, from 18–27 April 1994;

Considering that, at its Fifth Ordinary Session held in Benghazi (Libya), in April 1989, the Commission decided to link the 3 petitions registered under Nos. 16/88, 17/88 and 18/88 at the Secretariat due to their inter-relation;

Considering that the 3 petitions were declared inadmissible and that notification thereof was made to the parties concerned on 14 March 1990, 17 November 1990, 16 November 1992, 12 August 1993 and 20 January 1994;

Considering that during this same session, the Commission declared the 3 petitions admissible, in application of Articles 56 and 57 of the Charter and Rules 114 and 117 of the Rules of Procedure;

Considering that by letter dated 18 March 1994 the state of Benin acknowledged receipt of all the notifications and informed the Commission of the dispatch of the requisite documents and information;

Considering moreover that it was a result of a letter from Mr. Diawara to the Commission dated 12 April 1994 that the political and judicial authorities took into consideration the requests of Mr. Diawara by referring the matter to the examining magistrate and the President of the Republic of Benin;

Considering that prior to any substantive consideration, the communications must be referred to the Sixteenth Session of the Commission, pursuant to Rule 115 of the Rules of Procedure;

DECIDES to refer the matter to the Sixteenth Session for decision on the admissibility and consideration of the communication at its Sixteenth Session.

16. 19/88 International PEN v Malawi, Ethiopia, Cameroon, Kenya

Communication on wrongful imprisonment dated 30 August 1989.

"The African Commission on Human and Peoples' Rights, established under Article 30 of the African Charter on Human and Peoples' Rights;

Meeting at its Sixth Ordinary Session held from 23 October to 4 November 1989;

Considering that the communication is directed against States non-parties to the African Charter on Human and Peoples' Rights;

DECLARES the communication inadmissible." (Article 101 of the Rules of Procedure.)

17. 20/88 Austrian Committee Against Torture v Morocco

Communication about wrongful arrests and false imprisonment.

"The African Commission on Human and Peoples' Rights, established under Article 30 of the African Charter on Human and Peoples' Rights;

Meeting at its Sixth Ordinary Session held from 23 October to 4 November 1989;

Considering that the communication is directed against a state non-party to the African charter on Human and Peoples' Rights;

DECLARES the communication inadmissible." (Article 101 of the Rules of Procedure.)

18. 21/88 Centre Haitien des Libertés Publiques v Ethiopia

Communication on extra-judicial executions dated 20 January 1989.

"The African Commission on Human and Peoples' Rights, established under Article 30 of the African Charter on Human and Peoples' Rights;

Meeting at its Sixth Ordinary Session held in Banjul, The Gambia, from 23 October to 4 November 1989;

Considering that the communication is directed against a State non-party to the African Charter on Human and Peoples' Rights;

DECIDES the communication inadmissible." (Article 101 of the Rules of Procedure.)

19. 22/88 International PEN v Burkina Faso

Communication on alleged wrongful detention (not dated).

"The African Commission on Human and peoples' Rights, established under Article 30 of the African Charter on Human and Peoples' Rights;

Meeting at its Fifteenth Ordinary Session held in Banjul, The Gambia, from 18–27 April 1994;

Considering that Mr. Ernest N. Ouedraogo has been released on 4 August 1989;

DECIDES that the file be closed." (Article 56 of the Charter.)

20. 24/89 Union Nationale de Liberation de Cabinda v Angola

Communication on alleged denial of self-determination dated 2 April 1988.

"The African Commission on Human and Peoples' Rights, established under Article 30 of the African Charter on Human and Peoples' Rights;

Meeting at its Fifth Ordinary Session from 3–14 April 1989;

Considering that the communication is directed against a State non-party to the African Charter on Human and Peoples' Rights;

DECLARES the communication inadmissible." (Article 101 of the Rules of Procedure.)

21. 26/89 Austrian Committee Against Torture v Burundi

Communication about mass arrests, detention, torture, etc. dated 31 March and 19 June 1989.

"The African Commission on Human and Peoples' Rights, established under Article 30 of the African Charter on Human and Peoples' Rights;

Meeting at its Sixth Ordinary Session held in Banjul, The Gambia, from 23 October to 4 November 1989;

Considering that the communication is directed against a State non-party to the African Charter on Human and Peoples' Rights;

DECLARES the communication inadmissible." (Decision of 4 November 1989; Article 101 of the Rules of Procedure.)

22. 28/89 Association Internationale des Juristes Democrates v Ethiopia

Communication on alleged false imprisonment, destruction of property, etc.

"The African Commission on Human and Peoples' Rights, established under Article 30 of the African Charter on Human and Peoples' Rights;

Meeting at its Sixth Ordinary Session from 23 October to 4 November 1989;

Considering that the communication is directed against a State non-party to the African Charter on Human and Peoples' Rights;

DECLARES the communication inadmissible." (Article 101 of the Rules of Procedure.)

23. 29/89 Commission Française Justice et Paix v Ethiopia

Communication on denial of the right to life dated 3 March and 19 June 1989.

"The African Commission on Human and Peoples' Rights established under Article 30 of the African Charter on Human and Peoples' Rights;

Meeting at its Sixth Ordinary Session from 23 October to 4 November 1989;

Considering that the communication is directed against a State non-party to the African Charter on Human and Peoples' Rights;

DECLARES the communication inadmissible." (Article 101 of the Rules of Procedure.)

24. 33/89 Simon B. Ntaka v Lesotho

Communication on infringement of the right to free movement dated 14 January 1974.

"The African Commission on Human and Peoples' Rights, established under Article 30 of the African Charter on Human and Peoples' Rights;

Meeting at its Fourth Ordinary Session from 17–26 October 1988;

Considering that the communication is directed against a state non-party to the African Charter on Human and Peoples' Rights;

DECLARES the communication inadmissible." (Article 101 of the Rules of Procedure.)

25. 35/89 Seyoum Ayele v Togo

Communication on alleged deprivation of nationality dated 12 December 1987.

Decision:

The author complains that an alleged victim was impliedly denied his nationality by the action of his own State.

The Commission decided that the allegation was vague and the communication inadmissible under Article 56 of the Charter.

26. 37/90 Georges Eugene v USA, Haiti

Alleged ill-treatment by USA and Haiti dated 23 March 1990.

"The African Commission on Human and Peoples' Rights, established under Article 30 of the African Charter on Human and Peoples' Rights;

Meeting at its Seventh Ordinary session from 18–28 April 1990 in Banjul (The Gambia);

Has taken the following decision:

At its Fifth sitting held on Wednesday 25 April 1990;

Considering that the communication is directed against States non parties to the African Charter;

DECLARES the communication inadmissible." (Article 101 of the Rules of Procedure.)

27. 38/90 Wesley Parish v Indonesia

Alleged illegalities committed by Indonesia.

"The African Commission on Human and Peoples' Rights, established under Article 30 of the African Charter on Human and Peoples' Rights;

Meeting in its Seventh Ordinary Session held from 18–28 April 1990;

Considering that the communication is directed against State non-party to the African Charter on Human and Peoples' Rights;

DECLARES the communication inadmissible." (Article 101 of the Rules of Procedure.)

28. 41/90 Andre Houver v Morocco

Communication on alleged political imprisonment and other wrongdoing dated 28 March 1990.

"The African Commission on Human and Peoples' Rights, established under Article 30 of the African Charter on Human and Peoples' Rights;

Meeting at its Seventh Ordinary Session held from 18–28 April 1990 in Banjul (The Gambia);

Has taken the following decision:

At its Fifth sitting held on Wednesday 25 April 1990;

Considering that the communication is directed against a State non-party to the African Charter

DECLARES the communication inadmissible." (Article 101 of the Rules of Procedure.)

29. 42/90 International PEN v Malawi

Communication on denial of the right to life, etc. dated 12 March 1990.

"The African Commission on Human and Peoples' Rights, established under Article 30 of the African Charter on Human and Peoples' Rights;

Meeting at its Seventh Ordinary Session held in Banjul, The Gambia, from 18–28 April 1990;

Has taken the following decision:

At its Fifth sitting held on Wednesday 25 April 1990;

Considering that the communication is directed against a State non-party to the African Charter on Human and Peoples' Rights;

DECLARES the communication inadmissible." (Article 101 of the Rules of Procedure.)

30. 43/90 Union des Scolaires Nigerians – Union Generale des Etudiants Nigerians au Benin v Niger

Communication on alleged denial of right to life, etc. dated 14 February 1990.

"The African Commission on Human and Peoples' Rights, established under Article 30 of the African Charter on Human and Peoples Rights;

Meeting at its Fifteenth Ordinary Session held in Banjul, The Gambia, from 18–27 April 1994;

By petition dated 14 February 1990 registered at the Secretariat of the Commission under No. 43/90, the Union des Scolaires Nigerians and Union Generale des Etudiants Nigerians au Benin wrote to the Commission to denounce human rights violations allegedly committed by the State of Niger during the events of 9 February 1990 in that country, pursuant to to the provisions of Article 55 of the Charter;

Considering that the communication had been brought to the knowledge of the State of Niger vide letters of 6 November 1990 and 12 August 1993, pursuant to Article 57 of the Charter;

Considering that since the matter was referred to the Commission, no additional information has been received by the Secretariat, in spite of several reminders;

Considering that the 4 month deadline given to the parties at the Fourteenth Session of the Commission held in Addis Ababa, Ethiopia, in December 1993, has expired;

Considering that none of the conditions relating to form, time-limit or procedure laid down under Article 56 of the Charter and Rule 114 of the Rules of Procedure has been complied with;

Considering that the communication is therefore inadmissible;

DECIDES to declare the communication of the Union des Scolaires Nigerians et l'Union des Etudiants Nigerians au Benin against the State of Niger inadmissible pursuant to Article 55 of the Charter and Rule 114 of the Rules of Procedure.

31. 45/90 Civil Liberties Organization v Nigeria

Communication on wrongful eviction of inhabitants dated 4 October 1990.

Final Decision:

"The Commission decides that local remedies have not been exhausted as required by Article 55 of the Charter and 114 of the Rules of Procedure and declares the communication inadmissible."

32. 53/90 Alberto T. Capitao v Tanzania

Communication on recovery of money dated 26 March 1991.

Final Decision:

"The Commission decides that local remedies have not been exhausted as required by Article 56 of the Charter and 114 of the Rules of Procedure and declares the communication inadmissible."

33. 55/91 International PEN v Chad

Communication on alleged false imprisonment dated 27 March 1991.

Final Decision:

"Following the withdrawal of the communication dated 31 August 1993 following the release or the death of the prisoner concerned, the Commission closes the case." (Article 114 of the Rules of Procedure; Article 56 of the Charter.)

34. 57/91 Tanko Bariga v Nigeria (not dated)

Communication on demand of sums of money and other privileges.

Final Decision:

The demand is incoherent and uncoordinated and inadmissible under Article 55(2) of the African Charter on Human and Peoples' Rights.

35. 63/92 Congress for the second republic of Malawi v Malawi dated 5 April 1991

A communication on the general political situation Malawi.

Final Decision:

The information is noted and as it is not a complaint, no further action is necessary and accordingly the matter is closed. (Article 114 of the Rules of Procedure; Article 56 of the Charter.)

36. 66/92 Lawyers Committee for Human Rights v Tanzania

Communication on alleged false imprisonment dated July 1991.

The complainant Mr. Seif Hamad having been granted bail and subsequently the charges against him having been struck out by the Court, there is nothing further to proceed with, and the matter is accordingly closed. (Article 55 of the Charter.)

37. 67/91 Civil Liberties Organization v Nigeria

Communication on alleged wrongful detention dated 25 February 1992.

Final Decision:

The Commission obtains information by letter Co. 128/T/24 dated 19 May 1992 from the Government of Nigeria and other independent sources that the affair was being amicably resolved and therefore closes the file. (Article 50 of the Charter.)

38. 64/92 Krishna Achuthan v Malawi dated 10 October 1991
68/92 Amnesty International v Malawi dated 2 March 1992
78/92 Amnesty International v Malawi dated 6 October 1992

Communication on alleged wrongful detentions and denial of rights.

Final Decision:

The Commission finds that the state is in breach Articles 4, 5 and 7 of the African Charter on Human and Peoples' Rights and decides to refer the situation to the Assembly of Heads of State and Government under Article 58(1) of the Charter on Human and peoples' Rights.

39. 69/92 Amnesty International v Tunisia

Communication on alleged wrongful detention and torture dated 4 March 1992.

Final Decision:

"The African Commission on Human and Peoples' Rights, established under Article 30 of the African Charter on Human and Peoples' Rights;

Meeting at its 13th Ordinary Session, from 29 March to 7 April 1993 in Banjul, The Gambia;

Considering Articles 55 and 56 para. 7;

DECIDES to declare the communication of Amnesty International against the Republic of Tunisia inadmissible pursuant to the relevant provisions of Article 56 para. 7 which stipulate that the communications submitted within the framework of Part II, Chapter III of the African Charter on Human and Peoples' Rights should necessarily not deal with cases which have been settled in accordance with the principles of the Charter of the United Nations or the Charter of the Organization of African Unity or the provisions of the present Charter."

40. 72/92 Bamidele Aturu v Nigeria

Communication about denial of right to education dated 21 February 1992.

Final Decision:

Author fails to exhaust local remedies. The Commission considers the application to be inadmissible under Article 56(5) of the Charter.

41. 70/92 Ibrahim Dioumessi, Sekou Kande, Ousmane Kaba v Guinea (not dated)

Communication on detention without trial.

Final Decision:

"The African Commission on Human and Peoples' Rights, established under Article 30 of the African Charter on Human and Peoples' Rights;

Meeting at its Fifteenth Ordinary session held in Banjul, The Gambia, from 18–27 April, 1994;

Recalling the provisions of Article 57 of the Charter and those of Rules 110 and 115 of the Rules of Procedure which stipulate that prior to any substantive consideration, all communications must be brought to the knowledge of the State concerned;

NOTES that the said communication was brought to the attention of the State of the Republic of Guinea on 13 November 1992, 12 April 1993 and 12 March 1994;

REQUESTS the Guinean Government of submit additional information relating to the issue within 2 months of the receipt of a new notification, facing which this matter shall be considered during the Sixteenth Session." (Articles 110 and 115 of the Rules of Procedure.)

42. 73/92 Mohamed L. Diakite v Gabon

Communication on wrongful expulsion and deprivation of property dated 17 April 1992.

Decision:

"The African Commission on Human and Peoples' rights, established under Article 30 of the African Charter on Human and Peoples' Rights;

Meeting at its Fifteenth Ordinary Session held in Banjul, The Gambia, from 18–27 April 1994;

Recalling the provisions of Article 57 of the Charter and those of Rules 110 and 115 of the Rules of Procedure which stipulate that prior to any substantive consideration, all communications must be brought to the attention of the State concerned;

NOTES that the said communication was brought to the knowledge of the state of Gabon on 11 November 1992 and 12 April 1993;

DECIDES to enquire from the author of the complaint, pursuant to the decision of the Thirteenth Session, whether he intends to take up this matter with the Gabonese judicial authorities and requests him to submit a response within 4 months of the receipt of this decision;

DIRECTS that substantive consideration of the matter be undertaken during the Sixteenth Session." (Articles 1110, 115 and 117 of the Rules of Procedure.)

43. 83/92 Jean Y. Degli (on behalf of Bikagni) v Togo

Linkage with 88/93 and 91/93 of 1 March 1993.

Communication on unlawful detention.

"The African Commission on Human and Peoples' Rights, established under Article 30 of the African Charter on Human and Peoples' Rights;

Recalling the provisions of Article 57 of the Charter and those of Rules 110 and 115 of the Rules of Procedure which stipulate that prior to any substantive consideration, all communications must be brought to the knowledge of the State concerned;

NOTES that the said communication was brought to the attention of the State of Togo on 11 November 1992;

CONFIRMS the interim measures taken during the Fourteenth Session geared towards ensuring the security of Corporal Nikabou Bikagni to avoid any irreparable prejudice inflicted on the victim of the alleged violations." (Articles 110 and 115 of the Rules of Procedure; Article 57 of the Charter.)

44. 88/93 Union Interafricaine des droits de l'Homme v Togo

Communication on the human rights situation in Togo.

"The African Commission on Human and Peoples' Rights, established under Article 30 of the African Charter of Human and Peoples' Rights;

Recalling the provisions of Article 57 of the Charter and those of Rules 110 and 115 of the Rules of Procedure which stipulate that prior to any substantive consideration, all communications must be brought to the knowledge of the State concerned;

DECIDES to bring the communication to the knowledge of the Government of Togo and to request it to submit a response within two months of the receipt of the notification.

A substantive consideration of the matter shall be undertaken at the Sixteenth Session." (Articles 110, 115 and 117 of the Rules of Procedure; Article 57 of the Charter.)

45. 91/91 Commission Internationale de Juristes v Togo

Communication on the situation of human rights in Togo, etc. dated 1 March 1993.

Combined with No. 88/93 (43 above).

46. 93/93 International PEN v Ghana (not dated)

Communication on the freedom of expression.

Upon the request by the author on 24 March 1993, the communication is marked withdrawn and the file is closed." (Article 56 of the Charter.)

47. 97/93 John K. Modise v Botswana

Communication on denial of nationality dated 3 March 1993.

Final Decision:

It was decided to write to the author stressing the need for exhaustion of local remedies as required by Article 56 of the Charter. He should also be advised to contact the NGO Botswana Centre for Human Rights which enjoys observer status with the Commission for assistance. (Article 56(5) of the Charter.)

48. 104/93 Centre for the Independence of Judges and Lawyers v Algeria dated 12 August 1992

Communication on the general political situation in Algeria.

Final Decision:

This communication provides a general information to the Commission and deals with no specific breaches of the Charter. The file is closed accordingly. (Article 56 of the Charter.)

49. 106/93 Amuh Joseph Vitrine v Cameroon dated 16 September 1993

Communication on wrongful persecution.

Final Decision:

Mr. Amuh Joseph Vitrine wants the Commission to save his life and prevail on his Government to stop the hunt against him. He also wants the Commission to appeal to the Governments of Senegal and Niger to grant him refugee status.

The Commission applied Article 55 and decided not to take up the communication.

50. 107/93 Academic Staff Nigerian Universities v Nigeria

Communication on breach of agreement, threats, etc. dated 27 July 1993.

Final Decision:

From the evidence adduced by the author, local remedies have not been exhausted. The communication is therefore inadmissible. The Commission calls the attention of the author to the provisions of Article 56 of the Charter.

51. 131/94 Ousman Manjang v The Gambia

Communication on wrongful detention and confiscation of papers.

Final Decision:

Article 56(5) requires that the author exhausts local remedies before the Commission takes up his complaint. In the absence of that, the communication is declared inadmissible. (Article 56 of the Charter.)

52. 47/90 Lawyers Committee for Human Rights v Zaire

Communication on violations of human rights by the Government of Zaire including arbitrary arrests, detention, torture, etc. dated 16 October 1990.

Final Decision:

The Commission admits evidence of the existence of a series of serious or massive violations of human and peoples' rights and decides under Article 58(1) of the African Charter to call the attention of the Assembly of heads of State and Government to the situation. (Article 58(1) of the Charter.)

ANNEX X

Resolution on Human and Peoples' Rights Education

The African Commission on Human and Peoples' Rights at its 14th Ordinary Session in Addis Ababa, 1–10 December 1993:

Acknowledging that education in human and peoples' rights is a prerequisite for the effective implementation of the African Charter on Human and Peoples' Rights and other international human rights instruments,

Bearing in mind that the African Charter on Human and Peoples' Rights provides in Article 17(1) for the right to education and that Article 25 of the African Charter calls upon States parties to the Charter to promote human and peoples' rights through teaching, education and publication,

Recalling the Resolution on the African Commission on Human and Peoples' Rights, AHG/Res. 227 (XXIX), published in the Commission's 6th Annual Activity Report, 1992–1993, which all States parties are requested to "ensure among other things (a) that human rights are included in the curriculum at all levels of public and private education and in the training of all law enforcement officials, and (b) that education,of human rights and democracy should involve every organ of the society as well as the media",

Taking note of the UNESCO Plan of Action adopted at the International Congress on Education for Human Rights and Democracy in Montreal during March 1993, which laid the foundation for the recommendation adopted at the World Conference on Human Rights in Vienna for a Decade of Human Rights Education to be declared,

Noting also the Declaration at the World Conference on Human Rights, Vienna 1993, encouraging all Governments to include in the formal sector, curricula on the study of human rights in primary, secondary and tertiary institutions as well as those in the administration of justice, and for governments to be encouraged to undertake the promotion of human rights in the informal sector,

Taking into consideration the Program of Activities of the African Commission on Human and Peoples' Rights, 1992–1996, adopted at the 11th Session, March 1992,

Recognizing the importance of education as an active vehicle of inculcating the values and corresponding behaviours in a civil society based on full respect for human and peoples' rights, democracy, tolerance and justice,

Emphasizing the importance of propagating the principle of human rights law as well as international humanitarian law,

Taking into consideration further the great efforts made by the African Non-Governmental Organizations to promote and implement human and peoples' rights through education on both formal and informal levels, using popular participatory methods and through the media,

Having considered the item on human rights education upon the request of a number of Non-Governmental Organizations,

1. REITERATES its request for States parties to include the study of human and peoples' rights in the curriculum at all levels of public and private education, including at law schools to ensure, inter alia, that education and information regarding human and peoples' rights are included in the training of law enforcement personnel, civil or military, as well as medical personnel, public officials and other persons who may be involved in the custody, interrogation or treatment of any individual subjected to any form of arrest, detention of imprisonment;

2. DECIDES to intensify the co-operation between the African Commission and the African Non-Governmental Organizations on human and peoples' rights

education, bearing in mind in particular the activities contained in the Commission's Program of Activities, 1992–1996;

3. UNDERLINES the importance of education, through appropriate means and techniques, being geared among other things to the need of specific groups such as women, children, refugees and internally displaced persons, victims of armed conflicts and other disadvantaged groups;

4. ENCOURAGES Governments to take advantage of the activities of the Non-Governmental Organizations in the field of human and peoples' rights education and to facilitate such efforts;

5. WELCOMES the initiative taken by Non-Governmental Organizations to organize a workshop on human and peoples' rights education with a special reference to popular participation and non-formal education during 1994, and any further initiatives which would strengthen the long term activities of the African Commission and Non-Governmental Organizations in the field of human rights education.

ANNEX XI

Resolution on the Promotion and the Respect of International Humanitarian Law and Human and Peoples' Rights

The African Commission on Human and Peoples' Rights Rights Meeting in its 14th Ordinary Session in Addis Ababa, from 1–10 December 1993;

Considering that human rights and international humanitarian law (IHL) have always, even in different situations, aimed at protecting human beings and their fundamental rights,

Noting the competence of the International Committee of the Red Cross (ICRC) to promote the respect of the international humanitarian law,

Recalling the resolution CM/Res. 1059 (XLIV), adopted at the 44th Ordinary Session of the Council of Ministers of the OAU, which reaffirmed the determination of the OAU to support the ICRC in its activities and to grant it the necessary facilities to carry out its mandate,

Recalling also the conclusions of the seminar held in Banjul, October 1992, following the 12th Session of the African Commission on Human and Peoples' Rights on the national implementation of the African Charter of Human and Peoples' Rights, which underscored the need to disseminate and implement the provisions of international humanitarian law applicable in time of armed conflicts,

Considering the Resolution on Human and Peoples' Rights Education adopted by the African Commission on Human and Peoples' Rights at its 14th Session, December 1993,

Recognizing the need for close cooperation in the field of dissemination of international humanitarian law and human and peoples' rights,

1. INVITES all African States Parties to the African Charter on Human and Peoples' Rights to adopt appropriate measures at the national level to ensure the

promotion or the provisions of the international humanitarian law and human and peoples' rights;

2. STRESSES the need for a specific instruction of military personnel and the training of the forces of law and order in international humanitarian law and human and peoples' rights respectively;

3. STRESSES FURTHER the importance of regular exchange of information between the African Commission on Human and peoples' Rights, the International Committee of Red Cross and human rights non-governmental organizations, on the teaching and dissemination activities undertaken on the principles of human and peoples' rights and international humanitarian law, in the schools, universities and all other institutions;

4. DECIDES to participate, as much as possible, in the seminars, conferences or technical sessions organized by the ICRC on questions of mutual interest and urges the ICRC to reciprocate, or the activities or the Commission.

ANNEX XII

Resolution on the Situation in Rwanda

The African Commission on Human and Peoples Rights, meeting in its 15th Ordinary Session in Banjul, The Gambia, from 18 to 27 April 1994,

Deeply concerned about the alarming human rights situation in Rwanda characterised by serious and massive human rights violations,

Noting the OAU Secretary General's very energetic condemnation of the wanton killing of civilians and heinous acts perpetrated in this country,

Bearing in mind the recommendations made by the UN Special Rapporteur on extrajudicial, summary or arbitrary executions following his visit to Rwanda in 1993,

1. CONDEMNS very strongly the cycle of violence and the massacre of innocent civilians by the different armed factions;

2. URGES the parties to the conflict to immediately cease hostilities and work towards a peaceful settlement through dialogue between all the Peoples of Rwanda;

3. CALLS ON all parties to respect the African Charter on Human and Peoples' Rights, the principles of International Humanitarian Law as well as the activities of humanitarian organizations operating in the field;

4. INVITES the Special Rapporteur on extra-judicial summary or arbitrary executions to pay special attention to the situation in Rwanda and report back to the 16th Session.

ANNEX XIII

Press Release

The African Commission on Human and Peoples' Rights during its 15th Session from 18–27 April 1994 in Banjul,

Informed of the massacres and the outbursts of violence in Rwanda following the plane crash of 6 April 1994 in which the President of Rwanda, General Juvenal Habyarimana and the President of Burundi, His Excellency Cyprien Ntaryamira were killed,

Apprised of the Security Council's decision to withdraw UN troops from Rwanda because of the flare up of violence in that country,

Considering that this measure comes at a time when the Rwandan people is more in need of being protected and its survival ensured,

Considering that solidarity and interdependence amongst peoples and states require that every effort be made to avoid the recurrence of more serious disturbances in Rwanda,

DEPLORES the decision taken by the Security Council;

URGES the United Nations Organization to request for the withdrawal of the decision taken by the Security Council;

APPEALS to OAU Heads of State for increased assistance to Rwanda to put an end to the sufferings of its people.

ANNEX XIV

Resolution on South Africa

The African Commission on Human and Peoples' Rights, meeting in its 15th Ordinary Session in Banjul, The Gambia, from 18–27 April 1994,

Noting the violence that has taken place in South Africa and the loss of lives that has assumed alarming proportions,

Reiterating the importance of protecting human lives and creating a climate conducive to a free and fair elections,

Welcoming the positive developments that have emerged towards a consensus for holding the forthcoming election,

1. URGES all the parties concerned to cease the violence and create a peaceful atmosphere;

2. URGES the concerned parties in South Africa to take all necessary steps to create an atmosphere conducive to free and fair election;

3. URGES all political parties and others concerned in South Africa to accept the results of the election if it is declared to be substantially free and fair by the Independent Electoral Commission;

4. URGES the new government to ratify the African Charter on human and Peoples' Rights and to ensure the protection of the human rights of all South Africans in accordance with the said African Charter and other relevant treaties and standards.

ANNEX XV

Resolution on the African Commission on Human and Peoples' Rights

The Assembly of Heads of State and Government of the Organization of African Unity, meeting in its Thirtieth Ordinary Session, in Tunis, Tunisia, from 13–15 June 1994,

Considering the Seventh Annual Activity Report of the African Commission on Human and Peoples' Rights presented by its Chairman Professor Isaac Nguema, in accordance with Article 54 of the African Charter on Human and Peoples' Rights,

Recalling that the African Charter on Human and Peoples' Rights entered into force on 21 October 1986, and that 49 OAU Member States have already acceded to the Charter,

Recalling also that Article I of the African Charter on Human and Peoples' Rights stipulates that States Parties shall recognize the rights, duties and freedoms enshrined in the Charter and shall undertake to adopt legislative or other measures to give effect to them,

Recalling further the entry into force on 12 May 1994, on the Treaty Establishing the African Economic Community which complements the African Charter on Human and Peoples' Rights,

Bearing in mind that the African Charter recognizes the right to development as a Human Right,

Aware of the need to strengthen the African mechanism for the promotion and protection of Human and Peoples' Rights,

Concerned by the situation obtaining in the area of human and peoples' rights.

Finally recalling the provisions of Resolution AHG/Res. 227 (XXIX) Rev. 1 adopted at its Twenty-ninth Ordinary Session held in Cairo, Egypt, from 28–30 June 1993,

1. REAFFIRMS the need for Member States to ensure respect for Human and Peoples' Rights and thereby further promote peace, stability and development in Africa;

2. CONSEQUENTLY CALLS ON States Parties to the Charter to take concrete measures towards the effective implementation of the provisions of the African Charter on Human and Peoples' Rights;

3. REAFFIRMS the relevance of all the provisions of resolution AHG/Res. 227 (XXIV) Rev. 1 and APPEALS to all the concerned parties and people to scrupulously conform to these provisions particularly those relating to endowing the African Commission with adequate resources to enable it to accomplish its mission and to the submission of periodic reports by the States Parties;

4. REQUESTS the OAU Secretary-General to convene a meeting of government experts to ponder in conjunction with the African Commission on Human and Peoples' Rights over the means to enhance the efficiency of the Commission in considering particularly the establishment of an African Court of Human and Peoples' Rights;

5. CONGRATULATES the African Commission on Human and Peoples' Rights for having appointed its Vice-Chairman as Special Rapporteur on extra-judiciary, summary of arbitrary executions;

6. CALLS UPON the States Parties to the Charter to cooperate with the Special Rapporteur in carrying out his mandate;

7. APPEALS to Member States to ratify the said Charter as early as possible if they have not yet done so;

8. STRONGLY ENCOURAGES the African Commission on Human and Peoples' Rights to continue to pursue its activities aimed at promoting and protecting the rights recognized and guaranteed by the Charter;

9. TAKES NOTE WITH SATISFACTION of the Seventh Annual Activity Report of the African Commission on Human and Peoples' Rights and AUTHORIZES its publication.

Final Communiqué of the Fourteenth Ordinary Session of the African Commission on Human and Peoples' Rights

Addis Ababa, 1–10 December 1993

1. The African Commission on Human and Peoples' Rights held its 14th Ordinary Session at the OAU (Organization of African Unity) Headquarters in Addis Ababa, Ethiopia, from 1–10 December 1993.

2. The Session was preceded by the fifth Workshop on NGO participation in the work of the African Commission on Human and Peoples' Rights organized by the International Commission of Jurists in collaboration with the African Commission from 28–30 November 1993.

3. The following Commissioners attended the Session:

(i) Prof. Isaac Nguema, Chairman;
(ii) Dr. Mohammed Hatem Ben Salem, Vice Chairman;
(iii) Mr. Atsu-Koffi Amega;
(iv) Mr. Emmanuel Victor Oware Dankwa;
(v) Mr. Sourahata B. Semega Janneh;
(vi) Mr. Robert H. Kisanga;
(vii) Mrs.Vera Valentina Duarte-Martins;
(viii) Mr. Youssoupha Ndiaye;
(ix) Dr. Ibrahim A. Badawi El -Sheikh;
(x) Prof. U. O. Umozurike.

4. Mr. Alioune Blondin Bèye could not attend and sent his apologies.

5. The opening Session took place at 10 a.m. on 1 December 1993 at the Hilton Hotel in the presence of His Excellency, Salim Ahmed Salim, Secretary-General of the OAU, Mr. Adama Dieng, Secretary-General of the International Commission of Jurists and Ambassador Haggag, Assistant Secretary-General of the OAU. Also present at the opening ceremony were:

- Ambassadors and Heads of Diplomatic Missions;
- Representatives of Intergovernmental and Non-Governmental Organizations;
- Members of the press and other guests.

6. In his introductory Statement, Dr. Ibrahim Ali Badawi El-Sheikh, outgoing Chairman of the African Commission, welcomed the three new members of the African Commission, Mr. Atsu-Koffi Amega, Mrs. Vera Valentina Duarte-Martins and Mr. Emmanuel Victor Oware Dankwa. Dr. Badawi also congratulated Mr. Youssoupha Ndiaye for his re-election to the African Commission. He then called upon his Excellency, Dr. Salim Ahmed Salim, Secretary-General of the OAU to address the opening meeting of the 14th session.

7. In his address, His Excellency Salim Ahmed Salim congratulated the Commissioners elected during the last Summit of the OAU Assembly of Heads of States and Government. He also extended a special welcome to Mrs. Vera Valentina Duarte-Martins, the first woman to be elected to the Commission.

8. The OAU Secretary-General urged the members of the Commission to discharge their duties impartially and faithfully as they are enjoined to do by the solemn declaration they made upon assuming their functions as Commissioners.

9. The Secretary-General pointed out that the 14th Session convenes at a critical stage in the history of Africa. He noted that the changed world political circumstances have brought challenges to African States to adjust the systems of governments to respond to the new needs of society, particularly in the field of human and peoples' rights.

10. The OAU Secretary-General further noted that the new wave imposes a heavy duty on the African Commission as the human rights ombudsman in Africa. He called on the Commission to challenge governments to protect and promote human rights through dialogue and not through confrontation.

11. In conclusion, the OAU Secretary-General stated that in order to achieve the objective of promoting and protecting human rights, Africa must continue the struggle for a world order which is sensitive to the legitimate aspirations for economic and social development of Africans which is an essential element of human rights. The Secretary-General pledged to cooperate with the African Commission on the discharge of its functions.

12. In his opening address, the outgoing Chairman, Dr. Ibrahim Ali Badawi El-Sheikh thanked the OAU Secretary-General for his address and stated that the Commission will take into account the Secretary-General's message during its deliberations.

13. Dr. Badawi El-Sheikh noted that the 14th Session convenes at a time when the Central Organ for the Prevention, Management and Resolution of Conflicts in Africa meets at the level of Heads of State. Dr. Badawi El-Sheikh pointed out that many conflicts in Africa stem from human rights breaches.

14. Dr. Badawi El-Sheikh referred to the accomplishments and difficulties of the African Commission since its inception. In particular, he referred to the Commission's relations with NGOs, the Commission's examination of State reports and individual and NGOs complaints, as well as the Commission's 1992–96 programme of activities.

15. Dr. Badawi El-Sheikh, stressed the need for the OAU to increase the administrative capacity of the Commission's Secretariat as well as the Commission's budget so as to increase the effectiveness of the Commission.

16. Dr. Badawi El-Sheikh also referred to the importance of Coordinating with the OAU, the activities of the African Commission relevant to the work of the former. In particular, activities on the rights of the child, women and refugees.

17. In conclusion, Dr. Badawi El-Sheik stressed the importance of promoting and ensuring respect for human rights in Africa as a prerequisite for development, peace and stability.

18. After the opening ceremony the newly elected members of the Commission made a solemn declaration to discharge their duties impartially and faithfully.

19. Pursuant to Article 42 of the African Charter and Rule 7 of the Rules of Procedure, the Commission elected its Chairperson and Vice Chairperson for a renewable two-year period. Mr. Isaac Nguema was elected Chairman. Mr. Mohammed Hatem ben Salem was elected Vice Chairman.

20. During its proceedings the Commission dealt mainly with the following:

(i) Consideration of applications for Observer Status;
(ii) Consideration of Periodic Reports;
(iii) Consideration of Communications;
(iv) Consideration of Promotional activities;
(v) Administrative and financial matters.

21. The following non-governmental Organizations were granted Observer Status:

(i) International Federation of Women Lawyers (FIDA) Kenya Chapter;
(ii) Organisation nationale des droits de l'homme du Sénégal;
(iii) National Justice and Peace Commission, Catholic Mission;
(iv) Collectif des ligues et associations de défense des droits de l'homme au Rwanda (CLADHO);
(v) International Work for Indigenous Affairs;
(vi) Centre for Human Rights, Faculty of Law, University of Pretoria;
(vii) Ligue des Droits de la Personne dans la Region des Grands Lacs (LDGL);
(viii) International Commission of Jurists (Kenya Section);
(ix) Foundation for Human Rights Initiative;
(x) Media Rights Agenda;
(xi) Inter-African Network for Human Rights;
(xii) International Alert;
(xiii) University of Namibia;
(xiv) Ligue camerounaise des droits de la personne;
(xv) Ethiopian Human Rights Council.

22. The following non-governmental Organizations were granted Observer Status subject to the provision of additional basic documents:

(i) Penal Reform International;
(ii) AZADHO (Association de defense des droits de l'homme – Zaïre);
(iii) Association des journalistes du Cap-Vert;
(iv) Association pour la défense des droits de l'homme et des libertés.

23. These increase to 129 the number of non-governmental Organizations in Observer Status with the African Commission.

24. The granting of Observer Status to la Societé internationale pour les droits de l'homme (Zaïre) was postponed pending the submission of a complete set of documents.

25. At the beginning of its proceedings, the Commission heard Statements from several African and International NGO representatives including:

(i) Nana Ghartey, Ghana Committee on Human and Peoples' Rights;
(ii) Mr. Shadrack Gutto, Network of Activists and Researchers on Integrated Human Rights in Africa (NARIHRA);
(iii) Mrs. Tokunbo Ige, Legal Research and Resource Development Centre;
(iv) Mr. Christopher Hall, Amnesty International;
(v) Ms. Mona Rishmawi, International Commission of Jurists; and
(vi) Mr. Anslem Odinkalu, Interights (The International Centre for the Legal Protection of Human rights).

26. During the proceedings, the Commission considered the initial periodic report of Ghana. Mr. Kobina Wudu, Ghana's Chargé d'affaires in Ethiopia, presented the report on behalf of the Government of Ghana.

27. The purpose of periodic State reports is to encourage States to implement voluntarily their human rights obligations.

28. The Commission thanked the Government of Ghana and its representative for submitting the report. The Commission urged the Government of Ghana and its representative to submit in writing additional information and response to questions which could not be answered.

29. The Commission appealed to States Parties which have not yet done so to submit their reports as soon as possible.

30. With regards to protective activities, the Commission considered 60 communications from NGOs and individuals. These included 7 new communications. The Commission noted that some of these cases apparently relate to special cases which reveal the existence of serious and massive violations of human and peoples' rights.

31. The Commission noted with concern the situation of massive violations of human rights in a number of African countries which cause human suffering and death. Accordingly, the Commission appeals to all concerned to find ways and means to put an end to such unfortunate situations.

32. As regards promotional activities, the Commission decided to organize the following seminars:

(i) The status of women under the African Charter in relation to specific socio-economic problems;
(ii) Refugees and displaced persons in Africa;
(iii) Right to fair trial to be organized by the Arab Lawyers Union;
(iv) Popular participation and informal education.

33. In order to give effect to the rights set forth in the African Charter, the Commission also adopted two resolutions, one the Right to Human Rights Education and another on the Promotion and Respect of Human Rights and International Humanitarian Law.

34. During its deliberations, the Commission received information that President Houphouët Boigny of the Ivory Coast had passed away. The Commission noted with regret that the death of President Houphouët Boigny is a great loss to Africa. The Commission observed a minute of silence and decided to send its condolences to the Government of the Ivory Coast.

35. The Commission reiterated its decision to continue to encourage African States to recognize 21 October as African Human Rights Day.

36. The Commission calls upon Ethiopia, Swaziland and Eritrea to adhere to the African Charter on Human and Peoples' Rights.

37. The Commission decided to hold its 15th Ordinary Session from 18–27 April 1994 in Banjul, The Gambia.

Issued in Addis Ababa, 10 December 1993

Final Communiqué of the Fifteenth Ordinary Session of the African Commission on Human and Peoples' Rights

Banjul, 18–27 April 1994

1. The African Commission on Human and Peoples' Rights held its 15th Ordinary Session at its Headquarters in Banjul, Gambia from 18–27 April 1994 under the chairmanship of Professor Isaac Nguema.

2. The Session was preceded by the sixth Workshop on NGO participation in the work of the African Commission on Human and Peoples' Rights organized by the International Commission of Jurists in collaboration with the African Commission and the African Centre for Democracy and Human Rights Studies.

3. The following Commissioners attended the Session:

(i) Prof. Isaac Nguema, Chairman;
(ii) Dr. Mohammed H. B. Vice Chairman;
(iii) Prof. Emmanuel V. O. Dankwa;
(iv) Mr. Sourahata B. S. Janneh;
(v) Mr. Robert H. Kisanga;
(vi) Mrs. Vera Valentina B. S. Duarte-Martins;
(vii) Mr. Youssoupha Ndiaye;
(viii) Dr. Ibrahim Ali Badawi El-Sheikh;
(ix) Prof. U. Oji Umozurike.

4. Mr. Alioune Blondin Bèye and Mr. Atsu Koffi Amega could not attend and sent apologies.

5. The opening ceremony took place at 10 a.m. on 18 April 1994 at the Kombo Beach Novotel in the presence of the Honourable Mariama Alaba Mboge, Parliamentary Secretary, Ministry of External Affairs, the Gambia and Mr. Adama Dieng, Secretary-General of the International Commission of Jurists. Also present at the opening ceremony were:

- Ambassadors and Heads of Diplomatic Missions;
- Government officials;
- Representatives of Intergovernmental and Non-Governmental Organizations;
- Members of the press and other guests.

6. Prof. Isaac Nguema and Mr. Adama Dieng addressed the opening Session.

7. In his address, Mr. Nguema deplored the poor human rights situations in a number of African countries and in particular addressed the question of summary executions. He considered various theories on the origin of violence and dismissed the

notion that violence is inevitable in Africa. He, however, expressed the view that ethnic rivalry and poverty are the main causes of violence in Africa.

8. In view of the widespread problems in Africa, Prof. Nguema recognized the need for the African Commission to be seen as a forum for action, solidarity, responsibility, a forum of liberty and truth, dialogue and tolerance.

9. In his address, Mr. Adama Dieng stressed the need to strengthen cooperation between the African Commission and NGOs. He emphasized the importance of NGO involvement in the work of the Commission as NGOs provide information on human rights and urged the Commission to continue to make use of NGO resources.

10. Mr. Adama Dieng described the last sixth months as a period of despair because of the systematic and serious violations of human rights in African countries, notably Rwanda and Burundi. He also referred to the issue of extra judicial executions in Africa. On behalf of the NGOs attending the Session, Mr. Dieng called on the African Commission to interpret the African Charter in a dynamic way in order to ensure the enjoyment of fundamental rights in Africa.

11. During its proceedings, the Commission dealt mainly with the following:

(i) the situation in Rwanda and South Africa;
(ii) consideration of communications;
(iii) consideration of promotional activities;
(iv) administrative and financial matters;
(v) examination of Extra Judicial Executions;
(vi) cooperation with the United Nations in the promotion and protection of human rights in Africa;
(vii) consideration of applications for Observer Status;
(viii) preliminary Discussion of the question of establishing and African Human Rights Centre.

12. The following Non-Governmental Organizations were granted Observer Status:

(i) Community Legal Resource and Advice Centre;
(ii) the Botswana Centre for Human Rights was granted Observer Status subject to the provision of additional documents.

13. These increase to 131 the number of NGOs in Observer Status with the African Commission.

14. At the beginning of its proceedings, the Commission heard Statements from several African and International NGO representatives including:

(i) Dr. Philip Amoah, International Commission of Jurists (ICJ);
(ii) Mrs. Bernadette Palle, Coordinatrice du Réseau sous-regional femmes africaines et droits humains (REFAD);
(iii) M. Aref Mohamed Aref, Association pour la défense des droits de l'homme et des libertés;
(iv) Mrs. Florence Butegwa, Women in Law and Development (WILDAF);

(v) Mr. Salem Mezhoud, Anti-Slavery International;
(vi) Mrs. Dorcas Coker-Appiah, International Federation of Women Lawyers (FIDA), Ghana;
(vii) Mr. Kolawole Olaniyan, Constitutional Rights Project;
(viii) Mrs. Ndouré Mbam Diarra, Association malienne des droits de l'homme;
(ix) Dr. Majhoub Tijani, Sudan Human Rights Organization;
(x) Mr. Anslem Odinkalu, Interights; and
(xi) Mr. Kwasi Gyan-Apenteng, African Topics.

15. Dr. Philip Amoah, ICJ Legal Officer for Africa presented the conclusions and recommendations of the NGO workshop. In addition, the NGO workshop presented a number of draft resolutions for consideration by the African Commission.

16. During its deliberations, the Commission noted with regret that it could not consider the periodic report of Mozambique as scheduled because the leader of the delegation of Mozambique who had the mandate to present the report could not turn up, although two members of the said delegation were in attendance.

17. The purpose of periodic State reports is to encourage States to implement voluntarily their human rights obligations, and State Parties are encouraged to ensure that their representatives are present to present their reports.

18. Furthermore, the Commission appealed to States Parties which had not yet done so to submit their reports as soon as possible.

19. As regards protective activities, eight new communications were submitted to the Commission. The Commission also considered 70 communications out of a total a of 134 communications which have so far been submitted to it.

20. The Commission noted with concern the situation of massive violations of human rights in Rwanda. In this regard, the Commission appointed its Vice Chairman as Special Rapporteur for extra-judicial executions in Africa, and the Rapporteur has been requested to address the situation in Rwanda as a matter of urgency.

21. The Commission also noted with concern, the United Nations Security Council's withdrawal of peace keeping troops from Rwanda. The Commission issued a press communiqué deploring the Security Council's decision and urged the United Nations to send peace keeping troops to protect the people of Rwanda. The Commission also called on the OAU Heads of State to increase assistance to Rwanda in an effort to bring a speedy end to the sufferings of the people of Rwanda.

22. The Commission also passed a resolution calling for the cessation of violence and for a free and fair election in South Africa.

23. With respect to promotional activities, the Commission reiterated its decision to organize the following seminars:

(i) The status of women under the African Charter in relation to specific socio-economic problems (Scheduled to be held in Banjul, Gambia in October 1994);
(ii) The right to fair trial and legal assistance to be convened in Cairo, Egypt;
(iii) The implementation of the African Charter with particular reference to the reporting procedure (for French, Arabic and Portuguese speaking African countries) to be held in Tunis;

(iv) Human Rights Education in South Africa in collaboration with Lawyers Association for Human Rights;
(v) Informal education and popular participation.

24. The Commission accepted an invitation from the United Nations to participate in a regional seminar on the drafting and preparation of periodic reports, scheduled to be held in Abidjan, from 20–24 June 1994.

25. A report on a Seminar on African Refugees and internally displaced persons which was successfully held in Harare from 16–18 February 1994 was presented to the Commission.

26. The Commission considered in a preliminary way the question of establishing an African Court on Human Rights, and one Commissioner was entrusted to prepare for the 16th Session a Draft Resolution on the future possible action by the Commission on the matter.

27. The Commission calls upon Ethiopia, Eritrea and Swaziland to ratify the African Charter on Human and Peoples' Rights.

28. The Commission calls upon Ethiopia, Eritrea and Swaziland to ratify the African Charter on Human and Peoples' Rights.

29. The Commission decided to hold its 16th Ordinary Session from 31 October to 9 November 1994 in Banjul, the Gambia.

Issued in Banjul, 27 April 1994

Eighth Annual Activity Report of the African Commission on Human and Peoples' Rights 1994–1995

Adopted on 22 March 1995
Covering the 16th and 17th Ordinary Sessions in Banjul (25 October to 3 November) and Lome (12–22 March)
ACHPR/RPT/8TH

I. ORGANISATION OF WORK

A. Period Covered by the Report

1. The Seventh Annual Activity Report of the African Commission on Human and Peoples' Rights was adopted by the Thirtieth Ordinary Session of the Assembly of Heads of State and Government of the Organization of African Unity through its resolution AHG/Res. 230 (XXX). The present report, the Eighth Annual Activity Report, covers the Sixteenth and Seventeenth Ordinary Sessions held in Banjul, The Gambia, from 25 October to 3 November 1994 and in Lome, Togo, from 13–22 March 1995 respectively.

B. Status of Ratification

2. By the 17th Ordinary Session of the Commission, all the members of the OAU, with the exception of Eritrea, Ethiopia, South Africa and Swaziland, had ratified or acceded to the African Charter on Human and Peoples' Rights. The list of States and dates of signature, ratification/accession and deposit of instruments is attached as Annex I of this report.

C. Sessions and Agenda

3. The Commission held two Ordinary Sessions since the adoption of its 7th Annual Activity Report

- the 16th Ordinary Session held in Banjul, The Gambia, 25 October to 3 November 1994;
- the 17th Ordinary Sessions held in Lome, Togo, 13–22 March 1995;
- the Agenda for each of the two sessions is contained in Annexes II and III respectively.

D. Composition and Participation

4. The following commissioners attended the 16th Session:

(1) Prof. Isaac Nguema, Chairman
(2) Dr. Mohamed H. Ben Salem, Vice Chairman,
(3) Prof. Emmanuel V. O. Dankwa,
(4) Mr. Sourahata B. Semega Janneh,
(5) Mr. Robert H. Kisanga,
(6) Dr. Vera V. B. S. Duarte-Martins,
(7) Dr. Ibrahim A. Badawi El--Sheikh,
(8) Prof. U. Oji Umozurike.

Messrs. Alioune Blondin Beye, Atsu Koffi Amega and Youssoupha Ndiaye apologized for their inability to attend the 16th Session

5. The representatives of the following States attended the Session: Benin, Burundi, Cape Verde, Côte d'Ivoire, The Gambia, Niger, Swaziland and Togo.

6. The following Commissioners attended the 17th Session:

(1) Prof. Isaac Nguema, Chairman,
(2) Dr. Mohamed H. Ben Salem, Vice Chairman,
(3) Prof. Emmanuel V. O. Dankwa,
(4) Mr. Sourahata B. Semega Janneh,
(5) Mr. Robert H. Kisanga,
(6) Dr. Vera V. B. S. Duarte-Martins,
(7) Dr. Ibrahim A. Badawi El-Sheikh,
(8) Prof. U. Oji Umozurike,
(9) Mr. Atsu Koffi Amega.

Messrs. Alioune Blondin Beye, Atsu Koffi Amega and Youssoupha Ndiaye apologized for their inability to attend the 17th Session.

7. This 17th Session was also attended by the representatives of the following states: Algeria, Botswana, Burkina-Faso, Burundi, Central African Republic, Mali and Togo.

8. Many Non-Governmental Organizations attended these two sessions.

E. Adoption of the 8th Annual Activity Report

9. At its sitting of 22 March 1995, the Commission considered and adopted its 8th Annual Activity Report.

II. ACTIVITIES OF THE COMMISSION

A. Consideration of Periodic Reports

10. Under Article 62 of the African Charter on Human and Peoples' Rights, each State had undertaken to submit a report every two years, on the legislative and other measures it is taking to give effect to the rights and freedoms guaranteed by the Charter.

The initial reports of Benin and Cape Verde as well as the second periodic report of The Gambia were presented by the representatives of the States and examined by the Commission at its 16th Session. The Commission acknowledged the preparedness of the States concerned to cooperate with it and expressed its appreciation for The Gambia's second report.

11. The reports of Mauritius, Mozambique and Seychelles were scheduled for discussion at the 17th Session but there were no State representatives to present them. These States were accordingly requested to send representatives at the next session. Mauritius sent a note to explain that its representative could not attend due to the cyclone which swept through the country on 11 and 12 March 1995.

12. By the 17th Session the following States had submitted their reports: Libya, Rwanda, Tunisia (9th Session), Egypt and Tanzania (11th Session), The Gambia, (12th and 16th Sessions), Senegal and Zimbabwe (12th Session), Togo and Nigeria (13th Session), Benin, Ghana, Cape Verde and Mozambique (14th Session), Mauritius and Seychelles (17th Session). 34 States are yet to submit their reports (Annex IV).

III. PROMOTIONAL ACTIVITIES

(i) Report of the Chairman

13. The Chairman's Activity Report covered his attendance at various symposia and seminars, his work in connection with the Commission's publications, especially with regard to the third volume of the Review of the African Commission on Human and Peoples' Rights. He also reported on the mission to Togo which he conducted with the Vice-Chairman.

During the 17th Session, the Chairman Isaac Nguema, Vice Chairman, Mohamed H. Ben Salem, Commissioner S. S. B. Semega Janneh and the Secretary to the Commission, Mr. Germain Baricako were received in audience by the President of the Republic of Togo, His Excellency Mr. Gnassingbe Eyadema.

The discussion focused mainly on the global issue of the democratic process and human rights in Togo, and particularly on the application of the recently promulgated amnesty law, the organization of by-elections and the establishment of constitutional institutions.

These three issues were contained in a document that had earlier on been presented to the Commission by a delegation of the Action Commission for Renewal of Togo (CAR).

The Commission took note of the document and promised to discuss it with the President of the Republic if the latter accepted its mediation.

President Eyadema assured the Commission's delegation of his determination to foster national reconciliation, encourage direct and sincerely dialogue with all segments of the socio-political spectrum and to ensure that the democratic process is conducted in accordance with the aspirations and in the best interests of the Togolese people. Moreover, the President of the Republic highlighted a number of actions already carried out and others to be undertaken in this respect.

The Presidential delegation also indicated that the document given to the Commission by CAR was not genuine and promised to provide the Commission with the authentic document, which was done. The Commission's delegation expressed satisfaction at the efforts deployed by the Togolese President and Government to enhance the normalization of the socio-political situation in Togo and encouraged the latter to persevere in this direction.

The Commission's delegation informed the Action committee for Renewal (CAR) of the outcome of the audience with the President of the Republic. The CAR was requested to await the report of the national body charged with dealing with these contentious issues and the position of the President on the report.

(ii) Activities of Other Members of the Commission

14. During the intersession period, the other Commissioners also attended Conferences, Symposia and Seminars in and outside Africa and were involved in other promotional activities. The allocation of African countries for promotional activities is attached as Annex VIII.

(iii) The Commission Organized or Participated in the Organization of the Following Seminars:

15.

(a) Seminar on Human Rights Education in South Africa organized in collaboration with the South African Lawyers Committee for Human Rights, 24–27 September, Durban, South Africa;

(b) Seminar on the Rights of the African Woman and the African Charter on Human and Peoples' Rights, Lome Togo, on 8 and 9 March 1995, organized in collaboration with WILDAF. This seminar was organized through the financial assistance of the United Nations Centre for Human Rights;

c) Seminar on the Participation of NGOs in the work of the African Commission on Human and Peoples' Rights, Lomé, Togo 10–12 March 1995, organized by the International Commission on Human and Peoples Rights and the Association for the Promotion of the Rule of Law (APED), based in Togo.

(iv) Forthcoming seminars and conferences

16. The Commission decided to organize the following seminars/conferences:

(1) Legal Assistance and Fair Trial;
(2) Popular participation and Non-formal Education;
(3) Human rights in the New South Africa;
(4) Contemporary Forms of Slavery in Africa;
(5) The Peaceful Resolution of Ethnic and Social Conflicts from a Human Rights Perspective;
(6) The Right to Education: Essential Condition for Development in Africa;
(7) Economic, Social and Cultural Rights and the Right to Development;
(8) Conditions of Prisons in Africa;
(9) The problem of impunity in Africa.

The Commission decided to seek the support of international organizations and NGOs for the seminars/conferences and appointed Commissioners to be responsible for them.

III. REPORT OF THE SPECIAL RAPPORTEUR ON EXTRA-JUDICIAL EXECUTIONS IN AFRICA

17. At the 16th Ordinary Session, Dr. Mohammed Hatem Ben Salem, Special Rapporteur on extra-judicial, summary and arbitrary executions briefed the Commission on the outcome of his reflection on the terms of reference and methods of work.

18. In the light of the information provided, the Commission decided that, on account of the work already done by the United Nations System on the issue, the Special Rapporteur of the Commission should avoid duplication and concentrate on some aspects of the problem, viz:

(a) compensation of families of victims of such executions;
(b) responsibility of instigators and authors of such executions.

19. The Commission also considered the issue of the terms of reference of the Special Rapporteur and decided to study the matter thoroughly and finalize it at its next Session

20. At the 17th Session, the Special Rapporteur presented a preliminary document to the Commission containing proposals on:

(a) the scope of his mission;
(b) the area of investigation;
(c) the duration of his mission;
(d) the method of work;
(e) the presentation of reports;
(f) the budget estimates for 1995 and 1996.

21. The Commission approved these proposals as well as the draft terms of reference submitted to it for consideration.

IV. PUBLICATIONS

22. The Chairman of the Commission, Professor Isaac Nguema is charged with the supervision of the publication of the Review of the African Commission on Human and Peoples' Rights. The third edition of the Review was published in October 1994. Work on the fourth edition is in progress. This review is published through the financial assistance of the Raoul Wallenberg Institute and the African Society for International and Comparative Law.

23. The Vice-Chairman, Dr. Mohammed H. Ben Salem reported on plans for the publication of the Commission's Newsletter.

V. FORTHCOMING MISSIONS

24. The Commission decided to send missions to Nigeria, Sudan, Mauritania, Senegal and Zaire. The Government of Algeria invited the Commission while the Governments of Sudan and Senegal responded favourably to the Commission's request to visit.

VI. RELATIONS WITH OBSERVERS

25. During the two sessions the Commission granted observer status to 23 NGOs, bringing the number of organizations that enjoy observer status with the Commission to 154.

VII. PROTECTIVE ACTIVITIES

26. The Commission received 6 new communications during the two sessions and concluded work on 23 communications. The list of concluded communications and the decisions/recommendations is attached as Annex VI.

VIII. ADMINISTRATIVE AND FINANCIAL MATTERS

A. Administrative Matters

(i) Personnel Needs

27. At the 16th and 17th Ordinary Sessions, the Commission looked into the inadequate staffing situation of its Secretariat.

It noted that in spite of the volume and the importance of the work assigned to the Secretariat, the latter is staffed by only one professional officer, who is the Secretary to the Commission. The legal officer in charge of matters relating to the protection of human and peoples' rights left the Organization in August 1993 and is yet to be replaced.

The officer who was to be in charge of promotional matters was never recruited in spite of persistent demands by the Commission.

The Commission set up Documentation Centre in 1992 through assistance from the United nations Centre for Human Rights which agreed inter alia to take care of the salary of the documentalist pending the OAU taking over. The contract of this documentalist which has been renewed twice expired on 30 April, 1995.

As the OAU has not still appointed an officer to take care of the Centre, the Secretariat is compelled to close it down in spite of its capital importance to the Commission.

The Commission has decided to make another appeal to the OAU General Secretariat for an urgent resolution of this matter.

(ii) Equipment Needs

28. The volume and nature of the work of the Secretariat of the Commission call for the use of computers. The collection and management of data relating to human rights, promotional and protective activities cannot be effectively carried out within the required periods with the Secretariat's present logistics which is outdated.

The Secretariat therefore needs at least three (3) computers. The Commission has decided to take up this matter with the OAU General Secretariat.

(iii) Medical Cover and Insurance

29. The Commission once again looked into the issue of medical cover for Commissioners during sessions. The Commissioners are of the view that medical expenses incurred during sessions or official missions should be borne by the OAU.

Moreover, the Commissioners are required to undertake missions on behalf of the Commission which may expose them to certain risks. This is why they have requested that they be provided with an insurance cover for the duration of their missions.

These issues were raised at the 13th Session and a formal request made to the OAU General Secretariat which promised that the matter would be promptly addressed.

At its 17th Session the Commission felt that there was an urgent need to take up the matter again with the Secretary-General of the OAU, given the climate of insecurity prevailing in several countries that the Commissioners have to visit on official assignments for the Commission.

B. Financial Matters

30. At its 16th and 17 Sessions as in previous sessions, the Commission could not consider all the items on its agenda due to the fact that the duration of Sessions was reduced from 15 to 10 days for budgetary reasons.

The Commission therefore decided to appeal to the Secretary General of the OAU requesting him to take into account this serious handicap and restore the duration of sessions to 15 days.

The Commission also noted the fact that the same budgetary constraints forced members of the Commission to give up the idea of organizing promotional activities such as seminars, visits, etc. in State Parties. In this respect, the Commission renewed its appeal to the OAU Secretary General requesting him to contemplate the possibility of providing it with the necessary financial resources for the fulfilment of its mandate in accordance with the provisions of the Charter.

(i) The OAU Budget

31. The budget allocated by the OAU to the Commission for the period 1994–96 biennium is as shown in Table on p. 374.

(ii) Subventions from the United Nations Centre for Human Rights

32. The Commission received on 30 August 1994 the second tranche of 36,300 dollars as part of the 71,300 dollars subvention provided by letter of 22 July 1993 for the following activities:

(a) Strengthening of the Documentation Centre

  (1) Library
  (2) Printing of the Charter

(b) Seminars
(c) Support staff

33. The United Nations Centre also allocated an additional sum of 42,400 dollars from the Organization of the Seminar on the Rights of the African Woman and the African Charter on Human and Peoples' Rights held in Lome, Togo on 8 and 9 March 1995.

34. The same United Nations Centre is currently studying a project proposal submitted to it by the Commission for the computerization of the Secretariat and strengthening of promotional and protective activities.

(iii) Subventions from the Raoul Wallenberg Institute

35. The Raoul Wallenberg Institute continues to provide assistance to the Commission for:

- promotional activities;
- publication of the Commission's Review;
- funding of means of communications between the Commission's Secretariat, the Commissioners and partners of the Commission.

1	2	3	4	5			6	7
Code	Description	Appropriations 1993/94	Actual Expenditure 1990/93 (3 yrs average	Appropriation 1994/96			Increase Decrease	P/age Increase
				(a) Grand Total	(b) 1994/95	(c) 1995/96	(5b-4)	(6/4)
100	Basic Salary	101,771	80,563	199,248	98,429	100,819	17,866	22.18
101	Post Adjustment Allowance	21,182	25,282	45,303	22,406	22,897	(2,876)	(11.38)
102	Temporary Assistance	1,500	1,263	3,000	1,500	1,500	237	18.76
103	Overtime Payment	250	301	500	250	250	(51)	(16.94)
104	Commission's Honorarium	33,000	19,633	66,000	33,000	33,000	13,367	68.08
204–212	Common Staff Costs	79,098	69,405	186,794	104,630	82,164	35,225	50.75
300	Official Missions	20,000	22,739	30,000	15,000	15,000	(7,739)	(34.03)
401–406	Maintenance Costs	16,500	10,833	33,000	16,500	16,500	5,667	52.31
501–504	Communications Costs	6,500	4,309	13,000	6,500	6,500	2,191	50.85
600–610	Supplies and Services	16,000	21,243	32,000	16,000	16,000	(5,243)	(24.68)
800	Meetings	135,000	194,177	360,000	180,000	180,000	(14,177)	(7.30)
900	Research and Joint Projects	0	0	32,000	17,000	15,000	17,000	0.00
	Total	430,801	449,748	1,000,845	511,215	489,630	61,467	13.67

IX. RESOLUTIONS ADOPTED AT THE 16TH AND 17TH SESSIONS

36. The Commission adopted the first five Resolutions at the 16th Session and the other five at the 17th (Annexes VII and VIII). The list of these resolutions is hereafter:

(1) Resolution on the Military;
(2) Resolution on Nigeria;
(3) Resolution on Rwanda;
(4) Resolution on The Gambia;
(5) Resolution on the Human Rights Situation in Africa;
(6) Resolution on Sudan;
(7) Resolution on Nigeria;
(8) Resolution on The Gambia;
(9) Resolution on Anti-Personnel Mines;
(10) Resolution on conditions in the prisons of Africa.

X. ADOPTION OF THE REPORT BY THE ASSEMBLY OF HEADS OF STATE AND GOVERNMENT

37. Following consideration of this Report, the Assembly of Heads of State and Government adopted a resolution that took note of it and authorized its publication. (Annex IX)

ANNEX I

African Charter on Human and Peoples' Rights
List of Countries which have Signed, Ratified or Acceded to the Charter

No.	Country	Date of Signature	Date of Ratification/ Adhesion	Date Deposited
1.	Algeria	10/04/86	01/03/87	20/03/87
2.	Angola		02/03/90	09/10/90
3.	Benin		20/01/86	25/02/86
4.	Botswana		17/07/86	22/07/86
5.	Burundi		28/07/80	30/08/89
6.	Burkina Faso	05/03/84	06/07/84	21/09/84
7.	Cameroon	23/07/87	20/06/89	18/09/89
8.	Cape Verde	31/03/86	02/06/87	06/08/87
9.	Central African Republic		26/04/86	27/07/86

No.	Country	Date of Signature	Date of Ratification/ Adhesion	Date Deposited
10.	Chad	29/05/86	09/10/86	11/11/86
11.	Comoros		01/06/86	18/07/86
12.	Congo	27/11/81	09/12/82	17/01/83
13.	Côte d'Ivoire		06/01/92	31/03/92
14.	Djibouti	20/12/91	11/11/91	20/12/91
15.	Egypt	16/11/81	20/03/84	03/04/84
16.	Equatorial Guinea	18/08/86	07/04/86	18/08/86
17.	Eritrea			
18.	Ethiopia			
19.	Gabon	26/02/82	20/02/86	26/06/86
20.	Gambia	11/02/83	08/06/83	13/03/83
21.	Ghana		24/01/89	01/03/89
22.	Guinea	09/12/81	16/02/82	13/05/82
23.	Guinea-Bissau		04/12/85	06/03/86
24.	Kenya		23/01/92	10/02/92
25.	Lesotho	07/03/84	10/02/92	27/02/92
26.	Liberia	31/01/83	04/08/82	29/12/82
27.	Libya	30/05/85	19/07/86	26/03/87
28.	Madagascar		09/03/92	19/03/92
29.	Malawi	23/02/90	17/11/89	23/02/90
30.	Mali	13/11/81	21/12/81	22/01/82
31.	Mauritania	25/02/82	14/06/86	26/06/86
32.	Mauritius	27/02/92	19/06/92	07/07/92
33.	Mozambique		22/02/89	07/03/90
34.	Namibia		30/07/92	16/09/92
35.	Niger	09/07/86	15/07/86	21/07/86
36.	Nigeria	31/08/82	22/06/83	27/07/83
37.	Rwanda	11/11/81	15/07/83	22/07/83
38.	Sahrawi Arab Dem. Rep.	10/04/86	02/05/86	23/05/86
39.	Sao Tome & Principe		23/05/86	28/07/86
40.	Senegal	23/09/81	13/08/82	25/10/82
41.	Seychelles		13/04/92	30/04/92
42.	Sierra Leone	27/08/81	21/09/83	27/01/84
43.	Somalia	26/02/82	31/07/85	20/03/86
44.	Sudan	03/09/82	18/02/86	11/03/86
45.	Swaziland			
46.	Togo	20/02/82	05/11/82	22/11/82
47.	Tunisia		16/03/83	22/04/83
48.	Uganda	18/08/86	10/05/86	27/05/86
49.	Tanzania	31/05/82	18/02/84	09/03/84
50.	Zaïre	23/07/87	20/07/87	28/07/87
51.	Zambia	17/01/83	19/01/84	02/02/84
52.	Zimbabwe	20/02/86	30/05/86	12/06/86
53.	South Africa			

ADOPTED: by the 18th Session of the Assembly of Heads of State and Government, June 1981

REQUIRES: ratification or accession by a simple majority of Member States, to come into force
ENTERED INTO FORCE: 21st day of October 1986
DEPOSITED: with the United Nations on 10 September 1991, No. 26363

ANNEX II

Agenda of the Sixteenth Ordinary Session

1. Opening Ceremony
2. Adoption of Agenda
3. Organization of Work Observers
   (a) Consideration of Application for Observer Status
   (b) Relationship with Observers and Statements of Observers
5. Consideration of Periodic Reports
   Initial Reports of – Benin
   – Cape Verde
   – Mozambique
   Second Report of The Gambia
6. Promotional Activities
   (a) Activity Reports by Commissioners (as well as that on the colloquia and seminars)
   (b) Examination of Extra-judicial Executions
   (c) Establishment of an African Human Rights Court (Resolution AHG/230 (XXX) of the Assembly of Heads of State and Government of the OAU on the Creation of an African Human Rights Court)
   (d) Report on Regional Seminar on the Drafting and Preparation of Periodic Reports held in Tunis in May 1994
   (e) Report on Seminar on the African Woman and the African Charter on Human and Peoples' Rights
   (f) Dakar Preparatory Regional Conference on Women (November 1994) and 4th World Conference on Women (Beijing 1995)
   (g) Organization of Forthcoming Conferences and Seminars
   (h) Publication of the Review and the Newsletter of the Commission
   (i) Follow up of Decisions and Recommendations Adopted by the World Conferences on Human Rights (Vienna and Montreal Conferences)
7. Protective Activities
8. Question of the Head Quarters of the Commission
9. Administrative and Financial Matters
   (a) Report of the Chairman
   (b) Report of the Secretary

(c) Implementation of the Recommendations of the Previous Session
(d) Draft Rules on Contracts and Consultants
(e) Funding for the Translation of Periodic Reports
(f) Situation of the Documentation Centre

10. Methods of Work of the Commission

(a) Consideration of Amendments to the Rules of Procedure
(b) Examination of Article 58 of the Charter
(c) Question of interns within the Secretariat of the Commission

11. OAU activities relevant to the Commission
12. Dates, Place and Agenda of the 17th Session
13. Any Other Business
14. Preparation of:

(a) Sessional Report
(b) Final Communique

15. Adoption of the Report of the 16th Session
16. Final Communiqué and Closing Ceremony

ANNEX III

Agenda of the Seventeenth Ordinary Session

1. Opening Ceremony
2. Adoption of Agenda
3. Organization of Work
4. Adoption of the Report of the 16th Session
5. Observers

(a) Consideration of Application for Observer Status
(b) Relationship with Observers and Statements of the Latter

6. Consideration of Periodic Reports of the following Member States:

- Mauritius
- Mozambique
- Seychelles

7. Promotional Activities:

(a) Activity Reports by Commissioners
(b) Examination of Extra-judicial Executions
(c) Report on the Implementation of Resolution AHG/230 (XXX) on the Establishment of an African Human Rights Court
(d) The Situation in the Prisons in Africa

(e) Report on Seminar on the African Woman and the African Charter on Human and Peoples' Rights
(f) Dakar Preparatory Regional Conference on Women (November 1994) and 4th World Conference on Women (Beijing 1995)
(g) Organization of Forthcoming Seminars and Conferences
(h) Publication of the Review and the Newsletter of the Commission
(i) Follow-up of the Decisions and Recommendations (The Vienna and Montréal Conferences)
(j) Report of the African Mission of the Embargo Evaluation of the UN on Libyan Populations – February, 1995 (Proposed by the Cameroonian League for Human Rights)

8. Protective Activities
9. Question concerning the Headquarters of the Secretariat of the Commission
10. Administrative and Financial Matters

(a) Report of the Chairman of the Commission
(b) Report of the Secretary to the Commission
(c) Implementation of the Recommendations of the Previous Sessions
(d) Draft Rules on Contracts with Consultants
(e) Financing of the Translation of Summaries and Periodic Reports
(f) Situation of the Documentation Centre of the Commission
(g) Draft Cooperation Agreement Between the Commission and Interights
(h) Distribution of States Parties between the members of the Commission for promotional activities

11. Methods of Work of the Commission.

(a) Consideration of Amendments to the Rules of Procedure
(b) Examination of Article 58 of the Charter
(c) Amendment of Article 12 of the Rules of Procedure

12. OAU Activities Relevant to the Commission
13. Dates, Place and Agenda of the 18th Session.
14. Any Other Business
15. Preparation of:

(a) Sessional Report
(b) 8th Annual Activity Report
(c) Final Communiqué

16. Adoption of the Report of the 17th Session and the Annual Activity Report
17. Final Communiqué and Closing Ceremony

ANNEX IV

Status of Submission of Periodic Reports by States Parties

In accordance with Article 62 of the Charter reports are due from States Parties on the following dates:

No.	State Party	First Report	Second Report	Third Report
1.	Algeria	20/06/89	1991	1993
2.	Angola	09/01/92	1994	1996
3.*	Benin	21/10/88	1990	1992
4.	Botswana	21/10/88	1990	1992
5.	Burundi	30/11/91	1993	1995
6.	Burkina Faso	21/10/88	1990	1992
7.	Cameroon	18/12/91	1993	1995
8.*	Cape Verde	06/11/89	1991	1993
9.	Central African Republic	21/10/88	1990	1992
10.	Chad	11/02/89	1991	1993
11.	Comoros	21/10/88	1990	1992
12.	Congo	21/10/88	1990	1992
13.	Côte d'Ivoire	01/07/94	1996	1998
14.	Djibouti	20/03/93	1995	1997
15.*	Egypt	21/10/88	1990	1992
16.	Equatorial Guinea	18/11/88	1990	1992
17.	Ethiopia	–	–	–
18.	Eritrea	–	–	–
19.	Gabon	21/10/88	1990	1992
20.†	Gambia	21/10/88	1990	1992
21.*	Ghana	01/06/91	1993	1995
22.	Guinea	21/10/88	1990	1992
23.	Guinea Bissau	21/10/88	1990	1992
24.	Kenya	10/05/94	1996	1998
25.	Lesotho	27/05/94	1996	1998
26.	Liberia	21/10/88	1990	1992
27.*	Libya	26/06/89	1991	1993
28.	Madagascar	19/06/94	1996	1998
29.	Malawi	23/05/92	1994	1996
30.	Mali	21/10/88	1990	1992
31.	Mauritania	21/10/88	1990	1992
32.*	Mauritius	07/10/92	1994	1996
33.*	Mozambique	07/06/92	1994	1996
34.	Namibia	16/12/94	1996	1998
35.	Niger	21/10/88	1990	1992
36.*	Nigeria	21/10/88	1990	1992
37.	Rwanda	21/10/88	1990	1992
38.	SADR	21/10/88	1990	1992
39.	Sao Tome & Principe	21/10/88	1990	1992
40.*	Senegal	21/10/88	1990	1992

No.	State Party	First Report	Second Report	Third Report
41.*	Seychelles	30/07/94	1996	1998
42.	Sierra Leone	21/10/88	1990	1992
43.	Somalia	21/10/88	1990	1992
44.	Sudan	21/10/88	1990	1992
45.	Swaziland	21/10/88	1990	1992
46.*	Tanzania	21/10/88	1990	1992
47.*	Togo	21/10/88	1990	1992
48.†	Tunisia	21/10/88	1990	1992
49.	Uganda	21/10/88	1990	1992
50.	Zaire	28/10/89	1991	1993
51.	Zambia	21/10/88	1990	1992
52.*	Zimbabwe	21/10/88	1990	1992
53.	South Africa			

* has presented its preliminary report
† has presented its preliminary report and second periodic report

ANNEX V

Distribution of Countries by Members of the Commission for Promotional Work as at 10 December 1993

1. **Mr. Atsu-Koffi Amega**
   Togo
   Central African Republic
   Burundi
   Tchad
   Gabon
   Djibouti

2. **Dr. Ibrahim A. Badawi El-Sheikh**
   Comoros
   Seychelles
   Mauritius
   Madagascar
   Egypt

3. **Mr. Alioune Blondin Beye**
   Benin
   Equatorial Guinea
   Côte d'Ivoire
   Mauritania

4. **Mr. Emmanuel Victor Oware Dankwa**
   Ghana
   Zimbabwe
   Malawi

5. **Mr. Sourahata Baboucar Semega Janneh**
   Gambia
   Liberia
   Sierra Leone
   Botswana
   Namibia

6. **Mr. Robert Habesh Kisanga**
   Ethiopia
   Kenya
   Somalia
   Uganda
   Tanzania
   Zambia

7. **Mrs. Vera V. D. M. Duarte Martins**
   Cape Verde
   Mozambique
   Angola
   Guinea Bissau
   Sao Tome & Principe

8. **Mr. Youssoupha Ndiaye**
   Mali
   Niger
   Senegal
   Republic of Guinea

9. **Prof. Isaac Nguema**
   Zaire
   Burkina Faso
   Congo
   Rwanda

10. **Prof. Mohammed H. Ben Salem**
   Tunisia
   Algeria
   Libya
   Sahrawi Arab Democratic Republic
   Sudan
   Eritrea

11. **Prof. U. Oji Umozurike**
   Nigeria
   Cameroon
   Lesotho
   Swaziland
   South Africa

ANNEX VI

Communications

1. 8/88 Nziwa Buyingo v Uganda

Complaint:
The author of the communication, Mr. Nziwa Buyingo, citizen of Zaire, alleges that he was on 28 December 1987, subjected to arrest, arbitrary detention, torture and extraction of money by Ugandan soldiers in Kisoro, Uganda.

He alleges that his rights under Articles 5, 6, 12 and 14 under the African Charter on Human and Peoples' Rights have been violated.

Finding:
The Commission has since 1988 failed to get any response from the complainant on whether or not he has had recourse to local remedies as required by Article 56(5) of the Charter and Rule 103(1)(f) of the Rules of Procedure. The Commission accordingly declares the communication inadmissible.

2. 16/88 Comite Cultural pour la Democratie au Benin v Benin, joined with 17/88 Hilaire Badjogoume v. Benin and 18/88 El Hadj Boubacare Diawara v Benin

Complaint:
The communication, No. 16/88, submitted by "Comite Culturel pour la Democratie au Benin", alleges serious violations of various articles of the African Charter,

committed by the Benin Government. They refer to the detention of hundreds of citizens without charge or trial, torture, and the murder of a Mr. Akpokpo.

The communication requests full and unconditional liberation of all political prisoners. A letter submitted by the Government on 9 May 1994 states that all political prisoners were released after the new Government's take over in 1990.

Finding:
Notices of hearing was sent to the parties, but only the representative of the Government of Benin appeared. The Government representative was duly given the opportunity to present his case at the end of which the Commission, after due consideration decided that the present Government of Benin has satisfactorily resolved the issue of violations of human rights under the previous administration. This decision was communicated to the authors of the communication. In the absence of a response, the Commission confirms that the issue had been satisfactorily resolved.

3. 17/88 Hilaire Badjogoume v Benin, joined with 16/88 and 18/88

Complaint:
The communication No. 17/88, was submitted by Mr. Hilaire Badjogoume. He complained of being arbitrarily detained for two years, from 5 April 1988 to 10 January 1990.

Decision:
Notices of hearing were sent to the parties, but only the representative of the Government of Benin appeared. The Government representative was duly given the opportunity to present his case at the end of which the Commission after due consideration decided that the Government of Benin has settled the complainant's claim administratively.

This decision was communicated to the complainants and in absence of response the Commission confirms its decision.

4. 8/88 El Hadj Boubacare Diawara v Benin, joined with 16/88 and 17/88

Complaint:
The communication No. 18/88, was submitted by Mr. El Hadj Boubacare Diawara. He had been detained without charge or trial from 18 February 1982 for a period of more than 7 years. Furthermore, he reports the arbitrary detention of 7 others, one of whom died in prison 11 months after imprisonment. All detainees, he claimed, were tortured while imprisoned.

Finding:
Notice of hearing were sent to the parties, but only the representative of the Government of Benin appeared. Since the complainant has referred his complaint to the courts in Benin, where it is now pending, the Commission declared the communication inadmissible for want of exhaustion of local remedies, under Article 56(5) of the Charter and Rules 103(1)(f) of the Rules of Procedure.

5. 31/89 Maria Baes v Zaire

Complaint:
The communication was submitted by a Danish national, Maria Baes, on behalf of her colleague Dr. Shambuyi Naiadia Kandola, of the University of Kinshasa, Zaire. she alleges that her colleague was detained without charge in April 1988 for purely political reasons, in breach of Articles 6 and 7 of the African Charter on Human and Peoples' Rights.

Finding:
The author has failed to respond to inquiries from the Commission which learns that the detained person had since been released. The author shows no interest in pursuing the case. The Commission decides to close the file since the author has no interest in proceeding with the case.

6. 39/90 Annette Pagnoule/Cameroon

Complaint:
This communication was submitted by Annette pagnoule of Amnesty International and concerns one Abdoulaye Mazou, a Cameroonian national who continues to be held in prison, despite completing, in April 1989, a five-year prison term.

Decision:
The Commission decides to close the file because the victim has been released and the issue satisfactorily resolved.

7. 53/91 Alberto Capitao v Tanzania

Complaint:
Alberto Capitao is a businessman and a former citizen of Zaire, presently resident in Angola. He sued the Tanzanian Film Company, a state-owned company, in a Zairian court, and won a judgment of $500,000 on 4 July 1994. The Embassy of Tanzania in Kinshasa was sued simultaneously with the Tanzanian Film Company. As of January 1985, no appeal in the case had been filed. The Tanzanian Film Company failed to pay the judgement debt. The Tanzanian Film Company has no property in Zaire; the only property of the Tanzanian State is Embassy of Tanzania in Kinshasa, which is exempt from seizure under the tradition of diplomatic immunity. The complainant sought the intervention of the Foreign Ministries of Zaire and Angola where he now resides, but to no avail.

The complainant argues that he has been deprived of justice and in essence of the right to have his cause heard, since as an individual holding a judgment against a foreign State which refuses to pay, he has no recourse.

Decision:
The Commission decided that the case was inadmissible on account of lack of exhaustion of local remedies. The case can be resubmitted when the local remedies have been properly exhausted or if the complainant proves that local remedies are unavailable, ineffective or unreasonably prolonged.

8. 59/91 Embga Mekongo Louis v Cameroon

Complaint:
Embga Mekongo, a Cameroonian citizen, alleges false imprisonment, miscarriage of justice and damages for which he claims the sum of $105 million.

Finding:
The Commission finds that the author had been denied due process, contrary to Article 7 of the African Charter and had in fact suffered damages. Being unable to determine the amount of damages, the Commission recommends that the quantum should be determined under the law of Cameroon.

9. 60/91 Constitutional Rights Project v Nigeria (in respect of Wahab Akamu, G. Adeaga and others)

The facts:
(1) Communication 60/91 was brought by the Constitutional Rights Project, a Nigerian NGO, on behalf of Wahab Akamu, Gbolahan Adeaga and others sentenced to death under the Robbery and Firearms (Special Provision) Decree No. 5 of 1984. This decree creates special tribunals, composed of one serving or retired judge, one member of the armed forces and one member of the police force. The decree does not provide for any judicial appeal of sentences. Sentences are subject to confirmation or disallowance by the governor of a State.
(2) Wahab Akamu was convicted and sentenced to death on 12 August 1991 and Gbolahan Ageaga was convicted and sentenced on 14 August 1991. Both were sentenced by Robbery and Firearms Tribunal 1, Lagos. The complaint alleges that both were tortured to extract confessions while they were in custody.

Argument:
(3) The communication argues that the prohibition on judicial review of the special tribunals and lack of judicial appeals for judgements of these tribunals violates the right to an appeal to competent national organs against acts violating fundamental rights, guaranteed by Article 7, paragraph 1(a) of the African Charter.
(4) The communication also argues that the practice of setting up special tribunals, composed of members of the armed forces and police in addition to judges, violates the right to be tried by an impartial tribunal guaranteed by Article 7, paragraph 1(d).

Law:

Admissibility:
(5) The case was decided admissible at the 14th Session of the Commission on the following grounds:

The case raises the question of whether the remedies available are of a nature that requires exhaustion.

The Act complained of in Communication No.60/91 is the Robbery and Firearms (Special Provisions) Act, Chapter 398, in which Section 11, paragraph 4 provides:

> "No appeal shall lie from a decision of a tribunal constituted under this Act or from any confirmation nor dismissal of such decision by the Governor."

The Robbery and Firearms Act entitles the Governor to confirm or disallow the conviction of the Special Tribunal.

This power is to be described as discretionary extraordinary remedy of a non-judicial nature. The object of the remedy is to obtain a favour and not to vindicate a right. It would be improper to insist on the complainants seeking remedies from sources which do not operate impartially and have no obligation to decide according to legal principles. The remedy is neither adequate nor effective.

Therefore, the Commission is of the opinion that the remedy available is not of a nature that requires exhaustion according to Article 56, paragraph 5 of the African Charter.

The merits:

(6) The Robbery and Firearms (Special Provisions) Act, Section 11, Sub-section 4 provides:

> "No appeal shall lie from a decision of a tribunal constituted under this Act or from any confirmation of dismissal of such decision by the Governor."

(7) A "decision of a tribunal constituted under this Act or any confirmation or dismissal of such decision by the governor" may certainly constitute an "act violating fundamental rights" as described in Article 7.1(a) of the Charter. In this case, the fundamental rights in question are those to life and liberty provided for in Articles 4 and 6 of the African Charter. While punishments decreed as the culmination of a carefully conducted criminal procedure do not necessarily constitute violations of these rights, to foreclose any avenue of appeal to "competent national organs" in criminal cases bearing such penalties clearly violates Article 7.1 (a) of the African Charter, and increases the risk that severe violations may go unredressed.

(8) The Robbery and Firearms (Special Provisions) Act, Section 8(1), describes the constitution of the tribunals, which shall consist of three persons: one judge, one officer of the Army, Navy or Air Force and one officer of the Police Force. Jurisdiction has thus been transferred from the normal courts to a tribunal chiefly composed of persons belonging to the executive branch of government, the same branch that passed the Robbery and Firearms Decree, whose members do not necessarily possess any legal expertise. Article 7.1(d) of the African Charter requires the court or tribunal to be impartial. Regardless of the character of the individual members of such tribunals, its composition alone creates the appearance, if not actual lack of impartiality. It thus violates Article 7.1(d).

For the above reasons, the Commission:

declares that there has been a violation of Article 7.1(a), (c) and (d) of the African Charter; and

recommends that the Government of Nigeria should free the complaints.

At the 17th Session, the Commission decided to bring the file to Nigeria for the planned mission in order to verify that the complainants have been released.

10. 62/91 Committee for the Defence of Human Rights v Nigeria, in respect of Ms. Jennifer Madike

Complaint:
The case concerned an individual detained on charges of drug dealing. The complainant committee alleged that the detention was politically motivated. The Commission received information that the detainee was freed and subsequently inquired of the complainant if it wished to pursue the case.

Finding:
These inquiries went unanswered despite two reminders. The Commission therefore decided that the file be closed because of loss of contact with the complainant.

11. 64/92 Krischna Achutan (on behalf of Aleke Banda, 68/92 Amnesty International on behalf of Orton and Vera Chirwa 78/92 Amnesty International on behalf of Orton and Vera Chirwa v Malawi

The facts:

(1) In communication no. 64/92 Krischna Achutan appealed to the Commission on behalf of his father-in-law, Aleke Banda, a prominent political figure who at the time of the communication had been imprisoned for over 12 years without legal charge or trial. Mr. Achutan had met with two successive heads of intelligence of Malawi who said that there was no case pending against Mr. Banda, but he was being held "at the pleasure of the Head of State.

(2) In communications nos. 68/92 and 78/92 Amnesty International petitioned the Commission on behalf of Orton and Vera Chirwa. Orton Chirwa had been a prominent political figure in Malawi before independence, but had been living in exile in Zambia with his wife since 1964 because of differences with Malawi's President Banda. In 1981, the Malawi security officials took them into custody and they were subsequently sentenced to death for treason at a trial in the Southern Regional Traditional Court. They claimed at this trial that they had been abducted from Zambia. They were denied legal representation. The sentences were upheld by the national traditional Appeals Court, although the Appeals Court criticized many aspects of the conduct of the trial.

(3) After international protest, the sentences were commuted to life imprisonment. The Chirwas were held in almost complete solitary confinement, given extremely poor food, inadequate medical care, shackled for long periods of time within their cells and prevented from seeing each other for years.

(4) In its supplemental communication consisting of a report on Malawi for March–July 1992, Amnesty International described the arrests of many office workers in 1992 because of suspicions that the equipment used in their work, such as computers and fax machines, could be used to disseminate propaganda of the pro-democracy movement. The report also described extremely poor

prison conditions, including overcrowding and torture consisting of beatings and electric shocks.

(5) The communication also described the detention and intimidation of Roman Catholic bishops. Trade Union leaders were imprisoned, and peacefully striking workers were shot and killed by the police. Police also raided student dormitories and arrested students who were beaten and tortured.

Law:

(6) Article 4 of the African Charter reads:

> "Every human being shall be entitled to respect for his life . . ."

Shootings by police officers are a violation of this right.

(7) Article 5 of the African Charter provides as follows:

> "All forms of . . . torture, cruel, inhuman or degrading punishment and treatment shall be prohibited."

The conditions of overcrowding and acts of beating and torture that took place in prisons in Malawi contravened this Article. Aspects of the treatment of Vera and Orton Chirwa such as excessive solitary confinement, shackling within a cell, extremely poor quality food and denial of access to adequate medical care, were also in contravention of this Article.

(8) Article 6 of the African Charter reads:

> "Every individual shall have the right to liberty and to the security of his person. . . ."

The massive and arbitrary arrests of office workers, trade unionists, Roman Catholic Bishops and students violated this Article. The arbitrary detention of Mr. Aleke Banda is likewise a violation of Article 6.

(9) Mr. Banda was not allowed recourse to the national courts to challenge the violation of his fundamental right to liberty as guaranteed by Article 6 of the African Charter and the constitution of Malawi. Furthermore, Aleke Banda was detained indefinitely without trial. The Commission finds that Mr. Banda's imprisonment violated Article 7, paragraph 1 (a) and (d) of the African Charter.

(10) Vera and Orton Chirwa were tried before the Southern Region Traditional Court without being defended by a counsel. This constitutes a violation of Article 7, paragraph 1(c) of the African Charter.

(11) The Commission notes that Malawi has undergone important political changes after the submission of the communications. Multiparty elections have been held, resulting in a new Government. The Commission hopes that a new era of respect for the human rights of Malawi's citizens has begun.

(12) Principles of international law stipulate, however, that a new government inherits the previous government's international obligations, including the responsibility for the previous government's mismanagement. The change of Government in Malawi does not extinguish the present claim before the Commission. Although

the present Government of Malawi did not commit the human rights abuses complained of, it is responsible for the reparation of these abuses.

For these reasons, the Commission:
holds that there has been a violation of Articles 4, 5, 6 and 7 paragraph 1(a), (c) and (d) of the African Charter.

12. 75/92 Katangese Peoples' Congress v Zaire

The facts:

(1) The communication was submitted in 1992 by Mr. Gerard Moke, President of the Katangese Peoples' Congress requesting the African Commission on Human and Peoples' Rights to:

- recognize the Katangese Peoples' Congress as a liberation movement entitled to support in the achievement of independence for Katanga;
- recognize the independence of Katanga;
- help secure the evacuation of Zaire from Katanga.

Law:

(2) The claim is brought under Article 20(1) of the African Charter on Human and Peoples' Rights. There are no allegations of specific breaches of other human rights apart from the claim of the denial of self-determination.

(3) All peoples have a right to self-determination. There may however be controversy as to the definition of peoples and the content of the right. The issue in the case is not self-determination for all Zaireans as a people but specifically for the Katangese. Whether the Katangese consist of one or more ethnic groups is, for this purpose immaterial and no evidence has been adduced to that effect.

(4) The Commission believes that self-determination may be exercised in any of the following – independence, self-government, local government, federalism, confederalism, unitarism or any other form of relations that accords with the wishes of the people but fully cognizant of other recognized principles such as sovereignty and territorial integrity.

(5) The Commission is obliged to uphold the sovereignty and territorial integrity of Zaire, a member of the OAU and a party to the African Charter on Human and Peoples' Rights.

(6) In the absence of concrete evidence of violations of human rights to the point that the territorial integrity of Zaire should be called to question and in the absence of evidence that the people of Katanga are denied the right to participate in Government as guaranteed by Article 13(1) of the African Charter, the Commission holds the view that Katanga is obliged to exercise a variant of self-determination that is compatible with the sovereignty and territorial integrity of Zaire.

For the above reasons, the Commission:
declares that the case holds no evidence of violations of any rights under the African Charter. The request for independence for Katanga therefore has no merit under the African Charter on Human and Peoples' Rights.

13. 83/92, 88/93, 91/93 (joined) Jean Yaovi Degli (au nom du Caporal N. Bikagni), Union Interafricaine des Droits de l'Homme, Commission International de Juristes/Togo

The facts:
The first communication no. 83/92, concerns Corporal Nikabour Bikagni, who the communication alleges was arrested on 7 October 1992 in Lome and who was subject to torture and maltreatment. Under this duress, he made a confession that he was planning a coup against the Government of Togo.

The second communication no. 88/93, consists of a report of a mission sent to Togo by the Union Interafricaine des Droits de l'Homme from 23 to 29 December 1992. This report includes information on the attempt on the life of opposition leader Gilchrist Olympio, the assassination of the driver of the Prime Minister in December 1992, extortion and killings in villages in the north of Togo, the shooting incident of 25 January 1993 which resulted in at least 14 deaths, and the shooting incident of 26 January which resulted in at least 4 deaths. The communication also mentions the discovery of more than 15 bodies which were found, mutilated and bound, in the waters around Lome.

The report also provides a general overview of the political and economic situation in Togo, including irregularities with respect to how elections are conducted.

The third communication no. 91/93, alleges that on 30 January 1993 the Togolese military shot and killed 20 peaceful demonstrators in Lome. This was related to a general breakdown of law and order which resulted in numerous violations of human rights by the security forces. Abuses by the security forces caused 40,000 Togolese to flee the country

Complaint:
The complainants allege grave and massive violations of various rights protected by the African Charter.

Finding:
The Commission sent a delegation to Togo and was adduced that these acts were committed under a previous administration. The Commission is satisfied that the present administration has dealt with the issues satisfactorily.

14. 86/93 M. S. Ceesay v The Gambia

The facts:
The complainant was a Corporal in The Gambia National Army and was on 14 June 1991 – according to the complainant – randomly selected as one of seven men to see the Commander in order to discuss the problems of the Contingent sent to Liberia under ECOMOG. When the seven men had gathered they were immediately surrounded by armed personnel who attempted to arrest them. They managed to flee to the State House but were arrested, subsequently suspended and discharged allegedly because of state mutiny but without charge or trial.

According to the Attorney General, Mr. Ceesay and others were marching in the streets protesting because of lack of payment. The protesters were disrupting the peace and were charged with mutiny. A commission of Enquiry was set up to decide on the cases and the mutineers were eventually dismissed, the most inferior sanction available against mutiny.

Complaint:
The complainant asks the Commission to order re-instatement or to compel the Gambian authorities to issue the complainant with a certificate of discharge.

Decision:
The Government notified the Commission that the complainant had not had recourse to the local remedies. At its 16th Session the Commission declared the communication inadmissible.

15. 87/93 the Constitutional Rights Project (in respect of Zamani Lakwot and 6 others) v Nigeria

The facts:

(1) Communication 87/93 was brought on behalf of seven men – Zamani Lekwot, James Atomic Kude, Yohanna Karau Kibori, Marcus Mamman, Yahaya Duniya, Julius Sarki Zamman Dabo and Iliya Maza – sentenced to death under the Civil Disturbances (Special Tribunal) Decree No. 2 of 1987 from Nigeria. This decree does not provide for any judicial appeal against the decisions of the special tribunals and prohibits the courts from reviewing any aspect of the operation of the tribunal.

(2) The communication also alleges that the accused and their counsel were constantly harassed and intimidated during the trial, ultimately forcing the withdrawal of the defence counsel. Despite the lack of defence, the tribunal condemned the accused to death for culpable homicide, unlawful assembly and breach of the peace.

Argument:

(3) The communication argues that the prohibition on judicial review of the special tribunals and lack of judicial appeals of judgments of these tribunals violates the right to an appeal to competent national organs against acts violating fundamental rights, guaranteed by Article 7, paragraph l(a) of the African Charter.

(4) The communication complains that the conduct of the trials before these tribunals, which included harassment of defence counsel, and deprivation of defence counsel, violated the right to be defended by counsel of one's choice, guaranteed by Article 7, paragraph l(c).

(5) The communication finally complains that the practice of setting up special tribunals, composed of members of the armed forces and police in addition to judges, violates the right to be tried by an impartial tribunal guaranteed by Article 7, paragraph 1(d).

Law:

Admissibility:

(6) The case was declared admissible at the 14th Session of the Commission on the following grounds:

The case raises the question of whether the remedies available are of a nature that requires exhaustion.

The Act complained of in Communication No. 87/93 is the Civil Disturbances (Special Tribunal) Act, in which Part IV, Section S(1) provides:

> "The validity of any decision, sentence, judgment, . . . or order given or made, . . . or any other thing whatsoever done under this Act shall not be inquired into in any court of law."

The Civil Disturbances Act empowers the Armed Forces Ruling Council to confirm the penalties of the Tribunal.

This power is a discretionary, extraordinary remedy of a non-judicial nature. The object of the remedy is to obtain a favour and not vindicate a right. It would be improper to insist on the complainant seeking remedies from a source which does not operate impartially and has no obligation to decide according to legal principles. The remedy is neither adequate nor effective.

Therefore, the Commission is of the opinion that the remedy available is not of a nature that requires exhaustion according to Article 56, paragraph 5 of the African Charter.

Merits:

(7) The Civil Disturbances (Special Tribunal) Act, Part IV, Section 8(1) provides:

> "The validity of any decision, sentence, judgment, . . . or order given or made, . . . or any other thing whatsoever done under this Act shall not be inquired into in any court of law."

(8) A "decision, sentence, judgment . . . order given or made . . . or any other thing whatsoever done under" the Civil Disturbances Act may certainly constitute an "Act violating fundamental rights in question are those to life and liberty provided for in Articles 4 and 6 of the African Charter. While punishments decreed as the culmination of a carefully conducted criminal procedure do not necessarily constitute violations of these rights, to foreclose any avenue of appeal to "competent national organs" in criminal cases bearing such Charter, and increases the risk that even severe violations may go unredressed.

(9) The communication alleges that during the trials the defence counsel for the complainants was harassed and intimidated to the extent of being forced to withdraw from the proceedings. In spite of this forced withdrawal of counsel, the tribunal proceeded to give judgment in the matter, finally sentencing the accused to death. The Commission finds that defendants were deprived of their right to defence, including the right to be defended by counsel of their choice, violation of Article 7.1(c) as cited above.

(10) The Civil Disturbances (Special Tribunal) Act, Part II, Section 2 (2) says that the tribunal shall consist of one judge and four members of the Armed Forces. As such, the tribunal is composed of persons belonging largely to the executive branch of government, the same branch that passed the Civil Disturbances Act.

Article 7.1(d) of the African Charter requires the court or tribunal to be impartial. Regardless of the character of the individual members of such tribunals, its composition alone creates the appearance, if not actual lack of impartiality. It thus violates Article 7.1 (d).

For the above reasons, the Commission:
declares that there has been a violation of Article 7(a), (c) and (d) of the African Charter; and
recommends that the Government of Nigeria should free the complaints.

At the 17th Session the Commission decided to bring the file to Nigeria for a planned mission in order to make sure that the violations have been repaired.

16. 90/93 Paul S. Haye v The Gambia

Facts:
In November 1987, the complainant hired Edward Gomez, an attorney, to register a company for him. Complainant paid to Mr. Gomez a sum of D7,150 in fees, but the company was never registered. In March 1990, complainant sued Mr. Gomez for the return of the money. Mr. Gomez filed a counter-claim, but before the suit could be heard the judge who had been scheduled to hear the case resigned. After inquiries to discover when the suit would be heard, complainant was told to await notice by the court.

On 2 October 1991, a mini van belonging to the complainant was seized. He was informed that after failure to appear in court on 28 May 1991, a default judgment was entered in favour of Mr. Gomez, and the mini van was seized to satisfy the judgment. Complainant filed a motion for leave to appeal the judgment to the Gambia Court of Appeal on the grounds that he never received notification of the 28 May court date. This motion was heard by the same judge who made the original judgment, and was denied. Therefore the complainant alleges that he has no further domestic remedies available.

Argument:
Complainant alleged violation of his rights under Article 7 to have his cause heard. The Supreme Court judge had absolute discretion to disallow an appeal of his own judgement.

Questions also arise over the adequacy of the procedure of service (notification of hearing date).

Decision:
At its 16th Session, the Commission declared the case inadmissible for non-exhaustion of local remedies. The complainant by reason of his own default and/or negligence, did not seek to appeal to the court of Appeal of the Gambia against the

decision of the Supreme Court referring his application for leave to appeal to the Court of Appeal. Upon the complainant being notified of this decision he wrote back urging the Commission to review its decision on the same grounds he had advanced before. As no new grounds are raised or shown, the Commission finds no reasons to disturb its previous decision which is accordingly re-affirmed.

17. 92/93 International Pen vs Sudan (in respect of Kemal al-Jazouli)

The facts:

(1) The communication concerns one Kemal al-Jazouli, who was held incommunicado without charge from March to June 1992. During this period he had no opportunity to challenge his detention in a court of law.

Complaint:

(2) The complaint alleges violation of Articles 6 and 7 of the African Charter.

Decision:

(3) The Commission is of the opinion that none of the information given whether taken individually or together can constitute exhaustion of local remedies. The victim was tried in June 1992 and the complaint was lodged with the Commission in March 1993. He had ample freedom to exhaust local remedies before he approached the Commission. The fact that the Government has in general terms denied the existence of incommunicado detentions in Sudan does not amount to saying that the case has been tried in Sudanese courts.

For these reasons, the Commission:
declares the communication inadmissible for non-exhaustion of local remedies.

18. 101/93 Civil Liberties Organization in respect of the Nigerian Bar Association vs Nigeria

The facts:

(1) The communication is brought by the Civil Liberties Organization, a Nigerian non-governmental organization, in protest against the Legal Practitioners' Decree. This decree establishes a new governing body of the Nigerian Bar Association, namely the Body of Benchers. Of the 128 members of this body, only 31 are nominees of the Bar Association. The rest are nominees of the government.

(2) The functions of the Body of Benchers are (1) the prescription of practicing fees one tenth of which are payable every year to the Body and (2) the disciplining of legal practitioners.

(3) The decree excludes recourse to the Courts and makes it an offence 'to commence or maintain an action or any legal proceeding whatever relating to or connected with or arising from the exercise of any of the powers of the Body of Benchers". The decree is retrospective.

Argument:

(4) The communication argues that the prohibition on litigation violates Article 7 of the African Charter.

(5) The communication argues that the new governing body for the Nigerian Bar Association, established by governmental decree, violates Nigerian Lawyers' freedom of association guaranteed by Article of the African Charter.

Law:

(6) This communication was declared admissible at the 16th Session.

(7) The Legal Practitioners (Amendment) Decree 1993, Section 23A, Sub-section 1, reads:

> "No person shall commence or maintain an action or any legal proceeding whatsoever relating to, connected with or arising from:
>
> (a) the management of the affairs of the association; or
> (b) the exercise or preparation by the Body of Benchers for the exercise of the powers conferred upon it by this Act."

(8) A decision must be taken as to whether the above mentioned decree constitutes a violation of the African Charter.

(9) The Commission finds that the present case raises questions concerning Article –, the right to liberty, Article 7, the right to fair trail, and Article 10, the right to freedom of association.

(10) The above mentioned Legal practitioners (Amendment) Decree 1993, Section 23A, sub-section 3 reads:

> "A person who contravenes the sub-section (1) of this section commits an offence and is liable on, conviction to a fine N10,000 or to imprisonment for a term of one year to both such fine and imprisonment."

The Decree is retrospective since it was issue 18 February 1993 but was deemed to come into force on 31 July 1992.

(11) Article 6 of the African Charter reads:

> "No one may be deprived of his freedom, except for reasons and conditions previously laid down by law."

No retrospective law may deprive a person of his liberty. The wording of the decree therefore constitutes a violation of Article 6.

(12) Article 7(2) of the African Charter reads:

> "No one may be condemned for an act or omission which did not constitute a legally punishable offence for which no provision was made at the time it was committed."

The Commission is of the opinion that the retrospective effect of the decree constitutes a violation of Article 7(2) of the African Charter.

(13) Article 17(1) of the African Charter reads:

> "Every individual shall have the right to have his cause heard . . ."

The powers of the Body of Benchers include financial and disciplinary matters. The prohibition on litigation against these powers infringes the right to appeal to national organs, and violates Article 7(1) of the Charter.

(14) Article 10 of the African Charter reads:

> "1. Every individual shall have the right to free association provided he abides by the law . . ."

Freedom of association is enunciated as an individual right and is first and foremost a duty for the State to abstain from interfering with the free formation of associations. There must always be a general capacity for citizens to join, without State interference, in associations in order to attain various ends.

(15) In regulating the use of this right, the competent authorities should not enact provisions which would limit the exercise of this freedom. The competent authorities should not override constitutional provisions or undermine fundamental rights guaranteed by the constitution and international human rights standards.

(16) The Body of Benchers is dominated by representatives of the government and has wide discretionary powers. This interference with the free association of the Nigerian Bar Association is inconsistent with the preamble of the African Charter in conjunction with UN Basic Principles on the Independence of the Judiciary and thereby constitutes a violation of Article 10 of the African Charter.

For the above reasons, the Commission:
holds that there has been a violation of Articles 6,7 and 10 of the African Charter on Human and Peoples' Rights. The Decree should therefore be annulled.

19. 104/94, 109–126/94 Centre for Independence of Judges and Lawyers v Algeria, and others

The facts:

(1) The communication is in the form of a report published by the Center for the Independence of Judges and Lawyers of Geneva, Switzerland. It describes harassment and persecution of judges and lawyers in 53 different countries including 18 of the African countries party to the African Charter. The harassment and persecution described includes murder, torture intimidation and threats of all kinds. The report describes special features of court systems, such as military courts and special tribunals.

Complaint:

(2) The communication does not specify which of the facts it contains it regards as violations. Neither does it specify any sought remedy.

Law:

(3) Article 56 of the African Charter reads:

> "Communications . . . shall be considered if they:
> 1. Indicate their authors even if the latter requests anonymity . . ."

(4) Rule 114, section 3 the Rules of Procedure of the African Commission on Human and Peoples' Rights reads:

> "In order to decide on the admissibility of a communication . . . the Commission shall ensure:
> (b) that the author alleges to be a victim of a violation, . . . , that the communication is submitted in the name of an individual who is a victim (or individuals who are victims) who would be unable to submit a communication or to authorize it to be done".

(5) The reason for these provisions is that the Commission must receive communications with adequate information with a certain degree of specificity concerning the victims.

(6) The present report submitted by the CIJL does not give specific places, dates, and times of alleged incidents sufficient to permit the Commission to intervene or investigate. In some cases, incidents are cited without given the names of the aggrieved parties. There are numerous references to "anonymous" lawyers and judges. Thus, in this case the author is not an alleged victim, nor is the communication submitted in the name of a specific victim, nor does the complainant allege grave and massive violations. The information in the communication is insufficient to permit the Commission to take action.

For the above reasons, the Commission:
declares the communications inadmissible.

20. 127/94 Sana Dumbuya v The Gambia

The facts:
Mr. Dumbuya complains that he was working as a registry clerk for the Ministry for Local Government and Lands from January to July 1992. In July 1992 he was dismissed under unclear circumstances, allegedly for leaking official secrets.

Decision:
The complainant has failed or neglected to respond to two requests by the Commission for information whether all local remedies have been exhausted. In the circumstances the Commission during its 16th Session declared the communication inadmissible on account of lack of exhaustion of local remedies.

21. 136/94 William Courson v Zimbabwe

The facts:
The communication concerns the legal status of homosexuals in Zimbabwe. Domestic law of Zimbabwe criminalizes sexual contacts between consenting adult homosexual men in private. According to the complainant, this prohibition is currently being enforced in Zimbabwe, encouraged by statements against homosexuals by the President and by the Minister of Home Affairs.

The communication complaints of violations of the African Charter on Human and Peoples' Rights, namely Articles 1–6, 8–11, 16, 20, 22 and 24. The complainant points to Articles 60 of the Charter which states that the Commission shall draw inspiration from international law on human and peoples' rights and as Annex B to the communication the complainant has attached the views adopted by the Human Rights Committee in the case of Mr. Toonen vs. Australia. In this case the Committee was of the view that the criminalization of homosexuality in Tasmania was unreasonable and interfered arbitrarily with Mr. Toones's right to privacy under Article 17, paragraph 1 of the International Covenant on Civil and Political Rights (CCPR).

Finding:
The communication was withdrawn by the author. The Commission saw no need to continue with it.

22. 138/94 International PEN on behalf of Senn and Sangare v Côte d'Ivoire

The facts:
International Pen submitted the communication on behalf of two journalists – Senn and Sangare – who published an article that had appeared in Jeune Afrique about President Bedie. They were charged, imprisoned and fined while the appeal was pending. They were again detained, charged and imprisoned but subsequently released in an amnesty. In a subsequent letter to the Commission, the author insisted that the journalists were detained in violation of their rights.

Finding:
After reviewing the situation, the Commission held the view that if the author required any remedies, it should first resort to the legal system of Côte d'Ivoire, the amnesty having extirpated the legal effects of detention and from which the Commission could take note of.

23. 142/94 Muthuthirin Njoka v Kenya (previously 56/91)

The facts:
The communication was submitted by Muthuthirin Njoka who alleges that he was illegally admitted to Mathera Mental Hospital through Police duress and pressure. He alleges the wrong implementation of the Police Act 1961 and Mental Treatment Act 1949, which were both enacted by the colonial government. He also alleges wrongful detention and torture, the wrongful imprisonment of his sons and other members of his family, harassment of the members of his family and the confiscation of family property.

The communication was originally submitted in 1991 and designated No. 56/91. On 21 October 1993, the Commission decided that the communication was inadmissible because Kenya was not party to the African Charter on Human and Peoples' Rights at the time it was submitted.

Mr. Njoka was accordingly intimated but was also informed that he could resubmit his communication since Kenya had subsequently ratified the Charter. This, he did.

Applicable law:
The complainant alleges violations of his rights under Articles 5, 6, 7 and 21 of the Charter.

Recommendation:
The cause of the complaint arose at a time when Kenya was not a party to the Charter. There is no evidence of a continuing damage in breach of the Charter.
The communication is incoherent in several respects:

(1) The author alleges in a letter of 14 June 1994 to the Registrar of the High Court of Kenya that his suits had been pending in Court for 9 years. One was against Kenya claiming the sum of 7.5 billion Kenyan shillings for the wrongful implementation of colonial statutes and another claiming 12.5 billion British shillings for wrongfully passing those legislation.
(2) A letter of 20 March 1991 addressed to the World Health Organization is enclosed. The letter wants "the definition of mental capacity and the position of a living being."
(3) A letter of 31 May 1993 addressed to the Secretary-General of the OAU requires the Organization "to intercept this matter... quash the sentences imposed on my sons and set them free."

The author is incoherent and his complaints are vague. The communication is inadmissible.

For these reasons, the Commission:
declares the communication inadmissible.

ANNEX VII

RESOLUTIONS OF THE 16TH SESSION

Resolution on the Military Adopted 3/11/94 Rev. 1

The African Commission on Human and Peoples' Rights meeting at its 16th Ordinary Session held from 25 October to 3 November, 1994 in Banjul, The Gambia,

Recalling the intervention in African States by the military during the past three decades, and the fact that only very few states have escaped this phenomenon,

Affirming that the best government is one elected by, and accountable to the people,

Aware that the trend world-wide and in Africa in particular is to condemn military take-overs and the intervention by the military in politics,

Recognizing that the forcible take-over of government by Army civilian or military group contravenes Articles 13(1) and 20(1) of the African Commission on Human and Peoples' Rights,

Considering that such interventions stultify political development and antagonize relations between national groups,

CALLS UPON African military regimes to respect fundamental rights;

REMINDS them that they are entrusted with the national armouries solely for the purpose of national defence and the maintenance of internal order under the direction of the legitimate authorities;

CALLS UPON incumbent military governments to handover political power to democratically elected governments without prolonging their incumbencies and unnecessarily delaying the return to democratic civilian rule;

ENCOURAGES states to relegate the era of military interventions in government to the past in the interest of the African image, progress and development, and for the creation of an environment in which Human Rights values may flourish.

Resolution on Nigeria
Adopted 3/11/94 Rev. 1

The African Commission on Human and Peoples' Rights meeting at its 16th Ordinary Session held from 25 October to 3 November 1994 in Banjul, The Gambia,

Recalling that Nigeria has ratified the African Charter on Human and Peoples' Rights,

Believing that the restoration of democracy in Nigeria will be a positive step in African development,

REGRETS the annulment of the 12 June 1993 presidential election which was adjudged free and fair by national and international observers;

CONDEMNS the gross violations of Human Rights as evidence in:

(1) the exclusion of the African Charter on Human and People's Rights from the operation of decrees adopted by the military regime;
(2) the detention of pro-democracy activists and members of the press;
(3) the exclusion of the jurisdiction of courts over decrees;
(4) discarding of court judgements;
(5) the promulgation of laws without proper procedure of penal laws with retroactive effect;
(6) the closure of newspaper houses.

CALLS UPON the Nigerian military government to respect the right of free participation in government and the right to self-determination and hand over the government to duly elected representatives of the people without unnecessary delay;

RE-AFFIRMS the decision to send a delegation of Commission members to meet with the Nigeria Head of State, to express concern of the Commission about the gross violations of human rights and express the need for the Nigeria military government to urgently transfer power to a civilian government.

Resolution on Rwanda
Adopted 3/11/94 Rev. 1

The African Commission on Human and Peoples' Rights meeting at its 16th Ordinary Session held from 25 October to 3 November 1994 in Banjul. The Gambia,

Considering the appointment at the 15th Session of the Vice-Chairman of the African commission as Special Rapporteur on extra-judicial executions,

Considering the report of the United Nations Special Rapporteur indicating that genocide and massive human rights and international humanitarian law violations have been committed in Rwanda,

Considering the preliminary report of the UN Experts' Committee on Rwanda and its findings corroborating those of the UN Special Rapporteur,

Considering the UN Security Council's decision to approve the establishment of an international tribunal on Rwanda,

Considering the pledge of the Government of Rwanda and the International Community as expressed in the Hague Declaration of 18 September, 1994 to try the authors of the atrocious crimes committed in Rwanda:

1. CONDEMNS the inhuman and heinous crimes committed in Rwanda during the recent conflict;
2. EXPRESSES its support for the establishment of an international tribunal by the UN to try those responsible for the crimes;
3. CALLS FOR the convening by the OAU over the next few months in collaboration with African and international NGOs, a meeting of African and international experts to study long-term solutions to the problem of impunity in Africa with special reference to the case of Rwanda, and to formulate appropriate recommendations;
4. CALLS ON the OAU to explore ways and means of encouraging African jurists to participate in the process of reconstruction of the judicial machinery in Rwanda;
5. URGES the Government of Rwanda to prevent the perpetration of acts of reprisals and vengeance by the rapid establishment of a new police force and a local administration respectful of human rights and composed of members of all the ethnic groups of Rwanda.
6. EXHORTS the Government of Rwanda to ensure the rapid deployment of national and international human rights monitors as well as the strengthening of the interceding peace-keeping forces throughout Rwanda.
7. URGES international institutions and NGOs in general and African NGOs in particular to contribute to the effort of International solidarity and assist in the rapid reconstruction of Rwanda through the provision of technical and financial assistance especially by facilitating the resumption of the activities of local Human Rights NGOs in Rwanda.

Resolution on The Gambia Adopted 3/11/94 Rev. 1

The African Commission on Human and Peoples' Rights meeting at its 16th Ordinary Session held from 25 October to 3 November 1994 in Banjul, The Gambia,

Recalling the military take-over of the reins of government of the Gambia on 22 July 1994 which brought an end to an elected government and threatened the respect for Human Rights and the rule of law in that country,

Reaffirming the fundamental principle that all governments should be based on the consent of the people freely expressed by them and through their chosen representatives and that a military government is a clear violation of this fundamental principle of democracy,

Drawing attention to provisions of articles 13 of the Charter which provides, inter alia, that "Every citizen shall have the right to freely participate in the government of his country, either directly or through chosen representatives in accordance with the provisions of the law",

Convinced that the introduction of military rule is a clear setback to the cause of democracy and democratic development in The Gambia and Africa generally,

REITERATES that the military coup in The Gambia is a flagrant and grave violation of the right of the Gambian people to freely choose their government;

REQUESTS the Armed Forces Provisional Ruling Council to transfer power to freely elected representatives of the people;

CALLS UPON the military authorities to ensure that:

(i) the bill of Rights contained in the Gambian Constitution remains supreme over all other legislation emanating from the Ruling Council;
(ii) the dependence of the judiciary is respected;
(iii) during the transition period, the rule of law, as well as the recognized international standards of fair trial and treatment of persons in custody are observed;
(iv) all detainees should either be charged with the commission of offences or released forthwith and that meanwhile the rights of detainees to have access to their lawyers and members of their families are scrupulously respected.

Resolution on the Human Rights Situation in Africa Adopted 3/11/94 Rev. 1

The African Commission on Human and Peoples' Rights meeting at its 16th Ordinary Session held from 25 October to 3 November, 1994 in Banjul, The Gambia,

Acknowledging that the human rights situation in many African countries is characterized by the violations of economic, social, cultural, civil and political rights,

Alarmed by the possible resurgence of the illegal seizure of the reins of government in Africa,

Expressing concern over the persistent situation of refugees and internally displaced persons affecting the African Continent,

Seriously concerned with the continuous restrictions imposed on the right of freedom of expression by the arrest of journalists and the closure of newspapers in some African countries,

Considering that the persistent economic crisis in Africa has aggravated the human rights situation of vulnerable groups in Africa societies, in particular women and children,

Also concerned with the consequences of persistent ways in several African States, on the civilian population, which prevent the realization of the right to development,

Bearing in mind its role under the African Charter on Human and Peoples' Rights, to ensure the protection of Human and Peoples' Rights,

1. CONDEMNS the planning or execution of Coups d'Etat and any attempt to seize power by undemocratic means;
2. CALLS UPON all African Governments to ensure that elections and electoral processes are transparent and fair;
3. URGES all African countries to adopt the appropriate means to stop the phenomenon of refugees and internally displaced persons affecting the continent;
4. CONDEMNS all attempts at restricting the right to freedom of expression;
5. CALLS UPON all African Governments to adopt legislative and other measures to protect vulnerable groups of society, in particular women and children, against the consequences of the persistent economic crisis in Africa;
6. URGES all those parties engaged in war on the African continent, to abide by the provisions of International Humanitarian Law, particularly with regard to the protection of civilians and to undertake all efforts to restore peace.

ANNEX VIII

RESOLUTIONS OF THE 17TH SESSION

Resolution on Sudan
Adopted 22/3/95

The African Commission on Human and Peoples' Rights meeting at its 17th Ordinary Session, 13–22 March 1995, Lomé, Togo,

Recalling that Sudan is legally bound to comply with international human rights and international humanitarian law treaties it has ratified, including the African Charter on Human and Peoples' Rights, the International Covenant on "Civil and Political Rights, The International Covenant on Economic, Social and Cultural Rights, the Slavery Convention, the Supplementary Convention on the Abolition of Slavery, the Slave Trade and Institutions and Practices Similar to Slavery, the Convention on the Rights of the Child and the four Geneva Conventions of 1949,

Considering the consistent reports from United Nations experts, non-governmental organizations and others of continuing gross violations of human rights committed by the Government of Sudan,

Further considering that such reports also document gross abuses committed by factions of the Sudan People's Liberation Army (SPLA) and the South Sudan Independence Army (SSIA),

Mindful that the need for large scale humanitarian aid in parts of Sudan is principally a result of the continuing war and gross human rights abuses,

Alarmed by the large number of internally displaced persons and the continuing exodus of refugees, mainly from southern Sudan and the Nuba Mountain region:

1. EXPRESSED DEEP CONCERN at the continuing human rights abuses in Sudan;

2. CALLS on the government to take immediate steps to respect all human rights, including bringing law and practice into line with international human rights standards, carrying out prompt, impartial and independent investigations into reports of human rights violation and bringing to justice those responsible;

3. FURTHER CALLS on the Government of Sudan to give all detainees prompt and regular access to their family, lawyers and doctors;

4. CALLS on all parties to the armed conflict immediately to cease using military force to interfere with the delivery of humanitarian assistance to the civilian population and to allow such assistance to be delivered unhindered;

5. FURTHER CALLS on all factions of the SPLA and the SSIA to respect international humanitarian law, particularly Article 3 common to the four Geneva Conventions of 1949, including ending deliberate and arbitrary killings and the torture of detainees.

6. APPEALS to the Government of Sudan to support negotiations for a settlement to the conflict and ensure that any agreement includes strong guarantees for the protection of human rights;

7. CALLS for human rights monitors to be placed in Sudan and other locations to facilitate the monitoring and assessment of the human rights situation throughout the country.

Resolution on Nigeria
Adopted 22/3/95

The African Commission on Human and Peoples' Rights meeting at its 17th Ordinary Session held from 13–March 1995, Lome, Togo,

Guided by African Charter on Human and Peoples' Rights and other international human rights instruments of which Nigeria is a signatory,

Reaffirming that all Member States including Nigeria have the duty to fulfil the obligations they have undertaken under the various international human rights instruments, particularly the African Charter on Human and Peoples' Rights,

Recalling the resolution passed by the African Commission at its 16th Session in Banjul in November 1994 which condemned the gross violations of Human Rights in Nigeria by the military government,

Deeply concerned about the political, social, economic and general situation in Nigeria and the consequences that may result therefrom,

CONDEMNS the continued gross and massive violations of human rights in Nigeria and particularly:

(i) the arbitrary arrests and detention of human rights and pro-democracy activists, critics and opponents of military rule;
(ii) severe restriction on the rights to freedoms of expression, including the banning of several newspapers and news magazines;
(iii) circumscribing the independence of the judiciary and setting up military tribunals lacking independence and due process to try persons suspected of being opposed to the military regimes;
(iv) the abolition of habeas corpus with respect to political detainees;
(v) restrictions on the right to leave the country;
(vi) restrictions on the right to freedom of association;
(vii) promulgation of decrees and laws ousting the application of the African Charter on Human and Peoples' Rights and preventing the Courts from intervening in cases of human rights violations.

CALLS UPON the military government in Nigeria to ensure respect for human rights and the rule of law, and in particular to release all political prisoners, reopen all closed media and respect freedom of the press, lift arbitrarily imposed travel restrictions, allow unfettered exercise of jurisdiction by the courts and remove all military tribunals from the judicial system;

URGES the military government in Nigeria to respect the rights of minorities and all religions and ensure full respect for the right of association;

AGAIN CALLS UPON the military government in Nigeria to take immediate steps to return Nigeria to democratic rule.

Resolution on The Gambia
Adopted 22/3/95

The African Commission on Human and Peoples' Rights meeting at its 17th Ordinary Session held from 13–22 March 1995, Lomé, Togo,

Recalling the condemnation of the 22 July 1994 Coup d'Etat in The Gambia by the African Commission on Human and Peoples' Rights and the International community and the consequence of the military coup d'etat on the principles of democracy and the rule of law,

Taking note of the continued presence of the military in power in The Gambia, despite calls for an immediate handing over to a civilian government, as expressed in the resolution on The Gambia by the ACHPR during its 16th Ordinary Session held in Banjul in October 1994,

Taking note with great concern that there are allegations of serious violations of Human Rights in the period of military rule:

1. NOTES the reduction of the timetable of transition to civilian rule by the Armed Forces Provisional Ruling Council from 4 to 2 years and therefore recommends strongly that the international and Donor Communities lift the economic sanctions imposed on The Gambia;
2. INSISTS on the need for an independent Judiciary and due process of law in The Gambia under all circumstances;
3. RENEWS its demands on the AFPRC to accelerate the process of transition to constitutional rule and to abolish all decrees that infringe the freedom of The Gambia people individually and collectively, including the freedom of expression, the press, and the right of association and assembly.
4. CALLS UPON the AFPRC to set up an independent commission of inquiry to investigate all allegations of violation of Human Rights.

Resolution on Anti-personnel Mines
Adopted 22/3/95

The African Commission on Human and Peoples' Rights meeting at its 17th Ordinary Session held from 13 to 22 March 1995, Lomé, Togo,

Recalling the 1980 United Nations Convention on the use of certain conventional weapons which may be deemed to be excessively injurious or to have indiscriminate effects,

Considering Resolution CM/Res. 1726 (LX) adopted at the sixtieth session of the OAU Council of Ministers in Tunis (6–11 June 1994), calling upon Member States to ratify the above Convention and considering the holding of its next Review Conference in Vienna from 25 September to 13 October 1995,

Noting with regret the extremely limited number of African States parties to this Convention,

Considering the significant ravages caused by the indiscriminate use of anti-personnel mines, particularly in Africa where more than 30 million mines are scattered,

Noting with concern the consequences of the proliferation of mines in African countries, particularly the failure of efforts of rehabilitation in the affected areas and of reconstruction, in countries which emerged from wars,

Considering that this phenomenon constitutes a flagrant violation of the provisions of the African Charter on Human and Peoples' Rights and, more specifically, of its Article 4,

Further considering that one of the most adequate means to combat this calamity would be the extension of the 1980 United Nations Convention on situations of internal conflicts and, the adoption of effective provisions for the implementation of this Convention particularly aiming at the prohibition of restrictions on the use of mines;

Recalling the resolution on the promotion and respect of International Humanitarian Law and Human and Peoples' Rights, adopted in Addis Ababa by the

African Commission on Human and Peoples' Rights at its fourteenth session which recognized the competence of the International Humanitarian Law, and, the usefulness of a close cooperation in the dissemination of International Humanitarian Law and Human and Peoples' Rights,

Recognizing the importance of the NGOs in highlighting public awareness and, the need to strengthen their capacity in assisting mines victims:

1. ENCOURAGES African States to ratify, within the shortest possible time, the 1980 United Nations Convention on prohibitions or restrictions on the use of certain conventional weapons which may be deemed to be excessively injurious or to have indiscriminate effects;
2. URGENTLY REQUESTS African States to participate in large numbers in the review conference to press for the introduction of a clause on the prohibition or restriction of the use of mines in that Convention;
3. RECOMMENDS that concrete and effective steps be urgently taken to prohibit the manufacture of anti-personnel mines and to ensure that existing stocks are destroyed and an international control mechanism is set up;
4. APPEALS to the manufacturers of anti-personnel mines so that they may be conscious of the dangers and destruction caused by the use of their products;
5. REQUESTS that the provisions of the above Convention be extended to situations of internal conflicts;
6. CALLS UPON Member States to closely associate the NGOs with the implementation of the present resolution, and, particularly with the conception and execution of consciousness raising and mine victims rehabilitation programmes.

Resolutions on Prisons in Africa
Adopted 22/3/95

The 17th Ordinary Session of the African Commission on Human and Peoples' Rights held in Lomé, Togo, between 13–22 March, 1995,

Guided by the African Charter on Human and Peoples' Rights and, in particular, Article 45 of the Charter which defines the mandate of the Commission,

Considering that the rights established and guaranteed under the African Charter on Human and Peoples' Rights extend to all categories of persons including prisoners, detainees and other persons deprived of their liberty,

Considering also the leading role played by African States in the establishment of international norms and standards for the protection of human rights of prisoners including the International Covenant on Civil and Political Rights, the Convention Against Torture and other Cruel, Inhuman or Degrading Treatment or Punishment and the United Nations Standard Minimum Rules for the Treatment of Prisoners, among others, and that an overwhelming majority of the States Parties to the African Charter on Human and Peoples' Rights subscribe to the principles and rules contained in these international norms and standards,

Aware of Resolution 1984/87 of the United Nations Economic and Social Council which requests States to "inform the Secretary-General of the United Nations every five years of the progress made with the application of the Standard Minimum Rules for the Treatment of Prisoners and of the factors and difficulties, if any, affecting their implementation",

Concerned that the conditions of prisons and prisoners in many African countries are afflicted by severe inadequacies including high congestion, poor physical, health and sanitary conditions; inadequate recreational, vocational and rehabilitation programmes, restricted contact with the outside world, large percentages of persons awaiting trial, among others,

Conscious that States assume responsibilities to look after the welfare of persons who have been deprived for their liberty including prisoners and detainees;

Acknowledging that several States in Africa are presently experiencing economic difficulties,

Mindful of the obligation of the States parties to the African Charter on Human and Peoples Rights to improve prison conditions and protect the human rights of prisoners, detainees and other persons deprived of their liberty in Africa and efforts undertaken;

1. RESOLVES THAT prison conditions in many African countries do not conform with the articles of the African Charter on Human and Peoples' Rights and to the international norms and standards for the protection of the human rights of prisoners including the International Covenant on Civil and Political Rights and the United Nations Standard Minimum Rules for the Treatment of Prisoners, among others;

2. URGES States parties to the African Charter who have not yet ratified the United Nations Convention Against Torture and Other Cruel, Inhuman or Degrading Treatment to do so;

3. URGES States parties of the African Charter on Human and Peoples' Rights to include in the reports submitted to the Commission under Article 62 of the Charter information on human rights affecting the human rights of prisoners;

4. CALLS UPON States parties to the African Charter on Human and Peoples' Rights to comply with Resolution 1984/877 of the United Nations Economic and Social Council to submit periodic reports to the Secretary-General of the United Nations in compliance with the Standard Minimum Rules for the Treatment of Prisoners.

Final Communiqué of the Sixteenth Ordinary Session of the African Commission on Human and Peoples' Rights

Banjul, 25 October to 3 November 1994

1. The African Commission on Human and Peoples' Rights held its 16th Ordinary Session at its Headquarters in Banjul, The Gambia, from 25th October to 3rd November 1994.

2. The session was preceded by the sixth workshop on NGO participation in the work of the African Commission on Human and Peoples' Rights, organised by the International Commission of Jurists (ICJ) in collaboration with the African Commission and the African Centre for Democracy and Human Rights Studies.

3. The following Commissioners attended the Session:

(i) Prof. Isaac Nguema, Chairperson;
(ii) Dr. Mohammed H. Ben Salem, Vice Chairperson;
(iii) Prof. Emmanuel V. O Dankwa;
(iv) Mr. Sourahata B. S Janneh;
(v) Mr. Robert H. Kisanga;
(vi) Ms. Vera Valentina B. S. Duarte Martins;
(vii) Dr. Ibrahim Ali Badawi El-Sheikh;
(viii) Prof. U. Oji Umozurike.

4. Mr. Alioune Beye, Mr. Atsu Koffi Amega and Mr. Youssoupha Ndiaye could not attend and sent their apologies.

5. The opening ceremony took place at 10.00 a.m. on 25 October 1994 at the Kairaba beach hotel in the presence of the honourable Fafa E. Mbai, Attorney General and Minister of Justice of the Gambia, and Mr. Adama Dieng, Secretary General of the International Commission of Jurists.

6. Also present were:

- Ambassadors and heads of diplomatic missions;
- Government Officials;
- Members of the press and other guests;
- Representatives of inter-governmental and non-governmental organizations;
- Representatives of other States.

The Commission registered with satisfaction the participation for the first time of States Parties.

7. Prof. Isaac Nguema, Mr. Adama Dieng and the Hon. Fafa E. Mbai addressed the opening Session.

8. In his address, Prof. Nguema deplored the state of violence and the poor human rights situation in African countries. Prof. Nguema expressed that in order to resolve the crises in Africa new institutional structures should be established taking into account the present situation in Africa and the aspirations of the African people.

9. In accordance with these new model of society, Prof. Nguema called for a revision of the African Charter laying emphases on strengthening the mandate of the African Commission, amending the procedure for the consideration of complaints, and enhancing the logistics and the legal framework of the Commission.

10. In accordance with this new model of society, Mr. Adama Dieng expressed concern about 4 year transitional period which was announced by the present military government of Gambia. Mr. Dieng called upon the Commission to request the Gambian military government to shorten the transitional period.

11. Mr. Dieng referred to the NGO workshop preceding the Session and called on the Commission to adopt the resolutions submitted by the NGOs.

12. In his address, the Hon. Fafa Mbai congratulated the African Commission on the efforts it has made to execute its mandate and assured the Commission of his government's continued co-operation and support.

13. The Hon. Fafa Mbai stated that the co-operation which exists between the African Commission and NGOs is commendable and encouraged the two to nurture and sustain the relationship. The Hon. Fafa Mbai also noted that one of the fruits of co-operation between the African Commission and NGOs is the recent appointment by the Commission of a Special Rapporteur on Extra-judicial Executions. The Hon. Fafa Mbai stressed the need for NGOs, the African Commission and the OAU to give the Special Rapporteur the necessary support and assistance in the executions of this very important mandate.

14. During its proceedings the Commission dealt mainly with the following:

(i) the present military rule in The Gambia;
(ii) consideration of applications for observer status;
(iii) consideration of communications;
(iv) examination of periodic reports;
(v) examination of extra-judicial executions;
(vi) establishment of an African Human Rights Court;
(vii) administrative and financial matters.

15. The following non-governmental organisations were granted observer status:

(i) African Network for the Prevention and Protection against Child Abuse and Neglect (Kenya);
(ii) Centre for Justice and International Law (CEJIL) (United States);
(iii) DIH, Mouvement de Protestation Civique (France);
(iv) International Society for Human Rights (Zaire Section);
(v) Organisation Sénégalaise d'Appui au Développement (OSAD) (Senegal);
(vi) All African Conference of Churches (Kenya).

16. The following non governmental organisations were granted observer status subject to the provision of additional documents:

(i) Swedish NGO Foundation for Human Rights (Sweden);
(ii) English International Association of Lund (Sweden);
(iii) Centre for Applied Legal Studies, University of Witwaterstrand (South Africa).

17. The granting of observer status to the 9 NGOs increases to 140 number of NGOs which have observer status with the African Commission.

18. The Commission heard statements from representatives of the following States: Burundi, Côte d'Ivoire and Swaziland. The Commission also heard statements from several African and international NGO representatives including:

(i) Mr. Clement Nwanko, Constitutional Rights Project, Nigeria;
(ii) Mr. Motombo Mulami, All Africa Conference of Churches;
(iii) Mme Seny Diagne, Women in Law and Development (WILDAF)
(iv) Mme. Aissata Niang, Collectif des Veuves Mauritaniennes;
(v) Mr. Salem Mezhoud, Anti-Slavery International;
(vi) Mr. Aboubacry Mbodji, Rencontre Africain pour la Défense;
(vii) Mr. Harold Doe, International Society for Human Rights (Gambia)
(viii) Dr, K. G. Kwawang, Sudan Human Rights Organisation;
(ix) Ms. Mona Rishmawi, International Commission of Jurists;
(x) Prof. Shadrack Gutto, Centre for Applied Legal Studies;
(xi) Mr. Ahmed Motala, Lawyers for Human Rights;
(xii) Mr. Kouma Gopina, Association Tchadienne pour la protection des droits de l'homme;
(xiii) Mr. Akouete Akakpo Vidah, Centre International des Droits de l'Homme;
(xiv) Dr. Galal Ragab, Union des Avocats Arabes;
(xv) Mr. Julien Tobgadja, Union Internationale des Droits de l'Homme;
(xvi) Mr. Boudjema Ghechir, Ligue Algérienne des Droits de l'Homme;
(xvii) Mr. Moshen Awad, Arab Organisation for Human rights;
(xviii) Mr. Cheikh Tidjane, Collectif des Rescapés de Mauritanie;
(xix) Maître Diabira Maroufa, Association Mauritanienne de Droits de l'Homme;
(xx) Ms. Mona Rishmawi presented the Conclusions and Recommendations of the NGO workshop. The workshop welcomed the positive developments in the work of the African Commission and the publication of the Commission's 7th activity report which includes the communications that have been considered by the Commission. The Conclusions and Recommendations of the NGO workshop called on the Commission to begin the establishment of an African human rights jurisprudence. The Conclusions and Recommendations also draw the Commission's attention to the human rights situation in Africa and condemn the deteriorating human rights situations in a number of African countries. Accordingly, the

workshop presented for the consideration of the Commission's draft resolutions on the Gambia, Algeria, Nigeria, Rwanda, the Military, Contemporary forms of Slavery and the human rights situation in Africa.

20. The Côte d'Ivoire representative, the country's Ambassador to Senegal, the Gambia, Mauritania and Cape Verde congratulated the Commission for its work and assured the Commission of his country's support and co-operation.

21. The representative of Burundi, the Minister for Human Rights, Social Affairs and Promotion of Women's Rights, informed the Commission of the human rights situation in her country.

22. The representative from Swaziland, a Legal Adviser of the Ministry of Justice informed the Commission that his government has signed the African Charter and is considering its ratification. It sought advice from the Commission on the implications which ratification of the Charter could have on his country's monarchy.

23. The Commission considered the State reports of Benin, the Gambia and Cape Verde.

24. The purpose of State reports is to encourage States to implement voluntarily their human rights obligations; States parties are urged to ensure that their representatives are present to defend their reports before the Commission.

25. Benin sent its representative, a magistrate and an official of the Ministry of Justice to present its initial report to the Commission.

26. The Chairperson of the Commission thanked the government of Benin for presenting its report and for sending a representative to this Session. However, the Chairperson noted with concern that Benin's report was due in 1988 but was not submitted until 1992. Furthermore, the Commission could not examine the report until 1994 because Benin did not send a representative to present its report at previous sessions.

27. In this respect the Chairperson stressed that the purpose of the State reporting mechanism is to establish constructive dialogue between the Commission and States parties. The States are therefore required to inform the Commission about the legislative and other measures taken to protect human rights in their respective countries. The Commission on its part provides advice and assistance in areas where the States encounter difficulties in protecting human rights.

28. The representative of Benin informed the Commission that the African Charter has been incorporated in the Constitution of Benin. He also indicated that the human rights situation in Benin has improved since the end of the one party rule which lasted 17 years. He further informed the Commission of his government's efforts to protect human rights, as well as the difficulties encountered in areas such as education because of the country's limited resources.

29. After the presentation of Benin's report, several members of the Commission posed various questions regarding the realities of human rights in Benin. Members of the Commission also noted that the written report which was submitted in French was not translated in the other working languages of the Commission.

30. The representative responded to the question posed by the Commission. The

Commission requested the representative to submit the response to the questions in writing and thanked the representative and the government of Benin.

31. The Commission also examined the initial report of Cape Verde which was presented by a senior magistrate of the country.

32. The Chairperson thanked the government for submitting its report and sending a representative to present it to the Commission. It was noted that the initial report of Cape Verde was due in 1989 but was not submitted until 1992. The Commission could not examine the report until 1994 because Cape Verde did not send a representative to discuss the report in previous Sessions. The Commission also noted that the report was not translated in all three working languages of the Commission.

33. The representative of Cape Verde informed the Commission that the African Charter has direct applicability in Cape Verde because under the country's Constitution, international treaties ratified by Cape Verde have direct applicability. He informed the Commission that Cape Verde has abolished the death penalty. The representative also informed the Commission that Cape Verde has several rules governing the protection of human rights, but the main concern lies in the actual realization of the rights.

34. The representative stated that the full realization of economic, social and cultural rights are problematic and this was due to a lack of resources.

35. Several members of the Commission asked questions regarding the reality of human rights in Cape Verde. The representative responded to some of the questions. The Commission requested the representative to submit written answers to all the questions.

36. The Commission considered the second report of The Gambia. The Gambia sent a Parliamentary Counsel with the Ministry of Justice to present the report to the Commission. The Chairperson commended The Gambia for submitting a second report inspite of the recent Military take-over of 22 July 1994.

37. In his presentation, the representative stated that the former civilian government has been replaced by a military government through a peaceful coup. The representative informed the Commission that following the coup, certain parts of the Constitution have been suspended or modified, but these do not include the right to life. He informed the Commission of the government's effort to ensure many of the rights set forth in the Charter. The representative stated that the government is working towards the return of civilian rule and in the transitional period, it will ensure full respect of human rights.

38. The Commission asked several questions and made certain comments concerning the report. In particular, it found that some of the assertions made were contradictory and inconsistent with the present situation in the Gambia. The Commission also noted that the oral presentation addressed issues which were not dealt with in the report. Accordingly, the representative was requested to put those statements in writing as a supplement to the report. The Commission also expressed concern about the suspension of various parts of the Constitution by the military regime. In the meantime, the government was requested to ensure the respect of human rights with special reference to the rights of arrested and detained persons.

39. The representative responded to some of the questions and comments of the Commission. The Commission requested the representative to put the response in writing and thanked the government and representative for the report.

40. The report of Mozambique was scheduled for examination. Like the previous session, the Commission noted with regret that it could not proceed with the examination because Mozambique did not send a representative to present the report to the Commission.

41. The Commission considered the issue of the establishment of an African Human Rights Court and constituted a working group consisting of Commissioners Nguema, Badawi and Umozorike to discuss the proposed court.

42. The Commission considered the problem of extra-judicial executions. Commissioner Ben Salem, the Rapporteur for extra-judicial executions will present a draft on the terms of reference at the 17th Session on the basis of drafts prepared on this issue.

43. The Commission reiterated its decision to organize a Seminar on the right to fair trial and legal assistance.

44. The Commission noted with regret that the Seminar on the Status of Women Under the African Charter did not take place as planned. The Commission requested its Secretary to contact the other organisers in order to reschedule and inform the members of the Commission accordingly.

45. A member of the Commission presented a report on his seminar held in Tunis on the State Reporting procedure. This was the Francophone version of a seminar held earlier in Harare. Commissioner Dankwa was entrusted to examine the Commission's guidelines for the preparation of State reports taking into account the Conclusions and Recommendations of the two seminars.

46. The Commission considered and adopted resolutions on Algeria, the Gambia, Nigeria, Rwanda, the Military, Contemporary Forms of Slavery, and the Human Rights situation in Africa.

47. With respect to his protective activities, the Commission had before it 54 old communications and 8 new communications. The status of the communications is as follows:

- (i) Communications decided on the merits: 9;
- (ii) Communications declared admissible: 5;
- (iii) Communications declared inadmissible: 7;
- (iv) Communications withdrawn: 1;
- (v) Cases in which the Commission decided to send missions to the States concerned: 11;
- (vi) Cases in which decisions were deferred pending receipt of additional information: 8;
- (vii) Cases in which notification was to be sent to the government concerned for comments: 7;
- (viii) Cases in which the file was closed: 1;
- (ix) Communications which were not dealt with during the 16th Session due to time constraints: 13.

48. It should be pointed out that for the first time victims of human rights violations or their representatives came to defend their cause before the Commission.

49. The Commission welcomed the appointment of its new Secretary, Mr. Germain Baricako and noted with satisfaction the considerable improvement in the functioning of the Secretariat.

50. During this session, a delegation consisting of a Chairperson and Vice Chairperson of the Commission was received in audience by the Head of State of the Gambia. The delegation expressed the Commission's concern about the military takeover in the Gambia, the headquarters of the Commission.

51. The Commission calls on Algeria, Angola, Botswana, Burundi, Burkina Faso, Cameroon, Central African Republic, Comoros, Côte-d'Ivoire, Djibouti, Equatorial Guinea, Gabon, Guinea, Guinea-Bissau, Kenya, Lesotho, Liberia, Madagascar, Malawi, Mali, Mauritania, Mauritius, Namibia, Niger, Sahrawi Arab Democratic Republic, Sao Tome & Principe, Seychelles, Sierra Leone, Somalia, Sudan , Zaire and Zambia, to submit their initial reports as soon as possible.

52. The Commission calls on Eritrea, Ethiopia, South Africa and Swaziland to ratify the African Charter as soon as possible.

53. The Commission decided to hold its next Session from 6–17 March 1995 at a venue to be named.

Issued in Banjul, 3 November 1994

Resolution on Contemporary Forms of Slavery: Sixteenth Ordinary Session of the African Commission on Human and Peoples' Rights

Banjul, 25 October to 3 November 1994

Recalling Article 4 of the Universal Declaration of Human Rights, Article 8 of the International Covenant on Civil and Political Rights and Article 5 of the African Charter on Human and Peoples' Rights,

Considering that a number of international instruments prohibiting slavery in all its forms have been adopted. Among these are the Slavery Convention of 25 September 1926 and its amending Protocol, the Supplementary Convention on the Abolition of Slavery, the Slave Trade and Institutions and Practices Similar to Slavery of 7 September 1956, the Convention for the Suppression of the Traffic of Persons and of the Exploitation of the Prostitution of Others of 1949,

Noting with great concern that slavery and practices similar to slavery continue to exist throughout the African continent,

Noting in particular with alarm that the exploitation of children and child labour, and forced early, servile marriage destroying the lives of millions of women and children in Africa,

Recalling that by its Resolution 843 (IX) of 17 December 1954 the United Nations General Assembly declared that certain customs, ancient laws and practices relating to marriage and the family are inconsistent with the principles set forth in the Charter of the United Nations and the Universal Declaration of Human Rights,

RECOMMEND:

1. All Member States of the Organization of African Unity ratify, if they have not done so, all existing international legal instruments relating to slavery, the slave trade, sale and traffic of human beings, and other institutions and practices similar to slavery;
2. That OAU Member States effectively implement, and monitor the implementation of these instruments;
3. That African Government adopt legislation and take measures to prohibit all forms of slavery.

Press Release

23 January 1995
ACHPR/PRESS/A075 (25)

Following an invitation extended by the Togolese authorities, Professors Isaac Nguema and Mohamed Hatem Ben Salem, Chairman and Vice-Chairman, respectively, of the African Commission on Human and Peoples' Rights, undertook a working visit to Togo, from 10–18 January 1995.

During this visit, the delegation of the African Commission on Human and Peoples' Rights had talks with the Togolese authorities on the achievements already registered in the field of human rights, on the efforts made by the new government as well as the remaining task to be fulfilled in the said field.

The delegation has ascertained that the darkest era of human rights violations has long gone although a few cases of personalised human rights violations have been recorded.

The Togolese authorities have availed themselves to set up and to demonstrate an exemplary policy in the field of human rights.

Moreover, the Togolese authorities have freed during the course of the visit of the delegation of the Commission, Mr. Martin Akpé Gnenouba, a journalist who was sentenced to one year imprisonment with hard labour.

In addition, the Togolese authorities have invited the Commission to hold its 17th Session in Lomé, Togo.

The Commission has accepted the invitation to hold its 17th Ordinary Session from 13–22 March 1995 soon after the Seminar on the African Charter on Human and Peoples' Rights and Women's Rights in Africa, to be held in Lomé, on 8 and 9 March 1995.

Done in Banjul, 23 January 1995

Final Communiqué of the Seventeenth Ordinary Session of the African Commission on Human and Peoples' Rights

Lome, 13–22 March 1995
ACHPR/COM.FIN/XVII/Rev. 3

1. The African Commission on Human and Peoples' Rights held its 17th Ordinary Session in Lome, Togo upon the invitation of the Togolese government from 13–22 March 1995 under the chairmanship of Prof. Isaac Nguema.

2. The Session was preceded by a seminar on the African Charter on Human and Peoples' Rights and the Human Rights of Women in Africa, organized by the African Commission in collaboration with WILDAF (Women in Law and Development); as well as the 8th workshop on NGO participation in the work of the African Commission, organized by the International Commission of Jurists (ICJ) in collaboration with the African Commission and the Association pour la Promotion de l'Etat de Droit (APED), a Togolese NGO.

3. The following Commissioners attended the Session:

(i) Prof. Isaac Nguema, Chairman;
(ii) Dr. Mohammed H. Ben Salem, Vice Chairman;
(iii) Mr. Atsu Koffi Amega;
(iv) Dr. Ibrahim Ali Badawi;
(v) Prof. Emmanuel V. O Dankwa;
(vi) Ms. Vera Valentina B. S. Duarte Martins;
(vii) Mr. Sourahata B. S Janneh;
(viii) Mr. Robert H. Kisanga;
(ix) Prof. U. Oji Umozurike.

4. Mr. Alioune Beye, Mr. Atsu Koffi Amega and Mr. Yousoupha Ndiaye could not attend and sent their apologies.

5. The opening ceremony began at 10.00 a.m. on 13 March 1995 at the Hotel Sofitel 2 Février in the presence of the Hon. Djovi Gally, Minister for Human Rights and Rehabilitation responsible for Parliamentary Affairs of the Republic of Togo, representing the Prime Minister of the Republic; Mr. Dougan Beaca Jose Domingo, representing H.E. Mr. Ibrahima Fall, the Assistant Secretary General of the United Nations and Director of the UN Centre for Human Rights; and Mr. Adama Dieng, Secretary General of the International Commission of Jurists.

6. Also present were:

- Ambassadors and Heads of Diplomatic Missions in Togo;
- Officials of the Togolese government;

- Delegates of States parties to the African Charter;
- Representatives of inter-governmental and non-governmental organizations;
- Members of the Press; and
- Other guests.

7. Mr. Dougan Becca José Domingo, Mr. Adama Dieng, Prof. Isaac Nguema and the Hon. Djovi Gally addressed the opening ceremony.

8. In his address, Mr. Dougan Becca thanked the Commission for having invited the United Nations Centre for Human Rights to its 17th Ordinary Session. After having extended to the Commission the salutations and the wishes for its success of H.E. Mr. Ibrahim Fall, the Assistant Secretary General of the United Nations Centre for Human Rights and the Director of the said Centre, Mr. Dougan Becca assured the African Commission of the United Nations Centre for Human Rights' commitment to support the Commission in carrying out its mandate.

9. In his address, Mr. Adama Dieng referred to the financial difficulties and insufficient personnel of the Secretariat of the African Commission and assured the Commission of the International Commission of Jurists's commitment to support the latter in carrying out its functions. Mr. Dieng informed the Commission that the ICJ will very soon sponsor an African lawyer to work at the Commission's Secretariat for a period of 12 months.

10. Mr. Dieng congratulated the governments of Togo and Senegal for accepting the Commission's request to conduct on cite investigations in their countries.

11. Mr. Dieng referred to the need to create peace as well as the importance of strengthening the independence of the judiciary in Africa. The ICJ Secretary General also stated that those who commit serious breaches of human rights are often not brought to justice and noted the importance of addressing the problem of impunity.

12. In his address, Prof. Isaac Nguema thanked the ICJ for its commitment to attach a lawyer to the Commission's Secretariat. He discussed the origins of various problems facing Africa including ethnic and religious conflicts and the crimes that accompany military take-overs. Prof. Nguema also stressed the need to find an African solution to African problems.

13. In his address, the Hon. Djovi Gally stated that Togo is committed to the promotion and protection of human rights and noted that the country's Constitution incorporates the principles enshrined in international human rights treaties.

14. Mr. Gally stated that the African Charter should be seen as the Constitution of Africa. He referred to the various problems facing Africa and emphasized the necessity of education for the development of a democratic society.

15. During its proceedings, the Commission dealt mainly with the following:

(i) adoption of the Report of the 16th Session
(ii) consideration of Application for Observer status
(iii) promotional activities of the members of the Commission;
(iv) examination of extrajudicial executions;
(v) implementation of Resolution AHG/Res. 230 (XXX) on the Creation of an African Court on Human and People's Rights;

(vi) the situation of prisons in Africa;
(vii) report of the Seminar on the Rights of Women in Africa and the African Charter on Human and Peoples' Rights;
(viii) information on the Dakar Regional Preparatory Conference for the 4th World Conference on Women;
(ix) organization of forthcoming seminars and conferences;
(x) publication of the Review and the Bulletin of the Commission;
(xi) interpretation of Article 12 of Rules of Procedure of the Commission;
(xii) activities of the OAU relevant to the work of the Commission;
(xiii) administrative and financial matters;
(ix) consideration of Communications.

16. The following non-governmental organizations were granted observer status:

(i) Association Angolaise des Droits de l'Homme;
(ii) Human Rights Information and Documentation Systems (HURIDOCS);
(iii) Women Justice Program;
(iv) Association Mondiale pour les Orphelins et Enfants Abandonnés;
(v) Comité Africain pour le Droit et le Développement;
(vi) Association Mauritanienne des Droits de l'Homme;
(vii) Mouvement Mauritanian des Droits de l'Homme;
(viii) SOS Esclaves, Mauritanie;
(ix) Groupe d'Etudes et de Recherche sur la Démocratie et le Développement Economique et Social en Mauritanie;
(x) Tchad Non-Violence;
(xi) Human Rights Society, The Gambia;
(xii) FIDA (Uganda);
(xiii) Liberia Human Rights Chapter;
(xiv) Institut Africain pour la Démocratie.

17. The granting of observer status to the following organizations was postponed pending receipt of additional information:

(i) Initiatives et Développment – Afrique;
(i) Ligue Africaine des Droits de l'Homme et des Peuples;
(iii) Association pour le Progrès et la Défense des Droits des Femmes Maliennes;
(iv) International Movement for Development in Africa;
(v) Human Rights Defence Association for Peace in Central and Southern Africa.

18. The granting of observer status to the 14 NGOs increases to 154 the number of NGOs which have observer status with the African Commission.

19. Representatives of the States of Algeria, Botswana, Burundi, Burkina Faso, the Central African Republic, Mali and Togo attended the Session.

20. The representatives of Algeria, Burkina Faso and Mali addressed the Commission and informed the Commission of their countries' intention to present their State reports.

21. The Commission heard Statements from several African and International NGOs including:

(i) Mr. Ahmed Motala, Lawyers for Human Rights;
(ii) M. Alioune Tine, Rencontre Africaine pour la Défense des Droits de l'Homme;
(iii) M. Atondoko Guillaume Ngefa, AZADHO;
(iv) Mr. Salem Mezhoud, Anti-Slavery International
(v) Mrs. Tokunbo Ige, International Commission of Jurists;
(vi) M. Jean-Berckmans Kaburumdi, Ligue Burundaise des Droits de l'Homme (ITEKA);
(vii) Mr. Chidi Odinkalu, Interights;
(viii) Mrs. Gloria Scott, Association of Female Lawyers of Liberia;
(ix) Mme Marguerite Contat, Comité International de la Croix Rouge (CICR);
(x) Mr. Nicholas Howen, Amnesty International;
(xi) M. Jean-François Basse, Observatoire International des Prisons;
(xii) M. Agokla Mawuli, Defense of Children International;
(xiii) Mr. Clement Nwankwo, Constitutional Rights Project of Nigeria;
(xiv) Mr. Mohammed Moneib Genedy, Egyptian Organization for Human Rights;
(xv) M. Ahmed Othmani, Penal Reform International (PRI);
(xvi) Mr. Tite R. Gatabazi, Défense des Enfants International;
(xvii) Sister Marie Gonzaga J., Action des Chrétiens pour l'Abolition de la Torture (ACAT) – Togo.

22. Mrs. Tokunbo Ige of the ICJ presented the Conclusions and Recommendations of the 8th NGO workshop and put particular emphasis on the following questions:

(a) the necessity to appoint a Special Rapporteur on Prison Conditions in Africa;
(b) the study on the implementation of Economic, Social and Cultural Rights in Africa;
(c) the existence of systematic and gross violations of human rights in a number of African Countries;
(d) the fight against impunity in Africa.

23. The Commission notes with regret that the State reports of Mozambique, Mauritius and Seychelles could not be considered as scheduled because the States did not send their representatives to discuss the reports with the Commission. On the other hand, the Commission took note of the apologies of Mauritius, which could not send their representative due to the cyclone which swept through the country on 12 and 13 of March 1995.

24. Members of the Commission presented reports on promotional activities which they undertook during the inter-sessional period.

25. The Special Rapporteur on Extrajudicial, Summary or Arbitrary Executions presented a draft proposal of revised terms of reference after considering draft terms of from the Commission and NGOs. After consideration, the Commission adopted the terms of reference presented by the Special Rapporteur.

26. The Commission's Secretary informed the Commission that the OAU Secretary General in consultation with member States and the ICJ will convene a meeting of experts in May 1995 regarding the establishment of an African Court on Human and Peoples' Rights.

27. The Commission considered the question of penal reform and prison condition in Africa. The Commission decided to organize a seminar on penal reform in collaboration with Penal Reform International.

28. Commissioner Vera Valentina B. S. Duarte Martins presented the Conclusions and Recommendations on the seminar on the Rights of Women in Africa and the African Charter on Human and Peoples' Rights. The main recommendations are as follows:

(i) an additional protocol on the rights of women should be prepared;
(ii) pending the adoption of this additional protocol, some interim measures should be taken by the State parties in order to allow women to enjoy fully their rights;
(iii) the Commission should recommend to the OAU the nomination of a special rapporteur to the Commission who would be responsible for the protection of women's rights.

29. The Commission approved the first two recommendations relative to the additional protocol and to the interim measures.

30. The Commission entrusted two of his members, Dr. Duarte Martins and Prof. Dankwa to initiate work on an additional protocol on the rights of women.

31. The Commission reiterated its decision to organize the following seminars:

(i) The Right to Fair Trial and Legal Assistance;
(ii) Popular Participation and Non-formal Education;
(iii) Human Rights in a New South Africa.

32. The Commission also decided to organize the following seminars:

(i) Contemporary Forms of Slavery in Africa;
(ii) Peaceful Resolution of Ethnic and Social Conflicts;
(iii) The Right to Education as an Essential Condition for Development in Africa;
(iv) Freedom of Movement and the right to Asylum in Africa;
(v) The Problem of Impunity in Africa;
(vi) Conditions in African Prisons;
(vii) Economic, Social and Cultural Rights and the Right to Development.

33. The Commission considered and adopted the report and the resolutions of the 16th Session. These are resolutions on The Gambia, Nigeria, Rwanda, the Military, Contemporary Forms of Slavery and the Human Rights Situation in Africa.

34. The Commission also adopted new resolutions on Sudan, The Gambia, Nigeria, Anti-personnel Mines, and the situation of prisons in Africa.

35. With respect to its protective activities, the Commission examined 53 old communications and 1 new communication. The status of the communications is as follows:

(i) Communications on which a decision on the merits was taken: 3;
(ii) Communications declared admissible: 8;
(iii) Communications declared inadmissible: 4;
(iv) Cases in which the Commission decided to send missions to the States concerned: 23;
(v) Cases in which decisions were deferred pending receipt of additional information: 10;
(vi) Cases in which the Commission is to effect amicable settlement: 2;
(vii) Cases in which the file was closed: 4.

36. During this Session, the Commission was received in audience by the President of the Republic of Togo, General Gnassimbe Eyadema as well as by the Prime Minister, H.E. Mr. Edem Kodjo.

37. The closing ceremony was addressed by his Excellency, Edem Kodjo, Prime Minister of the Republic of Togo.

38. The Commission calls on Algeria, Angola, Botswana, Burundi, Burkina Faso, Cameroon, Central African Republic, Comoros, Congo, Côte-d'Ivoire, Djibouti, Equatorial Guinea, Gabon, Kenya, Lesotho, Liberia, Madagascar, Malawi, Mali, Mauritania, Namibia, Niger, Sahrawi Arab Democratic Republic, Sao Tome & Principe, Sierra Leone, Somalia, Sudan, Zaire and Zambia to submit their initial State reports as soon as possible.

39. The Commission urgently calls on Eritrea, Ethiopia, South Africa and Swaziland to ratify the African Charter as soon as possible.

40. The Commission decided to hold its 18th Ordinary Session in Cape Verde from 6–15 October 1995.

Issued in Lome, Togo, 22 March 1995

Ninth Annual Activity Report of the African Commission on Human and Peoples' Rights 1995–1996

Adopted on 3 April 1996
Covering the 18th and 19th Ordinary Sessions in Praia (2–11 October 1995) and Ouagadougou (26 March to 4 April 1996)
AHG/207 (XXXII)

I. ORGANIZATION OF WORK

A. Period Covered by the Report

1. The Eighth Annual Activity report of the ACHPR was adopted by the Thirty-first Ordinary Session of the Assembly of Heads of State and Government of the Organization of African Unity in its resolution AHG/Res. 240 (XXXI). The Ninth Annual Activity Report covers the Eighteenth Ordinary Session held in Praia, Cape Verde, from 2–11 October 1995, the Second Extraordinary Session held in Kampala, Uganda from 18–19 December 1995 and the Nineteenth Ordinary Session held in Ouagadougou, Burkina Faso from 26 March to 4 April 1996.

B. Status of Ratification

2. As of the 19th Ordinary Session of the Commission, all the members of the OAU, with the exception of Eritrea, Ethiopia and South Africa, had ratified or acceded to the Charter. The list of States and dates of signature, ratification/accession and deposit of instruments is attached (Annex I).

C. Sessions and Agenda

3. The Commission held two ordinary sessions and one extraordinary session since the adoption of the Eighth Annual Activity Report.

- the 18th Ordinary Session held in Praia, Cape Verde, 2–11 October 1995;
- the 2nd Extraordinary Session held in Kampala, Uganda, 18–19 December 1995.

D. Composition and Participation

4. The following Commissioners attended the 18th Session:

(1) Prof. Isaac Nguema, Chairman,
(2) Prof. Emmanuel V. O. Dankwa, Vice Chairman,

(3) Mr. Robert H. Kisanga,
(4) Dr. Mohamed H. Ben Salem,
(5) Dr. Vera V. Duarte Martins,
(6) Prof. U. Oji Umozurike,
(7) Mr. Atsu Koffi Amega,
(8) Mr. Kamel Rezzag-Bara,
(9) Mrs. Julienne Ondziel-Gnelenga,
(10) Mr. Youssoupha Ndiaye.
Mr. Alioune Blondin Beye was absent with apologies.

5. The representatives of the following States attended the Session and made statements before the Commission: Swaziland, Cameroon, Benin, Algeria, Zambia and Nigeria.

6. The following Commissioners attended the 2nd Extraordinary Session:
(1) Prof. Isaac Nguema, Chairman,
(2) Prof. Emmanuel V.O. Dankwa, Vice Chairman,
(3) Dr. Atsu Koffi Amega,
(4) Mr. Hatem Ben Salem,
(5) Mr. Robert H. Kisanga,
(6) Mr. Kamel Rezzag-Bara,
(7) Mrs. Julienne Ondziel-Gnelenga.

The following members of the Commission were absent with apologies:

Mr. Alioune Blondin Beye,
Mr. Youssoupha Ndiaye,
Dr. Vera Duarte Martins.

Prof. U. Oji Umozurike could not be contacted due to communication problems. The Extraordinary Session was addressed by representatives of Uganda, Nigeria and the OAU.

7. The following members of the Commission attended the 19th Session:

(1) Prof. Isaac Nguema, Chairman,
(2) Prof. Emmanuel V. O. Dankwa, Vice-Chairman,
(3) Mr. Robert Kisanga,
(4) Mrs. Julienne Ondziel-Gnelenga,
(5) Dr. Vera V. B. S. Duarte-Martins,
(6) Mr. Youssoupha Ndiaye,
(7) Mr. Kamel Rezzag-Bara,
(8) Prof. U. Oji Umozurike.

The following members of the Commission were absent with apologies:

(1) Mr. Alioune Blondin Beye,
(2) Mr. Atsu Koffi Amega,
(3) Dr. Hatem Ben Salem.

8. The representatives of the following States attended the 19th Session:

(1) Algeria,
(2) Burkina Faso,
(3) Egypt,
(4) Mauritania,
(5) Mozambique,
(6) Nigeria,
(7) Senegal.

9. The three sessions were attended by many non-governmental organizations.

E. Adoption of the Ninth Annual Activity Report

10. At its 3 April 1996 Session, the Commission considered and adopted its 9th Annual Activity Report.

II. ACTIVITIES OF THE COMMISSION

A. Consideration of Periodic Reports

11. Under Article 62 of the African Charter on Human and Peoples' Rights, each State undertakes to submit a report every two years on the legislative and other measures it takes to give effect to the rights and freedoms enshrined in the Charter.

The first periodic report of Tunisia was presented by the representatives of the State and was duly considered at the 18th Session. The Commission commended the representatives for a well prepared report which could serve as a model, reiterated its previous request that report should be submitted in the official languages of the OAU where possible, and called upon the Secretariat to translate reports into the other OAU languages.

12. The first periodic reports of Algeria and Mozambique were also considered at the 19th Session. The Commission took note of the high quality of the two reports.

13. As of the 19th Session the following States had submitted their reports: Libya, Rwanda, Tunisia (9th Session); Egypt and Tanzania (11th Session); The Gambia (12th and 16th Sessions); Senegal and Zimbabwe (12th Session); Togo and Nigeria (12th and 16th Sessions), Benin, Ghana, Cape Verde and Mozambique (14th Session); Mauritius and Seychelles (17th Session); Tunisia (18th Session); and Algeria and Burkina Faso (19th Session). 31 States parties have not yet submitted their periodic reports. This list is attached (Annex V).

B. Promotional Activities

(i) Report of the Chairman

14. The Chairman's Activity Report included his participation in various symposia and seminars within and outside Africa, work related to the Commission's publications and his participation in the 63rd Council of OAU Foreign Ministers. He also reported on his mission to Benin as the Chairman of the Francophone observer team of the 1996 elections.

(ii) Activities of Other Members of the Commission

15. The other members of the Commission also attended conferences, seminars and symposia in Africa as well as outside Africa, and carried out promotional activities in States parties. Two Commissioners who were part of the OAU observer teams presented reports on election in Tanzania and the Comoro Islands. The allocation of African countries for promotional activities is attached (Annex VI).

(iii) The Commission Co-sponsored and Participated in the Following Seminars:

(a) Workshop on NGO participation in the African Commission on Human and Peoples' Rights, which was organized by the International Commission of Jurists and held in Praia, Cape Verde, from 29 September to 1 October 1995.
(b) Impunity in Africa, held in Ouagadougou, Burkina Faso, 22–23 March 1996 and organized in collaboration with, among others, the International Centre for Human Rights and Democratic Development, based in Montreal, Canada.
(c) Workshop on NGO Participation in the African Commission, in Ouagadougou, Burkina Faso, from 23–25 March 1996. This workshop was organized in collaboration with the International Commission of Jurists, and the Burkinabe Movement for Human and Peoples' Rights (MBDHP).

C. Forthcoming Seminars and Conferences:

16. The Commission decided to organize seminars and conferences on:

(1) Human Rights in the New South Africa;
(2) Contemporary Forms of Slavery in Africa;
(3) Prison Conditions in Africa;
(4) The Right to a Fair Trial;
(5) Popular Participation and Non-Formal Education;
(6) Peaceful Resolution of Ethnic and Social Conflicts in the Context of Human Rights;
(7) Freedom of Movement and Asylum in Africa;
(8) Economic, Social and Cultural Rights and the Right to Development;

(9) Seminar for African Ambassadors based in Addis Ababa, Ethiopia on the Human Rights Promotion and Protection System.

The Commission sought the support of International Organizations and NGOs for the seminars/conferences and appointed Commissioners to follow up these matters.

III. SPECIAL RAPPORTEUR ON EXTRA-JUDICIAL EXECUTIONS IN AFRICA

17. At the 18th Session, the Commission considered and adopted the mandate of the Special Rapporteur and the budget estimates for the project. However, since the Special Rapporteur was absent from the 19th Session, the Commission could not discuss progress in work related to extra-judicial executions in Africa.

IV. SPECIAL RAPPORTEUR ON PRISON CONDITIONS IN AFRICA

18. The Commission agreed on the principle of appointing a Special Rapporteur on prison conditions in Africa, who will work under a designated Commissioner. The Commission called for the submission of CVs from suitable candidates and decided to seek the support of NGOs and other institutions in this project.

V. SPECIAL RAPPORTEUR ON THE RIGHTS OF WOMEN

19. The Commission decided to appoint at its next Session a Special Rapporteur on the rights of African women. The Special Rapporteur will work under Commissioners E. V. O. Dankwa and Vera V. B. S. Duarte-Martins who have experience in this field. The Session invited CVs of suitable candidates for consideration and decided to seek the support of NGOs and other institutions in this project.

VI. MISSIONS TO STATES PARTIES

20. The Commission reaffirmed its decisions to conduct missions to Nigeria, Senegal, Sudan, Mauritania, Burundi and Rwanda. It will consider with the States concerned communications brought against the latter which had been declared admissible. The final dates for the missions will be confirmed with the States concerned. The missions will be composed of the following Commissioners:

Nigeria:	Prof. I. Nguema
	Prof. E.V. O. Dankwa
	Prof. U. Oji Umozurike

Senegal:	Prof. I. Nguema
	Dr. V. Duarte-Martins
Sudan:	Mr. R. Kisanga
	Mr. Kamel Rezza-Bara
Burundi:	Prof. I. Nguema
	Mrs. Julienne Ondziel-Gnelenga
	Mr. Atsu Koffi Amega
Rwanda:	Prof. I. Nguema
	Mrs. Julienne Ondziel-Gnelenga
	Mr. Atsu Koffi Amega
Mauritania:	Prof. I. Nguema
	Mrs. Ondziel-Gnelenga
	Mr. Kamel Rezzag-Bara

VII. AMENDMENT TO THE RULES OF PROCEDURE

21. The Commission completed work on the amendments to its Rules of Procedure at its 18th Ordinary Session.

VIII. PUBLICATIONS

22. The Commission published two issues of its Review and is preparing the publication of its News Bulletin.

IX. RELATIONS WITH OBSERVERS

23. During the two Sessions, the Commission considered the application of, and granted observer status to 29 organizations. At present, the number of organizations with observer status is 183.

X. PROTECTIVE ACTIVITIES

24. The Commission received eleven new communications and concluded work on seven communications. Its recommendations and decisions are attached (Annex VII).

XI. ADMINISTRATIVE AND FINANCIAL MATTERS

A. Administrative Matters

(i) Staffing

25. During the financial year under review, the work of the Commission was affected by a number of administrative problems including the following:

26. The Secretariat is still suffering from a shortage of staff, in spite of numerous appeals made by the Commission. The Commission appeals again to the Secretary-General of the OAU for an early and appropriate solution to this problem.

27. The Secretary to the Commission is the only professional staff member who is entrusted with the technical and administrative duties of the Secretariat. In view of the Secretariat's volume of work, related to human rights promotional and protective activities, there is an urgent need to recruit four additional lawyers. There is also an urgent need to recruit a documentation officer to run the Documentation Centre which is currently closed because there is no staff member to run it.

(ii) Equipment

28. Due to the increase in the volume of work at the Secretariat, it is necessary to procure adequate and proper equipment. The Commission is appealing to the OAU Secretariat to provide the Commission's Secretariat with the equipment it needs to carry out its functions, including computers, photocopiers, electronic mail, etc.

(iii) Medical Coverage and Insurance

29. The problems of medical fees and the insurance of the Commissioners when travelling on duty for the Commission have still not been settled yet. The Commission is still waiting for the solution promised some years ago by the OAU Secretariat to materialize. The Commission is making an urgent appeal to the OAU Secretariat to look into this issue.

B. Financial Matters

30. During the financial year under review, the Commission was financed from the following resources:

(i) OAU Budget

31. Due to financial problems, facing the OAU, several projects of the Commission had to be suspended. This only made worse the situation of the Commission.

(ii) Subvention from UN Centre for Human Rights

32. The UN Centre for Human Rights provided the Commission with grants for its promotional activities.

(iii) Subvention from Raoul Wallenberg Institute

33. The Raoul Wallenberg Institute continued to finance the promotional activities of the Commission, including missions undertaken by Commissioners and the publishing of the Commission's Review.

(iv) Assistance from the African Society of International Comparative Law

34. The African Society provided the Commission with two jurists from 20 March for a period of 12 months.

XII. RESOLUTIONS ADOPTED AT THE 19TH SESSION

35. The Commission adopted the following resolutions at its 19th Session:

(1) Resolution on Liberia;
(2) Resolution on the Respect for and Strengthening of the Independence of the Judiciary;
(3) Resolution on the Role of Lawyers and Judges in the Integration of the Charter and the Strengthening of Commission's National and Sub-Regional Systems;
(4) Resolution on the Elections in Benin, Comoros and Sierra Leone;
(5) Resolution on Burundi.

These resolutions are attached (Annex VIII).

XIII. ADOPTION OF THE REPORT BY THE ASSEMBLY OF HEADS OF STATE AND GOVERNMENT

36. After considering this Report, the Assembly of Heads of State and Government adopted it in a resolution which took note of the Report with satisfaction and authorized its publication.

ANNEX I

African Charter on Human and Peoples' Rights List of Countries which have Signed, Ratified or Adhered to the Charter

No.	Country	Date of Signature	Date of Ratification/ Adhesion	Date Deposited
1.	Algeria	10/04/86	01/03/87	20/03/87
2.	Angola		02/03/90	09/10/90
3.	Benin		20/01/86	25/02/86
4.	Botswana		17/07/86	22/07/86
5.	Burundi		28/07/80	30/08/89
6.	Burkina Faso	05/03/84	06/07/84	21/09/84
7.	Cameroon	23/07/87	20/06/89	18/09/89
8.	Cape Verde	31/03/86	02/06/87	06/08/87
9.	Central African Republic		26/04/86	27/07/86
10.	Chad	29/05/86	09/10/86	11/11/86
11.	Comoros		01/06/86	18/07/86

No.	Country	Date of Signature	Date of Ratification/ Adhesion	Date Deposited
12.	Congo	27/11/81	09/12/82	17/01/83
13.	Côte d'Ivoire		06/01/92	31/03/92
14.	Djibouti	20/12/91	11/11/91	20/12/91
15.	Egypt	16/11/81	20/03/84	03/04/84
16.	Equatorial Guinea	18/08/86	07/04/86	18/08/86
17.	Eritrea			
18.	Ethiopia			
19.	Gabon	26/02/82	20/02/86	26/06/86
20.	Gambia	11/02/83	08/06/83	13/03/83
21.	Ghana		24/01/89	01/03/89
22.	Guinea	09/12/81	16/02/82	13/05/82
23.	Guinea-Bissau		04/12/85	06/03/86
24.	Kenya		23/01/92	10/02/92
25.	Lesotho	07/03/84	10/02/92	27/02/92
26.	Liberia	31/01/83	04/08/82	29/12/82
27.	Libya	30/05/85	19/07/86	26/03/87
28.	Madagascar		09/03/92	19/03/92
29.	Malawi	23/02/90	17/11/89	23/02/90
30.	Mali	13/11/81	21/12/81	22/01/82
31.	Mauritania	25/02/82	14/06/86	26/06/86
32.	Mauritius	27/02/92	19/06/92	07/07/92
33.	Mozambique		22/02/89	07/03/90
34.	Namibia		30/07/92	16/09/92
35.	Niger	09/07/86	15/07/86	21/07/86
36.	Nigeria	31/08/82	22/06/83	27/07/83
37.	Rwanda	11/11/81	15/07/83	22/07/83
38.	Sahrawi Arab Dem. Rep.	10/04/86	02/05/86	23/05/86
39.	Sao Tome & Principe		23/05/86	28/07/86
40.	Senegal	23/09/81	13/08/82	25/10/82
41.	Seychelles		13/04/92	30/04/92
42.	Sierra Leone	27/08/81	21/09/83	27/01/84
43.	Somalia	26/02/82	31/07/85	20/03/86
44.	Sudan	03/09/82	18/02/86	11/03/86
45.	Swaziland			
46.	Togo	20/02/82	05/11/82	22/11/82
47.	Tunisia		16/03/83	22/04/83
48.	Uganda	18/08/86	10/05/86	27/05/86
49.	Tanzania	31/05/82	18/02/84	09/03/84
50.	Zaïre	23/07/87	20/07/87	28/07/87
51.	Zambia	17/01/83	19/01/84	02/02/84
52.	Zimbabwe	20/02/86	30/05/86	12/06/86
53.	South Africa	–	–	–

ADOPTED: by the 18th Session of the Assembly of Heads of State and Government, June 1981

REQUIRES: ratification or adherence by a simple majority of Member States to come into force

ENTERED INTO FORCE: 21st day of October 1986
DEPOSITED: with the United Nations on 10 September 1991, No. 26363

ANNEX II

Agenda of the Eighteenth Ordinary Session

1. Opening Ceremony
2. Oath by the Newly Elected Members of the Commission
3. Election of the Chairman and the Vice-Chairman of the Commission
4. Adoption of Agenda
5. Organization of Work
6. Observers

   (a) Consideration of Application for Observer Status;
   (b) Relationship with Observers and Statements of the Latter

7. Consideration of Periodic Reports of the following Member States:

   - Mauritius
   - Mozambique
   - Seychelles
   - Tunisia

8. Methods of Work of the Commission

   (a) Consideration of amendments to the Rules of Procedure;
   (b) Examination of Article 58 of the Charter

9. Promotional Activities

   (a) Activity Reports by Commissioners
   (b) Examination of Extra-judicial Executions
   (c) Report on the Implementation of Resolution AHG/230 (XXX) on the Establishment of an African Human Rights Court
   (d) Report on the 4th World Conference on Women (Beijing, 1995)
   (e) Amendments of the Guidelines on the Preparation of the Periodic States' Reports
   (f) OAU Participation in Monitoring Elections in Member States
   (g) Organization of Forthcoming Seminars and Conferences
   (h) Publication of the Review and the Newsletter of the Commission
   (i) Follow-up of the Decisions and Recommendations from the International Conferences on Human Rights (the Vienna and Montreal Conferences)
   (j) Prison Conditions in Africa
   (k) Elaboration of the Draft Additional Protocol on African Women's Rights

10. Protective Activities
11. Administrative and Financial Matters:
    (a) Report of the Chairman of the Commission
    (b) Report of the Secretary to the Commission
    (c) Implementation of the Recommendations of the Previous Sessions
    (d) Draft Rules on Contracts with Consultants
    (e) Financing of the Translation of Summaries and Periodic Reports
    (f) Situation of the Documentation Centre of the Commission
    (g) Appraisal of the Work of the Commission and its Future Prospects
    (h) Distribution of States Between the Members of the Commission for Promotional Activities
12. Question Concerning the Headquarters of the Secretariat of the Commission
13. OAU Activities Relevant to the Commission
14. Date, Place and Agenda of the 19th Session
15. Any Other Business
    – Holding of Extraordinary Sessions.
16. Preparation of:
    (a) Sessional Report
    (b) Final Communiqué

ANNEX III

Agenda of the Second Extraordinary Session

1. Opening Ceremony
2. Adoption of the Agenda (Doc. II/ES/ACHPR/1)
3. Organization of Work
4. Human Rights Report on the Situation in Nigeria
    (a) Arbitrary and Summary Executions (Doc. II/ES/ACHPR/3)
    (b) Compatibility between Nigeria's Internal Legislation and the Provisions of the African Charter on Human and Peoples' Rights (Doc. II/ES/ACHPR/4)
5. Study of some Emergency Situations on Human Rights in Africa especially in Burundi (Doc. II/ES/ACHPR/5)
6. Study of Practical Measures to be Taken in the Prevailing Situation in Nigeria (Doc.II/ES/ACHPR/6)
7. Adoption of the Session's Report
8. Closing Ceremony

ANNEX IV

Agenda of the Nineteenth Ordinary Session

1. Opening Ceremony
2. Adoption of Agenda
3. Organization of Work
4. Adoption of the Report of 18th Ordinary Session, held in Praia, Cape Verde, 2–11 October 1995
5. Adoption of the Report of the 2nd Extraordinary Session (18–19 December, 1995, Kampala, Uganda)
6. Observers

   (a) Consideration of Applications for Observer Status
   (b) Relationship with Observers and Statements of the Latter
   (c) Statements by State Delegates

7. Consideration of Periodic Reports of the Following States:

   – Mozambique
   – Algeria
   – Mauritius
   – Seychelles

8. Amendment to the African Charter on Human and Peoples' Rights
9. Brainstorming on the Setting-up of an Early Warning Mechanism in Case of Massive Human Rights Violations
10. Promotional Activities

    (a) Activity Reports by Commissioners;
    (b) Examination of the Report of the Special Rapporteur on Summary, Arbitrary, and Extra-judicial Executions
    (c) Report on the Implementation of Resolution AHG/Res. 230 (XXX) on the Establishment of an African Human Rights Court
    (d) Human Rights Situation in Africa
    (e) Amendments of Guidelines on the Preparation of the Periodic Reports
    (f) Organization of Forthcoming Seminars and Conferences
    (g) Publication of the Review and the Newsletter of the Commission
    (h) Follow-up of the Decisions and Recommendations from the International Conferences on Human Rights (the Vienna and Montreal Conference' as well as Beijing Conference on Women)
    (i) Prison Conditions in Africa
    (j) Elaboration of the Draft Additional Protocol on African Women's Rights

11. Protective Activities
12. Administrative and Financial Matters

(a) Report of the Chairman of the Commission
(b) Report of the Secretary to the Commission
(c) Implementation of Recommendations of the Previous Sessions
(d) Draft Rules on Contracts with Consultants
(e) Financing the Translation of Summaries and Periodic Reports
(f) Situation of the Documentation Centre of the Commission
(g) Appraisal of the Work of the Commission and its Future Prospects
(h) Celebration of the 10th Anniversary of the entry into force of the African Commission on Human and Peoples' Rights

13. Question of the Headquarters of the Secretariat of the Commission
14. Participation of the Commission in Some Activities of the OAU
15. Date, Place and Agenda of the 20th Ordinary Session
16. Any Other Business
17. Preparation of

- 9th Annual Activity Report
- Sessional Report
- Final Communiqué

ANNEX V

Status of Submission of Periodic Reports by States Parties

In accordance with Article 62 of the Charter reports are due from States Parties on the dates listed in Table on pp. 437–438.

ANNEX VI

Distribution of Countries for Commissioners of the African Commission of Human and Peoples' Rights for Promotional Activities as at January 1996

1. **Prof. Isaac Nguema**
   Gabon
   Equatorial Guinea
   Zaire
   Burkina Faso

2. **Prof. E. V. O. Dankwa**
   Ghana
   Zimbabwe
   Malawi
   Botswana
   Namibia.

No.	State Party	1st Report to be submitted on	2nd Report to be submitted on	3rd Report to be submitted on	4th Report to be submitted on	5th Report to be submitted on	Report submitted in
1.*	Algeria	20/06/89	20/06/91	20/06/93	20/06/95	20/06/97	1995
2.	Angola	09/01/92	09/01/94	09/01/96	09/01/98	09/01/2000	
3.*	Benin	21/10/88	21/10/90	21/10/92	21/10/94	21/10/96	
4.	Botswana	21/10/88	21/10/90	21/10/92	21/10/94	21/10/96	
5.	Burundi	30/11/91	30/11/93	30/11/95	30/11/97	30/11/99	
6.*	Burkina Faso	21/10/88	21/10/90	21/10/92	21/10/94	21/10/96	1996
7.	Cameroon	18/12/91	18/12/93	18/12/95	18/12/97	18/12/99	
8.*	Cape Verde	06/11/89	06/11/91	06/11/93	06/11/95	06/11/97	
9.	Central African Republic	21/10/88	21/10/90	21/10/92	21/10/94	21/10/96	
10.	Chad	11/02/89	11/02/91	11/02/93	11/02/95	11/02/97	
11.	Comoros	21/10/88	21/10/90	21/10/92	21/10/94	21/10/96	
12.	Congo	21/10/88	21/10/90	21/10/92	21/10/94	21/10/96	
13.	Côte d'Ivoire	01/07/94	01/07/96	01/07/98	07/01/2000	01/07/2002	
14.	Djibouti	20/03/93	20/03/95	20/03/97	20/03/99	20/03/2001	
15.*	Egypt	21/10/88	21/10/90	21/10/92	21/10/94	21/10/96	
16.	Equatorial Guinea	18/11/88	18/11/90	18/11/92	18/11/94	18/11/96	
17.	Ethiopia (1)						
18.	Eritrea (1)						
19.	Gabon	21/10/88	21/10/90	21/10/92	21/10/94	21/10/96	
20.*	Gambia	21/10/88	21/10/90	21/10/92	21/10/94	21/10/96	
21.*	Ghana	01/06/91	01/06/93	01/06/95	01/06/97	01/06/99	
22.	Guinea	21/10/88	21/10/90	21/10/92	21/10/94	21/10/96	
23.	Guinea-Bissau	21/10/88	21/10/90	21/10/92	21/10/94	21/10/96	
24.	Kenya	10/05/94	10/05/96	10/05/98	10/05/2000	10/05/2002	
25.	Lesotho	27/05/94	27/05/96	27/05/98	27/05/2000	27/05/2002	
26.	Liberia	27/10/88	21/10/90	21/10/92	21/10/94	21/10/96	
27.*	Libya	26/06/89	26/06/91	26/06/93	26/06/95	26/06/97	

No.	State Party	1st Report to be submitted on	2nd Report to be submitted on	3rd Report to be submitted on	4th Report to be submitted on	5th Report to be submitted on	Report submitted in
28.	Madagascar	19/06/94	19/06/96	19/06/98	19/06/2000	19/06/2002	
29.	Malawi	23/05/92	23/05/94	23/05/96	23/05/98	23/05/2000	
30.	Mali	21/10/88	21/10/90	21/10/92	21/10/94	21/10/96	
31.	Mauritania	21/10/88	21/10/90	21/10/92	21/10/94	21/10/96	
32.*	Mauritius	07/10/92	07/10/94	07/10/96	07/10/98	07/10/2000	
33.*	Mozambique	07/06/92	07/06/94	07/06/96	07/06/98	07/06/2000	
34.	Namibia	16/12/94	16/12/96	16/12/98	16/12/2000	16/12/2002	
35.	Niger	21/10/88	21/10/90	21/10/92	21/10/94	21/10/96	
36.*	Nigeria	21/10/88	21/10/90	21/10/92	21/10/94	21/10/96	
37.*	Rwanda	21/10/88	21/10/90	21/10/92	21/10/94	21/10/96	
38.	SADR	21/10/88	21/10/90	21/10/92	21/10/94	21/10/96	
39.	Sao Tome & Principe	21/10/88	21/10/90	21/10/92	21/10/94	21/10/96	
40.*	Senegal	21/10/88	21/10/90	21/10/92	21/10/94	21/10/96	
41.*	Seychelles	30/07/94	30/07/96	30/07/98	30/07/2000	30/07/2002	
42.	Sierra Leone	21/10/88	21/10/90	21/10/92	21/10/94	21/10/96	
43.	Somalia	21/10/88	21/10/90	21/10/92	21/10/94	21/10/96	
44.	Sudan	21/10/88	21/10/90	21/10/92	21/10/94	21/10/96	
45.	Swaziland						
46.*	Tanzania	21/10/88	21/10/90	21/10/92	21/10/94	21/10/96	
47.*	Togo	21/10/88	21/10/90	21/10/92	21/10/94	21/10/96	
48.*	Tunisia	21/10/88	21/10/90	21/10/92	21/10/94	21/10/96	
49.*	Uganda	21/10/88	21/10/90	21/10/92	21/10/94	21/10/96	
50.	Zaire	28/10/89	28/10/91	28/10/93	28/10/95	28/10/97	
51.	Zambia	21/10/88	21/10/90	21/10/92	21/10/94	21/10/96	
52.*	Zimbabwe	21/10/88	21/10/90	21/10/92	21/10/94	21/10/96	
53.	South Africa (1)						

* has presented its preliminary report

† has presented its preliminary report and second periodic report

(1) not yet ratified the African Charter

3. **Mr. Atsu-Koffi Amega**
   Togo
   Rwanda
   Central African Republic
   Djibouti
   Seychelles

4. **Mr. Mohamed Kamel Rezzag-Bara**
   Algeria
   Comoros
   Sahrawi Arab Dem. Rep.
   Madagascar
   Egypt

5. **Mr. Justice Robert Habesh Kisanga**
   Tanzania
   Ethiopia
   Kenya
   Somalia
   Uganda
   Zambia

6. **Mme V. V. D. M. Martins**
   Cape Verde
   Mozambique
   Angola
   Guinea Bissau
   Sao Tome & Principe

7. **Mme J. Ondziel-Gnelenga**
   Congo
   Burundi
   Chad
   Mauritius

8. **M. Youssoupha Ndiaye**
   Senegal
   Mali
   Niger
   Republic of Guinea

9. **Prof. U. Oji Umozurike**
   Nigeria
   Cameroon
   Lesotho
   Swaziland
   South Africa

10. **Prof. Mohammed H. Ben Salem**
    Tunisia
    Libya
    Sudan
    Eritrea
    The Gambia

11. **M. Alioune Blondin Beye**
    Benin
    Côte d'Ivoire
    Mauritania
    Liberia
    Sierra Leone

ANNEX VII

Resolutions of the 19th Session

Resolution on Liberia

The African Commission on Human and Peoples' Rights at its 19th Ordinary Session held from 26 March to 4 April 1996 in Ouagadougou, Burkina Faso.

Recalling the Abuja Agreement singed by all the parties to the Liberian conflict under which the Heads of the Warring Factions were allocated seats on the Governing Council of State in the hope that such an arrangement would facilitate and ensure disarmament of their fighters, a prerequisite for free and fair election,

Taking note that the Council of State of the Liberia Transitional Government, created in pursuance of the Abuja Agreement, has been installed into office and that the Government including the Judiciary and the Legislature has been freely constituted and is now functional,

Considering however, that notwithstanding the establishment of the Council of State, the Warring Factions have refused to disarm, and that Liberia contrary to the Abuja Agreement, still remains fragmented and partitioned among warring factions, and hostilities still exist, all of which have the potential to derail the peace process and prolong the suffering of the Liberian people and the strain on the West African Sub-Region,

Considering further that if peace is to be restored to Liberia, a civil government installed through a free and fair elections, and democratic institutions established with respect for human and democratic institutions established with respect for human rights under the rule of law, Liberians themselves, and with the support of the International Community, must exert efforts to cease all hostilities, disarm their combatants, have them encamped, demobilized and re-integrated into civil society,

ENDORSES the Abuja Peace Accord as the best means for the cessation of hostilities and the restoration of peace to Liberia and calls upon all parties to this Agreement to cooperate in good faith in its implementation;

CALLS UPON the Warring Factions to take all necessary steps to disarm their fighters, cooperate with the West African Peace keeping Forces (ECOMOG) and United Nations Observer Mission in Liberia (UNOMIL) and have fighters encamped, demobilized and re-integrated into civil society society so as to pave the way for a free and fair general election;

CALLS ALSO upon the Council of State to extend its authority over the whole of Liberia and to guarantee genuine respect for the rights and liberties of all its citizens and residents, and in this regard to observe the independence of the Judiciary;

FURTHER CALLS UPON the Council of State to take all necessary measures to fight against impunity and ensure that all perpetrators of crimes against the Liberian people are brought to justice;

APPEALS to the International Community especially the United Nations, to facilitate Liberia's transition from war to peace by enhancing the capacity of the West African Peace-keeping Force to encamp all combatants and to keep the peace through the provision of financial and logistic support; and to alleviate the suffering and the daily struggle of the Liberian people for survival through the provision of humanitarian relief and medical supplies.

Resolution on the Respect and the Strengthening of the Independence of the Judiciary

The African Commission on Human and Peoples' Rights at its 19th Ordinary Session held from 26th to 4th April 1996 at Ouagadougou, Burkina Faso,

Noting that Justice is an integral part of human rights and a necessary condition for democracy,

Considering the importance and the role of the judiciary, not only in the quest for the maintenance of social equilibrium, but also in the economic development of African countries,

Recognizing the need for African countries to have a strong and independent Judiciary enjoying the confidence of the people for sustainable democracy and development,

Considering the need to train lawyers in human rights in order to enable them apply judiciously international human rights instruments,

1. CALLS UPON African countries to:

- repeal all their legislation which are inconsistent with the principle of respect of the independence of the Judiciary, especially with regard to the appointment and posting of judges;
- provide, with the assistance of the international community, the Judiciary with sufficient resources in order to enable the legal system fulfil its function;
- provide judges with decent living and working conditions to enable them maintain their independence and realize their full potential;
- incorporate in their legal systems universal principles establishing the independence of the Judiciary, especially with regard to security of tenure;
- refrain from taking any action which may threaten directly or indirectly the independence and the security of judges and magistrates.

2. URGES African judges to organize nationally and regionally periodic meetings in order to exchange experience and evaluate efforts undertaken in various countries to bring about an efficient and independent judiciary.

Resolution on the Role of Lawyers and Judges in Integration of the Charter and Enhancement of the Commission's Work in National and Sub-regional Systems

At the 19th Ordinary Session of the African Commission on Human and Peoples' Rights held from 26 March to 4 April 1996 at Ouagadougou, Burkina Faso,

Noting the central role that lawyers play in advocacy in the Judicial and other adjudicative processes in national legal systems and considering further how such roles can be used to promote reference to and reliance on the Charter in the Judicial and other adjudicative processes,

Considering the mandate and judicial competence of judges to base their reasoning and judgements on all relevant human rights instruments, either as applicable authoritative laws or as persuasive aids to interpretation of constitutional and legislative provisions on fundamental rights, freedoms and duties,

Recognizing the importance of specialized and continuing training in human and peoples' rights for legal practitioners, judges, magistrates and the Commissioners,

Appreciating the initiative of the Commonwealth judges to incorporate and further develop Human Rights instruments and principles in their work,

1. URGES Judges and magistrates to play a greater role in incorporating the Charter and future jurisprudence of the Commission in their judgements thereby promoting and protecting the rights and freedoms guaranteed by the Charter;
2. CALLS UPON lawyers to place greater reliance on the Charter and other international and regional human rights instruments in their various legal advocacy roles;
3. URGES law societies, legal and human rights, Non-Governmental Organizations with Observer Status with the Commission, associations or organizations of judges and magistrates to initiate specialized and comprehensive training for judicial officers, lawyers at national and sub-regional levels.

Resolution on Electoral Process and Participatory Governance

The African Commission on Human and Peoples' Rights meeting at its 19th Ordinary Session held in Ouagadougou, Burkina Faso from 26 March to 4 April 1996,

Having taken note of the report on recent elections in the Republic of Benin,

Taking note of the report on the smooth organization of elections in the Comoro Islands,

Further noting the satisfactory manner in which the Presidential Elections were held recently in the Republic of Sierra Leone,

1. ASSERTS that elections are the only means by which the people can elect democratically the Government of their choice in conformity to the African Charter on Human and Peoples' Rights;
2. COMMENDS the Governments and the people of the Republic of Benin, the Comoros and the Republic of Sierra Leone for having organized successfully free and

fair elections and hopes that their example will encourage and motivate other countries in transition to democratic rule;

3. EMPHASIZES that it is the duty of States Parties to the Charter to take the necessary measures to preserve and protect the credibility of the electoral process. These measures should include the presence of national and international observers during the elections and guarantee them access to the electoral process and personal safety to enable them to fulfil their mission and prepare their report on elections in a proper manner;

4. FURTHER EMPHASIZES that it is the responsibility of State Parties to provide electoral commissions and other organs entrusted with the task of organizing elections in their countries with adequate material, resources and any items necessary for the preparation and holding of elections;

5. REAFFIRMS the importance of African countries and institutions to participate in observation of elections in States Parties; and reasserts its willingness to place at the disposal of States Parties and other institutions its expertise and that of its members in observing elections.

Resolution on Burundi

The African Commission on Human and Peoples' Rights, at its 19th Ordinary Session held from 26 March to 4 April 1996, in Ouagadougou, Burkina Faso,

Extremely concerned with the serious human rights violations and abuses occurring in Burundi, especially extrajudicial executions by some members of the security forces, armed gangs and militias,

Considering that impunity is one of the main causes of the worsening human rights situation in Burundi,

Considering that the independence of the judiciary is the cornerstone of the effective struggle against human rights violations in general and impunity in particular,

Concerned with the plight of refugees and displaced persons and their vulnerability to human rights violations and abuses,

Considering that the Burundi crisis is made worse by the hate media and that the high point of the message of hatred was reached with the launching of "Radio Democratie la Voix du Peuple",

1. URGES the Government of Burundi to:

(a) conduct transparent and impartial investigations into all human rights violations and abuses;
(b) take the necessary steps to guarantee the independence of the judiciary by ensuring, inter alia, that there is no interference in its functioning by the executive and that judges and magistrates are protected in the carrying out of their duty;
(c) ensure that persons accused of human rights violations and abuses are tried in compliance with international fair trial standards;
(d) improve the living conditions of refugees and displaced persons, ensure their safety and security and create conditions to enable them to return to

their homes in collaboration with International Governmental and Non-Governmental Organizations;

(e) allow the Mission Internationale d'Observation au Burundi (MIOB), human rights monitors and special rapporteurs from the United Nations, African Commission on Human and Peoples' Rights and other International Bodies freedom of movement throughout the country and take adequate and effective steps to guarantee their safety and security without compromising their independence;

2. FURTHER URGES the Government of Burundi and the concerned political parties to respect the spirit and the letter of the Government Agreement which they signed in 1994 in the supreme national interest of Burundi;

3. CALLS UPON the OAU to strengthen MIOB and to include human rights monitoring in its mandate;

4. REQUESTS the UN to provide adequate resources to enable its Commission of inquiry sent to Burundi to function efficiently and to complete its tasks as soon as possible;

5. CALLS UPON the International Community to assist the Governments of Burundi and neighbouring countries to rid the sub-region of media which propagate hatred and fuel communal conflict in Burundi especially the Radio Station "Radio Democratie, la voix du Peuple" or "RUTOMORANGINGO";

6. DECIDES to involve itself more in efforts to resolve the crisis afflicting Burundi by, among other things, sending a mission to Burundi and participating actively in the process of national reconciliation.

ANNEX VIII

Communications

1. 25/89, 47/90, 56/91, 100/93 (Joined) Free Legal Assistance Group, Lawyers' Committee for Human Rights, Union Interafricaine des Droits de l'Homme, Les Temoins de Jehovah/Zaire

The facts:

(1) Communication 25/89 is filed by the Free Legal Assistance Group, the Austrian Committee Against Torture, and the Centre haitien des Droits et Libertes, all members of the World Organization Against Torture (OMCT).

The submission of the Free Legal Assistance Group was dated 17 March 1989, that of the Austrian Committee Against Torture dated 29 March 1989, that of the Centre Haitien dated 20 April 1989.

The Communication alleges the torture of 15 persons by a Military Unit, on or about 19 January 1989, at Kinsuka near the Zaire river. On 19 April 1989 when several people protested their treatment, they were detained and held indefinitely.

(2) Communication 47/90, dated 16 October 1990, is filed by the Lawyers' Committee for Human Rights in New York.

It alleges arbitrary arrests, arbitrary detentions, torture, extra-judicial executions, unfair trials, severe restrictions placed on the right to association and peaceful assembly, and suppression of the freedom of the Press.

(3) Communication 56/91 is submitted by the Jehovah's Witnesses of Zaire and dated 27 March 1991.

It alleges the persecution of the Jehovah's Witnesses, including arbitrary arrests, appropriation of church property, and exclusion from access to education.

(4) Communication 100/93 is submitted by the Union Interafricaine des Droits de l'Homme and dated 20 March 1993.

It makes allegations of torture, executions, arrests, detention, unfair trials, restrictions on freedom of association and freedom of the press. It also alleges that public finances were mismanaged; that the failure of the Government to provide basic services was degrading; that there was a shortage of medicines; that the universities and secondary schools had been closed for two years; that freedom of movement was violated; and that ethnic hatred was incited by the official media.

(5) The African Commission, when it determined that the communications, taken together, evidenced a grave and massive violation of human rights in Zaire, brought the matter to the attention of the Assembly of the Heads of State of the Organization of African Unity, in December 1995.

(6) The Commission also requested that a mission consisting of two members of the Commission be received in that country, with the objective of discovering the extent and cause of human rights violations and endeavouring to help the government to ensure full respect for the African Charter. The government of Zaire has never responded to these requests for a mission.

Procedure before the Commission:

(7) Communication 25/89 was received by the Commission in June 1989. The Commission was seized of the communication at its 11th Session in October 1989 and the State of Zaire was notified on 14 March 1990.

(8) Between 1990 and 1993, numerous reminders were sent by the Secretariat to the Government of Zaire, but no response was received.

(9) The Secretariat also sent the complainants regular updates on the status of the communications.

(10) On 23 September 1993, the Ministry of Justice of Zaire wrote that no copy of the communication had ever been received.

(11) A copy was sent on 3 March 1994 by registered post to the Embassy of Zaire in Dakar but no response was forthcoming.

(12) At the 16th Session, held in April 1994, the Commission decided to send a mission to Zaire in order to create a dialogue.

(13) At the 17th Session, held in March 1995, the Communications against Zaire were declared admissible.

(14) The Government of Zaire was notified of this decision on 26 April 1995.

(15) At the 18th Session, held in October 1995, the Commission decided to apply Article 58(1) of the Charter and to draw the attention of the Heads of State and Government to the serious and massive violations of human rights in Zaire.

(16) On 12 January 1996, a note verbale was sent to the Ministry of Foreign Affairs of Zaire informing the Ministry of the proposed mission to Zaire to be undertaken by Commissioner Nguema and Ben Salem.

(17) Communication No. 47/90 was received by the Commission in October 1990.

(18) On 20 October 1990, at its 8th Ordinary Session in Banjul, the African Commission was seized of the communication and decided to notify the State of Zaire of the complaint and invite its written comments on the admissibility.

(19) On 6 November 1990, the Secretariat of the Commission informed the Ministry of Zaire of this decision by registered post. No response was forthcoming.

(20) At its 11th Ordinary Session, the Commission decided to send a reminder to Zaire. The Secretariat sent this reminder on 30 March 1992. No response was forthcoming.

(21) At its 12th Ordinary Session, held in Banjul in October 1992, the Commission declared the communication admissible and decided that it would be examined on the merits.

(22) The notice of this decision was sent on 16 November 1992. No response was forthcoming.

(23) In 1993 and 1994, the Secretariat sent several reminders to the government of Zaire. No response was received.

(24) From August 1994 to the present, the correspondence in respect of this communication is identical with that in the communication 25/89, above.

(25) Communication No. 56/91 was received by the Commission in Summer 1991.

(26) The Commission was seized of the communication at its 10th Session in October 1991 and a notification was sent to the state on 14 November 1991. No response was forthcoming.

(27) Two reminders were sent by the Secretariat to the Government of Zaire in 1992.

(28) In a letter dated 14 September 1993, the Ministry of Justice of Zaire claimed that a copy of the communication had never been received.

(29) A copy of the communication was sent 3 March 1994 by registered post to the Embassy in Dakar, but no response was received.

(30) From August 1994, the correspondence in respect of this communication is identical with that in communication 25/89, given above.

(31) Communication No. 100/93 was received by the Commission in April 1993.

(32) The Commission was seized of the communication at its 13th Session in April 1993 and it was brought to the attention of the State on 12 April 1993. No response was forthcoming.

(33) In 1993 and 1994, reminders were sent to the Government of Zaire but no response was forthcoming.

(34) As from August 1994, the correspondence in respect of this communication is identical with that in communication 25/89, given above.

Law:

Admissibility:

(35) After deliberations, as envisioned by Article 58 of the African Charter, the Commission considered that communications 25/89, 47/90, 56/91 and 100/93 against Zaire reveal the existence of serious and massive violations of human rights.

(36) Article 56 of the African Charter requires that complainants exhaust local remedies before the Commission can take up a case, unless these remedies are as a practical matter unavailable or unduly prolonged. The requirement of exhaustion of local remedies is founded on the principle that a government should have notice of a human rights violation in order to have the opportunity to remedy such violations before being called before an international body. In this case, the government has had ample notice of the violation.

(37) The Commission has never held the requirement of local remedies to apply literally in cases where it is impractical or undesirable for the complainant to seize the domestic courts in the case of each violation. This is the situation here, given the vast and varied scope of the violations alleged and the general situation prevailing in Zaire.

(38) For the above reasons, the Commission declared the communications admissible.

Merits:

(39) The main goal of the communications procedure before the Commission is to initiate a positive dialogue, resulting in an amicable resolution between the complainant and the State concerned, which remedies the prejudice complained of. A pre-requisite for amicably remedying violations of the Charter is the good faith of the parties concerned, including their willingness to participate in a dialogue.

(40) In the present case, there has been no substantive response from the Government of Zaire, despite the numerous notifications of the communications sent by the African Commission. The African Commission, in several previous decisions, has set out the principle that where allegations of human rights abuse go uncontested by the government concerned, even after repeated notifications, the Commission must decide on the facts provided by the complainant and treat those facts as given.[1] This principle conforms with the practice of other international human rights adjudicatory bodies and the Commission's duty to protect human rights. Since the Government of Zaire does not wish to participate in a dialogue, the Commission must, regrettably, continue its consideration of the case on the basis of facts and opinions submitted by the complainants alone.

(41) Article 5 of the African Charter prohibits torture and inhuman or degrading treatment. The torture of 15 persons by a military unity at Kinsuka, near the Zaire river, as alleged in communication 25/89, constitutes a violation of this article.

(42) Article 6 of the African Charter guarantees the right to liberty and security of person. The indefinite detention of those who protested against torture, as described in communication 25/89, violates Article 6.

[1] See, e.g. the Commission's decisions in communications 59/91, 60/91, 87/93 and 101/93.

(43) Article 4 of the African Charter protects the rights to life. Communication 47/90, in addition to alleged arbitrary arrests, arbitrary detention and torture, alleges extrajudicial executions which are a violation of Article 4.

(44) Article 7 of the African Charter specifies the right to have one's cause heard. The unfair trials described in communication 47/90 constitute a violation of this right.

(45) Article 8 of the African Charter protects freedom of conscience. The harassment of the Jehovah's Witnesses, as described in communication 56/91, constitutes a violation of this article, since the government has presented no evidence that the practice of their religion in any way threatens law and order. The arbitrary arrests of believers of this religion likewise constitutes a contravention of Article 6, above.

(46) The torture, executions, arrests, detention, unfair trials, restrictions on freedom of association and freedom of the press described in communication 100/93 violate the above Articles.

(47) Article 16 of the African Charter states that every individual shall have the right to enjoy the best attainable state of physical and mental health, and that States Parties should take the necessary measures to protect the health of their people. The failure of the Government to provide basic services such as safe drinking water and electricity and the shortage of medicine as alleged in communication 100/93 constitutes a violation of Article 16.

(48) Article 17 of the Charter guarantees the right to education. The closures of universities and secondary schools as described in communication 100/93 constitutes a violation of Article 17.

For these reasons, the Commission:
holds that the facts constitute serious and massive violations of the African Charter, namely of Articles 4, 5, 6, 7, 8, 16 and 17.

Taken at the 18th Ordinary Session, Praia, Cape Verde, October 1995.

2. 70/92 Ibrahima Dioumessi, Sekou Kande, Ousmane Kaba/Guinea

The facts:

(1) The communication was submitted by Ibrahima Dioumessi, Sekou Kande, Ousmane kaba, and received by the Commission on 15 November 1991. It contains no mailing address for the complainants.

(2) The communication alleges that following the coup d'etat of 4 July 1984 in Guinea, the complainants were arrested, tortured and incarcerated for three years without charge or trial.

(3) The complainants allege violation of the right to security of persons and the right to fair trial. The former detainees request compensation for the moral and material prejudice they have suffered.

Procedure before the Commission:

(4) The Commission was seized of the communication at its 12th Session in November 1992.

(5) The Ministry of Foreign Affairs of Guinea was notified on 13 November 1992. The Secretariat also requested the complainants' address.

(6) In 1993 and 1994, numerous reminders were sent by the Secretariat to the Government of Guinea, but no response was received.

(7) On 21 October 1994, the Guinean Government sent a note verbale to the Commission requesting that the Commission delay consideration of the communication until the 17th Session, in order to allow the government to submit its memorandum in response.

(8) At the 17th Session in March 1995, the memorandum of the Government of Guinea had not been received, but it was decided to wait for it, and in the meanwhile to ask the complainants if they had exhausted all domestic remedies.

(9) All attempts to get the addresses of the complaints were of no avail.

(10) At the 18th Session, the memorandum of the Government of Guinea still had not been received.

Law:

(11) The problem posed here is one of admissibility. To be admissible, a communication must fulfil all the conditions of Article 56 of the Charter, in particular, the identity of the complainants so that they may be sent notifications.

(12) In the present case, the Secretariat has not been able to remedy this lack of the complainants' address.

For these reasons, the Commission:
declares the communication inadmissible.

Done in Praia, Cape Verde, October 1995.

3. 74/92 Commission Nationale des Droits de l'Homme et des Libertes/ Chad

The facts:

(1) The communication is brought by La Commission Nationale des Droite de l'Homme et des Libertes de la Federation Nationale des Unions de Jeunes Avocats de France. The complaint alleges several massive and severe violations in Chad.

(2) The complaint alleges that journalists are harassed, both directly and indirectly. These attacks are often by unidentified individuals who the complainants claim to be security service agents of the Government. The Government denies responsibility.

(3) The complaint alleges the arbitrary arrest of several people, among those four members of the opposition party, R.D.P., by the security services. These people were never brought before a court, although they were eventually set free. 15 more people were illegally detained, but have now been liberated.

(4) There are several accounts of killings, disappearances and torture. 15 people are reported killed, 200 wounded, and several persons tortured as a result of the civil war between the security services and other groups.

(5) The communication alleges the assassination of Bisso Mamadou, who was attacked by armed individuals. The Minister responsible was warned of the danger to Mr. Bisso, but he refused to issue protection. Subsequently, the Minister did not initiate investigation into the killing.

(6) The communication also alleges the assassination of Joseph Betudi, Vice-President of Ligue Tchadienne des Droits de l'Homme. It also contains allegations of inhuman treatment of prisoners.

Procedure before the Commission:

(7) The communication is dated 11 May 1992 and includes a report based on an observation mission to Chad made by the Association "Agir ensemble pour les droits de l'Homme" and the Federation Nationale des Unions de Jeunes Avocats.

(8) The Commission was seized of the communication at its 12th Session and on 16 November 1992 the Government of Chad was notified of the communication.

(9) On 10 March 1993, the Ministry of Justice responded to the communication.

(10) On 12 April 1993, the Chairman of the Commission wrote to the Ministry of Foreign Affairs and requested its permission to conduct an on-the-spot investigation in Chad.

(11) The Government did not reply to that letter, nor to the following reminders.

(12) A letter was sent to the Government on 3 February 1995, and to the complainant on 17 February 1995, stating that the communication would be considered at the 17th Session.

(13) At the 17th Session in March 1995, the communication was declared admissible. The Government and complainant were informed of that decision.

(14) On 1 September 1995, a letter was sent to the Government stating that the communication would be heard on its merits at the 18th Session of the Commission and inviting the Government to send a representative.

(15) At the 18th Session, the Commission heard Ms. Febiene Trusses-Naprous, de la Federation Nationale des Unions de Jeunes Avocats, Commission Nationale des Droits de l'Homme et des Libertes of France. She reiterated the information in the original communication, both verbally and by way of a memoire. This memoire, in addition to summarizing the information in the original communication, affirmed that the human rights situation in Chad has not seen improvement to the present day. The Commission decided the communication on the merits, resolving that there was evidence of serious and massive violations of human and peoples' rights. Article 58 was invoked to draw the attention of the Assembly of Heads of State and Government of the OAU to this fact.

(16) On 27 November 1995 a letter was received from the Ministry of External Affairs of Chad with regard to the Secretariat's letter of 1 September 1995. This letter stated that the National Human Rights Commission of Chad could find no record of the communication.

Law:

(17) Article 1 of the African Charter reads:

> "The Member States of the Organization of African Unity parties to the present Charter shall recognize the rights, duties and freedoms enshrined in this Charter and shall undertake to adopt legislative or other measures to give effect to them."

(18) In this case, the complainant claims that not only did Government agents commit violations of the African Charter, but that the state failed to protect the rights in the Charter from violation by other parties.

(19) The Government claims that no violations were committed by its agents, and that it had no control over violations committed by other parties, as Chad is in a state of civil war.

(20) The Charter specifies in Article 1 that the States Parties shall not only recognize the rights duties and freedoms adopted by the Charter, but they should also "undertake . . . measures to give effect to them". In other words, if a state neglects to ensure the rights in the African Charter, this can constitute a violation, even if the State or its agents are not the immediate cause of the violation.

(21) The African Charter, unlike other human rights instruments,[2] does not allow for states parties to derogate from their treaty obligations during emergency situations. Thus, even a civil war in Chad cannot be used as an excuse by the State violating or permitting violations of rights in the African Charter.

(22) In the present case, Chad has failed to provide security and stability in the country, thereby allowing serious and massive violations of human rights. The national armed forces are participants in the civil war and there have been several instances in which the Government has failed to intervene to prevent the assassination and killing of specific individuals. Even where it cannot be proved that violations were committed by government agents, the government had a responsibility to secure the safety and the liberty of its citizens, and to conduct investigations into murders. Chad therefore is responsible for the violations of the African Charter.

(23) The complainant claims that the events in Chad constitute violations of Articles 4 (Right to Life), Article 5 (Prohibition of Torture, Inhuman and Degrading Treatment), 6 (Right to Life and Security of Persons), 7 (Right to a Fair Trial), and 10 (Right to Freedom of Expression).

(24) In the present case, there has been no substantive response from the Government of Chad, only a blanket denial of responsibility.

(25) The African Commission, in several previous decisions, has set out the principle that where allegations of human rights abuse go uncontested by the Government concerned, Commission must decide on the facts provided by the complainant

[2] E.g. the European Convention on Human Rights, Article 15, the Inter-American Convention on Human Rights, and the International Covenant on Civil and Political Rights.

and treat those facts as given.[3] This principle conforms with the practice of other international human rights adjudicatory bodies and the Commission's duty to protect human rights. Since the Government of Chad does not wish to participate in a dialogue, that the Commission must, regrettably, continue its consideration of the case on the basis of facts and opinions submitted by the complaints alone.

(26) Thus, in the absence of a substantive response by the Government, in keeping with its practice, the Commission will take its decisions based on the events alleged by the complainants.

For these reasons, the Commission:
finds that there have been serious and massive violations of human rights in Chad;
finds that there have been violations of Articles 4, 5, 6, 7.

Taken at the 18th Ordinary Session, Praia, Cape Verde, October 1995.

4. 129/94 Civil Liberties Organization/Nigeria

The facts:

(1) The communication is filed by the Civil Liberties Organization, a Nigerian NGO. The communication alleges that the military government of Nigeria has enacted various decrees in violation of the African Charter, specifically the Constitution (Suspension and Modification) Decree No. 107 of 1993, which not only suspends the Constitution but also specifies that no decree promulgated after December 1983 can be examined in any Nigerian Court; and the Political Parties (Dissolution) Decree No. 114 of 1993, which in addition to dissolving political parties, ousts the jurisdiction of the courts and specifically nullifies any domestic effect of the African Charter.

(2) The communication complains that the ousting of the jurisdiction of the courts in Nigeria to adjudicate the legality of any decree threatens the independence of the judiciary and violates Article 26 of the African Charter.

(3) The communication also complains that this ouster of the jurisdiction of the courts deprives Nigerians of their right to seek redress in the courts for government acts that violate their fundamental rights, in violation of Article 7(1)(a) of the African Charter.

Procedure before the Commission:

(4) The complaint is dated 31 December 1993.

(5) On 29 July 1994 a copy of the communication was sent to the State concerned for its comments.

(6) At the 16th Ordinary Session of the Commission, the communication was declared admissible.

(7) On 10 January 1995, the parties were informed of the admissibility decision.

[3] See, e.g., the Commission's decisions in communications 59/91, 60/91, 64/91, 87/93 and 101/93.

Law:

Admissibility:

(8) The communication meets all the specifications for admissibility set out in Article 56 of the Charter. With specific reference to Article 56 (5), the Commission accepted the complainant's argument that since the decrees complained of oust the jurisdiction of the courts to adjudicate their validity, "it is reasonable to presume that domestic remedies will not only be prolonged but are certain to yield no results".

Merits:

(9) Article 7 of the African Charter provides:

> "1. Every individual shall have the right to have his cause heard. This comprises:
> (a) the right to an appeal to competent national organs against acts violating his fundamental rights as guaranteed by conventions, law, regulations and customs in force."

(10) The Constitution (Suspension and Modification) Decree 1993, (5) reads:

> "No question as to the validity of this Decree or any other Decree made during the period 31st December 1983 to 26th August 1993 or made after the commencement of this Decree or of an Edict shall be entertained by a court of law in Nigeria."

(11) The Political Parties (Dissolution) Decree 12993, 13 (1) reads:

> "Notwithstanding anything contained in the Constitution of the Federal Republic of Nigeria 1979, as amended, the African Charter on Human and Peoples' Rights (Ratification and Enforcement) Act or any other enactment, no proceeding shall lie or be instituted in any court for or on account of any act, matter or thing done or purported to be done in respect of this Decree."

(12) The reference in Article 7(1)(a) to "fundamental rights as guaranteed by conventions . . . in enforce" signifies the rights in the Charter itself, among others. Given that Nigeria ratified the African Charter in 1983, it is presently a convention in enforce in Nigeria. If Nigeria wished to withdraw its ratification, it would have to undertake an international process involving notice, which it has not done. Nigeria cannot negate the effects of its ratification of the Charter through domestic action. Nigeria remains under the obligation to guarantee the rights of Article 7 to all of its citizens.

(13) The ousting of jurisdiction of the courts of Nigeria over any decree enacted in the past ten years, and those to be subsequently enacted, constitutes an attack of incalculable proportions on Article 7. The complaint refers to a few examples of decrees which violate human rights but which are now beyond review by the courts. An attack of this sort on the jurisdiction of the courts is especially

invidious, because while it is a violation of human rights in itself, it permits other violations of rights to go unredressed.

(14) Article 26 of the African Charter reiterates the right enshrined in Article 7 but is even more explicit about States Parties' obligations to "guarantee the independence of the Courts and . . . allow the establishment and improvement of appropriate national institutions entrusted with the promotion and protection of the rights and freedoms guaranteed by the present Charter". While Article 7 focuses on the individual's right to be heard, Article 26 speaks of the institutions which are essential to give meaning and content to that right. This Article clearly envisions the protection of the courts which have traditionally been the bastion of protection of the individual's rights against the abuses of State power.

(15) The communication notes that Nigeria fully incorporated the African Charter upon ratification in 1983. The African Charter upon ratification in 1983. The African Charter (Ratification and Enforcement Act) specified:

> "1. As from the commencement of this Act, the provisions of the African Charter on Human and Peoples' Rights . . . shall, subject as thereunder provided, have force of law in Nigeria and shall be given full recognition and effect and be applied by all authorities and persons exercising legislative, executive or judicial powers in Nigeria."

It is this Act that is repealed by clause 13(1) of the Political Parties Dissolution Decree.

(16) Any doubt that may exist as to Nigeria's obligations under the African Charter is dispelled by reference to Article 1 of the Charter, which reads:

> "The Member States . . . Parties to the present Charter shall recognize the rights, duties and freedoms enshrined in this Charter and shall undertake to adopt legislative or other measures to give effect to them."

(17) The African Commission has to express its approval of Nigeria's original incorporation of the Charter, an incorporation that should set a standard for all Africa, and its sadness at the subsequent nullification of this incorporation. The Commission must emphasize, however, that the obligation of the Nigerian government to guarantee the right to be heard to its citizens still remains, unaffected by the purported revocation of domestic effect of the Charter. The Charter remains in force in Nigeria, and notwithstanding the Political Parties Dissolution Decree, the Nigerian government has the same obligations under the Charter as if it had never revoked. These obligations include guaranteeing the right to be heard.

For the above reasons, the Commission:

holds that the Decrees in question constitute a breach of Art. 7 of the Charter, the right to be heard;

holds the ouster of the courts' jurisdiction constitutes a breach of Art. 26, the obligation to establish and protect the courts;

finds the act of the Nigerian Government to nullify the domestic effect of the Charter constitutes a serious irregularity.

Taken at the 17th Session, Lome, March 1995

5. 135/94 Kenya Human Rights Commission/Kenya

The facts:

(1) The university academic staff from the four public universities in Kenya (University of Nairobi, Kenyatta University, Moi University and Egerton University) met and resolved to form an Umbrella Trade Union to represent their interests in negotiations with their respective employers. They decided to call their union, the Universities Academic Staff Union (UASU).

(2) On 25 May 1992, they submitted an application for registration to the Registrar of Trade Unions. The Registrar acknowledged the receipt of the application documents the same day. However, there was no further replies from either the Registrar General, or the Attorney General.

(3) In June 1993, the UASU interim officials wrote to the Attorney General seeking audience with him to discuss UASU's registration. The Attorney General did not reply to this letter.

(4) Due to the lack of response, the UASU decided in November 1993 to go on strike 29 November 1993. The notice of the intended strike was issued to the Attorney General, the Registrar and the Vice-Chancellors of the public universities. A copy of notice was also delivered to Kenya's President Daniel Moi, who is also the Chancellor of all the public universities.

(5) On 24 November 1993 the Registrar refused to register UASU on the grounds that "the union is used for unlawful purposes and as such peace, welfare and good order in Kenya would otherwise be likely to suffer prejudice . . ."

(6) The strike began on 29 November 1993 and court proceedings initiated on 23 December 1993, challenging the Registrar's decision to reject their application for registration as a trade union.

(7) On 27 December 1993, during the swearing-in of two newly appointed judges of the High Court of Kenya President Moi, who is also the Chancellor of the public universities, stated that the government would never register UASU despite the fact that the matter was already in court. He reiterated the government's position on 31 December in a public statement. He again repeated that the government would not allow the registration of UASU on 25 February 1994 and further stated that the government would take stern action against the leaders of the UASU.

(8) Justice A. B. Shah, one of the new judges sworn in on 27 December 1993, and who was previously the President's lawyer, heard an application filed by University of Nairobi UASU chapter officials seeking to restrain eviction from their university housing until the cases against the Registrar challenging the rejection of registration, and their purported dismissal from the university were fully determined. Justice A. B. Shah rejected the application.

(9) All the national officials of UASU have been arrested and harassed since the strike begun in November 1993. On 10 December 1993, the national interim officials were arrested while proceeding to Egerton University for a meeting. No charges were pressed and the officials were released the following day. Dr Korwa Adar was again arrested on 25 February 1994 from his house after the President warned that action will be taken against UASU leaders. Dr. Adar was charged with inciting students and colleagues to violence.

Procedure before the Commission:

(10) The communication is dated 8 March 1994 and was received by the Commission on 2 May 1994.

(11) The Commission was seized of the communication at its 16 Session in October 1994 and it was decided that the Government of Kenya should be notified of the complaint against it for comments.

(12) On 10 January 1995, a letter was sent to the complainant asking what had been the outcome of the court case respecting the refusal of the Government to register the union in question. On the same date a notification was sent to the Government informing it of the seizure of the communication during the 16th Session and that the admissibility of the communication would be considered at the 17th Session.

(13) At the 17th Session the 3 month period given to the Government of Kenya to respond to the communication had not yet elapsed. The case was therefore deferred to the 18th Session.

(14) On the 20 April 1995, letters were sent to both the complainant and the Government of Kenya, stating that the case would be considered at the 18th Session and requesting the Government of Kenya's response to the communication and information from the complainant on the pending court case.

Law:

(15) Article 56 of the African Charter reads:

> "Communications . . . shall be considered if they:
>
> . . .
>
> (5) Are sent after exhausting local remedies, if any, unless it is obvious that this procedure is unduly prolonged . . ."

(16) The most recent information the Commission has, provided by the complainants themselves, states that the communication is still pending before the courts of Kenya. The complainant has therefore not exhausted all available local remedies.

For the above reasons, the Commission:

declares the communication inadmissible without making any judgements as to the merits.

18th Session, Praia, Cape Verde, October 1995.

Final Communiqué of the Eighteenth Ordinary Session of the African Commission on Human and Peoples' Rights

Praia, 2–11 October 1995

1. The African Commission on Human and Peoples' Rights held its 18th Ordinary Session in Praia, Cape Verde from 2–11 October, 1995 at the invitation of the Government of the Republic of Cape Verde. The session was chaired by Professor Isaac Nguema.

2. The session was preceded by the 9th ICJ workshop on the participation of NGOs in the meetings of the African Commission on Human and Peoples' Rights. The Workshop, which took place from 29 September to 1 October, 1995, had been organized by the International Commission of Jurists (ICJ) in collaboration with the African Commission on Human and Peoples' Rights.

3. The following Commissioners attended the session:

- Professor Isaac Nguema – Chairman;
- Dr. Hatem Ben Salem – Vice Chairman;
- Mr. Atsu Koffi Amega;
- Professor Emmanuel V. O. Dankwa;
- Dr. Vera Valentina B. S. Duarte Martins;
- Mr. Youssoupha Ndiaye;
- Professor U. Oji Umozurike;
- Mr. Robert Habesh Kisanga;
- Mr. Kamel Rezzag-Bara; and
- Mrs Julienne Ondziel-Gnelenga.

4. Apologies for absence were received from Mr. Alione Blondin Beye.

5. The opening ceremony was held on 2 October 1995 at 10 a.m on the premises of the National Assembly of Cape Verde and was presided over by His Excellency the President of the Republic of Cape Verde, Mr. Antonio Mascarenhas Monteiro. The ceremony was also graced with the presence of Mr. Amilcar Spencer Lopes, the Speaker of the National Assembly, Mr. Carlos Veiga, the Prime Minister, Mr. Pedro Freire, the Minister of Justice and other members of the Government of Cape Verde.

6. The opening ceremony of the 18th Ordinary Session of the Commission was also attended by Ambassadors, Consuls and Heads of diplomatic missions accredited to Cape Verde, delegates of OAU member States, representatives of inter-governmental and non-governmental organizations, members of the press and invited guests.

7. The following dignitaries spoke at the opening ceremony:

- Honourable Pedro Freire, Minister of Justice of Cape Verde;
- Mrs. Tokungo Ige, the ICJ legal officer for Africa; representing Mr. Adama Dieng, Secretary-General of ICJ;
- Professor Isaac Nguema, Chairman of the African Commission on Human and Peoples Rights; and
- His Excellency the President of the Republic of Cape Verde, Mr. Antonio Mascarenhas Monteiro.

(a) In his speech, the Minister of Justice Mr. Pedro Freire, extended a warm welcome to members of the African Commission on Human and Peoples' Rights and to members of the NGOs taking part in meetings of the Commission to Cape Verde. Mr. Freire reaffirmed Cape Verde's commitment to preserving democratic values, the rule of law and the respect of human rights.

(b) Speaking on behalf of Mr. Adama Dieng, the ICJ Secretary-General, Mrs.Tokungo Ige, the ICJ Legal Officer for Africa, wished the Commission's meeting success and emphasized the need for cooperation between the Commission and NGOs in order to – in particular – consolidate the independence of the Judiciary in Africa and to eliminate impunity of perpetrators of serious violations of human rights.

(c) Professor Isaac Nguema, Chairman of the African Commission on Human and Peoples' Rights condemned the coup d'Etat which had taken place on the previous day in the Comoro Islands and called upon France to subdue Bob Denard, a French national who masterminded the overthrow of the Government of Comoro. Professor Nguema stressed the need to give greater priority to issues related to the development of Africa. Analyzing political development in Africa, Professor Nguema argued that Africa needs a new approach to society – a project based on, among other things, the rule of law, human rights, the independence of the Judiciary and freedom of opinion and expression.

(d) In his address, His Excellency the President of the Republic of Cape Verde, Mr Antonio Mascarenhas Monteiro asserted that the African Charter on Human and Peoples' Rights was a significant step forward for the people of Africa. President Monteiro said that current development in democratization gave rise to the hope of the establishment in the near future of an African Court on Human and Peoples' Rights. The President emphasized the fact that democracy should not be limited to institutional mechanisms only, but should rather bring about – through economic and social progress – a genuine human rights culture. In conclusion, President Monteiro declared the 18th Ordinary Session of the African Commission on Human and Peoples' Rights open and wished it success.

8. After the official opening ceremony, two new members of the Commission, Mr. Kamel Rezag-Bara and Mrs Julienne Ondziel-Gnelenga, took the oath of office.

Each one of them swore as follows "I swear to carry out my duties well and faithfully in all impartiality".

9. The Commission then proceeded to elect its office bearers. There were three candidates – Commissioners Isaac Nguema, Hatem Ben Salem and U. O. Umozurike – for the post of Chairman of the Commission. The incumbent Chairman of the Commission. The incumbent Chairman, Professor Isaac Nguema, was re-elected.

10. Professor E. V. O. Dankwa, the sole candidate for the post, was elected Vice-Chairman of the Commission.

11. During its deliberations, the Commission discussed mainly, the following items:

- consideration of applications for observer status;
- review of periodic reports of countries;
- consideration of amendments to the Rules of Procedure;
- review of Article 58 of the Charter;
- activity report of the Commissioners;
- consideration of the issue of extra-judicial, summary and arbitrary executions;
- report on the implementation of resolution AHG/Res. 230 (XXX) on the establishment of an African Court on Human and Peoples' Rights;
- organisation of forthcoming seminars and conferences;
- publication of the review and newsletter of the Commission;
- prison conditions in Africa;
- protection activities;
- administrative and financial matters;
- the situation of the documentation centre of the Commission; and
- dividing States parties among members of the Commission for promotional activities.

12. Observer status was granted to 13 new non-governmental organisations. The list of these NGOs is available at the Secretariat. The number of NGOs with Observer status has therefore increased from 154 to 167.

13. Representatives of the Governments of Algeria, Benin, Cameroon, Nigeria, Togo, Swaziland, Tunisia and Zambia took part in the Session.

14. The representative of the Government of Algeria announced that, among other things, he had submitted to the Secretariat the first report of this country which will be examined at the 19th Ordinary Session of the Commission.

15. Representatives of Benin, Cameroon, Togo and Swaziland asserted the willingness of their governments to cooperate with the Commission.

16. Furthermore, Swaziland's delegate announced that Swaziland had already ratified the African Charter on Human and Peoples' Rights and that the instrument of ratification had been sent to the office of the Secretary General of the OAU.

17. During its session of 3 October 1995, the Commission discussed Tunisia's first periodic report which was presented by two delegates of the Government of Tunisia, namely Mr. Ali Benmalek, chargé de missions in the Ministry of Affairs and Mr. Habib Cherif, an Advisor in the Ministry of Justice.

18. The Commission expressed satisfaction with the quality of the report presented by Tunisia and with the interest demonstrated by the Tunisian Government in keeping its commitment to the provisions spelt out in the African Charter on Human and Peoples' Rights.

19. The Commission noted with regret that it could not discuss the country reports of Mozambique, Mauritius and Seychelles as indicated on the Agenda because these countries had not sent delegates to the session to present their reports to the Commission.

20. The Commission heard speeches delivered by representatives of the following African and international non-governmental organizations:

- Mr. Ahmed Motala, Amnesty International;
- Mr. Alione Tine, Rencontre Africaine pour la Défense des Droits de l'Homme;
- Mr. Salah Zeghidi, Ligue Tunisienne pour la Défense des Droits de l'Homme;
- Mr. Ahmed Othmani, Penal Reform International;
- Mr. Aref Mohamed Aref, Association des Droits de l'Homme de Djibouti;
- Mr. Chidi Odinkalu, Interights;
- Mr. Jamai Abderrahim, Union des Avocats Arabes;
- Mr. Fernandez Gomez, Forum des ONG des Pays Lusophones;
- Mr. Massalbaye Tenebaye, Union Inter-Africaine des Droits de l'Homme;
- Mr. Kaudis Ouffoumou, Association Internationale pour la Démocratie en Afrique;
- Mrs Mariama Bayard Gamatie, Rassemblement Démocratique des Femmes du Niger;
- Mr. Sylver Ntukamazina, Ligue Burundaise des Droits des l'Homme – (ITEKA);
- Mr. Benedict Sannoh, Centre for Democracy and Human Rights – Liberia;
- Mr. Oberleitner, World University Service;
- Mrs. Bernadette Palle, Coordinator of the "Femmes Africaines et Droits Humains" Network;
- Mrs: Ayodele Atsenuwa, Legal Research and Resource Development – Nigeria;
- Mr. Joseph Henry Joof, African Centre for Democracy and Human Rights Studies – Gambia;
- Mr. Eze Onyekpere, Civil Liberties Organisation.

21. Mr. Ahmed Cassin Motala presented the resolutions and recommendations of the 9th Workshop of NGO's participating in the meetings of the African Commission. Mr. Motala highlighted the following issues:

(a) the role of NGOs in strengthening the African Commission;
(b) the human rights situation in a good number of African countries;
(c) the role of the Special Rapporteur on extra-judicial, summary and arbitrary executions;
(d) the monitoring of the respect of economic, social and cultural rights in Africa.

22. On behalf of Penal Reform International, Mr. Ahmed Othmani presented a draft resolution on appointing a special rapporteur of the African Commission on Human and Peoples' Rights who would look into prison conditions in Africa.

23. Mrs. Ige Tokunbo, the International Commission of Jurists' (ICJ) Legal Officer for Africa presented a draft resolution on appointing a special rapporteur to the African Commission who would deal with the rights of women in Africa. Mrs Ige also mentioned the preparation of a draft additional protocol to the African Charter on Human and Peoples' Rights on the issue of the rights of women.

24. Members of the Commission presented their reports on promotional activities undertaken during the intercession.

25. The Commission discussed and adopted amendments to its Rules of Procedure.

26. Members of the Commission exchanged their points of view on the interpretation of Article 58 of the African Charter on Human and Peoples' Rights.

27. With regard to protection activities, the Commission reviewed 41 communications.

28. The Secretary to the Commission presented to the Commission the report of his activities during the intercession. The Commission considered, in particular, matters pertaining to finance, the organisation of the Documentation Centre and the preparation and publication of the Commission's Review.

29. The Commission reiterated its decision to organize the following seminars:

- The right to fair trial and to legal assistance;
- Popular participation and non-formal education;
- Human rights in the new South Africa;
- Freedom of movement and issues related to refugees and displaced people in Africa;
- Prison conditions in Africa;
- Peaceful resolution of ethnic and social conflicts in Africa;
- Contemporary forms of slavery;
- Impunity;
- The rights of women;
- Economic, social and cultural rights in Africa.

30. The Commission distributed States parties among its members for promotional activities.

31. The Commission reviewed thematic resolutions as well as resolutions on countries made by the 9th ICJ Workshop which had been held just before the 18th Ordinary session of the Commission. In view of the importance and relevance of most of the points raised in those resolutions and in view of time constraint, the Commission decided to postpone deliberations thereon to its 19th Ordinary session. This will enable the Commission to discuss the resolutions in detail.

32. Due to its heavy schedule, the Commission decided to postpone to its next session discussion on criteria for granting observer status to NGOs and conditions pertaining to the status.

33. On 6 October 1995, the Commissioners were invited by His Excellency the President of the Republic of Cape Verde, Mr. Antonio Mascarenhas Monteiro to lunch at the State House.

The Commissioners were also invited to dinner by the Honourable Minister of Justice, Mr. Pedro Freire on 11 October 1995.

34. The Commission called upon Angola, Botswana, Burundi, Burkina Faso, Cameroon; Central African Republic, Comoro Islands, Congo, Cote d'Ivoire, Djibouti, Equatorial Guinea, Gabon, Kenya, Lesotho, Liberia, Madagascar, Malawi, Mali, Mauritania, Namibia, Niger, the Saharan Arab Democratic Republic, Sao Tome and Principe, Sierra Leone, Somalia, Sudan, Zaire and Zambia to present their initial reports as soon as possible.

35. The Commission called upon Ethiopia, Eritrea and South Africa to ratify the African Charter on Human and Peoples' Rights as soon as possible.

36. The closing ceremony of the 18th session was held on 11 October 1995 on the premises of the National Assembly of the Republic of Cape Verde. The Honourable Minister of Justice of Cape Verde, Mr. Pedro Freire, presided over the ceremony.

37. The Chairman of the Commission held a press conference after the closing ceremony.

38. The Commission decided that its 19th Ordinary session will be held in Ouagadougou, Burkina Faso in March 1996 at the invitation of the Government of Burkina Faso.

Issued in Praia, Cape Verde, 11 October 1995

Final Communiqué of the Second Extraordinary Session of the African Commission on Human and Peoples' Rights

Kampala, 19 December 1995
ACHPR/FINCOMM/2nd EXTRA ORDINARY/XX

1. The African Commission on Human and Peoples' Rights held its second extraordinary session from the 18–19 December 1995 in Kampala (Uganda) under the Chairmanship of Professor Isaac Nguema and centred principally on the examination of the human rights situation in Nigeria.

2. Present at the session were the following Commissioners:

- Prof. Isaac Nguema – Chairman;
- Prof. Emmanuel V. O. Dankwa – Vice Chairman;
- Dr. Hatem Ben Salem;
- Mr. Atsu Koffi Amega;
- Justice Robert-Habesh Kisanga;
- Mr. Kamel Rezzag-Bara;
- Mrs. Julienne Ondziel-Gnelenga.

3. Absent with apology:

- Mr. Alioune Blondin Beye;
- Mr. Youssoupha Ndiaye;
- Mrs. Vera Duarte Martins;
- Prof. O. Umozurike.

4. The opening ceremony was held on 19 December 1995 at 9:30 a.m. at the International Conference Centre – Kampala in the presence of Honourable Ruhakana Rugunda, Minister of Foreign Affairs of Uganda, Col. Kahinda Ottafire, Chairman of the Pan-African Movement and Mrs. Tokumbo Ige, representative of the Secretary General of the International Commission of Jurists.

5. Also present were official representatives of the Federal Republic Government of Nigeria, led by His Excellency the High Commissioner of Nigeria to Uganda, Ambassadors and Heads of Diplomatic Missions accredited to Uganda, representatives of inter-governmental and non-governmental organizations, representatives from the Press and invited guests.

6. The formal opening session was marked by a welcome address by Prof. Isaac Nguema, Chairman of the African Commission on Human and Peoples' Rights who asked the audience to observe a moment of silence in memory of the late Grace Ibingira, former member of the Commission who died recently.

7. The floor was given to Col. Kahinda Ottafire, Chairman of the Pan-African Movement, who recalled briefly the history of the movement whose evolution is linked to the long struggle of the African continent against colonialism, apartheid and exploitation. Talking about the situation of human rights in Africa, the Speaker insisted on the necessity of holding frank and open discussions concerning the sovereignty of states and peoples' freedom.

8. On behalf of the Secretary General of the International Commission of Jurists, Mrs. Tokumbo Ige, Legal Officer for Africa delivered a message expressing the support of the International Commission of Jurists to the holding of this extraordinary session centred on the examination of the human rights situation in Nigeria.

Talking about the continuing serious violation of human rights in Nigeria, Mrs. Tokumbo Ige recalled the decisions taken to that effect by Commonwealth states, the European Community and the UN and wished that the African Commission use all legal means at its disposal to help improve the human rights situation in that country in order to restore democracy and good governance.

9. In his opening remarks Prof. Isaac Nguema, Chairman of the African Commission on Human and Peoples' Rights recalled the emotion expressed by African and world opinion leaders towards the execution of playwright Ken Saro-Wiwa and his 8 comrades of the Movement for the Survival of the Ogoni People. Talking about some burning events concerning the human rights situation in Africa, Prof. I. Nguema indicated that the extraordinary session should give the continent the occasion to express itself of the modalities to develop in the framework of the principles of universality and indivisibility of human rights.

10. Honourable Ruhakana Rugunda, Ugandan Minister of Foreign Affairs delivered a message in which he recalled the mandate of the African Commission on Human and Peoples' Rights in the protection and promotion of human rights. Observing that the African continent had never accorded enough attention to this issue, the Minister regretted the persistent political tensions in Africa principally due to the absence of democracy and good governance.

On the major focus of the holding of the extraordinary session, the Minister indicated that his Government had condemned recent events which took place in Nigeria regarding human rights violations and recalled that the Commissions attention should equally spread to other regions of the continent where gross violations take place and wished that through dialogue, we can establish peace and stability in Africa.

11. The Commission adopted the following agenda:

(i) opening ceremony;
(ii) adoption of the agenda;
(iii) organisation of proceedings;
(iv) state of human rights in Nigeria:

(a) summary and arbitrary executions
(b) compatibility between internal legislation in Nigeria and certain articles of the African Charter on Human and Peoples' Rights;

(v) examination of practical measures to take faced with the prevailing situation in Nigeria;
(vi) examination of certain urgent situations concerning human rights in Africa, notably in Burundi;
(vii) adoption of the Session report;
(viii) closing ceremony.

12. The Commission nominated Commissioner Kisanga rapporteur of the session and Commissioner Rezzag-Bara to write the final communiqué.

13. In the course of the afternoon session on 18 December 1995, His Excellency the Ambassador Ahmed Haggag, Assistant Secretary General of the OAU delivered a message on behalf of the Secretary General, indicating the preoccupation of the continental Organisation on the situation of human rights in Nigeria. He recalled the recent visit undertaken by His Excellency Salim Ahmed Salim, Secretary General of the OAU in Nigeria, as well as the Special Summit held in Pretoria by SADC member states. Ambassador A. Haggag indicated that the OAU intends to do everything possible to give Nigeria all the help it needs in order to diffuse the crisis now shaking Nigeria, and to apply the transitional programme towards democracy, as announced by the Federal Government of Nigeria on 1 October 1995.

14. The Commission heard in presence of the official delegation of the Nigerian Government interventions from non-governmental organisations on human rights violations in Nigeria.

15. The Nigerian High Commissioner to Uganda, on behalf of the Nigerian Government, also addressed the Commission. He insisted on the promise made by the Nigerian authorities to start off from 1 October 1995 a transitional programme towards a civil and democratic government.

Emphasizing the will of the Nigerian Government to cooperate with the Commission, the Nigerian delegation promised to submit a written response to all the concerns expressed during the action before the Commission's 19th Ordinary Session. He also drew the Commission's attention to slanderous campaigns against Nigeria on the issue of human rights by assuring the Commission that it was honouring its international obligations and legal principles as well as the rule of law.

The Nigerian Delegation extended an invitation to the Commission to pay them a visit during the month of February 1996.

16. A fruitful exchange was established between members of the Commission and Nigeria's Government representatives on major preoccupations of which the forthcoming trial of the "19 Ogoni people" and the compatibility of the Nigerian legislation with the provisions of the African Charter on Human and Peoples' Rights were the major issues discussed.

The members of the Commission expressed their serious concern on the situation of human rights in Nigeria and their worry on measures which could aggravate the situation.

17. At the end of its deliberations, the Commission decided to take the following practical measures concerning the situation of human rights in Nigeria.

(i) Taking note of the readiness and will of the Nigerian Government cooperation, the Commission decided to ask the current President of OAU and the Secretary General to express to the Nigerian Authorities that no irreparable prejudice is caused to the 19 Ogoni detainees whose trial is pending.

(ii) In order to intensify the dialogue between the Commission and the Nigerian Authorities, a delegation composed of the Chairman, Vice-chairman, and the Special Rapporteur on summary and arbitrary executions shall undertake a mission to Nigeria from 16–21 February 1996.

(iii) The report of the extraordinary session shall be submitted to the Current Chairman of the OAU, the United Nations Secretary General and the United Nations High Commissioner for Human Rights.

(iv) The Commission shall write a statement to the UN Commission on Human Rights during its next session on the evolution of the situation of human rights in Nigeria in light of the results of its extraordinary session and its proposed mission.

(v) During its 19th session, the Commission will consider the mission's report on the human rights situation in Nigeria as well as the Special Rapporteur's report on summary and arbitrary executions.

(vi) The Commission invites the Government of Nigeria to submit in conformity with Article 62 of the Charter, its periodic report on the measures taken to ensure compliance with the rights and liberties recognised and guaranteed in the Charter, relevant past resolutions and decisions of the Commission as well as with the provisions of the Charter, relating to the independence of the Judiciary, the safety of persons and property, the freedom of opinion and expression and social rights of workers.

18. The Commission heard a Communication on the prevailing situation in Burundi where armed bandits cause permanent insecurity provoking assassinations and massive displacement of the civilian population.

The Commission's attention was drawn to the urgent need to assist in improving the judicial system, prison administration and the national reconciliation process.

19. The debate that followed allowed the Commission to express its fears on the rapid deterioration of the situation in Burundi. This issue will be further considered at the 19th session.

20. In the light of the human rights situation in Africa, the Commission decided to analyze in depth the idea of putting into place an early warning mechanism in case of emergencies and called upon the NGO community to render assistance in that field.

21. The closing ceremony took place on 19 December 1995 at the International Conference Centre in Kampala, Uganda in the presence of Hon. Joseph Ekemu, Minister of Justice of Uganda who addressed the meeting.

Done in Kampala, 20 December 1995

Account of Internal Legislation of Nigeria and the Dispositions of the Charter of African Human and Peoples' Rights

Second Extraordinary Session
Kampala, 18–19 December 1995
DOC. II/ES/ACHPR/4

COMPATIBILITY OF NATIONAL LAWS WITH THE AFRICAN CHARTER

As described above, all the laws promulgated in Nigeria for over a decade have been military decrees. These decrees have largely superseded the provisions of the Constitution. In addition to the troubling fact that decrees are necessarily laws made without the contribution of the peoples' elected representatives, Nigerian decrees have two chief features which have a negative effect on human rights. One of these is the very common "ouster" clauses, which prevent the courts from entertaining challenges to the legality of the decrees. The other is the establishment, by decree, of many special tribunals, separate from the ordinary courts, and the many crimes transferred to their jurisdiction.

Both ouster clauses and special tribunals have been the subjects of communications before the African Commission. The Commission carefully considered these communications, and ultimately adopted final decisions condemning both ouster clauses and special tribunals. Details of these cases and the Commission's decisions appear below.

OUSTER CLAUSES

Decisions in Communications 129/94 and 101/93

Section 5 of the Constitution (Suspension and Modification) Decree of 1993 reads:

> "No question as to the validity of this Decree or any other Decree made during the period 31st December 1983 to 26th August 1993, or made after the commencement of the Decree or of an Edict shall be entertained by court of law in Nigeria."

Section 13(1) of the Political Parties (Dissolution) Decree of 1993 reads:

> "Notwithstanding anything contained in the Constitution of the Federal Republic of Nigeria 1979, as amended, the African Charter on Human and

Peoples' Rights (Ratification and Enforcement) Act or any other enactment, no proceeding shall lie or be instituted in any court for or on account of any act, matter or thing done or purported to be done in respect of this Decree."

These Decrees were both at issue in Communication 129/94. Firstly, they create an important question of admissibility. Article 56(5) of the African Charter requires that before a communication can be considered on the merits by the Commission, the complainant must have exhausted all domestic remedies, unless such remedies are proven to be ineffective or unduly prolonged. Domestic remedies are understood to be those normally available in the domestic court system, and excluding those available only as a purely discretionary matter from the executive.

The Commission accepted the argument of complainants that the above ouster decrees create a situation in which "it is reasonable to presume that domestic remedies will not only be prolonged but are certain to yield no results" (ACHPR 129/94: 8).

In its conclusion on the merits, the African Commission turned to Article 7, which provides that everyone has the right to have his cause heard before an impartial tribunal, where the matter concerns fundamental rights recognized in treaties, laws and customs in force.

In its decision on communication 129/94, taken at its 17th Session, the Commission found that ouster clauses such as these constitute "[A]n attack on incalculable proportions on Article 7 [of the African Charter] . . . An attack of this sort on the jurisdiction of the courts is especially invidious, because while it is a violation of human rights in itself, it permits other violations of rights to go unredressed' (ACHPR 129/94: 12).

In its conclusion, the Commission found that "ouster of the court's jurisdiction constitutes a breach of Article 26, the obligation to establish and protect the courts" (ACHPR 129/94: 16.2).

Almost all decrees promulgated by the military government contain ouster clauses. Further, the Constitution (Modification and Suspension) specifies that no decrees can be challenged, so even decrees that may lack an ouster clause cannot be challenged. Thus, Nigerians face huge legal obstacles in challenging any new law.

In the Legal Practitioners (Amendment) Decree, amendment of 23A.-(1) reads:

"No person shall commence or maintain an action or any legal proceeding whatsoever relating to, connected with or arising from –

. . .

(b) the exercise of powers conferred . . . by this Act.

(2) Any action of the type mentioned in subsection (1) of this section which . . . is pending in any court as well as any such action which may be brought by any person after the commencement of this section . . . shall abate, be made null and void and of no effect whatsoever.

(3) Any person who contravenes the provisions of subsection (1) of this section commits an offence and is liable on conviction to a fine of N10,000 or to imprisonment for a term of one year or to both such fine and imprisonment."

This Decree was at issue in Communication No. 101/93. The attempt to challenge the decree is itself made a crime, and the decree is retroactive. The Commission decided at its 17th session that the retroactive character of the decree violates Article 7(2).

The ouster clauses create a legal situation in which the judiciary can provide no check on the executive branch of government. A few courts in the Lagos district have occasionally found that they have jurisdiction; in 1995 the Court of Appeal in Lagos, relying on common law, found that courts should examine some decrees notwithstanding ouster clauses, where the decree is "offensive and utterly hostile to rationality". It remains to be seen whether any Nigerian courts will be courageous enough to follow this holding, and whether the government will abide by their ruling should they do so. On their face, ouster clauses remove the right of courts to examine laws.

Since there is no legislature in existence in Nigeria, the Constitution can be overridden at will, and the domestic effect of the African Charter has been suspended, the pervasive ouster clauses mean that the military government operates without any significant counterbalance to its power. In its decision on communication 129/94, the Commission emphasizes that "the obligation of the Nigerian government . . . remains, unaffected by the purported revocation of domestic effect of the Charter" (ACHPR 129/94: 15). Thus, the decisions of the African Commission are legally binding on the Government of Nigeria, as are the provisions of the Charter itself.

SPECIAL TRIBUNALS

Decisions on Communications 60/91 and 87/93

Another prominent feature of the legal landscape in Nigeria is the existence of special tribunals. Many common and political crimes have been withdrawn from the jurisdiction of the court system and placed before small (usually 3-person) tribunals, composed of sitting judges and members of the military or police force who are chosen by the executive branch. Often the penalty mandated is death.

Ostensibly set up to increase efficiency in the trying of cases, these tribunals share the common characteristic that they provide for no appeal, only confirmation or clemency from the executive branch. In its decision on communication 60/91, the African Commission found that the power of the state Governor to confirm or disallow a conviction of the Robbery and Firearms Tribunal:

> "may be described as a discretionary, extraordinary remedy of a non-judicial nature. The object of the remedy is to obtain a favour and not to vindicate a right.
>
> . . .
>
> 21. Therefore, the Commission is of the opinion that the remedy available is not of a nature that requires exhaustion according to Article 56, paragraph 5 of the African Charter" (ACHPR 60/91: 20–21).

The same statement of principle appears in paragraphs 18 and 19 of decision ACHPR 60/91. It was on this basis that both communications were declared admissible.

In its decision on the merits, the Commission turned once more to Article 7, which comprises also the right to defence and the right to be tried within a reasonable time by an impartial court or tribunal. In its decision on communication 60/91, concerning the Robbery and Firearms Tribunal, the Commission found:

"[T]he tribunals . . . consist of three persons: one Judge, one officer of the Army, Navy or Air Force and one officer of the Police Force. Jurisdiction has thus been transferred from the normal courts to a tribunal chiefly composed of persons belonging to the executive branch of government, the same branch that passed the Robbery and Firearms Decree, whose members do not necessarily possess any legal expertise . . . Regardless of the character of the individual members of such tribunals, its composition alone creates the appearance, if not actual lack, of impartiality. It thus violates Article 7.1(d)" (ACHPR 60/91: 25).

The identical principle is stated in the decision on communication 87/93, adopted on the same day, concerning the Civil Disturbance Tribunal, which is composed of one judge and four other members, one of whom is from the armed forces. The Commission declined to consider the fairness of the particular trial at issue in the communication, or the impartiality of the particular individuals sitting on the tribunal in the case at hand. Instead, it held that the principle of impartiality enshrined in the Charter had necessarily been violated by the composition of the tribunal alone. The Commission found that all those convicted under such tribunals in both cases should be freed. In case 87/93, the death sentences passed on the subjects were commuted to five years' imprisonment. The fate of the subjects of communication 60/91 is not known.

RESPONSE OF THE NIGERIAN GOVERNMENT TO THE ABOVE DECISIONS

The delegation which attended the Commission's 18th Session presented a response entitled 'Response to Communications 105/93, 128/94, & 130/94". While the title of this document is puzzling in light of the fact that the decisions taken by the Commission are in cases 60/91, 87/93, 101/93 and 129/94, the content of the response is fully applicable to the decisions taken.

The response of the Nigerian Government begins with a reaffirmation of the commitment of the government to the principles and objectives of the African Charter, and the work of the African Commission. The response notes that Nigeria's early ratification, its extensive Ratification and Enforcement Act, and its sending of a delegation to the 18th Session embody this commitment. The response highlights that a National Human Rights Commission has recently been established in Nigeria to assist in implementation of the Charter, educate the public and investigate alleged abuses. The response goes on to refer to the political situation leading to the present administration.

Most important, the response acknowledges that:

"rights of individuals or groups are not subject of domestic law exclusively. We are aware that individuals are subjects of international law as much as states are especially in the area of recognition, respect for and enforcement of Human rights." (p. 4)

The Commission welcomes this recognition on the part of the Nigerian Government. It demonstrates that the government is well aware that its obligations towards its citizens exist on the international as well as national level.

The government's response goes on to criticize several aspects of the Commission's procedure and decisions. Many of these criticisms have already been answered above, but as the Commission wants to give full weight to the government's objections and to further its dialogue with the government, all arguments are discussed and reiterated below.

FAIR HEARING

The first objection made is on the grounds of fair hearing: the government objects that the requirements of due process were violated by the fact that the Commission's decisions were taken without the Nigerian government ever appearing to state its case. It states that in no legal tradition may an adverse finding be made against a party which has not had an opportunity to state its case.

In fact, the Nigerian Government had numerous opportunities to submit its case in writing or send a delegation to the Commission's sessions. It merely declined to do so. It is clear that the government had notice of the communications because in one instance the Ministry of Justice even responded. For the Commission to postpone decisions indefinitely while waiting for the government to send a representative would be to make the communications procedure hostage to governments, and effectively place in the government's hands the ability to prevent any decisions. These consequences have been recognized by other international human rights bodies such as the Inter-American Commission on Human Rights, and the African Commission was inspired by their example.

ASSAULT ON SOVEREIGN RIGHTS

The Nigerian Government argues that it is an assault on the sovereignty of Nigeria that certain decrees should be annulled. The response refers to paragraph 17 of decision 105/93, but the proper reference is to the last paragraph of decision 101/93, which concerns the Nigerian Bar Association. In this decision, the commission holds that in light of the violation of Articles 6, 7 and 10 of the Charter, "The Decree should therefore be annulled". In any case, the repeal of certain decrees is surely implied in all the decisions where the Commission finds that system of special tribunals, or the ouster of the courts, is incompatible with the African Charter.

As has been made clear above, Nigeria is bound by the African Charter. The Commission is likewise bound by the Charter, to consider communications fully, carefully, and in good faith. When the Commission concludes that a communication describes a real violation of the Charter's provisions, its duty is to make that clear and indicate what action the government must take to remedy the situation. Naturally the Commission could not make such judgments with regard to states outside its jurisdiction. But in ratifying the African Charter without reservation, Nigeria voluntarily submitted itself to the Commission's authority in this regard.

LACK OF JUDICIAL CAPACITY

Closely tied to the above objection is that the Commission has acted in a "judicial role in pronouncing on the validity of domestic laws and interpreting various provisions of the Charter" (p. 7). It is true that the communications procedure, as set out in Article 55 of the Charter, is quasi-judicial, in that communications are necessarily adversarial. Complainants are complaining against some act or neglect of a government, and the Commission must ultimately, if it is unable to effect a friendly settlement, decide for one side or the other.

These actions of the Commission are clearly required by the stipulations of Articles 55–59 of the African Charter. Article 45(3), cited by the government, is inapposite, reflecting only that the Commission must interpret all provisions of the Charter when requested by States Parties or the OAU. While, by promulgating the Charter, the OAU has indirectly "requested" the Commission's interpretation through the communications procedure, the procedure more properly falls under Article 45(2) "Ensure the protection of human and peoples' rights under conditions laid down by the present Charter". This charge to ensure protection clearly refers to the Commission's duties under Article 55 *et seq.*, to protect the rights in the Charter through the communications procedure. The Commission therefore cannot accept the government's contention that, in deciding communications, it has acted outside its capacity.

BREACH OF CONFIDENTIALITY

The Nigerian Government protests what it calls the violation of the confidentiality requirement of Articles 58 and 59. First of all, only Article 59 refers to confidentiality, to quote:

> "All measures taken within the provisions of the present Chapter shall remain confidential until such time as the Assembly of Heads of State and Government shall otherwise decide."

The resolution on Nigeria adopted on 22 March 1995 is not a "measure taken" within the meaning of this article. The "present chapter" refers to Chapter III of the Charter, dealing with communications. The resolution on Nigeria does not refer to communications in any way. There is no bar on resolutions of the Commission being disseminated however the Commission sees fit.

The decisions taken on communications were conveyed to the Government of Nigeria and to the complainants soon after they were taken. However, they were not disseminated publicly by the Commission in any way until they were approved by the Assembly of Heads of State and Government as part of the Commission's 8th Annual Activity Report, a public document. This fully complies with the requirement for a decision of the Heads of State and Government. Indeed, Article 59.3 goes further and stipulates that the Activity Report should be published after it is considered by the Assembly. This has not yet been done, although the Activity Report has been made available to the public.

Thus, the Commission cannot agree that it has committed any breach of the Charter's requirements of confidentiality.

EXHAUSTION OF LOCAL REMEDIES

The Nigerian Government complains that in the decisions made by the Commission, local remedies had not been exhausted. But the communications cited are not those for which decisions were adopted. As explained in reference to the decisions above, the Commission deemed that the complainants were left without meaningful domestic remedies either because of clauses ousting jurisdiction of the courts or because there is no regular appeal from special tribunals.

UNCONVENTIONAL PROCEDURES ADOPTED

The response of the Nigerian Government states that the Commission has violated Articles 60 and 61 in failing to draw guidance and inspiration from "the well-known procedural rules applied by various specialized Agencies of the OAU, the UN and other similar Committees". No specific examples are given of which procedural rules the Nigerian Government objects to. The African Commission stands by its record, satisfied that it has faithfully and in good conscience followed the African Charter, its highest authority, as well as having reference to the practice of other international bodies. The African Commission reaffirms its commitment to the task of drawing from existing international law while interpreting the Charter in a way that reflects the unique and precious facets of African culture and tradition.

Human Rights Report on the Situation in Nigeria

Second Extraordinary Session
Kampala, 18–19 December 1995

CHRONOLOGY OF COMMUNICATIONS BETWEEN THE AFRICAN COMMISSION AND NIGERIA SINCE THE 18TH ORDINARY SESSION

1. Note verbale addressed to A. H. Yadudu, the Special Advisor (Legal) to the Head of State of Nigeria, requesting dates for the mission to Nigeria.
2. Note verbale addressed to the Ministry of Foreign Affairs of Nigeria, invoking Rule 111 (provisional measures) as regards the Saro-Wiwa communications.
3. Note verbale from the Nigerian High Commission regarding the Saro-Wiwa communications.
4. Note verbale to the Nigerian High Commission requesting a copy of the judgment in the Saro-Wiwa case.
5. Note verbale to the Nigerian High Commission requesting copies of decrees relevant to the communications before the Commission.
6. Brief from the Office of the Special Advisor to the Head of State regarding the Saro-Wiwa cases, signed H. A. Tahir, Assistant Director, Legal.

1. NOTE VERBALE TO A. H. YADUDU REQUESTING DATES FOR MISSION TO NIGERIA

The Secretariat of the African Commission on Human and Peoples' Rights presents its compliments to the Head of State of the Federal Republic of Nigeria. The Commission expresses its appreciation for the commitment the Federal Republic of Nigeria has demonstrated to the work of the African Commission and the goals of the African Charter, evidenced by the presence of its delegation at the Commission's 18th Ordinary Session, held in Praia, Cape Verde, from 2–11 October 1995.

This delegation, headed by A. H. Yadudu, Special Advisor (Legal) to the Head of State, honored the Commission by extending to it an official invitation to send a mission to visit the Federal Republic of Nigeria in order to conduct a study of the human rights situation there.

The month of February was suggested by the delegation of Nigeria as an opportune time for such a mission to undertake its visit. The duration of the mission is envisaged as approximately one week. The Office of the Head of State is requested to inform the Secretariat of the Commission as soon as possible if any particular dates are preferred.

The Secretariat of the Commission seizes this opportunity to assure the Government of the Federal Republic of Nigeria of its highest consideration.

A. H. Yadudu
Special Advisor (Legal) to the
Head of State
State House
Aso Rock Villa
Abuja

2. NOTE VERBALE TO MINISTER OF FOREIGN AFFAIRS REGARDING SARO-WIWA COMMUNICATIONS

The Secretariat of the African Commission on Human and Peoples' Rights presents its compliments to the Ministry of Foreign Affairs of the Federal Republic of Nigeria and has the honor to inform the latter that the African Commission has been seized of communications no. 137/94 and 139/94 submitted on behalf of mr. Ken Saro-Wiwa and others by two human rights organisations, International PEN and Constitutional Rights Project, against the Federal Republic of Nigeria.

The Government of Nigeria has been duly notified of the two cases on 9 November 1994.

At its 18th Session, the Commission was happy to receive the Nigerian delegation – headed by Dr. A. H. Yadudu, Special Advisor (Legal) to the Head of State – which assured the latter of the full cooperation of the Nigerian Government in the work of the Commission in general and in the settlement of the communications against Nigeria in particular.

The Commission has decided then to examine, among others, these two communications during the mission to be undertaken in February 1996 at the invitation of the Nigerian Government.

The Secretariat of the African Commission has been informed that Mr. Ken Saro-Wiwa has been sentenced to death by a special tribunal of Nigeria.

The objective of this message is to request the Government of Nigeria not to execute the said sentence until the Commission has discussed the cases with the competent authorities.

It will be noted that, in accordance with Rule 111 of its revised Rules of Procedure (former rule 109), the Commission, by note verbale ACHPR/COMMU/AO44(201) of 13 February 1995, had requested the Government of Nigeria not to take any action resulting in irreparable prejudice to Mr. Ken Saro-Wiwa and his co-defendants.

The African Commission has high hopes that this appeal will be considered favorably.

The Secretariat of the African Commission on Human and Peoples' Rights avails itself of this opportunity to renew to the Ministry of Foreign Affairs of the Federal Republic of Nigeria, the assurances of its highest consideration.

1 November 1995

The Ministry of Foreign Affairs
of the Federal Republic of Nigeria
PMB 130
GARKI, Abuja
Nigeria

3. NOTE VERBALE FROM NIGERIAN HIGH COMMISSION REGARDING SARO-WIWA COMMUNICATIONS

Note No. 92/95
The High Commission of the Federal Republic of Nigeria presents its compliments to the African Commission for Human and Peoples' Rights and has the honour to acknowledge, with thanks, the receipt of latter's Note Ref. No. ACHPR/COMMU/AO44(6), dated 1 November 1995 and to enclose herewith, for information and records, photocopies of press interview given by the Acting High Commissioner and a release, all based on the actual facts of the case of the issue of Mr. Kenule Beeson Saro-Wiwa and fellow Ogoni activists. These do not substitute for the record of judgement of the Hon. Justice Ibrahim Auta's Special tribunal on the issue.

It is unfortunate that because of the cancellation of the 12 June 1993 Presidential election coupled with the military nature of the Nigerian Government, there is a full blast Western propaganda war on Nigeria aimed at damaging the credibility of the government and therefore a lot of facts on the issue have been misrepresented. It is hoped that the Human Rights Commission would formally request for the judgement of the tribunal to enable it to have a better picture of what transpired. It is pertinent to observe that:

(a) The tribunal is not a military one. It was presided over by a judge of the Nigerian Court of Appeal, Hon. Justice, Ibrahim Auta;
(b) Tribunals are part of the Nigerian judicial system properly constituted to deal with specific issues and for speedier dispensation of justice;
(c) The trial is not a witch-hunt and its fairness further subsists in the fact that it also discharged and acquitted the Vice President of the Movement for the Survival of Ogoni People (MOSOP), Barrister Ledum Mitee and five others;
(d) Evidences placed before it were thoroughly, carefully and exhaustively considered before judgement. It is therefore fair and just, etc.;
(e) The trial was open and its sittings held in public;
(f) The four prominent Ogoni sons, Mr. Albert Badey, Chief Edward N. Kobani, Samuel Orage and T. B. Orage who Ken Saro-Wiwa excited (counselled) youths to murder and were so murdered were equally human beings whose human rights should be protected as it is the duty of any responsible government to protect life and property within its territory. Otherwise, there would be a complete break down of law and order;

(g) Whatever the merit and the moral high grounds of Saro-Wiwa's course, it may not be out of place to state that it was wrong for him and his group to excite people to murder and or cause the murder of other innocent citizens;
(h) The loss of lives in this matter is deeply regretted but Nigeria has not abolished the death penalty having not acceded to the Second Optional Protocol of the United nations;
(i) No criminal justice system could hardly be said to be fair and just if it is inclined more towards the protection of the criminal or the offender rather than the protection of the rights of both parties to a dispute.

The High Commission of the Federal Republic of Nigeria avails itself of this opportunity to renew to the African Commission for Human and People's Rights the assurances of its highest consideration.

Banjul, 20 November 1995

The African Commission
for Human & Peoples' Rights
Kairaba Avenue
Pipeline

THE CONVICTION OF KEN SARO-WIWA

1. On 8 November 1995, the Provisional Ruling Council (PRC) upheld the death sentences passed on Mr. Ken Saro-Wiwa, and eight others on 30 and 31 October 1995, by the Ogoni Civil Disturbances Tribunal headed by Justice Ibrahim Auta, a renowned Judge of the Federal Court of Appeal, for the gruesome murder of four prominent Ogoni sons, on 21 May 1994. Six other accused persons were freed, including Ledum Mitee, the Vice-President of MOSOP. Since the sentences were passed, there have been both local and international reactions to the verdict. While some of the reactions have been pleas for clemency, others have been full of vitriolic fulminations, designed to trivialise a very serious murder charge which claimed the precious lives of four prominent Ogoni sons, in a most barbaric, inhuman and despicable manner.

2. It is true that Ken Saro-Wiwa is a foremost writer of international repute, who during the Nigerian civil war served as one of the youngest Commissioners in the Executive Council of Navy Commander Alfred Diete Spiff, the then Governor of Rivers State. It is also true that the four prominent Ogoni sons who were murdered on 21 May 1994, had equally enviable credentials or pedigree. Mr. Albert Badey was a one-time Permanent Secretary, State Commissioner and later, Secretary to the Rivers State Government; Chief E. N. Kobani was a former State Commissioner, former Deputy President of MOSOP, and former National Publicity Secretary of the defunct Social Democratic party (SDP); Chief Samuel Orage was a one-time State Commissioner and Chief T. B. Orage was Secretary to the Gokana Council of Chiefs.

3. What is more? These four prominent sons of Ogoniland were among the *founders* of the Movement for the Survival of Ogoni People (MOSOP), which was formed in 1990 and originally conceived as a pressure group that would use non-violent methods to protect the Ogoni people from the environmental degradation caused by oil exploitation and exploration in their areas. In fact, its first President, Dr. Garrick Leton, a former Federal Commissioner escaped being killed because he was not present at the scene of the barbaric murder. Otherwise, nearly all the foundation founders would have been completely wiped out by a group of terrorists and bandits under the umbrella of the National Youth Council of Ogoni People (NYCOP) formed by Saro-Wiwa as the Youth Wing of MOSOP.

4. Ken Saro-Wiwa who is now being widely acclaimed as the leader of MOSOP was not among its original founders. It was after its formation that he requested to be made its spokesman/ambassador in charge of Public Affairs to enable him to deal with the press, given his wide contacts with the local and international media. Together, they produced the Ogoni bill of rights. But Ken Saro-Wiwa had his own agenda, unknown to the foundation members. In 1993, he mooted the idea of forming a youth wing within the movement but this was widely opposed by other members. Despite their opposition, he unilaterally formed the youth wing which he called the National Youth Council of Ogoni People, promising its impressionable young members a lot of el dorado, such as huge bank accounts, palatial mansions and luxurious cars. The Youth Wing not only became militant in their approach to issues, they became a law unto themselves and unleashed a reign of terror as well as campaigns of calumny, blackmail, vilification and destruction on the whole of Ogoniland, mounting over 150 road blocks.

5. Despite admonitions from the elders, which included those murdered in cold blood, that the Youth Wing which had illegally constituted itself into a vigilante group and a private Army of Ken Saro-Wiwa, be much more restrained and follow the movement's original methods of dialogue which the MOSOP had used effectively in the past, they continued their reign of terror with the promptings of Ken Saro-Wiwa, their Commander-in-Chief. When it became clear that the group had not only become uncontrollable but owed their loyalty only to Ken Saro-Wiwa, the original founders parted ways with him and from then on he declared war on them and hijacked the leadership of MOSOP. It was this war that culminated in the gruesome murder of 4 prominent Ogoni sons during a meeting in the palace of their revered king. The only sin of the great 4 was that they disagreed with Ken Saro-Wiwa over tactics, and were later to pay dearly with their own lives. The build up to their tragic end was written, sealed and delivered by Ken Saro-Wiwa.

6. For instance, inflammatory exchanges between Ken and the big four also showed clearly that deep-seated animosity existed amongst them. For instance, on 27 November 1993, Chief Edward Kobani who was one of those murdered, in a letter addressed to the Rt. Rev. Bishop J. B. Poromon of the Methodist Church wrote en quote "Ken Saro-Wiwa has a formidable army of trained thugs and hoodlums who are terrorising the whole of Ogoniland, destroying the lives and property of those he does not like in the attempt to emerge as the one and only Ogoni leader".

Ken Saro-Wiwa replied in a letter dated 15 December 1993 en quote "I have noted how far your stock has fallen in the Ogoni Market. When will you accept responsibility for your failure. I cannot stop you from envying my achievements. I invite you to copy my ways and you will find that which you desire most, Ken Saro-Wiwa image. Good advice and it's free". Such deep feelings of hatred were manifested in other correspondences between Ken Saro-Wiwa and other members killed on 21 May 1994.

7. It was therefore not surprising when Justice Auta stated while sentencing Ken Saro-Wiwa to death that he (Saro-Wiwa) did not only counsel others to kill, he also prepared the grounds for the killing and organised NYCOP and some elements in MOSOP to carry out the dastardly murder of 4 prominent Ogoni sons. He added that his utterances, activities and actions before the killings, were well rehearsed actions to carry out the killings for which he and his accomplices were, consequently, convicted.

8. There are so many truths being twisted by some misguided elements to discredit the Federal Government. First, before the brutal, unconscionable and condemnable murder of the four prominent Ogoni citizens, no single Ogoni man was being held for the non-violent expression of his views. To the contrary, the Federal Government in keeping with its policy of Freedom of Speech and association, allowed Saro-Wiwa and MOSOP to thrive as a pressure group which expressed its views freely from time to time. The views were sometimes, considered on their own merit and taken into account by the Federal Government in Oil Policy formulations. Second, Ken Saro-Wiwa and others being tried were allowed access to the Counsels of their choice. Their defence team which comprised sly human rights activists such as Femi Falana and Gani Fawehitmal, known to be more disposed towards melodrama than the actual defence of their clients inexplicably withdrew from the Special Tribunal at a crucial stage of the trial in order to either play to the gallery or delay and frustrate the trial process. Their withdrawal accounted for the delay encountered by the Tribunal. In accordance with the law, Government lawyers were picked to defend the accused persons.

9. Third, they were never tried by either a special military tribunal nor a court-martial as was being bandied about. They were tried by a Special Tribunal recognised in law, and headed by a renowned Judge of the Federal Court of Appeal. In fact, it is a cardinal legal principle that laws should be interpreted as they are and not as they should be to meet selfish interests. Special Tribunals are recognised under the Nigerian Judicial system and function like normal courts. Their principal purpose is to speed-up the dispensation of justice.

10. Ken Saro-Wiwa's life is no more precious than the lives of the 4 prominent Ogoni citizens murdered in cold blood simply because they disagreed with Ken Saro-Wiwa over the tactics of achieving their goals. The families of the four slain Ogonis expect justice to be done in the same way Ken Saro-Wiwa's family is calling for justice, albeit, for the latter's selfish ends. Ken Saro-Wiwa was not sentenced to death because of his quest for a fair deal for his people or for environmental matters, he was sentenced to death for the cruel murder of four prominent Ogoni sons. Those who were murdered on 21 May 1994 are no lesser beings than Ken Saro-Wiwa.

11. The attempt by some critics to compare the fate of the coup plotters with that of the convicts by Justice Auta's Ogoni Civil Disturbances Tribunal is misguided.

The two cases are completely different. The Saro-Wiwa case is clearly criminal, involving murder. The penalty for such an offence which was not made by the Military but has always been part of Nigeria's statute-book is clear. The penalty has been duly imposed. And there is no apology to offer anyone. It is true that many countries today like South Africa have removed the death penalty from their statute-book, Nigeria has not yet done so. Consequently, for a country to seek to impose its own legal system on another smacks of undue interference and until the death sentence is removed from Nigeria's statute-book, the confirmation of the death sentences passed by the Tribunal is in order and well deserved.

9 November 1995

4. NOTE VERBALE TO THE NIGERIAN HIGH COMMISSION REQUESTING COPY OF JUDGMENT IN SARO-WIWA CASE

The Secretariat of the African Commission on Human and peoples' Rights presents its compliments to the high Commission of the Federal Republic of Nigeria in Banjul and has the honour to request the official judgment of the Hon. Justice Ibrahim Auta's Special tribunal in the case of Mr. Kenule Saro-Wiwa and his fellow Ogoni activists, mentioned in your note verbale of 20 november 1995.

The Secretariat of the African Commission on Human and Peoples' Rights would like to take this opportunity to renew to the High Commission of the Federal Republic of Nigeria in Banjul the assurances of its highest consideration.

Banjul, 21 November 1995

The High Commission of the
Federal Republic of Nigeria
Banjul
The Gambia

5. NOTE VERBALE TO NIGERIAN HIGH COMMISSION REQUESTING COPIES OF DECREES RELEVANT TO COMMUNICATIONS BEFORE THE COMMISSION

The Secretariat of the African Commission on Human and Peoples' Rights presents its compliments to the High Commission of the Federal Republic of Nigeria in Banjul and has the honour to request the latter to supply it with the following decrees:

- Decrees nos. 39–43 of 1993
- Decree no. 48 of 1993
- Decree no. 103 of 1993
- Decree no. 14 of 1994
- Decree no. 18 of 1995

This information would substantially help the African Commission to prepare its mission to Nigeria.

The Secretariat of the African Commission on Human and peoples' Rights avails itself of this opportunity to renew to the High Commission of the Federal Republic of Nigeria in Banjul the assurances of its highest consideration.

Banjul, 9 October 1995

The High Commission of the
Federal Republic of Nigeria
Banjul
The Gambia

6. BRIEF FROM OFFICE OF SPECIAL ADVISOR TO HEAD OF STATE REGARDING SARO-WIWA CASE

On the Saro-Wiwa Matter

We feel constrained to have to write to you on the above matter. I am sending you what is evidently government's understanding of the matter.

It is regrettable that the West and Human Rights groups the world over view Saro-Wiwa's matter as one involving an attempt by a "repressive" regime eager to muzzle dissent. Nothing could be further from the truth.

Knowing as we do the circumstances under which the gruesome murder of very prominent and highly respected elders of the Ogoni took place and in which Saro-Wiwa has played a pivotal role, we feel utterly amazed at the gullibility of all those who have chosen to view the matter as such.

I am aware that I am not entirely a disinterested party in the matter. Be that as it may, I do hope that the enclosed will give you another angle to the issues involved.

13 November 1995

H. A. Tahir
Assistant Director, Legal

ON THE SENTENCES OF OGONI CIVIL DISTURBANCES TRIBUNAL

On 21 May 1994, during a meeting called by the Council of Chiefs in Giokoo, Gokana, Rivers State, four prominent Ogoni chiefs were brutally murdered by the riotous youths who had been instigated and actively supported by the leadership of MOSOP. The deceased persons were Chiefs Kobani, Badey, T. Orage and A. Orage. The four were bludgeoned to death by the rampaging youths with sticks, matchets and rakes, stripped naked, dragged through the market and their corpses carried in a car which was later, presumably, burnt together with the bodies.

What led to their brutal murder could briefly be summarized as follows. A couple of years ago the Movement for the Survival of the Ogoni (MOSOP) was founded to peacefully champion the cause of all Ogoni people. It initially had Dr. G. B. Leton and Chief E. Kobani, the deceased, as President and Vice President respectively. Mr. Kenule Saro-Wiwa was its first Publicity Secretary. When MOSOP was becoming violent, especially as evidenced from the activities of its youth wing, the NYCOP during the WILBROS riots, and in the wake of MOSOP's decision to boycott the Presidential elections of 1993, Dr. Leton and Chief Kobani resigned from its leadership. Saro-Wiwa became the President.

Ever since assuming the mantle of leadership of MOSOP, Saro-Wiwa had chosen the destructive path. He masterminded the emergence of several other subversive wings of MOSOP. He preferred confrontation to conciliation. He opposed the re-absorption of Leton and Kobani, describing them as "cultures" or paid agents of various oil companies, the OMPADEC or the Federal Government of Nigeria. Under his leadership, the MOSOP and NYCOP orchestrated attacks on some identified Ogoni elders pejoratively described as "cultures". In concert with others, he made no secret of MOSOP's avowed intention to eliminate about 14 such "vultures" identified to be in Giokoo and other parts of Gokana and listed in a publication called "Newsflash" which he caused to be widely distributed amongst the youths.

Although not a bona fide candidate and he had opposed participation in the exercise, Mr Saro-Wiwa and his co-conspirators used the campaign period for the Constitutional Conference elections and the scheduled reconciliation meeting arranged by the local chiefs to carry out their avowed intention to eliminate the identified "cultures". On 21 May 1994, the youths descended on the Gbenemene Palace, venue of the meeting and brutally but selectively murdered the "vultures" present.

Following the civil disturbances of that day, investigations were carried out which led to several arrests made. Consequently, the Head of State, in the exercise of powers conferred on him by section 2(1) of the Civil Disturbances (Special Tribunal) Act, Cap 53 (hereinafter referred to as the Act), constituted the Ogoni Civil Disturbance (Special) Tribunal with Justice I. N. Auta, of the Federal High Court, as Chairman and Justice E. E. Arikpo, and Lt. Col. H. I. Ali as members. Under section 3 of the Act, the Tribunal has jurisdiction to try any person charged with offences listed in the First schedule and to impose any penalty provided for the offence in the Criminal Code or the Penal Code. Under section 3(2), any person who acts in concert or conspired with another or knowingly took part, to any extent, in the commission of the offence shall be treated in like manner as the person who is actually charged with committing the offence. Also under section 1(2) any person or group, who by conduct or negligence caused or in any way contributed to the breaking out of a civil disturbance shall be answerable for the consequence of such a disturbance.

Having sat for over 8 months, the Tribunal has now concluded its exercise. Delivering its judgements on 30 and 31 October 1995, the Tribunal was satisfied that the prosecution had proved the charges preferred against the two batches of accused persons beyond reasonable doubt:

Charge No. OCDT/PH/1/95

1. Mr. Kenule Saro-Wiwa

As President of MOSOP and founder of the NYCOP, he masterminded and led the riots of 21 May under the pretext of holding a Constitutional Conference rally on a day that the law did not permit and which exercise he had earlier directed members of MOSOP and NYCOP to boycott and in which he was not a bona fide candidate. He had orchestrated the campaign to eliminate the "vultures". He was heard on the day of riots to have said that he was not blaming those who had prevented him to go to the rally ground because they were sent by the "vultures" meeting in Giokoo. A prosecution witness, whose house has been burnt down by members of NYCOP, testified that when she complained to Mr. Saro-Wiwa about this, he cautioned her that a revolution was taking place and that "heads would roll in Gokana".

2. Dr. Barinem Nubari Kiobel

A serving commissioner in Rivers state and member of the Steering Committee of MOSOP, he was invited to attend the conciliatory meeting but kept coming in and out of the venue of the meeting. He was later seen by an eye-witness at a shrine, another venue for the murders of that day, giving orders, in low tones, to youths to deal with the "vultures". He covered the number place of his official vehicle with leaves to conceal his identity. He could not give a proper account of his suspicious movements of that day.

3. Mr. John Kpuinen

As a member of NYCOP, he participated in the decision to eliminate the "vultures". he also played a key part in the planning of the riots of 21 May 1994.

4. Mr. Baribor Bera

More than 3 eye-witnesses positively identified him as the person who led the rioting youths to attack the palace at which the conciliatory meeting was taking place. He gave orders to the youths as to whom to kill at the meeting, even characterizing a prosecution witness as "a small vulture" who should be spared.

Charge No. OCDT/PH/2/95

1. Saturday Dobee

He was positively identified by two eye-witnesses who testified he was one of the attackers at the palace. Although he attempted to put up an alibi, he could not account for his whereabouts on that day between 6 a.m. and 2 p.m. when the riots and mayhem took place.

2. Felix Nwate

He was positively identified by an eye-witness who testified that he was one of the attackers at the palace. The witness identified him at a filling station where he was arrested. Although he attempted to put up an alibi, this was considered highly unreliable and as an afterthought.

3. Nordu Eawo

He was positively identified by two eye-witnesses who testified that he was one of the attackers at the palace. Although he attempted to put up an alibi, he failed to call either his wife or another person who he said he had been with on the farm that day, to testify. He therefore could not account for his whereabouts on that day. All he could offer was that one of the witnesses framed him because of a disagreement he had had with him.

4. Paul Levura

He was positively identified by a witness who knew him very well to be among some people seen on the fateful day pushing a Beetle car with a dead body inside. Although he called two witnesses to vouch for his alibi, none could say that he saw the accused person on the fateful day.

5. Daniel Gbokoo

He was positively identified by an eye-witness to be the person who used a matchet to kill Chief Kobani. He did not offer any alibi and could not account for his whereabouts on that day.

The foregoing 9 accused persons were found guilty of murder contrary to section 316 of the Criminal Code as incorporated in section 3 of the Civil Disturbances (Special Tribunal) Act and item 13 in the First Schedule to the Act. Each one of them was sentenced to death by hanging.

The following have been discharged and acquitted for want of satisfactory proof of the commission of the alleged offences charged. Accordingly the Tribunal directed that they were free to go.

Charge No. OCD/PH/1/95

1. **Mr. Ledum Mitee**

Charge No. OCD/PH/2/95

1. **Pogbara Afa**
2. **Monday Dowin**
3. **Joseph Kpante**
4. **Michael Vizor**
5. **Albert Kagbara**

Confirmation of Sentences

Section 7(1) of the Act requires that:

(a) where the Tribunal passes a guilty verdict, it shall forward the records of proceedings to the confirming authority (the PRC);
(b) any sentences imposed by the Tribunal shall not be carried out until conviction or sentence is confirmed;

(c) the confirming authority may confirm or vary the sentence of the Tribunal.

Under section 11 of the Rules of Procedure used by the Tribunal, the Tribunal may, in addition to its sentence, make appropriate recommendations as to mercy but in any such case, *it shall give reasons for such recommendations.*

Observations

Following a thorough review of the two judgements of the Tribunal, the following observations could be made.

1. A considered assessment of this matter has been made based on copies of the two judgements read by the Tribunal. The full records of proceedings are not yet available. Although a more informed view may emerge from a review of the entire records, the two judgements contain accurate account of the testimony of all witnesses and those of the accused persons who gave evidence. They also convey very lucid review of the body of evidence against and the role played by each of the accused persons.

2. Based upon a thorough review and assessment of the prosecution case from the judgement read, it would appear that the trial has been fairly conducted in accordance with the provisions of the Act. The accused persons were given all the rights and every opportunity recognized by the Act and other laws of the land to defend themselves in person or by counsel of their choice. While some availed themselves of such opportunities others declined to.

3. Regrettably, counsel to some of the accused persons, contrary to all known principles of professional responsibility and decorum, chose to abandon their clients midstream during the trial advising them, wrongly, not to give evidence thereafter. Following a conviction of their clients, some of these lawyers have chosen to rationalize their action. It is instructive to note that Mr. Mitee, one of the accused persons and a legal practitioner who conducted his own defence, secured an acquittal from the tribunal as did 5 others.

4. Those who do not have the slightest respect for our judicial system use double standards while judging us. They have no qualms brow-beating us to make a mockery of all judicial processes known to our laws. The Ogoni Civil Disturbance Tribunal is *not* a Military court martial. It has two serving High Court judges. It is governed by due process known to our law of evidence and procedure. Its proceedings were openly conducted and watched by national and international press crews. It allowed to the accused persons all rights and privileges recognized under our laws. Above all, it has tried suspects arraigned before it in connection with similar disturbances in Kafanchan (1987), Tafawa Balewa (1991) and Zangon Kataf (1992). A similar tribunal was recently set up to try suspects arrested from the Kano civil disturbances of May 1995.

5. The Civil Disturbances engaged in by the accused persons led to brutal murder of highly respected citizens of Rivers state. it also did pose serious security risks to peace, order and good government in the state and the entire nation. The various activities of the perpetrators also did pose a serious threat to national security.

6. While none of the convicts in the first charge namely Saro-Wiwa & Co has pleaded for mercy, Counsel to the convicts in the second charge namely Saturday Dobee & Co did plead for mercy for their clients. In the case of the latter group, who pleaded for mercy, the Tribunal did, at page 106 of its judgement, indicate that, having heard their pleas, ". . . it will make the necessary recommendations". The Tribunal did not, however, make any such undertakings in respect of the Saro-Wiwa batch of convicts. Even in the case of those it undertook to make necessary recommendations, it has not made any specific recommendations.

7. It is clear from the testimonies of eye-witnesses to the events of 21 May 1994, that the convicts had planned a premeditated murder of highly respected and elderly members of their own people, the Ogoni, for whose "survival" MOSOP had been established and instigated riotous youths to carry out their designs. Since disagreeing with Ken Saro-Wiwa over strategies, chief Kobani and others who shared his views had been earmarked as vultures to be eliminated. 21 May 1994 was the appointed day. Certainly no responsible government can, under whatever pretext, countenance condoning such a cowardly murder of citizens who simply disagreed with MOSOP's new leadership and were meeting, at the invitation of their royal fathers, to reconcile their differences. The Western world and other misguided citizens could choose to characterize the perpetrators as celebrated playwrights and environmental crusaders. In this case the celebrated playwright and his co-conspirators happened to be murder suspects also and were treated accordingly.

Final Communiqué of the Nineteenth Ordinary Session of the African Commission on Human and Peoples' Rights

Ouagadougou, 26 March to 4 April 1996

1. The African Commission on Human and Peoples' Rights held its 19th Ordinary Session in Ouagadougou, Burkina Faso from 26 March to 4 April 1996. The Session was chaired by Professor Isaac Nguema.

2. The opening ceremony was attended by members of the Commission, members of the government of Burkina Faso, members of the diplomatic corps, representatives of governmental and non-governmental organizations, members of the national and international press and invited guests.

3. At the opening ceremony, speeches were delivered by Professor Isaac Nguema, Chairman of the African Commission on Human and Peoples' Rights, Mr. Halidou Ouedraogo, Chairman of the Inter-African Union for Human Rights, Mrs. Tokunbo Ige, representing the Secretary General of the International Commission of Jurists and Hon. Hermann Yameogo, Minister of State for African Integration and Solidarity.

4. The Commission adopted the agenda comprising 21 items.

5. The Commission examined and adopted the report of its 18th Ordinary Session held from 2–11 October 1995 in Praia, Cape Verde.

6. The Commission examined and adopted the report of the 2nd Extraordinary session held on the 18 and 19 December 1995, in Kampala, Uganda, on the human rights situation in Africa, in general, and Nigeria and Burundi, in particular.

7. The Commission granted observer status to 16 NGOs. The list of these NGOs is available at the Secretariat.

8. The report of the resolutions and recommendations of the ICJ workshop was submitted to the Commission. The workshop's emphasis was on the human rights situation in Africa, the independence of the judiciary and the incorporation of the provisions of the African Charter in the national legislation of States Parties.

9. Representatives of the government of Nigeria, Mauritania, Egypt and Senegal delivered messages to the Commission, underscoring the willingness of their countries to respect the provisions of the African Charter and reiterated their commitment to cooperate with the Commission.

10. With regard to the consideration of periodic State reports, the Commission examined the initial reports of Algeria and Mozambique. Government delegates presented State reports. During discussion following the presentation of the reports, the Commission urged countries to observe the provisions of the African Charter and to respect human rights.

11. The Commission heard statements delivered by African and international NGOs taking part in the Session.

12. The Commission examined the possibility of revising the African Charter. Following fruitful discussion, in open session, participants noted that there is a need to update the Charter.

13. Participants also asserted that there is a need to strengthen the current early-warning mechanisms and to develop a mechanism for prompt and urgent intervention in order to prevent massive human rights violations.

14. With regard to promotional activities Commissioners presented their activity reports for the intercession period.

15. With regard to the establishment of the African Court of Human and Peoples' Rights, the Secretary informed the Commission that the OAU Secretariat had sent a draft protocol as well as a report adopted in Cape Town by inter-governmental experts to all member States. The OAU Secretariat has invited members states and all interested parties to send to it their comments.

16. The human rights situation in Africa was examined in relation to Burundi, Angola, Nigeria and Sudan. The Commission confirmed its decision to send missions to these countries.

17. The Commission adopted a resolution commending democratic elections in Sierra Leone, Benin and the Comoro Islands. The Commission also adopted resolutions on Nigeria, Burundi and Comoros, the independence of the judiciary and the incorporation of the provisions of the African Charter in the legislation of States Parties.

18. The Commission reiterated its decision to organise the following seminars:

- The right to a fair trial;
- Popular participation and non-formal education;
- Human rights in the new South Africa;
- The peaceful resolution of ethnic and social conflicts within the context of human rights;
- Contemporary forms of slavery in Africa;
- The right to education: an essential condition for development in Africa;
- Freedom of movement and the right to asylum in Africa;
- Prison conditions in Africa;
- Economic, Social and Cultural rights and the right to development.

19. A seminar on impunity was held on 22 and 23 of March in Ouagadougou, Burkina Faso, at the initiative of the Commission in collaboration with the International Centre for Human Rights and Democratic Development (based in Canada), IUHR, ICJ, GERDES AF and WILDAF. A plan of action was drawn up and adopted at the end of the seminar.

20. In order to promote the review of the Commission, the Chairman urged participants to send articles for publication. He also called upon magistrates and judges to publish decisions related to human rights in order to establish an African jurisprudence on this subject.

21. The Commission deplored the inhuman conditions in most African prisons and agreed on the principle of appointing a special rapporteur on prisons in Africa.

22. The Commission also agreed on the principle of appointing a special rapporteur on the rights of women in Africa.

23. Concerning protection activities, the Commission examined, in close session, twenty-one communications and received seven new communications. The Commission took three decisions on seisin and five decisions on admissibility. The Commission has also reiterated its decision to send missions to Mauritania, Rwanda and Senegal.

24. Outside the regular session, the Commission was received by His Excellency Blaise Compaore, President of Burkina Faso, Mr. Kadré Désiré Ouedraogo, the Prime Minister, Hon. Ablassé Ouedraogo, Minister of Foreign Affairs and Mr. Larba Yarga, Minister of Justice.

25. The closing ceremony at the 19th Session of the Commission took place on 4 April 1996 in the Conference Hall of the Ministry of Foreign Affairs. Hon. Hermann Yaméogo, Minister of State for African Integration and Solidarity presided over the ceremony.

26. The Commission decided that its 20th Session, coinciding with the tenth Anniversary of the coming into effect of the Charter, will be held in Mauritius in October 1996 at the invitation of the Government of Mauritius.

27. After the closing ceremony, the Chairman of the Commission held a press conference.

Draft Terms of Reference for the Special Rapporteur on the Rights of Women in Africa

The decision relating to the appointment of a Special Rapporteur on the rights of women in Africa was adopted at the 19th session of the Commission in Ouagadougou in March 1996 (see Report). This appointment was postponed to this session to define the terms of reference and the profile of the Rapporteur.

I. JUSTIFICATION

In the implementation of the African Charter on Human and Peoples' Rights, the Commission has always put forward diverse conditions concerning the specificity of the situation of the rights of women in Africa.

The Commission has noted that the provisions of the Charter do not ensure an effective protection of the fundamental rights of women.

It is worth noting that the Vienna Conference of 1993 has reaffirmed that the rights of women form an integral part of human rights, and that the pertinent recommendations of this Conference have been the foundation of the conclusions of the Dakar and Beijing Conferences of 1994 and 1995 respectively.

Taking into account the aforesaid, and in order to assist the Commission in the effective implementation of its mandate with regard to women, in conformity with Article 45 of the Charter, it is necessary to appoint a Special Rapporteur on the rights of Women in Africa.

1. Mandate

(a) To carry out a study on the situation of the human rights of women in Africa.

(b) To draw up guidelines on the drafting and examination of States parties reports on the rights of women in Africa.

(c) Ensure or make a follow up on the implementation of the Charter by States parties. In this vein, the Special Rapporteur will prepare a report on the situation of violations of women's rights and propose recommendations to the Commission.

(d) The Special Rapporteur will assist African governments in the development and implementation of their policies of promotion and protection of women's rights in Africa.

(e) He or she will encourage and work with NGOs in the field of promotion and protection of women's rights.

(f) He or she will serve as a link between the Commission and inter-governmental and nongovernmental organisations at regional and international levels in order to harmonise the initiatives on the rights of women.

(g) In this regard, the Special Rapporteur will collaborate with Special Rapporteurs from the UN and other regional systems.

2. Duration of the Mandate

The initial duration of the mandate of the Special Rapporteur will run up to the year 2002. However, he or she will have a period of two years to submit his/her interim report and proposals for the future.

3. Area of Investigation

All OAU member States parties to the African Charter. Any other State hosting any organ likely to have information on women's rights in Africa.

4. Report

The Special Rapporteur shall inform the Commission at each session about the progress of his or her work and the difficulties encountered.

He or she will prepare an annual report which shall be annexed to the Commission's Report to the Assembly of Heads of State and Government of the OAU.

NB The elaboration of the financial provisions for the fulfilment of the Special Rapporteur's mandate for 1998–2000 remains to be done.

II. CRITERIA FOR APPOINTMENT OF SPECIAL RAPPORTEUR

(a) Must be a citizen of a State party to the Charter.
(b) Must have a high consideration and competence in matters of women's rights, particular consideration will be given to a person with legal experience.
(c) Must accept and be committed to execute, within the time allowed, the duty as defined in the terms of reference and is wholly responsible to the Commission.

III. APPOINTMENT PROCEDURE

The working group was mandated to propose a candidate for the position to the Commission.

NB At its last meeting held in January 1998 in Banjul, the Gambia, the working group has decided to propose Mrs. Julienne Ondziel-Gnelenga for the position of Special Rapporteur on the Rights of Women in Africa.

Tenth Annual Activity Report of the African Commission on Human and Peoples' Rights 1996–1997

Adopted on 24 April 1997
Covering the 20th and 21st Ordinary Sessions in Mauritius (21–31 October 1996) and Nouakchott (15–24 April 1997)

I. ORGANIZATION OF WORK

A. Period Covered by the Report

1. The Ninth Annual Activity report of the African Commission on Human and Peoples' Rights was adopted by the Thirty-second Ordinary Session of the Assembly of Heads of State and Government of the Organization of African Unity in its resolution AHG/Res. 250 (XXXII). The Tenth Annual Activity Report covers the Twentieth Ordinary Session held in Grand Bay, Mauritius, from 21–31 October 1996 and the Twenty-first Ordinary Session held in Nouakchott, Mauritania from 15–24 April 1997.

B. Status of Ratification

2. As of the 21st Ordinary Session of the Commission, all the member states of the OAU, with the exception of Eritrea and Ethiopia had ratified or acceded to the Charter. The list of States and dates of signature, ratification/accession and deposit of instruments is attached (Annex I).

C. Sessions and Agenda

3. The Commission held two Ordinary Sessions since the adoption of the Ninth Annual Activity Report:

- the 20th Ordinary Session held in Grand Bay, Mauritius, 21–31 October 1996;
- the 21st Ordinary Session held in Nouakchott, Mauritania, 15–24 April 1997.

D. Composition and Participation

4. The following Commissioners attended the 20th Session:

(1) Prof. Isaac Nguema, Chairman,
(2) Prof. Emmanuel V. O. Dankwa, Vice Chairman,

(3) Mr. Robert H. Kisanga,
(4) Dr. Mohamed H. Ben Salem,
(5) Dr. Vera V. Duarte Martins,
(6) Prof. U. Oji Umozurike,
(7) Mr. Atsu Koffi Amega,
(8) Mr. Kamel Rezzag-Bara,
(9) Mrs. Julienne Ondziel-Gnelenga,
(10) Mr. Youssoupha Ndiaye,
(11) Mr. Alioune Blondin Beye.

5. The representatives of the following States attended the Session and made statements before the Commission:

(1) Cameroon,
(2) Burkina Faso,
(3) Senegal,
(4) Sudan,
(5) Tunisia,
(6) Nigeria,
(7) Mozambique,
(8) Burundi,
(9) South Africa,
(10) Egypt,
(11) Ethiopia.

6. The following members of the Commission attended the 21st Session:

(1) Prof. Isaac Nguema, Chairman,
(2) Prof. Emmanuel V. O. Dankwa, Vice-Chairman,
(3) Mrs. Julienne Ondziel-Gnelenga,
(4) Mr. Youssoupha Ndiaye,
(5) Mr. Kamel Rezzag-Bara,
(6) Mr. Prof. U. Oji Umozurike,
(7) Dr. Hatem Ben Salem.

The following members of the Commission were absent with apologies:

(1) Dr. Vera V.B.S. Duarte-Martins,
(2) Mr. Robert Kisanga,
(3) Mr. Alioune Blondin Beye,
(4) Mr. Atsu Koffi Amega.

7. The representatives of the following States attended the 21st Session:

(1) Togo,
(2) Chad,
(3) Tunisia,
(4) Zimbabwe,

(5) Sudan,
(6) Senegal,
(7) Nigeria,
(8) Mozambique,
(9) Mauritania,
(10) Gabon,
(11) South Africa,
(12) Algeria,
(13) Burkina Faso,
(14) Cameroon,
(15) Côte d'Ivoire,
(16) Egypt,
(17) Gambia,
(18) Ghana,
(19) Sahrawi Arab Democratic Republic.

8. The two sessions were attended by many non-governmental organizations and National Human Rights Institutions.

E. Adoption of the Tenth Annual Activity Report

9. At its 24 April 1997 sitting, the Commission considered and adopted its Tenth Annual Activity Report.

II. ACTIVITIES OF THE COMMISSION

A. Consideration of Periodic Reports

10. Under Article 62 of the African Charter on Human and Peoples' Rights, each State Party undertakes to submit a report every two years on the legislative and other measures it takes to give effect to the rights and freedoms enshrined in the Charter.

11. The first periodic report of Mauritius was presented by the representatives of the State and was duly considered at the 20th Session. The Commission commended the representative for a well prepared report.

12. The second and third periodic reports of Zimbabwe were considered at the 21st Session. The Commission commended the representative for well prepared reports which could serve as a model.

13. The first periodic report of Sudan was also considered at the 21st Session. The Commission thanked the representative for the presentation.

14. As of the 21st Session the following State Parties had submitted their reports: Libya, Rwanda, Tunisia (9th Session); Egypt and Tanzania (11th Session), The Gambia (12th and 16th Sessions); Senegal (12th Session); Zimbabwe (12th and 21st Session); Togo and Nigeria (12th and 16th Sessions); Benin, Ghana, Cape Verde and

Mozambique (14th Session); Tunisia (18th Session); and Algeria (19th Session); Mauritius (20th Session); Sudan (21st Session); 33 States parties have not yet submitted their periodic reports. Their list is attached (Annex IV).

15. Seychelles has submitted it's report to the Secretariat (18th Session), but has not yet presented it formally to the Commission.

B. Promotional Activities

(i) Report of the Chairman

16. The Chairman's Activity Reports included his participation in various symposia and seminars within and outside Africa, work related to the Commission's publications and his participation in the 64th OAU Council of Ministers. He also reported on his mission to Madagascar to observe elections.

(ii) Activities of Other Members of the Commission

17. The other members of the Commission also reported on their inter-sessional activities.

(iii) The Commission Co-sponsored and Participated in the Following Seminars:

(a) Prison Conditions in Africa, Kampala, Uganda, 19–21 September 1996 with Penal Reform International.
(b) Mechanism for Early Warning in Emergency Situations under Article 58, Nairobi, Kenya 23–25 July 1996 with Interights.
(c) Draft Protocol on the Establishment of an African Human Rights Court, Nouakchott, Mauritania 11–14 April 1997 with the International Commission of Jurists.
(d) Draft Protocol concerning the Right of Women, Nouakchott, Mauritania, 13–15 April 1997 with the International Commission of Jurists.

III. SPECIAL RAPPORTEUR ON EXTRA-JUDICIAL EXECUTIONS IN AFRICA

18. At the 20th Session, Dr. Ben Salem, the Special Rapporteur submitted a report on the progress on his work. The report of the Special Rapporteur can be found in Annex VI.

At the 21st Session the Commission considered a report on Extra-judicial, Summary and Arbitrary Executions and commended the Special Rapporteur for the work he had done so far.

IV. SPECIAL RAPPORTEUR ON PRISON AND DETENTION CONDITIONS IN AFRICA

19. At the 20th Session Prof. Dankwa was appointed Special Rapporteur on Prison and Detention Conditions in Africa. At the 21st Session the Special Rapporteur submitted the first report on his work to the Commission (See Annex VII). The Special Rapporteur had among other things conducted a mission to Zimbabwe. The Commission commended the Special Rapporteur for the work he had done so far.

V. SPECIAL RAPPORTEUR ON THE RIGHTS OF WOMEN

20. The Commission appointed three Commissioners, Mrs. Julienne Ondziel-Gnelenga, Dr. Vera V. B. S. Duarte-Martins and Prof. E. V. O. Dankwa to work on a draft Protocol on the Rights of Women.

VI. MISSIONS TO STATES PARTIES

21. The Commission conducted missions to the following member states:

Senegal (1–7 June 1996). The mission was composed of the Chairman Prof. Nguema and Commissioner Duarte-Martins.
Mauritania (19–27 June 1996). The mission was composed of the Chairman Prof. Nguema, Commissioner Ondziel-Gnelenga and Commissioner Rezzag-Bara.
Sudan (1–7 December 1996). The mission was composed of the Vice-Chairman Professor Dankwa, Commissioner Kisanga and Commissioner Rezzag-Bara.
Nigeria (7–14 March 1997). The mission was composed of the Vice- Chairman Professor Dankwa and Commissioner Amega.

Staff members of the Secretariat assisted the delegation to these missions.

22. Mission reports were submitted on Senegal and Mauritania and were discussed by the Commission.

23. Reports on Sudan and Nigeria were to be submitted to the next session.

IX. RELATIONS WITH OBSERVERS

24. During the two Sessions, the Commission considered the application of, and granted observer status to 23 organizations. At present, the number of organizations with observer status is 205.

X. PROTECTIVE ACTIVITIES

25. The Commission completed consideration on 8 communications during the 20th and 21st sessions. These are attached as appendix X.

XI. ADMINISTRATIVE AND FINANCIAL MATTERS

A. Administrative Matters

26. During the financial year under review, the work of the Commission was affected by a number of administrative problems including the following:

(i) Staffing

27. The Secretariat is still suffering from a shortage of staff, in spite of numerous appeals made by the Commission. The Commission appeals again to the Secretary-General of the OAU for an early and appropriate solution to this problem.

28. The Secretary to the Commission is the only professional staff member who is entrusted with the technical and administrative duties of the Secretariat. In view of the Secretariat's volume of work, related to human rights promotional and protective activities, there is an urgent need to recruit four additional lawyers. There is also an urgent need to recruit a documentation officer to run the Documentation Centre as well as press and information officer.

(ii) Equipment

29. Due to the increase in the volume of work at the Secretariat, it is necessary to procure adequate and proper equipment. The Commission is appealing to the OAU Secretariat to provide the Commission's Secretariat with the equipment it needs to carry out its functions, including computers, photocopiers, electronic mail, etc.

(iii) Medical Coverage and Insurance

30. The problems of medical fees and the insurance of the Commissioners when travelling on duty for the Commission have still not been settled yet. The Commission is still waiting for the solution promised some years ago by the OAU Secretariat to materialize. The Commission is making an urgent appeal to the OAU Secretariat to look into this issue.

B. Financial Matters

31. During the financial year under review, the Commission was financed from the following resources:

(i) OAU Budget

32. Due to financial problems, facing the OAU, several projects of the Commission had to be suspended. This only made worse the situation of the Commission.

(ii) Subvention from Raoul Wallenberg Institute

33. The Raoul Wallenberg Institute continued to finance the promotional activities of the Commission, including missions undertaken by Commissioners and the publishing of the Commission's Review.

(iii) Assistance from the African Society of International Comparative Law

34. The African Society provided the Commission with two jurists from 20 March for a period of 12 months.

(iv) Assistance from the Danish Centre for Human Rights

35. The Danish Centre for Human Rights provided one jurist for a period of 9 months from 1 September 1996.

Furthermore the Danish Centre assisted getting funding from the Danish Government for purchase of computer equipment and the recruitment of two legal officers, one documentation officer, one administrative officers, one press and information officer and one bilingual secretary for a period of three years.

XIII. ADOPTION OF THE REPORT BY THE ASSEMBLY OF HEADS OF STATE AND GOVERNMENT

36. After considering this Report, the Assembly of Heads of State and Government adopted it in a resolution which took note of the Report with satisfaction and authorized its publication.

ANNEX I

RATIFICATIONS

African Charter on Human and Peoples' Rights
List of Countries which have Signed, Ratified or Adhered to the Charter

The state of ratifications of the African Charter on Human and Peoples' Rights is the subject of the present annex.

Reminders have been sent to OAU member states which have not done so to ratify the Charter as soon as possible. Countries which have not yet ratified the Charter are Eritrea and Ethiopia.

Alongside the meeting of the OAU Council of Ministers in Tripoli, Libya, direct contacts were made with the delegates from these two countries, who indicated that the process of ratification of the Charter is at an advanced stage.

No.	Country	Date of Signature	Date of Ratification	Date Deposited
1.	Algeria	10/04/86	01/03/87	20/03/87
2.	Angola		02/03/90	09/10/90
3.	Benin		20/01/86	25/02/86
4.	Botswana		17/07/86	22/07/86
5.	Burundi		28/07/80	30/08/89
6.	Burkina Faso	05/03/84	06/07/84	21/09/84
7.	Cameroon	23/07/87	20/06/89	18/09/89
8.	Cape Verde	31/03/86	02/06/87	06/08/87
9.	Central African Republic		26/04/86	27/07/86
10.	Chad	29/05/86	09/10/86	11/11/86
11.	Comoros		01/06/86	18/07/86
12.	Congo	27/11/81	09/12/82	17/01/83
13.	Côte d'Ivoire		06/01/92	31/03/92
14.	Djibouti	20/12/91	11/11/91	20/12/91
15.	Egypt	16/11/81	20/03/84	03/04/84
16.	Equatorial Guinea	18/08/86	07/04/86	18/08/86
17.	Eritrea			
18.	Ethiopia			
19.	Gabon	26/02/82	20/02/86	26/06/86
20.	Gambia	11/02/83	08/06/83	13/03/83
21.	Ghana		24/01/89	01/03/89
22.	Guinea	09/12/81	16/02/82	13/05/82
23.	Guinea-Bissau		04/12/85	06/03/86
24.	Kenya		23/01/92	10/02/92
25.	Lesotho	07/03/84	10/02/92	27/02/92
26.	Liberia	31/01/83	04/08/82	29/12/82
27.	Libya	30/05/85	19/07/86	26/03/87
28.	Madagascar		09/03/92	19/03/92

No.	Country	Date of Signature	Date of Ratification	Date Deposited
29.	Malawi	23/02/90	17/11/89	23/02/90
30.	Mali	13/11/81	21/12/81	22/01/82
31.	Mauritania	25/02/82	14/06/86	26/06/86
32.	Mauritius	27/02/92	19/06/92	07/07/92
33.	Mozambique		22/02/89	07/03/90
34.	Namibia		30/07/92	16/09/92
35.	Niger	09/07/86	15/07/86	21/07/86
36.	Nigeria	31/08/82	22/06/83	27/07/83
37.	Rwanda	11/11/81	15/07/83	22/07/83
38.	Sahrawi Arab Dem. Rep.	10/04/86	02/05/86	23/05/86
39.	Sao Tome & Principe		23/05/86	28/07/86
40.	Senegal	23/09/81	13/08/82	25/10/82
41.	Seychelles		13/04/92	30/04/92
42.	Sierra Leone	27/08/81	21/09/83	27/01/84
43.	Somalia	26/02/82	31/07/85	20/03/86
44.	South Africa	09/07/96	09/07/96	09/07/96
45.	Sudan	03/09/82	18/02/86	11/03/86
46.	Swaziland		15/09/95	09/10/95
47.	Togo	20/02/82	05/11/82	22/11/82
48.	Tunisia		16/03/83	22/04/83
49.	Tanzania	31/05/82	18/02/84	09/03/84
50.	Uganda	18/08/86	10/05/86	27/05/86
51.	Zaire	23/07/87	20/07/87	28/07/87
52.	Zambia	17/01/83	19/01/84	02/02/84
53.	Zimbabwe	20/02/86	30/05/86	12/06/86

Charter on the Rights and Welfare of the African Child
List of Countries which have Signed or Ratified the Charter

No.	Country	Date of Signature	Date of Ratification
1.	Algeria		
2.	Angola		
3.	Benin	27/02/92	
4.	Botswana		
5.	Burundi		
6.	Burkina Faso	27/02/92	08/06/92
7.	Cameroon	16/09/92	
8.	Cape Verde	27/02/92	20/07/93
9.	Central African Republic		
10.	Chad		
11.	Comoros		
12.	Congo	28/02/92	
13.	Côte d'Ivoire		
14.	Djibouti	28/02/92	
15.	Egypt		
16.	Equatorial Guinea		

No.	Country	Date of Signature	Date of Ratification
17.	Eritrea		
18.	Ethiopia		
19.	Gabon	22/02/92	
20.	Gambia		
21.	Ghana		
22.	Guinea		
23.	Guinea-Bissau		
24.	Kenya		
25.	Lesotho		
26.	Liberia		
27.	Libya		
28.	Madagascar		
29.	Malawi		
30.	Mali		
31.	Mauritania		
32.	Mauritius	07/11/91	14/02/93
33.	Mozambique		
34.	Namibia		
35.	Niger		
36.	Nigeria		
37.	Rwanda	02/10/91	
38.	Sahrawi Arab Dem. Rep.	23/10/92	
39.	Sao Tome & Principe		
40.	Senegal	18/05/92	
41.	Seychelles	27/02/92	13/02/92
42.	Sierra Leone	14/01/92	
43.	South Africa		
44.	Somalia	01/06/91	
45.	Sudan		
46.	Swaziland	29/06/92	
47.	Togo	27/02/92	
48.	Tunisia	16/06/95	
49.	Tanzania		
50.	Uganda	26/02/92	17/08/94
51.	Zaire		
52.	Zambia	28/02/92	
53.	Zimbabwe	28/02/92	19/01/95

ANNEX II

Agenda of the Twentieth Ordinary Session

1. Opening Ceremony (Public Session)
2. Adoption of Agenda (Private Session)
3. Organisation of Work (Private Session)
4. Observers (Public Session)

(a) Statements of the States' Delegates
(b) Consideration of Applications for Observer Status;
(c) Relationship with Observers and Statements by Observers

5. Consideration of Periodic Reports of the Following States (Public Session)

– Mauritius
– Zimbabwe

6. The Setting up of an Early Intervention Mechanism in Case of Massive Human Rights Violations (Public Session)
7. Administrative and Financial Matters (Private Session)

(a) Report of the Chairman of the Commission
(b) Report of the Secretary to the Commission
(c) Functioning of the Secretariat
(d) Implementation of Recommendations of the Previous Sessions
(e) Draft Rules and Regulations on Contracts with Consultants
(f) Financing the Translation of Session and Periodic Reports
(g) The Situation of the Documentation and Information Centre
(h) Appraisal of the Work of the Commission and its Future Prospects; Examining the Draft Plan of Action for the Period 1996–2001
(i) Discussion of the Logo of the Commission (Public Session)
(j) Preparation of the Commemoration of the 10th Anniversary of the African Commission on Human and Peoples' Rights (Public Session)
(k) Distribution of the OAU Member States Among Members of the Commission (Private Session)

8. Promotional Activities (Public Session)

(a) Activity reports by Commissioners
(b) Consideration of the Report of the Special Rapporteur on Extra-judicial, Summary and Arbitrary Executions
(c) Report on the Implementation of Resolution AHG/Res. 230 (XXX) on the Establishment of the African Court on Human and Peoples' Rights
(d) The Human Rights Situation in Africa
(e) Amendments of Guidelines on the Preparation of Periodic Reports
(f) Organisation of Forthcoming Seminars and Conferences
(g) Publication of the Review and the Newsletter of the Commission
(h) Follow-up of the Decisions and Recommendations of the International Conferences on Human Rights (the Vienna and Montreal Conferences as well as the Beijing Conference on Women)
(i) Report on the Seminar on Prison Conditions in Africa (19–21 September 1996, Kampala, Uganda)
(j) Drawing up of the Draft Additional Protocol on Rights of Women in Africa

9. Revision of the African Charter on Human and Peoples' Rights; The Issue of Incapability of Commission Members (Private Session)
10. Protective Activities (Private Session)
11. Secretariat Building (Private Session)
12. Participation of the Commission on Some Activities of the OAU (Public Session)
13. Date, Venue and the Agenda of the 21st Ordinary Session (Private Session)
14. Any Other Business (Private Session)
15. Preparation of
    - Report of the Session;
    - Final Communiqué
    - Declaration.
16. Adoption of the Report of the 20th Session (Private Session)
17. Closing Ceremony; Final Communiqué and the Mauritius Declaration (Public Session)
18. Press Conference of the Commission

ANNEX III

Agenda of the Twenty-first Ordinary Session

1. Opening Ceremony (Public Session)
2. Adoption of Agenda (Private Session): Doc.OS/1(XXI)
3. Organisation of Work (Private Session): Doc.OS/2(XXI)
4. Observers (Public Session)
    (a) Statements of the States' Delegates;
    (b) Examination of Applications for Observer Status: Doc.OS/3(XXI)
5. Consideration of Periodic Reports of States Parties (Public Session)
    (a) Second and Third Periodic Reports of Zimbabwe: Doc.OS/4(XXI)
    (b) Initial Report of Sudan: Doc.OS/5(XXI)
6. The Setting-up of an Early Intervention Mechanism in Case of Massive Human Rights Violations (Public Session): Doc.OS/6(XXI)
7. Promotional Activities (Public Session)
    (a) Activity Reports by Commissioners: Doc.OS/7(XXI) Add.1
    (b) Examination of the Report of the Special Rapporteur on Extra-judicial, Summary or Arbitrary Executions: Doc.OS/7(XXI) Add.2
    (c) Report on the Implementation of Resolution AHG/Res. 230 (XXX) on the Establishment of an African Court on Human and Peoples' Rights: Doc.OS/7(XXI) Add.3
    (d) Human Rights Situation in Africa and Statements of Observers

(e) Amendments of Guidelines on the Preparation of the Periodic Reports: Doc.OS/7(XXI) Add.4
(f) Organisation of Forthcoming Seminars and Conferences: Doc.OS/7(XXI) Add.5
(g) Publication of the Review and the Newsletter of the Commission: Doc.OS/7(XXI) Add.6
(h) Report of the Special Rapporteur on Prisons: Doc.OS/7(XXI) Add.7
(i) Elaboration of the Draft Additional Protocol on African Women's Rights: Doc.OS/7(XXI) Add.8
(j) Strengthening the Cooperation between the Commission and National Human Rights Institutions (item proposed by Commissioner Rezzag-Bara): Doc.OS/7(XXI) Add.9

8. Participation of the Commission in Certain Activities of the OAU (Public Session): Doc.OS/12(XXI)
9. Protective Activities

(a) Missions of the Commission for Protective Activities (Public Session) (item proposed by Interights, RADDHO and the CLO): Doc.OS/9(XXI) Add.1
(b) Missions of the Commission
(c) Consideration of Communications (Private Session): Doc.OS/9(XXI) Add.2

10. Revision of the African Charter on Human and Peoples' Rights, the Issue of Incompatibility of the Members of the Commission (Private Session): Doc. OS/8(XXI) Add.9
11. Administrative and Financial Matters (Private Session): Doc.OS/10(XXI)

(a) Report of the Chairman of the Commission: Doc.OS/10(XXI) Add.1
(b) Report of the Secretary to the Commission: Doc.OS/10(XXI) Add.2
(c) Examination of the Project of the Logo of the Commission (Public Session): Doc.OS/10(XXI) Add.3
(d) Preparation of the Commemoration of the 10th Anniversary of the African Commission on Human and Peoples' Rights (Public Session): Doc.OS/10(XXI) Add.4
(e) Distribution of the OAU Member States Among Members of the Commission: Doc.OS/10(XXI) Add.5

12. Question Concerning the Headquarters of the Commission (Private Session): Doc.OS/11(XXI)
13. Dates, Venue and Agenda of the 22nd Ordinary Session (Private Session)
14. Any Other Business (Private Session)
15. Preparation of:

(a) the 10th Annual Activity Report
(b) the Session Report
(c) the Final Communiqué

16. Adoption of the Session Report, the Annual Activity Report and Final Communiqué (Private Session)
17. Reading of the Final Communiqué and Closing Ceremony (Public Session).
18. Press Conference

ANNEX IV

Agenda of the Twenty-first Ordinary Session

See Table on pp. 506–7.

ANNEX V

Distribution of States Parties among Commissioners for Promotional Activities

This distribution was adopted by the Commission at its 19th ordinary session held from 2–11 October in Praia, Cape Verde. At the 20th ordinary session this distribution was outlined but was not concluded.

1. **Prof. Isaac Nguema**
   Gabon
   Equatorial Guinea
   Zaire
   Burkina Faso

2. **Prof. E. V. O. Dankwa**
   Ghana
   Zimbabwe
   Malawi
   Botswana
   Namibia

3. **Mr. Atsu-Koffi Amega**
   Togo
   Rwanda
   Central African Republic
   Djibouti
   Seychelles

4. **Mr. Mohamed Kamel Rezzag-Bara**
   Algeria
   Comoros
   Sahrawi Arab Dem. Rep.
   Madagascar
   Egypt

5. **Mr. Justice Robert Habesh Kisanga**
   Tanzania
   Ethiopia
   Kenya
   Somalia
   Uganda
   Zambia

No.	State Party	1st Report to be submitted on	2nd Report to be submitted on	3rd Report to be submitted on	4th Report to be submitted on	5th Report to be submitted on	Reports submitted but not yet considered
1.*	Algeria	20/06/89	20/06/91	20/06/93	20/06/95	20/06/97	
2.	Angola	09/01/92	09/01/94	09/01/96	09/01/98	09/01/2000	
3.*	Benin	21/10/88	21/10/90	21/10/92	21/10/94	21/10/96	
4.	Botswana	21/10/88	21/10/90	21/10/92	21/10/94	21/10/96	
5.	Burundi	30/11/91	30/11/93	30/11/95	30/11/97	30/11/99	
6.	Burkina Faso	21/10/88	21/10/90	21/10/92	21/10/94	21/10/96	
7.	Cameroon	18/12/91	18/12/93	18/12/95	18/12/97	18/12/99	
8.*	Cape Verde	06/11/89	06/11/91	06/11/93	06/11/95	06/11/97	
9.	Central African Republic	21/10/88	21/10/90	21/10/92	21/10/94	21/10/96	
10.	Chad	11/02/89	11/02/91	11/02/93	11/02/95	11/02/97	
11.	Comoros	21/10/88	21/10/90	21/10/92	21/10/94	21/10/96	
12.	Congo	21/10/88	21/10/90	21/10/92	21/10/94	21/10/96	
13.	Côte d'Ivoire	01/07/94	01/07/96	01/07/98	07/01/2000	01/07/2002	
14.	Djibouti	20/03/93	20/03/95	20/03/97	20/03/99	20/03/2001	
15.*	Egypt	21/10/88	21/10/90	21/10/92	21/10/94	21/10/96	
16.	Equatorial Guinea	18/11/88	18/11/90	18/11/92	18/11/94	18/11/96	
17.	Ethiopia (1)						
18.	Eritrea (1)						
19.	Gabon	21/10/88	21/10/90	21/10/92	21/10/94	21/10/96	
20.†	Gambia	21/10/88	21/10/90	21/10/92	21/10/94	21/10/96	
21.*	Ghana	01/06/91	01/06/93	01/06/95	01/06/97	01/06/99	
22.	Guinea	21/10/88	21/10/90	21/10/92	21/10/94	21/10/96	
23.	Guinea-Bissau	21/10/88	21/10/90	21/10/92	21/10/94	21/10/96	
24.	Kenya	10/05/94	10/05/96	10/05/98	10/05/2000	10/05/2002	
25.	Lesotho	27/05/94	27/05/96	27/05/98	27/05/2000	27/05/2002	
26.	Liberia	27/10/88	21/10/90	21/10/92	21/10/94	21/10/96	
27.*	Libya	26/06/89	26/06/91	26/06/93	26/06/95	26/06/97	
28.	Madagascar	19/06/94	19/06/96	19/06/98	19/06/2000	19/06/2002	

29.	Malawi	23/05/92	23/05/94	23/05/96	23/05/98	23/05/2000	
30.	Mali	21/10/88	21/10/90	21/10/92	21/10/94	21/10/96	
31.	Mauritania	21/10/88	21/10/90	21/10/92	21/10/94	21/10/96	
32.*	Mauritius	07/10/92	07/10/94	07/10/96	07/10/98	07/10/2000	
33.*	Mozambique	07/06/92	07/06/94	07/06/96	07/06/98	07/06/2000	
34.	Namibia	16/12/94	16/12/96	16/12/98	16/12/2000	16/12/2002	
35.	Niger	21/10/88	21/10/90	21/10/92	21/10/94	21/10/96	
36.*	Nigeria	21/10/88	21/10/90	21/10/92	21/10/94	21/10/96	
37.*	Rwanda	21/10/88	21/10/90	21/10/92	21/10/94	21/10/96	
38.	SADR	21/10/88	21/10/90	21/10/92	21/10/94	21/10/96	
39.	Sao Tome & Principe	21/10/88	21/10/90	21/10/92	21/10/94	21/10/96	
40.†	Senegal	21/10/88	21/10/90	21/10/92	21/10/94	21/10/96	
41.*	Seychelles	30/07/94	30/07/96	30/07/98	30/07/2000	30/07/2002	
42.	Sierra Leone	21/10/88	21/10/90	21/10/92	21/10/94	21/10/96	
43.	Somalia	21/10/88	21/10/90	21/10/92	21/10/94	21/10/96	
44.	South Africa	07/07/98	09/07/2000	09/07/2002	09/07/2003	07/07/2006	
45.*	Sudan	21/10/88	21/10/90	21/10/92	21/10/94	21/10/96	Initial report
46.	Swaziland						
47.*	Tanzania	21/10/88	21/10/90	21/10/92	21/10/94	21/10/96	
48.*	Togo	21/10/88	21/10/90	21/10/92	21/10/94	21/10/96	
49.†	Tunisia	21/10/88	21/10/90	21/10/92	21/10/94	21/10/96	
50.	Uganda	21/10/88	21/10/90	21/10/92	21/10/94	21/10/96	
51.	Zaire	28/10/89	28/10/91	28/10/93	28/10/95	28/10/97	
52.	Zambia	21/10/88	21/10/90	21/10/92	21/10/94	21/10/96	
53.**	Zimbabwe	21/10/88	21/10/90	21/10/92	21/10/94	21/10/96	2nd & 3rd rep

* has presented its preliminary report

† has presented its preliminary report and second periodic report

** has presented its preliminary, and submitted its second and third report

(1) not yet ratified the African Charter

6. **Mme V. V. D. M. Martins**
   Cape Verde
   Mozambique
   Angola
   Guinea Bissau
   Sao Tome & Principe

7. **M. Youssoupha Ndiaye**
   Senegal
   Mali
   Niger
   Guinea

8. **Mrs. Ondziel-Gnelenga**
   Congo
   Burundi
   Chad
   Mauritius

9. **Mr. U. Oji Umozurike**
   Nigeria
   Cameroon
   Lesotho
   Swaziland
   South Africa

10. **Prof. Mohammed H. Ben Salem**
    Tunisia
    Libya
    Sudan
    Eritrea
    The Gambia

11. **M. Alioune Blondin Beye**
    Benin
    Côte d'Ivoire
    Mauritania
    Liberia
    Sierra Leone

ANNEX VI

Report on Extra-judicial, Summary or Arbitrary Executions

1. Introduction

This report is presented in compliance with the decision of the African Commission on Human and Peoples' Rights (ACHPR), unanimously adopted during its 16th ordinary session (October 1994), designating M. Hatem Ben Salem, member of the Commission, as Special Rapporteur on extra-judicial, summary or arbitrary executions.

Far from being the result of chance or circumstance, the decision of the ACHPR was taken with courage and determination, taken in spite of a paucity of means. As it concerns one of the essential questions in relation to fundamental human rights, the decision of the signifies the profound conviction of all the members of the Commission that there is nothing more irreparable and more irreversible than the taking, outside the law, of the right to life, expressly guaranteed by Article 4 of the African Charter on Human and Peoples' Rights. Each human being thus has the right to the respect for their life and the integrity of their person and no one can deprive them of these arbitrarily. This principle is widely recognised by international instruments, particularly the Universal Declaration of Human Rights (Article 3) and the International Covenant on Civil and Political Rights (Article 6). Unfortunately, the ratification of the African Charter on Human and Peoples' Rights or the adherence to other international human rights treaties and conventions has not prevented states, groups, or individuals from attacking this fundamental human right, the right to life. Africa has, sadly, become a sort of "continent of predilection" of such acts because, on the soil of one of its countries, a party to the Charter, was perpetrated a genocide of atrocity rarely equalled in the course of human history. Encouraged by a good number of African and international NGOs, the ACHPR therefore designated one of its members with a view to assuring this mission of investigation, analysis and recommendation.

II. Mandate of the Special Rapporteur

The ACHPR, in designating the special rapporteur on extra-judicial, summary or arbitrary executions, delimited his competence on the following fundamental points.

A. Mission

1. To propose the implementation of a reporting system on cases of extra-judicial, summary and arbitrary execution in African states, specifically by keeping a register containing all information as to the identity of the victims.
2. To follow up, in collaboration with government officials, or failing that, with international, national or African NGOs, all enquiries which could lead to discovering the identity and extent of responsibility of authors and initiators of extra-judicial, summary, or arbitrary executions.
3. To suggest the ways and means of informing the African Commission in good time of the possibility of extra-judicial, summary or arbitrary executions, with the goal of intervening before the OAU Summit.
4. To intervene with States for trial and punishment of perpetrators of extra-judicial summary or arbitrary executions, and rehabilitation of the victims of these executions.
5. To examine the modalities of creation of a mechanism of compensation for the families of victims of extra-judicial, summary or arbitrary executions, which might be doing through national legal procedures, or through an African compensation fund.

B. Field of Investigation

In his mission, the Special Rapporteur will have as a priority to produce a report on extra-judicial execution of children, of women, of demonstrators, and of human rights activists/political opponents of their governments. The Rapporteur can decide to chose a country where he believes the incidence of execution are the most frequent or massive.

C. Duration of the Mandate

The Special Rapporteur will have a period of at minimum two years to finalise his mission, if the Commission does not decide to extend this time.

D. Methods of action

The Special Rapporteur can, for the execution of his mandate, have recourse to all methods of investigation, specifically by requesting the assistance of states and national, international and African NGOs. He can be assisted in his mission by any person whom he judges competent to perform this task well.

E. The Report

The Special Rapporteur will inform the Commission at each session of the progress of his mission. He will make an annual report which will be annexed to the activity report of the Commission to the Conference of Heads of State and government of the OAU.

III. Implementation of the Mandate of the Special Rapporteur

It is only at the 18th session of the ACHPR, held at Praia, Cape Verde, in October 1995, that the mandate fixing the responsibilities of the Special Rapporteur was approved. This delay in the articulation of his duties was essentially due to the wish expressed by members of the Commission to begin this first experience on a solid foundation. In fact, from the beginning there was no question of creating a mechanism without concretising a specific role for it to play in the effective protection of human rights in Africa. Thus, all the parties together believed that it was imperative that the Special Rapporteur have minimum means, independent of the Secretary to the Commission, with the object of fulfilling his task in the best conditions.

These conditions were not fulfilled until the beginning of 1996, thanks to a clarification of the mandate of the Special Rapporteur and to the logistical support of the North-South Centre of the Council of Europe, and the Swiss Directorate of Cooperation in Development and Humanitarian Aid.

A. Mission of the Special Rapporteur

In conformity with point 1 of his mandate (cf. II of the present report) the Special Rapporteur should propose the implementation of a system permitting the cataloguing of cases of extra-judicial, summary or arbitrary executions in African countries, specifically through a register containing all information as to the identity of the victims.

(1) Idea of the register of extra-judicial executions

From the first contact with available information and in light of the breadth of the task assigned to the Special Rapporteur to focus his first investigation on Rwanda – where a genocide was perpetrated – the implementation of a database of information is clearly necessary. An assessment of specialised NGOs permitted the identification of HURIDOCS (Geneva) to assist in the conceptualisation of the register. Written correspondence and contacts to this effect with M. Najib Ghali are in progress with the object of adapting from the HURIDOCS system a database accessible to the Secretariat of the Commission as well as to the Special Rapporteur.

The idea for a computerised database must take into consideration all the elements to establish the proof of an extra-judicial execution, the date and place of execution or disappearance, the details of the circumstances of death, those state actors, paramilitaries or individuals responsible for the execution. It is also useful to include the address of families or next of kin even if they do not live any longer in the country where the executions took place. All inquiry or other form of investigation, whether they come from judicial or police authorities of the country of origin, must figure in the register of extra-judicial executions. With collaboration with the Special Rapporteur of the UN, a teaching outline will be available soon and will be the object wide dissemination among concerned NGOs. The Secretariat of the ACHPR must be asked to assist in this respect and use will be made of email to coordinate and make more effective possible actions of the Special Rapporteur in relation to governments and NGOs.

(2) Collection of information

The computerisation must be coupled with assistance in the collection of information. Contacts made have permitted the Special Rapporteur to undertake this task with Amnesty International. A meeting is expected very soon. Moreover, several African NGOs have been requested to furnish useful information to the Special Rapporteur. Correspondence has been addressed to this effect to the UIDH (Union Interafricaine des Droits de l'Homme), la RADDHO (Rencontre Africaine pour la Défense des Droits de l'Homme), whom the Special Rapporteur found very willing. It is envisioned that the next step will be to appeal to other NGOs (International Observatory of Prisons, Penal Reform International, Africa Watch). Permanent contacts will be maintained with the ICJ (Geneva) and the Special Rapporteur will try to identify sources of credible information, above all on Rwanda and Burundi.

The UN Special Rapporteur on extra-judicial, summary or arbitrary executions, M. Bacre Waly Ndiaye has been solicited and has demonstrated great willingness to cooperate.

Several meetings have been held at Dakar with the goal of indicating the field of investigation and means of action. The collection of information also requires material proof which can only be obtained by visits in loci, discussions with victims' families or eyewitnesses. On site visits can only take place with the agreement of the governments concerned. A strategy for making contact will government organs will be made in cooperation with the Secretary of the Commission.

The Special Rapporteur has found, in the case Rwanda, much reticence on the part of witnesses to extra-judicial executions, who fear reprisals against their families or friends.

If in the first place the case of Rwanda and of Burundi will be a priority for the collection of information and creation of the computer database, as a matter of course all available information on extra-judicial executions in other African countries will be registered, especially for Liberia. To do so, and to collect more testimony, the reports submitted to the organs of the UN as well as the OAU will be taken into consideration.

(3) Publication of information

The periodic publication of information collected should not pose a particular problem in the case of Rwanda. Actually, numerous reported cases have also been submitted to the General Prosecutor of the Criminal Tribunal for Rwanda and are the object of much publicity on the part of NGOs and Rwanda refugees living abroad. However, the question of state responses is risky to pose explicitly, since they wish to maintain confidentiality, and the testimony of families must not in any way be publicized for fear of putting the witnesses in danger. The solution adopted, in order to avoid all polemics, will be to publish a bulletin on the eve of each session of the Commission, which will serve to inform African and international public opinion and will be distributed to the members of the Commission, to the different organs of the OAU, to international organs, to NGOs and to individuals concerned with the problem of extra-judicial executions.

The bulletin will be able thus to focus attention on particular situations of grave attacks on the right to life, and will render an account of the work of the Special Rapporteur and his contacts with African states and with national and international NGOs, without threatening the investigative procedures and without prejudging their result.

B. Methods of Work

The success of the mission of the Special Rapporteur on extra-judicial executions can be significant only if he is able, thanks to specific information, to convince states that the cases he submits are well-founded, and guarantee implementation of his recommendations, specifically for the punishment of executions and the compensation of victims. It is for this reason chiefly that the greatest efforts must be focused on the credibility of sources of information. In order to do this, the allegations of executions or threats of executions must be based on unquestionable criteria for the evaluation of facts concerning the victim and the exact circumstances in which the facts were perpetrated. With the object of being able to indivated allegations of extra-judicial executions and act upon them, the criteria fixed by the UN Special Rapporteur must be reiterated, specifically:

(a) information concerning the victim: family name, age six, place of residence or origin, profession or activity, if it has a relation to the alleged execution or threat of extra-judicial execution; all other pertinent information, likely to aid in the identification of a person (for example, the certificate of a prisoner, or the number of his passport or identity card);

(b) information concerning the alleged facts: date, place, description of the circumstances in which the events occurred, in the case of the violation of the right to life in relation to capital punishment, specific information on the insufficiencies in guaranteeing the right to have one's cause heard, the provisions of relevant laws, the sentence and the recourse available;

(c) information concerning the alleged authors of the crime, including the reasons they are suspected: their name if it is known; if they are members of the security forces, their rank, their duties, the unit or service to which they belong, etc.; if they are members of a civil defense group, a paramilitary force or others, the relations between these groups or the government forces (for example, cooperation with the state security forces, especially hierarchical relationship; cooperation or toleration of the state with regard to their activities, etc.);

(d) information concerning the measures taken by the victims or their families in particular any complaints they brought (and the organ before which such a complain was brought); if they have not brought any complaint, why not;

(e) information concerning the measures taken by the authorities to inquire into the alleged violations of the right to life, or the measures adopted to protect endangered persons and to prevent such acts in the future, specifically: if a complainant was brought, the action undertaken by the competent organ which was seized; progress of the investigation at the present time or when the allegation was presented; if the results of the investigation are not yet satisfactorily completed, reasons for this dissatisfaction;

(f) information concerning the source of allegations: name and complete address of the organisation or particulars in view of facilitating obtaining details on unclear points and measures taken.

The Special Rapporteur will be charged with inquiring into all serious allegations of extra-judicial, summary or arbitrary executions or threat of executions which are submitted to him, which will form entries in the register, whether they are committed by known persons or those whose identity could not be revealed. The principle objective of the Special Rapporteur must be to verify the facts contained therein, using facts provided to him by the responses of States, with the object of identifying those responsible for the extra-judicial execution and to determine the degree of implication of the authors or initiators of such acts.

An essential work will be undertaken with the governments of countries concerned with extra-judicial executions and the goal of bringing to light the circumstances of the executions, on the basis of the above-mentioned criteria and to encourage the initiation of national judicial procedures with the goal of indemnifying the families of victims and punishing those responsible for these crimes.

If the Special Rapporteur cannot, in any way, substitute for the police and judicial organs of the concerned country, nor play the role of detective, it nevertheless remains that he must evaluate the adequacy of the means of inquiry made by national organs and the credibility of the conclusions adopted by national investigative organs, and make a report to the Commission to summarize his opinion and recommendations. All means of investigation tending to inform the Special Rapporteur should be implemented, among them direct contact with families of victims and NGOs involved in the collection of information. The inquiries of the Special Rapporteur can take the form of visits to the relevant places, with cooperation and acceptance of the authorities of the country concerned; these could also during missions of the Commission and in connection with other international organs or in an independent fashion. After the recommendation of the ACHPR, independent and internationally recognised experts as well as NGOs having observer status can assist the Special Rapporteur in its missions or with other aspects of its mandate.

The observations of states concerned by extra-judicial executions as well as their responses on specific cases which are submitted to them must have all required attention. When a government responds that an inquiry has been opened on a particular case, the Special
Rapporteur must take into account the following elements:

- the character of the inquiry (judicial or administrative) and its objectivity;
- the independence, impartiality and competence of the organ charged with the inquiry;
- the applicable procedures, particularly those what concern the collection and evaluation of elements of proof;
- the rights of victims or their families or of their representatives;
- the decisions that can be taken and the punishments which can be inflicted following and inquiry;
- the possibilities for victims or their families to obtain reparations;
- that the delay in which the inquiry has been begun and completed is not excessive.

It is probably that in cases submitted to the attention of the Special Rapporteur, the information provided by governments and other sources will be contradictory. In these cases, after analysis and verification, the Special Rapporteur will present his recommendation to the Commission which will decide what action to take on the case.

In the case of a government remaining silent in the fact of allegations transmitted to it, the situation in question will be transcribed in the report which the Commission submits to the Conference of Heads of State and Government of the OAU. The investigations of the Special Rapporteur will be most effective if an early warning mechanism is put in place in cooperation with NGOs having observer status. An instant information network must thus be functioning between NGOs, the Secretariat of the Commission and the Special Rapporteur with the goal of preventing an imminent execution, which will require urgent intervention with the state concerned. It is intended in this regard to hold an inclusive meeting with the interested NGOs on this question, to fix the contours of the system and reflect on the ways and means of implementing it.

Members of the Commission will be constantly informed by the bi-monthly bulletin of the Secretariat and the information bulletin of the Special Rapporteur. They can for their part communicate all useful information on the countries which they supervise and will be called to contribute either through their own investigations or their presence if this becomes necessary for the proper execution of on-site visits.

If a situation of urgency becomes known on the eve of sessions of the Commission, it will be integrated into the agenda of the session and debated by the whole Commission. Measures of safeguard can be decided upon in conformity with the provisions of the African Charter on Human and Peoples' Rights.

Taking into account the irreversible damage caused by an extra-judicial, summary or arbitrary execution, adequate means of compensation must be investigated with the object of sustaining the families of victims. This is the specific and chief duty of the Special Rapporteur inaugurated by the ACHPR. The possibility of creating a trust fund for compensation has been debated by the Commission and will perhaps be debated in more detail in the future.

The Special Rapporteur on extra-judicial, summary or arbitrary executions believes for his party that the idea of creation of the trust fund presages the evolution which the Commission must recognised by the African Commission in the wake of the 10th Anniversary of the African Charter on Human and Peoples' Rights. The direct implication of the Commission, through the basis of the question of extra-judicial executions, will be the best proof of the maturity of the Commission and a strong indication of its commitment to engage, in the context of its mandate, in a serious and beneficial effort to safeguard the interests of victims of human rights violations.

The conditions of implementation, of administration, of modalities of compensation will be the subject of a joint reflection with interested NGOs and a report will be submitted for the advice of the Commission, which will pronounce on this question.

C. Fields of Investigation

Due to the civil wars and ethnic conflicts which grip it, the African continent finds itself in the front line of extra-judicial executions. In fact, conflict areas have seen, in addition to the regular armed forces, an increase in paramilitary groups which have systematically resorted to massacre of the innocent civilian population. The Special Rapporteur has decided, from the beginning of his mission, to dedicate himself as a matter of priority to populations vulnerable to becoming victims of extra-judicial executions. These are women, children, prisoners, human rights activists and demonstrators. Special attention will also be paid to ethnic minorities. This choice is likewise dictated by a concern for effectiveness, with the goal of avoiding all duplication of effort with the mission of the UN Special Rapporteur.

The Special Rapporteur will make an appeal for testimony, especially before the specialised NGOs and those having observer status before the Commission, which will be called to furnish all information concerning an attack or a threaten attack on the right to life of the above-mentioned populations.

The ACHPR has already decided that Rwanda and Burundi, to which must be added Zaire, in light of the events which are occurring in the east of that country and which have the consequence of worsening the situation in Rwanda, must be the object of the first investigations of the Special Rapporteur. However, NGOs may submit all information at their disposal concerning extra-judicial executions in other African countries, notably Sudan, Nigeria and Liberia.

D. Duration of Mandate

The 20th session must decide to extend the mandate of the Special Rapporteur for two years, that is to say, until October 1998.

E. The Report

To the present report will be joined a note on the progress of the preliminary inquiry on Rwanda and Burundi which will be submitted for the advice of the Commission in the course of the 21st session (April 1997). If the Commission agrees, the report can be integrated into the annual activity report presented to the Summit of Heads of State and Government of the OAU.

IV. Budget

The 19th session of the Commission has approved the budget approved by the Special Rapporteur in collaboration with the Secretariat of the Commission. Thanks to person contacts of the Special Rapporteur with the North-South Centre of the Council of Europe, the Swiss Directorate of Cooperation for Development and Humanitarian Aide furnished the means to execute the first phase of the budget, to wit:

– a computer, a photocopier and accessories	\$7,000
– postage, telephone, fax, documentation, temporary secretariat, register and various expenses	\$9,000

For the second phase, the provisional budget is:

– visits and inquiries in situ	\$25,000
– running expenses, keeping of the register, telephone, fax, temporary secretariat	\$16,000

Annex
Progress of the Report on Extra-judicial, Summary or Arbitrary Executions: Rwanda, Burundi

The Special Rapporteur on extra-judicial, summary and arbitrary executions several months ago began to prepare his report on Rwanda and Burundi.

His work consisted, first, of the presentation of his mandate to potential partners. Each time it was possible, whether at the Lisbon Forum or the Congress of the UIDH in Dakar, the mission, the mandate of the Special Rapporteur was conveyed to all NGOs present and they were asked to support, above all with information, the work of the Special Rapporteur. Next, correspondence was initiated with Amnesty, the UIDH, and RADDHO. Amnesty sent two reports in August 1996 (index AI: AFR 47/13/96 – index AI: AFR 16/21/96), the two other organisation promised a close collaboration with the Special Rapporteur. In the meanwhile, contacts and meetings were organised the Rwandan refugees in Brussels, Abidjan, Bukav (Zaire) and Dakar. The following represented Rwanda:

- the government of Rwanda in exile (Ministry of Justice)
- the community of Rwandan refugees in Central Africa
- the Forces of Resistance for Democracy
- the Assembly for the return of refugees and Democracy in Rwanda
- the Association "Justice and Peace" for Reconciliation in Rwanda (AJPR)

For Burundi:

- representatives of the Giheta commune, Province Gitaga
- Parti Sahwanga Frodebu, Front pour la Démocratie au Burundi
- M. Norbert Ndihokubwayo, Deputy of the National Assembly of Burundi (dissolved after the coup d'etat of 25/96)

Lists of names of several dozen individuals extra-judicially executed were submitted to the attention of the Special Rapporteur of which was simultaneously also addressed to the Prosecutor General of the Criminal Court for Rwanda. It must be recognised, as a preliminary matter, that these lists were provided, for Rwanda as well as for Burundi, by one of the two parties to the conflict. This does not detract from the gravity of the facts, but it is imperative that the inquires into these executions be made with the greatest seriousness.

In order to do so, the Special Rapporteur has suggested that the Secretariat enter quickly into contact with the head of the Criminal Tribunal for Rwanda with the goal of informing it of the mandate of the Special Rapporteur and inviting it to enter into a close cooperation. In the second place, the Special Rapporteur has proposed a joint meeting with the ICJ, Amnesty, the UIDH and RADDHO in order to list the cases of executions in the context of the mandate. This action will permit the seizure of the government of Rwanda (and secondarily, Zaire) with the cases of extra-judicial executions thus catalogued and to organise, if need be, a mission to these two countries.

ANNEX VII

Report of the Special Rapporteur on Prisons and Conditions of Detention to the 21st Session of the African Commission on Human and peoples' Rights 15–14 April 1997 Nouakchott, Mauritania

Introduction

In compliance with the decision of the Commission at its 20th Ordinary Session held at Grand Bay, Mauritius from 21–31 October 1996, the Terms of Reference of the Special Rapporteur on the above subject have been revised, and a copy of the revised text is attached to this report as appendix I.

The Report comprises (i) Programme of Activities for the period January 1997–1999; (ii) Intersessional activities covering the 20th and 21st Sessions; and (iii) a budget for the period stated in (i) above.

It was thought neater to fix the commencement of the work of the Special Rapporteur from January 1997 since the intervening period from the time of his appointment by the Commission and January 1997 not much could be done because of the imperative need to attend to work which had piled up at home during the period of the 20th Session in Mauritius and the holidays in December.

I. Programme of Activities: January 1997 to January 1999

The above period is divided into intersessional periods with the main activities planned to be undertaken as follows:

(i) January to April 1997: Consultation on Revision of Terms of Reference and method of work. Planning and execution of first country visit.
(ii) May to October 1997: Senegal or Mali.
(iii) November 1997 to March 1998: Uganda or Mauritius.
(iv) May to October 1998: Mozambique or Sao Tomé and Principe.
(v) November 1998 to January 1999: Tunisia and South Africa.

The feasibility of a visit to a Central African country will be closely studied, and if positive undertaken.

In drawing up this programme account was taken of the importance of covering the main geographical areas of Africa, the main languages of the OAU, big and small countries as well as island and mainland countries.

II. Intersessional Activities: 20th to 21st Sessions.

With a view to thinking through the Terms of Reference of the Special Rapporteur, his mode of operation, his relationship with inter-governmental agencies, non-governmental organisations and related matters, the Chairman of Penal Reform International, Mr. Ahmed Othmani, the Secretary of the Commission, Mr. Germain Baricako and I had a consultation in Banjul, the Gambia from 8–12 January 1997. The consultation found it desirable for a country visit to be undertaken before the 21st Session.

Factors which were to be taken into account in selecting the first country were Language (ease in communication), likelihood of co-operation from both government and non-governmental organisations, good road network which will not make internal travel difficult, and similar matters.

Assurance was given that Penal Reform International (PRI) would support the work of the Special Rapporteur (SR) as far as possible. Towards this end, PRI would endeavour to mobilise resources at local and international levels for the work of the SR. In particular, PRI will be able to offer assistance in three areas:

(i) alternatives to imprisonment;
(ii) prison conditions and rehabilitation; and
(iii) the strengthening of regional, sub-regional and local NGOs working on prisons.

PRI will make available to the SR relevant data and other material.

The Secretary to the Commission gave assurance of Secretarial support to the work of the SR.

Following from this consultation, the SR selected Zimbabwe for his first country-visit. That arrangements for the visit were completed within a short time and the visit undertaken from 23 February to 3 March was due to the indefatigable work of Mr. Ahmed Othmani and the great co-operation and assistance of the Commissioner of Zimbabwe Prisons, Mr. L. Chigwida as well as other officials with responsibility for Prisons in Zimbabwe. To them all I am extremely grateful.

A separate report on this visit is attached to the present Report as Appendix II.

I took advantage of my participation in a conference on the Future of the United Nations System of Human Rights in Cambridge University, England 21–23 March to have consultation in Geneva with the United Nations Special Rapporteur on Torture, Prof. Nigel Rodley on his method of work. To Mr. Ahmed Othmani who facilitated this encounter, and the Association for the Prevention of Torture headed by Claudine Haenni which nicely arranged the Geneva end of my mission, I am very grateful.

BUDGET

(1) *Equipment*	
Computer, printer and accessories	$5,000
(2) *Secretarial support*	
Emolument	$2,400
Transport	$1,200
Telephone, fax, correspondence etc.	$3,000
Publication of Report	$2,000

(3) *Travel and related expenses*	$25,000
(4) *Miscellaneous*	$1,400
	$40,000

Submitted by Prof. E. V. O. Dankwa, Special Rapporteur on Prisons and Conditions of Detention in Africa.

TERMS OF REFERENCE FOR THE SPECIAL RAPPORTEUR ON PRISONS AND CONDITIONS OF DETENTION IN AFRICA

Mandate

1. In accordance with its mandate under Article 45 of the African Charter on Human and Peoples' Rights (the Charter) the African Commission on Human and Peoples' Rights (The Commission) hereby establishes the position of Special Rapporteur on Prisons and Conditions of Detention in Africa.

2. The Special Rapporteur is empowered to examine the situation of persons deprived of their liberty within the territories of States Parties to the African Charter on Human and Peoples' Rights.

Methods of Work

The Special Rapporteur shall

3.1 examine the State of the prisons and conditions of detention in Africa and make recommendations with a view to improving them;

3.2 advocate adherence to the Charter and international human rights norms and standards concerning the rights and conditions of persons deprived of their liberty, examine the relevant national law and regulations in the respective States Parties as well as their implementation and make appropriate recommendations on their conformity with the Charter and with international law and standards;

3.3 at the request of the Commission, make recommendations to it as regards communications filed by individuals who have been deprived of their liberty, their families, representatives, by NGOs or other concerned persons or institutions;

3.4 propose appropriate urgent action.

4. The Special Rapporteur shall conduct studies into conditions or situations contributing to human rights violations of prisons deprived of their liberty and recommend preventive measures. The Special Rapporteur shall co-ordinate activities with other relevant Special Rapporteurs and Working Groups of the African Commission and United Nations.

5. The Special Rapporteur shall submit an annual report to the Commission. The report shall be published and widely disseminated in accordance with the relevant provisions of the Charter.

Duration of Mandate

6. This mandate will last for an initial period of two years which may be renewed by the Commission.

7. The Special Rapporteur shall seek and receive information from States Parties to the Charter, individuals, national and international organisations and institutions as well as other relevant bodies on cases or situations which fall within the scope of the mandate described above.

8. In order to discharge his mandate effectively the Special Rapporteur should be given all the necessary assistance and co-operation to carry out on-site visits and receive information from individuals who have been deprived of their liberty, their families or representatives, form governmental or non-governmental organisations and individuals.

9. The Special Rapporteur shall seek co-operation with State Parties and assurance from the latter that persons, organisations, or institutions rendering co-operation or providing information to the special rapporteur shall not be prejudiced thereby.

10. Every effort will be made to place at the disposal of the Special Rapporteur resources to carry out his/her mandate.

Mandate priorities for the First Two years

11. In order to establish his/her mandate in the first two years, the Special Rapporteur shall focus on the following activities, while paying special attention to problems related to gender:

11.1 Make available an *evaluation of the conditions of detention in Africa* highlighting the main problem areas.

This should include areas such as: prison conditions; health issues; arbitrary or extra-legal detention or imprisonment; treatment of people deprived of their liberty; and conditions of detention of especially vulnerable groups such as: refugees, persons suffering from physical or mental disabilities, or children.

The Special Rapporteur shall draw on information and data provided by the States.

11.2 Make *specific recommendations* with a view to improving the prisons and conditions of detention in Africa, as well as reflect on possible early warning mechanisms in order to avoid disasters and epidemics in places of detention.

11.3 Promote *the implementation of the Kampala Declaration.*

11.4 *Propose revised terms of reference if necessary*, at the end of this two year period to the African Commission and an overall programme for the following stage.

REPORT ON VISIT TO PRISONS IN ZIMBABWE BY PROFESSOR E. V. O. DANKWA, SPECIAL RAPPORTEUR ON PRISONS AND CONDITIONS OF DETENTION

Introduction and Acknowledgement

At its 20th Ordinary Session which was held at Grand Bay, Mauritius from 21–31 October 1996 the African Commission on Human and Peoples' Rights appointed me as Special Rapporteur on the above subject and charged me with the responsibility of revising the Draft Terms of Reference of my office which was considered by the Commission at that session. Taken the view that a report to the 21st Session on my activities over 6 months which consisted of only procedural matters should be less that adequate. I decided to study the prison regime and related matters of one of the State Parties to the African Charter on Human and Peoples' Rights.

My decision for so doing stemmed from the fact that whatever controversy there might be on the text to be revised the study of prisons as contemplated by me would be incontrovertible function of my office. Whatever portions which are exercised from the original draft or amended, the study of prisons will remain.

I was further fortified in my decision by the unanimous decision of a Consultation on the Draft Terms of Reference and matters connected therewith held in Banjul, The Gambia from 8–12 January 1996 that a visit to the prisons of a country was a course of action worthy of pursuit.

Being the first visit, and having to be planned within a short time, I took into account, in the selection of country, factors such as language with which I am familiar, the likelihood of agreement from the relevant officials for my visit, the co-operation I was likely to get from the state officials and NGOs working in the area of my study as well as good communication and road network which would make possible the accomplishment of much within a relatively short time.

Mr. L. Chigwida, Commissioner of Prisons, Zimbabwe and other officials were ready to receive me within a very short time of notification of my interest in visiting prisons in Zimbabwe. They extended to me every assistance I needed, and thus eased the burden of my task considerably.

As he had done during my Promotional Visit to Zimbabwe in February 1995, the Attorney-General, Mr. P.A. Chiwamasa found time to have discussions with me, on the subject of my instant visit in particular and the Commission in general. Mr. Y. Omerjee, Secretary for Justice, Legal and Parliamentary Affairs briefed me about the open nature of Zimbabwean prisons especially its prisons regime including the efforts being made to sustain a humane penal system. My understanding of the subject of my study was broadened by meetings with J. G. Mutombikwa; Mr. Mhiribidi, Director of Social Welfare and one of his deputies Mrs. Dhiembeu who has responsibility for child welfare. The Deputy Commissioner of Prisons, Washington Chimbeza and Mr. T. Mahema, Chief Magistrate contributed in no small measure in this direction.

Generally non-governmental organisations provide additional perspectives to matters within their domain, and I found those in Zimbabwe no exception. Indeed it was my fortune to have found NGOs working in the area of penal reform. But I am indebted to Mr. Chigwida, Commissioner of Prisons, who scheduled meetings with the NGOs for me at which there were no government. I acknowledge the assistance I had from Samuel Myanibo and Ernest Maigwara, Chief Executive and President respectively of Zimbabwe Association for Crime Prevention and Rehabilitation of the Offender; Peter Mandianike, Executive Director of Prison Fellowship; and John Reid Rowland, Chief Legal Adviser of Legal Resources Foundation. To Officials of Harare, Chikurubi and Kadama Prisons and many others I express my gratitude.

Mr. Ahmed Othmani, Chairman of Penal Reform relied on his knowledge of personnel in the penal system in Zimbabwe to set in motion the planning of my visit, and I am extremely grateful to him.

Charter Basis for Appointment of Special Rapporteur

That prisons in Africa as elsewhere have serious problems was put beyond dispute by the First All-African Conference On Prison Conditions which was held in Kampala, Uganda from 19–21 September 1996. Restriction of the Liberty of the individual and problems arising out of it or related to it are par excellence human rights problems. Studies and researchers such as a Special Rapporteur will undertake, will contribute towards the solution of the problems. Therein lies the justification for the appointment to my present office, and Article 45.1(a) provides a legal basis, for the creation of the Office of Special Rapporteur on Prisons and Conditions of Detention:

"The functions of the Commission shall be:
1. To promote Human and Peoples' Rights and in particular:
(a) To collect documents, undertake studies and researches on African problems in the field of human and peoples' rights."

The Prisons

Zimbabwe has 40 prisons, and "the official holding capacity of all the prisons is 16,000" (E. Mupfiga, Characteristics of Criminal Offenders in Zimbabwe During 1991 (1993) p. 4). A recent amnesty reduced a prison population of 22,000 to 16,000, but the rising trend of criminality makes overcrowding an ever present problem for the 11 million people of Zimbabwe including 4,000 prison officers 300 of which are professionals such as doctors, nurses and artisans.

Consistent with a universal trend, female prisoners in Zimbabwe with their low figure have lesser fear of overcrowding. Although females constitute 51% of the national population they account for only 5% of the total prison population.

Indeed at Kadoma Prisons a small female section with a holding capacity for 30 had 17 prisoners with 8 officers. However this is to be contrasted with Chikurubi Female

Prison which had 375 inmates although its capacity is 287; and in 1991, Mupfiga calculated that female offenders admitted into prisons represented 8.6% of total admission (op. cit. p. 7). In terms of space, male prisoners at Kadoma Prisons had more room that planned for: 564 occupied space constructed for 670. They also had a staff of 160.

As partial solution to the problem of overcrowding a former military barracks with a holding capacity of 6,000 has been acquired.

Remand

Out of the total of 16,000 prisoners 4,500 of them were on remand. 4,000 of the latter figure may generally be on remand for 6 months, and the remaining 500 beyond six months. At Kadoma Prison while some prisoners on remand may stay for less that one year, others stay for 12 or 18 to 24 months. It was said that screening by psychiatrists to determine the mental state of entrants is not fast enough and it accounted in part for long demand; delay by the police and prosecutors being the other major contributory factor.

At Chikurubi Female Prison and Kadoma Farm Prison, prisoners on remand were distinguishable from those serving sentences by their uniform, and at the latter by sitting arrangement when I met and talked to them in a Hall about my assignment.

Labour, Trade and Skills

Harare Prison has an impressive set of workshops which provide training and working at known trades by the inmates. A mechanic section gives training in engine-tune ups, engine overhauls, suspension, steering overhauls, gearbox repairs, brakes overhaul, wheels, clutch overhauls, auto-electric and general service. A Prison Officer who is a qualified mechanic, and was assisted by five other officers with similar qualifications, was in charge of the mechanics section. Understudying the officers were 37 prisoners. Most of these had no previous knowledge of mechanics, but, as part of the scheme they would be trade-tested by the Ministry of Higher Education and the successful ones issued with certificates which would enhance their prospects of employment, or give them the confidence to start their own small trade.

Under a welding section were moulding and forging sectors. There were also a panel beating and spay painting section.

A carpentry section whose supply of logs comes from prison farms make filing shelves for the Ministry of Justice, and repair furniture of the Prisons, Army and Ministry of Justice. Corner stands, beds and display cabinets, chairs and doors are also made at this carpentry. 74 prisoners in the carpentry had 2 prison officers as supervisors. A prisoner with experience in carpentry shared his skills with his mates.

Television sets, wireless and iron were repaired at an electrical repair wing of the workshop.

Carving engaged the attention of some prisoners.

A large tailoring shop with 106 machines had 170 prisoners working in it. Some of the items sown were male and female prison Officers' uniforms, gowns for judges, magistrates and prosecutors. Others were prisoners' uniforms, computer covers, hospital theatre towels and nurse aid uniforms. The skills imparted to the prisoners went beyond sewing to repair of sewing machines.

A book binding section had upholstery and cobblers wings. Pneumatic tyres served as material for making sandals for prisoners. 75 prisoners worked under 2 officers with qualification in the trades being learnt. As regards the binding of books, the Ministry of Education supplied materials with which books of government schools were bound.

Built in 1928 the workshops must have served over the years to make the Harare Prison not only a place of detention but a setting where some appreciable measure of rehabilitation of the offender could be expected of those who worked there.

Chikurubi Female Prison which was established in 1967 has set up projects for the training of the inmates through on a small scale. Training is given in typing from the intermediate to the advanced stages. Computer literacy is also encouraged. Prison Officers also can take advantage of these projects to either learn or improve their skills in the above areas.

A sewing section was under two officers, and uniforms of female officers were sown here.

A knitting section produced jerseys, some of which were said to be worn by the inmates during the winter months of May–August.

It is noted that a clinic is attached to the female wing while the Chikurubi maximum security prison which began operation in 1979 has a hospital attached to it.

Chikurubi Farm Prison

Under the command of Superintendent Mutongi, a farm manager oversees dairy animals and piggery which provide food for inmates of Zimbabwe prisons.

Unlike the prisons at Chikurubi and in Harare, Kadoma Prison was built after the independence of Zimbabwe. With 122 hectares of arable land reduced under cultivation, farming is the main activity at this prison. It has also a diary of 70. The excess produce of the farm is made available to other prisons. Maize is the main crop grown here, but an orchard and a vegetable garden make a balance diet attainable.

Grass on the compound of government institutions is cleared by the inmates.

Young Offenders and Juveniles

Young Offenders (13–25 years old) who are sentenced to 3 or more years of imprisonment are sent to a prison at Gweriu called "Whawha Prison" where they are trained in skills such as welding, carpentry and mechanics. They are also encouraged to take the "O" and "A" Levels examination with the assistance of "teacher-prisoners".

In Zimbabwe juveniles are under the jurisdiction of the Social Welfare Department. Within this Department, a Deputy Director is responsible for child welfare. The Department has facilities for detention of juveniles before trial. Juveniles may appear before both criminal and juvenile courts but in the case of the former the hearing may be without the public. After trial juveniles are placed either in homes or reformatory. There are 8 government homes which accept the care of children while NGOs and Churches have 40. The latter are concentrated in the urban areas. Each of the 10 administrative provinces has at least one home. There are about 3,000 juveniles in all the institutions.

If a child under 18 is arrested, the Police refer the case to the Department of Social Welfare if investigation and custody when necessary. Reports on the child compiled by the Department help the court decide on an appropriate sentence for him/her. The 200 officers of the Department throughout the country are all probation officers. The release of the child to the parents may be recommended by the
Department get involved with the parents in the supervision of the child. One of the recommendations may be the caning of the child.

Juveniles are detained for a maximum of 3 years during which they will be educated. Those who are beyond the control of social workers are kept in a juvenile wing of prisons. Such must have been the case of 7 convicted juveniles who were at Kadoma Prison.

Community service currently in operation in Zimbabwe has not been extended to cover juveniles although the Social Welfare Department is involved in the community service with magistrates.

Community based care of children has been tried in Zimbabwe. 11,000 children have been identified within this context as requiring care. A prominent category among them are orphans. In a district in Mashingo Province the Department of Social Welfare tried to revive the community's interest in looking after children in need.

Community Service

Concerned about overcrowding in prisons resort was had to community service. It started in 1994, and a success rate of 90% is claimed, and the scheme is catching on. Opening the High Court Session in February 1997, Chidyausiku J. exhorted judges to impose non-custodial sentence as far as possible (*Sunday Mail*, 22 February 1997).

A National Committee on Community Service first constituted in 1992 by the Minister of Justice originally had representatives from a number of ministries. Presently it consists of a High Court Judge, the Commissioner of Prisons, a representative of ODA, Chief Magistrate of the biggest Magisterial district and representatives from the Ministry of Social Welfare, Police and non-governmental organisations such as Prison Fellowship, Zimbabwe Association for Crime Prevention and Rehabilitation of the Offender and Legal Resource Foundation.

The National Committee on Community Service meets once a month on the last Thursday in each month.

At a lower level a District Committee composed of the local or provincial magistrate, representatives of the Police, Prison, Local NGOs, Civil leaders as well as representatives from the Ministry of Social Welfare supervise the service.

Funded for the first 18 months with the funds from the European Union, ODA provided the funds for a similar period thereafter with effect from August 1997 the Government of Zimbabwe will take it over.

Community Service operates throughout the country, and relies for its successful implementation mainly on volunteers. A mark of its success is the request form its study from diverse countries like Swaziland, Lesotho, Malawi, Zambia, Kenya, Cambodia and the government of Trinidad.

New guidelines have been issued, in consultation with the judiciary as in the case of earlier ones to guide the courts in administering the scheme. There are guidelines for supervisors also. A training programme has been carried out for supervisors with a view to achieving uniformity of treatment of offenders who are sentenced to Community Service.

I visited two locations where Community Service was being performed.

Rutsanan Clinic

Located about 15 kilometres from Harare, the Sisters on charge of the clinic stated that first offenders are sentenced by the court to 60, 180 or 300 hours. An offender who reports for community service in counselled by the Sisters under whose supervision he/she signs for the hours done each day. One such offender was seen working in a garden of the clinic at the time of my visit.

As far as possible the skills of the offender are utilised: an electrician or painter will be assigned jobs in their areas of expertise. 18 offenders had been sent to the clinic of which number 3 defaulted.

Glenview Clinic

It is located about 20 kilometres from Harare. Offenders sent here work either 3 weekdays or 2 weekends.

Finally I attended a meeting of the National Committee which reviewed the past and looked into the future after foreign support ceases.

Training

Chikurubi Training Depot

It offers in-service training. Initial training, promotion and refresher courses.

Conversion Courses are also run by the depot. They enable technicians to join the Prison Service at the appropriate level.

The Depot also trains dogs for use within the prison service. Attached to the depot is an 800 acre maize farm which is under the headship of a female officer. 900 male prisoners work under the female prison officer's supervision.

Legal resources Foundation has been involved in training some Police Officers at the request of the Commissioner of Prisons. A Training of Trainees 5–10 May 1996.

It was limited to 20 senior Police Officers drawn from all over Zimbabwe because of limited financial resources. Three objectives were to be met by the Workshop (training): (a) human rights education; (b) trainees were to be equipped to train others; and (c) highlighting the rights of specific groups of prisoners – juveniles, women and the elderly.

Six months after the workshop an evaluation exercise was undertaken to assess the impact of the training.

A second workshop with in-depth training of techniques of human rights education and substantive human rights involving mere prison officers is being planned.

Prison Fellowship International

This NGO facilitates visits of relatives to prisoners. It also has an economic outreach, GEO-GLOBAL ECONOMIC OUTREACH. Under this scheme 104 families have been given loans. The scheme which was embarked upon on discovery of the plight of families of prisoners has been a success. In terms of repayment of loans, rate of over 80%.

Zimbabwe Association for Crime Prevention and Rehabilitation (ZACRO)

It has been registered as a charitable institution in 1968 with branches throughout the country. ZACRO works closely with the Police and Prison administration. It aims at the rehabilitation of the offender and the prevention of crime. ZACRO involves the community and individuals on the pursuit of its objectives. It also targets the youth, and organises street boys to sew and learn how to make soap. Thereafter they are placed in commercial entities. Those taught these trades are either ex- or non-offenders

In schools, ZACRO is concerned about drug and alcohol abuse.

ZACRO passes on to the governments complaints of prisoners. A noticeable change for the better resulted from making government aware of maltreatment by prison officers of those awaiting trial as well as convicts.

Poor quality plates were also replaced about five years ago when ZACRO brought it to the government's attention. ZACRO also claimed some credit for the extension of vocational training from male to female prisoners.

"Prison Talk, the Law versus the Practice": A Report on Prison Conditions in Zimbabwe by the Catholic Mission for Justice and Peace in Zimbabwe

I came across this work in the course of my study. Although undated, since work published in 1992 is cited in it, the report must have been prepared in or after that date.

A very frank and critical report, it states the prison population as 22,600 at the time of writing. It lists 41 prisons and refers to Bulawayo Prison to underscore the problem of overcrowding. Built to accommodate 445 prisoners on the occasion of the author(s) visit there were 758 inmates.

Problems

Officials of the Prison Service found overcrowding to be a problem. Consequently a judicial sentencing conference was held in 1996 to consider alternatives to imprisonment. The perennial problem of limited financial resources was also stated. While food and toiletries were available, replacement of equipment on workshops and the building of more workshops are beyond the means of the Prisons, a direct result of the financial constraints on the nation.

Sources outside official circles viewed the staying of children with their mothers throughout their sentences in prison as a serious problem. The problem is exacerbated by the fact that the immediate family are reluctant to take on the children of a convict, even is closely related to them. Some were if the view that the training of prison officers was too security oriented, and that the training should concentrate on rehabilitation. The Prison Administration Manual has to be revised for more humane provisions. Illustration of a regulation that ought to be amended for the better is the 20 minutes per month visit a prisoner is entitled to, or the one page letter per month which is the limit for a prisoner. Attempts should also be made to replicate the workshop at Harare at other prisons. To encourage society to accept convicts who are released, and to illustrate the rehabilitation of prisoners can be achieved, the Prison Administration should begin to employ ex-convicts who have acquired skills in prison.

Conclusion

For me to be able to visit the prisons in Zimbabwe that I did at a very short notice and for the author(s) of "Prisons Talks" etc. to have access to all the prisons on Zimbabwe speak volumes of the openness of the Prison regime in Zimbabwe.

The novel institution of community service which by the end of 1996 had seen 12,000 convicts going through the scheme will no doubt have an impact on overcrowding in prisons. That others beyond Africa, in Asia and the Americas will look to Zimbabwe for reform of their penal system is reason for satisfaction and justifiable pride. Equally co-operation between governmental organisations towards a more humane prison regime is worthy of commendation. For this very reason, criticisms from the later must be takes seriously.

Recommendations

1. The majority of the inmates (about 97% or so) were decently attired. A minority who nevertheless should not be dismissed were found in torn prison garments. That attempts were not made to spirit them out of sight is evidence that there was no stage management.

2. The observations and criticisms contained in the "Prisons Talks" should receive sober reflection, and wherever necessary remedial measures should be adopted.

3. The importance of reducing the period for which prisoners are remanded should be constantly raised by the Prison Service with the Police and Prosecution authorities with a view to the latter acting to achieve this goal.

4. The decision to revise the standing orders of the Commissioner of Prisons should be carried out as has been done in the case of Prison Act, Chapter 7:11 (revised edition 1996).

5. Human Rights Training of Prison officers which was organised in May 1996 and evaluated after six months should be continued as planned.

6. Supervision of the community Service Scheme should not be relaxed for the danger of increase in criminality is real if it is perceived by the public as a very soft option to fine or custodial sentence.

7. The prison service should help orient public attitude to accepting that rehabilitation does occur in the prisons of Zimbabwe by employing ex-convicts whenever there is the opportunity to do so.

8. The Department of Social Welfare should consider the appropriateness of extending community service to juveniles.

9.

(i) While welcoming the sentencing conference involving the judiciary in August 1996, a future conference involving the judiciary, police and prisons will advance further the redressing of the concerns which led to the former conference, and should therefore be seriously pursued.

(ii) Towards the same end a conference of the Bench, Bar, Faculty of Law, Police and Prison is likely to serve similar end, and the Prison Service is encouraged to take the initiative to bring it to fruition.

ANNEX VIII

Report on the Mission of Good Offices to Senegal of the African Commission on Human and Peoples' Rights (1–7 June 1996)

I. Objective

On 12 October 1992, the African Commission on Human and Peoples' Rights was seized by an NGO called, "Rencontre Africaine Pour la Défense des droits de l'Homme" (RADDHO). In its communication, brought against Senegal, it described grave and massive violations of human rights at Kaguitt, in Casamance, following a clash between the Senegalese army and the rebels of the Mouvement des Forces Démocratiques de la Casamance (MFDC).

At its 17th, 18th and 19th ordinary sessions, the African Commission decided to send a mission of good offices to Senegal, with a view to contributing to the amicable resolution of the conflict.

With the aim of attaining this objective by the appropriate ways and means, the mission went to Senegal, collected all useful information and interviewed the principle parties likely to bring significant clarification to the events of Casamance.

II. Duration and Composition of the Mission

Scheduled 1–7 June 1996 and conducted by Professor Isaac Nguema, Chairman of the African Commission, the mission also comprised Dr. Vera Valentina de Melo Duarte Martins and Mr. Marcel Buzingo, member and legal adviser to the Commission, respectively.

III. Implementation of the Mission

The mission took place at two locations: Dakar and Ziguinchor (Casamance).

A. Dakar

The mission was received for a meeting with:

(1) The President of the Constitutional Council, Mr. Yousoupha Ndiaye; the Guardian of Seals and Minister of Justice, Mr. Jacques Baudin; the General Secretary of Government, Mr. Ousmane Ndiaye; the Diplomatic Counsellor of the President of the Republic, Mr. Amadou Diop; the Legal Adviser to the President of the Republic, Mr. Yann Aguila.

(2) The Prime Minister, His Excellency Mr. Habib Thiam, who gathered for the occasion the Guardian of Seals and Minister of Justice, the General Secretary of Government, the Diplomatic and Legal Counsellors to the President of the Republic, and the Special Counsellor Minister of the Prime Minister, Mr. Daniel Kabou.

(3) The delegation of the Commission participated in a working session presided over by the Guardian of Seals and Minister of Justice, which encompassed the Minister of the Interior, Mr. Abdouahmane Sow; the Minister of the Armed Forces, Mr. Cheikh Hamidou Kane; Professor Assane Seck, President of the National Committee for the Administration of Peace in Casamance; the General Secretary of Government, Mr. Ousmane Ndiaye; Mr. B. Diallo, Diplomatic and Legal Counsellor to the President of the Republic.

(4) The Commission also had interviews with the following persons: The Honorable Deputy Landing Savane, leader of the opposition; His Eminence Cardinal Yacinthe Thiandoim; His Excellency Ambassador Moustapha Cissé, General Kaliph of Pire, Personal Counsellor of the Head of State for islamic affairs.

B. Ziguinchor

The delegation of the Commission was received and interviewed by:

(1) Mr. Famara Ibrahima Sagna, former Minister, President of the Economic and Social Council.
(2) The Regional Governor, Mr. Mame Sarr, accompanied by Colonel Boissy, responsible for the regional arm for the Administration of Peace in Casamance.
(3) Mr. Sidy Badji, former commander of the North Front, who was accompanied notably by two of his lieutenants from the bush.
(4) Father Diamacoune, accompanied by several of his followers, of whom some were former rebels
(5) Monseigneur Maixent-Coly, Bishop of the diocese of Ziguinchor.
(6) Two priests who are members of the clerical committee established to restore peace to Casamance.

IV. The Facts

(1) The Origin of the Conflict

Without going into details, the Casamance was occupied first by the Portuguese, who took possession of Ziguinchor in 1845. They ceded the territory to France forty years later, on 12 May 1886, in exchange for the north of Guinea-Bissau, as well as fishing rights at Terre-Neuve.

Covering 28,350 square km, one seventh of the area of Senegal, Casamance is situated between Gambia in the north, Guinea-Bissau and Guinea Conakry to the south, the Atlantic Ocean to the west and the Kouloutou, a tributary to the Gambia River, to the east.

Thus, it is isolated from the rest of Senegal.

In the course of its history, Casamance developed a cultural identity especially marked by resistance to different colonisations and foreign cultures.

In the economic sphere, the inhabitants of Casamance have traditionally practiced an economy of subsistence essentially based on fishing and agriculture.

Evoking notably arguments which he considers founded on the history of the territory, Father Diamacoune has not hesitated to affirm the existence of historical documents tending to justify the calling of Casamance to independence.

According to him, the administration of Casamance was conferred on Senegal by France, from which comes the following formulation used by this priest: "Casamance with Senegal, but not in Senegal".

(2) The Evolution of the Conflict

At demonstrations organised in December 1982 in Ziguinchor at the instigation of movements desirous of expressing the frustrations felt in Casamance to the central government (but not without separatist ulterior motives) the forces maintaining public order intervened when certain demonstrations lowered the national flag from public buildings.

Skirmishes followed, and further, loss of human life on both sides, which set off the beginning of violence and the joining with the rebels of separatist groups under the leadership of the Movement of Democratic Forces of Casamance (MFDC) having at its head Father Diamacoune as spiritual leader.

The conflict evolved unevenly, marked sometimes by grave violations of human rights by one side as by the other, sometimes by cessation of hostilities following cease-fires.

In this regard it is necessary to emphasize the unmistakable will of the Senegalese head of state, President Abdou Diouf, concerned to resolute the conflict through negotiated means, not by arms, while remaining first on respect for national unity and territorial integrity.

The following initiatives to this effect have been revealed:

- the creation of a National Committee for the Administration of Peace in Casamance;
- the liberation of a good number of persons arrested due to the conflict;
- the prosecution of elements of the army accused of having violated human rights;
- the adoption of the law bringing code of the local communities.

Further, it is important to consider as an initiative in the search for peace the unilateral cease-fire declaration of 3 December 1995, made by Father Augustin Diamacoune Senghor which declares itself "given for eternity, to place in the world truth, charity, justice and peace".

Even more, it is important to note that certain former warriors, such as Sidy Badji, commander of the North Front of the MFDC, have deposited their arms after having realised that the revelations of Father Diamacoune relating to the calling of Casamance to independence are without foundation.

This accords furthermore with the point of view contained in the CHARPY report made following the arbitration asked of France, in its capacity as former colonial ruler of Senegal.

According to the report, rejected by the separatist camp, "Casamance did not exist as an independent territory before colonisation".

In any case, this conclusion has not dampened the conviction of Father Diamacoune for whom "the independence of Casamance is a fixed idea" to use the words of a high personality who knows him well. Still less has it deterred the deputy Secretary General of the MFDC, Monsieur Nkruma Sane, who is presently a refugee in France. He has likewise persisted in developing the separatist platform, while opposing the declaration of unilateral cease-fire of 3 December 1995.

For their part, although they have responded favorably to this declaration of Father Diamacoune, the rebels of the South Front still remain in the bush, awaiting the outcome of these events.

(3) Present Situation

The present situation is characterised by four principal elements:

(1) The will affirmed by both sides to sit down at the negotiation table.
(2) This will is manifested by the departure abroad of elements of the separatist movement following the decision of the Senegalese government to grant their passports so that they might go meet with their activists exiled in Europe, in order to determine the object and place of the negotiations to be undertaken with the government.
(3) The mutual suspicion of each party as to the sincerity of the other.
    For its part, the government of Senegal fears being deprived of the present of the principle interlocutor, if Father Diamacoune leaves the country and remains abroad, like others who have left and have not yet returned.
    For its part, the MFDC does not believe the intention of the Senegalese authorities to negotiate because it notes that they have refused Father Diamacoune his passport to leave the country and even in Ziguinchor he is kept under surveillance.
(4) The existence of occult influences, difficult to identify, which pull the strings of the conflict on which they are based, and which have not, consequently, any interest in the return of peace.
(5) The divisions and inconsistency of the MFDC which is reflected in the contradictory and fluctuating declarations of its leaders.

It is in this general context that one fears that the cease fire will not be renewed, and the combatants will recommence with further violence and determination.

In consequence, the prospects for negotiations find themselves presently at an impasse. Only significant initiative, without equivocation, can renew the dynamic of peace, that which assumes a good comprehension and a deep analysis of the existing phenomena.

V. Analysis of the Facts

Upon analysis of the facts, two opposing themes appear.

(1) Separatist Position

The separatist thesis propounded by Father Diamacoune and his unconditional followers advocates the accession of Casamance to international sovereignty. They articulate a number of arguments, of which the following are notable:

(1) Historical legitimacy.
(2) Feelings of frustrations for having been deprived of their lands, being governed by outsiders, not truly sharing their cultural traditions or their aspiration (the example of a hotel constructed on the site of a former cemetery, which was destroyed for this purpose, was given).

(3) Revolt against living in poverty despite the natural riches of their region, these being neglected for many years by the central power which has only exploited them for the benefit of other regions.
(4) The will to put an end to the injustices that they continue to undergo, which make the rejects in a state whose sovereignty over Casamance they contest.
(5) The firm conviction of being able to live better in the future in a free and independent Casamance, occupied chiefly with the well-being of its population, with cooperation accords with other states, Senegal among them.

(2) Government Position

The authorities of the Senegalese state oppose this separatist position with a series of arguments of which these are the principals:

(1) No more than for other regions of Senegal does any historical argument support the separatist claims in Casamance, which was never an autonomous territory under colonisation.
(2) In the sociological plan, Casamance is composed of a mosaic of ethnic and cultural groups, while the MFDC rests its base on an ethno-cultural minority; thus this movement cannot legitimately claim to speak in the name of all Casamancais, the vast majority of whom, furthermore, do not want independence. According to this hypothesis, if independence came out, it would inevitably plunge the region into civil war without precedent.
(3) The principle of maintenance of national unity and territorial integrity cannot be questioned. Should Casamance by misfortune become independent, there would be no reason for the other regions of Senegal not to claim the benefits of the same status, using similar arguments.
(4) Senegal is a republic, respecting the principle of non-discrimination, equality for all its citizens and all national communities before the law. Casamance has never been the object of discrimination in relation to other regions. Much the contrary, it has received more investments than the others.

(3) Elements of Analysis of the Two Positions Presented

(1) Given the separatist position, it is easy to demonstrate that the reasons advanced are not unique to the Casamance, but can be invoked with a certain measure of profit by other regions of Senegal.
(2) Furthermore, it is not possible to rule out that the volume of investments from which Casamance has benefitted might be more important than those granted to other regions.
(3) As for the question of lands, of which certain natives have been deprived, it is important to emphasis this has in no way been the result of a conspiracy, but simply the consequence of the application of new legislation installing a system of private property.

(4) Also, this situation is explained by the drought which provided the movement of populations from the semi-arid zones of the north towards Casamance, better endowed by rain patterns and having more fertile land.
(5) The newly-arrived have practiced market economics while the natives limited themselves to an economy of subsistence. The former have thus become riches than the latter, and the frustrations felt at seeing these "strangers" coming from outside to make fortunes with the local lands and materials (agriculture, fishing, etc.) are not surprising.
(6) Furthermore, these migratory movements have naturally introduced other cultures into Casamance, particular Wolof culture, without imposing itself by force.
(7) As for the argument drawn from historical identity, without it being necessary to have reference to the study of CHARPY, it is simple to demonstrate that each people had in its history a cultural identity. Furthermore, the wise founders of the OAU in 1963 pronounced themselves in favour of territorial integrity and the immutability of the borders inherited from colonisation.
(8) In sum, the arguments developed to support the separatist positions lack pertinence. They cannot justify the grave attacks against human rights in the course of the conflict.
(9) Concerning the arguments developed by the government authorities, it is not sure that they are more pertinent. In effect, it is clear that Senegal has just endowed itself with a law on regionalisation, while at the moment that the conflict ignited in Casamance, the Senegalese state had a mechanical and static conception of national unity.
(10) Furthermore, the principle of territorial integrity and inviolability of borders seen to perpetuate the arbitrary and artificial divisions affected by the former colonial powers, without consulting the concerned populations.
(11) As for the principle of equality of citizens and communities, it is clear that this means not a mathematical equality, but above all an equality of participation in the administration of public affairs.
(12) In total, it appears that neither the position of the separatists, nor that of the state authorities, can be taken in its entirety. For this reason, a frank and constructive dialogue must be instituted between the two parties, from which a solution can emerge, a solution which will assure the cohesion and continuity of the people of the unified Senegalese state in a community of interest and destiny.

VI. Conclusions and Recommendations

With the goal of bringing about a constructive dialogue, it is recommended on the one hand that certain conditions be fulfilled, and on the other hand that certain objectives be aimed at.

A. Conditions Favorable for Negotiations

The Commission recommends:

(1) The Government should:

- consider lifting the measures which confine Father Diamacoune to his residence, to permit him to move freely and involve himself more easily in the negotiations and the search for peace;
- free all political prisoners detained for reasons connected to the conflict;
- assist all displaced persons and refugees, encouraging them to return to their homes by guaranteeing their security;
- fight impunity by prosecuting those implicated in torture and summary executions.

(2) The separatists should:

- ensure that their leaders based in Europe and abroad return to Senegal where guarantees of their safety will be given;
- accept that future negotiations will take place on African soil;
- work for coherence in statement of their positions.

(3) Both parties should:

- do their best to identify and isolate those who oppose a return to peace, who have made the conflict the foundation of their business.

B. Objectives of Negotiation

The Commission recommends that each of the parties put all in place to realise the following objectives:

- to resolve the problem on the ground;
- to post in Casamance so far as possible, officials native to the region;
- to elaborate a vast programme of investment with the object of further developing the region;
- to establish a system of social integration, to help unemployed youth, and encompassing demobilised rebels;
- to create a joint committee of follow-up to supervise the realisation of these objectives.

Before concluding this report, it is important to note the quality of facilities placed at the disposal of the mission by the Senegalese authorities.

The Commission maintains its expression of profound gratitude with the hope that the sincerity, the loyalty, and the transparency which the authorities demonstrated throughout the mission will contribute to reestablish peace, justice and well-being of the populations of Senegal in general and of the people of Casamance in particular.

ANNEX IX

Report of the Mission to Mauritania
Nouakchott, 19–27 June 1996

I. Introduction

(1) Mandate of the Mission

After receiving communications that revealed disturbing violations of human rights in Mauritania, the African Commission applied Article 46 of the Charter, according to which "the Commission may resort to any appropriate method of investigation". The Commission decided at the 19th ordinary session to send a fact-finding and investigation mission to Mauritania, with a view to finding an amicable resolution to put an end to the situation.

As the head of the mission repeated to all the individuals who were met in the course of the mission, the goal was not to decide whether what was encountered was wrong or right, but above all to listen to all sides with the objective of bringing clarification to the Commission in its contribution to the search for an equitable solution through dialogue.

(2) Duration and Composition of the Mission

Undertaken from 19–27 June 1996 and conducted by Prof. Isaac Nguema, Chairman of the African Commission, the mission comprised also Commissioners Julienne Ondziel-Gelenga and Rezzag-Bara, as well as Mr. Marcel Buzingo, members and legal adviser of the African Commission, respectively.

(3) Implementation of the Mission

The mission was undertaken in Nouakchott where the delegation had interviews with government officials and representatives of civil society.

(a) Government officials met:

- His Excellency Cheik El Avia Ould Khouna, Prime Minister;
- His Excellency Dieng Boubou Farba, President of the Senate;
- His Excellency Cheikh Sid Ahmed Ould Baba, President of the National Assembly;
- His Excellency Dah Ould Abdel Jilil, Minister of the Interior, of Mail and Telecommunications;
- His Excellency Lemrabott Sidi Mahmoud Ould Cheik Ahmed, Minister of Foreign Affairs and Cooperation;
- His Excellency Ahmed Salem Ould Dah, Minister of Justice;
- Dr. Mohamed Salem Ould Merzoug, Commissioner of Food Security;
- Mr. Skhna, Counsellor to the President of the Republic on Human Rights;

- Mr. Mouhamed-Lamine Dahi, Director General of Legislation;
- His Excellency the Mediator of the Republic;
- The Rector of the University of Nouakchott;
- Her Excellency the Secretary for Women, who met with Commissioner Juliene Ondziel-Gnelenga.

(b) NGOs and representatives of civil society met with:

- the Bar: the Batônnier of the Bar of Nouakchott;
- the Committee for Defense of the Republic (CDR): Professor Mohamed Kaber O/Hamoudi and Cheikh Ahmed O/Zahare, President and Secretary General, respectively;
- the Mauritanian Human Rights Association (AMDH): Mr. Kamara (President) and Mrs. Raki Kane;
- the National Committee for Struggle for the Eradication of Remnants of Slavery in Mauritania (CNESEM):
  - Cheikh Saad Bout Kamara (President)
  - Beibeni O/Ahmed Babou (Secretary General)
  - Saleck O/Sidi Mouhamed, Treasurer
  - Limam O/Sidi, Programme Secretary;
- the Mauritanian League for Human Rights (LMDH): Mr. Mine Abdel Kader Mohamedi (Secretary General) and Mr. Koita;
- the Collective of Survivors of the Repression of 1989–1991: Mr. Kebe Abdoulaye (Vice-President) and Mr. Wane Bechir (Secretary General);
- the National Independent Press Association (ANPI): Delegation led by the President of the Association;
- the Mauritanian League for the Defense of Women's Rights (LMDDF): represented notably by :
  - Mrs. Malado Coulibaly (Secretary General)
  - Mrs. Mintata Mint Hedeed
  - Mrs. Oum El Id Fall
  - Mrs. Aicha Mint Ghaddour;
- SOS Slavery: Mr. Yahya Ramdane, Mr. Oumar Ould Yali;
- the Widows' Collective:
  - Mrs. Houleye Sall (President)
  - Mrs. Maimouna Djibril (Vice-President)
  - Mrs. Barou Dia Aminata Alassane Sarr;
- the Collective of Former Civil Detainees of 1996;
- the Collective of Government Officials Victims of the Events of 1989: being notably present Mrs. Raby Diallo and Mrs. Nene Kane;
- the Collective of Deported Family: Delegation headed by Mrs. Sarr, née Diop Dewel;
- the Civil Initiative: Delegation headed by Dr. Mouhamoud Sahid.

II. General Context

A. Historical and Political Aspects

A former French colony, Mauritania became independent in 1960 and endowed itself in 1961 with its first constitution, consecrating the Islamic Republic, its population being one hundred percent Muslim.

The people of Mauritania are composed of four different ethnic groups, namely: the Moors or Arab-Berbers (75–80% of the population, according to certain estimates); the Peulaar (Peuls and Toucouleurs). the Soninkés and Wolofs, forming together the black Mauritanian group (20–25% of the population, estimated at 2.2 million inhabitants according to certain sources). This multi-ethnic composition constitutes the background which explains the political problems, struggles for influence and the phenomenon of exclusion which mark the history of the country, especially from 1986 when the attempted coup d'états and arrests occurred.

According to certain observers, the ethnic tensions have their roots in the birth of extremist movements, on one side Arab (pro-Irakian Baathists, Nasseristes), on the other side black Mauritanian, when the Front for the Liberation of the Africans of Mauritania (FLAM) was founded in 1985.

Following the publication of a manifesto, black Mauritanians were arrested in September and October 1986. They were principally accused of belonging to an illegal organisation and of having distributed a racist document which planned the destruction of a whole people. They were submitted to physical and moral torture.

As the result of trials which did not guarantee the right to defense, some of them were freed, others were condemned but reprieved, while others were condemned to prison terms together with loss of civil rights, heavy fines and banishment.

As a consequence of the harsh imprisonment to which they were subjected, some, such as the writer Tene Yousouf Gueye, died.

In 1987, an attempted coup, attributed to black Mauritanian elements in the army, was foiled.

After a series of arrests, following an abbreviated trial, severe penalties were pronounced, including the condemnation to death of three officers, who were immediately executed.

In 1988, another attempted coup d'état, led by Arab nationalists who wanted to create a Baathist state, was crushed. However, their trial did not result in any death sentences, and this was resented by certain black Mauritanians as a double standard.

In 1989, in the quarrel over land, an incident occurred between Mauritanian Peul herders and Senegalese Soninké farmers at Diawara, in the Senegal River valley. Lives were lost and the incident provoked an unprecedented crisis between Mauritania and Senegal.

In effect, on 24 and 25 April 1989, a collective murderous madness took place. Moorish Mauritanians living in Senegal were killed and hunted, while Senegalese and black Mauritanians suffered the same fate in Mauritania. In the face of the atrocities and the gravity of the crisis, the two governments concluded an exchange of endangered populations. Thus 60 to 70 thousand black Mauritanians arrived in Senegal, while 240 to 250 thousand Arab Berbers made the reverse trip.

Naturally, this situation exacerbated inter-ethnic tensions in Mauritania.

In effect, from November 1990 to April 1991, under the pretext that there was a conspiracy engineered from abroad to provoke civil massacres and seize power, the government arrested 503 soldiers and black Mauritanian civilians. Nearly all of them were subsequently killed.

All of these periods were marked by a totalitarian military regime under a single party.

B. Socio-cultural and Economic Aspects

To better understand the problem of ethnic and cultural tensions in Mauritania, it is necessary to recall the differences between the Moors of the north of the country, whose traditional way of life is nomadic, and the blacks, pastoralists and sedentary farmers living along the Senegal River in the south. In spite of their cultural homogeneity, the Moors are divided into several tribal groups and are composed of two groups of distinct racial origin, the white Moors called Beydanes, and the black Moors. The majority of the black Moors are Haratine, which means literally, "those who have been freed" although certain families of black Moors have never been subject to slavery. The "white Moors", of whom the majority have dark skin due to mixing with the groups of black Africans south of the Sahara, are chiefly found in government, in business and in the professional community.

For their part, the Peulaar, the Wolofs and the Soninké are concentrated in the southern part of the country. They are under-represented in the military and security sectors.

At the level of culture, the Constitution stipulates that Arabic, Peulaar, Soninké and Wolof are the national languages of Mauritania. Nevertheless, the regimes which have come to power, civilian as well as military, have pursued several policies of arabisation at the level of schools and workplaces, which have been the object of protest on the part of non-Arabic-speaking ethnic groups.

The difficult economic situation across Mauritania also nourishes the abovementioned ethnic tensions.

In effect, the drought has provoked migratory movements and pushed considerable numbers of nomads to become sedentary.

Also, it struck with full force the masters who had slaves in their service, because in most cases they could no longer retain them and were forced to let them go.

All these disturbances had placed part of the population in an economic dependance which naturally engendered frustrations with all their consequences of ethnic tensions.

C. Aspects Connected to the Respective Internal difficulties of Mauritania and Senegal

The crisis of 1989 which occurred between Senegal and Mauritania is not strange in light of the situation which prevailed in each of the two states.

In effect, according to certain sources, in light of the successive coups d'etat and their consequent repressions that provoked divisions in the population, the Mauritanian government needed an external crisis in order to gain breathing space and to unify behind it all the people to fight an external enemy.

Furthermore, the legitimacy of the regime of President Abdou Diouf was being contested by opposition leaders whom he threw into prison, and the internal political situation in Senegal appeared unstable.

Also, some were advocating the creation of a new port at Nouakchott, which would free Mauritania from its dependance on the port of Dakar, and this disturbed certain Senegalese interests.

In the economic sphere, both countries were characterised by the deterioration of social conditions for large numbers of peoples following structural adjustment programmes. This was a factor favoring the exacerbation of tensions.

III. Analysis of Communications Brought Against Mauritania

A. The Complaints and their Authors

The violations of human rights in Mauritania were the object of four communications introduced before the African Commission respectively on 16 July 1991 by the Malawi African Association, 21 August 1991 by Amnesty International, 12 March 1993 by Madame Sarr Diop, 30 March 1993 by the Rencontre Africaine pour la Defense des Droits de l'Homme, the Interafrican Union of Human Rights and the Mauritanian League for Human Rights. Thus, only one of the communications was submitted by an individual person; the others were presented by NGOs.

Concerning the object of the communications, the first concerns the massacres perpetrated against black Mauritanians. It concerns murders perpetrated by soldiers against unarmed villagers, and alleges also the expulsion of black Mauritanians from their lands, and the denial of their right to speak their local languages.

The second communication describes the death in detention of certain black Mauritanian prisoners following torture or extra-judicial executions.

The allegations contained in this communication are notably: the regular torture undergone by political detainees, the arbitrary judgments of which they were victims, without the opportunity to be defended by lawyers, the incapacity of specifying the confessions extracted by force.

The third communication denounces the deportation of black Mauritanians towards Senegal and Mali, forcing them to live in refugee camps; the arrest and arbitrary detention of black Mauritanians; the denial of the right to a fair trial, the use of torture and inhuman treatment during detention, and the summary execution of certain prisoners.

The last complaint deals with expulsion of thousands of black Mauritanians towards Senegal and Mali. Numerous deportees (55,000) found themselves thus in extremely difficult conditions, their goods having been confiscated or pillaged. In this same period, Mauritanian and Senegalese citizens were massacred, others disappeared. In November 1990, on the pretext of the discovery of an attempted coup, thousands of black Mauritanians were arrested, tortured and executed. It was established that 502 persons died in extra-judicial executions.

B. The Problems of Victims

With regard to the facts related, which denote grave violations of human rights, it is important to dwell on the subject of refugees, on the different categories of victims of the events of 1986, 1989 and 1990–1991, without forgetting to inquire into "slavery" or the problem of remnants of slavery.

Before finishing the examination of the democratic development opened by the new Mauritanian constitution, the violations of human rights undergone by women will be the object of particular consideration.

(i) The problem of Mauritanian refugees in Senegal after the events of 1989

After the tragic Senegal-Mauritania conflict occurred in 1989, close to 70,000 black Mauritanians were expelled by Mauritania, or fled. It is estimated that 20,000 of these have returned to their country.

Concerning the return of the others, the position of the refugees, specially expressed by the Association of Mauritanian Refugees in Senegal (ARMS) conflicts with that of the Mauritanian Government.

(a) Position of the refugees: To return to Mauritania, the refugees want a collective return organised on the basis of an agreement with the UN High Commissioner for Refugees (UNHCR), with Senegal taking part. In this context, they ask for the fulfilment of the following demands:

- Restoration of the goods lost, or failing that, the benefit of an indemnification.
- The recovery of all their rights (citizenship, government jobs, reintegration of officials and workers).
- The recovery of traditional lands and the inauguration of a national committee of welcome and reintegration.

Timed to coincide with the day of the African Refugee, the Association of Mauritanian Refugees in Senegal announced that the first contingent of 5,112 refugees were ready for self-repatriation on 20 June 1996. The return did not take place: the authorities of the association declared two days before the appointed date, the UNCHR which had guaranteed the logistics transporting the refugees up to the Senegal River had retracted its guarantee with explanation.

In truth, officials of the UNCHR expressed their astonishment at these statements, because they had never been involved in the preparations for the return, which they learned of at the last minute, like everyone else.

Finally, the Association of Mauritanian Refugees in Senegal maintains the position that there should be an organised, collective (rather than individual) return, and an officially mediated repatriation.

(b) Government thesis: It is necessary to recall above all that the Mauritanian government denies the existence of Mauritanian refugees as defined in the Geneva Convention.

According to the Mauritanian government, all the doors are open to every Mauritanian who wants to return. It is not acceptable to recognise refugee status because no one can reasonably believe that they have fear of persecution.

The government authorities prefer a voluntary return, non-politicized and not mediated. They insist that more than 15,000 persons have returned and been successfully integrated in the local population. Individuals and even complete villages have thus returned, without making it a formal act.

Invoking the UNHCR as a witness, the government adds that it makes efforts to assist returnees, issuing them identity cards, restoring their lands, houses and even personal possessions when these can be recovered and identified.

In truth, although some have not yet received their identity cards, it must be recognised that these delays relate to the structure of the government and to the few resources available for administration.

(ii) The problem of indemnification and the rehabilitation of survivors

The Survivors' Collective: According to the representatives met, the surviving former black Mauritanian political prisoners who constitute the Collective continue to be the object of systematic exclusion seven years after their liberation and complete amnesty which took place in 1991.

In fact, former government employees for the most part, they have been completely excluded from the public sector and despair of ever recovering their jobs, given the hostility of the public authorities towards them. Moreover, their Arab counterparts who were liberated at the same time were rehabilitated in 1989 and 1990, and reintegrated into their work. What is more, some of them were given responsibilities in the government even before the general amnesty.

Faced with their distressing situation, the former detainees organised themselves into a "survivors' collective" with the goal of getting the Mauritanian authorities to pay attention to their fate and take positive measures assuring their rehabilitation, their reintegration in government service or other governmental organisations, with obvious benefit of a reconstituted career including the rights and privileges pertaining to it.

In addition to these demands, they ask that there be an inquiry into the reasons for their arrest and that the authors of maltreatment and torture be brought to justice. The government's position in this regard will be described below.

(iii) The problem of widows

Widows' collective: One will recall that between November 1990 and March 1991, hundreds of soldiers, of whom the majority were Halpeulaar, were arrested, killed, tortured or mutilated following allegations of an attempted coup d'etat. The military has never made public the results of its internal inquiry on the subject, done in 1991; nevertheless, in 1993, the National Assembly approved an amnesty law which excluded any possibility of judicial prosecution of the members of the armed forces or any other citizen implicated in the abuses committed in the period January 1990 to April 1992.

The refusal of the government to prosecute the officers having committed extra-judicial killings and other abuses contributed to the feelings of frustration of families of those who disappeared who never saw the bodies or the graves of their loved ones. The widows of these victims formed a collective.

In addition to all other reparation, this collective affirmed to us their will, above all, to see the prosecution of the members of the armed forces implicated in the massacres.

On the basis of information collected from several rare, surviving witnesses to these killings, the collective affirmed knowing the identity of the authors of the executions. Some of these have even been compensated and benefitted from promotion in their jobs, or seen to be given other responsibilities.

It is important to note that the mothers of unmarried soldiers who disappeared in these tragic events form part of the collective. Also, the collective claims for pensions. As for the indemnities given by the government, some members of the collective affirmed that they had refused them, because in their belief, accepting such a compensation would be like drinking their relatives' blood.

(iv) Position of the Government on victims of events of 1986, 1989 and 1990–1991

According to the Mauritanian Government, most of the questions brought up had already found solutions, while others were in the process of being resolved. Thus, as for the claims of the surviving government employees, the authorities asserted that most of them had already regained their jobs. As for those who were in the collective, the government said, it could not be ruled out that their actions resulted from manipulations for the opposition, with the object of opposing government action.

Likewise, concerning the problem of widows, the government affirmed that under the terms of the law adopted in June 1993, it had proceeded to award indemnities in July 1993, to benefit widows and families of the persons killed.

With the exclusion of members of soldiers' families who were not married, "as of law", all those entitled had received their pensions; the widows who were not legally married (common law marriages) and the children of these unions remained a subject of concern, because they were without means of subsistence.

To all those who asked for judicial prosecution of the soldiers who might be found guilty of torture, killings and other atrocities inflicted on their colleagues, the government repeated that it had been an affair internal to the army, that the army had carried out an investigation, by which the appropriate sanctions had been taken against those soldiers found guilty.

Finally, the government recalled that by virtue of the amnesty law voted by the National Assembly in 1993, all legal prosecution of the authors of abuses committed in the given period was definitively excluded. Justifying the sound foundation of this law, the authorities suggested that civilians had benefitted from an amnesty law in

1991, so the military wanted to obtain the same favours, and after all, they had ceded power by permitting the holding of presidential elections in 1992 and elections for the legislature in 1993.

IV. The Problem of "Slavery" or its Remnants

Although legal slavery in all forms may have been definitively abolished on all territory of the Islamic Republic of Mauritania (Ordinance no. 81-234 of 9 November 1981), its existence remains a contested question to this day.

In this respect, two positions clash. One affirms its existence, while the other considers that there exists only remnants.

A. Affirmation of the Existence of Slavery

According to the members of "SOS-Slavery" (an NGO created in 1995 but having no legal recognition), slavery continues to exist in Mauritania and affects 60% of the population, Arab-Berbers as well as black Mauritanians. SOS-Slavery affirms the existence of men, women and children belonging to other human beings, who dispose of their persons and their lives.

Thus, "SOS-Slavery" refutes the official version of the government according to which there are no longer slaves in Mauritania, but merely remnants of slavery (see below).

To support their position, the members of this NGO articulated the following arguments:

1. Nature of the relationship between masters and slaves

The relations between masters and slaves are not always overtly conflictual. These relations depend on the state of ideological, economic and cultural alienation in which the slaves find themselves, and this depends on where they live (in the countryside or in the city).

In the country, relationships of domination are more clear and thus more constraining than in the city.

(a) Ideological alienation: Religion, monopolised by the masters, is used to justify slavery, perpetuate domination and contain any vague impulse to revolt or desire for liberation. In fact, it is inculcated in the slave that his health depends on the master, that his happiness is tied to obedience to the master. Thus, the submission of the slave is constructed as religious duty.

(b) Economic and political alienation: In Mauritania, according to the members of "SOS-Slavery", masters are known and openly claim their status as masters. They exercise their "rights" over their slaves chiefly in the countryside. The master possesses several slaves that he maintains under a domination that may be subtle (in cities) or open (in the countryside, but in the city as well), assured of total impunity by the public powers. The master disposes of the person and goods of his slave, it is he who decides on his work, on his food, and on his liberty or manumission.

In the countryside, the masters are owners of sources of water and control access to the traditional lands of the tribe. In the cities, constituting the heart of the managerial class, they control access to employment.

(2) Illustration of the submission of slaves to their masters

According to the leaders of "SOS-Slavery", domination of masters over their slaves is demonstrated in several realms, notably:

(a) Work: A slave, whether man, woman, or child, is obligated to perform all duties without compensation, any consent, or any form of written or verbal contract. The food he takes from his master can in no way be considered as a salary in exchange for the work performed. So far as land goes, the division of the products of agriculture is done according to the master's will.

The surplus of slaves not utilised or sold by the master appear to live in a free and independent fashion. For some, this apparently autonomous way of life dates far back in history, while for others this arrangement dates to the economic dislocation of the long drought. Yet, essentially, they remain closely tied to their master, who grants them all their rights: to be well received and maintained, they adopt what pleases him. The master decides if slaves shall have the opportunity to vote, and for whom.

In the countryside, the slave cultivates the land of the master, tends his palm groves, guards his herds, undertakes all the work that the master judges useful to himself. The slave can be the object of maltreatment and physical or moral torture each time the master is not satisfied with the services rendered.

(b) Seizing and holding of children: Incapable of enduring any longer the maltreatment and torture and longer, some slaves (men, women and children) flee their masters and take refuge in towns. They can sometimes be made to return by force, occasionally with the complicity of certain authorities who intimidate, threaten and terrorise the "recalcitrants". The masters can also exercise pressure over the fugitive slaves by taking their children hostage to force them to return, and thus to have slave labour at their disposal.

(c) Loans, inheritance and renting of slaves: The master can lend his slaves or their children to relatives and friends as he might bequeath them to his young married daughters who are setting up their households; it is a common form of gift, constituting a contribution to the equipping of a new household. This practice exists even in the capital of the country, and in the houses of government leaders. Slaves can be rented to other persons, and the pay for their work and services is given to the master. Children can thus be used, either in cities or the countryside, for watching herds and after a time be exported to certain countries of the Middle East.

(d) Deprivation of property: By law, the slave does not possess any property. All the fruit of his labor belongs as of right to the master; the land which he has cleared and made useful belongs to the master. When a slave dies, the master is, according to tradition, his sole heir at law.

(e) Kidnapping and sale of slaves: To recapture their slaves who have fled, masters resort to kidnapping. Furthermore, cases of kidnapping are still indications to maintain or renew slave labour.

Slaves are still sold today in Mauritania; most "officially" when the sales are controlled by the religious authorities.

(f) Marriage: The master decides on the marriage of his slaves. He may take female slaves as wives, according to his wish, without asking the consent of the woman, and abuse her.

(3) Behavior of government authorities in the face of slavery

Members of "SOS-Slavery" allege that the administrative and judicial authorities manifest different attitudes and behavior when faced with slavery. The official discourse tries to obscure it to give a positive image to international opinion. It is thus that one can speak of "remnants" of slavery.

The state hides behind ordinance No. 81-234 of 9 November 1981 abolishing slavery, and the constitution, which refers to the UN Charter.

But according to "SOS-Slavery", the highest authorities of the country today maintain that this ordinance is without purpose because according to them there have been no slaves in Mauritania for a very long time. It is perhaps for this reason, the NGO thinks, that the decree of application of this law has never been made, and no campaign of explanation or information has been undertaken by the state, so much through the official media as in the discourse of leaders of popular meetings, political meetings and other gatherings.

Thus, the above-mentioned ordinance, like the implicit abolition which preceded or followed it, remains theoretical, without significant effect.

The judicial void reinforces slaveholders and certain authorities from feudal, slaveholding families.

In cases of conflict, conclude the activists of SOS-Slavery, the state has never punished the perpetrator of any seizure or holding of slaves, dispossession of inheritance or goods. Some officials have sent fleeing slaves back to their masters, other have contested their impotence in the face of the legal void, although others try timidly to resolve certain conflicts without leaving any traces that might attest to the existence of slavery.

B. The Existence of Vestiges of Slavery

Contrary to the affirmations of the activists of SOS-Slavery, several state officials and members of NGOs whom we met with maintained the positions that there was no longer slavery as such, but rather its remnants, in the form of dependence as much psychological as economic, deeply anchored in the ancestral traditions of Mauritanian society.

In fact, according to our interlocutors and other sources who swore by this thesis, of the tens of thousands of persons whose ancestors were slaves find themselves still in states of servitude or quasi-servitude, even if such practices as coercive servitude and commerce in slaves appears to have virtually disappeared. In the majority of cases, those who find themselves still in a state of non-compensated servitude are bound in this situation by lack of viable alternatives or by lack of knowledge of their correct legal status. Some freed slaves (Haratine) have decided, it may be, to remain with the former master, to be rejoined with him and thus continue to furnish their work in exchange for room, board and the covering of other necessities.

Others live independent of their former master, but continue, in symbiosis, to maintain relations with them, in effect, from time to time a non-salaried work in exchange for provisions, clothes and medical care. There exist no reliable statistics on the number of Haratines who continue to work for the same family that they served before the abolition law of 1981, whether they are salaried or not. The case of reports of involuntary servitude are rare because, having been abolished, the administrative authorities and courts repress it when it presents itself.

To sum up, the Mauritanian public authorities refuse to apply the idea "slavery", which they believe is derogatory and likely to sow confusion in the minds of western partners who understand it in the classical sense.

C. Confrontation of the Two Positions

To hold, like "SOS-Slavery", that slavery remains a living reality which touches 60% of the population of Mauritania is not credible. If one can admit the existence of several rare cases in the remote countryside, isolated from the competent authorities, it is insufficient to support such a thesis. That which is common and conforms with reality, is the persistence of vestiges of slavery. The executive and judicial powers cannot be reasonably accused of not acting in conformity with the spirit and the letter of the 1981 abolition law.

By way of example, the disputes over inheritance between the Haratines and the descendants of their former masters have often been heard and been resolved in court. Although the resolution of these cases is rests on the principles dictated by the law and practice, that is the transmission of an inheritance to the descendants of former slaves, the independent press brought to light one case of a decision taken in 1994 at Néma by a qadi, in favour of the former master. The execution of this decision was stayed, thus permitting the descendants of the former slave to make an appeal to the competent court. In another case, the Supreme Council of the Magistrature removed a magistrate from his position for having violated the law by a decision attributing the estate of a slave to his former master instead of his descendants.

In its concern to eradicate the vestiges of slavery, and above all ignorance and extreme poverty, the executive branch has already initiated measures in the right direction, but which must be amplified and deepened.

It is relevant to cite the following:

- participation of former slaves in the exercise of high political, administrative, military and trade union activities;

- raising the level consciousness of former slave by means of priority schooling of children in their dialects, and literacy for adults;
- agrarian reform, envisioning a better exploitation of the land for the benefit of those who till it.

Finally, the argument for the existence of remnants of slavery mobilises civil society with a view to finding a solution. Thus, for example, the El Hor (literally, "free man") movement continues to pursue its programme with the aim of eradicating the last vestiges of slavery and the mentality inherent in it, prevailing among former slaves as well as their masters. A new NGO, the National Committee for the Fight against the Vestiges of Slavery in Mauritania was created in 1995 to promote the rights of ex-slaves.

V. The Question of Rights of Women

Although they appear to be in decline, the traditional forms of treatments of women remain serious causes of concern, in most cases in isolated, rural communities. Such treatment comprises the feeding by force of adolescent girls and female genital mutilation.

These practices are widely condemned by international health experts because their effects are harmful to the physical and psychological health of their subjects.

Thus, for example, because obesity is considered a traditional form of beauty, feeding by force of adolescent girls consists of feeding them on a schedule, and exaggerated with foods intended to make them fat as quickly as possible during their adolescence, with a view to early marriage. This practice is dangerous for the health because it causes hypertension, diabetes, etc.

As for female genital mutilation most often practiced on young girls, it continues to be widespread among all the ethnic groups of the country, with the exception of the Wolofs. It is estimated that 95% of Soninké and Peulaar women and 30% of Moorish women are subjected to these practices.

Also, the problems linked to early marriage, polygamy and divorce constitute a source of concern for the protection of women's rights in Mauritania where the traditions of the family prevail.

As for the enjoyment of the right to non-discrimination, Mauritanian women are participating in the economic sector of the country (they hold 80% of small commerce, including industries, indeed small manufacturing) and in teaching they are the majority.

By contrast, although they represent 51% of the population, they are notable for their absence in political and legal life. In fact, there is not a single woman at the centre of government, while the National Assembly and Senate have not a single female member. Likewise is the judiciary, which has not a single woman judge.

In sum, the promotion of women's rights is deficient in the country, and merits a particular attention.

VI. Conclusions and Recommendations

1. The Commission rejoices in the total willingness of the Mauritanian government to cooperate with it, in conformity with the principles of the African Charter on Human and Peoples' Rights.

2. The Commission appreciates the willingness of the Mauritanian authorities to reinforce democratic evolution in a pluralism context.

3. The Commission deplores all the tragic events that have occurred in Mauritania and their consequences. It recommends that all might be implemented so that the effects of these events might be repaired, with a view to the reconciliation of all elements of Mauritanian society.

4. The Commission calls on the sense of responsibility among the socio-political organisations and civil society to reinforce democratic equilibrium and construction.

5. The Commission finds that in spite of the amnesty laws of 1991 and 1993 adopted by the government to repair the prejudice caused, there still exists a certain number of unresolved matters, such as the situation of widows and black Mauritanian survivors.

The Commission recommends to the government to put into place mechanisms and procedures likely to accelerate the process of indemnification and reparation in a satisfactory manner and to maintain a dialogue with the organisation of civil society.

6. The delegation thanks the Mauritanian authorities for the warmth of their welcome and the quality of the hospitality which was accorded to them.

ANNEX X

Communications

1. 27/89, 46/91, 49/91, 99/93 Organisation Mondiale Contre La Torture and Association Internationale des juristes Democrates) Commission Internationale des Juristes (C.I.J) Union Interafricaine des Droits de l'Homme/Rwanda

The facts:

(1) Communication 27/89 alleges the expulsion from Rwanda of Burundi nationals who had been refugees in Rwanda for many years (Bonaventure Mbonuabucya, Baudouin Ntatundi, Vincent Sinarairaye and Shadrack Nkunzwenimana). They were told on 2 June 1989 that they had a month to leave the country. The reason given for their expulsion was that they were a national security risk due to their "subversive activities". The refugees were not allowed to defend themselves before a competent court.

(2) Communication 46/90 alleges arbitrary arrests and summary executions have occurred in Rwanda.

(3) Communication 49/91 alleges the detention of thousands of people in various parts of the country by the Rwandan security forces. These arrests have been

made on the basis of ethnic origin and peaceful political activities. The communication states that over 1000 people including women, children and the aged are held in deplorable conditions. A large number of villages have been destroyed and villagers, mostly Tutsis, have been massacred.

(4) Communication 99/93 alleges serious and massive violations between October 1990 and January 1992. A report was submitted at the same time detailing such violations as widespread massacres, extra-judicial executions and arbitrary arrests against the Tutsi ethnic group.

Procedure:

(5) Communication 27/89 was submitted on 22 June 1989 by Organisation Mondiale contre la Torture and Association Internationale des Juristes Démocrates. The letter of the Free Legal Assistance Group was dated 17 March 1989, that of the Austrian Committee against Torture dated 29 March 1989, that of the Centre Haitien dated 20 April 1989.

(6) The Commission was seized of the communication at the 6th Ordinary Session in October 1989.

(7) On 14 March 1990 the Secretariat of the Commission notified the Ministry of Foreign Affairs of Rwanda.

(8) From 1990 to 1995, the Commission attempted unsuccessfully to send a mission to Rwanda in order to carry out investigations on this cases.

(9) Communication 46/90 was submitted by the International Commission of Jurists on 16 October 1990.

(10) On 6 November 1990 a notification was sent to the Ministry of Foreign Affairs by registered mail.

(11) At the 10th Ordinary Session, in October 1991, the communication was declared admissible. The Ministry of Foreign Affairs was notified on this decision on 23 October 1991.

(12) Communication 49/91 was submitted by the Organisation Mondiale Contre la Torture (OMCT) on 28 November 1990.

(13) Communication 99/93 was submitted by Union Interafricaine des Droits de l'Homme on 20 March 1993.

(14) From 1993 to 1995, various letters and notifications were sent to Rwanda, to which there was no response from the government.

Law:

Admissibility:

(15) It appears as stated under Article 58 of the African Charter, the communications 27/89, 46/90, 49/91 and 99/93 against Rwanda reveal the existence of a series of serious or massive violations of the provisions of the African Charter.

(16) Article 56 of the African Charter requires that complainants exhaust local remedies before the Commission can take up a case, unless these remedies are, as a practical matter, unavailable or unduly prolonged. The requirement of exhaustion of local remedies is founded on, amongst others, the principle that a

government should have notice of a human rights violation in order to have the opportunity to remedy such violations before being called before an international tribunal.

(17) In accordance with its earlier decisions on cases of serious and massive violations of human rights, and in view of the vast and varied scope of the violations alleged and the large number of individuals involved, the Commission holds that remedies need not be exhausted and, as such, declares the communications admissible.

(18) For the above reasons, the Commission declared the communications admissible.

Merits:

(19) The main goal of the communications procedure before the Commission is to initiate a positive dialogue, resulting in an amicable resolution between the complainant and the state concerned, which remedies the prejudice complained of. A pre-requisite for amicably remedying violations of the Charter is the good faith of the parties concerned, including their willingness to participate in a dialogue.

(20) In the present case, there has been no substantive response from the Government of Rwanda, despite the numerous notifications of the communications sent by the African Commission.

The African Commission, in several previous decisions, has set out the principle that where allegations of human rights abuse go uncontested by the government concerned, even after repeated notifications, the Commission must decide on the facts provided by the complainant and treat those facts as given (See, for example, the decisions of the Commission on communications 59/91, 60/91, 64/91, 87/93 and 101/93). This principle conforms with the practice of other international human rights adjudicatory bodies and the Commission's duty to protect human rights. The fact that the Government of Rwanda does not wish to participate in a dialogue obliges the Commission to continue its consideration of the case regrettably on the basis of facts and opinions submitted by only one of the parties.

(21) Article 2 of the Charter reads:

> "Every individual shall be entitled to the enjoyment of the rights and freedoms recognised and guaranteed in the present Charter without distinction of any kind such as race, ethnic group . . . national or social origin . . ."

(22) There is considerable evidence, undisputed by the government, that the violations of the rights of individuals have occurred on the basis of their being Burundian nationals or members of the Tutsi ethnic group. The denial of numerous rights to individuals on account of their nationality or membership of a particular ethnic group clearly violates Article 2.

(23) Article 4 of the Charter reads:

> "Human beings are inviolable. Every human being shall be entitled to respect for his life and the integrity of his person. No one may be arbitrarily deprived of this right."

(24) The massacre of a large number of Rwandan villagers by the Rwandan armed forces and the many reported extra judicial executions for reasons of their membership of a particular ethnic group is a violation of Article 4.

(25) Article 5 of the Charter reads:

> "Every individual shall have the right to the respect of dignity inherent in a human being . . . torture, cruel, inhuman or degrading punishment and treatment shall be prohibited."

(26) The conditions of detention in which children, women and the aged are held violates their physical and psychological integrity and therefore constitutes of violation of Article 5.

(27) Article 6 of the Charter reads:

> "Every individual shall have the right to liberty and security of his person. No one may be deprived of his freedom except for reasons and conditions previously laid down by law. In particular, no one may be arbitrarily arrested or detained."

(28) The arrests and detentions of the Rwandan Government based on grounds of ethnic origin alone, in light of Article 2 in particular, constitute arbitrary deprivation of the liberty of an individual. These acts are clear evidence of a violation of Article 6.

(29) Article 12 of the African Charter reads:

> "3. Every individual shall have the right, when persecuted to seek and obtain asylum in other countries in accordance with laws of those countries and international conventions."
> 4. A non-national legally admitted in a territory of a State Party to the present Charter, may only be expelled from it by virtue of a decision taken in accordance with the law."

(30) This provision should be read as including a general protection of all those who are subject to persecution, that they may seek refuge in another state. Article 12.4 prohibits the arbitrary expulsion of such persons from the country of asylum. The Burundian refugees in this situation were expelled in violation of Articles 2 and 12 of the African Charter.

(31) Article 12.5 of the African Charter reads:

> "The mass expulsion of non-nationals shall be prohibited. Mass expulsion shall be that which is aimed at national, racial, ethnic or religious groups."

(32) There is ample evidence in this communication that groups of Burundian refugees have been expelled on the basis of their nationality. This constitutes a clear violation of Article 12.5.

(33) Article 7.1 of the Charter reads:

> "Every individual shall have the right to have his case heard. This comprises:

(a) The right to an appeal to competent national organs against acts violating his fundamental rights . . ."

(34) By expelling these refugees from Rwanda, without giving them the opportunity to be heard by the national judicial authorities, the government of Rwanda has violated article 7.1 of the Charter.

(35) The African Commission is aware of the fact that the situation in Rwanda has undergone dramatic change in the years since the communications were introduced. Furthermore, the Commission has to rule on the facts which were submitted to it.

For the above reasons, the Commission:

holds that the facts constitute serious or massive violations of the African Charter, namely of Articles 4, 5, 6, 7, 12.3 and 12.4 and 12.5 of the Charter.

urges the government of Rwanda to adopt measures in conformity with this decision.

Taken at the 20th Ordinary Session, Grand Bay, Mauritius, October 1996.

2. 39/90 Annette Pagnoulle (on behalf of Abdoulaye Mazou)/Cameroon

The facts:

(1) This communication was submitted by Annette Pagnoulle of Amnesty International and concerns Abdoulaye Mazou, a Cameroonian national. Mr. Mazou was imprisoned in 1984 by a military tribunal without trial, without witnesses, and without right to defence. He was sentenced to 5 years imprisonment for hiding his brother who was later sentenced to death for attempted coup d'etat. Even after he had served his sentence in April 1989, he continued to be held in prison and was only freed by the intervention of Amnesty International on 23 May 1990. He continued to be under detention at his residence until the law of amnesty of 23 April 1991.

(2) Although Mr. Mazou has now been freed, he has not been reinstated in his position as a magistrate. The complainant therefore requests action be continued on his behalf.

(3) The government was represented by a delegation at the 20th session of the Commission held in Mauritius in October 1996, which asked that the communication should be declared inadmissible because it was still pending at the Supreme Court.

(4) The alleged victim petitioned the President of the Republic in order to solicit his reinstatement as a magistrate. He then submitted an out of court settlement to the Ministry of Justice. When no response from the President or the Ministry was forthcoming the alleged victim made a submission for a legal settlement to the Administrative Chamber of the Supreme Court which rejected his case in principle. He submitted further petitions to the Supreme Court and seized the Ministry of Justice for reinstatement in his position. He has also undertaken to bring political pressure, jointly with others, to reclaim his profession. As yet, none of these actions has produced any result.

Procedure:

(5) The Commission was seized of the communication at the 7th Session in April 1990.

(6) On 31 May 1990, the Secretariat of the Commission notified the state of Cameroon of the communication and asked it for its views on admissibility.

(7) On 1 March 1995, the Secretariat informed the complainant that the Commission takes note of the release of Mr. Mazou. The complainant was advised to inform the Commission whether or not his release was satisfactory reparation for Mr. Mazou no later than 1 July 1995.

(8) On 8 June 1995, a fax was received from the complainant stating that although the victim, Mr. Abdoulaye Mazou, had been released he had not been reinstated in his position as a magistrate, to which he is legally entitled.

(9) At the 19th session, in March 1996, the communication was declared admissible. The parties were notified of this decision.

(10) At the 20th Session, held in October 1996, a delegation of the government of Cameroon was present and submitted a written response to the effect that the communication was inadmissible. The delegation also admitted, however, that the conditions under which Mr. Mazou was tried by a military tribunal fell short of the standards provided for in the African Charter, but that the laws governing such tribunals had since been changed. The delegation promised to forward to the Commission the written judgement of the Military Tribunal, any judgement concerning the alleged disciplinary measures against Mr. Mazou, a document proving the existence of recourse as concerns disciplinary measures and the law after which Mr. Mazou was condemned.

The Commission decided to postpone consideration of the case to the 21st session.

(11) On 24 March the Secretariat received received a letter from the Ministry of Foreign Affairs of Cameroon informing the Secretariat that the question had been dealt with in the Administrative Chamber of the Supreme Court and that all interested parties had the possibility of exhausting local remedies. The Ministry also sent the Supreme Court judgment, the ordinance no 304 which placed Mr. Mazou under surveillance, ordinances no 72/5 and 72/20 concerning the competence of the military court and law no. 74/4 modifying ordinance no. 72/5, the judgment of the military court, ordinance no. 72/13 concerning state of emergency, ordinance 72/6 concerning the organisation of the Supreme Court and law no. 76/28 modifying this ordinance, Decree no. 80/276 concerning the nomination of Secretary Generals of Ministries and Decree no. 82/467 relating to the judiciary.

Law:

Admissibility:

(12) Article 56 of the African Charter reads:

> "Communications . . . shall be considered if they:
>
> . . .
>
> 5. Are sent after exhausting local remedies, if any, unless it is obvious that this procedure is unduly prolonged . . ."

(13) In this case, the alleged victim petitioned the President of the Republic in order to solicit his reinstatement as a magistrate. He then submitted an out of court settlement to the Ministry of Justice. When no response from the President or the Ministry was forthcoming the alleged victim made a submission for a legal settlement to the Administrative Chamber of the Supreme Court. He submitted further petitions to the Supreme Court and seized the Ministry of Justice for reinstatement in his position. In light of the above actions taken by the victim and their failure to yield any results the Commission holds that local remedies have been duly exhausted.

Merits:

(14) Article 6 of the Charter reads:

> "No one may be deprived of his freedom except for reasons and conditions previously laid down by law. In particular, no one may be arbitrarily arrested or detained."

(15) In conformity with Article 65 of the Charter, the Commission cannot pronounce on the equity of court proceedings that took place before the African Charter entered into force in Cameroon on 20 September 1989 (see the Commission's decision on communication 59/91). If however irregularities in the original sentence has consequences that constitute a continuing violation of any of the Articles of the African Charter, the Commission must pronounce on these.

(16) Mr. Mazou was held in prison after the expiration of his sentence in April 1989 until 23 May 1990. After his release, he was placed under house arrest. The delegation of Cameroon at the 20th session stated that: "After serving his sentence he was released, but the problem is that he was the subject of purely administrative measures based on existing laws at that time. These laws were however abrogated only in 1989".

(17) All parties agree that Mr. Mazou was held beyond the expiry of his sentence. No judgment was passed to extend his sentence. Therefore the detention is arbitrary, and the Commission finds that this constitutes a violation of Article 6.

(18) Article 7 of the African Charter reads:

> "1. Every individual shall have the right to have his cause heard.
> This comprises:
>
> . . .
>
> (b) the right to be presumed innocent until proved guilty by a competent court or tribunal;
>
> . . .
>
> (d) the right to be tried within a reasonable time by an impartial court or tribunal."

(19) Mr. Mazou has not yet had a judgment on his case brought before the Supreme Court over 2 years ago, without being given any reason for the delay. At the 20th

session the delegation held that the case might be decided upon by the end of October 1996, but still no news of it has been forwarded to the Commission. Given that this case concerns Mr. Mazou's ability to work in his profession, two years without any hearing or projected trial date constitutes a violation of article 7.1(d) of the African Charter.

(20) At the 20th session, the delegation of Cameroon stated that "the administrative detention had not for its reason the fact that sentenced Mazou, it was not linked to the trial. When the state believes that an individual who is free can trouble public order we can take preventive measures, and this explains why he was detained administratively. This can be renewed at any time when the administrative authorities deem that there is a risk and therefore they deem need of preventive measures".

(21) Detention on the mere suspect that an individual may cause problems is a violation of his right to be presumed innocent.

(22) Article 15 of the African Charter reads:

> "Every individual shall have the right to work under equitable and satisfactory conditions . . ."

(23) Article 2 of the Amnesty Law of 23 April 1992 reads:

> "Have been amnestied:
> – All persons sentenced of subversion to penalty of imprisonment and/or fined;
> – All persons sentenced a punishment of detention or serving an penalty of detention;
> – All persons authors of offences of a political nature, condemned to death penalty."

(24) Article 3 of the Amnesty Law of 23 April 1992 reads:

> ". . . the persons condemned who have been granted amnesty and who had public employment will be reintegrated . . ."

(25) Still after the Amnesty Law of 23 April 1992, Mr. Mazou has been denied reinstatement by the government in his former professional capacity as a magistrate.

(26) The delegation of the government which appeared at the 20th session claimed the reason to be that he is not covered by the Amnesty law of 23 April 1992, because he has not been judged of subversion or sentenced to detention. It also stated that disciplinary action was taken against Mr. Mazou because of his sentence.

(27) Although according to the delegation, Mr. Mazou was judged for an ordinary criminal offence in Cameroon, he was still judged by a Military Tribunal. The delegation answered the Commission's questions about this as follows: "Why he was tried by a Military Tribunal? Everybody knows that when you are involved in a problem which includes the attempt to violently, using arms, overthrow a government and a president, then you are actually taking actions in political acts,

something of a political nature. The coup plotters of 1984 were judged by the Military Tribunal and since Mr. Mazou hid for some time a brother of his who was involved, then there was, there could have been a connection between the coup attempt and the fact that Mr. Mazou had accepted to hide his brother."

(28) To the Commission it still seems peculiar that Mr. Mazou was tried by a Military Tribunal like the coup plotters and that afterwards he is not given amnesty like them. The delegation promised to forward to the Commission the written judgement of the Military Tribunal. This has not yet happened.

(29) The Commission finds that by not reinstating Mr. Mazou in his former position after the Amnesty Law, the government has violated Article 15 of the African Charter, because it has prevented Mr. Mazou to work in his capacity of a magistrate even though others who have been condemned under similar conditions have been reinstated.

For the above reasons, the Commission:

declares the violations of Articles 6, 7.1(b), 7.1(d) and 15;

recommends that the government of Cameroon draw all the necessary legal conclusions to reinstate the victim in his rights.

Taken at the 21st Ordinary Session, Nouakchott, Mauritania, April 1997.

3. 44/90 Peoples' Democratic Organisation for Independence and Socialism/The Gambia Report on an Amicable Resolution

The facts:

(1) The complaint alleges that voter registration in the constituencies of Serrekunda West, Serrekunda East and Bakau was defective because those registering were not required by the law to give an address or identification. It argues that there was no control over voter registration since no documents have to be shown to the registration officer. The voter may be asked his name and citizenship, but there is no requirement to produce an address or compound number. Furthermore, the witness is not required to identify himself. The complainant argued that the absence of a requirement to produce an address or compound number makes it possible for the voter to forge his right to vote in the constituency, or to vote several times.

(2) In the rural areas the registration of the voters and the voting procedure itself are controlled by the headman, the registration officer, representatives of different political parties, and village elders. In the urban areas the control is only done by the registration officer, who does not know the people. Without the street address or compound number it is impossible for the registration officer to control the identity of the voter, even though they must sign a form of registration and enclose a photograph, because the signature could be forged and the lack of communication between different constituencies could make it possible for the voter to register in several stations.

(3) The complainant argues that the registration by street address/compound number is possible, since most urban areas in the Gambia have street address or compound number.

(4) The complainant argues that, based on its observations of voter registration, there is widespread fraud.

According to the Government:

(5) The government argued firstly that the case was inadmissible because it could be taken through the courts to the level of the (British) Privy Council.

(6) The complainant pointed out that the (Gambian) Elections Act, Section 22(5), states that the judgment of the Gambian Supreme Court shall be final and conclusive; thus, appeal to the Privy Council is impossible.

(7) As to the merits, the state originally claimed that the Gambia does hold free and fair elections. In the urban areas a form was signed and address/compound number, occupation, constituency and photo, were included wherever possible. These were checked by the registration officer both at registration and at the elections, providing adequate protection against fraud. Likewise, in the rural areas, the personal identification by the village headman took place both at registration and at the elections.

(8) The state claimed that it is almost impossible in a developing country like the Gambia to ensure control by street addresses/compound number. Many dwellings in the Gambia, including in the urban areas, do not have street addresses/compound numbers, but are registered in the names of the owners. It is therefore impossible to make this requirement absolute.

(9) The state further argued that it is impossible to require showing of identity papers at the time of registration and election as a high percentage of the population does not have identification papers. It was not before 1985 that a National Identity Card was introduced and now not more than 50% of the population has been registered.

(10) In July 1994 there was a change of government in The Gambia. The present government strongly condemns the claims of the previous government that the streets of Serrekunda were not named with sufficient specificity to permit making an street address a mandatory requirement for voter registration. The present government calls this claim "inexcusable and indefensible".

(11) The present government, by its "Admission of Communication No. 44/90 from the Peoples Democratic Organisation for Independence and Socialism-PDOIS Against the State of the Gambia" concedes that the grievances expressed by the complainants are valid and logical. It expressed its intent to change the current system to correct the present "anomalies".

Procedure:

(12) The communication is dated 19 June 1990. The Commission was seized of the communication at the 8th Session and the government of The Gambia was notified on 6 November 1990.

(13) From 1990 to 1995, the Commission proceeded to verify the exhaustion of local remedies.

(14) At the 17th session the communication was declared admissible on the basis that exhaustion of local remedies had been unduly prolonged.

(15) On 20 April 1995 a letter was sent to the complainants and the Gambian Government, stating that the communication was admissible.

(16) The Commission received a letter from the Attorney General's Chambers and Ministry of Justice of The Gambia, conceding that the grievances expressed by the complainants are valid and logical, and that the present electoral law is being reviewed with the objective of curing the present anomalies.

(17) On 20 December 1995, the complainant was informed of this response with the specification that if the Secretariat does not receive arguments to the contrary before the 1 February 1996, the Commission would consider the communication to have been resolved amicably.

Law:

Admissibility:

(18) The PDOIS argued that it was beyond the jurisdiction of the judiciary to order Parliament to change defective procedures and laws; thus, recourse to the courts was not an option. The complainant alleged that, while the Elections Act provides for objections to voter lists to be made before a revising officer appointed by the Supervisor of Elections, the fact that the voter lists posted did not include a list of addresses made effective scrutiny impossible. The complaint noted that numerous letters had been addressed to the Supervisor of Elections and the President of the Republic as early as 1987 with no response.

(19) The Government noted that in July 1990, the complainant did file a Notice of Objection and sent it to the Commissioner of Western Division. The document was forwarded to the Revising Court. No action appeared to have been taken by the court.

(20) On the basis of these facts the communication was declared admissible.

(21) Article 13 of The African Charter reads:

> "Every citizen shall have the right to participate freely in the government of his country, either directly or through freely chosen representatives in accordance with the provision of the law".

(22) In 1994 there was a change of government in The Gambia. The present government recognizes that it has inherited the previous government's rights and obligations under international treaties.

(23) The present government has a different view of voter registration. It concedes that the grievances expressed by the complainants are valid and logical. It describes that it is in the process of establishing an independent electoral commission and has commissioned a team of experts to review the present electoral law.

(24) The African Commission welcomes the acceptance of the complainant's contentions and the government's stated determination to review the current electoral law, in order to ensure that elections are regular, free and fair.

For these reasons, the Commission:
holds that the above communication has reached an amicable resolution.

Taken at the 20th Ordinary Session, Grand Bay, Mauritius, October 1996.

4. 65/92 Ligue Camerounaise des Droits de l'Homme/Cameroon

The facts:

(1) The complaint is in two parts. The first, submitted by the Ligue Camerounaise des Droits de l'Homme, alleges a number of serious and massive violations in Cameroon committed by the present government. The Ligue alleges that the prison conditions in Cameroon constitute cruel, inhuman and degrading treatment and that many people have been arbitrarily arrested and detained in these conditions. Between 1984 and 1989 at least 46 persons were tortured and deprived of food in the Central Prison of Yaoundé. Further violations consist in the repression of freedom of expression, creation of special tribunals, denial of fair hearing, ethnic discrimination, and massacres of the civil population.

(2) The second part relates to the situation of Mr Joseph Vitine, an ex-police officer. He stated that he has been persecuted by his former colleagues since March 1990. Subsequent to this submission Mr. Vitine re-submitted his case as a separate communication, no. 106/93.

(3) The government of Cameroon responded in writing that the case of Mr. Vitine should be declared inadmissible because the author did not appear to be in possession of his full mental faculties. The government responded orally that the allegations of the Ligue Camerounaise should be declared inadmissible because they are posed in disparaging and insulting language.

Procedure:

(4) The communication is not dated but was received from the Ligue Camerounaise just before March 1992. The Commission was seized of the communication at the 11th Session.

(5) The government of Cameroon was notified of the communication on 8 April 1992. No response was forthcoming.

(6) On 13 November 1992 another notification was sent.

(7) As of the 19th session, no information had been received from the government. The Commission declared the communication as regards Mr. Vitine inadmissible.

(8) On 17 May 1996 the Commission sent a letter to Mr. Vitine informing him that his communication had been declared inadmissible at the 19th session.

(9) At the 20th session, a delegation of the government of Cameroon was present and submitted a written response to the communication, dealing with the portion of the communication submitted by Mr. Vitine, which had already been declared inadmissible. The government delegation made an oral presentation concerning the allegations of the Ligue Camerounaise. The Commission decided to request more information from both the government and the complainant, and to postpone a decision on the merits of the case.

(10) On 10 December 1996 the parties were informed of this decision.

Law:

Admissibility:

(11) Article 55.2 of the Charter reads:

> "A communication shall be considered by the Commission if a majority of its members so decide."

(12) This power of the Commission to consider communications naturally includes the lesser power to decline to hear them.

(13) The allegations submitted by Mr. Vitine were in 1993 submitted separately to the Commission and registered as communication 106/93. The information in this communication did not give evidence of prima facie violations of the African Charter. For this reason the Commission declared the communication inadmissible.

(14) Article 56.3 of the Charter reads:

> "Communication relating to Human and Peoples' Rights referred to in Article 55 received by the Commission, shall be considered if they:
>
> . . .
>
> 3. are not written in disparaging or insulting language directed against the State concerned and its institutions or to the Organisation of African Unity."

(15) The allegations submitted by the Ligue Camerounaise are of a series of serious and massive violations of the Charter. The communication contains statements such as: "Paul Biya must respond to crimes against humanity", "30 years of the criminal neo-colonial regime incarnated by the duo Ahidjo/Biya", "regime of torturers", and "government barbarisms". This is insulting language.

(16) In addition to the requirements of form, the Commission has a clear precedent that communications must contain a certain degree of specificity, such as will permit the Commission to take meaningful action. (See the Commission's decision on communication 104/94, 109–126/94 Center for the Independence of Judges and Lawyers/Algeria et al.)

For these reasons, the Commission:
declares the communication inadmissible.

Taken at the 21st Ordinary Session, Nouakchott, Mauritania, April 1997.

5. 71/92 Rencontre Africaine pour la Defense des Droits de l'Homme/Zambia

Facts:

(1) The complaint is presented by a Senegalese NGO, Rencontre Africaine pour la Defense des Droits de l'Homme, on behalf of 517 West Africans who were expelled from Zambia on 26 and 27 February 1992, on grounds of being in

Zambia illegally. Prior to their expulsion, most of the individuals had been subject to administrative detention for more than 2 months. The deportees lost all the material possessions they had in Zambia, and many were also separated from their Zambian families.

(2) The communication was submitted on 28 February 1992. The Commission was seized of it at the 12th Session.

(3) On 13 November 1992, the text of the communication was sent to the Zambian Ministry of Justice and ministry of External Affairs by registered post. No reply has been forthcoming.

(4) At the 16th Session, the communication was declared admissible and the parties were informed that the merits of the case would be considered at the 17th Session.

(5) At the 18th session in October 1995, a delegation of the Zambian government appeared and presented additional information dated 29 September 1995.

(6) The complainant also appeared and presented a reply to the government's arguments.

(7) The Commission decided to pursue an amicable resolution to the communication, which would involve further details being given to the Zambian government so that reparations might be effected.

(8) On 2 August 1996, the Commission informed the Government of Zambia of its intention to continue the efforts towards an amicable resolution of the case.

Law:

Admissibility:

(9) The Zambian government argues that the communication must be declared inadmissible because domestic remedies have not been exhausted.

(10) Article 56 of the African Charter provides as follows:

> "Communications shall be considered if they:
>
> . . .
>
> 5. are sent after exhausting local remedies, if any, unless it is obvious that these procedures are unduly prolonged . . ."

(11) The rule requiring the exhaustion of local remedies as a condition of the presentation of an international claim is founded upon, amongst other principles, the contention that the respondent state must first have an opportunity to redress by its own means within the framework of its own domestic legal system, the wrong alleged to have been done to the individual.

(12) This does not mean, however, that complainants are required to exhaust any local remedy which is found to be, as a practical matter, unavailable or ineffective.

(13) When the Zambian government argues that the communication must be declared inadmissible because the local remedies have not been exhausted, the government then has the burden of demonstrating the existence of such

remedies. The government of Zambia attempts to do so by referring to the Immigration and Deportations Act which provides for appeal of expulsion orders. The government states that actions for loss of property likewise can be brought under Zambian law.

(14) The question is therefore whether, in the circumstances alleged, the Immigration and Deportation Act constitutes an effective and adequate remedy in respect to the complaints.

(15) The mass nature of the arrests, the fact that victims were kept in detention prior to their expulsions, and the speed with which the expulsions were carried out gave the complainants no opportunity to establish the illegality of these actions in the courts. For complainants to contact their families, much less attorneys, was not possible. Thus, the recourse referred to by the government under the Immigration and Deportation Act was as a practical matter not available to the complainants. This was confirmed by the complainants during their arguments before the Commission, as well as by expert testimony. (See "Réplique du RADDHO a la Réponse du Gouvernement Zambien", p. 3; also letter of Executive Director of Afronet Zambia, 7 October 1995.)

(16) The Zambian government argues that the victims were remiss in not taking advantage of the legal aid system in Zambia ("Additional Information", p.6.) However, complainants make clear, in their "Réplique" and through expert testimony contained in the file, that if the victims of deportation were in fact illegal as the government argues, they would be ineligible for legal aid. (See "Réplique", p. 3; see also the letter of Chakota Beyani, Refugee Studies Program, Oxford University, p. 1.)

(17) For the above reasons the Commission holds the communication admissible.

Merits:

(18) Given that the process of arriving at an amicable resolution can take a substantial period of time, the Commission believes it is important to make a statement on the question of law raised by this communication.

(19) Article 12, paragraph 5 of the Charter provides:

> "The mass expulsion of non-nationals shall be prohibited. Mass expulsion shall be that which is aimed at national, racial, ethnic or religious groups."

(20) Clearly, the drafters of the Charter believed that mass expulsion presented a special threat to human rights.

(21) The Charter makes this point clearly in Article 2, which states:

> "Every individual shall be entitled to the enjoyment of the rights and freedoms recognized and guaranteed in the present Charter without distinction of any kind such as race, ethnic group, colour, sex, language, religion, political or any other opinion, national and social original, fortune, birth or other status."

(22) This imposes an obligation on the contracting state to secure the rights protected in the Charter to all persons within their jurisdiction, nationals or non-nationals.

(23) The government of Zambia argues that the expulsion of the west African was justified because they were in Zambia illegally, and that the African Charter does not abolish visa requirements and borders between African states. It is true that the African Charter does not bar deportations per se, but Zambia's right to expel individuals does not justify the manner in which it does so.

(24) The victims on whose part RADDHO seized the Commission were all from West Africa, some from Senegal, some from Mali, Guinea Conakry, and other West African countries. The government of Zambia, in its "Additional Information" presented to the Commission at the 18th Session, argues that the expulsion was not discriminatory because nationals of several West African countries and other foreign countries were all subject to the same treatment. (See "Additional Information", p. 1; list of aliens repatriated between 25 November 1991 and 16 January 1992, attached.)

(25) The complainants respond that they are concerned only with the expulsion of West Africans, because it is these persons who appealed to them for help, but that simultaneous expulsion of nationals of many countries does not negate the charge of discrimination. Rather, the argument that so many aliens received the same treatment is tantamount to an admission of a violation of Article 12.5. ("Réplique," pp .1–2.)

(26) It is clear from the government's own list of repatriated aliens, however, that after excluding nationals Zambia's immediate neighbors, Tanzania and Zaire, West Africans constitute the majority of those expelled.

(27) The Zambian government disputes the characterization of the expulsions as "en masse" by arguing that the deportees were arrested over a two-month period of time, at different places, and served with deportation orders on different dates. (Additional Information, p. 4, pp iii.) Zambia, however, cannot prove that the deportees were given the opportunity to seek appeal against the decision on their deportation.

(28) Zambia maintains that the two months during which some of the deportees were held were necessary to verify their nationality in some cases, and also that complainants might have used this time to contact their lawyers. The facts of this communication show that West Africans were arrested and assembled over time, with a view to their eventual expulsion. The deportees were kept in a camp during this time, not even an ordinary prison, and it was impossible for them to contact their lawyers.

(29) Article 7 of the Charter specifies:

> "Everyone shall have the right to have his cause heard.
> This comprises:
>
> . . .
>
> a. the right to an appeal to competent national organs against acts violating his fundamental rights as recognized and guaranteed by conventions, law, regulations and customs in force."

In holding this case admissible the Commission has already established that none of the deportees had the opportunity to seize the Zambian courts to challenge their detention or deportation. This constitutes a violation of their rights under Article 7 of the Charter and under Zambian national law.

(31) The African Commission will not dispute that the Zambian state has the right to bring legal action against all persons illegally residing in Zambia, and to deport them if the results of such legal action justify it. However, the mass deportation of the individuals in question here, including their arbitrary detention and deprivation of the right to have their cause heard, constitute a flagrant violation of the Charter.

For the above reasons, the Commission:

decides that the deportations constitute a violation of Articles 2, 7.1(a), and 12(5) of the African Charter

resolves to continue efforts to pursue an amicable resolution in this case.

Taken at the 20th Ordinary Session, Grand Bay, Mauritius, October 1997.

6. 97/93 John K. Modise/Botswana

The facts:

(1) The complainant claims citizenship of Botswana under the following circumstances: His father was a citizen of Botswana who went to work in South Africa. While in South Africa, he married and the complainant was an issue of that marriage. Complainant's mother died shortly after birth and complainant was sent to Botswana where he grew up. Complainant therefore claims Botswana citizenship by descent.

(2) The complainant alleges that in 1978 he was one of the founders and leaders of the Botswana National Front opposition party. He alleges it was as a result of these activities that he was declared a "prohibited immigrant" by the Botswana government.

(3) On 17 October 1978, complainant was arrested and handed over to the South African Police, without being brought before any tribunal. He already had a court action in process in Botswana concerning a Temporary Occupation Permit, but due to his deportation was unable to attend the hearing.

(4) When he returned to Botswana, he was arrested and deported again without hearing. After his third entry back into Botswana he was charged and convicted of unlawful entry and being a prohibited immigrant. He was serving a ten-month sentence and appealing his conviction when he was deported for a fourth time to South Africa, before his last appeal could be heard.

(5) Because the complainant was not a citizen of South Africa, he was forced to live in the "homeland" of Bophuthatswana. He remained there for seven years, until the government of Bophuthatswana issued a deportation order against him, which landed him in the no-man's land between Bophuthatswana and Botswana, where he remained for five weeks before he was admitted to Botswana on a humanitarian basis. He lived there on three-month resident permits, renewable at the absolute discretion of the minister concerned, until June 1995.

(6) Complainant does not possess, nor has he ever possessed, a South African passport or Bophuthatswanan nationality.

(7) Complainant alleges he has suffered financial losses, since much of his property and possessions was confiscated by the government. He cannot work because he is not permitted to, and is in constant danger of being deported. Complainant has made several efforts to assert his Botswana nationality and an appeal from his prison sentence is still pending, but has not been heard. He presently has no funds to continue in the courts.

(8) He is asking the Government of Botswana to recognise him as a citizen by birth.

Procedure:

(9) The communication is dated 3 March 1993 and is sent by John K. Modise.

(10) At the 13th Session in March 1993, the Commission was seized of the communication.

(11) On 12 April 1993, a notification of the communication was sent to the Botswana government.

(12) At the 17th session the communication was declared admissible. It was found to be a fit subject for settlement by the Commissioner responsible for Botswana, that is, Commissioner Janneh. The parties were notified of this decision.

(13) The government of Botswana was invited to consider the possibility of an amicable resolution.

(14) On 19 October 1995 the Commission received a note verbale by fax from the Ministry of Foreign Affairs of Botswana, stating that Mr. Modise had been granted citizenship by the President. The citizenship certificate was posted to him on 26 June 1995.

(15) On 30 November 1995 a copy of this note verbale was sent to Mr. Odinkalu with a letter asking if the granting of citizenship could be considered an amicable resolution of the case.

(16) On 14 December 1995 the Commission received a letter from Mr Chidi Odinkalu, the complainant's counsel, indicating that he did not consider that a friendly settlement had been reached and requesting further action on the part of the Commission.

(17) On 9 October 1996 the Secretariat of the Commission received a fax from Interights with a copy of a letter from Mr. Modise stating that all local remedies have been exhausted, and that even though the Government of Botswana had promised Commissioner Dankwa that they would issue a passport to Mr. Modise, his application to get a passport had still not been approved by the authorities.

Law:

Admissibility:

(18) Article 56.5 of the African Charter requires that communications shall be admissible only if the complainant has exhausted the remedies available domestically, provided these are not unduly prolonged. Other international human rights instruments have similar provisions.

(19) The complainant affirms that he has been trying without success to establish his Botswana nationality legally since 1978 and his final appeal is still pending, 16 years later.

(20) In this case the complainant brought his first action over 16 years ago, and the legal process was repeatedly interrupted the summary deportations of which he was the victim. The national legal procedures were willfully obstructed.

(21) All the preceding elements lead to the conclusion that the complainant has exhausted all local remedies.

(22) For all these reasons the Commission declared the communication admissible.

Merits:

(23) The Republic of Botswana ratified the African Charter on 17 July 1986. Although some of the events described in the communication took place before ratification, their effects continue to the present day. The current circumstances of the complainant is a result of a present policy decision taken by the Botswana government against him.

(24) The complainant argues that he has been unjustly denied Botswana citizenship. In the brief submitted by the complainant's representative, it is explained that the complainant was born in Cape Town to a father and mother both from the Goo-Modultwa Ward in Kanye of the Bangwaketse in the former Protectorate of Bechuanaland.

(25) The complainant furthermore alleges that in 1978 he was one of the founding members and leaders of the opposition party, National Front of Botswana. As a consequent of his activities he was declared an prohibited immigrant and expelled to South Africa, which also expelled him several times, with all the disturbing consequences described above.

(26) Botswana became an independent country in 1966. Section 20 of its Constitution states:

> "Every person who, having been born in the former Protectorate of Bechuanaland, is on 29 September 1966, a citizen of the United Kingdom and Colonies or a British protected person shall become a citizen of Botswana on 30th September, 1966."

(27) The complainant thus alleges that as a matter of law, by birth, he is a citizen of Botswana. The Government has nowhere contested the facts on which the complainant bases his claim.

(28) Article 7 of the African Charter specifies:

> "1. Every individual shall have the right to have his cause heard. This comprises:
> (a) the right to an appeal to competent national organs against acts of violating his fundamental rights as recognized and guaranteed by conventions, laws, regulations and customs in force; . . ."

(29) To this day, no court has remedied the effects of the complainant's original deportation, which constitutes a flagrant violation of Article 7.

(30) The complainant's defence against deportation rests on the fact that he is by law a citizen of Botswana. In his trial for illegal re-entry into Botswana, this defence was not considered by the court. To this day, there is no resolution in the courts of this essential issue. This constitutes another violation of Article 7.

(31) Article 5 of the African Charter states:

> "Every individual shall have the right to the respect of the dignity inherent in a human being and to the recognition of his legal status. All forms of exploitation and degradation of man particularly . . . torture, cruel, inhuman or degrading punishment and treatment shall be prohibited."

(32) The complaint was deported to South Africa and was forced to live for eight years in the "homeland" of Bophuthatswana, and then for another seven years in "No-Man's Land", a border strip between the former south African Homeland of Bophuthatswana and Botswana. Not only did this expose him to personal suffering, it deprived him of his family, and it deprived his family of his support. Such inhuman and degrading treatment offends the dignity of a human being and thus violates Article 5.

(33) The Government of Botswana, without acknowledging any responsibility did take some steps to remedy the complainant's situation by granting him a certificate of citizenship in June 1995, under section 9(2) of the Citizenship Act of Botswana.

(34) However, subsequent information from the complainant indicates that the citizenship granted is in several ways inferior to citizenship by birth. Citizenship by birth is a right which cannot be taken away, whereas citizenship by registration is a privilege that is granted only at discretion of state officials.

(35) When the complainant applied for an international passport to enable him to travel abroad for medical treatment, the Government of Botswana issued him a "Local Passport", #L213968, on 6 July 1995. This passport restricted his travelling to countries on mainland Africa south of Latitude 15 South. It expired on 5 January 1996.

(36) Furthermore, a person who acquires citizenship under section 9(b) of the citizenship act, rather than by birth, is considered a citizen from the time of granting only. This means that prior to his registration the complainant was a stateless person, and his children are in the same situation.

(37) Article 13 of the African Charter stipulates:

> "1. Every citizen shall have the right to participate freely in the government of his county, either directly or through freely chosen representatives in accordance with the provisions of the law.
> 2. Every citizen shall have the right of equal access to the public service of his country."

(38) Citizens by registration cannot be candidates for the presidency of the Republic. Taken together with his first deportation, soon after he founded an opposition political party, it appears that this is an action designed to hamper his political

participation. Granting the complainant citizenship by registration has effectively deprived him of what is for him, one of the most valuable rights that Botswana citizenship affords.

(39) Elements in the file show that the complainant did obtain Botswana nationality, but he is not satisfied. The Commission considers, however, that the other rights which the complainant is seeking, could be obtained through local judicial action.

(40) If issues related to the acquisition of full citizenship are not resolved by competent domestic judicial authorities, or in the event of new facts coming to light, Mr. Modise can resort once more to the Commission.

For the above reasons, the Commission

takes note of the granting of Botswana citizenship to Mr. Modise

calls upon the Government of Botswana to continue with its efforts to amicably resolve this communication in compliance with national laws and with the provisions of the African Charter on Human and Peoples' Rights.

7. 103/93 Alhassan Abubakar/Ghana

The facts:

(1) Alhassan Abubakar is a Ghanaian citizen, presently residing in Côte d'Ivoire. He was arrested on 16 June 1985 for allegedly cooperating with political dissidents. He was detained without charge or trial for 7 years until his escape from a prison hospital on 19 February 1992.

(2) After his escape, his sister and his wife, who had been visiting him, were arrested and held for two weeks in an attempt to get information on the complainant's whereabouts. The complainant's brother has informed him that the police have been given false information about his return, and have on several occasions surrounded his house, searched it, and subsequently searched for him in his mother's village. In the early part of 1993 the UNHCR in Côte d'Ivoire informed the complainant that they had received a report on him from Ghana assuring that he was free to return without risk of being prosecuted for fleeing from prison. The report further stated that all those detained for political reasons had been released.

(3) Complainant on the other hand holds that there is a law in Ghana which subjects escapees to penalties from 6 months to 2 years imprisonment, regardless of whether the detention from which they escaped was lawful or not.

Procedure:

(4) The communication is dated 26 July 1993. The complainant was sent a questionnaire concerning communications on 11 August 1993 and returned it completed. The Commission was seized at the 14th Session and the communication was sent to the state concerned on 6 January 1994. No response was forthcoming.

(5) The Commission tried without success to resolve this communication amicably.

Law:

Admissibility:

(6) Article 56.5 of the Charter requires that all local remedies be exhausted before the Commission can consider the communication, unless the procedure is unduly prolonged. In this case the complainant is residing outside the state against which the communication is addressed and thus where the remedies would be available. He escaped to Côte d'Ivoire from prison in Ghana and has not returned there. Considering the nature of the complaint it would not be logical to ask the complainant to go back to Ghana in order to seek a remedy from national legal authorities. Accordingly, the Commission does not consider that local remedies are available for the complainant.

(7) As the communication fulfils all the other requirements of Article 56, the Commission declares the communication admissible.

Merits:

(8) Article 6 of the Charter reads:

> "Every individual shall have the right to liberty and security of his person. No one may be deprived of his freedom except for reasons and conditions previously laid down by law. In particular, no one may be arbitrarily arrested or detained."

(9) The complainant contends he was arrested by the Government for alleged collaboration with dissidents to overthrow the administration. He was arrested under section 2 of the Preventive Custody Law of 1992 (P.N.D.C.L. 4) in the interest of national security. However, the complainant states he was never charged with this offence nor brought to trial.

(10) The Government failed to provide further details of the relevant laws on request, merely stating that "if the complainant has violated some laws, he must stand trial for them in the national courts". It is by now well-settled law before the Commission that where no substantive information is forthcoming from the government concerned, the Commission will decide on the facts as alleged by the complainant (see, e.g., decisions on communications 25/89, 59/91, 60/91, 64/92, 87/93 and 101/93).

(11) Article 7.1 of the Charter reads:

> "1. Every individual shall have the right to have his case heard. This comprises:
>
> . . .
>
> (d) the right to be tried within a reasonable time . . ."

(12) The complainant was detained in prison for seven years without trial before his escape. This period clearly violates the "reasonable time" standard stipulated in the Charter.

(13) Article 12.2 of the Charter reads:

"2. Every individual shall have the right . . . to return to his country. This right may only be subject to restrictions, provided for by law, for the protection of national security, law and order, public health or morality."

(14) The complainant alleges the existence of a law in Ghana permitting the detention of escapees on their return to the country. The Government has denied that the complainant would be imprisoned on grounds of escape on his return, but concedes that he could be tried for any criminal offences that he may have committed. The government has stated that all political prisoners have been released, but the complainant provides evidence of other escapees who were arrested on their return to Ghana and that there is some indication that he would also be subject to the same treatment.

(15) The facts provided are insufficient to find that the complainant's right to return to his country has been violated.

For these reasons, the Commission:
holds there has been a violation of Articles 6 and 7.1(d) the Charter
urges the Government to take steps to repair the prejudice suffered.

Taken at the 20th session, Grand Bay, Mauritius, October 1996.

8. 108/93 Monja Joana/Madagascar

The facts:

(1) The complainant was a citizen of Madagascar, who was a prominent political figure and had been a candidate for president. He was arrested on 1 June 1993 under a special decree, which provided for his detention for an indefinite period of time without being told the reason and without the right to appear before a judge. His sons were also arrested.

(2) According to the court judgment of 17 December 1993, the complainant is guilty of trespass in government buildings and acquisition of arms without authorization. He was given a one-year suspended sentence. His sons were acquitted. The communication does not include his address.

Procedure:

(3) The communication is dated 20 July 1993. The state concerned was notified by mail on 6 January 1994.

(4) The Commission proceeded to examine the necessary facts in order to be sure that the United Nations Human Rights Committee had not been seized of the same communication and in order to try to know the address of the complainant.

(5) The information received revealed that this case had not been submitted to the United Nations and that the complainant had died.

Law:

Admissibility:

(6) Article 56.1 of the Charter requires that communications presented pursuant to Article 55 indicate their author, even if the author has requested anonymity. The

Commission must be in communication with the author, to know his identity and status, to be assured of his continued interest in the communication and to request supplementary information if the case requires it. This is reflected in Rule 104 of the Rules of Procedure of the Commission.

(7) In the past, the Commission made decisions on the admissibility in the case where the requirements of Article 56.1 had not been fulfilled.

(8) The Commission closed communication 62/92 (Committee for the Defence of Human Rights in respect of Ms Jennifer Madike /Nigeria) because two letters of reminder to the complainant had gone unanswered. The Commission interpreted this prolonged silence on the part of the complainant as "loss of contact with the complainant".

(9) In its decision on communication 70/92 (Ibrahima Dioumessi, Sekou Kande, Ousmane Kaba/Guinea), the Commission declared the communication inadmissible because the complainant had included no address and the address could not be located through other means.

(10) In the present case, the Commission has not had contact with the complainant since the case was brought.

(11) The Commission has tried various means in an attempt to contact the complainant through other individuals. The address of the complainant's family reached the Commission in the same letter as news of the complainant's death. Efforts made to contact the deceased's legal successor have not borne results.

For these reasons, the Commission
declares the communication inadmissible.

Taken at the 20th session, Grand Bay, Mauritius, October 1996.

ANNEX XI

Resolutions of the African Commission on Human and Peoples' Rights

RESOLUTION ON ZAIRE

The African Commission on Human and Peoples' Rights meeting at its 21st ordinary session in Nouakchott,Mauritania between 15–24 April 1997 views with grave concern the massive violations of human rights that continue to be perpetrated in Zaire by conflicting parties,

Desiring an immediate end to the harrowing suffering of people from various ethnic backgrounds and all walks of life,urgently appeals to all parties in the conflict in Zaire to respect the human rights of all peoples in Zaire, especially non-combatants, refugees and internally displaced persons,

FURTHER CALLS UPON the various political leaders to resolve their differences peacefully, and thereby avoid the inevitable bloodshed that an assault on Kinshasa and President Mobutu's Headquarters would entail,

EXPRESSES its appreciation for the efforts made at the level of the UN, the OAU and the International Community at seeking a peaceful resolution to the conflict in Zaire and urges them not to relent in their efforts to achieve this goal.
24 April 1997

RESOLUTION ON THE PROTECTION OF THE NAME, ACRONYM AND LOGO OF THE AFRICAN COMMISSION ON HUMAN AND PEOPLES' RIGHTS.

The African Commission on Human and Peoples' Rights, meeting at its 21st Ordinary Session in Nouakchott, Mauritania, from 15–24 April 1997,

Recalling the relevant provisions of the African Charter on Human and Peoples' Rights, particularly Articles 30 and 45 (1-a and 2),

Noting with satisfaction the enthusiasm demonstrated by the civil society in Africa in the promotion of human and peoples' rights,

Considering, however, the misuse by some NGOs of the name, logo and acronym of the Commission,

Recalling the need to avoid any confusion which may result in an uncontrollable use of names, acronyms, logos or other external signs bearing resemblance to those belonging to the African Commission on Human and Peoples' Rights;

CALLS UPON States Parties to do everything, in collaboration with the OAU Secretariat, to ensure the protection of the name, acronym and logo of the Commission throughout their countries,

CALLS ON States Parties to refuse granting registration to NGOs whose names, acronyms or symbols could cause confusion prejudicial to the Commission,

FURTHERMORE CALLS UPON organisations concerned to proceed to make the necessary rectification in conformity with the present resolution.

Final Communiqué of the Twentieth Ordinary Session of the African Commission on Human and Peoples' Rights

Mauritius, 21–31 October 1996

1. The 20th Ordinary Session of the African Commission on Human and Peoples' Rights was held in Grand Bay, Mauritius, from 21–31 October 1996 and was chaired by Professor Isaac Nguema. It was preceded by the Eleventh NGOs Workshop jointly organised by the International Commission of Jurists and the African Commission on Human and Peoples' Rights.

2. This session started with the commemoration of the 10th anniversary of the entry into force of the African Charter on Human and Peoples' Rights.

3. The opening ceremony was attended by all the Members of the Commission; the Prime Minister of the Republic of Mauritius, H.E. Mr Navinchandra Ramgoolam, accompanied by Members of his government; by Mr. Mr Salem Ahmed Salim, Secretary General of the OAS; H.E. Mr Ayala Lasso, office of the UN Human Rights Commissioner; States-Parties delegates; Members of the Diplomatic Corps accredited in Mauritius; Representatives of governmental and non-governmental organisations; Representatives of the national and international press as well as other distinguished invitees.

4. At the opening ceremony, after the presentation of the draft Plan of Action of the Commission for the next five years by the Vice-Chairman of the Commission, Professor E. V. O. Dankwa, speeches were delivered by the Chairman of the African Commission; the Prime Minister of the Republic of Mauritius; the Secretary-General of the OAU; the UN Human Rights High Commissioner; the Minister of Justice and Human Rights of the Republic of Togo and the Secretary-General of the International Commission of Jurists.

5. The Commission held a meeting with the Secretary-General of the OAU who indicated his comprehension of the issues raised before him. On this occasion, the Commission responded favourably to the invitation extended by the Secretary General to participate in monitoring the elections in Gambia and Zambia.

6. The Commission considered applications for observer status and granted it to 15 NGOs. The list of these NGOs is available at the Secretariat.

7. The report on the conclusions of the 11th NGOs Workshop was submitted to the Commission. Briefly, the Workshop emphasised the future of the human rights' system in Africa and the need to provide assistance to the African Commission in the elaboration of a plan of action for the years 1996–2001.

8. The Representatives of the governments of South Africa, Burundi, Ethiopia, Egypt, Burkina Faso, Cameroun, Equatorial Guinee, Mozambique, Nigeria, Senegal,

Sudan and Tunisia delivered statements underscoring the willingness of their countries to respect the provisions of the African Charter and reiterated their commitment to cooperate with the Commission.

9. The Commission, the statements delivered by the Representatives of the United Nations Centre for Human Rights, the ICRC and African and international organisations, as well as representatives from national Commissions on Human Rights who participated in the session.

10. Concerning the consideration of periodic state reports, the Commission examined the initial reports of Mauritius presented by His Excellency Mr. Razack Peeroo, the Minister of Justice. A discussion followed, thus giving the Commission the opportunity to congratulate Mauritius for its interest in the African Charter and its respect for human rights.

11. The setting up of an Early Warning Mechanism in case of massive human rights violations in Africa was a significant issue of concern to the Commission which appointed three commissioners following the report presented by Professor Umozurike on behalf of a working group that addressed this issue during the meeting in Nairobi.

12. The Commission considered and adopted its Plan of action for 1996–2001.

13. The Commission decided to commemorate its 10th Anniversary on 2 November 1997 held at its 22nd Ordinary Session.

14. The Commissioners presented their reports on their promotional activities during the intersession.

15. The Commission considered the report of Commissioner Ben Salem, the Special Rapporteur on extra-judicial, summary or arbitrary executions and decided to extend his mission up to the end of his mandate in the Commission.

16. The Commission was informed by its Secretary that most States had not yet submitted their comments on the first draft of the protocol establishing the African Court on Human and Peoples' Rights. Therefore this issue was deferred to the forthcoming Ordinary Session of the OAU Council of Ministers in February 1997.

17. With respect to human rights situation in Africa, the Commission heard from various participants who highlighted the disturbing situations in Kenya, Zaire, Burundi and Liberia. They raised among others, issues of refugees and internally displaced persons, independence of the judiciary and the need to establish independent electoral commissions.

18. The Commission considered the report prepared after following the Seminar on Prison Conditions in Africa (Kampala, 19–21 September 1996) and decided to appoint Commissioner E. V. O. Dankwa, Vice-Chairman of the Commission as Special Rapporteur on prison conditions in Africa.

19. The Commission reiterated its commitment to elaborate the additional protocol on the rights of African women and to appoint a Special Rapporteur and has decided to consider the proposals pertaining to this issue in its forthcoming session as will be submitted by its working group.

20. The Commissioner took cognizance of the progress achieved in the preparation of the planned seminars and decided to hold other seminars.

21. With regard to protectional activities, the Commission received five new communications and examined fourteen communications against Zaire, Tanzania, Uganda, Rwanda, Kenya, Zambia, Angola and Benin. For the cases concerning Nigeria and Sudan, the Commission designated missions which will visit these countries, and examine, at the same time, different communications which relate to them. The Commission equally considered and adopted the reports presented by the two delegations sent respectively to Senegal and Mauritania following the previous decisions taken during the examination of communications concerning these countries. Recommendations were addressed to the two countries.

22. During the session, the Commission was respectively received by:

- H.E. President, C. Uteem, President of the Republic of Mauritius;
- H.E. Mr. N. Ramgoolam, the Prime Minister;
- H.E. Mr. P. Bérenger, Deputy Prime Minister and Minister of Foreign Affairs;
- H.E. Mr. R. Peeroo, Minister of Justice.

23. The Commission decided to hold its 21st Ordinary Session from 15–24 April 1997 in a country to be determined later.

24. The closing ceremony of the 20th Ordinary Session took place on 31 October 1996 and was officiated by H.E. Mr P. Bérenger, Deputy Prime Minister and Minister of Foreign Affairs.

25. The Chairman of the Commission held a press conference after the closing ceremony.

Done in Grand Bay, Mauritius, 31 October 1996.

The Mauritius Plan of Action 1996–2001

INTRODUCTION

At the end of the first decade (21 October 1996) since the African Charter on Human and Peoples' Rights came into effect, the Commission adopted a five-year Plan of Action with the aim of attaining, in as far as possible, the fundamental objectives of the Charter.

The paramount mission of the African Charter is the promotion and protection of human and peoples' rights in Africa.

A preliminary Plan of Action had been adopted in 1988 in order to launch the activities of the Commission. A Plan of Action of the African Commission on Human and Peoples' Right for 1992–1996 was adopted later. The Commission evaluated the implementation of its activities which were based on these two Plans. The Plans were implemented only partially because of the serious resource constraints facing the Commission. It was noted that much remains to be done.

The present Plan of Action which is more of a continuity than an innovation, takes into account all previous problems and attempts – in as much as possible – to find solutions to those problems.

Basically, this Plan of Action is pursuing the same objectives as the previous Plans. It has been enriched by the experience of the past ten years and contribution of the various partners of the Commission, especially the resolutions and recommendations of the NGO fora which, since the Tenth Ordinary Session in 1991, meet for three day periods prior to each ordinary session of the Commission to look into ways of contributing to the work of the African Commission on Human and Peoples' Rights.

This Plan also takes into account new developments in Africa especially in the political, social, economic and cultural spheres which add new dimensions to the work of the Commission which has to be in a position of meeting all new challenges.

Apart from the Commission's main tasks of the promotion and protection of human rights in Africa, the present Plan of Action will also make cooperation a key area. The universal character of human rights requires close collaboration between the African Commission and its partners within and outside Africa.

The implementation of the present Plan of Action will therefore not be the task of the African Commission only. The Plan's application is rather a system of partnership in which the role of the African Commission will be, among others, to encourage and coordinate the various initiatives taken in the different programmes for the promotion and protection of human rights. The African Commission, therefore, counts on the cooperation of all its partners.

I. FRAMEWORK

1. The current Plan of Action (1992–1996) includes activities which had been planned for the previous Programme of Action but which were not implemented or which were implemented partially.

2. These activities will be expanded and readjusted in view of the situation in Africa and the various contributions received and according to developments of the past several years.

3. The Plan of Action will be based on the various missions of the Commission while duly taking into account the priority requirements of Africa.

4. During the coming five years, all the activities of the Commission as well as those initiated in collaboration with other partners will concentrate on implementing the Plan of Action.

5. In this regard, all human rights organizations and institutions in Africa are invited to work with the Commission so as to combine their efforts and harmonize their activities with the aim of achieving maximum results in the promotion and protection of human and peoples' rights in Africa.

II. PROMOTIONAL MISSION OF THE AFRICAN COMMISSION

A. Information Activities of the African Commission

6. The information activities are being structured into different programmes which bring together a number of relevant targeted projects.

(1) Promotion of the African Charter and Dissemination of Information on the Work of the African Commission

7. The lack of informative documentation on the work of the African Commission is a problem which needs to be solved urgently. The Commission intends to put at the disposal of interested users session reports on the activities of the Commission which are not confidential. It is also envisaged that a Newsletter of the Commission will be published monthly. This will enable the Commission to make its communiques, session reports and activities known to the public. The annual activity reports will be published immediately after their adoption by the Conference of Heads of State and Government and distributed at the sessions of the Commission.

8. With regard to publications, only the African Charter is actually available for distribution. Efforts will be made to print more publications.

9. Special emphasis will be placed on the following projects:

A wider dissemination of the African Charter in the four working languages of the OAU (English, French, Arabic and Portuguese) as well as the various documents and publications of the African Commission;
the translation and distribution of the Charter in African languages.

(2) Dissemination of the African Charter and the Activities of the Commission by the Press, Radio and Television (Media Programme)

10. The following projects are envisaged:

- Presence of journalists at the African Commission sessions and other meetings;
- Workshop for journalists to promote the African Charter;
- Production of television programmes on the African Charter;
- Discussion and interviews on radio and television and in the print media during missions and meetings organised by the Commission.

11. As planned in the previous Programme of Action, it will be useful to envisage undertaking "a feasibility study on the cooperation of the African Commission with the media with the aim of strengthening the promotion of human rights in Africa"; this will include, among other things, drawing up a list of obstacles encountered and solutions proposed to improve the relationship of the Commission with the media as well as concrete projects on the way and means of popularising the African Charter through the press, radio, cinema and television.

(3) Human Rights Education with Special Emphasis on the African Charter

12. Under this programme the following activities are planned:

- Developing curricula on Human Rights Education for primary and secondary education in collaboration with the UN Commission for Human Rights, UNESCO, OAU and other partners;
- Developing a course for adults;
- Developing a course on human rights for various professional groups;
- Establishing a Human Rights Award: in its 1988 Programme of Action, the African Commission had envisaged "instituting an award-winning competition on Human Rights". This prize could be awarded to people at different levels of education, professional groups, civil servants as well as politicians. The Commission could decide to award its prize to students of different levels by organizing an essay competition on the theme of human rights in Africa, as well as to individuals who have distinguished themselves in the field of Human Rights. The prize could be money or otherwise.

(4) Publications

13. The Commission plans to carry out the following activities:

- Printing of the Charter;
- Printing of booklets/leaflets on the Charter and the work of the African Commission;

- Publication of the activity reports of the African Commission;
- Publication of the African Review on Human and Peoples' Rights;
- Printing of the reports of seminars, workshop and other activities of the Commission;
- Publication of studies undertaken by or for the African Commission;
- Publication of the Commission's Newsletter;
- Publication of a compendium of decisions and resolutions adopted by or on the African Commission;
- Publication of a compendium of final decisions of the Commission on communications.

B. Documentation and Research Activities of the African Commission

(1) Documentation Activities

14. The documents of the African Commission as well as all relevant OAU documents should be catalogued, and made available in sufficient copies in order to cater to the needs of the African Commission observers and the public. They should also be integrated in a data base as is the case today in all institutions. Translation of documents has to be done. With regard to the documentation of other Human Rights institutions, the Commission receives documents and publications from various intergovernmental and non-governmental organizations, and it intends to establish a mechanism for a systematic exchange of documents and publications.

(2) Documentation Centre

15. The documentation Centre will have to acquire a basic collection of literature on human rights, international law, African law, general reference, African constitutions, legislation and jurisprudence relating to human rights and major African and international journals dealing with human rights. The Centre should list all publications on research and studies on human rights.

(3) Studies and Research

16. There is a need of studies and research on issues relating to the African Charter and to human rights in Africa in general. The Commission will identify subjects contributing to the advancement of its work, comparative studies of the principles and practice of other Human Rights instruments and bodies so as to determine the probable impact of the "applicable principles" stipulated in Articles 60 and 61 of the Charter, customary law and human rights in Africa, study of researches being carried out in Africa and on Africa with relation to human rights, the role of and difficulties facing African human rights NGOs, etc. Other themes will be dealt with in workshops and seminars. It will be possible to undertake research projects in collaboration with other institutions.

17. The Commission will do everything possible to acquire means of communication for the dissemination of information as well as for the publication of documents.

C. Promotional Workshops, Seminars and Training Courses of the African Commission

18. The Commission has made a list of major themes for the workshops, seminars and training courses. Below are some of the seminars and training courses which will be given priority in the coming years:

- Comparison of the African Charter Protection system with other regional systems;
- The setting up in the African Commission of a mechanism country rapporteurs and rapporteurs for main themes;
- Freedom of expression, association and assembly in Africa;
- Economic, social and cultural rights: the respect by states parties of obligations defined in the African Charter;
- Relevance of peoples' rights in African Charter, especially the right to development, the right to have a clean and safe environment, peace, security and the right to self determination;
- The rights of the child in Africa;
- Freedom of movement and the right to asylum in Africa;
- Clawback clauses in the African Charter;
- The African Commission and the national structures for protection and promotion of human and peoples' rights;
- Ethnic conflict resolution in a human rights context;
- The problem of a mass expulsions in Africa.

19. Training courses on the obligation to present reports in compliance with the African Charter (article 62) will continue to be organised. Each training course will be based on the ways and means of applying and/or improving the adopted guiding principles on the preparation and presentation of reports. A guideline on how to present reports in compliance with Article 62 of the African Charter which brings together experts' views and contains a synthesis of the various training courses is being finalised. The Commission intends to pursue this exercise so as to make the booklet available to users in the Commission's working languages.

20. Other training courses will be organised for government officials in various departments including the Ministry of Justice, Foreign Affairs, Home Affairs, Defence, Education, Information Social Affairs and so on.

21. Training courses for representatives of civil society, religious organisations, professional groups and human rights activists and other groups will be jointly organised in collaboration with other institutions.

D. Other Promotional Activities of the African Commission

(1) General Promotional Activities of the Commission

(a) Discussion on main issues

22. Discussion on major issues will be organised in order to improve knowledge of the Charter and to sensitize outside observers and the media on human rights issues.

23. Rapporteurs will be appointed to follow up the results of the proceedings and to submit a report to the Commission. They would make a synergy of the various issues and carry on with their work between sessions. These rapporteurs need not necessarily be members of the Commission; they could be African Researchers and experts who can make a useful contribution to the work of the African Commission.

(b) The Additional Protocol on the Rights of Women in Africa

24. At its 31st Ordinary session, the Conference of Heads of State and Government of OAU countries approved the recommendation of the African Commission on the drawing up of an additional protocol on the rights of women in Africa and directed the Commission to undertake this work and to present a report to the Conference of Heads of State and Government.

25. It was noted that the African Charter does not cover all the concerns of African women. There is a need therefore to fill in the existing gaps in the Charter. The Commission will proceed with consultations for the preparation of a draft additional protocol in collaboration with other partners and present it for adoption to the Conference of Heads of State and Government as soon as possible.

(c) The African Charter 18(b) on the Rights and Welfare of Children

26. This Charter which was adopted the OAU Conference of Heads of State and Government in July 1990 has not come in force because the minimum required number of countries (15) have not yet ratified it.

27. The Commission is proposing that a sensitization campaign be undertaken with the aim of obtaining the ratification and the coming into force, as soon as possible, of this important instrument. The Commission plans to carry out this task with the cooperation of its partners.

(d) Periodic reports

28. Periodic reports play a promotional and a protective role. The dialogue initiated by the Commission with governments will most certainly result in an improvement of national legislation or practice related to human rights. This dialogue should be maintained. Public discussions of periodic reports also provide an opportunity for NGOs to make their contribution to the process of dialogue.

29. A systematic translation of the State Reports in the Commission's working languages is envisaged in order to ensure their efficient use.

(2) Promotional Activities of Members of the African Commission

30. The objective of promotional activities or visits by members of the Commission to member States is to popularise the African Charter and the Commission in all African countries. The Commission also takes advantage of such visits to asses the human rights situation through discussion with Governments officials and local NGOs in the relevant country.

31. This Plan of Action will maintain the system of distributing African countries among Commissioners and means will be sought to enable them to effectively cover the countries allocated to them. Member states, the OAU Secretariat and other partners will be informed of this distribution.

32. In order to enhance efficiency, and in as far as practical, members of the Commission will be accompanied during their promotional missions by member of the Secretariat's staff who will provide the necessary technical back-up in such missions and in the preparation of reports. Local partners will be involved in the collection of information and contribution to the missions.

33. In this regard, written reports will have to be submitted to the Commission at each session, according to clear and specific guidelines to be decided by the Commission.

III. PROTECTION ACTIVITIES

A. Communications

34. The protective activities of the African Commission are provided for in Article 45 (2) of the Charter which states that the Commission has the mission "to ensure the protection of human and peoples' rights under conditions laid down by the present Charter".

35. It has been noted that in the past, some cases of violation of human rights called for an urgent intervention on the part of the Commission. The Commission should reflect on the possibilities, provided for by the Charter, of possessing adequate response to emergency situations.

36. The consideration of communications takes a long time because of various reasons, especially because of lack of means, non-cooperation from the concerned states and due to some provisions of the Charter which places heavy procedural constraints on the Commission's work.

37. The present Plan of Action aims at finding ways and means of considering communications in as short a period as possible. The Commission therefore plans to have extraordinary sessions and group working meetings.

38. It is envisaged that more thought will be given to the possibility of conducting enquiries in a more diligent and efficient way to enable reported cases to be considered in as short a period as possible. Fact finding missions will be sent to countries concerned by communications in order to try and settle matters amicably.

39. Due to intensification of the Commission's efforts to promote and disseminate the Charter and its activities, it is expected that the public will become more aware of the need to report to the Commission any case of violation of human rights in Africa.

40. To this end, the Commission intends to seek the assistance of active NGOs and other local bodies and to organise them into "networks of correspondents" of the Commission which will work in a more coordinated and efficient manner. Each member of the Commission will have a list of active NGOs in his or her area of jurisdiction. Further feasibility studies will have to be carried out on this approach.

B. Emergency Cases

41. Experience has shown that the Commission is often powerless when faced with cases of massive and serious violations of human rights which require a rapid intervention.

42. Currently, the Commission has neither the means nor any power under its rules to deal with such situations. This adversely affects the Commission's credibility and efficiency.

43. The establishment of a rapid intervention mechanism has already been considered. However, more thought will be given to this question and conclusions could be expected soon. Ways of acting in the shortest possible period before the convening of extra ordinary sessions or meetings of small groups will be envisaged.

44. The Commission will do its best to establish its presence in States Parties where human and peoples' rights are either under threat or are being violated.

C. African Court of Human and Peoples' Rights

45. The draft document for the establishment of an African Court of Human and Peoples' Rights is being prepared and is in its final stage. A draft protocol was prepared at a meeting of experts jointly organised by the OAU, the International Commission of Jurists and the African Commission which took place in South Africa in September 1995.

46. This draft protocol was sent out to all OAU member States for comments. The OAU Council of Ministers intends to examine it at its 65th Ordinary Session in February 1997. Consideration of the draft protocol by the Conference of Heads of State and Government is scheduled for June 1997. The African Commission will work towards its early adoption and ratification. The Commission, working in collaboration with NGOs and other partners, will also work towards the sensitization of States Parties on this particular subject.

IV. COOPERATION

47. In fulfilling its mission, the Commission has to co-operate in promotion and protection of human and peoples' rights, with States parties, international, regional

and national institutions as well as non-governmental and inter-governmental organisations in its activities for the promotion and protection of human and peoples' rights in order to attain its objectives in as short a period as possible.

48. To this end, the Commission will also strengthen its cooperation with all its members and parties likely to contribute towards the realisation of its objectives.

49. The Commission will cooperate with:

(a) States parties;
(b) OAU Secretariat;
(c) International and regional organisations;
(d) Human rights NGOs;
(e) National Institutions and Associations;
(f) Funding partners;

A. States Parties

50. The African Charter on Human and Peoples' Rights and the African Commission emanate from decisions of the Conference of Heads of State and Government of the Organisation of African Unity (OAU). Consequently, the accomplishment of the mission of the African Commission cannot be conceived outside OAU member States.

51. The attainment of the objectives of human rights promotional and protective activities is possible only with the sustained cooperation of OAU member States.

52. Furthermore, the voluntary contribution Fund – envisaged in the present Plan of Action to supplement the inadequate budgetary allocations from the OAU Secretariat for the work of the Commission – will for the most part receive resources from member states willing to provide financial and technical assistance to an institution which was established by the countries themselves.

53. The Commission will work towards achieving and strengthening this cooperation which is indispensable to the fulfilment of its mission.

B. OAU Secretariat

54. The Commission intends to enhance the OAU Secretariat's involvement in its activities related to human and peoples' rights with regard to, among other things, conflict prevention and management, refugees and displaced people, observation of elections and the establishment of the African Economic Community.

55. The African Commission has already initiated dialogue with the OAU Secretary General on this subject and will look into ways of setting up practical modalities of cooperation.

C. International and Regional Organisations

56. The present Plan of Action covers cooperation activities between the Commission and various inter-governmental and non-governmental organisations at international and regional levels. This cooperation is very important because the African Commission may benefit from the experience of these organisations which have existed for some of them since several decades.

57. In the past the Commission initiated meetings with other human rights organisations and institutions such as the United Nations Centre for Human Rights, the Friedrich Naumann Foundation, the Commission and the European Court for Human Rights, the Inter-American Court for Human Rights and the Inter-American Institute for Human Rights, the Danish Centre for Human Rights, the Raoul Wallenberg Institute for Human Rights, the International Institute for Human Rights, UNESCO and the North-South Centre.

58. Those contacts have contributed considerably to strengthening the relationship between the Commission and these organisations and institutions.

59. In the next five years the Commission intends to revive these initiatives and strengthen its relationship with these organisations. The Commission will place special emphasis on the coordination of its activities with those of the institutions of the United Nations system and of other organisations which are active in Africa.

D. Human Rights NGOs

60. With regard to African non governmental organisations, the Commission intends to start consultations for the establishment of an exchange and communication network, thereby creating an appropriate mechanism for promotional and protection activities in Africa.

61. Since the Commission counts very much on the widest possible participation of NGOs in the realisation of its objectives, it will set up a system of Communication/Cooperation which would operate both vertically and horizontally, thus permitting the NGOs to cooperate among themselves and at the same time with the Commission. This programme could be considered to be quite urgent.

62. In the past, the Commission established excellent relationship with a number of African NGOs. With their collaboration, it has been able to implement a good number of its projects.

63. In the next five years, the Commission plans to strengthen these links and seek the contribution of NGOs as well as other new partners in the implementation of the present Plan of Action.

E. National Human Rights Institutions and Associations

64. Article 26 of the Charter states that the Commission has the duty to "allow the establishment and improvement of appropriate national institutions entrusted with the promotion and protection of the rights and freedoms guaranteed by the present Charter". To this effect, the Commission has already recommended to the Conference of Heads of State the creation of national committees and human rights institutes. Over the last few years, with the advance of democracy in Africa, a number of human rights organisations have emerged.

65. The African Commission will endeavour to establish and strengthens regular working relationship with existing organisations in order to develop concrete programmes for the promotion and protection of human rights.

66. Within the framework of its promotional mandate, the Commission will also encourage the establishment of national human rights associations and institutions.

67. These national institutions and associations could serve as a basis for initiatives for human rights in the respective countries, and will help the Commission to disseminate the African Charter and to fulfil its educational mission on human and peoples' rights in general. They may also contribute to protective activities by providing the Commission with information on human rights violations and by assisting the victims of such violations.

68. The Commission intends to set up a cooperation framework between national human rights associations and institutions in order to promote the exchange of information and experience thus assisting them to enhance their efficiency.

F. Cooperation with Partners

69. According to Article 41 of the Charter, the Commission functions with the staff, services and funds provided to it by the Organisation of African Unity. Nevertheless, in view of the wide range of activities pertaining to the Commission's mandate, the funds placed at its disposal are insufficient. For this reason, since its inception, the Commission has been forced to seek extra budgetary funding to implement a number of projects. In the past, many organisations and states have favourably considered requests from the Commission.

70. For the implementation of the present Plan of Action, the Commission will need considerable technical, material and financial assistance from its partners. The Commission is planning to launch a campaign on sensitization and resource mobilisation.

71. Reflection has already been initiated with the participation of other partners on the setting up of a system of resource mobilisation. The establishment of a resource mobilisation committee composed of members of the Commission and other partners is an idea which should be looked into and transformed into reality as soon as possible.

72. Furthermore, the Commission should follow up the contacts already made with donors and try to diversify as much as possible the sources of funding.

73. Funding projects which have already been presented to the relevant parties will be submitted again and new funding requests will be prepared and presented within the context of this Plan of Action.

74. States, international and regional institutions and non-governmental organisations will be requested to contribute to these efforts.

V. STRENGTHENING OF THE SECRETARIAT OF THE AFRICAN COMMISSION

75. Article 41 of the Charter stipulates that the General Secretariat of the OAU provides the Commission with the necessary human, material and financial means for the effective exercise of its functions.

It is important and a matter of urgency to strengthen the Secretariat of the Commission by providing it with adequate human, financial and other resources for the efficient and effective implementation of its activities.

76. Currently the Secretariat is still seriously understaffed and its equipment is inadequate and inappropriate. The implementation of the present Plan of Action requires adequate human and material resources. The OAU Secretariat could adopt a consistent system and ensure that adequate human, financial and material resources are provided to the Commission in order to enable the Commission to meet the Human and Peoples' rights needs of Africa.

77. In this regard, a list of essential needs of the Secretariat has been submitted to the OAU Secretariat. Alongside the request for these needs, the strengthening of the Commission's Secretariat by the OAU will require the following staff composition:

(1) Secretary to the Commission;
(2) Section in charge of promotion (2 people);
(3) Section in charge of protection (2 people);
(4) Research and training department (3 people);
(5) Press and information department (1 person);
(6) Documentation Centre (1 person);
(7) Support staff:

   (a) Administration and finance (2 people);
   (b) Registry (1 person);
   (c) Secretariat (4 people).

78. Even if this proposal for restructuring was to be adopted in its entirety by the deciding organs of the OAU, the Commission would still need additional staff to properly implement the various activities set out in the present Plan of Action.

79. In the spirit of the African Charter and in view of the present Plan of Action, the African Commission should become a centre of coordination of all activities pertaining to human and peoples' rights in Africa. The Commission, therefore, has to have a solid, efficient and flexible administrative and technical structure which will enable it to fulfil the role assigned to it.

80. It is in view of this objective that proposals have been elaborated and submitted to donors. Some of them are in the process of being finalized while others need to be renewed within the present Plan of Action. The projects cover practically all priority areas identified within the framework of the present Plan of Action and require adequate human and financial resources for their effective implementation.

81. In this report, the Commission will need the support of States Parties, friendly countries as well as its various partners. Contacts will be made to this effect. Voluntary contribution fund proposed by the present Plan of Action should be operational as early as possible in order to enable the Commission to overcome some of its constraints and to fulfil its mission effectively.

82. To this end, a resource mobilisation committee will be established as early as possible in order to support the Secretariat in it effort to raise funds. This Committee shall be made up of members of the Commission members of staff of the Secretariat and other partners.

83. With regard to equipment, the Secretariat has up to now benefited from the support of certain donors. Apart from the fact that the equipment is inadequate, it should be noted that the Secretariat needs material to fully meet present technological needs. These include computers, printers, communication modules, photocopying machines, equipment for the documentation Centre and the press and information unit.

84. The Commission has already received pledges in this regard, but even these will not be sufficient to cover all its needs. Resource mobilisation activities will take into account this problem. The actual staff and equipment needs are shown in a draft appended to the present Plan of Action.

VI. CONCLUSION

85. The present Plan of Action contains various activities pertaining to the different missions of the Commission and selected according to priorities.

86. It is not an exhaustive list of projects to be implemented, rather it is a conceptual framework which will guide the Commission during the next five years.

87. An outline of the requirements for the implementation of this Plan of Action has also been presented.

88. The implementation of the present Plan of Action is not exclusively the task of the Commission. The African Commission depends on the support of its partners for the effective realisation of its objectives.

89. The Commission intends to involve fully member States, the OAU Secretariat, the NGO Community as well as national, regional and international organisations and institutions in this exercise so as to mobilize all its partners and channel all efforts towards the realization of this common objective.

90. In conclusion, the Commission is appealing to all those who are sensitive to the cause of human rights to devote themselves fully to the implementation of the present Plan of Action.

Final Communiqué of the Twenty-first Ordinary Session of the African Commission on Human and Peoples' Rights

Nouakchott, 15–24 April 1997

1. The 21st Ordinary Session of the African Commission on Human and Peoples' Rights was held in Nouakchott, Mauritania from 15–24 April 1997 at the kind invitation of the Islamic Republic of Mauritania and was chaired by Professor Isaac Nguema. It was preceded by the second Governmental Legal Experts meeting on the establishment of an African Court of Human and Peoples' Rights and the Experts meeting on the preparation of a Draft Additional Protocol on the Rights of Women to the African Charter on Human and Peoples' Rights Workshop jointly organized by the International Commission of Jurists and the African Commission on Human and Peoples' Rights.

2. The opening ceremony was attended by Members of the Commission, the Prime Minister of the Islamic Republic of Mauritania, Hon. Cheik El Avia Ould Mohamed Khouna, officials of the government of Mauritania, H.E. Ambassador Mamadou Bah represented the Secretary General of the Organization of African Unity (OAU) and the Secretary General of the International Commission of Jurists, Mr. Adama Dieng. Also present at the opening ceremony were members of the diplomatic corps, representatives of governmental and non-governmental organisations, members of the local and international press, and other dignitaries.

3. At the opening ceremony, speeches were delivered by Professor Isaac Nguema, the Chairman of the African Commission on Human and Peoples' Rights, the Secretary General of the International Commission of Jurists, the Representative of the Secretary General of the OAU and the Prime Minister of the Islamic Republic of Mauritania. The various speakers emphasized the importance of human and peoples' rights and asserted their commitment to support the Commission in its work of attaining its desired goals and fulfilling its promotional and protective mandate.

4. The Commission heard delegates of the governments of Sudan, Nigeria, Mauritania and The Gambia who delivered messages emphasizing the commitment of their countries to comply with the provisions of the African Charter and reiterating their commitment to co-operate with the Commission.

5. Statements were made by representatives of various African and international non-governmental organisations namely; International Commission of Jurists (ICJ) WILDAF, Organisation Nationale des Droits de l'Homme du Senegal (ONDH), Rencontre Africaine Pour la Défense des Droits de l'Homme (RADDHO), Anti-Slavery International, Human Rights Watch/Africa, Association of Mauritanian Refugees in Senegal, Gerddes Mauritanie, SOS Esclaves, Association Mauritanienne

des Droits de l'Homme and International Centre for Human Rights and Democratic Development.

6. The Commission considered applications for observer status and granted it to eight NGOs. The list of those NGOs is available at the Secretariat.

7. Concerning the consideration of periodic reports of the States Parties, the Commission examined the initial report of Sudan presented by Mr. Sirajuddin H. Yousif, the head of Sudan's delegation. The presentation was followed by a discussion of the report. This gave the Commission the opportunity to examine the human rights situation in that country and its compliance with the provisions of the Charter. The second and third periodic reports of Zimbabwe were presented by H.E. Chimbi E. C. Sanyangare, Ambassador of Zimbabwe in Dakar and Mrs Antonia Guvava, from the Legal Affairs Division at the Ministry of Justice, After a fruitful debate, the Commission commanded Zimbabwe for the good quality of the report

8. The Commission heard a report presented by three members who were entrusted with the task of examining the establishment of a rapid response mechanism in the event of serious massive human rights violations. Discussions on the report will continue at the next session of the Commission.

9. The Commissioners presented their reports on their promotional activities during the intersession.

10. The Commission considered the report of Commissioner Ben Salem, the Special Rapporteur on extra-judicial, summary and, arbitrary executions, The Commission agreed with the rapporteur that publicly identifying those responsible for extra-judicial executions and their prosecution is a form of restitution and contributes to the fight against impunity Consequently, the Commission encouraged the Special Rapporteur to continue with his investigation work.

11. The Special Rapporteur on Prison Conditions in Africa, Commissioner Dankwa presented his first report on his visit to prisons in Zimbabwe and his contact with the UN Special Rapporteur on Torture.

12. The draft protocol on the African Court of Human, and Peoples' Rights was discussed by the Commission, 25 NGOs made statements expressing their concern with some provisions of the document as well as the discrepancy between the French and English versions. The Commission will submit comments made by NGOs to the OAU General Secretariat for appropriate action.

13. The Draft Protocol on the Rights of Women drafted by a group of experts in Nouakchott before the session on the basis of a document prepared by the Vice-Chairman Prof Dankwa who worked in collaboration with two other Commissioners was discussed. On examining the report, the Commission requested each of its members to send their remarks to the Secretariat who will in turn send them to the Commissioners assigned to deal with the issue namely, Dankwa, Duarte and Ondziel-Gnelenga.

14. The Commission examined the subject of strengthening national human rights institutions which was proposed and presented by Commissioner Rezzag-Bara, The Commission decided to discuss this subject at length at a later date, especially the issue of granting special status to such institutions.

15. With regard to the human rights situation in Africa, the Commission heard reports from various participants who highlighted human rights violations in Zaire and Nigeria as well as the situation prevailing in Mauritania and Cameroon. The delegates of the governments of, Mauritania and Cameroon expressed their views on statements concerning their countries.

16. The Commission urged NGOs to take part actively in the preparation of seminars and conferences organized by Commissioners.

17. The issue of missions undertaken by the Commission was raised by INTERIGHTS, Civil Liberties Organization and RADDHO. These organizations emphasized the importance for the Commission's delegations to have a clear and specific mandate and to preserve their independence from governments of the states visited.

18. Concerning protective activities, the Commission examined fourteen communications brought against Cameroon, Tanzania, Zaire, Uganda, Zambia, Rwanda, The Gambia, Gabon, Djibouti, Equatorial Guinea, Angola, Botswana, Egypt and Nigeria.

19. The Commission undertook missions to Senegal, Nigeria, Mauritania and Sudan. The mission's reports on Senegal and Mauritania were examined by the Commission. The examination of the reports on Nigeria and Sudan was deferred to the next session.

20. The Commission adopted a press release on Zaire and a resolution on the protection of the name, acronym and logo of the African Commission on Human and Peoples' Rights.

21. The Commission's Bureau was received by H.E. Maaouya Ould Sidi Ahmed Taya, President of the Islamic Republic of Mauritania.

22. The dates and venue of the 22nd Ordinary Session will be determined at a later date.

23. The closing ceremony of the 21st Ordinary Session took place on 24 April 1997. It was officiated by H.E. Sidi Ould Khalifa, Minister of Foreign Affairs and Cooperation.

24. The Chairman of the Commission held a press conference after the closing ceremony.

Done at Nouakchott, Mauritania, 24 April 1997.

Eleventh Annual Activity Report of the African Commission on Human and Peoples' Rights 1997–1998

Adopted on 29 April 1998
Covering the 22nd and 23rd Ordinary Sessions in Banjul
(2–11 November 1997 and 20–29 April 1998)

I. ORGANIZATION OF WORK

A. Period Covered by the Report

1. The Tenth Annual Activity report of the African Commission on Human and Peoples' Rights was adopted by the Thirty-third Ordinary Session of the Assembly of Heads of State and Government of the Organization of African Unity in its decision AHG/DEC 123 (XXXIII) taken during its meeting in Harare, Zimbabwe, from 2–4 June 1997. The Eleventh Annual Activity Report covers the Twenty-second and Twenty-third Ordinary Sessions held in Banjul, Gambia, from 2–11 November 1997 and from 20–29 April 1998 respectively. The addendum to this document concerns the part of the report covering the Twenty-third session.

B. Status of Ratification

2. All the Member States of the OAU, with the exception of Eritrea and Ethiopia have ratified or acceded to the African Charter on Human and Peoples' Rights. Annex I contains the list of States parties to the African Charter on Human and Peoples' Rights indicating inter alia the dates of signature, ratification or accession, as well as the date of deposit of the instruments of ratification or accession as the case may be.

C. Sessions and Agenda

3. The Commission held two ordinary sessions since the adoption of the Tenth Annual Activity Report in June 1997:

- the 22nd Ordinary Session held in Banjul, The Gambia, the Headquarters of the Commission, from 2–11 November 1997;
- the 23rd Ordinary Session held in Banjul, from 20–29 April 1998. The agenda of each of these sessions is attached to this report.

D. Composition and Participation

4. The following Commissioners attended the 22nd Session:

(1) Mr. Youssoupha Ndiaye, Chairman,
(2) Dr. Vera V. Duarte Martins, Vice Chairman,
(3) Dr. Mohamed Hatem. Ben Salem,
(4) Prof. Emmanuel V. O. Dankwa,
(5) Dr. Nyameko Barney Pityana,
(6) Dr. Ibrahim Badawi El Sheikh,
(7) Mrs. Julienne Ondziel-Gnelenga,
(8) Mr. Kamel Rezzag-Bara,
(9) Prof. Isaac Nguema

Messrs Alioune Blondin Beye and Atsu Kofi-Amega were absent from the proceedings However, Mr. Blondin Beye sent an apology.

5. The representatives of the following States attended the 22nd Session and made statements before the Commission:

(1) Burundi,
(2) Cameroun,
(3) Libya,
(4) Mauritania,
(5) Nigeria,
(6) Niger,
(7) Togo,
(8) Gambia,
(9) Burkina Faso.

6. A number of Non-Governmental Organizations (NGOs) and a national human rights institution also attended the proceedings.

7. Swearing in

8. The newly elected members of the Commission were sworn in. They are:

- Mr. Ben Salem,
- Dr. Nyameko Barney Pityana,
- Dr. Ibrahim Badawi El Sheikh.

9. Commissioners Youssoupha Ndiaye and Vera Valentino De Melo Duarte Martins were elected Chairman and Vice Chairman of the Commission respectively at the 23rd session.

10. The following members of the Commission attended the 23rd ordinary session:

(1) Mr. Youssoupha Ndiaye, Chairman,
(2) Dr. Vera V. Duarte Martins, Vice Chairman,
(3) Prof. Isaac Nguema, member,
(4) Prof. Emmanuel V. O. Dankwa, member,

(5) Dr. Mohamed Hatem Ben Salem , member,
(6) Mme Julienne Ondziel-Gnelenga, member,
(7) Mr. Kamel Rezzag-Bara, member,
(8) Dr. Nyameko Barney Pityana, member,
(9) Dr. Ibrahim Badawi El Sheikh, member.

11. Messrs. Atsu-Koffi Amega and Alioune Blondin Beye were absent with apologies.

12. The representatives of the following States participated in the proceedings of the 23rd session and some of them made statements:

(1) Gambia,
(2) Mauritania,
(3) Burkina Faso,
(4) Sudan,
(5) Namibia,
(6) the Republic of Guinea,
(7) Nigeria,
(8) Mozambique.

13. Many Non Governmental Organizations (NGOs) and National Institutions also took part in the proceedings of the 23rd session.

E. Adoption of the 11th Annual Activity Report

14. The Commission considered and adopted the eleventh annual activity report at its sitting of 29 April 1998.

II. ACTIVITIES OF THE COMMISSION

A. Consideration of Periodic Reports

15. Under Article 62 of the African Charter on Human and Peoples' Rights, each State Party undertakes to submit a report every two years on the legislative and other measures it takes to give effect to the rights and freedoms enshrined in the Charter.

16. The Republic of Chad and the Republic of Seychelles sent their periodic reports to the Secretariat, but these were not considered by the Commission as there were no official delegations to present them.

17. The periodic reports of the Republic of Namibia and the Republic of Guinea were presented at the 23rd session. The Commission praised the quality of the reports and thanked the representatives for their presentation.

18. The Commission considered several proposals for improving the operation of the reporting system and examined a draft amendment of the guidelines on the preparation of the said periodic reports.

19. As at the 22nd session, thirty-three (33) State parties had not yet submitted their periodic reports.

B. Promotional Activities

20. The Chairman met with the OAU Secretary General in Addis Ababa in December 1997 and discussed with him administrative, financial and other matters.He also met with the President of the Republic of The Gambia in January 1998 and discussed with him the question of the Headquarters of the Commission. The Chairman further intervened with the Governments of Mauritania and Djibouti in emergency situations.

21. All the members reported on the human rights promotional and/or protective activities they participated in during the intersession.

22. The Commission co-sponsored or organized the following meetings, seminars and international conferences:

(1) The second workshop on the improvement of the regional human rights systems, 17–18 November 1997, Lisbon, Portugal;
(2) International Conference on Community Work, 24–28 November 1997, Kadoma, Zimbabwe with Penal Reform International (PRI);
(3) The meeting of government experts on the establishment of an African Human and Peoples' Rights Court, 8–12 December 1997, Addis Ababa, Ethiopia;
(4) The African contexts of the rights of the child, 12–14 January 1998, Harare, Zimbabwe, with CODESRIA, Redd Barna-Zimbabwe and the Centre for Family Research of the University of Cambridge;
(5) Working Group on the additional protocol to the African Charter on women's rights, 26–28 January 1998, Banjul, The Gambia, with the African Centre for Democracy and Human Rights Studies and the International Commission of Jurists (ICJ);
(6) International Conference on HIV/AIDS in African Prisons, 16–18 February 1998, Dakar, Senegal, with the International Observatory of Prisons (OIP);
(7) Regional Seminar on Economic, Social and Cultural Rights, 9–12 March 1998, in Abidjan, Côte d'Ivoire.

23. The Commission heard the statements of several NGOs on the human rights situation in Rwanda, Burundi, Congo (Brazzaville), Mauritania, Algeria, Gambia, Sierra Leone, Sudan, Nigeria, Democratic Republic of Congo and Cameroon.

24. Among the issues raised were those concerning women's rights in general, female genital mutilation, refugees, prison conditions, slavery, extrajudicial executions, restriction of the freedom of association, assembly, expression, torture, poverty, unemployment, discrimination.

25. Following the information provided by representatives of Amnesty International on the imminent execution of 23 persons in Rwanda accused of participation in the genocide of 1994, the Commission immediately requested the Rwandan government to stay this execution in order to enable it to take a position on the matter on the basis of the complaint submitted by Amnesty.

26. The Commission discussed the Celebration of the 50th anniversary of the Universal Declaration of Human Rights of the United Nations, as well as the preparation of the next Ministerial Conference on Human Rights in Luanda.

27. The Commission also discussed the distribution of States parties among its members for the purpose of promotion, organisation of seminars and conferences, the establishment of the International Criminal Court, the publication of its Review and other aspects of promotional work.

28. The resolution adopted by the Commission on the International Criminal Court is attached as an annex.

III. REPORT OF THE SPECIAL RAPPORTEUR ON EXTRA-JUDICIAL EXECUTIONS IN AFRICA

29. At the 23rd session, Commissioner Ben Salem presented the final report on the summary, arbitrary and extrajudicial executions in Rwanda, Burundi, Chad, Comoros, and the Democratic Republic of Congo. This report contains the names of people about whom the special rapporteur is expecting information from the States concerned.

IV. REPORT OF THE SPECIAL RAPPORTEUR ON PRISON AND DETENTION CONDITIONS IN AFRICA

30. Commissioner E. V. O. Dankwa, Special Rapporteur on Prison and Detention Conditions in Africa submitted his second report. He spoke about his activities during the intersession when he attended various symposia and visited several detention centres inter alia in Mozambique and Madagascar.

31. The special rapporteur visited inter alia the prisons in Mali and studied the prison conditions of this country. His recommendations for the improvement of the Malian prison conditions will be submitted to the government. The special rapporteur expressed appreciation for the assistance rendered to him by the NGO Penal Reform International (PRI).

32. At the 23rd session, Commissioner Dankwa presented his third report. In it he mentions his visits to prisons and other places of detention, meetings with government authorities, participation in seminars on African prisons.

V. SPECIAL RAPPORTEUR ON THE RIGHTS OF WOMEN

33. The working group already set up for the elaboration of an additional protocol to the Charter on the rights of women met from 26–28 January 1998. The group was expanded to include the International Commission of Jurists and the African Centre for Democracy and Human Rights Studies. The said group prepared the terms of reference of the special rapporteur and presented a report at the 23rd session. Upon its proposal, Mme Julienne Ondziel-Gnelenga was appointed special rapporteur on the rights of women. She is expected to present an interim report at the 24th session.

VI. MISSIONS TO STATES PARTIES

34. The Commission deferred to the 23rd ordinary session consideration of the reports on the missions undertaken in Sudan and Nigeria. This session discussed Commissioner Dankwa's report on Sudan.

VII. RELATIONS WITH OBSERVERS

35. At the 23rd session, observer status was granted to nineteen Non Governmental Organizations (NGOs), which brings the number of NGOs with observer status to 224. The 23rd session granted such status to 7 NGOs. This gives a total of 231.

36. With regard to the relations with National Human Rights Institutions, the Commission deferred the consideration of applications for observer status from National Human Rights Institutions.

37. On the same issue of relations between the Commission and observers, it was noticed that only thirty percent of observers complied with the obligation to submit reports on their activities to the Commission every two years. The Commission further noticed that some of these NGOs cut off all contact with it once they obtained observer status. The Commissions decided to review the criteria for granting observer status.

VIII. PROTECTIVE ACTIVITIES

38. The Commission considered seventy-two communications. It made a ruling on the merits of four of them. For the others, it acknowledged receipt or ruled on their admissibility .

In this regard, the Commission invited reflection on the reasons for the reduction in the number of communications submitted to it. It also noted that the non compliance by some States parties with the Commission's recommendations affects its credibility and may partly explain that fewer complaints are submitted to it.

IX. ADMINISTRATIVE AND FINANCIAL MATTERS

A. Administrative Matters

39. The Commission examined the resources at its disposal for its functioning and expressed satisfaction at the improvement of its working conditions thanks to the additional human and financial resources provided by its partners.

The Commission also expressed its appreciation for the measures taken by the Council of Ministers of the OAU at its 67th Ordinary Session with a view to implementing the decisions and resolutions of the Assembly of the Head of States and Government of the OAU directing that the African Commission be provided with adequate financial, human and material resources for its efficient functioning.

B. Financial Matters

40. During the financial year under review, the Commission obtained funding from the following sources:

(i) OAU Budget

41. Due to financial problems facing the OAU, several projects of the Commission had to be suspended. This only slowed down the activities of the Commission and worsened its situation.

(ii) Assistance from the African Society of International Comparative Law

42. The African Society provided the Commission with two jurists from 30 August 1997 for a renewable period of one year. It also provided two computers and a printer. This somewhat improved the working conditions in the Secretariat.

(iii) Assistance from the Danish Centre for Human Rights

43. The Danish Centre for Human Rights provided a computer expert for a period of 9 months. He is responsible for the setting up of a computerised data base on the Commissions jurisprudence, the management of its relations with States parties and NGOs with observer status, the dissemination of information on human rights in Africa for the general public, etc.

(iv) Assistance from the European Union

44. The European Union in collaboration with the African Society for International Comparative Law provided the Commission with a jurist responsible inter alia for the dissemination of the African Charter on Human and Peoples' Rights, the human rights promotional activities, the organization of sensitization seminars intended for target groups across the continent, etc.

(v) Assistance from the United Nations High Commission for Human Rights

45. The United Nations High Commission for Human Rights granted financial assistance to the African Commission on Human and Peoples' Rights for the preparation of a Protocol on the African Court on Human and Peoples' Rights, the organisation of the Ministerial Conference on Human Rights in Africa to he held in November 1998 in Luanda, Angola, the preparation of human rights training manuals, of training courses and seminars on human rights, as well as for the improvement of the system for handling communications and periodic reports of States parties, etc.

(vi) Assistance from the Friedrich Naumann Foundation

46. The Friedrich Naumann Foundation assists the Commission in its fund raising efforts with foreign partners, as well as in the strengthening of its relations with the latter.

47. The Commission considered several proposals for improving working methods.

X. ADOPTION OF THE REPORT BY THE ASSEMBLY OF HEADS OF STATE AND GOVERNMENT

48. After considering this Report, the Assembly of Heads of State and Government adopted it by a resolution which took note of the Report with satisfaction and authorized its publication.

ANNEX I

African Charter on Human and Peoples' Rights List of Countries which have Signed, Ratified or Adhered to the Charter

No.	Country	Date of Signature	Date of Ratification/ Accession	Date Deposited
1.	Algeria	10/04/86	01/03/87	20/03/87
2.	Angola		02/03/90	09/10/90
3.	Benin		20/01/86	25/02/86
4.	Botswana		17/07/86	22/07/86
5.	Burkina Faso	05/03/84	06/07/84	21/09/84
6.	Burundi		28/07/80	30/08/89
7.	Cameroon	23/07/87	20/06/89	18/09/89
8.	Cape Verde	31/03/86	02/06/87	06/08/87
9.	Central African Republic		26/04/86	27/07/86
10.	Comoros		01/06/86	18/07/86
11.	Congo	27/11/81	09/12/82	17/01/83
12.	Congo (RD)	23/07/87	20/07/87	28/07/87
13.	Côte d'Ivoire		06/01/92	31/03/92
14.	Djibouti	20/12/91	11/11/91	20/12/91
15.	Egypt	16/11/81	20/03/84	03/04/84

No.	Country	Date of Signature	Date of Ratification/ Accession	Date Deposited
16.	Equatorial Guinea	18/08/86	07/04/86	18/08/86
17.	Eritrea		14/01/99	15/03/99
18.	Ethiopia		15/06/98	22/06/98
19.	Gabon	26/02/82	20/02/86	26/06/86
20.	Gambia	11/02/83	08/06/83	13/03/83
21.	Ghana		24/01/89	01/03/89
22.	Guinea	09/12/81	16/02/82	13/05/82
23.	Guinea-Bissau		04/12/85	06/03/86
24.	Kenya		23/01/92	10/02/92
25.	Lesotho	07/03/84	10/02/92	27/02/92
26.	Liberia	31/01/83	04/08/82	29/12/82
27.	Libya	30/05/85	19/07/86	26/03/87
28.	Madagascar		09/03/92	19/03/92
29.	Malawi	23/02/90	17/11/89	23/02/90
30.	Mali	13/11/81	21/12/81	22/01/82
31.	Mauritania	25/02/82	14/06/86	26/06/86
32.	Mauritius	27/02/92	19/06/92	07/07/92
33.	Mozambique		22/02/89	07/03/90
34.	Namibia		30/07/92	16/09/92
35.	Niger	09/07/86	15/07/86	21/07/86
36.	Nigeria	31/08/82	22/06/83	27/07/83
37.	Uganda	18/08/86	10/05/86	27/05/86
38.	Rwanda	11/11/81	15/07/83	22/07/83
39.	Sahrawi Arab Dem. Rep.	10/04/86	02/05/86	23/05/86
40.	Sao Tome & Principe		23/05/86	28/07/86
41.	Senegal	23/09/81	13/08/82	25/10/82
42.	Seychelles		13/04/92	30/04/92
43.	Sierra Leone	27/08/81	21/09/83	27/01/84
44.	Somalia	26/02/82	31/07/85	20/03/86
45.	South Africa	07/07/96	09/07/96	09/07/96
46.	Sudan	03/09/82	18/02/86	11/03/86
47.	Swaziland			
48.	Tanzania	31/05/82	18/02/84	09/03/84
49.	Chad	29/05/86	09/10/86	11/11/86
50.	Togo	20/02/82	05/11/82	22/11/82
51.	Tunisia		16/03/83	22/04/83
52.	Zambia	17/01/83	19/01/84	02/02/84
53.	Zimbabwe	20/02/86	30/05/86	12/06/86

ADOPTED: by the 18th Session of the Assembly of Heads of State and Government, June 1981
REQUIRES: ratification or adherence by a simple majority of Member States to come into force
ENTERED INTO FORCE: 21st day of October 1986
REGISTERED: with the United Nations on 10 September 1991, No. 26363

ANNEX II

Communications

1. 40/90 Bob Ngozi Njoku/ Egypt

Facts as alleged by the complainant:

(1) The communication is submitted by a Nigerian student who was in transit from New Delhi to Lagos. He complains that at the Cairo airport, on 20 September 1986, while he was waiting for his connecting flight, Colonel Mohamed El Adile of the Egyptian police stamped a false entry visa for Egypt on his travel papers.

(2) As a consequence, his luggage was searched. A suitcase bearing another person's name, of a different weight than that recorded on his ticket, and for which he had no key, was ascribed to him. The Egyptian police did not ask the airline to identify the owner of the suitcase. Drugs were found in the suitcase.

(3) In the presence of two Nigerian diplomats, Mr. Njoku denied that the suitcase was his. A police officer wrote down a statement in Arabic, which the three signed, without it having been translated for them. The subsequent trial was held behind closed doors, without a translator being present for the defendant.

(4) Apparently, the Arabic statement signed by the complainant contained the admission that the suitcase was his. The complainant did have a lawyer, but complains that the lawyer was ineffective and appeared afraid of the judge. The trial lasted only 5 minutes and there was no translator present. The complainant was given a life sentence under a law specifying this punishment for importers of drugs who have visas for Egypt, whose final destination is Egypt and who cross into Egyptian territory. The complaint argues that none of these three conditions applies to him, as he was a transit passenger with no Egyptian visa who wished to remain in the airport. The complainant's appeal was rejected.

(5) Article 33 of the Egyptian criminal code prohibits the searching of transit passengers. The complainant argues that the interception and search of transit passengers is a common practice by the Egyptian police, and has been condemned by Dr. Adwar Gali of the Legal Commission of Egypt. The former director of the Drug Enforcement Agency has stated that the Egyptian criminal code nowhere provides for transit related cases and that Egypt is intercepting people only because of international conventions on drug abuse.

(6) The complainant argues that the judge who sentenced him, Mr. Anwe Gebali, believed the testimony of the police colonel who forged the Egyptian visa in the complainant's passport. The complainant exhausted his last appeal in March 1991.

Facts according to the government of Egypt:

(7) The government agrees that on the date in question the complainant was arrested in the transit lounge at Cairo airport, and that the visa for Egypt was stamped in his passport only so that he could be admitted into Egypt for investigations of the case, but that the time at which he acquired the visa was found

irrelevant by the courts. The government representative stated at the 19th session that the transit area is "a free zone for customs only", not for crime, and under the anti-drug convention of New York states parties may not permit individuals to carry drugs into another state party.

(8) The government states that the validity of the complainant's arrest in the transit lounge was raised by his lawyer during his trial, and that this was his first grounds for overturning his conviction on appeal, but the Supreme Court refused his appeal and the conviction became final.

(9) The government states that the complainant then availed himself of a special process by which appeal to the attorney general is possible, and raised the point that the confession attributed to him was not valid. The government said that in the attorney general's review of the case it was found that the court did recognise that the complainant had denied guilt in the case; no confession was used.

(10) The government states that the complainant had access to all the protections of Egyptian law, that during the investigations he was represented by a private attorney, a representative of the Nigerian consulate, and during the trial he had a lawyer chosen by the bar association and paid for by the court. As evidenced by the appeals brought before the high court, the supreme court, and the court of cassation, the lawyer did a competent job.

(11) The government states that the complainant was tried and convicted under the 1961 Egyptian drug law, which was in force in 1986. This law was revised in 1995, but the changes made the law more harsh and would not be to the advantage of the complainant.

(12) The government further claims that the communication is inadmissible because the Working Group of the Sub-Commission on Prevention of Discrimination and Protection of Minorities of the UN decided not to take any action in respect of a communication from Mr. Njoku.

Procedure:

(13) The communication is dated 10 October 1989. It was originally sent to the Secretary General of the OAU, who forwarded it to the Commission. It was received on 12 April 1990.

(14) The Commission was seized of the communication at the 7th Ordinary Session, and the Ministry of External Affairs and Ministry of Justice of Egypt were notified on 31 May 1990. The complainant was also notified of this decision.

(15) Between 1990 and 1995, several letters were exchanged between the Secretariat and the parties to ascertain the various issues raised by the protagonists as well as the exhaustion of local remedies.

(16) At the 17th session, held in March 1995 the Commission declared the Communication admissible and it was decided that the case should be heard on its merits at the 18th session.

(17) On 31 March 1995, a letter was sent to the complainant stating that his case had been declared admissible at the 17th session.

(18) On 31 March and 20 May 1995 letters were sent to the government of Egypt requesting further information.
(19) On 23 June 1995 copies of the letter of 31 March and decision were sent to him.
(20) On 1 September 1995, a letter was sent to the complainant requesting him for further information with regard to the legal basis for the sentence he received.
(21) On 11 September the complainant responded to the Secretariat's letter of 1 September.
(22) On 30 November 1995 the Secretariat sent a note verbale to the Ministry of Foreign Affairs of Egypt informing it that it would examine the case at the 19th session.
(23) On 19 December 1995 a letter was sent to the complainant acknowledging receipt of his previous three letters, and informing him that his case would be heard on its merits at the 19th session.
(24) On 20 December 1995 the complainant wrote to the Secretariat with details on a court judgement relating to transit cases, enclosing a photocopied newspaper article describing the judgement, and a translation of it that he had made.
(25) On 23 January 1996, the Secretariat of the Commission sent a copy of the complainant's 20 December 1996 letter and a copy of the newspaper article to the Ministry of Foreign Affairs of Egypt.
(26) On 13 February 1996 the Commission received a letter, dated 6 February 1996, from the Embassy of Egypt in Dakar with a copy of the government's submission on the case.
(27) At the 19th session, in March 1996, the Commission heard the representative of the Egyptian Government, but deferred taking a final decision, pending receipt from the Egyptian Government of the Egyptian law or laws under which the complaint was dealt with.
(28) On 26 July 1996 the Secretariat received a letter from the complainant acknowledging receipt of the letter of 8 May 1996 and stating that as he could not appear in person at the session in October 1996, he requested that the Secretary or an NGO represent him.
(29) On 1 August 1996 a copy of the Secretariat's last letter to the complainant was sent to the priest indicated by the complainant. With it was sent a summary of the presentation of the government at the 19th session.
(30) On same date a copy of the Secretariat's letter of 8 May 1996, requesting copies of laws, was sent to the government of Egypt. With it was sent a summary of the presentation of the government at the 19th session, for the government's approval.
(31) On 13 August 1996 the Secretariat acknowledged receipt of the letter dated 22 June and informed the complainant that as neither the Secretary nor the Commission could represent him at the session, a list of NGOs was attached whom he could contact.
(32) On 13 August 1996 the Secretariat sent a letter to the Egyptian Organisation for Human Rights requesting that they represent Mr. Njoku at the session.
(33) On 13 August 1996 the Secretariat received a letter from the complainant informing it that he had already contacted the Egyptian Human Rights Organisation who had agreed to represent him at the session.

(34) On 27 August 1996 the Secretariat received a letter from the complainant giving the names of the two lawyers who would be representing him at the 20th session, in their private capacities.

(35) On 23 September 1996 the Secretariat received a letter from the Egyptian Organisation for Human Rights with the complainant's power of attorney.

(36) On 8 October 1996 the Secretariat received a letter from the complainant stating that his punishment was harsher than authorised by Egyptian law.

(37) On 9 October 1996 the Secretariat received a note verbale from the Embassy of Egypt in Dakar giving additional information and asking whether it would still be necessary to send a representative to the 20th session of the Commission.

(38) The same date, the Secretariat sent a letter to the Embassy of Egypt in Dakar acknowledging receipt of the latter's note verbale of the 9 October 1996 and answering that the Secretariat still found it important that Egypt send a representative to the 20th session.

(39) On 21 October 1996 the Secretariat received a letter from the representative of the complainant asking the Commission to postpone the consideration of the communication because of new information.

(40) At the 20th session held in Grand Bay, Mauritius, October 1996, the Commission decided to postpone the decision to the following session.

(41) On 10 December 1996 a note verbale to this effect was sent to the government. The note verbale also asked the government to send relevant laws to the Secretariat.

(42) On the same date, the Secretariat sent a letter to the complainant, informing him of the decision of the Commission to postpone the consideration of the Communication.

(43) On 10 January 1997 the Secretariat sent a letter to Mr. Monieb, informing him of the decision taken by the Commission at its 20th Session.

(44) On 23 January 1997 the Secretariat received a note verbale from the Embassy of Egypt in Dakar, informing the Secretariat that the Working Group on Communications of the Sub-Commission on Prevention of Discrimination and Protection of Minorities of the UN had decided not to take any action in respect of a communication submitted by Mr. Njoku.

(45) On 31 January 1997 the Secretariat received a letter from Mr. Njoku summarising his case and giving examples of Egyptian case-law in drug related cases.

(46) On 3 February 1997 the Secretariat sent an acknowledgement of receipt to Mr. Njoku, enclosing a copy of the Embassy's letter of 23 January 1997.

(47) On 11 February 1997 the Secretariat sent a letter to the Embassy of Egypt in Dakar informing it that all relevant information would be taken up by the Commission at its 21st session and requesting it once more to send copies of the relevant laws.

(48) On 8 April 1997, the Secretariat received letters from the complainant reiterating the facts of the case and indicating cases of individuals prosecuted on similar grounds and who, according to the complainant, received lighter sentences.

(49) On 23 April 1997, the Secretariat renewed its request to the Embassy of Egypt in Senegal for the provision of the relevant legislative enactment against drug trafficking, as well as examples of case-law dealing with passengers on transit charged with drug trafficking. The Embassy was also informed of cases presented to the Secretariat by Mr. Ngozi Njoku.

(50) On 21 May 1997, the Secretariat received a note verbale from the Embassy of Egypt in Senegal forwarding copies of the legislative instruments in force relating to drug trafficking in Arabic (as well as amendments made thereto) as requested by the Commission. The Note verbale also underscored that there was no special law applicable to passengers on transit in Egypt and therefore that the latter were subject to the same law.

(51) On 28 May 1997, the Secretariat informed the complainant of the defendant's response.

(52) On 9 July 1997, the Secretariat acknowledged receipt of the complainant's last letter and on the same day sent a note verbale to the Embassy of Egypt seeking the reaction of its government to the information provided by Mr. Ngozi Njoku.

(53) At the 22nd Ordinary Session held in Banjul (The Gambia) from 2–11 November 1997, the Commission took a decision on the merits of the case.

Law:

Admissibility:

(54) Article 56, paragraph 7 of the African Charter on Human and Peoples' Rights stipulates inter alia that "communications . . . shall be considered if they do not deal with cases which have been settled in accordance with the principles of the Charter of the United Nations, or the Charter of the Organization of African Unity or the provisions of the present Charter".

(55) The defendant state maintains that the communication should be declared inadmissible on the grounds that the working group of the United Nations subcommission on the prevention and protection of minorities seized of the matter by Mr. Ngozi Njoku decided not to entertain the case.

(56) The Commission, considering the provisions of the above-mentioned article, observes that the said text talks about "cases which have been settled". It is therefore of the view that the decision of the United Nations sub-commission not to take any action and therefore not to pronounce on the communication submitted by the complainant does not boil down to a decision on the merits of the case and does not in any way indicate that the matter has been settled as envisaged under Article 56 paragraph 7 of the African Charter on Human and Peoples' Rights. The Commission therefore rejected the arguments of the defendant.

(57) On the issue of exhaustion of local remedies as provided for by Article 56 paragraph 5, the Commission observes that the complainant has exhausted all local remedies provided for by Egyptian Law, including the possibility of having the

case reviewed. Moreover, the government has not indicated existence of remedies other than those used by the complainant.

(58) For all these reasons, the Commission declared the communication admissible.

Merits:

(59) Both the complainant and the defendant (State) admit that Mr. Ngozi Njoku was arrested in the transit zone of Cairo airport on 20 September 1986, whilst he was on his way to Lagos from New Delhi. They also admit that drug was found in a suitcase which was alleged to belong to the Complainant, the latter was tried and sentenced to life imprisonment, that he was provided with the services of a Lawyer and that he exhausted all local remedies in 1991.

(60) Apart from these points of convergence, the rest of the communication contains serious divergences as regards the information provided by the parties. It does not however behove the Commission to judge the facts. This is the responsibility of the Egyptian courts.

(61) The role of the Commission in such a case is to ensure that during the process from the arrest to a the conviction of Mr. Ngozi Njoku, no provision of the African Charter on Human and Peoples' Rights was violated. It is also incumbent on it to ensure that the defendant state respected and indeed enforced its own law in total good faith. To all these questions, the Commission responded in the affirmative.

For these reasons, the Commission:

considers that no provision of the African Charter on Human and Peoples' Rights has been violated and therefore declares the communication closed;

gives mandate to Commissioner Isaac Nguema to pursue his good offices with the Egyptian government with a view to obtaining clemency for Mr. Ngozi Njoku on purely humanitarian grounds.

Taken at the 22nd Ordinary Session, Banjul (Gambia) on 11 November 1997.

2. 144/95 William A. Courson/Equatorial Guinea

Complainant's allegations:

Facts as submitted by the author:

(1) The complainant alleges that one Mr. Moto Nsa, along with 12 others, both military and civilian personnel, was tried and sentenced on charges of attempting to overthrow the Government of Equatorial Guinea and high treason. He was sentenced to imprisonment rather than the death penalty as an act of lenience on the part of the court.

(2) Mr. Moto Nsa was officially arrested on 6 March 1995, but had already been imprisoned for two and a half years on charges of insulting the President. At the time of his arrest, Mr. Moto Nsa was planning to participate in Equatorial Guinea's planned May 1995 municipal elections, after having led an opposition boycott of the country's first multiparty national elections, which were criticized

by United Nations and European Union observers for lack of transparency and impartial administration.

(3) From the time of his arrest until the trial he was denied the right to consult with the defense counsel and not permitted to examine the evidence against him.

(4) Although the victim has now been released as a result of a presidential pardon, the complainant wishes the Commission to declare that Mr. Nsa's conviction and imprisonment were violations of the African Charter.

The Government's Version

(5) In its response to the accusations levelled against it, the Equato-Guinean government asserts that human rights are fully protected by the country's constitution and according to the Government, the complainant's accusation are based on unfounded information. It agrees that Equatorial Guinea has a legislation governing the activities of political parties, freedom of religion, freedom of assembly and freedom of the press.

(6) Furthermore, government maintains that all ethnic groups in Equatorial Guinea live in harmony, without any discrimination; the Prime Minister as well as other members of the government belong to ethnic groups different from that of the Head of State. The impartiality of the Courts, according to him, are fully guaranteed by the laws of Equatorial Guinea. He further asserted that the law on the press and information was recently revised by the Parliament. It henceforth authorizes private individuals and associations to possess their own papers and radio and television stations. According to the government all political parties have access to the media during electoral campaigns and political meetings are freely organized throughout the country.

(7) According to the government, Mr. Moto was assisted by three "great" lawyers during his trial. And pursuant to the practice in Equatorial Guinea, when there are loopholes in the domestic law, to ensure a proper administration of justice, the courts resort to Spanish law. It further asserted that in spite of being the leader of The Progress Party, one of the fourteen recognized political parties in Equatorial Guinea, Mr. Moto was tried as an ordinary citizen and convicted for "insults and endangering state security and the form of government". Finally, the Government emphasized that Mr. Moto Nsa appealed against the sentence, of twenty-eight years' imprisonment imposed on him and after serving only three months in prison "he was granted an amnesty". In view of the foregoing, the Government concludes that the complainant's accusations have no legal basis.

Procedure before the Commission:

(8) The Communication is dated 5 May 1995. It was filed by Mr. William Andrew Courson, member of Magnus F. Hirschfeld Centre for Human Rights, an organisation based in the US. The matter was brought before the Commission on 23 May of the same year and on 30 May, it wrote to the Equato-Guinean Government to inform it of the Communication.

(9) On 22 September 1995, the complainant wrote to the Secretariat of the Commission to inform it that Mr. Moto Nsa had been released following a presidential amnesty. He however requested that his qualification of the facts, that is, the arrest and detention of Mr. Moto constitute a violation of the provisions of the Charter, be maintained. In other words, he requested the Commission not to close the matter. He further requested that the Commission orders the payment of damages to Mr. Moto for the period spent in detention.

(10) At its nineteenth session held in March 1996, the Commission declared the communication admissible and decided to rule on its merits at its twentieth session; the complainant and government have been informed accordingly.

(11) At its twentieth Session, after hearing from an official delegation from Equatorial Guinea, the Commission deferred the consideration of the case on its merits to its 21st Session and requested for additional information on the exhaustion of local remedies.

(12) During its twenty first Session, the Commission decided to postpone the consideration of the case on its merits pending the outcome of the appeal that Mr. Moto, according to the Government, is reported to have lodged against the decision sentencing him to a prison term.

(13) At its 22nd Session held from 2–11 November 1997 in Banjul (Gambia), the Commission ruled on the merits of the communication.

Law:

Admissibility:

(14) Article 56 paragraph 5 of the Charter requires that Communications be brought before the Commission only "after exhausting local remedies, if any, unless it is obvious that this procedure is unduly prolonged".

(15) What the complainant is seeking is a ruling by the Commission that Mr. Moto's arrest and detention constitute a violation of the Charter. As for the government, it maintains that Mr. Moto has appealed against the two charges for which he was prosecuted. The Commission notes that the outcome of this appeal remains unknown.

(16) Moreover, given that Mr. Moto has been granted amnesty, it appears most unlikely for any domestic court to entertain this appeal as this would only be a purely theoretical exercise. However, certain elements of the case seem to indicate procedural of laws during the trial and the Commission would like these issues clarified to enable it come to a valid decision on the case. On these grounds, the Commission declares the communication admissible.

Merits:

(17) The complainant invokes the violation of Articles 2 (enjoyment of the rights and freedoms recognized and guaranteed in the Charter without discrimination), 9, paragraph 2 (the right to express disseminate has opinions), 10, paragraph (the right to free association), 13, paragraph 1 (the right to participate freely in the government of his country) and 20, paragraph 1 (to right to self determination).

(18) All these allegations are founded on the assertion that Mr. Moto Nsa was arrested, detained, tried and sentenced because of his political opinion. The Commission is of the view that, although this could be the case, the communication does not however contain elements likely to reasonably lead to such a conclusion.

(19) The information relating to the arrest of another opposition leader contained in the complainant's submission are rather circumstantial and does not enable the commission to clearly establish that Mr. Moto was arrested because of his political opposition to the government of the day. The information does not also indicate how Mr. Moto allegedly tried to express his political opinions or set up associations with other persons. In view of the foregoing, the Commission is of the view that the violation of the above-mentioned provisions of the Charter has not been established.

(20) The complainant then goes on to base his complaint on certain provisions of Article 7 of the Charter, which stipulates that:

> "1. Every individual shall have the right to have his cause heard. This comprises:
>
> (a) The right to an appeal to competent national organs against acts of violating his fundamental rights as recognized and guaranteed by conventions, laws, regulations and customs in force;
> (b) the right to be presumed innocent until proved guilty by a competent court or tribunal;
> (c) the right to defence, including the right to be defended by counsel of his choice;
> (d) the right to be tried within a reasonable time by an impartial court or tribunal.
>
> 2. No one may be condemned for an act or omission which did not constitute a legally punishable offence at the time it was committed. No penalty may be inflicted for an offence for which no provision was made at the time it was committed. Punishment is personal and can be imposed only on the offender."

(21) The Commission notes that the submission made by the complainant contains certain elements outlining the circumstances of the trial of Mr. Moto. It notes that as regards the right to defence that the latter includes the right to be informed of the charges against him, as well as the evidence of the said charges; all sorts of elements required to prepare his defence, if all these elements were not brought to the knowledge of the accused (as alleged by the complainant) then Article 7, paragraph 1-C of the Charter had been violated.

(22) The Commission recalls that the right to defence, including the right to a counsel is exercised not only during the trial, but also during detention. Unfortunately, once again, the information at its disposal does not allow it to clearly establish whether Article 7, paragraph 1-C has been violated.

(23) Moreover, the Commission deplores the silence maintained by the parties in spite of its repeated request for information relating to the exhaustion of local remedies and other procedural aspects of the case. It is of the view that such lack of co-operation does not help the Commission to have a clear and precise understanding of the case brought before it.

On these grounds, the Commission:
decides that no provision of the African Charter on Human and Peoples' Rights has been violated.

Taken at the 22nd Ordinary Session, Banjul (Gambia), on 11 November 1997.

3. 162/97 Mouvement des Réfugiés Mauritaniens au Sénégal v Sénégal

The facts:

(1) The complainant alleges that during the operations carried out from 16–29 October 1996 in the region of Podor, Mauritanian refugees established there were the main targets of the Senegalese security forces. Refugees were reportedly arrested and subjected to all sorts of humiliating treatment during identity checks. The green cards the Senegalese State had issued to them were allegedly not regarded as valid by the security forces who considered them expired.

(2) The complainant further alleges that a group of individuals described as Mauritanian refugees were arrested by the Senegalese gendarmerie in Mboumba and on the Island of Morphil in October 1996.

(3) The communication finally alleges that these Mauritanian refugees are still being held at the Central Prison in Saint Louis, whilst Senegalese nationals arrested together with them have been set free.

(4) In a note verbale dated 24 July 1997, addressed to the Secretariat of the Commission, the Senegalese Ministry of Foreign Affairs and Expatriate Senegalese maintains that since the month of December 1995, when the United Nations High Commission for Refugees stopped distributing food, the majority of Mauritanian refugees voluntarily returned to Mauritania and those who remained are moving about freely, that they are shuttling between Rosso/Senegal and Rosso/Mauritania trying to reach an agreement with the Waly of Trarza in order to arrange for their final repatriation. The Ministry of Foreign Affairs insists that, in spite of the fact the refugees do not carry green cards they are nevertheless free to go about their business on both sides of the common border.

(5) The Ministry of Foreign Affairs also claims that the following four Mauritanian refugees: Samba Mbare, Alassane Bodia, Oumar Bodia and Balla Samba arrested by the Senegalese gendarmerie for allegedly taking part in the murder of an officer of the Mauritanian gendarmerie, were set free for lack of evidence. The Ministry of Foreign Affairs therefore argues that the communication should be declared inadmissible on the grounds that the allegations it contains are unfounded.

(6) In reaction to the arguments of the defendant State, the complainant reiterated the facts alleged and rejected the Senegalese government's claim that the refugees voluntarily returned to their home country. According to the complainant, the refugees decided to return not individually but as a group and only after obtaining assurances about their security and reintegration into Mauritanian society.

(7) The complainant claims that those refugees who left for Mauritania returned to Senegal because of threats they faced from Mauritanian authorities, the lack of assistance and the undisguised indifference of Mauritarians concerning their situation. The complainant reiterates that the refugees continue to be handicapped by the fact that they do not possess green cards. The lack of this document prevents them for example from applying for employment within the Senegalese civil service.

(8) The communication, however, does not indicate the provisions of the African Charter of Human and Peoples' Rights the defendant State may have violated.

Procedure:

(9) The communication was received by the Secretariat on 9 January 1997.

(10) On 16 January 1997, the Secretariat informed the defendant State by note verbale about the substance of the communication. On the same day, it wrote to the complainant requesting it to state whether the information contained in its letter of 4 November 1996 was to be considered as a communication under the terms of Article 55 of the Charter.

(11) On 21 January 1997, the complainant replied in the affirmative to the question asked by the Secretariat.

(12) On 27 February 1997, the Secretariat informed the complainant that its complaint had been recorded under number 162/97 and that it would be submitted to the Commission for a decision on its admissibility at the 21st ordinary session scheduled for April 1997.

(13) On the same day, a note verbale was addressed to the defendant, informing it that the communication had been recorded and requesting it to submit its views about its admissibility.

(14) On 19 March 1997, the Secretariat received a note verbale emanating from the Senegalese High Commission in the Gambia, acknowledging receipt of its note of 16 January 1997 and informing it that the dossier had been referred to the competent Senegalese authorities.

(15) At the 21st session, the Communication was submitted to the Commission which decided to postpone consideration of its admissibility until the 22nd session to be held in November 1997.

(16) On 13 June 1997, the Secretariat addressed a note verbale to the Ministry of Foreign Affairs of Senegal , informing it of the Commission's decision and requesting it to send its government's observations and arguments concerning this matter.

(17) On 24 July 1997, the Secretariat received a note verbale from the Ministry of Foreign Affairs of Senegal containing the observations and arguments of its government on this matter.
(18) On 25 July 1997, the Secretariat wrote to the complainant sending it a copy of the defendant's reply and requesting its own response. This response was received by the Secretariat on 6 October 1997.
(19) At the 22nd session held from 2–11 November 1997, the Commission reached a decision on the question of admissibility.

Law:

Admissibility:
(20) The Commission recalls that under the terms of the provisions of Article 56 paragraph 5, communications shall be considered by the Commission if they "are sent after exhausting local remedies, if any, unless it is obvious that this procedure is unduly prolonged".
(21) In this case, it should be noted that the complainant avoids saying that it has not used the remedies supposed to be available to it under the legal system of the defendant State. Further, it simply presents facts which, prima facie, do not show that the Senegalese State may be responsible.
(22) Further, the complainant does not mention the provisions of the Charter which the Senegalese State may have violated.

On these grounds, the Commission:
declares the communication inadmissible.

Taken at the 22nd session, Banjul (The Gambia), 11 November 1997.

4. 159/96 Union Inter Africaine des Droits de l'Homme, Federation Internationale des Ligues des Droits de l'Homme, Rencontre Africaine des Droits de l'Homme, Organisation Nationale des Droits de l'Homme au Sénégal and Association Malienne des Droits de l'Homme au Angola

Facts
(1) The communication is jointly filed by UIDH, FIDH, RADDHO, ONDH and AMDH. All these NGOs are acting in this case on behalf of certain West African nationals expelled from Angola in 1996. According to the complainants, between April and September 1996, the Angolan government rounded up and expelled West African nationals on its territory. These illegal expulsions were preceded by acts of brutality committed against Senegalese, Malian, Gambian, Mauritanian and other nationals. Those affected lost in the process their belongings.
(2) The complainants maintain that the Angolan State violated the provisions of Articles 2, 7 paragraph 1(a), 12 paragraphs 4 and 5 of the African Charter on human and Peoples' Rights.

Procedure:

(3) The communication is not dated, but it was received during the 20th session of the Commission, held in Grand Bay, Mauritius in October, 1996.

(4) On 24 October 1996 the Secretariat acknowledged receipt of the communication.

(5) On 19 December 1996 the Secretariat notified the Angolan government of the communication.

(6) During its 21st Session in Nouakchott (Mauritania) in April 1997, the Commission declared the communication admissible.

(7) The government and the complainants were informed of this decision on 23 June 1997.

(8) At the 22nd Session in November 1997, the Commission ruled on the merits of the case.

Law:

Admissibility:

(9) The Commission considered the issue of admissibility of this communication on the basis of information furnished by the complainants. It deplores the fact that the defendant State did not respond to the notification sent to it on 19 December 1996, following the decision of the seizure of the Commission.

(10) Article 57 of the Charter implicitly indicates that the State Party to the said Charter against which allegation of human rights violations are levelled is required to consider them in good faith and to furnish the Commission with all information at its disposal to enable the latter to come to an equitable decision. In this case, in view of the defendant State's refusal to co-operate with the Commission, the latter can only give more weight to the accusations made by the complainants and this on the basis of the evidence furnished by them.

(11) The evidence show that between April and September 1996, the government of the Republic of Angola embarked on mass expulsion of aliens from its territory, and that these expulsions were illegal and arbitrary, and in violation of Article 12, paragraphs 4 and 5 of the African Charter on Human and Peoples' Rights.

(12) According to information at the disposal of the Commission, it appears that those expelled did not have the possibility to challenge their expulsion in court. In communication No: 71/92 "Rencontre Africaine pour la Défense des Droits de l'Homme vs Zambia "(20th Session, October 1996), the Commission was of the view that "the massive nature of the arrests, the fact that the victims were kept in detention before the expulsions and the pace with which they were carried out did not leave any opportunity to the complainants to establish the illegality of these acts before the Courts". In view of the foregoing, the Commission notes that local remedies were not accessible to the complainants.

(13) On these grounds, the Commission declared the communication admissible.

Merits:

(14) Article 12, paragraph 4 stipulates that a non national legally admitted in a territory of a State party to the present Charter, may only be expelled from it by virtue of a

decision taken in accordance with the law. Paragraph 5 of the same article stipulates that "the mass expulsion of non nationals shall be prohibited. Mass expulsion shall be that which is aimed at national, racial, ethnic or religious groups".

(15) In communication 71/92 cited here above, the Commission indicated that "mass expulsion was a special threat to human rights. A government action specially directed at specific national, racial ethnic or religious groups is generally qualified as discriminatory in the sense that, none of its characteristics has any legal basis or could constitute a source of particular incapacity".

(16) The Commission concedes that African States in general and the Republic of Angola in particular are faced with many challenges, mainly economic. In the face of such difficulties, States often resort to radical measures aimed at protecting their nationals and their economic from non-nationals. Whatever, the circumstances may be however, such measures should not be taken at the detriment of the enjoyment of human rights. Mass expulsions of any category of persons, whether on the basis of nationality, religion, ethnic, racial or other considerations "constitute a special violation of human rights".

(17) This type of deportations calls into question a whole series of rights recognized and guaranteed in the Charter; such as the right to property (Article 14), the right to work (Article 15), the right to education (Article 17, paragraph 1) and results in the violation by the State of its obligations under Article 18, paragraph 1 which stipulates that "the family shall be the natural unit and basis of society. It shall be protected by the State which shall take care of its physical and moral health". By deporting the victims, thus separating some of them from their families, the defendant State has violated and violates the letter of this text.

(18) Article 2 of the Charter emphatically stipulates that "Every individual shall be entitled to the enjoyment of the rights and freedoms recognized and guaranteed in the present Charter without distinction of any kind such as race, ethnic group, colour, sex, language, religion, political or any other opinion, national and social origin, fortune, birth or other status". This text obligates States Parties to ensure that persons living on their territory, be they their nationals or non nationals, enjoy the rights guaranteed in the Charter. In this case, the victims rights to equality before the law were trampled on because of their origin.

(19) It emerges from the case file that the victims did not have the opportunity to challenge the matter before the competent jurisdictions which should have ruled on their detention, as well as on the regularity and legality of the decision to expel them by the Angolan government.

(20) The Commission does not wish to call into question nor is it calling into question the right of any State to take legal action against illegal immigrants and deport them to their countries of origin, if the competent courts so decide. It is however of the view that it is unacceptable to deport individuals without giving them the possibility to plead their case before the competent national courts as this is contrary to the spirit and letter of the Charter and international law.

On these grounds, the Commission:
declares that the deportation of the victims constitute a violation of Articles 2, 7 paragraph 1(a), 12, paragraphs 4 and 5 as well as Articles 14 and 18 of the African Charter on Human and Peoples' Rights.

with regards to damages for prejudice suffered, it *urges* the Angolan government and the complainants to draw all the legal consequences arising from the present decision.

Taken at the 22nd Ordinary Session, Banjul (Gambia), 11 November 1997.

ANNEX III

Status of Submission of Periodic Reports by States Parties

No.	State Party	1st Report to be submitted on	2nd Report to be submitted on	3rd Report to be submitted on	4th Report to be submitted on	5th Report to be submitted on	Reports submitted but not yet considered
1.	Algeria	20/06/89	20/06/91	20/06/93	20/06/95	20/06/97	
2.	Angola	09/01/92	09/01/94	09/01/96	09/01/98	09/01/00	
3.	Benin	21/10/88	21/10/90	21/10/92	21/10/94	21/10/96	
4.	Botswana	21/10/88	21/10/90	21/10/92	21/10/94	21/10/96	
5.	Burundi	30/11/91	30/11/93	30/11/95	30/11/97	30/11/99	
6.	Burkina Faso	21/10/88	21/10/90	21/10/92	21/10/94	21/10/96	
7.	Cameroon	18/12/91	18/12/93	18/12/95	18/12/97	18/12/99	
8.	Cape Verde	06/11/89	06/11/91	06/11/93	06/11/95	06/11/97	
9.	Central African Republic	21/10/88	21/10/90	21/10/92	21/10/94	21/10/96	
10.	Chad	11/02/89	11/02/91	11/02/93	11/02/95	11/02/97	
11.	Comoros	21/10/88	21/10/90	21/10/92	21/10/94	21/10/96	
12.	Congo	21/10/88	21/10/90	21/10/92	21/10/94	21/10/96	
13.	Côte d'Ivoire	01/07/94	01/07/96	01/07/98	07/01/00	01/07/02	
14.	Djibouti	20/03/93	20/03/95	20/03/97	20/03/99	20/03/01	
15.	Egypt	21/10/88	21/10/90	21/10/92	21/10/94	21/10/96	
16.	Equatorial Guinea	18/11/88	18/11/90	18/11/92	18/11/94	18/11/96	
17.	Ethiopia (1)						
18.	Eritrea (1)						
19.	Gabon	21/10/88	21/10/90	21/10/92	21/10/94	21/10/96	
20.	Gambia	21/10/88	21/10/90	21/10/92	21/10/94	21/10/96	
21.	Ghana	01/06/91	01/06/93	01/06/95	01/06/97	01/06/99	
22.	Guinea	21/10/88	21/10/90	21/10/92	21/10/94	21/10/96	
23.	Guinea-Bissau	21/10/88	21/10/90	21/10/92	21/10/94	21/10/96	
24.	Kenya	10/05/94	10/05/96	10/05/98	10/05/00	10/05/02	
25.	Lesotho	27/05/94	27/05/96	27/05/98	27/05/00	27/05/02	
26.	Liberia	27/10/88	21/10/90	21/10/92	21/10/94	21/10/96	
27.	Libya	26/06/89	26/06/91	26/06/93	26/06/95	26/06/97	

No.	State Party	1st Report to be submitted on	2nd Report to be submitted on	3rd Report to be submitted on	4th Report to be submitted on	5th Report to be submitted on	Reports submitted but not yet considered
28.	Madagascar	19/06/94	19/06/96	19/06/98	19/06/00	19/06/02	
29.	Malawi	23/05/92	23/05/94	23/05/96	23/05/98	23/05/00	
30.	Mali	21/10/88	21/10/90	21/10/92	21/10/94	21/10/96	
31.	Mauritania	21/10/88	21/10/90	21/10/92	21/10/94	21/10/96	
32.	Mauritius	07/10/92	07/10/94	07/10/96	07/10/98	07/10/00	
33.	Mozambique	07/06/92	07/06/94	07/06/96	07/06/98	07/06/00	
34.	Namibia	16/12/94	16/12/96	16/12/98	16/12/00	16/12/02	
35.	Niger	21/10/88	21/10/90	21/10/92	21/10/94	21/10/96	
36.	Nigeria	21/10/88	21/10/90	21/10/92	21/10/94	21/10/96	
37.	Rwanda	21/10/88	21/10/90	21/10/92	21/10/94	21/10/96	
38.	SADR	21/10/88	21/10/90	21/10/92	21/10/94	21/10/96	
39.	Sao Tome & Principe	21/10/88	21/10/90	21/10/92	21/10/94	21/10/96	
40.	Senegal	21/10/88	21/10/90	21/10/92	21/10/94	21/10/96	
41.	Seychelles	30/07/94	30/07/96	30/07/98	30/07/00	30/07/02	Initial report
42.	Sierra Leone	21/10/88	21/10/90	21/10/92	21/10/94	21/10/96	
43.	Somalia	21/10/88	21/10/90	21/10/92	21/10/94	21/10/96	
44.	South Africa	07/07/98	09/07/00	09/07/02	09/07/03	07.07/06	
45.	Sudan	21/10/88	21/10/90	21/10/92	21/10/94	21/10/96	Initial report
46.	Swaziland	15/09/97	15/09/99	15/09/01	15/09/03	15/09/05	
47.	Tanzania	21/10/88	21/10/90	21/10/92	21/10/94	21/10/96	
48.	Togo	21/10/88	21/10/90	21/10/92	21/10/94	21/10/96	
49.	Tunisia	21/10/88	21/10/90	21/10/92	21/10/94	21/10/96	
50.	Uganda	21/10/88	21/10/90	21/10/92	21/10/94	21/10/96	
51.	Zaire	28/10/89	28/10/91	28/10/93	28/10/95	28/10/97	
52.	Zambia	21/10/88	21/10/90	21/10/92	21/10/94	21/10/96	
53.	Zimbabwe	21/10/88	21/10/90	21/10/92	21/10/94	21/10/96	2nd & 3rd reports

* has presented its preliminary report
† has presented its preliminary report and second periodic report
** has presented its preliminary, and submitted its second and third report
(1) not yet ratified the African Charter

ANNEX III

Resolution on the International Criminal Court

The African Commission on Human and Peoples' Rights meeting at its 23rd Ordinary Session held from 20 to 29 April 1998 in Banjul, the Gambia,

Recalling the provisions of the African Charter which, inter alia, indicate that all peoples shall have the right to national and international peace and security,

Recalling also the rules and principles of international law in general and the international humanitarian law in particular,

Bearing in mind the African and international efforts aspiring at the establishment of an International Criminal Court,

Stressing the importance of the independence of such court with a view to enabling to try crimes of genocide, crimes against humanity and serious violations of humanitarian law and to ensure a fair trial:

RECOMMENDS to the Council of Ministers and Assembly of Heads of State and Government of the OAU to intensify and co-ordinate the African efforts during the Diplomatic Conference in Rome, Italy (15 June–17 July 1998) in support of the establishment of an International Criminal Court on the basis of the principles endorsed by many African countries in the 1997 Declaration by the Southern Africa Development Community (SADC) and in the 6 February 1998 Decalration in Dakar;

REQUESTS the Chairman to the African Commission to ensure its representation at the Diplomatic Conference in Rome and to report to it for appropriate follow-up.

Final Communiqué of the Twenty-second Ordinary Session of the African Commission on Human and Peoples' Rights

Banjul, 2–11 November 1997

1. The Opening Ceremony of the 22nd Ordinary Session of the African Commission on Human and Peoples' Rights was held in Banjul, The Gambia on 2 November, 1997 under the Chairmanship of Professor Isaac Nguema, outgoing Chairman of the Commission. The Session was preceded by the 12th International Commission of Jurists (ICJ) Workshop on Participation in the work of the African Commission on Human and Peoples' Rights.

2. The Opening Ceremony of the Session which was graced with the presence of His Excellency the President of the Republic of the Gambia, Colonel (Rtd.) Yahya A. J. J. Jammeh, was also attended by officials of the Government of The Gambia, His Excellency Ambassador Papa Louis Fall, the Acting Dean of the African Diplomatic Corps accredited to the OAU in Addis Ababa, Ethiopia and Mrs. Tokunbo Ige, the ICJ Legal Officer for Africa representing the ICJ Secretary General.

3. The Opening Speech was delivered by His Excellency Col. (Rtd.) Yahya A. J. J. Jammeh, President of the Gambia. Prior to the opening speech, Professor Isaac Nguema, the outgoing Chairman of the African Commission on Human and Peoples' Rights, His Excellency Ambassador Papa Louis Fall, the Acting Dean of the Diplomatic Corps accredited to the OAU in Addis Ababa, Ethiopia and Mrs. Tokunbo Ige, representing the ICJ Secretary General, Mr. Adama Dieng addressed the session.

The speakers emphasized the importance of human and peoples' rights, noting that these rights have to be guaranteed by more efficient and effective regional instruments and mechanisms for the promotion and protection of human rights. In this respect, they asserted their commitment to support the Commission in the pursuit of its objectives.

4. After the adoption of the agenda, members of the Commission elected Mr. Youssoupha Ndiaye as Chairman of the Commission and Mrs. Vera Duarte as Vice Chairperson for a period of two years.

5. Statements were delivered by representatives of the governments of Sudan, Nigeria, Niger, Togo, Burundi and Mauritania.

6. Statements were also delivered by, among others, representatives of the following African and international NGOs: the International Commission of Jurists, Women in Law and Development in Africa (WILDAF), the Algerian Committee on Human and Peoples' Rights, Service International des Droits de l'Homme, Association Zaïroise des Droits de l'Homme (AZADHO), Inter-African Network for

Human Rights and Development, International Society for Human Rights Campaign, Human Rights Watch, Amnesty International, African Centre for Democracy and Human Rights Studies, Malawi Career, Femmes Africa Solidarity, Association pour la Prévention de la Torture, Penal Reform International, Fédération Internationale des Jeunes Avocats de France.

7. Mr. David Padilla, the Assistant Executive Secretary of the Inter-American Commission on Human Rights, who was a special guest of the African Commission at the Session, spoke on behalf of the Inter-American Commission and underscored the need to strengthen the relationship between the two institutions.

Mr. Ali Bouhedma, a former member of the Commission and Chairman of the Libyan Human Rights Committee requested the support of the African Commission to have the embargo against Libya lifted and deplored the suffering inflicted on the people of Libya.

The Minister for Human Rights, Institutional Reforms and Relations with the National Assembly of Burundi as well as some NGOs deplored the suffering inflicted on the people of Burundi by the embargo against their country.

8. The Commission granted observer status to 18 NGOs. The list of the NGOs granted observer status with the Commission is available at the Secretariat.

9. The Commission postponed the consideration of the periodic report of Chad because of the failure of the Government of Chad to send a representative to the Session.

10. Mr. Hatem Ben Salem, Special Rapporteur on Extra-judicial, Summary and Arbitrary Executions and Professor E. V. O. Dankwa, Special Rapporteur on Prison Conditions in Africa presented their reports to the Commission.

11. The Commission also discussed the implementation of Resolution AHG/ Resolution 230 (XXX) of the Assembly of Heads of State and Government of the OAU recommending the establishment of an African Court on Human and Peoples' Rights. In this respect, the Secretariat informed members of the Commission that a meeting of experts will be held in Addis Ababa from 8–11 December and will be followed by the Conference of Ministers of Justice from 12–13 December 1997.

12. A group of experts co-ordinated by Commissioner E. V. O. Dankwa presented a progress report on the draft Additional Protocol on the Rights of African Women. After discussion, it was decided to expand the group to include two more NGOs, the ICJ and the African Centre for Democracy and Human Rights Studies.

The Commission also recalled its resolution on the appointment of a Special Rapporteur on Women's Rights in Africa adopted at its 19th Ordinary Session in Ouagadougou, Burkina Faso.

13. The Commission considered the agenda item on the strengthening of co-operation with national human rights promotion and protection institutions. Commissioners Rezzag-Bara and Pityana were entrusted with the task of studying the matter.

14. As regards the human rights situation in Africa, the Commission heard various NGO representatives who cited inter alia cases of human rights violations in the Democratic Republic of Congo, Sudan and Nigeria as well as the situation prevailing in Cameroon and Mauritania.

The Commission also deplored the massive and serious violations of human rights in Congo (Brazzaville). The representatives of the Governments of Mauritania, Sudan, and Nigeria expressed their opinion on these statements.

15. The Commission discussed in detail the issue of its participation in OAU activities relevant to human rights and highlighted the importance of its participation in such activities.

16. The Commission reiterated its decision to organise the following seminars:

- The right to a fair trial and legal aid;
- Popular participation and Non-formal education;
- Human rights in the new South Africa;
- Peaceful Resolution of ethnic and social conflicts within the framework of human rights;
- Contemporary forms of slavery in Africa;
- The right to education: a prerequisite for development in Africa;
- Freedom of movement and right to asylum in Africa;
- Economic, Social and Cultural Rights and right to development.

17. On protective activities, the Commission decided to defer consideration of the mission reports on Sudan and Nigeria to the next session. The Commission also considered 75 communications and took appropriate action on each of them.

18. The Commission considered the report of the Secretary and took note of the strengthening of the Secretariat through the kind assistance of its partners. The Commission also discussed the preparation of the African Ministerial Conference on Human Rights scheduled for November 1998 in Angola and decided to be fully involved.

The Commission has also expressed the wish to see the Secretary General of the OAU making plans to readjust the budget allocated to the Commission

19. The Commission also examined the proposal for the institution of a Tri-continental Conference of the Commissions of Human Rights of the Council of Europe, the Organisation of American States and the Organisation of African Unity.

20. The Commission decided that the 23rd Session be held in April 1998 in South Africa, the 24th Session in November 1998 in Angola and the 25th Session in April 1999 in Algeria.

21. The Closing Ceremony took place on 11 November 1997 at the Kairaba Hotel under the Chairmanship of Mr. Youssoupha Ndiaye. The Session was closed by the Attorney General and Secretary of State for Justice of The Gambia, Her Excellency Mrs. Hawa Sisay Sabally.

22. After the Closing Ceremony, the Chairman of the Commission, Mr. Youssoupha Ndiaye gave a press conference.

Issued in Banjul, Gambia, 11 November 1997

Prisons in Mali
Report of the Special Rapporteur on Prisons and Conditions of Detention

Report on a Visit 20-30 August 1997
By Prof. E. V. O. Dankwa
Series IV No. 2

INTRODUCTION

This report covers two main activities undertaken after the 21st Session of the Commission held in Nouakchott, Mauritania from 15–24 April 1997.

At the invitation of the Association for the Prevention of Torture (APT), I participated in a one-day workshop on modalities For Missions And Visits To Places of Detention which APT organised in collaboration with Penal Reform International (PRI) in Geneva on 24 May 1997.

In pursuit of activities which I presented to the Commission at its last session, I visited prisons[1] *in Bamako, Tombouctou, Goundam, Mopti, Baguineda and Kati in Mali from 20–30 August 1997.*

ACKNOWLEDGEMENTS

My task was made easier by the supply of background materials on Mali in general and its prison regime in particular by PRI. APT also kindly shared with me their report on a recent visit to some prisons in May by a member of its staff. The efforts of mr. Ahmed Othmani, Chairman of PRI helped in getting me permission to visit prisons in Mali. Audrey Pascaud of the same body removed the language barrier between me and the respondents I interviewed or from whom I gathered relevant information. They are too numerous to mention, but for being crucial for the success of my mission I must thank Mr. Cheikhna Detteba Kamissoko, Minister of Justice, who gave me permission to visit any prison or place of detention. Mr. Bourouma Sidibe, National Director of Prisons and his deputy, Mr. Toure who briefed me on prisons and their administration in Mali. Mme Diarra Assétou Loite, Head of Division of Detention, Regulation and Rehabilitation and Administrative Management, her Deputy Mr. Kamara; Amadon Balma Karembe, Head, Division de l'Education Surveillée and her deputy Diotié Togola; and Suzanne Hofstetter, Chief of the ICRC Delegation in Mali added to the background knowledge useful for my mission. Madam Ouattara and M. Diarra

[1] Wherever the context demands it "prisons" should be understood to include places of detention.

of the Malian Association of Human Rights organised a meeting of NGOs where we shared information and ideas. I am much obliged to all of them.

THE COUNTRY

Covering an approximate area of 1,241,000,000 sq. km, Mali is one of the two biggest countries in Africa with a population of about 10 million. It became independent in 1960 under its first President Modibo Keita. He was overthrown in a coup d'état in 1968. Imprisoned after his overthrow Modibo Keita spent the rest of his life in detention giving up the ghost in 1977. The military officer who took over power Moussa Traoré was himself overthrown after a long reign of 23 years, and is now in prison after conviction of crimes. 108 people had been killed and 708 injured when his security forces brutally suppressed demonstrators seeking democracy. His first head of government, Capt. Yoro Diakité died in detention in 1973. Mrs. Keita spent time in prison after the overthrow of her husband, and Mrs. Traore is in detention. Also in detention were Almany Sylla, leader of the Opposition and some of his colleagues following allegations of their involvement in the death of a security personnel. About 4000 people of low status in society are in prisons in Mali. The conditions under which people are imprisoned or detained must, therefore, be of concern to the low and high alike in Mali as elsewhere.

In a statesmanlike fashion, General Amadou Toumani Touré who became the new head of State after Moussa Traoré organised a constitutional referendum, municipal and presidential elections in just over a year; and handed over power to the winner of the presidential election, Alpha Oumar Konaré. He is still the Head of State after recent elections, aspects of which were questioned by the opposition.

The government of President Konaré identified education and health as priority areas and consequently allocated 24% and 7% respectively of the annual budget to these sectors.

Conditions in prisons which were visited may indicate the attention which has been and should be paid to this subject by government.

MEETINGS AND PRISONS

Bamako

21 August 1997
Direccion Nationale de l'Administration Pénitentiaire et de l'Education Surveillée (DNAPES)[2]

At this headquarters of the prison administration the National Director and his Deputy named above briefed me about the penal regime in Mali and the problems his

[2] Literal translation into English is National Direction of Prison Administration and Supervised Education.

administration was encountering. Until 1990 the prison regime was governed by colonial legislation. DNAPES was established in 1990 under legislation which is appended to this report as Annex I. DNAPES consists of two divisions:

(i) The Division for Detention, Rehabilitation and Regulation; and
(ii) The Division of Supervised Education.

For financial reasons subdivisions provided for under the legislation have not been set up, an example of the gap between the letter of the law and practice. There are prisons termed "Maisons Centrales d'Arrêt", farm prisons known as "pénitenciers agricoles" and a rehabilitation centre referred to as "Centre de Rééducation" which is situated at Bollé and which is close to Bamako. Juveniles are kept at this Centre.

Food

Until 1993 feeding of prisoners posed a big problem to the administration. But in 1993/94 Parliament doubled the budgetary allocation for food. In Bamako central prison prisoners have three meals a day. In the rest of the prisons inmates were fed twice. The meals consist of millet, rice and beans; and occasionally maize. Maladministration is the big problem now, but as soon as such as issue is brought to the attention of the Director corrective action is taken. Illustrative of this stance is the dismissal of the registrar of Koulikoro prison two days earlier. While the food allocated to the prison there should have provided two meals a day for the prisoners there was a day when they had none.

Health

While the Ministry of health has been providing medicine for the prisons, the supplies are inadequate except for Bamako Central prison which receives the quasi-totality of the medicine needed to treat the detainees. Sick prisoners are brought to Bamako prison where there is a clinic, and in serious cases they are sent to hospital. The judiciary and local administration supplement the allocation from the Ministry of health. Local churches and religious organisations also offer assistance.

Training and activities in prison

Each prison is engaged in some agricultural activity but except for 4 prison farms, it is not well organised. Prison farms are organised as open establishments with minimum security measures. Inmates at the farms have background in agriculture. Additionally, those who are about to complete their sentence are sent there. Started 4 years ago, prison farms have not shown encouraging results in terms of output and escape. With an eye on improvement, greater care was being taken in the selection of the inmates. Registrars (those in charge of prisons) were also being trained.

There is the interesting case of two prisoners sentenced to long terms of imprisonment who agreed to work in a prison farm and were living with their respective families. They cultivate their own plot part of the time, and work on the prison farm the rest of their working time. They are on the Monségéla and Baguinéda prison farms.

Workshops

Before 1991 all prisons were supplied with sewing machines, and most prisons had workshops where inmates were trained. Bamako Prison had the most advanced workshop, but they were either destroyed or rendered inoperative in two uprisings in 1991 and 1992.

State of buildings

The Tuareg rebellion and resultant fighting destroyed some prisons in the northern part of Mali and generally delayed development programmes. However, since 1991 the Ministry of Justice has been allocated money for the building of 2 to 3 new prisons a year each with a capacity of 40–50 inmates. 10 prisons have been built since 1991. These are at Bla, Koulikorom Kenielba, Banamba, Kati, Diéma, Bougoni, Kangaba and Diola. The last one is still under construction and it is air-conditioned. Rehabilitation of prisons also commenced in 1991.

Multiplicity of authority

No one ministry or authority controls prisons and the prison staff. Prison cells are under Territorial Administration while the Gendarmerie is under the Ministry of Defence and prisons under the Ministry of Justice. Prison guards are from the Gendarmerie and Registrars or Directors are selected from the Civil Service.

Gender and children

Prisons so not have separate parts or wings for men and women. By law women with children under 6 months should not be sent to prison. The practice, however, is different. In Bamako prison mothers with children are kept in a separate wing. Juveniles are detained in most prisons with adults. The only institution providing special care in Bolle rehabilitation centre, where also a new prison is being built for women and juveniles. In the new prisons women, men, juveniles, remand and convicts are kept in separate wings.

Personnel

Lack of training of Registrars and prison staff was acknowledged. Efforts were, however, being made to address the problem. 13 people were undergoing a 6 months course in Dakar so that they could replace untrained registrars. 466 former guards from the National Guards Body have also been recruited by DNAPES and given a one month course at the Institut National de Formation Judiciaire under the supervision of the Deputy Director of Prisons for the purpose of their replacing the guards from the National Guards Body. Unlike the guards currently at post, the new recruits would be under the direct authority of DNAPES. The existing situation of personnel in prison answering to different authorities created problems in efficiency and discipline.

Remand

It is a serious problem. The estimate is that 80% of the inmates in Bamako central prison are on remand, and this figure would be as high as 90% in other prisons. The remand period could last up to 6 years. Examining magistrates (juges d'instruction) did not have the means to visit detainees. They also felt insecure and requested the State to convey prisoners to Court.

Although DNAPES did not have sufficient means of transport this did not prevent detainees from being taken to court. Outside Bamako transport is not a problem because the courts are not far from the prisons and gendarmerie can requisition vehicles to transport detainees to court.

Visit to Ministry of Justice

Present at this meeting were:

Mr. Cheikhna Dettaba Kamissoko, Minister of Justice;
Mr. Mamadou K. Cissouma, Secretary-General;
Mr. Baba Sylla, Technical Adviser on Prisons;
Mr. Amadou Ousmane Toure, Chef de Cabinet and Secretary General of the National Consultative Commission on Human Rights.

Welcoming me to his office, the Minister emphasised that democracy and human rights are priority concern of the government. The judiciary has to be independent so that there will not be arbitrary use of power by either the state or the citizen. Humane treatment of prisoners and their rehabilitation is one of the concerns of government. The current government, therefore, welcomes international bodies monitoring the observance of human rights like the International Committee of the Red Cross.

An open forum on democracy was held in Mali in December 1996. Assessment of the extent to which recommendations from the forum have been implemented would take place in September.

He appealed to the African Commission on Human and Peoples' Rights to co-operate with the government. He also encourages the Special Rapporteur to make the necessary recommendations to Government. He gave the assurance that such recommendations would be taken seriously by government.

22 August 1997
DNAPES, Division of Detention, Rehabilitation and Regulation

Mme. Diarra, head of Division of Detention, rehabilitation and regulation explained that DNAPES would like to make conditions in all prisons humane. It, however, lacked the human and financial means to attain this goal. Nevertheless social rehabilitation constituted their priority, and DNAPES had appealed to funding agencies for assistance. DNAPES has not recovered from the damage caused by the 1991 and 1992 mutinies in prisons. The workshops which were destroyed in the disturbances have not been rebuilt.

What was required to ensure humane conditions were identified by her as: improvement in health conditions; education of inmates; professional training (trades and skills for prisoners); improvement in the training of prison personnel; and rebuilding of prisons.

Mme Diarra added that her Division was responsible for the administrative matters of detainees from their arrival to their release. Drawing up of prison programmes and projects were also their responsibility. Present at the meeting was Mme Diarra's Deputy, Mr. Camara.

DNAPES, Division of Supervised Education

Present were mr. Amadou Karambe, Head and Mr. Diotié Togola, Deputy Head.

Although the statute providing for the establishment of the division was passed in 1990 it was not until 1992 that it was set up. The work of the Division was geared towards juveniles in prison (Bollé and Bamako) and crime prevention among the youth, especially street children.

The Division has organised a training session for 40 young girls from Bollé village, and they were taught sewing and dyeing. It had encouraging results. 25 of the trainees went through the whole course. Such courses will be replicated if there is the financial means to do so.

Visit to Baquinéda Prison Farms

The Registrar in charge is Sergeant Chef Mory Sidibé.

The farm is located 30 km from Bamako; and it is 5 km off the Bamako-Segou road.

It was opened in 1970, closed in 1987, and reopened in 1994. There were 12 inmates although the prison farm could accommodate 15. The inmates had served the greater part of their sentences elsewhere. They were also petty offenders.

The farm covered an area of 9.5 hectares, 4 hectares of which were cultivated (3 hectares for millet produced 1.4 tonnes in 1996, 1 hectare mangoes). 5.5 hectares are used for grazing.

The prisoners worked on the prison farm for part of the time, and on their own plots for some of the time.

Family visits were allowed, and the inmates could correspond with the outside world.

As regards food DNAPES had supplied 2 tons of millet, 1 ton of rice and another ton of beans to provide the inmates with 3 meals each day.

Relationship with the local community

The local population, the registrar stated, were not happy with the location of the prison. They feared that prisoners could steal from the village and escape. He admitted that lack of sensitisation accounted for this attitude of the local community.

There had not been positive results as far as the rehabilitation of prisoners was concerned. Most of the inmates had tried to escape from the farm. While they were not satisfied with their conditions they recognised that those conditions were better than those in the regular prisons.

Private discussion with prisoners

They complained bitterly about their conditions of life: their living conditions were bad, they were overcrowded and had neither blankets nor clothes (they were not naked though); their supply of soap was not sufficient; and they had no cleaning material. The small structure which housed them had poor ventilation. From their viewpoint DNAPES did not pay sufficient attention to their conditions of life because they were perceived as already enjoying a privileged regime of partial release. They also complained that they were excluded from consideration by the selection committee for presidential pardon.

In Mali there is no judge who reviews the terms and conditions of a prisoner's sentence. Sentences are reviewed and reduced at the mercy of the president.

They get nothing from working for the administration. They work for the administration in the morning, and in the afternoon for themselves (whenever they have the means to buy seeds) or offer their services to the villagers.

Visit to Bamako Central Prison

The Director of the Prison Amadou Diarra is an officer of the Gendarmerie. He introduced some officers of the prison, Mme Diarra, a social worker and Major Attouhen Ag. Acheikh, Chief of the guards.

Built for 400 inmates, there were 1025 inmates made up of 1003 males and 22 women. Among the males were 30 juveniles. 64 of the inmates arrived when they were juveniles. The youngest juvenile was 15 years old. The oldest inmate was 60 years old. Of the total number in prison 922 were on remand with some having been in that status for five years. There are different wings for women, juveniles, those on remand and convicts. Slow dispensation of justice accounts for the long remands.

Guards and administrators number 30.

The Director had not found transport a problem in getting prisoners to court. By his account, daily visits to inmates posed no difficulty and were unrestricted from 8 a.m.–3 p.m. Between 15 August and 22 August more than 19,900 visits had been registered. Correspondence with the outside world was allowed, and only incoming mail was censored.

Meals were served 3 times each day (rice and millet). There was no prison uniform. Prisoners wore their own clothes but those without clothes were supplied with some. Soap and washing powder were distributed once a month.

The assistance to the prison of organisations such as CICR, ENDA and the Red Cross was acknowledged.

Sanitation posed a major problem to the prison. The drainage system was faulty, and so dirty water could not be drained easily out of the prison.

The prison had sections with a total room number of 23. Each section has a tap and toilets, one school but no library. Sewing workshops were out of use, and the same was true of carpentry and mechanics.

Magistrates could, but rarely did, visit detainees.

The Director took me on a tour of the Prison. It has two main parts. One section was once reserved for convicts, but because of the high increase in the number of remand prisoners, only a section of it now serves that function.

Juveniles section

Juveniles were housed on one yard with a tap and 10 rooms measuring about 4 × 2 metres each. There were 2 toilets. The roof leaked, and seeping water produced stagnant water on the floor of all the cells. The stench of urine was quite pungent, and a little more cleanliness would have been welcomed. 33 juveniles in fact occupied the cells. They expressed the desire to sleep in the open yard adjacent to their cells so that they could have fresh air instead of the heat in their cells. Were their desire to be granted, the nuisance of mosquitoes in their cells would still have persisted in their preferred abode since a large section of it is not roofed.

The juveniles confirmed receiving 3 meals each day, but wished the administration would provide them with clothes. Some of them went to school from their cells. Most of them had no visit from their families since they either had none or had lost contact with them. Essential medicine was the only medication they received from the administration in case of ill health.

The remand section

Citing security as the reason, the Registrar counselled against entry. Communication with the inmates was through iron bars which separated us.

There were some who appeared young enough to be juveniles. Each section consisted of a yard and rooms which opened onto the yard. There were a tap and toilet in each yard. They complained about lack of blankets, mats, clothes and soap. They also complained about the poor quality of the meals served to them. Since most of them had lost contact with their families the rights of visit and correspondence were not of use to them.

They were bitter that some of them had been no remand for more than 5 years.

Convicts section

As in the case of those on remand, the Registrar did not allow us to go inside the section for convicts for security reasons. Communication with the prisoners was carried out as had been done with the juveniles.

20 of them were inside this section while the rest were working outside the prison. Those present had similar complaints as the juveniles. Additionally, they complained that their remand period had not been taken into account during their sentencing.

The tap here was defective, and water had to be brought from another tap in the central yard of the prison.

General remarks about the atmosphere in the prison

The detainees were tense, and not relaxed at all. This must explain why the Registrar feared for security when I asked to be allowed into the remand and convicts sections. It partially explains, most probably, why there had been two revolts in this prison. Kept in such tense circumstances over a long period the danger of escape, riot or revolt is ever present. The escape of 100 inmates from Kayes prison on 17 August 1997 must also have concentrated the mind of the Registrar most wonderfully on the question of security.

The Chief guard appeared nervous during the visit, and was observed beating one inmate who was on his way to fetch water from the yard.

The second half of the prison

This part looked quieter, neater and better kept. The inmates wore better and cleaner clothes. Food parcels coming into the prison for inmates were kept together at an entrance of the prison before being distributed to the donees.

Inmates walked freely about in the yard. They were not locked into their cells and rooms as in the case of those in the first half of the prison.

The Registrar explained that elderly detainees and "civil servants" were held in this half of the prison. The cells looked much nicer and cleaner and quite comfortable with fans, games, mats and books. This section was generally dry.

Among the inmates were foreigners from Nigeria, The Gambia, Liberia and Ghana.

The women's section was located in this part of the prison. All the guards and almost all other personnel were men. The female section was locked, and only members of the administration could enter it.

29 August 1997

Meeting with NGOs Working in the Areas of Detention or Prevention of Crime

Ms. Camara, a social worker at Bamako central prison who had worked in that capacity for five years outlined her duties as follows: reception of detainees, re-establishment and preservation of family links, follow up of court files, protection against violence and corporal punishment, welfare of juveniles, workshops and co-operation with NGOs.

ENDA Tiers Monde

Representatives of this NGO recounted their activities as including organising training workshops for juveniles who had been released from prison. They also collaborate with the international Catholic office for children. Subjects of study at their workshops have been carpentry, metal works, shoe repair and indigo dyeing.

ADEP

They organise training sessions for street children to enable them to stay off the streets.

APDE

The representative stated that their organisation works towards the promotion and defence of women's and girls' rights. They fight against all forms of degrading treatment of females. In 1992 they conducted a survey in the women's section of Bamako central prison. Cases of rape, bad treatment and poor conditions of detention cropped up. The organisation plans to launch a basic education programme.

The meeting was informed that the association has branches in Ségou, Mopti, Diré and Kidal.

AMDH

Mr. Amadou Diarra, a lawyer and member of the above organisation observed that there was a gap between regulations and practice as far as detention was concerned. He also noted that in practice common prisoners and political detainees were separated but there was no legal provision which sanctioned this practice.

Commission for the Promotion of Women and Children

Ms. Fatoumata Diarra of the above Commission gave the year of its establishment as 1996. It has visited Bamako central prison and Bollé rehabilitation centre. Following these visits, seminars were organised in collaboration with the Ministry of Justice, and various recommendations were made to the Ministry as regards the welfare of women in prison. A sports field was being planned and external assistance would be solicited for the project.

Clinique juridique Demeso

Speaking for his organisation, jean Dembele stated that they undertook a one year study of prisons, and issued a report with recommendations. These were discussed with officials from the Ministry of Justice. The organisation has also set up a legal aid scheme for detainees. It intends to focus more attention on the social rehabilitation of offenders.

In conclusion, the Special Rapporteur suggested to the NGOs that they should coordinate their activities for maximum effect.

Meeting with Tiébile Drame, Member of Parliament and Former Minister of Arid and Semiarid Zones

He is also a leading member of PAREMA one of the parties in coalition with President Alpha Oumar Konare

From the above gentleman I had a refreshing and instructive perspective of the penal regime in Mali. My only regret is that our meeting took place at the end instead of the beginning of my mission.

Tombouctou

25 August 1997

Meeting with Brahima Kone, Commandant de Cercle[3]

The above official explained the administrative structure of Mali up to the regional level as follows:

Level	*Head*
Village	Chief
Arrondissement	Chief of arrondissement
Cercle	Commandant
Region	Governor

[3] Head of the territorial administration at the "cercle" level.

Prison registrars are appointed by DNAPES on the recommendation of the Commandant of a Cercle. Factors taken into account in the selection of registrars are moral uprightness, dedication to prison work, managerial ability and a balanced disposition especially in relation to prisoners. The registrar is a civilian usually a civil servant of category 8 but in the absence of suitable persons from this grade persons with basic education can be appointed from category C.

The Police are responsible for the maintenance of law and order in Tombouctou while the Gendarmerie take care of the areas outside Tombouctou.

There should be a Committee at the Cercle level to monitor and supervise prison administration. Membership of the Committee is drawn from the judiciary, the Health Services, the administration, and the registrar. Among other things, the Committee is required to pay attention to the conditions of detention and the health of prisoners; and make recommendations on prisoners who should enjoy Presidential pardon.

The Committee has not functioned since the Tuareg rebellion.

The Registrar now recommends prisoners for pardon or mercy.

Thieves and robbers are excluded from pardon or mercy, and they do not, therefore, have any incentive to be of good behaviour in prison.

In 1985 the Commandant of the Cercle participated in a human rights training workshop. A workshop on the same subject was held for magistrates and registrars in 1996.

He identified the poor state of the building as the main problem facing the prison in Tombouctou. What is required is a new building and not renovation of the existing one.

The Judiciary

Tombouctou has a magistrate Court Grade I which is under the Court of Appeal in Mopti. There are seven magistrates in the Tombouctou Cercle, three at the public prosecutor's department (Parquet) and four on the bench (Siège).

The Special Rapporteur met 4 of the above and a Court Clerk who stated that the penal procedure code made provision for bail with or without guarantee. Limitation periods for offences ranged from 1 year for infraction of the law (misdemeanour); to 10 years in the case of murder.

The Public Prosecutor; Christian Idrissa Diassana

He granted me permission to visit Police and Gendarmerie cells in Tombouctou Brigade of Gendarmerie of Tombouctou Sandogo, Head of Station.

Brigade of Gendarmerie of Tombouctou Sandogo, Head of Station

The second official above explained to me that the Gendarmerie, commanded by a Captain was based in Goundam (regional headquarters). The gendarmerie acted as the police of the judiciary and were entitled to keep people in custody for questioning. But there were no detainees that day, and the Agent Chef asserted that they were not kept beyond the legal limit of 72 hours.

The one cell I visited was about 1.5 metres × 4 m. It was a very warm day, and it felt so inside the cell. A guard stated that it was either very warm (day) or very cold (night). They therefore tried to avoid detaining people there. The cell had neither blankets, mats nor toilets.

Visit to a Detainee Transferred to Hospital

In the company of the Registrar of Tombouctou prison, I visited a prisoner who had been transferred to the regional hospital from prison not long before my visit, it would appear.

The Registrar stated that he received no medicine from DNAPES. Their only source of medicine was private mainly ICRC. It appeared, however, that the hospital was in charge of the medicine for the prison.

On my visit to the prison, the inmates stated that they had to pay for their medicine.

Police Post, Commissioner Bougadany Touré

On the first visit, I was asked to come back later.

On the latter occasion the Commissioner informed me that the Police did not keep more than 10 persons per month in custody. The 72 hours' limitation period was always respected.

A detainee at the post, however, informed me that he had been detained there for 9 days. he did not find the conditions in the cell satisfactory.

In visiting the cell it was noticeable that there was no toilet and that a corner of the room was used as a toilet. There was neither mat nor blanket in the cell which measured about 2 × 3 metres with poor ventilation.

Visit to Tombouctou Prison

DNAPES had informed the Registrar of my visit. After a short discussion with the registrar, he took me round the prison. A meeting with the inmates alone concluded the visit. The prison was built in 1925 with a maximum capacity of 500. But because sections of it collapsed, and the remainder may soon do so, it now has a very reduced capacity. Prisoners were no longer being brought from Bamako.

At the time of the visit there were 36 inmates of whom only 3 had been tried and convicted. The rest were on remand. The prison staff comprised 2 guards (soldiers) and the registrar (civil servant).

Each of the two guards works one week of 7 days for 24 hours each day. Each guard does so twice a month.

There were no women in the prison, and what used to be the women's wing was being used by men because it was not secure enough. Whenever there were any female prisoners they were kept in the adjutant's house. Because of lack of space women were rarely arrested. Whenever women were detained the authorities endeavoured to release them as soon as possible.

There being no water in the prison, it was fetched from outside.

4 juveniles were among the 36 inmates, and the convicts mixed among those on remand.

Practices to avoid

One of the inmates was in leg irons or chained by the legs, but in my presence he was unchained. The Registrar explained that the poor state of the prison made escape easy and so strong preventive measures like chaining was resorted to. The chained prisoner had tried to escape on two occasions.

The prisoners complained that their visitors had not been allowed to see them. They also complained about lack of mats and blankets as well as the quality of food served (2 to 3 meals per day). They had no soap, and what ICRC brought for their use had not all been distributed (e.g. out of 36 blankets brought only a few were in the cells).

The remand prisoners also complained about the slow nature of the judicial system.

On inquiry, the Registrar responded that he had been queried about slack security measures, and had therefore demanded authorisation from the Prosecutor before visits. This had not, it appeared, been explained to the visitors.

I took up the issue of family visits with the prosecutor who was not aware of the recent developments in the prison. He promised to facilitate the visits, and asked the Registrar in the presence of us three to do the same.

Detention of women

For the reasons stated above, women could not be detained in the prison. The authorities hesitated in arresting women because of the space problem. If arrested and detained for short periods, they were kept with the guards at the entrance of the prison, and not inside with the male inmates. In the case of longer detention for females, they were accommodated in the house of the head of the guards. The authorities endeavoured to release female detainees as soon as it was possible to do so.

Goundam

26 August 1997

This town is situated 95 km south east of Tombouctou.

I had discussions with Tiecoura Malle, Magistrate and Justice of the Peace who had assumed duty there 6 months previously.

As "Juge de paix" he acted as Chairman of the court and examining magistrate. he was the investigator, prosecutor and judge. He presided over a Magistrate Court Grade I. Justices of the peace are to be found in remote areas.

Due to budgetary constraints the Ministry of Justice could not appoint more magistrates, prosecutors and examining judges.

He informed me that he visited the prison once a week. At the time of my visit there were 7 detainees, 2 convicts, 1 on remand and 4 who had been arrested the previous day and were being kept in the prison because the police post had no cells. The remand period did not exceed one month in his jurisdiction. Criminality was low but had gone up slightly at the start of the farming season over disputes about land and crops. He also acted as mediator and conciliator to limit the number of detainees.

In 1992 Goundam was attacked by the Tuaregs. The judge and the prison guards were killed. The prisoners escaped and the military camp where the prison was located was destroyed except the prison building which itself did not entirely escape damage. The military camp was abandoned, and rebuilt further away. The prison is, however, still being used.

Problems

It is easy to escape from the prison because of its low structure. There were no toilets, buckets were used and emptied outside the prison. There was no telephone line connected to Goundam. The visit was, therefore, a surprise one.

Brigade of Gendarmerie

The gendarmerie did not have a cell and prisoners who had to be sent to police cells were sent to the prison. They were not kept beyond 72 hours. Because of the paucity of cases, interrogation was completed within short periods.

There was no police post at Goundam.

Visit to Goundam Prison

The guard on duty stated that he worked seven days 24 hours each day and was relieved by another guard who worked the same schedule. The two guards alternated on a weekly basis. The inmates ate once a day (rice on Saturday, beans on Sunday, millet the rest of the week). There was neither water, shower nor toilets within the prison. Water was obtained from about 200 metres outside the prison. But the magistrate himself does not have water in his house, he informed me. Many parts of the building were cracked, and it could collapse. A section of the building had been abandoned because the walls crumbled.

In a private discussion with the inmates, they complained about not getting food, blankets, mats, family visits as well as the dangerous state of the building. One inmate came from Segou. He was arrested in Goundam, and his family was not aware of it. He had not had any family visit. But they had no complaint about the guards; they had a good relationship with the guards, they said.

Mopti

27 August 1997
Mopti Prison

Baréma Karambaye, Registrar, Moussa Traoré, Chief of guards and Deputy Sergent Sidi Mohammed.

They responded to my questions and conducted me through the prison.

They were 92 inmates, 64 of whom were on remand. The prison had two guards.

Female prisoners

There were 3 women who had been sentenced to life, 20 years and 15 years' imprisonment respectively for murder and sorcery. Two of them were mother and daughter, and all three belonged to the same family. They had served more than six years of their sentences.

They were not detained in the prison but were accommodated by the Counsellor for administrative affairs of the territorial administration. They worked for him and he maintained them. presidential pardon had been sought for them, but it had not been granted.

Discussion with the women outside the prison

They were fed by their employer but were not paid. The youngest had had a baby with a prison guard but would not say much about it. The oldest claimed to be 80 years old.

Inside the prison

Parts of it were falling apart. Half of it, I was informed, collapsed in 1994/95. The prisoners had one meal of millet a day, and rice on Sunday. Some of the inmates were locked up in their cells (cells 1 and 2) 24 hours a day while others (cells 3, 4 and 5) were allowed to stay in the yard day and night.

Discussion with detainees of cell 1

The heat in the room was unbearable, and it could well have accounted for the ill-health of some of them. One of them claimed that he had been beaten up by a guard the previous week for attempting to escape. Wounds and marks which could well have been the result of assault with belt, as the victim claimed had been used by the guard, were very visible on the back and abdomen of this prisoner.

They also complained that the guards demanded money before allowing visitors to see them. Two of the inmates complained that for two years they had been kept 24 hours a day in that cell without being brought before a court. Out of the 17 inmates in this cell only 3 were convicts. All of them were allowed out only to have a shower or go to toilet. They also complained that the guards had asked them for money so that they could be allowed to change to cells 3, 4 and 5. 5 of those in this cell were juveniles. One of them. Amadou Saye (16 years old) had been there for 6 months while a 15 year old had spent a longer period than Amadou. Sometimes for 2 months, they complained, they would not get soap.

Discussion with detainees in cell 2

Of the 24 inmates only one was a convict. 2 alleged that they had been beaten recently by a guard with belt. The wounds and marks on the bodies of Dramane Tambadou (17 years old) and Ibrahim Dembele (18 years old) could well have been the result of assault with belt. The conditions under which the inmates were detained were generally similar to those of the inmates of cell 1. 2 of the inmates stated that they had been on remand in this cell for 2 years. They ate once a day, and the food was small. They denied that they ate rice on Sunday. A juvenile was in leg iron and he stated that he had been in that condition 24 hours a day. They claimed that detainees who give money to the guards were allowed to escape. To be able to live outside this cell one had to pay the guards CFA 10,000. A Liberian prisoner Anson David, I was informed, died of starvation. A prisoner who was operated upon in December 1996 needed medication, but had none. He claimed that his urine and stool were bloody.

Ventilation in both cells was terrible, and there was very little light as well. It was not, therefore, surprising that when the doors of both cells were opened the inmates squinted. They were supplied with neither blankets nor clothes.

Final discussion with chief of guards

When asked why the inmates of cells 1 and 2 were kept indoors the whole day, he replied that it was to prevent their escape.

He frankly informed me that he had his own policy for dealing with prisoners as regards security. If a prisoner tried to escape or escaped he would be apprehended and put into leg irons for 8 days. On a second occasion, the prisoner's arms and feet would be chained for 8 days. A third attempt or escape would be followed with beating with belt and a wooden stick.

He was aware that his "bosses" from DNAPES would not approve of his practices since they were against corporal punishment for prisoners. But, according to him, if he was following the regulations he should order the guards to shoot prisoners who tried to escape. But he preferred to beat such prisoners. It was the only way to rehabilitate them and get them to obey prison regulations ("la seule maniere de leur faire comprendre et respecter le règlement est de les cogner").

He confessed that he feared being prosecuted for the escape of a prisoner. The prison buildings were falling apart, and the prisoners could easily escape if deterrent measures were not taken.

The registrar who had been away during my meeting with the Chief of guards then turned up to say that the two prisoners with marks on them had in fact been beaten by police officers during interrogation ("à la police ils ont des manières de les faire parler").

I witnessed the reception into prison of a new accused person. In an interview with him he stated that he had been detained at a police station for 24 hours. He was not maltreated, and he did not see any one being ill treated there. He had, however, not had any food during his detention.

28 August 1997
Governor of Mopti, Daouda Tangara

Present at a meeting with the governor was Bokary Boire, Civil Administrator.

The governor attributed the bad conditions of detention to harsh economic circumstances. He was aware that the prison was in a state of disrepair and was also overcrowded.

I urged the governor to visit the prison with a view to effecting improvement which was within his power; and also seeing things at first hand.

RECOMMENDATIONS

The recommendations below have been made in the full knowledge that Mali is a poor country which has recently begun on the road of parliamentary democracy. Its limited resources will slow measures which require a lot of capital, but other problems facing prisons need to be and can be addressed immediately.

1. Mopti prison requires urgent and early attention. Cells 1 and 2 where inmates are held 24 hours a day except when they go out for shower or toilet should have windows to let in light and air. This regime should be improved upon.
2. Chaining of prisoners, especially those in cells should cease.
3. Assault and battery of prisoners in Mopti prison should cease. An inquiry should be conducted into the conduct of the guards at Mopti in relation to their treatment of prisoners for the necessary action to be taken.

   Guards should be trained to avoid assaulting prisoners.
4. Serious attention should be paid to the question of the many inmates who are on remand with a view to giving them early trial or releasing them. Fewer prisoners will free resources to be used in the many areas crying for attention in the penal system of Mali.
5. Tombouctou, Goundam and Mopti prisons are in danger of caving in, and should receive urgent attention.
6. Admittedly, the huge expanse of the country does not make transportation easy, but keeping female prisoners in private houses is not satisfactory.
7. The new prisons under construction or yet to be built, should have separate sections for women and juveniles if separate structures cannot be built for them.
8. Remand prisoners should be separated from convicts.
9. Ways and means should be found to ease the tense atmosphere in what has been described as the first part or section of Bamako Central prison. The constant confinement of most of them may produce another disturbance.
10. A guard should not be made to work 24 hours, seven days continuously as seems to be the rule in Mopti, Tombouctou and Goundam. The temptation to adopt ruthless methods to ensure discipline is high.

11. Preferential treatment given to civil servants as was evidenced by their comfortable surroundings and privileges in Bamako Central Prison should be reviewed. There will be little or no incentive by civil servants to do what is in their power to improve the conditions of the ordinary prisoner knowing that neither he/she nor their kind will experience a harsh regime were they to find themselves in prison. Equal treatment should also be respected in prison.

12. For a similar reason, the policy of building an air-conditioned prison for political detainees does not make for a setting where there will be eagerness on the part of political authorities to work hard at improving prison conditions. The undoubtedly enormous resources which will go into the construction of such a luxury prison could be used in improving the conditions of a few prisons.

13. DNAPES should adopt guidelines which will enable it to know what assistance each prison gets from non-budgetary resources. It will then be able to monitor the use to which the donation is put.

This recommendation is made as a direct result of complaints from prisoners of how they do not receive all the donation, like blankets, which are made to them.

14. Efforts should be made to supply prisoners with basic needs such as mats, blankets, soap and clothing.

15. Reconsideration should be given to the issue of amnesty with a view to extending the category and number of those who have been benefiting from this exercise.

16. Female guards should be trained to take over guard duties for women prisoners.

17. NGOs should be encouraged to visit prisons and pass on their recommendations to government.

18. The recommendations contained in the report of Mr. Sanidié A. Touré, the Deputy Director following his visit to Mopti and other prisons should be carefully studied and implemented.

PRESS RELEASE

Bamako, 30 August 1997

Visit to Mali by the Special Rapporteur on Prisons and Conditions of Detention in Africa

Prof. E. V. O. Dankwa, Ghana, Vice-President of the African Commission on Human and Peoples' Rights and Special Rapporteur on Prison and Conditions of Detention in Africa arrived in Mali on 20 August 1997 for a ten-day visit.

The objective of his visit was to study the penitentiary system of Mali to establish if it is in conformity with the African Charter on Human and Peoples' Rights to which Mali is signatory.

To this end, the Special Rapporteur met with representatives of the States and NGOs. He visited Bamako Central Prison, Baguinéda Prison farm and prisons in

Timbuctu, Goundam and Mopti. In each of the prisons, he was able to discuss with the detainees in private. He also visited Kati prison where he met with all the detainees.

The Special Rapporteur will submit his report and recommendations to the Government in due course.

The Special Rapporteur took note of the policy for rebuilding prisons and training prison personnel he also took under consideration the obvious financial constraints which Mali is facing. However, some measures seem to him to be within the Government's capabilities.

In particular, the Special Rapporteur wishes to draw the Government's attention to the necessity to solve the problem of the high number of persons on remand. Moreover, waiting for its rebuilding, Mopti prison requires improvements which shall not represent an excessive burden for the Government.

Mali is the second country visited by the Special Rapporteur, the first one being Zimbabwe. The Special Rapporteur wishes to thank the prison authorities for their welcome.

And the permissions they granted him to visit the prisons and places of detention of his choice.

The Special Rapporteur wishes in particular to thank Mr. Cheikhna Dettebe Kamissoko, Minister of Justice, Mr. Buruma Sidibé, National Director of the Administration of Prisons and Supervised Education (DNAPES) and Mr. Sanidié Touré, Deputy Director of DNAPES.

PRI contributed to the preparation of the visit of the Special Rapporteur and helped him overcome the language barrier by putting Ms. Audrey Pascaud, from PRI, at his disposal. The Special Rapporteur is extremely grateful to them.

A meeting with NGOs was organised by Ms. Outtara from AMDH. The Special Rapporteur wishes to thank her deeply.

Prof. E. V. O. Dankwa
Special Rapporteur on Prisons and
Conditions of Detention in Africa
African Commission on Human and
Peoples' Rights

COMMENTS BY GOVERNMENT OF MALI

In its comments on the report, the Ministry of Justice stated that:

(i) presidential pardon had been granted to the three women prisoners in Mopti, who were mentioned in the report;
(ii) the Director and guards at Mopti prison have been changed. The last have also been trained to treat prisoners humanely.

OTHER ACTIVITY OF THE SPECIAL RAPPORTEUR

Workshop on Modalities for Missions and Visits to Places of Detention

On 24 May 1997, the Special Rapporteur joined members from regional, international and other organisations involved in missions and visits to prisons and places of detention to consider effective procedures for undertaking missions to the above institutions.

The result of the workshop appears in a 33 page Report entitled "Standard Operating Procedures of International Mechanisms for Carrying Out Visits to Places of Detention". The report was prepared by the Association for the Prevention of Torture (APT), which also hosted the workshop.

The workshop aimed at the sharing of experiences and ideas on the subject by the participants. Preparation for missions and visits, what to do and look for when in the field, duration of visit which will produce a well-informed account of the subject-matter, writing and submission of reports and related matters engaged the attention of the participants. The need for and adherence to a code of conduct was also discussed.

A descriptive account of how each institution represented at the workshop undertook its mission or visit was given by the participants.

I am grateful to APT and Penal reform International (PRI) for organising the workshop and for including me as one of the participants. I learnt a lot more than I know on the subject, and I am, therefore, equally grateful to the other participants who freely gave of their rich store of experience.

The other participants were:

M. Alain Aeschliman	Deputy Head of Central Tracing and Protection Division, International Committee of the Red Cross
M. Pascal Daudin	Head of Training Sector, International Committee of the Red Cross
M. Bacre W. N'Diaye	United Nations' Special Rapporteur on Extrajudicial, Summary or Arbitrary Executions
M. Joseph Exume	Member, Inter-American Commission on Human Rights
Prof. Walter Kälin	Professor of international law at the University of Bern, Vice President, APT and Chairman of the Workshop
M. Trevor Stevens	Secretary, European Committee for the Prevention of Torture
M. Ahmed Othmani	Chairperson, Penal Reform International
Mme. Bernath	APT
Mme. Anette Corbaz	APT
Mme. Anna Khakee	APT
Mme. Isabel Ricupero	APT

Prisons in Mozambique
Report of the Special Rapporteur on Prisons and Conditions of Detention

Report on a Visit 14–24 December 1997
By Prof. E. V. O. Dankwa
Series IV No. 3

ACKNOWLEDGEMENTS

Audrey Pascaud of Penal Reform International (PRI) provided invaluable administrative support. PRI also provided me with useful background material. Ingella Sthal of Raoul Wallenberg Institute made the Portuguese language intelligible to me.

The Raoul Wallenberg Institute provided important support.

Without the constant support of the Human Rights League of Mozambique, especially its Executive Director, Ms Mabote and Legal Officer, Danilo Nala, the mission would not have been successful. I was in constant touch with them, and the latter at my request accompanied me to some of the places I visited. members of the League in Nampula, in rain, walked with us from prison to prison.

To them all therefore, I am extremely grateful.

THE BACKGROUND

"Joaquim Gouveia [Frelimo guerrilla] recalls that when Kaulza's [Portuguese armed forces commander-in-chief in Mozambique] forces entered the areas where Frelimo was strongly implanted they killed anybody, children, old people, women – they were just killing, killing. And they were carrying away everything – hoes, machetes, pots, even mortars for pounding maize . . . Gouveia also recalls that planes were dropping 'incendiary bombs which burned everything they touched' and chemical weapons which had an even worse effect. 'They were dropping these bombs on farmland to destroy it and to ensure that there would be no crop the following year and so the people would go hungry . . .' " (p. 64).

"Father Cesare Bertull, the Regional Superior of the White Fathers (Roman Catholic) in Mozambique, described in detail the horrific tortures being inflicted on Mozambicans suspected of opposing the colonial regime." (p. 68).

"The Dragons of Death quickly showed their political stripe. They went to the capital's main prison and released about 200 PIDE (International Police for the Defence of the State) agents whom the post-coup Portuguese authorities had detained, pending inquiries into responsibility for the torture of political prisoners. Other supporters of the Dragons were touring the black township in open vehicles, shooting black Mozambicans at random." (p. 87)

"Partly because of the growing expense of the war and partly because almost all the technicians in the country had been Portuguese and had left, the Mozambicans would not be able to repair infrastructure destroyed in Rhodesian attacks. By flattening villages and destroying roads, bridges, railways and vital communications centres Smith's military chief, General Peter Walls was doing more than stressing the cost factor of war: he was pointing out that the Mozambicans were losing the little that they had inherited from the Portuguese and would soon have nothing." (p. 100)

"Mozambique did not have a modern, well-equipped regular army. The inherited guerrilla structure of independence days would appear inadequate in the face of big infantry and artillery invasions with strong air support. The Mozambicans would be obliged to invest heavily in military hardware, which would severely limit the government's ability to improve the standard of living of its citizens." (p. 100)

"Samora Machel never hesitated to support the Zimbabwe struggle. Mozambique became the home for Robert Mugabe and Zanu. It was this relationship between Machel and Mugabe that became the anvil for Zimbabwe's Independence. Machel was unstinting in his support, experiencing constant raids from Ian Smith's forces and infiltration from Selous Scouts." (David Owen) (p. 102)

"Mozambique is, and was then, a poor country. So recruiting mercenaries was not difficult. It became even less difficult after the Rhodesians and their surrogates destroyed schools, clinics and communications facilities, that had been established since independence. New villages with all these facilities were attacked and peasants were murdered." (p. 106)

"In the People's Republic of Mozambique we have witnessed systematic violations of legality: violations of the constitution, violations of laws and regulations and violations of our principles. A particularly serious aspect of this situation is that these violations are in many cases committed by members of the defence and security forces. They are committed by members of the Mozambique Armed Forces (FPLM), by members of the police force and militias and by personnel of the Ministry of Security (SNASP) . . .

Aggression and torture are used as a means of punishing mistakes, which are often imaginary, and as a means of making people confess to crimes, committed or not. [These abuses are] the result of the continued presence of values and practices from colonial-capitalist and tribal-feudal society, and mistakes and deviations from that are the result of our own failings." (Samora Machel at a mass rally in Maputo on 5 November 1981) (pp. 160–161)

"The President (Samora Machel) marched up and down the platform, speaking non-stop, agitated by old memories of friends who had been reduced to human wreckage before being butchered by the colonialists and their hirelings. The nurses at the hospital who had disappeared after being taken to the secret police dungeons. The Frelimo guerrillas who were captured wounded and refused to reveal secrets under excruciating torture.

Then memories emerged from the other side of the hall. Grim confessions of betrayal. Free from any threat of jail or hanging, men admitted to having been paid by the Secret police to infiltrate students' groups, discussion associations even conversations on railway trains, to get the names of African nationalists. These nationalists were then arrested and many were tortured to death in prison. A driver for the PIDE-DGS admitted taking the bodies to be thrown into the sea.

Two ex-commandos admitted having been present at the 1972 massacre of Winiyamu in Tete province, when hand grenades were thrown into a crowd of villagers. It took three days to bury the bodies." (p. 173)

(The above passages are reproduced from Iain Christie, *Samora Machel, A Biography* (PANAF, an imprint of Zed Press Ltd, London and New Jersey, 1989.)

Mozambicans value human rights. André Matzangaisse and Afonso Dhlakama would not deny this assertion. And it was for the promotion, protection and enjoyment of the rights of Mozambicans that Eduardo Mondlane, Marcelino dos Santos, Samora Machel, Joaquim Chissano, Alberto Chipande, Sebastiao Mabote and many others worked, fought and some of them died. From the home of Eduardo Mondlane in the then Lourenco Marques, now Maputo in 1961 through the formation of Frente de Libertacao de Mocambique (Frelimo) in 1962, the attainment of independence on 25 June 1975, the establishment of Resistencia Nacional Mocambicans (Renamo) and its conflict with the former, the General Peace Agreement in October 1992, presidential and legislative elections of 27–28 October 1994 to today the abiding concerns of Mozambicans have been the upholding of their dignity and their rights to self-determination and development. With these, the African Commission on Human and Peoples' Rights identify very closely.

It was to contribute towards the realisation of these goals that the Special Rapporteur on Prisons and Detention Centres in Africa visited Mozambique from 14–24 December 1977; a visit which took him to:

(i) Maputo (Central Prison and Civil Prison);
(ii) Beira (Central Prison and Police Station);
(iii) Nampula (Prison and Police Station);
(iv) Matola Open Prison;
(v) Xai-Xai (Prison and Police Station) and Macheva Prison.

MEETINGS

I had meetings with the Minister of Justice, Jose Ibraimo Abudo, the Chief of Cabinet of the Ministry of Justice, Charles Almasso, the National Director of Prisons, Antonio

Eduardo Munete, the Secretary General of the Ministry of Interior and officials of the Prison and Police Services. Summaries of some of the meetings follow.

15 December 1997
Ministry of Justice

The Chief of Cabinet of the Ministry of Justice informed me that his Minister was in Parliament to seek approval of a budget which had increased allocation to prisons. As at all the meetings, I outlined the purpose of my mission within the context of the ACHPR and my mandate, always reminding my listeners or hosts that the Commission aims at achieving its objectives through dialogue with States Parties.

Director of the Prison Service

At a meeting with the Director of the Prison Service under the Ministry of Justice on 16 December 1997 an idea was gained on issues such as prison population, the division of responsibility between the Ministries of Justice and Interior, detention of juveniles and women, health care, the judicial process, disappearances, discipline and punishment, remand, the state of prisons and plans for the future. Generally, questions and answers from me and by the Director respectively produced the account below. The Director also granted me written permission to visit places of detention which I had set out in my programme.

The Director welcomed my visit, which like those of other international human rights organisations, he pronounced as necessary. Violations of human rights which Mozambique has been accused of, he explained, were the result of poor conditions in prisons and detention centres, and not the result of the lack of will to implement international standards. He stated that it was difficult to control how prison and police cells were managed because of the lack of means for regular monitoring and control of these institutions.

Prison population

The total figure was about 11,000 out of a national population of 16 million. The Ministry of Interior had responsibility for about 5000 of these inmates while 5800 were under the authority of the Ministry of Justice. Of the last figure 3200 were awaiting trial or sentence. 995 people aged between 16 and 21 were in prisons under the Ministry of Justice. These also had 114 females. Exact figures could not be given about foreigners. What was known was that most of the foreign prisoners were in prisons close to the borders of Mozambique like Maninca, Tete and Nyassa. They had been arrested mostly for illegal entry into the country.

Overcrowding

This was a real problem. Maputo Central Prison, for instance, housed 1600 prisoners when it was built to accommodate 800. No prison had been built since the 1960s, and most of those which existed were old and had neither been rehabilitated nor maintained well. To this was added the problems of the lack of blankets and mattresses.

I suggested resort to Community Service and speedy trial as ways by which the prisons could be decongested. Open centres in the countryside where prisoners could cultivate crops to feed themselves were being considered as a way of dealing with the problem of overcrowding, according to the Director.

Ministries of Justice and Interior

Generally the Ministry of Interior has responsibility for pre-trial detention while accused persons are transferred to the Ministry of Justice prisons for trial but, specifically the latter's responsibility commenced when a suspect's file was transmitted to the prosecutor by the criminal investigation police. Within each ministry there is a National department which caters for those in places of custody and detention.

Guards under the Ministry of Interior are policemen while those under the Ministry of Justice are regular prison officers.

Remand

By law a person who is arrested should not be held in a police cell for more than 48 hours. Suspects may be held in Detention Centres of the Ministry of Interior for a maximum period of 90 days although it may be exceeded, in complex cases or where surety could not be provided, to 2 or several years.

If a magistrate knew that the process would last more than 90 days she could grant bail.

Judicial process

The courts are notorious for being slow. Many more judges and magistrates are needed than exist with the result that a magistrate, for instance, may find herself with responsibility for several sections instead of one.

Health

Prisons under the Ministry of Justice have Health Centres with nurses or paramedics. Inmates who are sick are treated in the health centres of the prisons by a medical officer or nurse twice, or thrice a week. Serious cases as well as those requiring specialized attention are referred to hospitals. The health centres do not have sufficient medicine.

Discipline

United Nations Standard Minimum Rules for the treatment of offenders are observed. National rules on the subject are in conformity with the UN Rules. Corporal punishment is outlawed. Prisoners are disciplined for infringement of regulations by being confined to cells but they are not to be given any inhuman or degrading treatment. The policy is that there should be no more punishment than the deprivation of liberty itself. Arbitrary punishment and disciplinary diet are outlawed.

Disappearances

This phenomenon is unheard of in the Ministry of Justice prisons. They occur in institutions under the Ministry of Interior, and they result from the escape of detainees from police stations where suspects can be kept for up to 48 hours.

Juveniles

A person under the age of 16 is not responsible in criminal law for his action. parents or guardians must prove the age of such a person, and he/she would be released to them. The problem is that some parents do not want their children to be released to them, and do not, therefore, present the necessary documents to establish their age. There is no specialised rehabilitation Centres to accommodate juveniles. As a result of overcrowding it has not been possible to separate young persons from the old.

Minister of Justice

On 17 December, the Minister of Justice granted me audience. He welcomed my mission, and saw it as an opportunity to learn more about the African Commission on Human and Peoples' Rights. It also provided an occasion to consider further necessary improvement in human rights. He stated that it is difficult to protect human rights in poor countries such as Mozambique because the general population itself suffer and do not have sufficient food. In this connection it is not easy to ensure that minimum standards are implemented in prisons.

Prisons in Gaza province and others in the countryside, outside the big cities are more open than those in Maputo which are overcrowded. Prisons in Gaza provide 3 meals a day for inmates while in Maputo it is one meal a day. The former produce part of their own food. When there are too many prisoners, the services provided by the administration become inadequate, and prison conditions can deteriorate very quickly.

Judicial process and lawyers

The slow court process accounts partly for the overcrowding and related problems. There are far fewer judges than what is needed. To take his own experience, when the Minister was the Chief Judge in Sofala, 4 judges served under him. Only two of these were trained lawyers, the other two had only rudimentary instruction in law. In the provinces there are judges who have had only one year training. The minister was also one of the first graduates of the Faculty of Law, which was established in 1975, and even before completing his degree he worked in the courts. Few nationals had the opportunity to study law in Portugal before lawyers started to be trained in Mozambique. Moreover locally trained lawyers prefer to work with private companies than in the courts. Prosecutors are also in short supply.

There is the need for 2 graduates in law in each court but in most courts there is not even one. Most of the court personnel had one year basic training. Graduates are concentrated in Maputo. Lawyers in the provinces, some of whom give legal aid, have had only one year training. But against the foregoing background provision of legal aid by government is a real problem.

Overcrowding

Although the weak judicial process contributes to this problem, the inability of government as a result of lack of means to construct more prisons is also a contributory factor. prisons built in colonial times cannot accommodate prisoners of a highly increased population.

The war added to the problem. For instance, Mabalame prison situated on 60 acres of land in Gaza province, produced food for itself and other prisons, but it was destroyed during the war.

Prison personnel

Lack of training for them does not make for or ensure respect of human rights.

In conclusion, the Minister saw lack of resources as the main reason why the government could not improve the conditions of imprisonment and detention. He also observed that the Commission was doing a good job in trying to protect human rights. Mozambique, he promised, would also do more to improve upon the situation.

23 December 1997
Secretary General of the Ministry of Interior

H.E. Almerinho Manhenji, Minister of Interior was unable to attend the meeting scheduled for the above date. The Secretary-General of the ministry, Armando Mario Correia therefore deputised for him. I informed him of two important concerns which must be treated as matters of priority and given the necessary attention: juveniles and pre-trial detention.

Juveniles

I expressed the concern that if nothing was done about persons whose conduct was excused on account of their age (under 16), many of them were likely to walk straight into jail when they reached the age of criminal responsibility. In response the Secretary-General stated that prevention programmes had been established with the ministries of Justice, Culture and Health with the aim of helping juveniles who had been made orphans by the war not to get involved in criminal activity. However not much had come out of this initiative. It was also stated that there was a court which protected the interest of minors when their parents were divorced. A tribunal also acted as a mediator between the victims of "crimes" of "juveniles" and the families of the latter.

Pre-trial detention

The Secretary-General stated that the maximum period of detention for the purpose of investigation was 84 days. However, the examining magistrate could extend the period of detention in the case of serious offences.

Prison officials were required by law to send sick detainees to hospital whenever it was necessary.

Conditional release was possible in the case of those sentenced to less than 8 years' imprisonment. Bail could also be granted at any stage of the criminal process, investigation and trial.

Difficulties with transportation from Beira and Xai-Xai prevented me from honouring, on two occasions, meeting with the President of the Bar Association.

On 23 December, I had a meeting with NGOs and journalists who learned about the work of the Commission including my mandate. To the extent permissible, I briefed them about my work in mozambique.

PRISON VISITS

16 December 1997
Maputo Central Prison (Under the Ministry of Justice)

Located in the northern section of Maputo, the prison has buildings which house the administration, the kitchen and workshops. Gardens, fruit trees and other trees adorn its large compound. present at a meeting which preceded a visit to the cells and other parts of the prison were:

(a) The Director, Mr. Aruerico Abilio Parruque who had worked in the prison for the past 33 years, the last 7 of which had been as its Director in prison administration;
(b) Mr. Jaime Ernesto Tivane, Secretary;
(c) Mr. Julio Sitoe, Chief of Guards;
(d) Mr. Laurenco Magul, Assistant for Social Affairs;
(e) Mr. Francisco Fulaho, Chief of penal control (discharge and discipline).

The prison was built in 1965 with a maximum capacity of 800 although at the time of the visit it housed 2059 prisoners, who were all male. As a result of limited space, women prisoners were kept in Maputo civil prison. 1018 of the inmates were awaiting trial. There were also 100 young adults. The youngest inmate was 17 years old while the oldest was 55. 180 guards man the prison. There were no political prisoners in Mozambique, I was informed.

Although according to the regulations prisoners should be housed according to age group, type of offence and status (remand or convict) separately, it was difficult to implement the rules because of limited space.

Food

By law, three meals should be provided for each inmate every day. Financial constraints have led to one meal being provided each day. It consists of maize flour, beans and sometimes fish and rice when the budget allocation permitted it.

Clothing

Inmates provide their own clothes. Non-governmental organisations supply clothes for those who do not have any.

Mail

There is no limit to the letters which inmates can write and receive. The Red Cross tries to unite inmates and families through correspondence.

Visits

Family members and friends can visit inmates. Each inmate is entitled to 2 visits per month.

Games

Inmates played football and chess. They also sang, danced and staged plays. But on the whole, there was a lack of equipment for games.

Health

Medical service was provided in the prison. Serious cases were referred to hospitals.

Vocational training

Both academic and vocational training was provided. The latter is in carpentry, ceramics, clothes-making and electricity. There was also opportunity to take part in agricultural activity: the growing and tending of corn, beans and vegetables. Young adults were given priority in vocational training.

Reading and writing lessons up to the 9th grade were given.

Exercise/stay in cells

Inmates who were not engaged in vocational training were allowed to be outside their cells two hours each day, one hour in the morning and another hour in the afternoon.

Riots

There had been riots by those on remand over food.

Relationship between guards and inmates

It was said to be good with the guards doing their work well and the inmates reciprocating.

Discipline and punishment

It was noticeable that unlike the other issues above, response to my inquiry on this topic took a long time before it was made, and when it did come it was from different directions not addressing the issue. Eventually isolation in disciplinary cells was given as the main punishment. These cells also housed detainees who were a security risk (those arrested for or convicted of armed robbery, for instance).

If a guard provoked a detainee the former would be punished. The main problems were, however, among the detainees.

Escapes

As a last resort, firearm was used to prevent prisoners from escaping.

Sanitary condition

The director spoke of an outbreak of cholera in the prison.

Visit to the premises

The prison had a very neat health centre with a nurse and assistants. part of the prison had been cordoned off for those suffering from cholera or being treated for it. Since the outbreak of the epidemic in november 1997, 2 inmates had died, 28 were still receiving treatment. 310 had contracted the disease while 285 had been treated at the Health Centre. Also those infected with the disease at Machava civil prison had been transferred to the Central prison for treatment. Médicins sans Frontières (MSF) was providing medical and material assistance to fight the epidemic. The water system, for instance, was being repaired by MSF.

Kitchen and dining hall

Food was cooked in a kitchen for all the inmates by some of them. They started work at 4 a.m.

Unfortunately, a nice dining hall with 26 cement tables each 3 metres long was in disuse because most of the tables and seats were in a state of disrepair.

Classes

A class on health matters was in progress at the time of my visit. Members of the class were expected to pass on the knowledge gained to the other inmates.

A church service with sonorous voices was also in progress at the time of the visit.

Discussion with detainees in private

Manuel Carlitas Massango: The apparent tender age of this inmate attracted me to him. He claimed to be 15 years old, and had been in prison for 15 months after having been sentenced to 3 years' imprisonment for stealing. He also claimed to have received soap only twice in 15 months. He had one visit since being confined to prison. The food was small, he complained.

Amando Domingo Macie: I was attracted to this inmate for the same reason as in the previous case. This remand prisoner claimed to be 15 years old although his file indicated that he was 19.

Workshops and fields

Due to limited equipment and raw materials only a few of the inmates were working in the workshops. Equipment in the carpentry needed repair. A shoe-making section had become a shoe repair shop because the machinery for the former was out of order.

An impressive orchard with many fruits was being cultivated by the inmates in a central area of the prison. Around the cells also a few fruit trees have been raised by the same. According to the Director the inmates who could pay for the fruits as well as the sick ones and those who worked in the orchard enjoyed the fruits.

The cells

Of the 10 buildings constructed to house prisoners, 8 of them were habitable.

One building housed 219 young adults. Most of these were on remand. The separation of young adults from adults did not extend to life outside the cells.

One cell had less than 25 beds for 53 persons. A small section of this cell was used as both bathroom and toilet. The inmates complained that they had no equipment to clean the toilet/bathroom and had to use their hands.

Another cell with 54 inmates had 16 beds. The youngest here was 16 years old. They were not supplied any soap, but they had the opportunity to bath every day. Most of them had had no visit from their families because they either had none or the families could not afford the visit or were not aware of their imprisonment.

Disciplinary cells

Those confined here forfeit their right to have visitors. They had not been supplied with soap. Alberto Junior had spent 5 months here for trying to escape from the cell for armed robbers. Inmates of the armed robbery cells got more food than those in the disciplinary cell.

Fernand José Cherinza had scars which were consistent with his claim that he was beaten by the guards when he tried to escape from the disciplinary cell. He had earlier on tried to escape from the cell for armed robbers. Other inmates of the disciplinary cells complained of having been beaten by the guards. They had been informed of my visit, and instructed not to speak about issues such as beating by guards. Some had been on remand for 2 years. Complaints were also made about the police demanding money for cases to be dropped.

The visit ended by going through the measures instituted by the Ministry of Health visitors: washing their hands with chlorinated water.

Maputo Civil Prison (Ministry of Interior)

The Director Diamantino Alfredo who had been notified about my visit, briefed me about the prison.

It is a prison for remand prisoners. Although required by law, it has no assistant director. There are 4 departments of the prison; security, rehabilitation, monitoring and administration as well as a female wing which is under the Ministry of Justice. Built to accommodate 250 inmates, it had 300 inmates.

Primary health care is available in the hospital prison.

Food

Different answers were given on the number of meals provided each day: one official put it at 2 daily though sometimes financial constraints led to only one meal while another official said that in principle there should be 3 meals each day but in fact it was 2 or 3. The diet consisted of beans, maize flour meal, fresh or dried fish and vegetables when in season.

Length of remand

The average was 34 days but some could extend to 90 days, and in rare cases beyond this period.

Punishment

The sanction for breach of regulations was isolation for 1 or 2 days though it could sometimes last for 10 days. Isolation was coupled with denial of visit.

Clothing

The prison authorities provided clothes for the inmates.

Visits

Every inmate was entitled to 2 visits each month lasting 3 hours per visit.

Correspondence

There was no limit to the number of letters which an inmate could write or receive.

Water and hygiene

It was sometimes a problem getting water but generally there was access to water three times daily. The sewerage system was in a state of disrepair. Soap was distributed twice a month whenever available.

Complaint procedure

Inmates could complain to the rehabilitation section which would pass it on to the appropriate authorities including the President of the Republic.

Visit to the premises

A long hall which overlooks a football field served as a reception for visitors. A transit ward housed new arrivals until they were transferred to other prisons or sections of Maputo Civil Prison. At the time of the visit all the inmates of the transit ware were policemen.

1st section of prison

With difficulty the officers agreed to a private discussion between the inmates and myself. The former wanted to be present. The inmates were served one meal a day in small quantity. They had beds and blankets. They complained about not getting visits: they only received messages informing them of the names of their visitors without seeing them. It is noted that the cholera outbreak led to a cancellation of visits. Beds and blankets were available, but they were given no soap. There were foreigners from Sierra Leone, Nigeria, Uganda and Portugal among the inmates.

The inmates complained bitterly about corruption among police officers who would destroy evidence on payment of money. One of the foreigners complained that although an order for his release had been given by a judge, he had stayed on for a week because he could not raise the money demanded by the police for his actual release. His embassy was also not aware of his detention.

Most of the inmates would not talk because, they informed me, they had been ordered not to talk.

2nd part of prison

One cell with 6 prisoners had one bed and two blankets. Some of them, therefore, slept on the bare floor. One would not talk to me because he feared what would happen to him on my departure.

A bathroom had water flowing without control although there were days when water did not flow.

Health centre

A health centre which was attended by men and women on different occasions was neat and tidy, as was the nurse.

Female section

The head of this unit was male. It had 67 women with 9 children between 1 and 4 months. One of them was born in prison three months earlier. The mother was said to have been imprisoned just before giving birth. The children ate the same food as their mothers, which consisted of maize and beans. They complained about the poor quality of the food. They were given no soap.

Most of them were on remand, some up to 1 year. Some had not even been charged. Others should have been kept in Maputo Central Prison but limited space there had ended them here. Convicts and remand prisoners lived in the same cell. They had no uniforms.

The cancellation of visits as a result of the outbreak of cholera was a sore point for them because it had dried up the source of improvement in their diet: food from visitors. Other complaints were inadequate medicine, lack of water containers and inability to get rid of waste water.

The cells looked better than those of the male prisoners. The female inmates had beds and blankets.

Disciplinary cells

Some of the cells had clothes, cup and toothbrushes which suggested that there were inmates there but none was seen inside.

The Director welcomed my visit and looked forward to whatever help the Commission could give towards improvement of conditions in the prison. He also apologised for the misunderstanding about discussion with inmates in private at the beginning of the visit. He had not received instruction to permit it.

17 December 1997
Beira Central Prison

The prison was situated within the town, and inmates could witness part of life outside prison through the windows. A wall of about 2 metres surrounded the prison.

Luis Seberto Tsueane, the Director seemed genuinely surprised to see us because he had had no notification of our visit. However, he welcomed us heartily and agreed to a discussion with him as well as a visit to the cells and other sections of the prison.

Constructed about 80 years ago, it had never been renovated. It was built to accommodate 150 prisoners, but held 626 inmates at the time of the visit. 17 of them were women. While the exact number of young adults (16–21) could not be given immediately, it was known that they formed the largest number because they were the most active criminal group. None of the inmates was below 16.

206 had not been charged; 218 were waiting to be tried while 202 were convicts. The average period of remand was 6 months to 1 year. All these categories of prisoners were mixed up: they did everything together as a result of limited space. The prison had a staff of 66 (guards and administrative personnel).

A new prison, which the Director was eager to show us, but which time constraint did not make it possible, when completed, would house all the inmates from Beira Central Prison. Located near Beira it would have been completed quite some time ago had there been the requisite funds.

Health

There was a health centre with a nurse. Serious cases were transferred to hospitals. Those who could afford it paid for the more expensive medicine as the centre had only basic medicine.

Food

It was a problem for the prison administration. Had there been a kitchen in the prison, the inmates would have had 2 meals each day. But because the food was prepared some distance away from the prison, what should have been eaten on two occasions was combined and prepared once (600 g per detainee).

Riot

There was a riot in 1993 when those on remand demanded an immediate trial.

Punishment

The only punishment was isolation in disciplinary cells. The gravity of the offence determined the length of confinement. Maximum period of confinement was 30 days but in rare cases (escape or attempt to escape), it could be 60 days. From the disciplinary cells one could go out only twice, and this to the bathroom.

Hygiene

The prison had no money to buy soap and cleaning material for the inmates. From October to December, therefore, there had been no supply of soap. Food was the priority concern. The Director expressed the hope that the new budget would enable the needs of the inmates to be met. He noted that he did not receive any assistance beyond the budget from anywhere.

Visits and correspondence

An inmate is allowed 2 visits per month although in cases of emergency extra visits are permitted. Inmates were allowed to write and receive letters without limit. Letters going out and coming in are, however, censored.

Training of guards

They were trained but their morale was getting low as their work got more difficult with the overcrowding and its attendant problems. The relationship between guards and inmates was generally good. But occasionally some guards beat the inmates. Whenever this happened the guards involved were disciplined.

Games

The prison was so small that no games were played in it.

In camera discussion with inmates

The Director was, at first, not disposed to allowing me to talk to the inmates alone since he had not received a programme for my visit. But eventually, he relented.

Female section

Only female guards worked there. The inmates complained that the food was not well cooked. Catholic nuns visited them, and gave them milk. One inmate had her young child with her. 96 prisoners had been transferred to an open prison the previous day, the Director states.

The general state of the building was very poor with stairs, banisters and ceilings threatening to collapse. The walls were extremely dirty and stagnant waste water was all over the small compound, and the scent it produced could be imagined.

Male section

Ground floor: Cell 1: you were hit with a pungent foul odour, on entering. A number of the 18 inmates were in tattered clothes. Thomas Sinamunda Chawasini, 55 complained that he needed surgery from an acute ailment with his stomach. An elderly looking inmate gave his age as 64. Another inmate was suffering from tuberculosis. Reserved for the sick, the inmates said sometimes they got medicine from the hospital, but on other occasions, they had nothing.

Cell 2 was also for sick inmates, and was in a similar state as Cell 1.

Disciplinary cell: There were 11 people in this small cell of approximately 8 sq metre. One inmate claimed to have been in confinement for 57 days for smoking hard drugs. A second person who allegedly tried to escape from the hospital had been in confinement for 40 days. They came out twice, to eat and bath. None of them had a blanket, and there was no light in the cell.

First floor: All the cells were extremely overcrowded. In none was there sleeping space for all of them. "Terrible" sums up the condition in the cells: it is unimaginable how all the inmates could fit into the cells.

In a final discussion with the Director of the prison on 18 December 1997, he indicated that the new prison should be ready in July 1998. It would be a modern prison with carpentry, mechanics and sewing workshops. It would also have a kitchen, a dining hall and a wing for farming. The Director wanted to know about prison conditions elsewhere. In response, I stated that the background and history of Mozambique should always be kept in mind but pointed out that it was nevertheless possible to adopt measures which would improve prison conditions.

My main worries were that:

(a) the majority of prisoners were young adults who had not been tried, but were mixed up with others who were criminals;
(b) the overcrowding was so acute that the inmates did not have sufficient space even to sit down comfortably although 96 of them had been transferred the previous day; and
(c) the disciplinary cell was most appalling; and it was not deserving of Mozambique to have a cell like that whatever its economic circumstances.

I suggested that, despite the work it would entail:

(a) untried detainees should be separated from convicts;
(b) outside exercise should be organised in shifts to avoid having all the inmates outside at the same time; and
(c) the disciplinary cell should be scrubbed, and the iron sheet barring the window should be removed to allow air and light to enter the cell.

An extremely attentive director replied that convicts could be sent to the provincial open centre if they behaved well. Those who were still in prison were those whose conduct was not consistent with the open centre's prison regime.

Finally, I expressed the hope of making a follow up visit in the not too distant future.

Beira Central Police Station

I briefed Mr. Francisco Chaneiro, Commander and Mr. Alberto Nete, Chief of Administration about my mission. This was after authorisation for my visit had been ascertained from the Ministry of Interior in Maputo.

Cells

There were 180 detainees in 5 cells at the time of the visit. They were given one meal per day. A transit cell where new arrivals were kept for not more than 24 hours was the scene of my first private discussion with the inmates at the station. The commander readily agreed to this type of discussion. Two of the inmates claimed to have been in this cell for 4 and 9 days respectively. They cleaned the toilet with their bare hands.

One cell with 72 inmates aged between 18 and 21 had no bed and almost no light. Most of them claimed to have been in the cell for more than 46 hours, some for 30 days or more. An inmate complained that he was under 16 but had no paper to prove it. This was disputed by the Police Officer in charge of criminal investigation. The inmates were allowed to go outside the cell thrice for 30 minutes each.

I went into two other cells, but there was nothing unusual to report.

19 December 1997
Nampula Central Prison

It was most helpful to have a member of the Mozambique League of Human Rights accompanying me on my rounds in Nampula, even during a heavy downpour.

Director José Ramote Fakira said he had nothing to hide and allowed me to see the organisational chart and the state of prisoners on the wall of his office. Under a Provincial director is a Chief of Guards. Two other officers were responsible for operations and administration. There were 5 guards.

A disciplinary cell did not hold any prisoner. The prison had a total number of 438 inmates. 286 of them were on remand while 152 were convicts. There were only 5 female inmates. The length of remand was given as between 90 to 120 days although the slow court process sometimes stretched it to 6 months with the longest being 8 months. Young adults were not separated from adults. Generally, convicts and remand prisoners were accommodated in different cells, and were also kept apart during outdoor exercise. Among the convicts there was no categorisation according to either length of sentence or the type of offence due to limited space.

Food

3 meals a day were served the inmates: maize meal with sugar for breakfast, maize flour and beans for lunch, and rice and dried fish for dinner. Additionally, the inmates could receive two meals each day from outside.

Health

A health centre provided medical care for the sick. Serious cases were referred to the hospital in Nampula.

Punishment

Confinement in a disciplinary cell was the only punishment known to the prison administration. A confined prisoner could come out in the morning for half an hour for a bath and fresh aid.

Visits

Both remand prisoners and convicts could have 2 visits each week.

Correspondence

Inmates could write letters twice a month but this right was hardly exercised. Mail was censored.

Hygiene

Water was accessible to the inmates. They were also given soap twice a month.

Pardon

The last amnesty granted was under the late President Samora Machel. Conditional release could be granted after 6 months for remand prisoners, and after half of the sentence in the case of convicted prisoners who were of good behaviour.

Open centre

One was located in the district of Rex for raising and rearing of crops and animals respectively. prisoners of good behaviour could be sent here.

Visit to cells

The inmates confirmed that they received 3 meals each day. Two complained that they had been in custody without trial since 1995. Three of them claimed that they were 15 years old. Twice a day for 1 hour each they could go outside the cells. There was not sufficient sleeping room (normal state) in the cells, and some of the inmates slept hunched up or simply sat. Some even slept in the bathroom.

Clothing

No uniform was provided by the authorities. Many inmates were in tattered clothes.

Security

Some of the inmates were cell leaders who had responsibility for order and security in their cells.

Cells

A spokesman for prisoners on remand complained about the length of remand. They had no problem with the guards and the prison administration whom the former thought were doing their best. He was incensed against the police who took unduly long time in their investigation resulting in long detention. Some of them were in detention, on such minor offences as stealing a hen or singlet. He invited the Governor to come and see things for himself.

Struck by the youth of most of the inmates in the remand cell, I inquired of how many had parents. More than half said they had none, victims of the war presumably. These orphans had no assistance from outside.

Foreigners

There were 2 Tanzanians among the remand prisoners.

Cell for convicts

As in the case of the remand cell, the overcrowding here was such that the prisoners could not sleep lying down, they just sat up.

There was one seriously ill prisoner lying on a veranda, who had not been taken to hospital, and no one seemed to care. Death did not seem far away.

Cell 3

Convicts were mixed up with remand prisoners. This cell was relatively spacious. The inmates, 23, had responsibility for various tasks in the prison.

Female cell

Of the 5 registered in the prison records, 3 had been sent to a prison farm, leaving only 2 in the cell.

The disciplinary cell had hardly a window. Up to 5 people were sometimes confined here though it was hard to imagine how it could contain even 2 people. It appeared to have faeces on the floor.

First Squadron Police Station, Nampula

There were 4 police stations in Nampula, and what I visited was the central one.

While waiting for permission to visit the cells, from the provincial commander, I saw a 13 year old boy who had been arrested for selling cassettes in the streets. Onlookers said he had been there for over an hour, and predicted that the police would seize the goods; and it came to pass. The boy was released without the tapes. 2 other persons, apparently above the age of 16 were also at the police station for a similar offence.

There were 133 detainees in the cells who had been there for 16–30 days although the legal limit was 48 hours.

On arrival, the commander stated that suspects spent 40–60 days at the police station before being transferred to the prison.

Punishment

The sanction for infringement of regulations was confinement to disciplinary cells. As a result of overcrowding, the disciplinary cell was used to accommodate suspects.

Food

One meal a day was served.

Clothing

The inmates were supplied with uniforms.

Visits

Twice a month an inmate could receive visitors.

The Commander did not allow me to have any private discussion with any of the inmates.

Cell A

Inmates complained that they removed faeces with their bare hands. Another complaint was that the uniforms were not washed although they were passed on from inmate to inmate. Most of them slept on the bare floor. They also ate the same food all the time.

One inmate, who looked it, said he was 14 years old. Selemane Mussa said that although he had been in custody for 4 days, he did not know what he had done.

20 December 1997

I was interviewed prior to our departure from Nampula for radio by Rafael D. Omar of Radio Mozambique who was also a member of the Mozambique League of Human

Rights. The interview centred around the Commission, my mandate, the mission to Mozambique and my findings. I indicated generally the efforts being made by the authorities; the financial and material constraints facing Mozambique; the openness of the authorities and their willingness to receive advice and not hide the prison conditions; but stressed that there were still certain things which could be done to improve the situation.

20 December 1997
Hanhane Open Centre, Matola

This was situated about 2 kilometres from Maputo. There were 2 of such centres within the environs of Maputo; and each of the 10 provinces of Mozambique would have at least one of them.

The National Director of Prisons under the Ministry of Justice and Danilo Nala from the Mozambican League of Human Rights accompanied us on this visit.

The Centre was established in 1986 for women but men have subsequently been added. At the time of the visit there were 6 women and 8 men although the centre had capacity to accommodate 25 inmates. The male and female inmates lived in different buildings. The women's was better than that of the men in sleeping conditions. The guards were all women.

The Director explained that inmates of open centres consisted generally of those who had served the greater part of their sentence and were about to be discharged. They must also have behaved well. The centre was also used to assess the suitability of inmates who had been earmarked for conditional release. A big idea behind the open centres was to help reintegration of inmates into society.

The two living quarters of the centre were almost surrounded by two farms with oranges, lemon, mangoes, pear, corn, beans, cassava and paw-paw trees.

21 December 1997

I had discussion with Miss Mabote Executive Director of LMDH. This organisation was the main local body working in the area of promoting and protecting the rights of prisoners. Some journalists and religious organisations also work in this area.

21 December 1997
Xai-Xai Provincial Prison

Xai-Xai is a small town in Gaza Province located 200 km north of Maputo. From Maputo it is just beyond the Limpopo River. One also crosses the Nkomati River on the way to Xai-Xai from Maputo.

Xai-Xai has a main road which is broad and well-tarred with pavement and trees on both sides.

The prison officials had been informed of my visit, and were waiting for me. As usual, a discussion with the Director, Domingo Chambal preceded a visit to the cells and other parts of the prison.

Discussion with the Director

A blackboard behind the Director's desk had vital statistics of the prison. 118 of the inmates were on remand while 53 were convicts making a total of 171. 166 of them were male while 5 were female. Three of the 5 were under the responsibility of the Ministry of Interior.

There was no record of the number of orphans in the prison; and it was not certain how many young adults had been imprisoned.

It was built in 1946 to hold 70 prisoners (information partly supplied by Director).

While male and female inmates were kept apart, the same was not true for convicts and those on remand because of limited space.

Food

3 meals a day were served to the inmates. They consisted of maize, rice, beans and fish. Asked how the prison authorities were able to provide 3 meals, the Director responded that the prisoners worked on farms for a fee. Gaza was also an agricultural province; and the prison had a farm. 46 of the inmates had gone to work on the prison farm on the day of the visit.

Although sited near the Limpopo river, water was a problem for the prison. The town itself did not have pipe-borne water.

Robbery, homicide and stealing were the common crimes in the area.

Religion

Members of churches preached in the prison on Sundays and Wednesdays.

Visits

Inmates were allowed 2 visits each month usually on the first and third Sundays in the month. Emergency visits were allowed on other days.

Correspondence

Inmates were allowed to write and receive letters at any time, but this right was rarely exercised. Most of the inmates came from the Province and were visited by their families.

Punishment

Those who infringed prison regulations were confined to disciplinary cells for up to 5 days. Inmates for whom maximum security was necessary (attempting to escape, for instance) were also confined here. But the latter were allowed some freedom to go outside in the day.

Visit to cells

8 of the 171 inmates did not sleep in the cells. They lived in their homes, and worked outside the prison. These were selected on the basis of their good behaviour; and this was an exercise in rehabilitation and to prepare them for their return to society.

Female section

It was very spacious. Of the 8 inmates here, two had gone to work outside the prison. One inmate complained about the poor quality of the food and sleeping conditions. Some slept on rice sacks without mattresses or blankets. Another complained that her family was not aware of her imprisonment.

One prisoner on remand had a 7 months old child which was one month old when the mother was imprisoned. They sometimes worked on farms, and the mother also worked with the child on her back.

Kitchen

The food being prepared was beans with fish.

Male section

There were 6 cells of unequal sizes and 2 disciplinary cells. Most of the cells did not have beds, and very little daylight penetrated into them.

Discussion with inmates without officers

The Director had encouraged them to speak without any inhibition. Despite this assurance two inmates said they were afraid to talk. Another said he had been on remand for 3 years, and did not know when his trial would take place. That the food was not well cooked was another complaint. It was a sore point to some that the Director did not go round the cells to find out the condition of both the inmates and the cell, even though the second in command did. No uniform was supplied to them. Soap was supplied once in three months. They were assaulted on the farm by the guards. There was a mental patient among the inmates.

Visits

It was not a problem. Families and certain NGOs visited them.

Xai-Xai Police Station

47 people were in the cells. Three of them were women. Length of stay varied from 48 hours to 3 months.

Food

Two meals a day of beans and maize were served to the inmates.

Clothing

Uniform was provided.

Correspondence

There was no limit to the letters which could be written or received.

Visits

Twice a month but emergencies were catered for.

Punishment

Corporal punishment was prohibited. 40 hours to 3 days confinement for infringement of prison regulations was imposed on offenders.

The sick

There was an extremely sick looking person who had been taken to hospital the previous day, but had been brought back, the Director informed me. In unison, the inmates denied that he had been taken anywhere. He slept in almost the open air throughout the day.

Cells

Two cells in a dungeon were lit by bulb in the day, and in the night they were turned off. Except for going for their food, they were in the cells all day. In the absence of the Director, however, the inmates said the lights were on the whole day.

One inmate had marks which were consistent with his claim that he had been assaulted by the police.

They had never been given soap, they maintained; and they had also not had water for 3 days.

Food was provided once a day, sometimes it was twice. Unless you paid the police, you were not allowed to be visited, the inmates maintained. When under interrogation, suspects were beaten by the police to extract confession.

I suggested that the lights should be put off in the night; and that all efforts should be made to provide medical attention to the sick.

The commander observed that the conditions of detention were the result of the general situation in the country. Most of the detention centres were built in the colonial era, and had not been rehabilitated.

23 December 1997
Machava Prison, Maputo
Discussion with Director his his Deputy

Mumar Tali, the Director had assumed duty only a week previously. Machava was a maximum security prison under the Ministry of Interior. The prison authorities had been notified by their National Director of my visit.

On roll were 422 inmates while it had a capacity for 600. All of the inmates were male. Maximum period of being here was given as 45 days.

Food

Twice a day the inmates were fed on rice, maize flour, beans and dry fish. Rice is frequent but they preferred maize.

According to the Director, the prison had a doctor and nurses. The prisoners were allowed to be outside in the day.

Health

One or two prisoners were sent to hospital every day. I urged the Director to keep an eye on the very sick with a view to sending them to hospital.

Visits

because of the outbreak of cholera, visits had been banned.

Before then visits were paid every day.

Correspondence

There was no limit to the number of letters which could be written or received.

Prisoners were grouped and housed according to considerations such as the nature of offences committed and age. Uniform was supplied by the authorities.

A church on the compound was used for worship on Sunday, Wednesday and Saturday. A library with booklets was manned by the inmates.

Soccer was played three times a week.

The light security arrangements did not make for attempt to escape.

Complaints of inmates

Money had to be paid before one was released. Some were denied the opportunity to play football. They were locked in cells for unduly long periods. They were assaulted by guards with batons, hand and feet. Those who do not have money to pay investigators did not have their cases investigated, and therefore stayed in detention for unduly long periods. The food provided by the authorities was badly prepared. Food brought by visitors did not all reach their owners. In the young adults section, for instance, the "chief" (of this group) took some of the food, and gave some to others. No soap was provided. A young adult who tried to escape when smoking hard drugs was shot at.

He had been at Machava for 3 months without being taken to the hospital.

In two of the bathrooms water flowed uncontrollably. Pipes for water in the yard were however being repaired.

Disciplinary cell

It would not be easy for the 4 people kept here to have sleeping room.

Dangerous prisoners section

Inmates here were not allowed to go outside their cells. One had been there since September 1996. Most of the inmates here were being kept at the request of the police. One was serving a 12 year term of imprisonment.

RECOMMENDATIONS

The recommendations which follow are made after having taken into account, the burdens which Mozambique bears as a result of the long war for independence and the internal struggle between FRELIMO and RENAMO.

1. Steps should be taken to expedite investigation of cases and trial of accused persons. This will reduce the burden on the state by reducing the number of inmates who are cared for by the State.

2. Urgent measures should be taken to set up regimes and programmes for dealing with delinquent juveniles. If this is not done these juveniles will "graduate" into prisons on the attainment of adulthood.

3. Alternative sentences, like community service should be explored and implemented to decongest the prisons and not disrupt social life of those who commit minor offences.

4. The allegation of corruption against the police and prison officers are worthy of investigation for disciplinary action to be taken.

5. Efforts should be made to discourage assault on prisoners, and guards responsible for it should be punished.

6. The distinct impression one gets of guards abandoning extremely sick prisoners to die should be dispelled by at least getting them to take such sick prisoners to the hospital.

7. The harsh realities of life make a second look at criminalising street vending imperative. While this activity goes on with wanton abandon and without criminal consequences visited even on the elderly in Maputo, it seems immoral for the wares of minors, struggling to eke out a living, to be confiscated in Nampula.

8. With a view to supplementing governmental efforts towards prison reform, Government should encourage NGOs to take an interest in prisons and prisoners.

9. Where prisoners grow and tend fruit trees and crops, as in Maputo Central Prison their diet should be supplemented by the produce of their labour.

10. The traditional method of making soap should be revisited with a view to manufacturing it for use in the prison. This can be produced at the Open Centres. It will also contribute towards the rehabilitation of prisoners at these Centres.

11. Simple implements like brooms and wooden shovels can be made, again by inmates at the Open Centres, for supply to prisons for clean-up work.

COMMENTS BY GOVERNMENT OF MOZAMBIQUE*

Professor E. V. O. Dankwa
Faculty of Law of the University of Ghana
Legon – Ghana

Maputo, 28 August 1988 382/SIC-GMJ/98

Subject: Report on the Mission concerning Prisons in Mozambique – 14-12-97

Esteemed Professor,

I acknowledge receipt of your letter dated 28 May 1998, reporting on the situation of the prison population in Mozambique.

* The original of these comments was in Portuguese.

By means of this letter I wish to express my thanks for the descriptive analysis of the report and your brief comments on the situations which you encountered.

As Your Excellency had the opportunity to verify, prisons in Mozambique lack substantial improvements in infrastructure, equipment, the inmates' diet, training of prison wardens in the treatment of prisoners, the introduction of alternative systems for serving sentences, strengthening of productive, educational and sports activities, and the rehabilitation of the inmates themselves. These situations are being remedied according to reforms that have been occurring in the field of prisons.

I also intend to explain to Your Excellency about the periods of remand in custody required by law, which Your Excellency mentioned in your report, but which require clarification. The Law authorizes different lengths of time for remand, according to whether it concerns remand with or without established guilt.

Thus in cases of remand in custody without established guilt, the Law establishes two periods of remand without established guilt, to wit:

(a) lasting up to the notification of charges to the accused or request for instructions to the contrary.

For the first period, we have the durations of remand set out in §1 of Article 380 of the Penal Code, which are as follows:

- 20 days, for crimes of fraud, for which the correctional prison sentence is over a year;
- 40 days, for crimes which may attract a longer sentence;
- 90 days, for crimes that are instructed exclusively by the Criminal Investigation Police (CIP) (i.e. forging of banknotes, drug trafficking, etc.) or in cases of ceded competence, in which competence may only be granted by the Public Prosecutor.

These remand periods start to count from the day of the arrest.

(b) that which goes from the indictment up to the time of sentencing.

For the second period, i.e. in cases of remand up to the time of sentencing, we have §2 of the same article, which establishes the following periods of remand:

- 3 months, if the offence is susceptible of receiving a sentence corresponding to a proceeding by the Criminal Investigation Police;
- 4 months, for crimes which may attract a sentence after trial.

These periods are counted, not from the day of the arrest, but from notification of the charges to the accused or the request for instructions to the contrary.

At the end of these delays, the Accused must be set free, being released on bail and subject to certain conditions determined by the judge.

In respect of release on bail and its inherent obligations, the law establishes a special period of remand for situations in which these conditions are not obeyed. Thus, if these conditions are not fulfilled, the period of remand depends on the offence.

There is an exception in cases where release on bail is inadmissible. In these cases, in a despatch giving his reasons and after hearing the Prosecution and the Defence, the judge may straight away set the date for the judicial proceedings which he deems indispensable for the conclusion of the instruction, and may extend the above mentioned periods for a time not exceeding 60 days.

In cases of remand with established guilt, if any accused persons are in detention, and the period of remand up to the trial has been longer than one year in the case of trial proceedings, six months in proceedings of the Criminal Investigation Police, and three months in the remaining forms of proceedings, the Prosecution will inform the Public Prosecutor of the fact, who will take or propose the appropriate measures, within the terms of Article 337 of the Penal Code, and may request the Supreme Court to set a date for the trial.

I finish by expressing my hope that your work, as Commissioner of the African Commission on Human and Peoples' Rights, will contribute positively towards the prison policies as a whole that are to be introduced and perfected by the Governments of our countries.

Please accept the expression of my highest consideration.

The Minister of Justice
José Ibraimo Abudo

TERMS OF REFERENCE FOR THE SPECIAL RAPPORTEUR ON PRISONS AND CONDITIONS OF DETENTION

Mandate

1. In accordance with its mandate under Article 45 of the African Charter on Human and Peoples' Rights (the Charter), the African Commission on Human and Peoples' Rights (the Commission) hereby establishes the position of Special Rapporteur on Prisons and conditions of detention in Africa.

2. The Special Rapporteur is empowered to examine the situation of persons deprived of their liberty within the territories of States Parties to the African Charter on Human and Peoples' Rights.

Methods of Work

3. The Special Rapporteur shall:

3.1 Examine the state of prisons and conditions of detention in Africa and make recommendations with a view to improving them;

3.2 Advocate adherence to the Charter and international human rights norms and standards concerning the rights of persons deprived of their liberty and the conditions in which they are held, examine the relevant national law and regulations in the respective States Parties as well as their implementation and make appropriate recommendations on their conformity with the Charter and with the Charter and with international law and standards;

3.3 Make recommendations to the Commission as regards communications submitted to it, by individuals who have been deprived of their liberty, by their families or representatives, by NGOs or other persons or institutions;

3.4 Propose appropriate urgent action.

4. The Special Rapporteur shall conduct studies into conditions or situations contributing to human rights violations of persons deprived of their liberty and recommend preventive measures. The Special Rapporteur shall co-ordinate activities with other relevant Special Rapporteurs and Working Groups of the African Commission and United Nations.

5. The Special Rapporteur shall submit an annual report to the Commission. The report shall be published and widely disseminated in accordance with the relevant provisions of the Charter.

Means of Implementing the Mandate

6. The Special Rapporteur shall seek and receive information from States Parties to the Charter, individuals, national and international organisations and institutions as well as other relevant bodies on cases or situations which fall within the scope of the mandate described above.

7. In order to discharge his mandate effectively the Special Rapporteur should be given all the necessary assistance and co-operation to carry out on-site visits and receive information from individuals who have been deprived of their liberty, their families or representatives, from governmental or non-governmental organisations and individuals.

8. The Special Rapporteur shall seek co-operation with States Parties and assurance from the latter that persons, organisations or institutions rendering or providing information to the Special Rapporteur shall not be prejudiced thereby.

9. Every effort will be made to place at the disposal of the Special Rapporteur resources to carry out his/her mandate.

Duration of the Mandate

10. This mandate will last for an initial period of two years which may be renewed by the Commission.

Mandate Priorities for the First Two Years

11. The Special Rapporteur shall focus on the following activities and in each case shall pay attention to problems related to gender:

11.1 Evaluate conditions of detention, highlighting the main problem areas including: prison conditions, health issues, arbitrary or extra-legal detention or imprisonment, treatment of people deprived of their liberty; and conditions of detention of especially vulnerable groups such as: refugees, persons suffering from physical or mental disabilities, or children. The Special Rapporteur shall draw on information and data provided by the States and other relevant sources.

11.2 Make specific recommendations with a view to improving prisons conditions and conditions of detention in Africa and establishing early warning mechanisms in order to avoid disasters and epidemics in places of detention.

11.3 Promote the implementation of the Kampala Declaration on Prisons and Conditions of Detention in Africa.

11.4 Propose revised terms of reference if necessary, at the end of the two-year period to the African Commission and an overall programme for the following stage.

Final Communiqué of the Twenty-third Ordinary Session of the African Commission on Human and Peoples' Rights

Banjul, 20–29 April 1998

1. The 23rd Ordinary Session of the African Commission on Human and Peoples' Rights was held from the 20–29 of April 1998, in Banjul, The Gambia.

2. The opening ceremony of the 23rd Ordinary Session of the African Commission on Human and Peoples' Rights took place in Banjul, the Gambia, on the 20 April 1998 under the Chairmanship of Mr. Youssoupha Ndiaye, Chairman of the Commission.

3. The opening ceremony was graced by the presence of the Chief Justice of the Supreme Court of The Gambia Hon. Justice Omar Alghali who delivered the opening speech.

4. The Session was also addressed by a representative of the NGOs, Mr. Mohamad Monieb of the Egyptian Organisation on Human Rights.

5. The issue of enhancing cooperation between NGOs and the Commission was deliberated upon. Statements were delivered by representatives of the governments of Sudan, Namibia and Mauritania, and also by representatives of various NGOs.

6. The Commission granted observer status to 7 NGOs. The list of the NGOs granted observer status is available at the Secretariat.

7. The Commission considered the initial report of Namibia which was presented by Mr. U. Daniel Nujoma, the Human Rights Coordinator of Namibia, on behalf of the government of Namibia; and the initial report of Guinea which was presented by Mr. Mamadou Bobo Diallo, the Legal Advisor, Ministry of External Affairs of the Republic of Guinea, on behalf of the government of Guinea.

8. In relation to the human rights situation in Africa, various NGO representatives deplored the situation in countries like the Democratic Republic of Congo, Algeria, Mauritania, Rwanda, Chad, Sudan, Cameroon, Eastern Sierra Leone and Nigeria. Special mention was made of female genital mutilation, which is one of the widespread violations of the rights of African women, in many African countries.

Other human rights violations highlighted were slavery, freedom of expression and association as well as forced deportations, extra-judicial executions, religious intolerance and political repression.

The representatives of the Governments of Mauritania, Burkina Faso, the Gambia and Namibia also expressed their opinions on the issue and on the statements made. The session was also later addressed by the representative of the government of Mozambique.

9. The Commission was notified by Amnesty International that the government of Rwanda had announced its decision to execute 22 people who had been charged

with committing genocide and convicted without fair trial, on 24 April. The Commission sent urgent messages appealing for a stay of execution as the intended executions would be in violation of the Charter. Upon confirmation that the executions were carried out in public, the Commission authorised the Chairman to write to the government of Rwanda and express the outrage of the Commission at this blatant disregard of the provisions of the Charter. A press release was issued on this matter.

10. The Special Rapporteur on summary, arbitrary and extra-judicial killings, Dr. Hatem Ben Salem and the Special Rapporteur for prison conditions in Africa, Prof. E. V. O. Dankwa, presented their reports to the Commission

11. The working group on the Draft Additional Protocol to the African Charter on the Rights of Women in Africa, coordinated by Commissioner E. V. O. Dankwa, presented a progress report on the said document.

Commissioner Julienne Ondziel Gnelenga was appointed as the Special Rapporteur on the Rights of Women in Africa.

12. The Commission and the NGOs present discussed various ways in which the African Commission for Human and Peoples' Rights could celebrate the 50th anniversary of the Universal Declaration on Human Rights. The Secretariat was requested to draw up a programme for the celebrations taking into consideration all the proposals that had been made.

13. The Commission discussed at length the issue of the periodic reporting of States and among other things, ways of improving the guidelines for State reporting.

The Commission decided to consider the reports of Seychelles and Chad at the 24th Ordinary Session.

14. The Commission discussed in detail the need for strengthening cooperation between the Commission and National Human Rights Institutions and considered the report of Commissioners Rezag-Bara and Pityana recommending the grant of affiliated institutions status to National Human Rights Institutions.

The Commission deferred its decision on this matter to the next Session and decided that National Human Rights Institutions could in the meantime be invited to attend the Commission's Sessions.

15. The Commission adopted a resolution supporting the establishment of an International Criminal Court.

16. The Commission continued its discussions on the establishment of an African Court on Human and Peoples' Rights. It was decided that each Commissioner would endeavour to sensitize Heads of States and governments of countries that had been assigned to them, on the need for this Court, and hence the need to ratify the Protocol on the establishment of an African Court on Human and Peoples' Rights as soon as possible.

17. The publication of the Review and Newsletter of the Commission was discussed and the Commission decided to ensure that the 6th edition of the Review and Newsletter was published as soon as possible.

18. The Commission reiterated its plans to organise and/or participate in the following seminars:

- Peaceful Settlement of Ethnic and Social Conflicts from a Human Rights Perspective;
- Contemporary Forms of Slavery in Africa;
- The Right to education: An Essential Condition for Development in Africa;
- Freedom of Movement and the Right to Asylum in Africa;
- Good Governance and Corruption in Africa;
- Seminar of African Ambassadors based in Addis Ababa on the Human Rights System in Africa;
- The Right to Fair Trial and Legal Assistance;
- Ministerial Conference on Human and Peoples' Rights in Africa;
- Diplomatic Conference on the International Criminal Court.

19. The Commission considered the Mission report on Sudan. Consideration of the Mission report on Nigeria was postponed to the 24th Session.

20. The Commission considered sixty-nine (69) complaints on human rights violations and made the necessary recommendations.

21. The African Commission expresses its profound gratitude to the Government of the Republic of The Gambia, which did not spare any effort to ensure the smooth running of the 23rd Ordinary Session of the Commission.

22. The Closing Ceremony took place on the 29 April 1998, at the Kairaba Hotel under the Chairmanship of Mr. Youssoupha Ndiaye and was closed by the President of the Court of Appeal of the Gambia, Mr Justice Chomba.

23. The Chairman of the Commission Mr. Youssoupha Ndiaye held a press conference after the closing ceremony.

Celebration of the Fiftieth Anniversary of the Universal Declaration of Human Rights

Twenty-third Ordinary Session
Banjul, 20–29 April 1998
DOC/OS/29 (XXIII)

1998: INTERNATIONAL HUMAN RIGHTS YEAR HOW TO CELEBRATE THE FIFTIETH ANNIVERSARY OF THE UNIVERSAL DECLARATION OF HUMAN RIGHTS?

Request for Proposals

1. The Fiftieth Anniversary of the Universal Declaration of Human Rights will be celebrated throughout the world on 10 December 1998. This celebration will take place concomitantly with the fifth anniversary of the 1993 Vienna Declaration and Programme of Action.

2. Since its adoption on 10 December 1948, the Universal Declaration has served as a beacon and a source of inspiration for the enactment and revision of national legislations as well as regional and international human rights instruments.

3. 1998 is the most appropriate occasion to take stock of actions undertaken and progress accomplished in the past so as to adequately prepare for the future. But far from being a simple inventory of the results obtained and a moment to boast of progress registered, this anniversary should serve as an appropriate framework for in-depth exchanges and concrete actions for the entrenchment of a genuine universal culture and the establishment of a real human rights society.

4. To celebrate this important event, the General Assembly and the United Nations Human Rights Commission have appealed to Governments, the entire United Nations System, Regional and International Organisations and Non-governmental Organisations to start preparing for the Fiftieth Anniversary by planning, proposing and implementing projects and concrete actions.

5. Africa, as a subject and actor, cannot remain indifferent to this solemn event. Through the African Charter on Human and Peoples' Rights and the African Commission which constitute the cornerstone and backbone of its human rights promotional and protective system, Africa has an important contribution to make to the world with respect to the full enjoyment of these rights by all.

6. This explains why the Secretariat of the African Commission welcomes and applauds the initiatives already made and actions taken so far throughout the continent and urges States Parties to the Charter, Non-governmental Organisations as well as African Civil Society as a whole to immediately start working on preparations for

the commemoration of the Fiftieth Anniversary of the Universal Declaration of Human Rights and initiate concrete actions in this respect (Symposia, Conference, Cultural activities, prizes, sensitization, educational and information campaigns on human and peoples' rights, publication of brochures, posters, Radio/TV round-tables).

7. Among other materials, the Secretariat recommends the following as sources of information:

- the African Commission's Information Kit;
- the Fiftieth Anniversary Periodic Information Kit published by the United Nations Human Rights Commission;
- the Special Information Kit prepared by the Public Information Department of the United Nations for the benefit of the Press; and
- the Brochure entitled: "Initiatives and Proposals for the Celebration of the Fiftieth Anniversary of the Universal Declaration of Human Rights" published in 1997 by the Arab Human Rights Institute (Tunis).

8. The active participation of Africa in the celebration of this Fiftieth Anniversary, barely two years after the tenth anniversary of the African Charter, affords us the opportunity to further reflect on the abuses and massive violations of human rights on the continent as well as on their causes and heighten awareness of Africans on the need to respect the rights of others and on ways of ensuring respect of theirs. Moreover, it would help us assess the contributions made by Africa at the international level in the area of human rights, identify the difficulties encountered and enter the new millennium with new ideas and new actions with a view to enhancing the promotion and protection of human rights in Africa.

9. The Conference of African Ministers scheduled to take place in Luanda (Angola) in October 1998, although very close to the event, will play a lead role in enhancing Africa's participation in the celebration of the Fiftieth Anniversary of the Universal Declaration of Human Rights.

Geographical Distribution of Countries Among Commissioners for Promotional Activities

DOC/OS/36e (XXIII)

1. The criteria proposed during previous sessions for revising the present distribution stemmed basically from:

(a) the nationality of the members of the Commission who should not cover their countries of origin; it has been observed at the 23rd Session that this criterion should not apply for Promotional activities;
(b) the language of the Commissioners and the countries to be covered, in order to improve efficiency;
(c) the distance between the countries to be covered and the countries of residence of the members of the Commission for pragmatic reasons (to cut down on time and financial resources).

2. In accordance with the proposals made by Commissioners at the 23rd Ordinary Session, the proposed distribution is as follows:

(1) Mr. Youssoupha Ndiaye:	Senegal, Niger, Guinea and the Gambia
(2) Mrs. Vera Duarte-Martins	Angola, Cape Verde, Mozambique, Guinea Bissau and Sao Tome and Principe
(3) Prof. Isaac Nguema:	Gabon, Equatorial Guinea, Democratic Republic of Congo, Burkina Faso, Congo (Brazzaville) and Cameroon
(4) Prof. E. V. O. Dankwa:	Ghana, Sierra Leone, Kenya, Uganda and Cameroon
(5) Mr. Atsu-Koffi Amega:	Togo, Central African Republic and Benin
(6) Mr. Kamel Rezzag-Bara:	Algeria, Comoros, Saharawi Arab Democratic Republic, Mauritania and Chad
(7) Dr. Ibrahim Ali Badawi:	Egypt, Tanzania, Ethiopia, Eritrea, the Sudan and Somalia
(8) Mr. Mohammed H. Ben Salem:	Tunisia, Libya, Djibouti, Mali, Liberia and Seychelles
(9) Mr. Alioune Blondin Beye:	Côte d'Ivoire and Angola
(10) Mrs. J. Ondziel-Gnelenga:	Burundi, Rwanda, Mauritius, Côte d'Ivoire and Madagascar

(11) Dr. Nyameko B. Pityana: South Africa, Zimbabwe, Zambia, Malawi, Botswana, Namibia, Lesotho and Swaziland (Nigeria temporarily)

NB: Both Prof. E. V. O. Dankwa and Mr. Isaac Nguema have been assigned to cover Cameroon because the country is bilingual.

Twelfth Annual Activity Report of the African Commission on Human and Peoples' Rights 1998–1999

Adopted on 5 May 1999
Covering the 24th and 25th Ordinary Sessions in Banjul
(26 April to 5 May 1999)

I. ORGANIZATION OF WORK

A. Period Covered by the Report

1. The Eleventh Annual Activity Report was adopted by the Thirty-fourth Ordinary Session of the Assembly of Heads of State and Government of the Organization of African Unity (OAU), meeting from 8–10 June 1998 in Ouagadougou, Burkina Faso, by Decision AHG/Dec. 126 (XXXIV). The Twelfth Annual Activity Report covers the Twenty-fourth and Twenty-fifth Ordinary Sessions of the Commission held respectively in Banjul, The Gambia, from 26 April to 5 May 1999.

B. Status of Ratification

2. All the OAU Member States have either ratified or acceded to the African Charter on Human and Peoples' Rights. Annex I contains the list of States Parties to the African Charter on Human and Peoples' Rights, stating, among others, the dates of the signing, the ratification or accession as well as the depositing of the instruments of ratification or accession.

C. Sessions and Agenda

3. The Commission held two Ordinary Sessions since the adoption in June 1998 of its Eleventh Annual Activity Report:

- Twenty-fourth Ordinary Session held in Banjul, The Gambia, Headquarters of the Commission, from 22–31 October 1998;
- Twenty-fifth Ordinary Session held in Bujumbura, Burundi, from 26 April to 5 May 1999;

The Agenda of each of these Sessions is attached as Annex II to this Report.

D. Composition and Attendance

4. The following members of the Commission participated in the deliberations of the 24th Session:

Mr. Youssoupha Ndiaye – Chairman,
Dr. Vera Valentino Duarte Martins – Vice-Chairman,
Mr. Atsu Koffi Amega,
Dr. Mohamed Hatem Ben Salem,
Professor E. V. O. Dankwa,
Professor Issac Nguema,
Mrs. Julienne Ondziel-Gnelenga,
Dr. Nyameko Barney Pityana,
Mr. M. Kamel Rezag-Bara.

5. Commissioner Ibrahim Ali Badawi El Sheikh was absent with apologies.

6. The Representatives of the following States Parties participated in the deliberations of the 24th Session and some of them made statements: Angola, Benin, Burkina Faso, Cameroon, Ethiopia, The Gambia, Mauritania, Nigeria, Rwanda, Senegal, The Sudan, Zambia.

Tribute to Mr. Alioune Blondin Beye

7. The Commission devoted part of the Fourth sitting of the 24th Session to remember the Late Commissioner Alioune Blondin Beye who was the victim in an air crash that occurred on 26 June 1998 in Cote d'Ivoire. Tribute was paid particularly by Messrs Alioune Tine of the "Rencontre Africaine pour La Defense des Droits de l'Homme" (RADDHO) and Christophe Compaore of the "Mouvement Burkinabe des Droits de l'Homme et des Peuples" (MBDHP) on behalf of the NGO community as well as by Commissioner Atsu Koffi Amega and Chairman Youssoupha Ndiaye: on behalf of the Commission. The speakers pointed out the major qualities of Late Alioune Blondin Beye whose studious and sociable youth, his professional competence, his love for work, his devotion to the cause of peace in Africa and in the work, his faithfulness and particularly his generosity towards his brothers and friends. The Commission decided to call the 24th Session "The Alioune Blondin Beye Session" and to establish a Human Rights Prize "Alioune Blondin Beye Prize".

8. The following members of the Commission participated in the deliberations of the 25th Ordinary Session:

Mr. Youssoupha Ndiaye – Chairman,
Dr. Vera Valentino Duarte Martins – Vice-Chairman,
Dr. Ibrahim Ali Badawi El-Sheikh,
Dr. Mohammed Hatem Ben Salem,
Professor E. V. O. Dankwa,
Professor Issac Nguema,

Mrs. Julienne Ondziel-Gnelenga,
Dr. Nyameko Barney Pityana,
Mr. Kamal Rezag-Bara.

9. Commissioner Atsu Koffi Amega was absent with apologies.

10. The Representatives of the following States participated in the deliberations of the 25th Ordinary Session and some of them made statements: Burkina Faso, Burundi, Chad, Egypt, Ethiopia, The Gambia, Mauritania, Mali, Rwanda, Senegal, South Africa, The Sudan, Zambia. The Secretary-General of the Organization of African Unity, Dr. Salim Ahmed Salim, graced the 25h Session and made a statement.

11. Many Non-Governmental Organizations (NGOs) and National Institutions also participated in the deliberations of the two Ordinary Sessions.

Adoption of Twelfth Annual Activity Report

12. The Commission considered and adopted the Twelfth Annual Activity Report at its sitting of 5 May 1999.

II. ACTIVITIES OF THE COMMISSION

A. Consideration of Periodic Reports

13. Under Article 62 of the African Charter on Human and Peoples' Rights, each State Party pledges to present every two years, as from the date of entry into force of the Charter, a Report on the legislative and other measures taken to give effect to the rights and freedoms guaranteed in the said Charter.

14. It was within that framework that the initial Report of Angola was considered by the Commission at its 24th Session and expressed satisfaction at the quality of the Report. It thanked the Representative of Angola for the efforts that his Government made in the field of human rights.

15. The initial Periodic Reports of the Republic South Africa, Burkina Faso and Chad were presented at the 25th Ordinary Session. Expressing satisfaction at the quality of the Reports submitted and the dialogue thus established, the Commission thanked the Representatives of the States concerned for their services and encouraged the said States to continue their efforts, to make the fulfilment of their obligations stated in the Charter a tangible reality.16. The Republic of Seychelles deposited its initial Report since the 17th Ordinary Session held from 13–22 March 1995 in Lome, Togo but still did not send anybody to present it despite the repeated reminders of the Commission. The latter deplored the negative attitude of Seychelles and had to adopt a Resolution (attached as Annex V to the Report) on this matter at the 25th Session.

17. The status of submission of Periodic Reports by the States is contained in Annex III attached to this Report.

18. The Commission strongly appeals to the States Parties that are still behind schedule with their Report to submit their Report as soon as possible and if necessary to compile all their Reports due into a single Report.

B. Promotional Activities

(i) Report of the Chairman of the Commission

19. The Chairman of the Commission presented his Activity Report and particularly pointed out that he had participated in the Sixty-ninth Ordinary Session of the OAU Council of Ministers, 19–23 March 1999, the First Ministerial Conference on Human Rights in Africa in Grand Bay, Mauritius, 12–16 April 1999, the Second Conference of National Human Rights Institutions in Durban, South Africa, 1–3 July 1998. He met with the United Nations High Commissioner for Human Rights and officials from other partner organizations of the Commission. The Chairman also met with the OAU Secretary-General, Ministers of various State parties and initiated contacts with the Governments of the Republic of Guinea and the Islamic Republic of Mauritania with regard to emergency situations. He also visited Mali following the demise of the late Alioune Blondin Beye and met with the family of the deceased and the authorities of the country.

(ii) Activities of Other Members of the Commission

20. All the members of the Commission presented reports on human rights promotion and/or protection related activities which they carried out during the inter-sessions.

(iii) Seminars and Conferences

21. The Commission was represented at the following meetings, seminars and conferences:

(a) Seminar organized by the United Nations High Commission's Office for Refugees (UNHCR) for officials of its offices in West and Central Africa, on African mechanism for the protection of human rights and the possibilities offered regarding the protection of refugees (Dakar, Senegal 1–4 December 1998);
(b) Meeting of a Group of Experts on the strategy to be adopted regarding the speedy ratification of the Protocol establishing the African Court of Human and Peoples' Rights, organized at the initiative of the International Commission of Jurists in Ouagadougou, Burkina Faso, from 7–9 December 1998 under the auspices of the OAU Current Chairman, H.E. Mr. Blaise Compaore, President of Faso;
(c) Meeting organized by the International Commission of Jurists on "Human Rights in Africa: challenges and prospects" as part of the activities marking the

celebration of the Fiftieth Anniversary of the Universal Declaration on Human Rights (Ouagadougou, Burkina Faso, 17–19 December 1998);

(d) Meeting with the partners of the Commission organized by SIDA in Lund, Sweden, from 11–13 January 1999 to explore possible ways of strengthening the capacity of the African Commission;

(e) Forum of NGOs to prepare the contribution to the meeting of the First Ministerial Conference on Human Rights in Africa (Nairobi, Kenya, 7–9 April 1999);

(f) First Ministerial Conference on Human Rights situation in Africa (Grand-Bay, Mauritius, 12–16 April 1999).

C. Forthcoming Seminars and Conferences

22. The Commission decided to organize the following seminars and conferences:

(a) peaceful resolution of ethnic and social conflicts from the human rights perspectives;

(b) contemporary forms of slavery;

(c) right to education: a sine qua non for development. The Commission decided that the Seminar on popular participation and informal education should be included in the seminar on the right to education;

(d) freedom of movement and right of asylum in Africa

(e) right to fair trial and legal assistance (Senegal, September 1999);

(f) the rights of the disabled.

23. The Commission enlisted the support of the international organizations and NGOs in the organization of the above-mentioned seminars and conferences, and appointed commissioners to oversee the organization.

III. REPORT OF THE SPECIAL RAPPORTEUR ON EXTRA-JUDICIAL, SUMMARY AND ARBITRARY EXECUTIONS IN AFRICA

24. Commissioner Ben Salem Special Rapporteur on Extra-judicial, Summary and Arbitrary Executions drew the Commission's attention to the new cases of extra-judicial executions in Chad, the Democratic Republic of Congo, Angola, the Comoros and Sierra Leone.

25. Commissioner Ben Salem presented a report to the 25th Ordinary Session on extra-judicial, summary and arbitrary executions in Rwanda, Burundi and Chad. The report makes mention of the difficulties encountered by the Special Rapporteur and the methodology used in the execution of his mandate.

IV. REPORT OF THE SPECIAL RAPPORTEUR ON PRISONS AND PRISON CONDITIONS IN AFRICA

26. Commissioner E. V. O. Dankwa, Special Rapporteur on Prisons and Conditions of Detention in Africa presented a succinct report on his missions to Kenya, Cameroon, Zimbabwe and Uganda.

27. The Special Rapporteur presented a report to the Twenty-fifth Ordinary Session in which he expressed satisfaction at the follow-up and evaluation mission to Mali.

V. REPORT OF THE SPECIAL RAPPORTEUR ON THE RIGHTS OF WOMEN IN AFRICA

28. Madam Julienne Ondziel-Gnelenga, Special Rapporteur on the Rights of Women in Africa, presented a preliminary report containing the proposed programme of activities, implementation strategies and draft budget.

29. She also presented a report on the activities she undertook within the purview of her mandate. She mentioned among other things the contacts she initiated to inform the various partners and mobilize the necessary resources for her activities.

VI. CONSIDERATION OF THE ADDITIONAL DRAFT PROTOCOL TO THE AFRICAN CHARTER ON THE RIGHTS OF WOMEN

30. Commissioner Dankwa presented a report on the work of the group charged to prepare the Additional Draft Protocol to the African Charter on the Rights of Women in Africa. The Commission asked the group to continue its work.

VII. RATIFICATION OF ADDITIONAL PROTOCOL TO THE AFRICAN CHARTER ON HUMAN AND PEOPLES' RIGHTS ESTABLISHING THE AFRICAN COURT OF HUMAN AND PEOPLES' RIGHTS

31. With regard to the strategy to be adopted for the rapid ratification of the Additional Protocol to the African Charter on Human and Peoples' Rights establishing the African Court of Human and Peoples' Rights, the Commission decided to continue with its efforts of sensitizing OAU Member States to the need to ratify the protocol as quickly as possible, and to involve the media in the campaign as well as all the actors who may contribute to its success.

VIII. MISSIONS TO THE STATES PARTIES

32. The Commission decided to publish the mission reports on Mauritania together with the observations of the government.

33. The 25th Ordinary Session considered the report on the mission to Nigeria and decided to send it to that country for its observations and comments.

IX. RELATIONS WITH THE OBSERVERS

34. For some time now, the NGOs have been pondering on how best to coordinate their activities in Africa in order to enhance the work of the African Commission.

35. For the first time, the NGOs organized themselves into geographical groups covering West Africa, Central Africa, Southern Africa, East Africa and North Africa and presented their declarations on the human rights situation to the Twenty-fifth Ordinary Session. The declarations dealt with human rights violations in the respective four sub-regions.

36. They also highlighted extra-judicial summary and arbitrary executions, arbitrary arrests and detentions, torture, inhuman prison and detention conditions, restrictions and breach of fundamental freedoms, of the right to participation in the democratic process as a result of military coups d'etat, forced disappearances, impunity, the situation of the vulnerable groups, women and children in particular, etc. These human rights violations are compounded by armed conflicts that are proliferating on the continent.

37. The NGOs urged the Commission to react fast to incidences of human rights violation.

38. The Commission commended the NGOs for the rationalization and quality of their contribution to the deliberation.

39. The Commission adopted a resolution conferring on National Human Rights Institutions the status of affiliated bodies, and decided to pursue consideration on the possibility of strengthening its cooperation with these institutions.

40. The Commission also adopted a resolution on the criteria, for granting observer status to and enjoyment of same by the NGOs which had submitted a request in these regards.

X. PROTECTION ACTIVITIES

41. A total of 114 complaints (eight (8) of which were new) were tabled before the Commission during its 24th and 25th Ordinary Sessions. Six (6) of these communications were fully actioned. The decisions relating thereto are to be found in Annex V.

XI. ADMINISTRATIVE AND FINANCIAL MATTERS

A. Administrative Matters

42. The Commission expressed satisfaction at the significant progress made by its Secretariat in recent years. It commended the Secretary of the Commission and his staff for the improved quality of the Secretariats' work despite limited resources, and urged them not to relent in their endeavours.

43. The Commission expressed profound appreciation both for the measures already taken by the OAU Secretary-General, and for those he plans to take to give effect to the decisions of the Assembly of Heads of State and Government of the OAU, stipulating that the Commission be endowed with adequate financial, human and material resources to enable it function effectively.

44. The African Commission was also appreciative of the assistance provided by its partners, which made possible the implementation of a considerable part of its activities.

B. Financial Matters

(i) OAU Budget

45. By virtue of Article 41 of the Charter, the functioning of the African Commission is ensured by the staff, facilities and services provided by Secretary-General of the OAU. Owing to the limited resources allocated to it by the OAU, the Commission had to have recourse to financial and material assistance from its partners.

(ii) Assistance from the African Society of Comparative International Law

46. With the assistance of the African Comparative International Law Society, the Secretariat secured the services of two (2) jurists for a period of one year. Publication of the Commissions Review was also ensured thanks to the technical assistance received from this society which was responsible for the publication's printing and distribution costs.

(iii) Assistance from the Danish Human Rights Centre

47. There has been notable improvement in the working conditions in the Secretariat thanks to the Danish assistance which made possible the recruitment of additional staff, procurement of computers with accessories and the funding of promotion activities such as documents production, and field missions by members of the Commission. The Danish Human Rights Centre is in the process of helping the Commission and its Commissioners with the planning of their activities and with the mobilization of resources for implementation of these activities. This assistance will last for three years.

(iv) Assistance from the European Union

48. The European Union made funds available to the Commission for, among other things, the production and dissemination of its documents and other human rights promotion activities throughout the Continent. The European Union has expressed readiness to continue providing this assistance.

(v) Assistance from the United Nations Commission for Human Rights

49. The United Nations Human Rights Commission extended financial aid to the African Commission for the elaboration of the Draft Protocol on the Rights of Women in Africa, for the organization of seminars on the right to fair trial, the preparation of human rights training manuals, and for the organization of training courses for two officials of the Secretariat on the processing of communications and periodic reports submitted by States Parties to the African Charter. This assistance which covers a period of twelve (12) months became effective from 1 April 1999.

(vi) Assistance from the Friedrich-Naumann Foundation

50. The Friedrich-Naumann Foundation has continued to undertake measures to mobilize resources in favour of the Commission, especially at the level of the European Union and other European partners.

(vii) Assistance from the Raoul Wallenberg Institute

51. Publication of the Commission's Review has been realised up to now, thanks to the grants accorded by the Swedish Government through the Raoul Wallenberg Institute. Promotion missions to States Parties are also catered for under this grant subject to the limits of the budget provided.

(viii) International Commission of Jurists

52. The International Commission of Jurists has continued to provide the African Commission with assistance towards implementation of numerous activities such as the elaboration of the Draft Protocol on the Rights of Women, a studies pertaining to strategies for speedy ratification of the Protocol on the African Court on human and Peoples' Rights, assistance to the Special Rapporteur on the Rights of Women, etc.

(ix) Other Partners

53. The Commission was beneficiary of various firms of assistance from several partners, both African and non-African thus enabling it, with sizeable degree of success to discharge its human and peoples' rights promotion and protection mission on the Continent.

54. The Commission plans to further strengthen this cooperation.

XII. ADOPTION OF THE REPORT BY THE ASSEMBLY OF HEADS OF STATE AND GOVERNMENT OF THE OAU

55. The Assembly of Heads of State and Government, after consideration, adopted the report by a resolution in which it expressed satisfaction at the Report and authorized its publication.

ANNEX I

African Charter on Human and Peoples' Rights List of Countries which have Signed, Ratified or Adhered to the Charter

No.	Country	Date of Signature	Date of Ratification	Date Deposited
1.	Algeria	10/04/86	01/03/87	20/03/87
2.	Angola		02/03/90	09/10/90
3.	Benin		20/01/86	25/02/86
4.	Botswana		17/07/86	22/07/86
5.	Burkina Faso	05/03/84	06/07/84	21/09/84
6.	Burundi		28/07/80	30/08/89
7.	Cameroon	23/07/87	20/06/89	18/09/89
8.	Cape Verde	31/03/86	02/06/87	06/08/87
9.	Central African Republic		26/04/86	27/07/86
10.	Comoros		01/06/86	18/07/86
11.	Congo	27/11/81	09/12/82	17/01/83
12.	Congo (RD)	23/07/87	20/07/87	28/07/87
13.	Côte d'Ivoire		06/01/92	31/03/92
14.	Djibouti	20/12/91	11/11/91	20/12/91
15.	Egypt	16/11/81	20/03/84	03/04/84
16.	Equatorial Guinea	18/08/86	07/04/86	18/08/86
17.	Eritrea		14/01/99	15/03/99
18.	Ethiopia		15/06/98	22/06/98
19.	Gabon	26/02/82	20/02/86	26/06/86
20.	Gambia	11/02/83	08/06/83	13/03/83
21.	Ghana		24/01/89	01/03/89
22.	Guinea	09/12/81	16/02/82	13/05/82
23.	Guinea-Bissau		04/12/85	06/03/86
24.	Kenya		23/01/92	10/02/92
25.	Lesotho	07/03/84	10/02/92	27/02/92
26.	Liberia	31/01/83	04/08/82	29/12/82
27.	Libya	30/05/85	19/07/86	26/03/87
28.	Madagascar		09/03/92	19/03/92
29.	Malawi	23/02/90	17/11/89	23/02/90

No.	Country	Date of Signature	Date of Ratification	Date Deposited
30.	Mali	13/11/81	21/12/81	22/01/82
31.	Mauritania	25/02/82	14/06/86	26/06/86
32.	Mauritius	27/02/92	19/06/92	07/07/92
33.	Mozambique		22/02/89	07/03/90
34.	Namibia		30/07/92	16/09/92
35.	Niger	09/07/86	15/07/86	21/07/86
36.	Nigeria	31/08/82	22/06/83	27/07/83
37.	Uganda	18/08/86	10/05/86	27/05/86
38.	Rwanda	11/11/81	15/07/83	22/07/83
39.	Sahrawi Arab Dem. Rep.	10/04/86	02/05/86	23/05/86
40.	Sao Tome & Principe		23/05/86	28/07/86
41.	Senegal	23/09/81	13/08/82	25/10/82
42.	Seychelles		13/04/92	30/04/92
43.	Sierra Leone	27/08/81	21/09/83	27/01/84
44.	Somalia	26/02/82	31/07/85	20/03/86
45.	South Africa	07/07/96	09/07/96	09/07/96
46.	Sudan		18/02/86	11/03/86
47.	Swaziland			
48.	Tanzania	31/05/82	18/02/84	09/03/84
49.	Chad	29/05/86	09/10/86	11/11/86
50.	Togo	20/02/82	05/11/82	22/11/82
51.	Tunisia		16/03/83	22/04/83
52.	Zambia	17/01/83	19/01/84	02/02/84
53.	Zimbabwe	20/02/86	30/05/86	12/06/86

ADOPTED: by the 18th Session of the Assembly of Heads of State and Government, June 1981
REQUIRES: ratification or adherence of a simple majority of Member States to come into force
ENTERED INTO FORCE: 21st day of October 1986
REGISTERED: with the United Nations on 10 September 1991, No. 26363

ANNEX II

Agenda of the Twenty-fourth Ordinary Session

1. Opening Ceremony (Public Session)
2. Adoption of the Agenda (Private Session)
3. Organisation of Work (Private Session)
4. Introductory Note of the Secretary on the Activities of the Commission (Public Session)
5. Observers (Public Session):
   - (a) Statements by State Delegates
   - (b) Relationship and Co-operation Between the Commission and NGOs

6. Periodic Reports
    (a) Amendment of Guidelines for the Preparation of State Parties' Periodic Reports (Public Session)
    (b) Consideration of Initial Reports (Public Session):
        (i) Chad
        (ii) Seychelles
7. The Setting-up of an Early Intervention Mechanism in Cases of Massive Human Rights Violations (Public Session)
8. Promotional Activities (Public Session)
    (a) Activity Report of Commissioners
    (b) Human Rights Situation in Africa
    (c) Examination of the Report of the Special Rapporteur on Summary, Arbitrary and Extra-judicial Executions
    (d) Examination of the Report of the Special Rapporteur on Prisons and Conditions of Detention in Africa
    (e) Examination of the Report of the Special Rapporteur on the Rights of Women in Africa
    (f) Discussion of the Draft Additional Protocol to the African Charter on the Rights of Women in Africa
    (g) Co-operation Between the Commission and the National Human Rights institutions
    (h) Celebration of the 50th Anniversary of the Universal Declaration of Human Rights
    (i) Organisation of Seminars and Conferences
9. Review of Some Provisions of the African Charter in the Light of the Protocol Establishing the African Court on Human and Peoples' Rights
10. Review and Newsletter of the African Commission on Human and Peoples' Rights
11. The issue of Incompatibility of the Membership of the Commission
12. Protective Activities (Private Session)
    (a) Consideration of the Mission report to Nigeria
    (b) Follow up of Mission Reports to Senegal, Mauritania and Togo
    (c) Consideration of Communications
13. Administrative and Financial Matters (Private Session)
    (a) Report of the Chairman
    (b) Financial Situation and Functioning of the Secretariat
    (c) The Issue of the Construction of the Headquarters
    (d) Participation of the Commission in Certain Activities of the OAU
14. Evaluation of the Implementation of the Mauritius Plan of Action (Private Session)

15. Logo of the Commission
16. Methods of Work of the Commission (Private Session)
17. Date, Venue and Provisional Agenda for the 25th Ordinary Session
18. Any Other Business
19. Preparation of:

    (a) The Session Report
    (b) The Final Communiqué

20. Adoption of the Session Report and the Final Communiqué (Private Session)
21. Reading of the Final Communiqué and Closing Ceremony
22. Press Conference

Agenda of the Twenty-fifth Ordinary Session

1. Opening Ceremony (Public Session)
2. Adoption of the Agenda (Private Session)
3. Organisation of Work (Private Session)
4. Introductory Note of the Secretary on the Activities of the Commission (Public Session)
5. Observers (Public Session):

    (a) Statements by State Delegates and Guests
    (b) Co-operation Between the Commission and the National Human Rights Institutions
    (b) Relationship and Co-operation Between the Commission and NGOs.

6. Consideration of Initial Reports:

    (i) Chad
    (ii) Seychelles
    (iii) South Africa
    (iv) Burkina Faso

7. The Setting-up of an Early Intervention Mechanism in Cases of Massive Human Rights Violations (Public Session)
8. Promotional Activities (Public Session)

    (a) Activity Report of the Chairman and Members of the Commission
    (b) Examination of the Report of the Special Rapporteur on Summary, Arbitrary and Extra-judicial Executions
    (c) Examination of the Report of the Special Rapporteur on Prisons and Conditions of Detention in Africa
    (d) Examination of the Report of the Special Rapporteur on the Rights of Women in Africa
    (e) Discussion of the Draft Additional Protocol to the African Charter on the Rights of Women (Progress)

- (f) Strategy for a Quick Ratification of the Additional Protocol to the African Charter on Human and Peoples' Rights on the Establishment of an African Court on Human and Peoples' Rights
- (g) Situation of Peoples with Disability
- (h) Organisation of Seminars and Conferences
- (i) Human Rights Situation in Africa
- (j) Situation of Indigenous People
- (k) Situation of the African Child
- (l) World Conference on Racism
- (m) Situation of Human Rights Defenders in Africa

9. Review of Some Provisions of the African Charter in the Light of the Protocol Establishing the African Court on Human and Peoples' Rights and Mainly the Issue of Incompatibility of the Membership of the Commission
10. Review and Newsletter of the African Commission on Human and Peoples' Rights
11. Protective Activities (Private Session)
    - (a) Consideration of the Mission Report to Nigeria
    - (b) Consideration of Communications
12. Administrative and Financial Matters (Private Session)
    - (a) Report of the Chairman
    - (b) Financial and Administrative Situation of the Secretariat
    - (c) The Issue of the Construction of the Headquarters
    - (d) Participation of the Commission in Certain Activities of the OAU
13. Methods of Work
14. Evaluation of the Implementation of the Mauritius Plan of Action (Public Session)
15. Logo of the Commission
16. Dates, Venue and Provisional Agenda for the 26th ordinary session
17. Any Other Business.
18. Preparation of:
    - (a) The Session Report
    - (b) The Twelfth Annual Activity Report
    - (c) The Final Communiqué
19. Adoption of the Session Report, the Twelfth Annual Activity and the Final Communiqué (Private Session)
20. Reading of the Final Communiqué and Closing Ceremony
21. Press Conference

ANNEX III

Status on Submission of Periodic Reports by States Parties

No.	State Party	1st Report to be submitted on	2nd Report to be submitted on	3rd Report to be submitted on	4th Report to be submitted on	5th Report to be submitted on	Reports submitted but not yet considered
1.	Algeria	20/06/89	20/06/91	20/06/93	20/06/95	20/06/97	
2.	Angola	09/01/92	09/01/94	09/01/96	09/01/98	09/01/00	
3.	Benin	21/10/88	21/10/90	21/10/92	21/10/94	21/10/96	
4.	Botswana	21/10/88	21/10/90	21/10/92	21/10/94	21/10/96	
5.	Burundi	30/11/91	30/11/93	30/11/95	30/11/97	30/11/99	
6.	Burkina Faso	21/10/88	21/10/90	21/10/92	21/10/94	21/10/96	
7.	Cameroon	18/12/91	18/12/93	18/12/95	18/12/97	18/12/99	
8.	Cape Verde	06/11/89	06/11/91	06/11/93	06/11/95	06/11/97	
9.	Central African Republic	21/10/88	21/10/90	21/10/92	21/10/94	21/10/96	
10.	Chad	11/02/89	11/02/91	11/02/93	11/02/95	11/02/97	
11.	Comoros	21/10/88	21/10/90	21/10/92	21/10/94	21/10/96	
12.	Congo	21/10/88	21/10/90	21/10/92	21/10/94	21/10/96	
13.	Côte d'Ivoire	01/07/94	01/07/96	01/07/98	07/01/00	01/07/02	
14.	Djibouti	20/03/93	20/03/95	20/03/97	20/03/99	20/03/01	
15.	Egypt	21/10/88	21/10/90	21/10/92	21/10/94	21/10/96	
16.	Equatorial Guinea	18/11/88	18/11/90	18/11/92	18/11/94	18/11/96	
17.	Ethiopia (1)						
18.	Eritrea (1)						
19.	Gabon	21/10/88	21/10/90	21/10/92	21/10/94	21/10/96	
20.	Gambia	21/10/88	21/10/90	21/10/92	21/10/94	21/10/96	
21.	Ghana	01/06/91	01/06/93	01/06/95	01/06/97	01/06/99	
22.	Guinea	21/10/88	21/10/90	21/10/92	21/10/94	21/10/96	
23.	Guinea-Bissau	21/10/88	21/10/90	21/10/92	21/10/94	21/10/96	
24.	Kenya	10/05/94	10/05/96	10/05/98	10/05/00	10/05/02	
25.	Lesotho	27/05/94	27/05/96	27/05/98	27/05/00	27/05/02	
26.	Liberia	27/10/88	21/10/90	21/10/92	21/10/94	21/10/96	
27.	Libya	26/06/89	26/06/91	26/06/93	26/06/95	26/06/97	

Cont./

No.	State Party	1st Report to be submitted on	2nd Report to be submitted on	3rd Report to be submitted on	4th Report to be submitted on	5th Report to be submitted on	Reports submitted but not yet considered
28.	Madagascar	19/06/94	19/06/96	19/06/98	19/06/00	19/06/02	
29.	Malawi	23/05/92	23/05/94	23/05/96	23/05/98	23/05/00	
30.	Mali	21/10/88	21/10/90	21/10/92	21/10/94	21/10/96	
31.	Mauritania	21/10/88	21/10/90	21/10/92	21/10/94	21/10/96	
32.	Mauritius	07/10/92	07/10/94	07/10/96	07/10/98	07/10/00	
33.	Mozambique	07/06/92	07/06/94	07/06/96	07/06/98	07/06/00	
34.	Namibia	16/12/94	16/12/96	16/12/98	16/12/00	16/12/02	
35.	Niger	21/10/88	21/10/90	21/10/92	21/10/94	21/10/96	
36.	Nigeria	21/10/88	21/10/90	21/10/92	21/10/94	21/10/96	
37.	Rwanda	21/10/88	21/10/90	21/10/92	21/10/94	21/10/96	
38.	SADR	21/10/88	21/10/90	21/10/92	21/10/94	21/10/96	
39.	Sao Tome & Principe	21/10/88	21/10/90	21/10/92	21/10/94	21/10/96	
40.	Senegal	21/10/88	21/10/90	21/10/92	21/10/94	21/10/96	
41.	Seychelles	30/07/94	30/07/96	30/07/98	30/07/00	30/07/02	Initial report
42.	Sierra Leone	21/10/88	21/10/90	21/10/92	21/10/94	21/10/96	
43.	Somalia	21/10/88	21/10/90	21/10/92	21/10/94	21/10/96	
44.	South Africa	07/07/98	09/07/00	09/07/02	09/07/03	07.07/06	
45.	Sudan	21/10/88	21/10/90	21/10/92	21/10/94	21/10/96	Initial report
46.	Swaziland	15/09/97	15/09/99	15/09/01	15/09/03	15/09/05	
47.	Tanzania	21/10/88	21/10/90	21/10/92	21/10/94	21/10/96	
48.	Togo	21/10/88	21/10/90	21/10/92	21/10/94	21/10/96	
49.	Tunisia	21/10/88	21/10/90	21/10/92	21/10/94	21/10/96	
50.	Uganda	21/10/88	21/10/90	21/10/92	21/10/94	21/10/96	
51.	Zaire	28/10/89	28/10/91	28/10/93	28/10/95	28/10/97	
52.	Zambia	21/10/88	21/10/90	21/10/92	21/10/94	21/10/96	
53.	Zimbabwe	21/10/88	21/10/90	21/10/92	21/10/94	21/10/96	2nd & 3rd reports

* has presented its preliminary report
† has presented its preliminary report and second periodic report
** has presented its preliminary, and submitted its second and third report
(1) not yet ratified the African Charter

ANNEX IV

Resolution on the Ratification of the Convention on Anti-personnel Mines

The African Commission on Human and Peoples' Rights, meeting at its 24th Ordinary Session from 22–31 October 1998 in Banjul, The Gambia,

Taking note of the various international and regional meetings ushering in the coming into force of the Ottawa Convention as September 1998, prohibiting the production, use, transfer and stockpiling of anti-personnel mines,

Emphasising that to date only five countries have ratified this Convention, and that more than 15 African Countries are yet to sign it,

Noting that the African continent remains the most heavily mined region of the world,

Observing that anti-personnel mines continue to kill and mutilate vast populations including a great number of women and children,

CALLS ON African States to sign and ratify without delay the Ottawa Treaty on the prohibition, production, use, transfer, stockpiling of anti-personnel mines;

WELCOMES the International campaign against anti-personnel mines urged by the Human Rights activists and contribute to the implementation of the various action plans against the use, production, transfer and stockpiling of anti-personnel mines.

Resolution on the Ratification of the Treaty on the International Criminal Court

The African Commission on Human and Peoples' Rights, meeting at its 24th Ordinary Session from 22–31 October 1998 in Banjul, The Gambia,

Considering that the 67th ordinary session of the OAU Council of Ministers, meeting at Addis Ababa in February 1998, adopted the Dakar Declaration on an International Criminal Court,

Considering that the 34th Assembly of Heads of State and Government of the OAU, meeting at Ouagadougou in June 1998, also adopted the Dakar Declaration on an International Criminal Court,

Considering that around 43 States Members of the OAU participated in the Diplomatic Conference on the International Criminal Court (ICC) in Rome, June/July 1998, and that African countries supported the creation of a permanent, independent, impartial and effective ICC,

Considering that the statute of the ICC was adopted at Rome on 16 July 1998 by 120 states, of which more than 40 were African Countries,

Considering that 19 African states have signed the statute, demonstrating the will of African countries to create an effective ICC,

Considering the serious and troubling situation of human rights in Africa, especially in zones of armed conflict, and taking note of the universal consensus to end impunity for crimes which shock the conscience of humanity,

CALLS ON all States Parties to the African Charter on Human and Peoples' Rights to carry out all the appropriate constitutional procedures to sign and ratify the Rome treaty on the International Criminal Court; and

INVITES THEM to take all necessary legislative and administrative steps to bring national laws and policies into conformity with the statute.

Banjul, 31st October 1998.

Resolution on Nigeria's Return to a Democratic System

The African Commission on Human and Peoples' Rights, meeting at its 24th Ordinary Session from 22–30 October 1998 in Banjul, The Gambia,

Considering paragraph two of the preamble to the African Commission on Human and Peoples' Rights which stipulates that "freedom, equality, justice and dignity are essential objectives for the achievement of the legitimate aspirations of the African peoples",

Recalling the firm conviction of the States Parties to the African Commission on Human and Peoples' Rights of their duty "to promote and protect human and peoples' rights and freedoms, taking into account the importance traditionally attached to these rights and freedoms in Africa",

NOTES with satisfaction the positive evolution in the field of human rights, the promises and democratic advances made by the Nigerian Government since the end of June 1998;

WELCOMES the release of the Ogoni prisoners and other detainees previously held in the Port Harcourt central prison and the gradual return to the country of numerous political exiles in favour of democratic transition in Nigeria;

EXHORTS the Government of Nigeria to persist in its efforts the course of democracy, respect for, and protection of human rights;

ASSURES the Government of its total support and readiness to help it in its task of rebuilding in Nigeria a democratic society which respects human rights.

Resolution on the Ratification of the Additional Protocol on the Creation of the African Court on Human and Peoples' Rights

The African Commission on Human and Peoples' Rights, meeting at its 24th Ordinary Session from 22–30 October 1998 in Banjul, The Gambia,

Recalling the adoption of the protocol by the 34th Ordinary Session of the Assembly of Heads of State and Government of the OAU, held from 8–10 June 1998, in Ouagadougou, Burkina Faso, and its signature by 32 African countries,

Considering that the protocol on the African Court has been ratified by only two States, out of the 53 States Parties to the African Charter,

Also considering the serious and troubling state of human rights in Africa, especially, in zones of conflict, and taking into account the need to guarantee and protect human rights by an effective, independent and impartial African Court, which would perfectly complement the mission of the African Commission,

APPEALS to the States Parties to the African Charter on Human and Peoples' Rights to activate the appropriate constitutional procedures in order for them to sign and ratify the protocol on the African Court of Human and Peoples' Rights within the shortest possible time.

Resolution on the Co-operation Between the African Commission on Human and Peoples' Rights and NGOs Having Observer Status with the Commission

Background

1. Article 45 of the African Charter on Human and Peoples' Rights maps out the mandate of the Commission as follows:

(i) to promote human rights;
(ii) to protect human rights;
(iii) to interpret provisions of the African Charter;
(iv) any other tasks that may be referred to the Commission by the OAU.

2. In the performance of its tasks and to enhance its efficiency, the Charter also makes provision for the Commission to work with other partners in the field of human rights. Article 45(1)(c) of the African Charter on Human and Peoples' Rights provides that the Commission shall co-operate with other African and International Institutions concerned with the promotion and protection of human and peoples' rights. In accordance with this article, the African Commission on Human and Peoples' Rights has since its inception granted observer status to 231 human rights NGOs.

3. The granting of this status enables the NGOs to participate directly in the Commission's activities. Rules 75 and 76 of the Rules of Procedure of the African Commission ensure this participation in the Commission's Sessions by requesting the Secretary to the Commission to inform all NGOs with observer status of the days and agenda of the forthcoming Session, at least four weeks before the Session. NGOs with observer status can then authorize their representatives to attend and participate in the public Sessions of the Commission and its subsidiary bodies. Participation can be in either written or oral forms.

4. Apart from participating in the sessions, all documents such as final communiqués of the session and other relevant documents have to be sent by the Secretariat to all NGOs with observer status.

5. Another benefit enjoyed by NGOs with observer status is the preparation of "shadow" reports on the human rights situation in their countries. These "shadow" reports enable the Commission to have a constructive dialogue with a State representatives when that country's periodic report is being considered.

6. During its 11th Ordinary Session held in Tunis, Tunisia, the Commission reiterated its desire to co-operate with NGOs in the promotion and protection of human and peoples' rights on the continent. In order to encourage and ensure reciprocal

commitment on the part of its NGO partners, it was decided that all NGOs that have observer status with the Commission should submit their activity reports once every two (2) years from the date the said status was granted.

7. The Commission's readiness to co-operate with national, regional and international Human Rights NGOs is further emphasized, and its importance stressed in the Mauritius Plan of Action 1996–2001, which was adopted at the Commission's 20th Session. The said Plan proposes the creation of an exchange and communication network, especially with regards to NGOs operating in Africa, to establish an appropriate mechanism for promotional and protective activities in Africa. This network is intended to enhance co-operation amongst NGOs and the Commission concurrently.

8. The present status of submission of the activity reports of NGOs in compliance with the decision taken at the 11th Session of the Commission, indeed leaves much to be desired. Out of 231 NGOs that had been granted observer status by October 1998, 197 were expected to have submitted all due and overdue reports. Out of this number, only 26 have submitted all their reports up to date, 48 have submitted some of the reports and 114 have submitted none at all. This clearly shows the extent of the lack of commitment on the part of these NGOs.

9. It is also clear that the Commission continues granting observer status to NGOs, while it is not adequately informed by most of them about what work they are doing in the sphere of human rights or how they are helping to promote and/or protect human rights in Africa. The very essence of having NGOs as partners in creating a culture of recognition of and respect for human rights on the African continent is thereby betrayed.

10. Note must also be taken of the fact that some of these NGOs on occasion, have been found to use their granted status to raise funds which is sometimes totally misused, or is used for purposes other than the promotion and protection of human rights. The fear, therefore, that some of them may have either changed their mandate or shifted their focus to issues other than human rights becomes legitimate.

11. To address this situation, it is hereby recommended that the Commission revise its criteria for granting and enjoying observer status.

12. The Conference of the Heads of States and Governments of the Organization of Africa (OAU), as its Thirty-Fourth Ordinary Session [AHG/Dec. 126 (XXXIV) para. 3], requested the African Commission to review its criteria for granting and enjoying observer status to NGOs.

Therefore, the African Commission on Human and Peoples' Rights, meeting at its 24th Ordinary Session from 22–31 October 1998, in Banjul, The Gambia,

Recalling that the African Charter on Human and Peoples' Rights, which entered into force on 21 October 1986, mandates the African Commission on Human and Peoples' Rights under Article 45(1)(c) to co-operate with other African national and international institutions concerned with the promotion and protection of human and peoples' rights,

Recalling further its decision taken during its Second Ordinary Session held in Dakar, Senegal, in February 1988, to grant observer status to NGOs working in the field of human rights in Africa,

Also recalling Rules 75 and 76 of the Commission's Rules of Procedure which further emphasise this co-operation,

Aware of the Mauritius Plan of Action which emphasises the importance of co-operation with NGOs,

Convinced that such co-operation will provide NGOs with the support and opportunity to work closely with the Commission, and recognising the invaluable role institutions such as NGOs can play in the enhancement of human rights in Africa,

Further convinced that for any meaningful co-operation to take place, there has to be commitment and reciprocity on the part of all parties,

Bearing in mind the decision taken at its 11th Ordinary Session requiring all NGOs having observer status to submit their activity reports to the Commission at least once every two years,

Convinced that the submission of activity reports by NGOs is a way of enhancing the protection of human rights, and the co-operation between the Commission and NGOs,

Firmly convinced that the said reports can be very invaluable not only to the Commission, but also to the ever increasing number of human rights workers around the world,

Considering the request of the Conference of Heads of State and Governments of the OAU to review the criteria for granting observer status to NGOs,

EXPRESSES its profound appreciation to those NGOs which have submitted their reports regularly;

NOTES WITH CONCERN the fact that the majority of NGOs whose reports are due have not done so, and have ceased communicating with the Commission;

DECIDES that representatives of NGOs that have applied for observer status should be present to be interviewed during the consideration of their application;

DECIDES ALSO to review, in conformity with the Decision AHG/Dec. 126 (XXXIV) by the Conference of the Heads of State and Government, the criteria for obtaining and enjoying observer status with the Commission;

INVITES NGOs which have observer status with the Commission but which have not yet submitted their overdue reports, to do so before the 27th Ordinary Session of the Commission;

DECIDES FINALLY to revoke observer status of any NGOs that do not submit any activity reports at the 27th Ordinary Session;

REQUESTS the Secretary to the Commission to submit a report on the implementation of this resolution at each Session.

Resolution on Granting Observer Status to National Human Rights Institutions in Africa

Background

In the preamble of the African Charter on Human and Peoples' Rights adopted at the 18th Conference of Heads of State and Government in Nairobi in June 1981, Member States of the Organization of African Unity reaffirmed

> "their adherence to the principles of human and peoples' rights and freedoms contained in the declarations, conventions and other instruments adopted by the Organization of African Unity, the Movement of Non-Aligned Countries and United Nations."

In the same preamble, African Countries pledged to "coordinate and intensify their cooperation and efforts to achieve a better life for the peoples of Africa and to promote international cooperation having due regard to the Charter of the United Nations and the Universal Declaration of Human Rights".

With the aim of concretizing this commitment, Article 26 of the African Charter on Human and Peoples' Rights stipulates that :

> "States Parties to the present Charter shall have the duty to guarantee the independence of the Courts and shall allow the establishment and improvement of appropriate national institutions entrusted with the promotion and protection of the rights and freedoms guaranteed by the present Charter."

The use of the word "allow" suggests not just encouraging and promoting the establishment of National Institutions but also developing a mutually cooperative relationship in order to "promote and ensure, through teaching, education and publication, respect for the rights and freedoms contained in the present charter" (Article 25).

National Institutions, therefore, are an essential partner in the implementation of the Charter at National Level. It is noted that the Mauritius Plan of Action (1996–2001) envisage workshops on national institutions as one of its promotional activities. It also seeks the cooperation of national institutions in fulfilling its mandate of promoting and protecting human and peoples' rights.

Finally, the 2nd Seminar of Ambassadors of African States to the OAU held in Addis Ababa, 8–9 September 1998 recognized the importance of National Institutions and urged Governments to accord them appropriate support.

African States in general and the African Commission on Human and Peoples' Rights in particular took an active part in the deliberations of the World Conference on Human Rights which was held in Vienna in June 1993. The Vienna Conference's Declaration and Programme of Action reaffirmed:

> "the important and constructive role played by national institutions for the promotion and protection of Human Rights, in particular in their advisory role to the competent authorities, their role at remedying human rights violations, in the dissemination of information and education in human rights."

The World Conference on Human Rights also encouraged: "the establishment and strengthening of national institutions" and recognized "that it is the right of each State to choose the framework which is best suited to its particular needs at the national level".

At this Conference a formal status was granted to the International Committee for Coordination of National Institutions as a statutory liaison instrument of the United Nations system. This Committee shall organize a biennial world meeting of national institutions.

At the International level, the United Nations Human Rights Commission approved by its Resolution 1992/54 of 3 March 1992 under the heading "Principles Relating to the Status of National Institutions", also known as the Paris Principles, rules which define the mandate of such institutions. The General Assembly of the United Nations endorsed these principles in its Resolution 48/144 of 20 December 1993.

The objective of these principles is to guarantee the independence of national institutions in their work and pluralism in their composition. The central mission of the national institutions is to play an advisory role to the government, parliament and other relevant bodies and authorities involved in giving opinion and making recommendations on all issues related to the promotion and protection of human rights.

In Africa, the trend to establish national institutions has continued to develop especially after 1991. At present Africa has more than twenty (20) national human rights institutions which are represented in the International Coordination Committee by Cameroon, Morocco, South Africa and Togo.

At the first conference of national human rights institutions in Africa held in Yaounde, Cameroon, from 5–7 February 1996 participants adopted the Yaounde Declaration which commended "the creation of new National Institutions in Africa" and expressed the hope that these institutions will be given "a proper representative status on the African Commission". At the 2nd Conference of African National Institutions held in Durban, 1–3 July 1998, the need for a clear relationship and a unique status in the African Commission were reiterated.

Since the Mauritius session, the issue of African national human rights institutions has always been included on the agenda of meetings of the Commission. A paper on this subject was presented by Commissioner K. Rezag-Bara at the 21st Ordinary Session of the Commission held in Nouakchott, Mauritania in April 1997. The Commission decided at its 22nd Session held in Banjul in November 1997 to entrust Commissioners K. Rezag-Bara and N. Barney Pityana with the task of preparing a draft resolution on the advisory status of national institutions in the African Commission on Human and Peoples' Rights. The matter was deferred for finalization at this session.

Therefore, the African Commission on Human and Peoples' Rights, meeting at its 24th Ordinary Session from 22–31t October 1998, in Banjul, The Gambia,

Considering the preamble of the African Charter on Human and Peoples' Rights which reaffirms the adherence of African States to "human and peoples' rights and freedoms contained in the declarations, conventions and other instruments adopted by the organization of African Unity, the Movement of Non-Aligned countries and the United Nations",

Considering that Article 26 of the African Charter on Human and Peoples' Rights stipulates that "States Parties to the present Charter shall have the duty to . . . allow the establishment and the improvement of appropriate national institutions entrusted with the promotion and protection of rights",

Considering the recommendation adopted in the Programme of Action of the World Conference on Human Rights held in Vienna, Austria in June 1993 and United

Nations resolutions on human rights, particularly resolution 1992/54 of 3 March 1992 of the Commission Human Rights and resolution 48/134 of 20 December 1993 of the United Nations General Assembly,

Considering the decisions, resolutions, recommendations and the final declaration adopted by the first conference of national human rights institutions in Africa held in Yaounde, Cameroon from 5–7 February 1996 and the 2nd Conference held in Durban, South Africa on 1–3 July 1998,

Convinced of the importance of the role of national institutions in the promotion and protection of human rights and in creating public awareness in Africa with regard to the institutional defense of human rights,

1. COMMENDS the increasing interests shown by African states in establishing and strengthening national institutions for the protection and promotion of human rights based on the principles of independence and pluralism;

2. RECOGNIZES that it is the right of each state to establish, according to its sovereign prerogatives and within the most appropriate legislative framework, a national institution charged with the promotion and protection of human rights according to internationally recognized norms;

3. NOTES WITH SATISFACTION the significant participation of African National Institutions in the deliberations of the sessions of the African Commission on Human and Peoples' Rights and registers positively the wish expressed by several institutions to be granted an observer status with the Commission;

4. DECIDES to grant special observer status to any African national institution established in Africa and functioning according to internationally recognized norms and standards.

(a) that the following criteria for the status of affiliated institution shall apply:

- the national institution should be duly established by law, constitution or by decree;
- that it shall be a national institution of a state party to the African Charter;
- that the national institution should conform to the Principles relating to the Status of National Institutions, also known as the Paris Principles, adopted by the General Assembly of the United Nations under Resolution 48/144 of 20 December 1993;
- that a National Institution shall formally apply for status in the African Commission;

(b) that such institutions shall have the following rights and responsibilities:

- be invited to sessions of the African Commission according to rule 6 of the Rules and Procedures;
- be represented in public sessions of the commission and its subsidiary bodies;
- participate, without voting rights, in deliberations on issues which are of interest to them and to submit proposals which may be put to the vote at the request of any member of the Commission;

(c) that any national institution shall be required to submit reports to the Commission every two years on its activities in the promotion and protection of the rights enshrined in the Charter; and

(d) that the National Institution will assist the Commission in the promotion and protection of human rights at national level.

Resolution on the Peace Process in Guinea Bissau

The African Commission on Human and Peoples' Rights meeting at its 24th Ordinary Session in Banjul, The Gambia, from 22–31 October 1998,

Concerned by the situation prevailing in Guinea Bissau and especially by the numerous violations of human rights resulting from the situation of war (conflict) in this country since June 1998,

Noting with satisfaction the favourable evolution of the conflict towards direct dialogue between the belligerents,

RECOGNIZES the efforts initiated by the Economic Community of West African States (ECOWAS) and the Portuguese speaking countries community (PSCC) in order to find a peaceful settlement of the Guinea Bissau conflict;

COMMENDS the continuation of negotiations between parties to the conflict and pays tribute to H.E. Colonel (Rtd) Yahya Jammeh, President of the Republic of the Gambia for his mediation;

EXPRESSES ITS SUPPORT to the ongoing peace process and calls on parties to the conflict and Member States of the ECOWAS and PSCC to take necessary measures to ensure restoration of peace in Guinea Bissau.

Resolution on the Criteria for Granting and Enjoying Observer Status to Non-Governmental Organisations Working in the Field of Human Rights with the African Commission on Human and Peoples' Rights

The African Commission on Human and Peoples' Rights, meeting in its 25th Ordinary Session, held in Bujumbura, Burundi, from 26 April to 5 May 1999,

Considering the provisions of Article 45 of the African Charter on Human and Peoples' Rights, which establishes the competence and determines the mandate of the Commission,

Considering the Grand Baie (Mauritius) declaration and plan of action, adopted at the 1st African Ministerial Conference on Human Rights (12–16 April 1999), which "recognises the contribution made by African NGOs to the promotion and protection of human rights in Africa",

Considering the provisions of Chapter XIII (Articles 75 and 76) of the Rules of Procedure of the Commission regarding representation of, and consultation with NGOs by the African Commission on Human and Peoples' Rights,

Considering that since its establishment in October 1987, 231 African and international non-governmental organisations have been granted observer status with the African Commission on Human and Peoples' Rights,

Considering the Decision AHG/Dec. 126 (XXXIV) of the Assembly of Heads of State and Government which requests the African Commission on Human and Peoples' Rights to "undertake a review of the criteria for observer status with the Commission, with a view to enhanced efficiency and co-operation, and to suspend the granting of the said status until the adoption of the new criteria",

Convinced of the need to strengthen its co-operation and partnership with NGOs working the field of human rights,

ADOPTS the new criteria for granting and enjoying observer status, the text of which is annexed to the present resolution;DECIDES that the new criteria shall immediately enter into force;REQUESTS the Secretary to the Commission to report at every Ordinary Session on the implementation of the present resolution.

Annex: Criteria for the Granting of and for Maintaining Observer Status with the African Commission on Human and Peoples' Rights

Chapter I:

1. All Non-Governmental Organisations applying for observer status with the African Commission on Human and Peoples' Rights shall be expected to submit a documented application to the Secretariat of the Commission, with a view to showing their willingness and capability work for the realisation of the objectives of the African Charter on Human and Peoples' Rights.

2. All organisations applying for observer status with the African Commission shall consequently:

(a) Have objectives and activities in consonance with the fundamental principles and objectives enunciated in the OAU Charter and in the African Charter on Human and Peoples' Rights;
(b) Be organisations working in the field of human rights;
(c) Declare their financial resources.

3. To this effect, such an Organisation shall be requested to provide:

(a) A written application addressed to the Secretariat stating its intentions, at least three months prior to the Ordinary Session of the Commission which shall decide on the application, in order to give the Secretariat sufficient time in which to process the said application;
(b) Its statutes, proof of its legal existence, a list of its members, its constituent organs, its sources of funding, its last financial statement, as well as a statement on its activities.

4. The statement of activities shall cover the past and present activities of the Organisation, its plan of action and any other information that may help to determine the identity of the organisation, its purpose and objectives, as well as its field of activities.

5. No application for Observer Status shall be put forward for examination by the Commission without having been previously processed by the Secretariat.

6. The Commission's Bureau shall designate a rapporteur to examine the dossiers. The Commission's decision shall be notified without delay to the applicant NGO.

Participation of Observers in Proceedings of the African Commission

Chapter II:

1.

(a) All observers shall be invited to be present at the opening and closing sessions of all Sessions of the African Commission;
(b) An observer accredited by the Commission shall not participate in its proceedings in any manner other than as provided for in the Rules of Procedure governing the conduct of sessions of the African Commission.

2. All observers shall have access to the documents of the Commission subject to the condition that such documents:

(a) shall not be of a confidential nature;
(b) deal with issues that are of relevance to their interests.

The distribution of general information documents of the African Commission shall be free of charge; the distribution of specialised documents shall be on a paid-for basis, except where reciprocal arrangements are in place.

3. Observers may be invited specially to be present at closed sessions dealing with issues of particular interest to them.

4. Observers may be authorised by the Chairman of the African Commission to make a statement on an issue that concerns them, subject to the text of the statement having been provided, with sufficient lead-time, to the Chairman of the Commission through the Secretary to the Commission.

5. The Chairman of the Commission may give the floor to observers to respond to questions directed at them by participants.

6. Observers may request to have issues of a particular interest to them included in the provisional agenda of the African Commission, in accordance with the provisions of the Rules of Procedure.

Relations Between the African Commission and Observers

Chapter III:

1. Organisations enjoying observer status shall undertake to establish close relations of co-operation with the African Commission and to engage in regular consultations with it on all matters of common interest.

2. NGOs enjoying observer status shall present their activity reports to the Commission every two years.

3. Administrative arrangements shall be made, whenever necessary, to determine the modalities of this co-operation.

Final Provisions

Chapter IV:

1. The provisions of the General Convention on the privileges and immunities of the OAU and those of the Headquarters Agreement of the African Commission shall not apply to observers except as regards the granting of visas.
2. The Commission reserves the right to take the following measures against NGOs that are in default of their obligations:

- non-participation in sessions;
- denial of documents and information;
- denial of the opportunity to propose items to be included in the Commission's agenda and of participating in its proceedings.

3. Observer status may be suspended or withdrawn from any organisation that does not fulfil the present criteria, after deliberation by the Commission.

Resolution on the Situation in Comoros

The African Commission on Human and Peoples' Rights, meeting in its 25th Ordinary Session, in Bujumbura, Burundi, from 26 April to 5 May 1999,

Recalling the military coup d'état which took place on 30 April 1999 in Comoros, which resulted in the overthrow of the Government of the interim President, Mr. Tadjeddine Bensaid by the Army Chief of Staff, Colonel Azali Assoumane,

Recalling its resolution on military regimes in Africa, adopted at its 16th Ordinary Session, held in Banjul (The Gambia), from 25 October to 3 November 1994,

Noting that the Declaration and Plan of Action of Grand Baie (Mauritius), adopted by the First Ministerial Conference on Human Rights in Africa (12–16 April 1999) recognises that the causes of human rights violations in Africa include unconstitutional changes of government,

Reaffirming the fundamental principle that for a government to be legitimate it must be freely chosen by the people and through democratically elected representatives,

Recognising that the take-over of power by force is contrary to the provisions of Articles 13(1) and 20(1) of the African Charter on Human and Peoples' Rights and that accession to power by military regimes through coups d'état constitutes an intolerable infraction of the democratic principles of the rule of law,

DECLARES that the military coup d'état in Comoros is a grave and unacceptable violation of the rights of the Comorian People to freely choose their government;

CALLS ON the de facto military authorities in this country to ensure that:

(1) The fundamental rights and freedoms contained in the constitutional provisions of Comoros are given pre-eminence over any other form of legislation that may emanate from the authorities in place.
(2) The independence of the judicial power, especially as regards its mission to guarantee inalienable human rights, is respected.
(3) The reinstatement of democratically instituted civilian rule is initiated without delay.

Resolution on the Situation in Niger

The African Commission on Human and Peoples' Rights, meeting in its 25th Ordinary Session, in Bujumbura (Burundi), from 26 April to 5 May 1999,

Recalling the military coup d'état which took place on 9 April 1999 in Niger, which during of President Ibrahim Mainassara Bare was assassinated and his Government overthrown by the Presidential Guard under the Command of Colonel Wanke,

Recalling its resolution on military regimes in Africa, adopted at its 16th Ordinary Session, held in Banjul (The Gambia), from 25 October to 3 November 1994,

Noting that the Declaration and Plan of Action of Grand Baie (Mauritius), adopted by the First Ministerial Conference on Human Rights in Africa (12–16 April 1999) recognises that the causes of human rights violations in Africa include unconstitutional changes of government,

Reaffirming the fundamental principle that for a government to be legitimate it must be freely chosen by the people and through democratically elected representatives,

Recognising that the take-over of power by force is contrary to the provisions of Articles 13(1) and 20(1) of the African Charter on Human and Peoples' Rights and that accession to power by military regimes through coups d'état constitutes an intolerable infraction of the democratic principles of the rule of law,

DECLARES that the military coup d'état in Niger is a grave and unacceptable violation of the rights of the Nigerian People to freely choose their government;

CALLS ON the de facto military authorities in this country to ensure that:

(1) The fundamental rights and freedoms contained in the constitutional provisions of Niger are given pre-eminence over any other form of legislation that may emanate from the authorities in place.
(2) The independence of the judicial power, especially as regards its mission to guarantee inalienable human rights, is respected.
(3) The reinstatement of democratically instituted civilian rule is initiated without delay.

Resolution on the Ratification of the African Charter on the Rights and Welfare of the Child

The African Commission on Human and Peoples' Rights, meeting in its 25th Ordinary Session, in Bujumbura, Burundi, from 26 April to 5 May 1999,

Taking note that the persistence of situations of war, famine and underdevelopment bring about particularly negative consequences for the African child population, especially their physical, intellectual and psychological development,

Considering that one of the consequences of this situation is manifested all over the continent, with thousands of displaced, refugee, handicapped, orphaned children, living in conditions of malnutrition, sickness, even misery, are obliged to do illegal labour, prostitution and delinquency, without any prospects,

Convinced that the promotion and defence of the rights of the child is the only way of safeguarding the future of the African continent,

Considering that the African Charter on the Rights and Welfare of the Child constitutes a prime legal framework towards this end, and that, consequently, its entry into force is urgent,

INSTANTLY CALLS ON all States Parties to the African Charter on Human and Peoples' Rights that are yet to do so to ratify the said Charter, to allow its entry into force without further delay.

Resolution on the Extension of the Mandate of the Special Rapporteur on Prisons and Conditions of Detention in Africa

The African Commission on Human and Peoples' Rights, meeting in its 25th Ordinary Session, in Bujumbura, Burundi, from 26 April to 5 May 1999,

Recalling its decision to designate Professor E. V. O. Dankwa to the post of Special Rapporteur on prisons and conditions of detention in Africa, taken at its 20th Ordinary Session,

Considering that the mandate of the Special Rapporteur is of two years' duration, subject to renewal,

Considering further that the initial term of two years of the Special Rapporteur comes to an end with the 24th Ordinary Session,

Emphasising the importance of the work of the Special Rapporteur as regards the search for solutions to the problems arising from the restriction of the freedom of the individual, in particular,

DECIDES TO EXTEND the mandate of the Special Rapporteur on prisons and conditions of detention in Africa for a period of two years, with effect from 31 October 1998.

Resolution on the Designation of a Special Rapporteur on the Rights of Women in Africa

The African Commission on Human and Peoples' Rights, meeting in its 25th Ordinary Session, in Bujumbura, Burundi, 26 April to 5 May 1999,

Recalling the United Nations Convention on the Elimination of all Forms of Discrimination against Women,

Recalling further the provisions of Article 18(3) of the African Charter on Human and Peoples' Rights,

Referring to the provisions of Article 45(1)(a) of the African Charter on Human and Peoples' Rights,

Recognising the need to place particular emphasis on the problems and rights specific to women in Africa,

Recalling further the decision taken by the Commission at its 23rd Ordinary Session, held in Banjul (The Gambia) to designate Mrs. Julienne Ondziel-Gnelenga to the post of Special Rapporteur on the Rights of Women in Africa,

DESIGNATES Mrs. Julienne Ondziel-Gnelenga to the post of Special Rapporteur on the Rights of Women in Africa for a period of two years, subject to renewal, with effect from 31 October 1998.

Resolution Concerning the Republic of Seychelles' Refusal to Present its Initial Report

The African Commission on Human and Peoples' Rights, meeting in its 25th Ordinary Session, in Bujumbura, Burundi, 26 April to 5 May 1999,

Considering that, in accordance with Article 62 of the Charter, the Republic of Seychelles has been summoned, at several occasions, to present at its 17th session, its initial report submitted on September 1994,

Considering that the Republic of Seychelles, despite repeated demands made to its Government, has refused, on several occasions, to abide by the Commission's request, under the pretext that the resources to implement such an obligation were not provided by the State,

Considering that such a persistent behaviour represents a deliberate violation of the Charter to which the Republic of Seychelles is party,

Considering that the Commission, at its 25th ordinary session in Bujumbura, Burundi, firmly condemned this unspeakable behaviour on behalf of an OAU Member State, party to the Charter,

INVITES the Heads of State and Government Conference to be held in Algiers, in July 1999, to express their disapproval of such a persistent refusal that amounts to a deliberate violation of the Charter by the Republic of Seychelles;

REQUESTS the Conference to invite Seychelles to abide by the Charter and to consider the appropriate measures to be taken against the Republic of Seychelles.

ANNEX V

Communications

1. 102/93 Constitutional Rights Project and Civil Liberties Organisation/ Nigeria

Rapporteur:
17th Session: Commissioner Umozurike
18th Session: Commissioner Kisanga
19th Session: Commissioner Umozurike
20th Session: Commissioner Dankwa
21st Session: Commissioner Dankwa
22nd Session: Commissioner Dankwa
23rd Session : Commissioner Dankwa
24th Session : Commissioner Dankwa

The facts as submitted by the author:

(1) On 12 June 1993 a presidential election was held in Nigeria. Both foreign and local election monitoring groups observed the conduct of the election and were generally satisfied that the elections was free and fair.

(2) Three days later, the National Electoral Commission began announcing the election results. The National Electoral Commission announced the results from 14 states including the Federal Capital Territory, Abuja, before it was restrained by an Abuja High Court from announcing the election results. On 23 June the Federal Military Government announced the annulment of the 12 June election results. Various reasons were given for this action. The communication alleges that these reasons included the fact that the military government was not happy that Abiola, the Social Democratic candidate, appeared to have won the election.

(3) Dissatisfied with the decision of the Federal Military Government to annul election results, Abiola, together with the Governors of all the States controlled by the Social Democratic Party, went to the Supreme Court to seek redress. Shortly thereafter the Federal Military Government promulgated several Decrees ousting the jurisdiction of the courts and restating the decision of the Nigerian government to annul the election results.

(4) Decree No. 41 of 1993 states in part:

> "Notwithstanding anything contained in the Constitution of the Federal Republic of Nigeria 1979, as amended, the African Charters on Human and Peoples' Rights (Ratification and Enforcement) Act or any other enactment, no proceeding shall lie or be instituted in any court for, or on account of any act matter or thing done or purported to be done in respect of this Decree."

(5) The other Decrees promulgated are Presidential Election (Basic Constitutional and Transitional Provisions) (Repeal) Decree No. 39, 1993; Transition to Civil

Rule (Disqualification and Prohibition of certain Presidential Aspirants) (Repeal) Decree No. 42 1993. These Decrees gave legal backing to the annulment of 12 June election results and ensure that the two presidential candidates were banned from contesting any Presidential elections in the country.

(6) When activists and journalists protested the annulment of the elections, the government arrested and detained many persons, several of whom are named in the communication.

(7) The government also seized thousands of copies of magazines. "The News" Magazine was proscribed by military decree in June 1993. Even prior to its proscription, copies of the magazine were seized by security agents and four of its editors declared wanted by the police. 50,000 copies of "Tempo", a weekly news magazine, were seized by security agents and the police.

State Party's response and observations:

(8) The government has made no written submission in respect of this case. In an oral submission before the Commission (31 March 1996, Ouagadougou, Burkina Faso, Chris Osah, Head of Delegation), the government stated that the elections were held in circumstances that "the government felt were not propitious". The representative of the government stated that "[A]nnulling the election and setting up a government, as was done, to all intents and purposes, was a coup". The government admitted that many people were arrested and detained at the time the elections were annulled, but that "many have now been released".

(9) The government contends that it was within its own constitutional rights to make laws for the order and good governance of the country, which it did in annulling the election results. The government felt that there were irregularities which may not have been detected by the observers and that although the elections may have been adjudged to be free and fair by all, there were fundamental problems which the government could not brush aside. In such circumstances the government decided that rather than put in place a government that was going to create more problems, it should form a different government. The government formed was in any case not a military government but an interim national government in which people from both parties were appointed to serve.

(10) The government maintains that these actions were justified because some people abandoned their offices and went to their villages, creating a chaotic situation. "What the government did was to salvage a situation that was bad. And whatever laws it made at that time, I want this Commission to look at it in terms of [the government] holding a solution to the problem, not as if this were geared to any particular group of people or human rights activities . . . The government felt that it had to avoid chaos and it restored an interim government, rather than even perpetuating its own regime. I think the Commission should look rather carefully into that because it was not an ordinary situation. I could say it was just a military coup." (See above statement of Chris Osah.)

The Complaint:

(11) The complainant alleges violation of the following Articles of the Charter 6 and 13.

Procedure before the Commission:

(12) The communication was received on 29 July 1993.

(13) On 6 January 1994 the Secretariat of the Commission notified the government of Nigeria.

(14) On 22 September 1994 the Secretariat of the Commission sent a reminder to the Ministry of Foreign Affairs.

(15) At the 16th Session, the Commission reiterated the need to send a mission to Nigeria. The Commission also decided to invoke Article 58 of the Charter by writing to the Chairman of the OAU, drawing his attention to the grave violations of human rights in Nigeria.

(16) At its 16th session, the Commission has decided that the communication should be added to the other files that its Members going to Nigeria were to discuss with the military authorities of this country.

(17) At the 17th session, held in March 1995, it was decided that the communication should be added to the cases to be taken up with the authorities by members of the mission to Nigeria.

(18) On 20 April 1995 the Secretariat of the Commission sent letters to both complainants to inform them of this decision.

(19) On 7 June 1995 the Secretariat to the Commission sent a letter to this effect to the Ministry of Foreign Affairs.

(20) At the 18th session, held in Praia, Cape Verde, the Commission renewed its decision to join this file with those to be considered by the mission to Nigeria.

(21) On 20 December 1995 the Secretariat of the Commission sent a letter to each complainant to this effect.

(22) On 20 December 1995 a letter was sent to the government of Nigeria to this effect.

(23) At the 19th session, held in March 1996, these cases were due for a decision on admissibility. The Commission heard Mr. Chidi Anselm Odinkalu who was duly instructed to appear for the complainants in all the cases except the International PEN, and heard Mr. Osah and Mr. Bello for the Nigerian Government in reply.

(24) At the end of the hearing the Commission took a general view on the cases and deferred taking final decision in each case pending the accomplishment of its proposed mission to Nigeria.

(25) The Commission declared the communication admissible. It further decided that all the ten files on Nigeria in respect of which the parties were heard during this session should be entrusted to its mission to Nigeria for consideration during the proposed visit.

(26) On 9 May 1996 a letter was sent to the Nigerian Government informing it that at the 19th session it renewed the decision taken at the 17th session to send a mission to the country. It also stated that the communication would be considered on the merits at the 20th session in October 1996.

(27) On 9 May 1996 letters were sent to both complainants informing them that the communication had been declared admissible at the 19th session and that the Commission had decided to undertake a mission to Nigeria. The merits of the case would be examined at the 20th session.

(28) At the 20th session held in Grand Bay, Mauritius, October 1996, the Commission decided to postpone the final decision on the merits of the case to the next session, awaiting the result of the planned mission to Nigeria.

(29) On 10 December 1996 the Secretariat sent a note verbale to this effect to the government.

(30) On 10 December 1996 the Secretariat sent letters to this effect to the complainants.

(31) On 29 April, the Secretariat received a letter from Mr. Olisa Agbakoba entitled Preliminary objections and observations to the Mission of the Commission which visited Nigeria from 7–14 March 1997. The document was submitted on behalf of Interights with regard to 14 communications, including this one.

(32) Among the objections raised and or observations made were: the neutrality, Credibility and Relevance; and composition of the Mission.

(33) At its 21st session held in April 1997, the Commission postponed taking decision on the merits to the next session, pending the submission of scholarly articles and court case by the complainants to assist it in its decision. The Commission also awaits further analysis of its report of the mission to Nigeria.

(34) On 22 May 1997, the complainants were informed of the Commission's decision, while the State was informed on 28 May 1997.

(35) At the 22nd Ordinary session, the Commission postponed taking a decision to the next session pending a discussion of the Nigerian Mission report.

(36) At the 23rd Ordinary session held in Banjul, The Gambia from 20–29 April 1998, the Commission postponed consideration of this case due to lack of time.

(37) On 25 June 1998, the Secretariat of the Commission sent letters to the parties involved informing them of the status of the case.

(38) During the 24th Ordinary session, the complainants furnished the Commission with a "supplementary submission on pending communications on Nigeria", basically urging the Commission to continue consideration of communications against Nigeria including the instant one because the violations have not abated, and the change in government following the death of General Sani Abacha has not changed any State responsibility of Nigeria.

Law:

Admissibility:

(39) Article 56 of the African Charter reads:

> "Communications . . . shall be considered if they:
> Are sent after exhausting local remedies, if any, unless it is obvious that this procedure is unduly prolonged, . . ."

(40) The annulment of the elections was brought before various Nigerian courts by various parties, as was the seizure of the magazines. None of these actions

resulted in a remedy of the prejudice alleged, either reinstatement of the election results or compensation for the confiscated magazines.

(41) Additionally, the jurisdiction of the courts to entertain these actions in the first place is in serious question. Decree No. 43, like almost all decrees promulgated by the military government, contains ouster clause which specifies that the Decree cannot be challenged in the national courts. The ouster clauses create a legal situation in which the judiciary can provide no check on the executive branch of government. A few courts in the Lagos district have occasionally found that they have jurisdiction; in 1995 the Court of Appeal in Lagos, relying on common law, found that courts should examine some decrees notwithstanding ouster clauses, where the decree is "offensive and utterly hostile to rationality". (Reprinted in Constitutional Rights Journal.) In a unanimous opinion the court of Appeal Holden at Lagos on 12 December 1996 in the case of Chief Gani Fawehinmi v General Sani Abacha, Attorney-General of the Federation, State Security Services, Inspector General of Police, held that the African Charter being the joint effort of States, no legislative body in Nigeria could oust its operation and application in Nigeria. Dr. A. H. Yadudu, Special Adviser (Legal Matters) to the head of State of Nigeria underscored the importance of this case in a written address to the members of the Commission to Nigeria on Friday, 14 March 1997. However, it is fair to state that at the time the case came before the Commission no effective legal remedy existed in Nigeria of which the appellants could avail themselves.

(42) Furthermore, the Constitution (Modification and Suspension) specifies that even decrees that may lack an internal ouster clause cannot be challenged. Thus, Nigerians face huge legal obstacles in challenging any new law.

(43) The Commission, in its decision on communication 129/94, decided that in this situation, "it is reasonable to presume that domestic remedies will not only be prolonged but are certain to yield no results." (ACHPR/S1/129/94: 8).

(44) For these reasons the Commission declared the communication admissible.

Merits:

(45) In his presentation at the 19th session, the representative of the complainants expressed his view that an amicable resolution of the alleged violation of Article 13, concerning the annulled elections, was impossible because the government had already indicated that the issue was not negotiable. The representative of the complainant requested the Commission to clarify the legal situation by indicating if there had been a violation of the Charter.

(46) The government of Nigeria, through its official representative, referred to "irregularities that may not have been detected by the [international] observers" and that "though the elections may have been adjudged free and fair by all", they were held in "circumstances that the government felt were not propitious". (See statement of Osah, above.) The government stated that "[A]nnulling the elections and setting up a government, as was done, to all intents and purposes, was a coup". These statements accord with the complainant's argument that the question of the election can no longer be the subject of meaningful negotiation.

(47) Although the present government contends that there were "irregularities" in the elections, it fails to explain what these were. The government acknowledges that international observers of the elections, applying international standards, judged them to be free and fair. Yet it discounted the judgement of these international observers and substituted its own, unsupported, judgment.

(48) A basic premise of international human rights law is that certain standards must be constant across national borders, and governments must be held accountable to these standards. The criteria for what constitutes free and fair elections are internationally agreed upon, and international observers are put in place to apply these criteria. It would be contrary to the logic of international law if a national government with a vested interested in the outcome of an election, were the final arbiter of whether the election took place in accordance with international standards. In the case the government does not even attempt to defend its decision to overrule the judgement of international observers.

(49) Article 13.1 of the Charter reads:

> "Every citizen shall have the right to participate freely in the government of his country, either directly or through freely chosen representatives in accordance with the provisions of the law."

(50) To participate freely in government entails, among other things, the right to vote for the representative of one's choice. An inevitable corollary of this right that the results of free expression of the will of the voters are respected; otherwise, the right to vote freely is meaningless. In light of this, the annulment of the election results, which reflected the free choice of the voters, is in violation of Article 13.1.

(51) Article 20.1 of the Charter provides: "[All peoples] shall freely determine their political status . . . according to the policy they have freely chosen."

(52) The right of a people to determine their "political status" can be interpreted as involving the right of Nigerians to be able to choose freely those persons or party that will govern them. It is the counterpart of the right enjoyed by individuals under Article 13.

(53) The election at issue here, held in conditions adjudged to be free and fair by international observers, was an exercise of the right of Nigerians to freely determine this political status. The subsequent annulment of the results by the authority in power is a violation of this right of the Nigerian people.

(54) Article 6 of the African Charter guarantees that:

> "Every individual shall have the right to liberty and to the security of his person. No one may be deprived of his freedom except for reasons and conditions previously laid down by law. In particular, no one may be arbitrarily arrested or detained."

(55) The government does not dispute that many people, including human rights activists and journalists, were detained without having charges brought against them and without the possibility of bail. The government maintains that "many"

of these individuals have since been released. Where individuals have been detained without charges being brought, particularly since the time of the elections, a period of now over three years, this constitutes an arbitrary deprivation of their liberty and thus violates Article 6.

(56) In the words of Article 9 of the African Charter:

> "1. Every individual shall have the right to receive information.
> 2. Every individual shall have the right to express and disseminate his opinions within the law."

(57) The government justifies its actions with regard to the journalists and proscription of publications by reference to the "chaotic" situation that transpired after the elections were annulled. The Commission decided, in its decision on communication 101/93, with respect to freedom of association, that "competent authorities should not enact provisions which limit the exercise of this freedom. The competent authorities should not override constitutional provisions or undermine fundamental rights guaranteed by the constitution and international human rights standards" (ACHPR/A/101/93:18).

(58) With these words the Commission states a general principle that applies to all rights, not only freedom of association. Government should avoid restricting rights, and take special care with regard to those rights protected by constitutional or international human rights law. No situation justifies the wholesale violation of human rights. In fact, general restrictions on rights diminish public confidence in the rule of law and are often counter-productive.

(59) Given that Nigerian law contains all the traditional provisions for libel suits, a governmental proscription of a particular publication, by name, is of particular concern. Ad hominem Legislation, that is laws made to apply to specifically one individual or legal entity raise the acute danger of discrimination and lack of equal treatment before the law guaranteed by Article 2. The proscription of "The News" thus constitutes a violation of Article 9. Equally, the seizure of 50,000 copies of "Tempo" and "The News" Magazine justified in the face of Article 9 of the Charter.

For the above reasons, the Commission

holds violations of Articles 1, 6, 9 and 13 of the African Charter;

appeals to the government of Nigeria to release all those who were detained for protesting against the annulment of the elections; and to preserve the traditional functions of the court by not curtailing their jurisdiction.

2. 105/93, 128/94, 130/94, 152/96 Media Rights Agenda, Constitutional Rights Project, Media Rights Agenda and Constitutional Rights Project/Nigeria

Rapporteur:
17th Session: Commissioner Janneh
18th Session: Commissioner Umozurike
19th Session: Commissioner Umozurike

20th Session: Commissioner Dankwa
21st Session: Commissioner Dankwa
22nd Session: Commissioner Dankwa
23rd Session: Commissioner Dankwa
24th Session: Commissioner Dankwa

The facts as submitted by the complainant:

(1) Communications 105/93, 128/94 and 130/94 state that after the annulment of the Nigerian elections of 12 June 1993, several decrees were issued by the government. These proscribed the publication of two magazines. State officials sealed the premises of the two magazines embarking upon frequent seizures of copies of magazines critical of its decisions and arrest of newspaper vendors selling such magazines.

(2) By decree, the government also proscribed 10 newspapers published by four different media organisations. The complainant alleges that the newspapers and their operators were not previously accused of any wrongdoing either publicly or before a court of law or given any opportunity to defend themselves before their premises were sealed up on 22 July and they were subsequently outlawed by Decree 48 of 1993, which was released on 16 August 1993.

(3) Constitution (Suspension and Modification) Decree no. 107 of 17 November 1993 Article 5 specifies: "No question as to the validity of this Decree or any other Decree made during the period 31st December 1983 to 26th August 1993 or made after the commencement of this Decree or of an Edict shall be entertained by a court of law in Nigeria".

(4) On 16 August 1993, the Government also announced the promulgation of the Newspaper Decree No. 43 of 1993. By virtue of Section 7 of the Decree, it is an offence, punishable with either a fine of N250.000 or imprisonment for a term of 7 years or both for a person to own, publish or print a newspaper not registered under the Decree. The registration of existing newspapers under a previously subsisting law (the Newspaper Act) is extinguished by the Decree.

(5) The decision whether or not to register a newspaper is vested exclusively in the Newspapers Registration Board set up under the Decree. Compliance with the formal pre-registration requirements stipulated in the Decree does not guarantee registration of a newspaper because the Newspaper Registration Board has total discretion to decide whether the registration of a newspaper is "justified having regard to the public interest". There are no procedures for challenging the Board's decision not to register a newspaper.

(6) If the Board decides to register a newspaper, N100.000 must be paid as registration fee. Furthermore, N250.000 must be deposited into a fund to meet the amount of any penalty imposed on or damages awarded against the owner, printer, or publisher of the newspaper by a court of law in the future. Under the Newspapers Act (now repealed by Decree 43), a bond for N500 with sureties was sufficient security for possible penalties or damages which might be imposed on or awarded against a newspaper.

(7) Although released by the Government on 16 August 1993, the Decree is given a retroactive commencement date to 23 June 1993 and persons intending to own, print or publish newspapers in Nigeria are obliged to apply for registration within three weeks of the commencement of the Decree (i.e. by 14 July 1993) after complication with pre-registration requirements, thus making all newspapers in Nigeria immediately "illegal", and owners, printers and publishers liable to be arrested and detained.

(8) Communications 128/94 and 130/94 deal specifically with the events of 2 January 1994 when 50,000 copies of TELL magazine were seized by heavily armed policemen and other security officers on the printer's premises. In addition, twelve films and fourteen plates, used for processing, were also confiscated. TELL is a popular weekly magazine whose aim is to promote and protect human rights in Nigeria. That week's issue was entitled: "The Return of Tyranny – Abacha bares his fangs". The story involved a critical analysis of certain legislation enacted by the military government which ousts the jurisdiction of the courts. The complainant stated that no remedies were available at the local level, the jurisdiction of the courts having been ousted in considering the validity of such actions.

(9) Communication 152/96 was submitted by Constitutional Rights Project. It states that on 23 December 1995 Mr. Nosa Igiebor, the Editor in Chief of TELL Magazine was arrested and detained. The Constitutional Rights Project alleges that he was not told the reason for his arrest and that no charge has been made against him. Furthermore, Constitutional Rights Project alleges that he has been denied access to his family, doctors and lawyers and that he has received no medical help even though his health is deteriorating.

(10) Constitutional Rights Project also claim that TELL Magazine was declared illegal and in violation of Decree No. 43 of 1993 which requires all newspapers to register with the Newspaper Registration Board and to pay a pre-registration fee of N250,000 and a non-refundable fee of N100,000. These payments would be put into a fund for payment of penalties from libel actions against the owner, publisher or printer. Constitutional Rights Project stated that Decree No. 43 of 1993 had been declared null and void by two different courts, namely the Ikeja High Court on 18 November 1993, and the Lagos High Court on 5 December 1993. The Nigerian Government did not appeal against these decisions.

(11) In his oral arguments before the Commission, the complainants' representative emphasised that the government's prerogative to make laws for peace and good government does not entitle it to evade its obligations under international law.

State Party's response and observations:

(12) The government has made no written submissions in respect of this communication. At the 19th session, held in March 1995 in Ouagadougou, Burkina Faso, the government sent a delegation of several persons. Mr. Chris Osah, Assistant Director General of the Legal and Treaties Department at the Ministry of Foreign Affairs, made the following statements in his presentation on the communication.

(13) He stated that "Decree No. 43 of 1993 was made to underscore not only the government's sovereign rights but also its policy of free enterprise. Registration fees are payable to an independent board. It is in the public interest that all newspaper providers or publishers should ensure registration of their enterprises. The government is convinced that such registration fees are reasonable and justifiable in any democratic society. In any case, many newspapers and magazines operate although they have not registered".

(14) On ouster of the jurisdiction of the courts, the government stated that "there is nothing particularly new about this. It is the nature of military regimes to provide for ouster clauses, the reasons being that for a military administration which has come in, the resources of litigation become too cumbersome for the government to do what it wants to do".

(15) As for retroactive effect, the government maintained that, although the decree technically did have retroactive effect, not a single newspaper was declared illegal or harassed for violating the decree.

Complaint:

(16) The communications allege violations of Articles 6, 7, 9, 14 and 16 of the Charter.

Procedure before the Commission:

(17) Communication 105/93 is dated 1 September 1993. The Commission was seized of the communication at the 14th Session. The state concerned was notified on January 1994.

(18) Communication 128/94 is not dated but was received at the Secretariat between January and April 1994. The Commission was seized of the communication at the 15th session. The text of the communication was sent to the state concerned on 29 July 1994.

(19) Communication 130/94 is dated 5 January 1994. The Commission was seized of the communication at its 15th session and the text was sent to the state on 29 July 1994. The procedure relating to these three cases is the same.

(20) On 14 September 1994 a letter was sent to the complainants concerning communications no. 105/93, 128/94 and 130/94, asking whether all domestic remedies had been exhausted and whether any further seizures of TELL Magazine has occurred since 2 January 1994.

(21) A reminder was sent by the Secretariat of the Commission to the government of Nigeria on 22 September 1994.

(22) At the 16th session, held in October 1994 in Banjul, The Gambia, the Commission declared the communications admissible.

(23) At the 17th session, held in March 1995 in Lomé, Togo, it was decided to delay final decision on the cases so that they might be taken up with the Nigerian authorities when the Commission undertook its mission to that country. It was also declared that the chairman of the OAU should be informed of the situation in Nigeria.

(24) On 20 April 1995, a letter was sent by the Secretariat of the Commission to the complainants stating that the communications were declared admissible, and

that a mission would be sent to Nigeria, and that a decision on the merits would be taken at the 18th session.

(25) On 7 June 1995, a letter was sent by the Secretariat of the Commission to the government of Nigeria stating that the communications were declared admissible and that a mission would be sent to Nigeria.

(26) On 1 September 1995, a letter was sent to the government of Nigeria stating that the communications would be heard on the merits at the 18th session of the Commission and inviting the government to send a representative.

(27) At the 18th session of the Commission it was decided that the communications would be taken up by the mission to Nigeria, and if the government did not facilitate the visit, the Commission would at the next session adopt a decision on the facts available.

(28) On 30 November 1995 a letter was sent to the complainants reflecting this decision.

(29) On 30 November 1995 a note verbale was sent to the government of Nigeria reflecting this decision.

(30) At the 19th session, the Commission heard Mr. Chidi Anselm Odinkalu, who was duly instructed to appear for all the complainants in all cases against Nigeria, except that brought by International PEN. The Commission heard Mr. Osah and Mr. Bello for the Nigerian Government in reply. At the end of the hearing the Commission took a general view on the cases and deferred taking final decision in each case pending the accomplishment of its proposed mission to Nigeria.

(31) On 9 May 1996 letters were send to the Nigerian Government, Constitutional Rights Project and Media Rights Agenda informing them of the Commission's renewed decision to take a mission to the country and that the three communications detailed above would be considered on their merits at the 20th session in October 1996.

(32) At the 20th session held in Grand Bay, Mauritius, October 1996, the Commission decided to postpone the final decision on the merits of the communications to the 21st session, awaiting the result of the planned mission to Nigeria.

(33) On 10 December 1996 the Secretariat sent a note verbale to this effect to the government.

(34) On 10 December 1996 the Secretariat sent letters to this effect to the complainants.

(35) Communication 152/96 is dated January 1996.

(36) On 5 February 1996 a letter was sent to the complainant acknowledging receipt of the communication and that the admissibility of the case would be examined at the 20th session in October 1996.

(37) At the 19th session the communication was not examined.

(38) At the 20th session held in Grand Bay, Mauritius October 1996, the Commission declared the communication admissible, and decided that it would be taken up with the relevant authorities by the planned mission to Nigeria. At the same time it was joined with communications 105/93, 128/94 and 130/94.

(39) On 29 April, the Secretariat received a letter from Mr. Olisa Agbakoba entitled Preliminary objections and observations to the Mission of the Commission which visited Nigeria from 7–14 March 1997. The document was submitted on behalf of Interights with regard to 14 communications including this one.

(40) Among the objections raised and or observations made were on: the neutrality, Credibility and Relevance; and, composition of the Mission.

(41) At its 21st session held in April 1997, the Commission postponed taking decision on the merits to the next session, pending the submission of scholarly articles and court case by the complainants to assist it in its decision. The Commission also awaits further analysis of its report of the mission to Nigeria.

(42) On 22 May, the complainants were informed of the Commission's decision, while the State was informed on 28 May.

(43) From this date on, the procedure in respect of the communication is identical to that in communication 105/93, 128/94 and 130/94, above.

(44) At the 22nd Ordinary session the Commission postponed taking a decision on the cases pending the discussion of the Nigerian Mission report.

(46) At the 23rd ordinary session held in Banjul, The Gambia, the Commission postponed consideration of the case to the next session due to lack of time.

(46) On 25 June 1998, the Secretariat sent letters to the parties concerned informing them of the status of the case.

Law:

Admissibility:

(47) Article 56 of the African Charter reads:

> "Communications . . . shall be considered if they: . . .
> Are sent after exhausting local remedies, if any, unless it is obvious that this procedure is unduly prolonged."

(48) Specifically, in the four decisions the Commission has already taken concerning Nigeria, Article 56.5 is analyzed in terms of the Nigerian context. Communication 60/91 (Decision ACHPR/60/91) concerned the Robbery and Firearms Tribunal; communication 87/93 (Decision ACHPR/87/93) concerned the Civil Disturbances Tribunal; communication 101/93 (Decision ACHPR/101/93) concerned the Legal Practitioners Decree; and communication 129/94 (ACHPR/129/94) concerned the Constitution (Modification and Suspension) Decree and the Political Parties (Dissolution) Decree.

(49) All of the Decrees in question in the above communications contain "ouster" clauses. In the case of the special tribunals, these clauses prevent the ordinary courts from taking up cases placed before the special tribunals or from entertaining any appeals from the decisions of the special tribunals. (ACHPR/ 60/91:23 and ACHPR/87/93:22). The Legal Practitioners Decree specifies that it cannot not be challenged in the courts and that anyone attempting to do so commits a crime (ACHPR/101/93:14–15). The Constitution Suspension and Modification legal prohibited their challenge in the Nigerian Courts (ACHPR/ 129/94:14–15).

(50) In all of the cases cited above, the Commission found that the ouster clauses render local remedies non-existent, ineffective or illegal. They create a legal situation in which the judiciary can provide no check on the executive branch of government. A few courts in the Lagos district have occasionally found that they have jurisdiction; in 1995 the Court of Appeal in Lagos, relying on common law, found that courts should examine some decrees notwithstanding ouster clauses, where the decree is "offensive and utterly hostile to rationality" (Reprinted in the Constitutional Rights Journal). It remains to be seen whether any Nigerian courts will be courageous enough to follow this holding, and whether the government will abide by their rulings should they do so.

(51) In communication 152/96 the complainant states that Decree no. 43 has been declared null and void by two different courts, but these decisions have not been respected by the government. This is a dramatic illustration of the futility of seeking a remedy from the Nigerian courts.

(52) For these reasons, consistent with its earlier decisions, the Commission declared the communications admissible.

Merits:

(53) Article 9 of the African Charter reads:

> "1. Every individual shall have the right to receive information.
> 2. Every individual shall have the right to express and disseminate his opinions within the law."

(54) This Article reflects the fact that freedom of expression is a basic human right, vital to an individual's personal development, his political consciousness, and participation in the conduct of public affairs in his country. The problem at hand is whether the decrees requiring the registration of newspapers, and prohibiting many of them, violate this Article.

(55) A payment of a registration fee and a pre-registration deposit for payment of penalty or damages is not in itself contrary to the right to the freedom of expression. The government has argued that these fees are "justifiable in any democratic society", and the Commission does not categorically disagree.

(56) However, the amount of the registration fee should not be more than necessary to ensure administrative expenses of the registration, and the pre-registration fee should not exceed the amount necessary to secure against penalties or damages against the owner, printer or publisher of the newspaper. Excessively high fees are essentially a restriction on the publication of news media. In this case, the fees required for registration, while high, are not so clearly excessive that they constitute a serious restriction.

(57) Of more concern is the total discretion and finality of the decision of the registration board, which effectively gives the government the power to prohibit publication of any newspapers or magazines they choose. This invites censorship and seriously endangers the rights of the public to receive information, protected by Article 9.1. There has thus been a violation of Article 9.1.

(58) Also of serious concern is the retroactivity of the decree. The government bases its defense on the non-enforcement of this aspect of the decree. The government representative offered this defense: "Article 7.2 of the Charter is very specific: 'no one may be condemned', and we are saying that no one has been condemned. Second, it says 'no penalty may be inflicted' we are also submitting that there has been no penalty inflicted . . . We are even going further to say that more than 3/4 of the newspapers in Nigeria have registered and yet nobody has taken them to court".

(59) While it is reassuring to hear that no one has suffered under the retroactivity clause of the Decree No. 43, the Commission must take a stand on the issue of justice underlying Article 7.2 and condemn the literal, minimalist interpretation of the Charter offered by the representative of Nigeria. Article 7.2 must be read to prohibit not only condemnation and infliction of punishment for acts which did not constitute crimes at the time they were committed, but retroactivity itself. It is expected that citizens must take the laws seriously. If laws change with retroactive effect, the rule of law is undermined since individuals cannot know at any moment if their actions are legal. For a law-abiding citizen, this is a terrible uncertainty, regardless of the likelihood of eventual punishment.

(60) Furthermore, the Commission unfortunately cannot rest total confidence in the assurance that no one and no newspaper has yet suffered under the retroactivity of Decree 43. Potential prosecution is a serious threat. An unjust but unenforced law undermines, as above, the sanctity in which the law should be held. The Commission must thus holds that Decree no. 43 violates Article 7.2.

(61) Communication 152/96 states that two different courts have declared Decree no. 43 null an void, without any result.

(62) This shows not only a shocking disrespect by the Nigerian government for the judgments of the courts, it is also a violation of Article 7.1. The right to have one's cause heard by competent and independent courts must naturally comprise the duty of everyone, including the state, to respect and follow these judgments.

(63) Decree No. 48 proscribes approximately 10 newspapers published by four different media organizations without having subjected them to the due process of the law. Decree No. 48 likewise permitted the newspapers and their operators to have their premises sealed without being given any opportunity to defend themselves and without previously being accused of any wrongdoing before a court of law.

(64) The Commission decided, in its decision on communication 101/93, with respect to freedom of association, that "competent authorities should not enact provisions which limit the exercise of this freedom. The competent authorities should not override constitutional provisions or undermine fundamental rights guaranteed by the constitution and international human rights standards" (ACHPR/A/101/93:18).

(65) With these words the Commission states a general principle that applies to all rights, not only freedom of expression. Governments should avoid restricting rights, and have special care with regard to those rights protected by constitutional

or international human rights law. No situation justifies the wholesale violation of human rights. In fact, general restrictions on rights diminish public confidence in the rule of law and are often counter-productive.

(66) According to Article 9.2 of the Charter, dissemination of opinions may be restricted by law. This does not mean that national law can set aside the right to express and disseminate one's opinions; this would make the protection of the right to express one's opinions ineffective. To allow national law to have precedent over the international law of the Charter would defeat the purpose of the rights and freedoms enshrined in the Charter. International human rights standards must always prevail over contradictory national law. Any limitation on the rights of the Charter must be in conformity with the provisions of the Charter.

(67) In contrast to other international human rights instruments, the African Charter does not contain a derogation clause. Therefore limitations on the rights and freedoms enshrined in the Charter cannot be justified by emergencies or special circumstances.

(68) The only legitimate reasons for limitations to the rights and freedoms of the African Charter are found in Article 27.2, that is that the rights of the Charter "shall be exercised with due regard to the rights of others, collective security, morality and common interest".

(69) The reasons for possible limitations must be founded in a legitimate state interest and the evils of limitations of rights must be strictly proportionate with and absolutely necessary for the advantages which are to be obtained.

(70) Even more important, a limitation may never have as a consequence that the right itself becomes illusory.

(71) The government has provided no evidence that the prohibition was for any of the above reasons given in Article 27.2. Given that Nigerian law contains all the traditional provisions for libel suits, so that individuals may defend themselves where the need arises, for the government to proscribe a particular publication, by name, is disproportionate and uncalled for. Laws made to apply specifically to one individual or legal personality raise the serious danger of discrimination and lack of equal treatment before the law, guaranteed by Article 3. The proscription of "The News" cannot therefore be said to be "within the law" and constitutes a violation of Article 9.2.

(72) Communications 128/94 and 130/94 allege that 50,000 copies of TELL magazine were seized without any possibility of having the decision judged by a court of law, because of an article critical of the government.

(73) In the present case, the government has provided no evidence that seizure of the magazine was for any other reason than simple criticism of the government. The article in question might have caused some debate and criticism of the government, but there seems to have been no information threatening to, for example, national security or public order in it. All of the legislation criticized in the article was already known to members of the public information, as laws must be, in order to be effective.

(74) The only person whose reputation was perhaps tarnished by the article was the head of state. However, in the lack of evidence to the contrary, it should be assumed that criticism of the government does not constitute an attack on the personal reputation of the head of state. People who assume highly visible public roles must necessarily face a higher degree of criticism than private citizens; otherwise public debate may be stifled altogether.

(75) It is important for the conduct of public affairs that opinions critical of the government be judged according to whether they represent a real danger to national security. If the government thought that this particular article represented merely an insult towards it or the head of state, a libel action would have been more appropriate than the seizure of the whole edition of the magazine before publication. The seizure of the TELL therefore amounts to a violation of Article 9.2.

(76) Article 14 of the Charter reads:

> "The right to property shall be guaranteed. It may only be encroached upon in the interest of public need or in the general interest of the community and in accordance with the provisions of appropriate laws."

(77) The government did not offer any explanation for the sealing up of the premises of many publications. Those affected were not previously accused in a court of law, of any wrongdoing. The right to property necessarily includes a right to have access to property of one's own and the right not for one's property to be removed. The Decrees which enabled these premises to be sealed up and for publications to be seized cannot be said to be "appropriate" or in the interest of the public or the community in general. The Commission holds a violation of Article 14. In addition, the seizure of the magazines for reasons that have not been shown to be in the public need or interest also violates the right to property.

(78) In his oral argument, the complainant specifically raised the ouster of the court's jurisdiction over the decrees at issue here, denying the alleged victims the right to challenge the acts which affected them. The government offered the surprising defense that "[I]t is in the nature of military regimes to provide for ouster clauses", because without such clauses the volume of litigation would make it "too cumbersome for the government to do what it wants to do".

(79) This argument rests on the assumption that ease of government action takes precedence over the right of citizens to challenge such action. It neglects the central fact that the courts are a critical monitor of the legality of government action, which no lawful government acting in good faith should seek to evade. The courts' ability to examine government actions and, if necessary, halt those that violate human rights or constitutional provisions, is an essential protection for all citizens.

(80) It is true that if national tribunals are not deprived of their powers, they will almost certainly eventually pronounce on the legality of military government itself. The government representative's argument implicitly admits what the Commission has already said in its decision on communication 102/93, which is

that military regimes rest on questionable legal ground. Government by force is in principle not compatible with the rights of peoples to freely determine their political future.

(81) A government that governs truly in the best interest of the people, however, should have no fears of an independent judiciary. The judiciary and the executive branch of government should be partners in the good ordering of society. For a government to oust the jurisdiction of the courts on a broad scale reflects a lack of confidence in the justifiability of its own actions, and a lack of confidence in the courts to act in accordance with the public interest and rule of law.

(82) The Commission must therefore reject the defense of "the nature of military regimes" offered by the government's representative, and holds that the ouster of the court's jurisdiction violates the right to have one's cause heard, under Article 7.1.

(83) Article 6 of the African Charter reads:

> "Every individual shall have the right to liberty and to the security of his person. No one may be deprived of his freedom except for reasons and conditions previously laid down by law. In particular, no one may be arbitrarily arrested or detained."

(84) Communication 152/96 alleges that Mr. Nosa Igiebor was arrested and detained without being told any reason and without any charges being made.

(85) The government has offered no substantive response to this allegation.

(86) The Commission, in several previous decisions, has set out the principle that where allegations of human rights abuses go uncontested by the government concerned, even after repeated notifications, the Commission must decide on the facts provided by the government at treat those facts as given (see, e.g., the Commission's decisions in communications 59/91, 60/91, 64/91, 87/91 and 101/93). Therefore the Commission finds that there has been a violation of Article 6.

(87) Article 7.1 (c) of the African Charter reads:

> "1. Every individual shall have the right to have his cause heard. This comprises:
>
> . . .
>
> (c) The right to defense, including the right to be defended by counsel of his own choice;"

(88) Constitutional Rights Project alleges that Mr. Nosa Igiebor was denied access to lawyers. The government has made no response to this allegation. Therefore the Commission must take a decision on the facts as presented by the complainant. To be denied access to a lawyers is a violation of Article 7.1(c) even if there were no charges against Mr. Igiebor. People who are detained in violation of the Charter must not have lesser rights that those detained in conformity with the rules in Article 7.

(89) Article 16 of the African Charter reads:

> "1. Every individual shall have the right to enjoy the best attainable state of physical and mental health.
> 2. States Parties to the present Charter shall take the necessary measures to protect the health go their people and to ensure that they receive medical attention when they are sick."

(90) Constitutional Rights Project alleges Mr. Nosa Igiebor was denied access to doctors and that he received no medical help even though his health was deteriorating through his detention. The government has made no response to this allegation. Therefore the Commission must take a decision on the facts as presented by the complainant.

(91) The responsibility of the government is heightened in cases where the individual is in its custody and therefore someone whose integrity and well-being is completely dependent on the activities of the authorities. To deny a detainee access to doctors while his health is deteriorating is a violation of Article 16.

For these reasons, the Commission:
holds a violation of Article 6, 9.1, 9.2, 7.1(c), 7.2, 14, and 16 of the African Charter;
requests that the Government of Nigeria take the necessary steps to bring its law into conformity with the Charter.

3. 137/94, 139/94, 154/96 and 161/97 International Pen, Constitutional Rights Project, Interights on behalf of Ken Saro-Wiwa Jr. and Civil Liberties Organisation/Nigeria

Rapporteurs:
17th Session: Commissioner Badawi
18th Session: Commissioner Kisanga
19th Session: Commissioner Kisanga
20th Session: Commissioner Kisanga
21st Session: Commissioner Dankwa
22nd Session: Commissioner Dankwa
23rd Session: Commissioner Dankwa
24th Session: Commissioner Dankwa

The facts as submitted by the authors:

(1) These communications were submitted to the African Commission by International Pen, the Constitutional Rights Project, Interights [and Civil Liberties Organisation] respectively. They were joined because they all concern the detention and trial of Kenule Beeson Saro-Wiwa, a writer and Ogoni activist, president of the Movement for the Survival of the Ogoni People. The communications 139/94 and 154/96 also complain of similar human rights violations suffered by Mr. Saro-Wiwa's co-defendants, also Ogoni leaders.

(2) The communications 137/94 and 139/94 were submitted in 1994 before any trial began. After the murder of four Ogoni leaders on 21 May 1994, following

riot during a public meeting organised by Movement for the Survival of the Ogoni Peoples (MOSOP) representing the rights of those who lived in oil producing areas of Ogoni land, Saro-Wiwa and many hundreds of others were arrested, Saro-Wiwa himself on 22 May 1994 and the vice-president of MOSOP, Ledum Mitee, shortly thereafter. Both communications allege that Mr Saro-Wiwa was severely beaten during the first days of his detention and was held for several days in leg irons and handcuffs. He was also denied access to his lawyer and the medicine he needed to control his blood pressure, at times prevented from seeing his family, and held in very poor conditions.

(3) In its communication, submitted on 9 September 1994, the Constitutional Rights Project included a list of 16 other Ogonis who had been held without charge or bail for what was at that time over three months. Both communications alleged that Mr. Saro-Wiwa had been detained because of his political work in relation to MOSOP. He had been detained five times for brief periods since the beginning of 1993, and released each time without charge, except on one occasion in mid-1993 where he was held for several weeks and charged with unlawful assembly.

(4) The State Military Administrator declared that Mr. Saro-Wiwa and his co-defendants had incited members of MOSOP to murder four rival Ogoni leaders, but no charges were brought until 28 January 1995. In the months between arrest and the beginning of the trial, the defendants were not allowed to meet with their lawyers, and no information on the charges was provided to the defence.

(5) In February 1995 the trial of the defendants began before a tribunal established under the Civil Disturbances Act. The three members of this tribunals were appointed directly by General Abacha in November 1994, although counsel for the Rivers State Administrator argued in August that the cases were within the exclusive jurisdiction of the Rivers State High Court, since Rivers State is where the offences occurred.

(6) In June 1995 the Constitutional Rights Project submitted a supplement to its communication, alleging irregularities in the conduct of the trial itself: harassment of defence counsel, a military officer's presence at what should have been confidential meetings between defendants and their counsel, bribery of witnesses, and evidence of bias on the part of the tribunal members themselves. In October 1995 PEN also copied to the Commission a letter it sent to General Abacha protesting the lack of concrete evidence and the unfair conduct of the trial.

(7) On 30 and 31 October 1995, Ken Saro-Wiwa and eight of the co-defendants (Saturday Dobee, Felix Nuate, Nordu Eawo, Paul Levura, Daniel Gbokoo, Barinem Kiobel, John Kpunien and Baribor Bera) were sentenced to death, while six others including Mr. Mitee were acquitted. The CRP submitted an emergency supplement to its communication on 2 November 1995, asking the Commission to adopt provisional measures to prevent the executions.

(8) The Secretariat of the Commission faxed a note verbale invoking interim measures under revised Rule 111 of the Commission's Rules of Procedure to the

Ministry of Foreign Affairs of Nigeria, the Secretary General of the OAU, the Special Advisor (Legal) to the Head of State, the Ministry of Justice of Nigeria, and the Nigerian High Commission in The Gambia. The note verbale pointed out that as the case of Mr. Saro-Wiwa and the others was already before the Commission, and the government of Nigeria had invited the Commission to undertake a mission to that country, during which mission the communications would be discussed, the executions should be delayed until the Commission had discussed the case with the Nigerian authorities.

(9) No response to this appeal was received before the executions were carried out.

(10) On 7 November 1995 the Provisional Ruling Council (PRC) confirmed the sentences of death and on 10 November 1995 all the accused persons were executed in secret at the Port Harcourt Prison. By section 7 of the Civil Disturbances (Special Tribunals) Decree No. 2 of 1987, under which the executed persons were tried, the PRC are required to receive the records of the trial Tribunal before confirmation of the decision is possible. These records were not prepared by the Tribunal and so were not available for the PRC.

(11) In 1996 the Secretariat received a communication from Interights representing Ken Saro-Wiwa Jr. It alleged that the condemned persons had been detained arbitrarily prior to and during the trial and that they had been subjected to torture in the Army camp. Furthermore it alleged serious irregularities concerning the conduct of the trial: that the tribunals that convicted the accused persons were not independent; that there was no presumption of innocence; that the accused persons had not been given time or facilities in which to prepare their defence; that they had been denied legal representation by a counsel of their choice; that there was no right of appeal and that following the sentencing the persons were held incommunicado. Interights asserted that they were tried, convicted and sentenced to death for the peaceful expression of their views and opinions on the violations of the rights of the Ogoni people.

(12) In December 1996 the Secretariat received a communication from the Civil Liberties Organisation, alleging that the Civil Disturbances (Special Tribunal) Decree is invalid because it was made without participation of the people; that it's composition with military officers and members of the Provisional Ruling Council meant that it could not be impartial; and that the lack of judicial review of the decisions of this tribunal amount to a violation of the right to appeal and fair trial. The communication alleges that the trial, conviction and sentencing of Ken Saro-Wiwa and others violated Articles 7.1(b)(c) and (d) of the African Charter, and that the execution of these persons violates Article 4. The communication alleges that the arraignment of 19 more alleged suspects constitutes another potential violation of the Charter.]

The Complaint:

(13) The Communications allege violation of Articles 1, 4, 5, 7, 9, 10, 11, 16 and 26 of the African Charter.

State Response and Observations:

(14) The government argues that its actions were necessary to protect the rights of the citizens who had been murdered; that the tribunal which tried Saro-Wiwa was competent because two of its three members were lawyers; that the process of confirmation by a state government was an adequate appeal; that the Civil Disturbances Decree had not been protested upon its enactment in 1987 and that it had been set up to deal with a crisis situation.

Procedure before the Commission:

(15) Communication 137/94 is dated 28 September 1994 and was submitted by International Pen.

(16) Communication 139/94 is submitted by Constitutional Rights Project and dated 9 September 1994.

(17) The Commission was seized of the communications at its 16th Session in October 1994, but deferred its decision on admissibility pending notification and receipt of additional information from the Nigerian Government.

(18) At the 16th session the Commission decided to merge the communications.

(19) On 9 November 1994, a notification of the two communications was sent to the Nigerian Government and Rule 109 of the Rules of Procedure was invoked, requesting the Nigerian Government not to cause irreparable prejudice to Mr. Saro-Wiwa.

(20) On 6 February 1995 a letter was received from International Pen stating that Mr. Saro-Wiwa was being ill-treated and that he was facing the death penalty.

(21) On 13 February a letter was sent to the Nigerian Government re-emphasising the need for Rule 109 to be applied.

(22) On 22 February 1995, a letter was received from complainants stating that Ken Saro-Wiwa had been charged and was scheduled to appear before a three person tribunal from which there was no right of appeal. The tribunal members are chosen by General Abacha in violation of international fair trial standards. The complainant recognised that local remedies had yet to be exhausted and announced its intention to present an update of the case to the Commission once the trial was completed.

(23) At the 17th session the Commission declared the communications admissible. They were to be heard on their merits at the 18th session.

(24) On 20 April 1995, letters were sent to the Government of Nigeria and the complainants informing them of this.

(25) On 28 June 1995 a letter was received from the Constitutional Rights Project describing developments in the case.

(26) On 1 September 1995, a letter was sent to the government of Nigeria stating that the communication would be heard on the merits at the 18th session of the Commission and inviting the government to send a representative.

(27) At the 18th session the Commission decided that the communications should be taken up by the mission planned for Nigeria.

(28) On 9 October 1995 a letter was received from PEN American Centre expressing concern for the state of health of Mr. Saro-Wiwa.

(29) On 1 November 1995, upon hearing that a death sentence had been passed on Mr. Saro-Wiwa and eight of his co-defendants, the Secretariat faxed a note verbale to the government of Nigeria, invoking the revised Rule of Procedure 111 (formerly 109) asking that the executions should be delayed until the Commission had taken its mission and spoken with the competent authorities. This note verbale was also faxed to the Secretary General of the OAU, the Nigerian High Commission in Banjul, and the Special Adviser (Legal) to the Head of State of Nigeria.

(30) On 2 November 1995 a letter was received from the Constitutional Rights Project notifying the Secretariat of the death sentences and requesting that provisional measures be invoked.

(31) On 9 November 1995 Commissioner Dankwa, hearing that the death sentence had been confirmed, wrote to the Secretariat requesting such action. He was faxed a copy of the note verbale.

(32) On 20 November 1995 the Secretariat received a note verbale from the Nigerian High Commissioner in Banjul, attempting to justify the executions.

(33) On 21 November 1995 the Secretariat wrote a note verbale to the Nigerian High Commission in Banjul, requesting the official judgement in the Saro-Wiwa case, which had been mentioned in the note verbale.

(34) On 30 November 1995 a letter was sent to the complainants stating that the communications would be taken up by the Commission's mission to Nigeria.

(35) On 13 December 1995, the Secretariat received a letter dated 13 November 1995 from the office of the Special Adviser to the Head of State, attempting to justify the executions.

(36) On 18 and 19 December 1995, the Commission held an extraordinary session on Nigeria in Kampala.

(37) On 26 January 1996 a letter was sent to the Constitutional Rights Project informing it of the interim measures taken with regard to Ken Saro-Wiwa.

(38) At the 19th session, held in March/April 1996 in Ouagadougou, Burkina Faso, the Commission heard statements from the government of Nigeria and the complainants. Mr. Chidi Anselm Odinkalu was duly authorised to appear for the complainants, and Mr. Osah and Mr. Bello appeared for the Nigerian Government. At the end of the hearing the Commission took a general view on the cases and deferred taking final decision in each case pending the accomplishment of its proposed mission to Nigeria. The Commission proposed May 1996 as the dates for the visit. The Nigerian delegation said they will communicate these dates to the Government of Nigeria for confirmation.

(39) On 8 May 1996 the Commission wrote to the Nigerian Government, Constitutional Rights Project and International PEN informing them that a decision had been taken at the 19th session to send a mission to the country where the cases would be taken up.

(40) At the 20th session held in Grand Bay, Mauritius, October 1996, the Commission decided to postpone the final decision on the merits of the

communications to the next session, awaiting the result of the planned mission to Nigeria. The Commission also decided to join communication 154/96 with these communications.

(41) On 10 December 1996 the Secretariat sent letters to the complainants informing them of the decisions of the Commission.

(42) On 10 December 1996 the Secretariat sent a note verbale to the government informing it of the decisions of the Commission.

(43) On 29 April, the Secretariat received a letter from Mr. Olisa Agbakoba entitled Preliminary objections and observations to the Mission of the Commission which visited Nigeria from 7–14 March 1997. The document was submitted on behalf of Interights with regard to 14 communications, including this one.

(44) Among the objections raised and or observations made were: the neutrality, credibility and relevance; and composition of the Mission.

(45) At its 21st session held in April 1997, the Commission postponed taking decision on the merits to the next session, pending the submission of scholarly article and court decisions by the complainants to assist it in its decision. The Commission also awaits further analysis of its report of the mission to Nigeria. It must be stated that Mr. Chidi Odinkalu did send the article mentioned above.

(46) On 22 May, the complainants were informed of the Commission's decision, while the State was informed on 28 May 28.

(47) Communication 154/96 is dated 6 November 1995 and received at the Secretariat on 4 March 1996.

(48) The communication requested the Commission to take interim measures to prevent the executions. A supplementary submission was sent with the communication informing the Commission that the executions had taken place on 10 November but that the communication was reaffirmed.

(49) On 13 November 1995 the Nigerian Government wrote to the Commission informing it of the Government's view of the situation.

(50) On 20 November 1995 the High Commission of Nigeria in the Gambia giving its opinion on the matter.

(51) On 21 November 1995 the Commission wrote to the High Commission of Nigeria in the Gambia requesting a copy of the Justice's judgement in the case.

(52) On 12 March 1996 a confirmation was sent to this effect by the complainant.

(53) At the 19th session in March 1996 the communication was not considered, but the Commission took a general view of all the communications against Nigeria and deferred any decision on cases pending the accomplishment of its proposed mission to Nigeria.

(54) On 13 August 1996 a complete copy of the communication was sent to the government of Nigeria.

(55) On 13 August 1996 a letter was sent to the complainant informing him of the status of the case.

(56) On 4 February 1997, the Secretariat received a letter entitled supplementary submissions with respect to communication No. 154/96.

(57) On 4 April, the Secretariat acknowledged receipt of the letter.

(58) On 29 April, the Secretariat received a letter from Mr. Olisa Agbakoba entitled Preliminary objections and observations to the Mission of the Commission which visited Nigeria from 7–14 March 1997. The document was submitted on behalf of Interights with regard to 14 communications, including this one.

(59) Among the objections raised and or observations made were: a) the neutrality, credibility and relevance; and composition of the Mission.

(60) At its 21st session held in April 1997, the Commission postponed taking decision on the merits to the next session, pending the submission of scholarly articles and court case by the complainants to assist it in its decision. The Commission also awaits further analysis of its report of the mission to Nigeria.

(61) On 22 May, the complainants were informed of the Commission's decision, while the State was informed on 28 May.

(62) On 27 May, the Secretariat received a letter from the complainant entitled Additional Information on Ouster Clauses in Nigerian Law in which he promised to furnish the Secretariat with the information requested by the Commission at its 21st session " within the next three weeks".

(63) From this day on the procedure is identical to communications 137/94 and 139/94.

(64) Communication 161/97 was received on 10 January 1997.

(65) On 14 January 1997 a note verbale with a copy of the communication was sent to the Ministry of External Affairs, copy to the Special Legal Adviser to the Head of State, the Nigerian High Commission, and the Embassy of Nigeria in Addis Ababa.

(66) On 23 January 1997 an acknowledgement of receipt was sent to the complainant.

(67) At its 21st session held in April 1997, the Commission postponed taking decision on the merits to the next session, pending the submission of scholarly articles and court case by the complainants to assist it in its decision. The Commission also awaits further analysis of its report of the mission to Nigeria.

(68) On 22 May, the complainants were informed of the Commission's decision, while the State was informed on May 28.

(69) At the 22nd Ordinary session, the Commission postponed taking a decision on the cases pending the discussion of the Nigerian Mission report.

(70) At the 23rd Ordinary session held in Banjul The Gambia, from 20–29 April 1998, the Commission was unable to consider the communication due to lack of time.

(71) On 25 June 1998, letters were sent from the Secretariat of the Commission to all parties concerned regarding the status of the communications.

Law:

Admissibility"

(72) Article 56 of the African Charter reads:

"Communications . . . shall be considered if they:

. . .

5. Are sent after exhausting local remedies, if any, unless it is obvious that this procedure is unduly prolonged, . . . "

(73) This is just one of the 7 conditions specified by Article 56, but it is that which usually requires the most attention. Because Article 56 is necessarily the first considered by the Commission, before any substantive consideration of communications, it has already been the subject of substantial interpretation; in the jurisprudence of the African Commission, there are several important precedents.

(74) Specifically, in the four decisions the Commission has already taken concerning Nigeria, Article 56.5 is analysed in terms of the Nigerian context. Communication 60/91 (Decision ACHPR/60/91) concerned the Robbery and Firearms Tribunal; Communication 87/93 (Decision ACHPR/87/93) concerned the Civil Disturbances Tribunal; Communication 101/93 (Decision ACHPR/101/93) concerned the Legal Practitioners Decree; and Communication 129/94 (ACHPR/129/94) concerned the Constitution (Modification and Suspension) Decree and the Political Parties (Dissolution) Decree.

(75) All of the Decrees in question in the above communications contain "ouster" clauses. In the case of the special tribunals, these clauses prevent the ordinary courts from taking up cases placed before the special tribunals or from entertaining any appeals from the decisions of the special tribunals (ACHPR/60/91: 23 and ACHPR/87/93: 22). The Legal Practitioners Decree specifies that it cannot not be challenged in the courts and that anyone attempting to do so commits a crime (ACHPR/101/93: 14–15). The Constitution Suspension and Modification legally prohibited their challenge in the Nigerian Courts (ACHPR/129/94: 14–15).

(76) In all of the cases cited above, the Commission found that the ouster clauses render local remedies non-existent, ineffective or illusory. They create a legal situation in which the judiciary can provide no check on the executive branch of government. A few courts in the Lagos district have occasionally found that they have jurisdiction; in 1995 the Court of Appeal in Lagos, relying on common law, found that courts should examine some decrees notwithstanding ouster clauses, where the decree is "offensive and utterly hostile to rationality" (Reprinted in the Constitutional Rights Journal). It remains to be seen whether any Nigerian courts will be courageous enough to follow this holding, and whether the government will abide by their rulings should they do so.

(77) In the present case, while the above reasoning was used in the initial decisions on admissibility, it is at the present time unnecessary. In light of the fact that the subjects of the communications are now deceased, it is evident that no domestic remedy can now give the complainants the satisfaction they seek. The communications are thus admissible.

Merits:

(78) Article of the Charter 5 reads:

> "Every individual shall have the right to the respect of the dignity inherent in a human being and to the recognition of his legal status. All forms of exploitation and degradation of man particularly slavery, slave trade, torture, cruel, inhuman or degrading punishment and treatment shall be prohibited."

(79) Article 5 prohibits not only torture, but also cruel, inhuman or degrading treatment. This includes not only actions which cause serious physical or psychological suffering, but which humiliate the individual or force him or her to act against his will or conscience.

(80) International PEN alleges that Ken Saro-Wiwa was kept in leg irons and handcuffs and subjected to ill-treatment including beatings and being held in cells which were airless and dirty, then denied medical attention, during the first days of his arrest. There was no evidence of any violent action on his part or escape attempts that would justify holding him in irons. Communication 154/96 alleges that all the victims were manacled in their cells, beaten and chained to the walls in their cells.

(81) The government has made no written submission in these cases, and has not refuted these allegations in its oral presentation. It is well-established jurisprudence of the Commission that where allegations go entirely unchallenged, it will proceed to decide on the facts presented (see, e.g., the Commission's decisions in communications 59/91, 60/91, 64/91, 87/93 and 101/93). Thus, the Commission holds a violation of Article 5 of the Charter.

(82) Article 6 of the African Charter reads:

> "Every individual shall have the right to liberty and to the security of his person. No one may be deprived of his freedom except for reasons and conditions previously laid down by law. In particular, no one may be arbitrarily arrested or detained."

(83) All the victims were arrested and kept in detention for a lengthy period under the State Security (Detention of Persons) Act of 1984 and State Security (Detention of Persons) Amended Decree No. 14 (1994), that stipulates that the government can detain people without charge for as long as three months in the first instance. The decree also states that the courts cannot question any such detention or in any other way intervene on behalf of the detainees. This decree allows the government to arbitrarily hold people critical of the government for up to 3 months without having to explain themselves and without any opportunity for the complainant to challenge the arrest and detention before a court of law. The decree therefore prima facie violates the right not to be arbitrarily arrested or detained protected in Article 6.

(84) The government has made no defence of this decree, either for its general validity or its justice as applied in this case. Thus, the Commission holds a violation of Article 6.

(85) Article 7 of the African Charter reads:

"1. Every individual shall have the right to have his cause heard. This comprises:

(a) The right to appeal to competent national organs against acts of violating his fundamental rights
(b) the right to be presumed innocent until proved guilty by a competent court or tribunal;
(c) the right to defence, including the right to be defended by counsel of his choice;
(d) the right to be tried within a reasonable time by an impartial court or tribunal."

(86) As regards the conduct of the trial itself, it is unnecessary for the Commission to delve into the specific circumstances, because by the Commission's own precedent the tribunal was defective. As will be recalled, in its decision on Communication 87/93, the Commission considered that special tribunals established under the Civil Disturbances Act violate Article 7.1(d) of the African Charter, because their composition is at the discretion of the executive branch. Removing cases from the jurisdiction of the ordinary courts and placing them before an extension of the executive branch necessarily compromises their impartiality, which is required by the African Charter. This violation of the impartiality of tribunals occurs in principle, regardless of the qualifications of the individuals chosen for a particular tribunal.

(87) The note verbale of the Nigerian High Commissioner in The Gambia points out that the tribunal was not a military one, but was presided over by a judge of the Nigerian Court of Appeal, and that tribunals are properly constituted in the Nigerian judicial system to deal with specific issues and for speedier dispensation of justice. The note verbale makes other specific points on the conduct of the trial, arguing for its fairness: the placement of evidence, its conduct in public, and the fact that some of the defendants were ultimately acquitted.

(88) In its oral presentation at the 19th session, the government argued that the confirmation of sentence given by the state governors is an adequate appeal.

(89) The Commission might cite opposing facts, casting doubt upon the fairness of the tribunal. For example, The Head of State personally chose its members consisting of three instead of the five persons required by the Civil Disturbances Act. When defence counsel wrote to the Chief Judge of the Federal High Court on 27 November 1994 for information on when the trial would begin, the judge responded, "This Court has nothing to do about the Tribunal. It is the responsibility of the Presidency".

(90) There is a great deal of information available from Nigerian and international sources on the day-to-day conduct of the tribunal and the significance of its legal rulings. Yet in reaching its decision, the Commission need only rely upon its earlier holding, made in less politically charged circumstances, that the special

tribunals established under the Civil Disturbances Act are in violation of the African Charter. As a result, it finds that Ken Saro-Wiwa and his co-defendants were denied the right to a fair trial, in violation of Article 7.1(d).

(91) Section 7 of the Civil Disturbances (Special Tribunals) Decree No. 2 of 1987 decides that the confirming authority of judgments given under the act is the PRC, that is the ruling council of the Federal Military government, the members of which are exclusively members of the armed forces.

(92) Section 8(1) of the same Decree stipulates:

> "The validity of any decision, sentence, judgement, confirmation, direction, notice or order given or made, as the case may be, or any other thing whatsoever done under this Act shall not be inquired into by any court of law."

(93) In this case, it is not safe to view the Provisional Ruling Council as impartial or independent. Section 8(1) effectively ousts all possibility of appeal to the ordinary courts. Thus, the accused persons had no possibility of appeal to a competent national organ, and the Commission finds a violation of Article 7.1(a).

(94) Article 26 of the African Charter reads: "States parties to the present Charter shall have the duty to guarantee the independence of the Courts".

(95) As stated above, the Special Tribunal and the Provisional Ruling Council are not independent. The Commission also finds that there is a violation of Article 26 of the African Charter.

(96) The government has not contradicted the allegations contained in communication 154/96 that at the conviction in October 1995 the Tribunal itself admitted that there was no direct evidence linking the accused to the act of the murders, but held that they had each failed to establish that they did not commit the crime alleged. Communication 154/96 has also affirmed that prior to and during the trial, leading representatives of the government pronounced MOSOP and the accused guilty of the crimes at various press conferences and before the United Nations. As the allegations have not been contradicted, the Commission find a violation of the right to be presumed innocent, Article 7.1(b).

(97) Initially, the accused were defended by a team of lawyers of their own choice. According to Communication 154/96 and Communication 139/94, this team withdrew from the case because of harassment, both in the conduct of the trial and in their professional and private lives outside. Communication 154/96 alleges that two of the lawyers were seriously assaulted by soldiers claiming to be acting on the instruction of the military officer responsible for the trial. On three occasions defence lawyers were arrested and detained and two of the lawyers had their offices searched. When these lawyers withdrew from the case, the harassment subsided.

(98) After the withdrawal of their chosen counsel, the accused were defended by a team assigned by the Tribunal. However, this team also resigned, complaining of harassment. After that, the accused declined to accept a new team appointed

by the Tribunal, and the court proceedings were closed without the accused having legal representation for the duration.

(99) Communication 154/96 also claims that the defence was denied access to the evidence on which the prosecution was based and that files and documents which were required by the accused for their defence were removed from their residences and offices when they were searched by security forces on different occasions during the trial.

(100) The government claims that: "Their [the accused] defence team which comprised sly human rights activists such as Femi Falana and Gani Fawehinmi, known to be more disposed towards melodrama than the actual defence of their clients, inexplicably withdrew from the Special Tribunal at a crucial stage of the trial in order to either play to the gallery or delay and frustrate the process".

(101) This statement does not contradict the allegations of Communication 154/96, that two different defence teams were harassed into quitting the defence of the accused persons; it merely attributed malicious motives to the defence. The government has not responded to the allegations of withholding evidence from the defence. The Commission therefore finds itself with no alternative but to conclude that a violation of Article 7.1(c) has occurred.

(102) Article 4 of the African Charter reads:

> "Human beings are inviolable. Every human being shall be entitled to respect for his life and the integrity of his person. No one may be arbitrarily deprived of this right."

(103) Given that the trial which ordered the executions itself violates Article 7, any subsequent implementation of sentences renders the resulting deprivation of life arbitrary and in violation of Article 4. The violation is compounded by the fact that there were pending communications before the African Commission at the time of the executions, and the Commission had requested the government to avoid causing any "irreparable prejudice" to the subjects of the communications before the Commission had concluded it consideration. Executions had been stayed in Nigeria in the past on the invocation by the Commission of its rule on provisional measures (Rule 109 now 111) and the Commission had hoped that a similar situation will obtain in the case of Ken Saro-Wiwa and others. It is a matter of deep regret that this did not happen.

(104) The protection of the right to life in Article 4 also includes a duty for the state not to purposefully let a person die while in its custody. Here at least one of the victims' lives was seriously endangered by the denial of medication during detention. Thus, there are multiple violations of Article 4.

(105) Article 11 of the African Charter provides: "Every individual shall have the right to assemble freely with others".

(106) Communication 154/96 alleges that Article 11 was violated because the murder trial directly followed public meetings of MOSOP. In its judgement, the Tribunal held that the condemned persons "created the fire that consumed the four Ogoni chiefs" by wrongfully organising election campaign rallies and

permitting a large crowd of fanatical MOSOP and NYCOP youths to congregate. It appears that the Tribunal holds the accused responsible for the murders because they organised the rally after which the murders took place, although Ken Saro-Wiwa for one was prevented by government officials from attending the rally. The Commission has considerable difficulty with this position as it can adversely affect the right to assembly.

(107) Article 10.1 of the African Charter reads: "Every individual shall have the right to free association provided that he abides by the law.".

(108) Communication 154/96 alleges that Article 10.1 was violated because the victims were tried and convicted for their opinions, as expressed through their work in MOSOP. In its judgement, the Tribunal held that by their membership in MOSOP, the condemned persons were responsible for the murders, guilt by association, it would seem furthermore that, government officials at different times during the trial declared MOSOP and the accused guilty of the charges, without waiting for the official judgement. This demonstrates a clear prejudice against the organisation MOSOP, which the government has done nothing to defend or justify. Therefore the Commission finds a violation of Article 10.1.

(109) Article 9.2 of the African Charter reads: "Every individual shall have the right to express and disseminate his opinions within the law".

(110) There is a close relationship between the rights expressed in the Articles 9.2, 10.1 and 11. Communication 154 alleges that the actual reason for the trial and the ultimate death sentences was the peaceful expression of views by the accused persons. The victims were disseminating information and opinions on the rights of the people who live in the oil producing area of Ogoniland, through MOSOP and specifically a rally. These allegations have not been contradicted by the government, which has already been shown to be highly prejudiced against MOSOP, without giving concrete justifications. MOSOP was founded specifically for the expression of views of the people who live in the oil producing areas, and the rally was organised with this in view. The Government's actions is inconsistent with Article 9.2 implicit when it violated Articles 10.1 and 11.

(111) Article 16 of the Charter reads:

> "1. Every individual shall have the right to enjoy the best attainable state of physical and mental health.
> 2. States parties to the present Charter shall take the necessary measures to protect the health of their people and to ensure that they receive medical attention when they are sick."

(112) The responsibility of the government is heightened in cases where an individual is in its custody and therefore someone whose integrity and well-being is completely dependent on the actions of the authorities. The state has a direct responsibility in this case. Despite requests for hospital treatment made by a qualified prison doctor, these were denied to Ken Saro-Wiwa, causing his

health to suffer to the point where his life was endangered. The government has not denied this allegation in any way. This is a violation of Article 16.

(113) Nigeria has been a State Party to the African Charter for over a decade, and is thus bound by Article 1 of the African Charter.

(114) The Commission assists States parties to implement their obligations under the Charter. Rule 111 of the Commission's Rules of Procedure (revised) aims at preventing irreparable damage being caused to a complainant before the Commission. Execution in the face of the invocation of Rule 111 defeats the purpose of this important rule. The Commission had hoped that the Government of Nigeria would respond positively to its request for a stay of execution pending the former's determination of the communication before it.

(115) This is a blot on the legal system of Nigeria which will not be easy to erase. To have carried out the execution in the face of pleas to the contrary by the Commission and world opinion is something which we pray will never happen again. That it is a violation of the Charter is an understatement.

(116) The Nigerian Government itself recognises that human rights are no longer solely a matter of domestic concern. The African Charter was drafted and acceded to voluntarily by African States wishing to ensure the respect of human rights on this continent. Once ratified, States Parties to the Charter are legally bound to its provisions. A state not wishing to abide by the African Charter might have refrained from ratification. Once legally bound, however, a state must abide by the law in the same way an individual must.

For the above reasons, the Commission:

decides that there has been a violation of Articles 5 and 16 in relation to Ken Saro-Wiwa's detention in 1993 and his treatment in detention in 1994 and 1995;

decides that there has been a violation of Articles 6 in relation to the detention of all the victims under the State Security (Detention of Persons) Act of 1984 and State Security (Detention of Persons) Amended Decree no. 14 (1994). The government therefore has the obligation to annul these Decrees;

reiterates its decision on communication 87/93 that there has been a violation of Article 7.1(d) and with regard to the establishment of the Civil Disturbances Tribunal. In ignoring this decision, Nigeria has violation Article 1 of the Charter;

decides that there has been a violation of Articles 4 and 7.1 (a), (b) (c) and (d) in relation to the conduct of the trial and the execution of the victims;

holds that there has been a violation of Articles 9.2, 10.1 and 11, 26, 16;

holds that in ignoring its obligations to institute provisional measures, Nigeria has violated Article 1.

4. 198/97 S.O.S. – Esclaves v. Mauritania

Rapporteur:
22nd session: Commissioner Ondziel-Gnelenga
23rd session: Commissioner Ondziel-Gnelenga
24th session: Commissioner Ondziel-Gnelenga
25th session: Commissioner Ondziel-Gnelenga

Facts as presented by the Complainant:

(1) SOS – Esclaves alleges that slavery remains a common practice in Mauritania, regardless of its prohibition under the law. According to this NGO, in a considerable number of cases, the Mauritanian government is informed about these practices, and in some of those cases, it occasionally supports the authors of those practices. SOS – Esclaves cites some concrete examples in support of its allegations.

(2) In its report of March 1996, SOS – Esclaves provides the following illustrations:

- ten Mauritanian adults sold and bought as slaves (M'barka mint Said, Temrazguint mint M'Barek, Nema mint Ramdane, Aïchana mint Abeid Boïlil, Mbarka mint Meriéme, Zgheilina, Bakary, Abeid, Aïcha mint Soélim, Kneïba);
- children from four families enslaved by the masters of their parents (the daughter of M'barka mint Meriéme, the five children of Aïchana mint abeid Boïlil, the daughter of Messaoud ould jiddou, and the two sons of Fatma mint Mama);
- four other children sold as slaves (Baba ould Samba, Houssein, Mohamed Ould Maoulould, Sidi ould Matallah); two Mauritanian women married to their masters against their will (Aïchetou mint M'Boyrik and Temrazguint mint M'Bareck);
- finally, six Maritanians and their families dispossessed of their ancestral property by the masters of their parents, following the death of the latter (Mohamed ould Bilal, Oum El Hella mint Bilal, Bah ould Rabahl, Biram ould Abd Elbarka and M'Boyrik would Maouloud).

(3) SOS – Esclaves requested the Mauritanian government to carry out investigations into these acts and to take necessary measures for their eradication. However, its request was never followed up.

Complaint:

(4) The communication alleges violation of Articles 2, 3, 4, 5, 6, 7, 9, 11 and 15 of the African Charter.

Procedure:

(5) The communication is dated 11 April 1997 and was received by the Commission meeting at its 21st Ordinary Session, which was seized of the matter.

(6) On 7 July 1997, a letter of notification was addressed to the Mauritanian government informing it of the content of the communication and requesting it to give its reaction.

(7) On 7 July 1997, a letter was sent to the complainant acknowledging receipt of the complaint.

(8) At the 22nd ordinary session held from 2–11 November 1997, the Commission decided to defer action on all communications submitted against Mauritania until the 23rd session. This was due to the fact that it was still awaiting the reaction of the government to the mission report that had been given to it during the 21st session.

(9) At the 23rd session, the Commission determined that some of the information contained in the report submitted in conjunction with the communication did not help it to establish conclusively whether internal remedies had been exhausted. In particular, the Commission emphasised that SOS – Esclaves should supply copies of all judicial decisions on all the cases that it brings up in its report, and to point out those cases that were still pending before Mauritanian jurisdictions. This would enable it to decide on a firm basis of knowledge as the admissibility of the communication.

(10) On 25 April 1998, a copy of the communication and the letters requesting additional information on internal procedure were given to the Mauritanian representative at the 23rd session.

(11) On 19 August 1998, correspondence was dispatched to the complainant communicating the Commission's position to it.

(12) At its 24th ordinary session, the Commission deferred consideration of the this communication to the following session.

(13) On 12 November 1998, the Secretariat addressed letters to both parties informing them of this decision.

Law:

Admissibility:

(14) In terms of the provisions of article 56, 5 of the African Charter on Human and Peoples' Rights:

> "communications . . . relating to Human and Peoples' Rights received by the Commission, shall be examined if they . . . are sent after exhausting local remedies, if any, unless it is obvious that this procedure is unduly prolonged."

(15) The facts alleged in the communication submitted by SOS – Esclaves are very grave and from all appearances, contrary to the provisions of the African Charter on Human and Peoples' Rights, in particular Articles 2, 3 and 5. However, the complainant, having indicated that there are internal procedures initiated by the supposed victims, does not say anything regarding the status of those procedures. Hence, the Commission is unable to determine whether the said procedures have been concluded or otherwise; nor whether they have allowed the supposed victims to have their rights restored.

(16) To enable it to reach an objective determination, the Commission requested the complainant to supply the additional information it required. Faced with the silence observed by the latter, it is unable to form a precise opinion regarding the facts of which it has been seized. This would seem to indicate that the internal remedies have not been exhausted; the Commission is of the view that if they had been, the complainant would have made it known.

For these reasons, the Commission:

(17) *Declares* the communication inadmissible due to non-exhaustion of internal remedies;

(18) It however acknowledges that the complainant still enjoys the opportunity to seize the Commission again once the conditions of Article 56, 5 have been fulfilled.

5. 212/98 Amnesty International/Zambia

Rapporteur:
23rd session: Commissioner Pityana
24th session: Commissioner Pityana
25th session: Commissioner Pityana

Facts:

(1) The communication is submitted by Amnesty International on behalf of William Steven Banda and John Lyson Chinula.

(2) Complainant alleges that Zambia has violated the provisions of African Charter in that:

(a) Mr. William Steven Banda was served with a deportation order on 10 November 1991. The reason given was that "in my opinion by his presence he (is) likely to be a danger to peace and good order in Zambia". He contested the order through the courts of Zambia.

(b) On 25 October 1994, William Steven Banda was deported to Malawi unlawfully, wrongfully and out of political malice. He alleges that he was blindfolded and drugged, driven by Zambian immigration service and para-military police officers. He entered Malawi through Mchinji border post and later dumped at Lilongwe Police station.

(c) John Luson Chinula was removed from his home in Ndola on 31 August 1994. He was driven to Lusaka International Airport with the intention of deporting him. He was served with a deportation order signed by the Minister of Home Affairs alleging that he was a threat to Zambia's peace and security. He was forcibly sedated and later found himself at Lilongwe Police station in Malawi. His Warrant of Deportation also alleged that he was "by his presence, likely to be a danger to peace and good order in Zambia". No reason in law or in fact was advanced for this finding.

(d) Both complainants were prominent political figures in Zambia. They were leading members of UNIP, the party that had been in power since Independence in 1964. UNIP was defeated by MMD in the first multi-party elections of November 1991.

(3) William Steven Banda exhausted all domestic remedies in that, his matter went to the Supreme Court of Zambia. John Lyson Chinula could not effect any remedies through the Zambian courts because he was deported and was given no opportunity to approach the Zambian courts.

(4) It is alleged by the complainant that prior to his forcible expulsion from Zambia under order of deportation, William Banda exhausted local remedies through his appeal to the High Court of Zambia in 1992 and the Supreme Court of Zambia in 1994.

(5) Complainant alleges that the Zambian government's deportation of the two men amounted to "forcible exile".

(6) Complainant alleges that attempts to seek redress through existing national legal remedies both in Zambia and in Malawi have been futile.

(7) Complainant also charges that John Chinula was not allowed recourse to the national courts of Zambia. He was prevented from returning to Zambia by threats of imprisonment by the Zambian authorities.

(8) Complainant states that Banda and Chinula have obtained two judgements at the High Court of Malawi confirming that they were not citizens of Malawi. The government of Malawi has failed to comply with the judgement of the Court which ordered that they be assured to return to Zambia. They have therefore exhausted all available local remedies at their disposal.

(9) Complainant prays that the Commission adopt interim measures to allow the deportees to return to Zambia immediately.

Complaint:

(10) Complainant alleges that Articles 2, 5, 7(1)(a), 8, 9, 9(2), 10, 12(2), 13(1), 18(1), 18(2) of the African Charter have been violated.

Procedure:

(11) Communication is dated 6 March 1998 and was sent by mail.

(12) On 18 March 1998, a letter was sent to the complainant acknowledging receipt.

(13) At its 23rd ordinary session held in Banjul, The Gambia, the Commission decided to be seized of this matter and declared the communication admissible. The Commission also requested that provisional measures be adopted by the Government of Zambia, namely to allow the burial of Mr. John L. Chinula, in Zambia and the return of Mr. William S. Banda to his family in Zambia pending the finalization of the matter by the Commission.

(14) On 10 July 1998, the Secretariat of the Commission wrote to the Ministry of Foreign Affairs, Zambia, informing them of the decision of the 23rd Ordinary Session, drawing attention to the request for provisional measures to be taken by the government of Zambia.

(15) A copy of the Note was also sent to the Embassy of Zambia in Addis Ababa. When there was no reply, the Secretariat sent a reminder on 17 September 1998. The Embassy replied on 21 September that the Note Verbale was received but did not enclose the communication referred to.

(16) The representative of the Government of Zambia appeared before the Commission on 26th and 27th of October 1998 at the 24th ordinary session. He presented a statement in response to the communication.

(17) At the 24th ordinary session, the Commission postponed consideration of this for a decision on the merits to the next session.

(18) On 26 November 1998, the Secretariat conveyed the decision of the Commission to the parties concerned.

(19) In preparation for a hearing on this matter, the Rapporteur for this communication requested the parties to address only some of the critical matters he had

identified. Mr. Ahmed Motala represented Amnesty International. Mr. Clifford Msika of the Centre for Human Rights and Rehabilitation, Lilongwe, Malawi, assisted him. Mr. William Steven Banda was also present. The Zambian Government was represented by Mr. Palan Mulonda, Senior State Advocate in the Ministry of Legal Affairs accompanied by Mr. K.K. Nsemukila, Deputy Permanent Secretary, Home Affairs Department and Ms. Lucy M. Mungoma of Foreign Affairs Department with responsibility for Africa and OAU relations. The Commission also heard testimony from Mr. William Steven Banda.

Argument:

(20) Mr. Motala argued that Zambia was bound by the African Charter which it ratified in 1984. It, therefore, was obliged to extend the rights in the Charter to "every individual" except where political rights are specifically indicated as in Article 13 for example. He argued that Zambia was in violation of Article 12 especially sub article 2 which provides that "every individual" has a right to leave one's country and to return. It also says that a "non-national legally admitted in a territory of a State Party may only be expelled from it by virtue of a decision taken in accordance with the law". He alleged discrimination on the basis of ethnic group and social origin (Article 2) and on the basis of political opinion. The treatment the complainants received violated the victims rights to human dignity and freedom of movement. In the case of Chinula, he was deprived of the right to have his cause heard (Article 7). He insisted that the actions against complainants were politically motivated. They have been left in a strange country destitute.

(21) Mr. Mulonda, for the government, stated that the government did not act with political malice. It acted within the law. The investigations against Banda began in 1976 and against Chinula in 1974 long before the present regime came into power. He denied that the deportees were drugged and dumped across the border. He stated that the Malawi authorities received them. The government of Zambia was acting within its sovereign rights in ordering its internal affairs, regulating immigration and was within the provision or limitation of the right stipulated in Article12: "This right may only be subject to restriction as provided for by law for the protection of nation security, law and order, public health and morality".

Law:

Admissibility:

(22) Admissibility of communications under the African Charter is governed by Article 56, which sets out conditions that must be met before they are considered by the Commission.

(23) Article 56 of the Charter reads:

> "Communications . . . shall be considered if they: . . .
> (5) are sent after exhausting local remedies, if unless it is obvious that this procedure is unduly prolonged."

(24) This provision of the Charter is necessarily first considered before any substantive consideration of a complaint.

(25) In the present case all local remedies have been exhausted and there is documentary evidence made available to the Secretariat of the Commission in support of this claim. As already stated in the case of Chinula, the arbitrary deportation prevented him from exercising this right.

(26) The complainant has attached to the communication copies of the following judgements/orders obtained by William Banda and John Chinula;

- Consent Order of 13 March 1995, High Court of Lilongwe, in Miscellaneous Cause No. 2 of 1995;
- Judgement of 30 June 1997, High Court of Malawi in Lilongwe, in Miscellaneous Cause No. 2 of 1995;
- Judgement No. 16 of 1994, Supreme Court of Zambia in Lusaka, in Banda vs. Chief Immigration Officer and Attorney General;
- Judgement No. JH/12 of 1991, High Court of Zambia in Chipata, in Banda vs Chief Immigration Officer and Attorney General.

For these reasons the Commission declares the communication admissible.

Merits:

(27) Zambia ratified the African Charter on Human and Peoples' Rights in January 1984.

(28) A number of supporting documents were submitted: On Banda, the transcript of the judgement by Kakusa J in the High Court of Zambia held at Chipata; the judgement on appeal by Bweupe DCJ in the Supreme Court in Lusaka. The various decisions of the Malawi Court and affidavits submitted in support. The Government also submitted documents on Banda and Chinula.

(29) Regarding William Steven Banda, the judgement of Justice Kakusa in the High Court is instructive. The judge found that there was no evidence, on a balance of probabilities, to prove that Banda was born in Zambia of Zambian parents. He found that Banda was an unreliable witness. He, however, refused to rule as to where Banda originated from. He dismissed all evidence that suggested that Banda was from Malawi, as inadmissible and hearsay. He also noted that the government had failed to produce the alleged Malawian father of Banda. The judge also made the following obiter dictum without justifying his opinion, that "once it is shown on a balance of probabilities that a petitioner is not a citizen of this Republic he becomes a deportable person even if the country to which he must proceed is unknown . . . possession of a National Registration Card . . . does not confer citizenship" (at p. J25). It appears that the authorities relied on this statement in deporting William Steven Banda.

(30) The judge also expressed himself in sympathy with Banda's predicament. He said "the petitioner has been in Zambia for a long time and has, in his own way, contributed in the political arena . . . Zambia has become almost the petitioner's only home – a de facto situation – upon which the executive may exercise its discretion and, maybe, consider normalising the status of petitioner should he apply

. . . If this court were empowered to declare persons like petitioner be Zambians, the petitioner would have received a favourable declaration considering his long stay in Zambia and the role he played" (p. J25).

(31) It is not denied that on the day of the judgement, William Steven Banda was taken into custody and deported to Malawi. In addition, Banda charges that his pleas that he be taken to South Africa were ignored including his request for a five-day stay of execution of the warrant.

(32) It is evident that the Malawi Courts are irrelevant for purposes of deciding this matter against Zambia. The fact that they declared complainants not to be Malawi citizens is neither here nor there. Secondly, the Commission is not competent to substitute the judgements of the Zambian courts, especially on matters of fact. It must be accepted that the legal processes were appropriate and conducted in a manner that showed respect for the rule of law. The legal processes in Zambia did not violate the principles of the Charter. The Commission must, therefore, accept that William Steven Banda was not a Zambian by birth or descent.

(33) This does not mean, however, that the Commission should not raise questions of law especially as the Zambian courts did not consider the obligations of Zambia under the African Charter. The court also failed to rule on the alleged reason for the deportation, namely, that his presence was likely "to endanger peace and good order in Zambia". There was no judicial inquiry on the basis in law and in terms of administrative justice for relying on this 'opinion' of the Minister of Home Affairs for the action taken. The fact that Banda was not a Zambian by itself, does not justify his deportation. It must be proved that his presence in Zambia was in violation of the laws. To the extent that neither Banda nor Chinula were supplied with reasons for the action taken against them means that the right to receive information was denied to them (Article 9(1)).

(34) The Rapporteur invited the parties to give guidance on the authority of the Charter where it was in contradiction to domestic law. That seems relevant because Zambia ratified the Charter by Executive Act. That means that there is legislative process that domesticates international human rights treaties. Mr. Mulonda affirmed Zambia's commitment to abide by the treaties it is party to. He also confirmed that Zambia operated a dual legal system and that the Charter is not considered to be a self executing measure. Nonetheless, Zambia accepted the binding character of the Charter in Zambia.

(35) By all accounts, though, Banda was in possession of Zambian national registration certificate and a passport. For many years he freely used these without challenge. Immediately following the verdict of the Supreme Court, he voluntarily presented himself to the police but he was forcibly deported. This meant that he was denied the opportunity to pursue the option of applying for citizenship by naturalisation in terms of the Citizenship Act. Granted, the government argues that Banda had obtained the documents of registration and Passport by making false claims about his place of birth. He could not therefore, be approaching the court with clean hands. The unstated implication being that the chances of his

obtaining naturalisation were negligible. In truth, of course, the Court did not say that Banda was an illegal immigrant. It simply disputed his claims to being Zambian by birth. It was not proved, therefore, that Banda was in Zambia illegally.

(36) Zambia has contravened Article 7 of the Charter in that he was not allowed to pursue the administrative measures, which were opened to him in terms of the Citizenship Act. More importantly, Zambia is in breach of Article 7(2) which says that "no one may be condemned for an act or omission which did not constitute a legally punishable offence at the time it was committed . . ." By all accounts, Banda's residence and status in Zambia had been accepted. He had made a contribution to the politics of the country. The provisions of Article 12(4) have been violated.

(37) The allegations of violations of Articles 2, 4, 5, 6, 9 and 10 may now be addressed. The evidence that William Steven Banda was a political opponent of the ruling MMD cannot be lost sight of. The manner in which he was treated was demeaning of the dignity and status of somebody of his standing in society. It appears that he was singled out for action because of his ethnic origin, which incidentally, is also found in Zambia. The authorities insisted on deporting him to Malawi even though, he told them that he knew nobody there. There was no compelling evidence that he had roots in Malawi having lived in Zambia, by their own admission, since about 1964. Counsel for Zambia argued that Banda was "accepted" by the Malawi immigration authorities. Whatever may have been the "legal" basis for such "acceptance", Malawi courts have ruled that they were not citizens of Malawi. In addition, unlawful deportation could not be said to obliterate their rights in Zambia.

(38) John Lyson Chinula was in an even worse predicament. He was not given any opportunity to contest the deportation order. Surely, government cannot say that Chinula had gone underground in 1974 having overstayed his visiting permit. Chinula, by all account, was a prominent businessman and politician. If government wished to act against him they could have done so. That they did not, does not justify the arbitrary nature of the arrest and deportation on 31 August 1994. He was entitled to have his case heard in the Courts of Zambia. Zambia has violated Article 7 of the Charter. Having made that finding, the findings in para 30 of above also obtain in this circumstance.

(39) The Commission had requested provisional measures in terms of Rule 111 of the Rules of Procedure. Zambia must be required to allow the return of William Steven Banda with a view to making application for citizenship by naturalisation. No evidence was led before the Commission for compensation. The evidence is that Banda had lost his job as governor after the 1991 elections. No award for compensation is called for.

(40) John Lyson Chinula died in Malawi. He was a prominent businessman. His deportation must have caused prejudice to his business interests. His family is requesting the return of his body for burial in Zambia. The Government of Zambia should be required to grant that wish.

(41) The Government of Zambia has relied on the "claw-back" clause of Article 12(2):

> "This right may only be subject to restrictions, provided for by law for the protection of national security, law or order, public health or morality . . ."

(42) The deportation order also stated that the deportees were considered " a danger to peace and good order to Zambia". The Commission is of the view that the "claw-back" clauses must not be interpreted against the principles of the Charter. Recourse to these should not be used as a means of giving credence to violations of the express provisions of the Charter. Secondly, the rules of natural justice must apply. Among these are in the audi alterm partem rule, the right to be heard, the right of access to the Court. The Court in Zambia, in Banda's case failed to examine the basis of administrative action and as such, it has not been proved that the deportees were indeed a danger to law and order. In any event the suggestion that they were "likely" to be a danger was vague and not proved. It is important for the Commission to caution against a too easy resort to the limitation clauses in the African Charter. The onus is on the state to prove that it is justified to resort to the limitation clause. The Commission should act bearing in mind the provisions of Articles 61 and 62 of the Charter.

(43) Article 2 of the Charter reads:

> "Every individual shall be entitled to the enjoyment of the rights and freedoms recognised and guaranteed in the present Charter without distinction of any kind such as race, ethnic group, colour, sex, language, religion political or any other opinion, national and social origin, fortune, birth or other status."

(44) By forcibly expelling the two victims from Zambia, the State has violated their right to enjoyment of all the rights enshrined in the African Charter. This Article imposes an obligation on the Zambian Government to secure the rights protected in the African Charter to all persons within their jurisdiction irrespective of political or any other opinion. This obligation was reaffirmed by the Commission in Rencontre Africaine pour la Défense des Droits de l'Homme / Zambia (Communication 71/92). The arbitrary removal of one's citizenship in the case of Chinula cannot be justified.

(45) Article 9(2) states:

> "Every individual shall have the right to express and disseminate his opinions within the law".

(46) Both Banda and Chinula were leading politicians and businessmen. Both had lived in Zambia for decades. Even if deportation action had been initiated against them in 1974 and 1976, it can be safely assumed that the action had been advanced unless it is proved that that was due to unlawfulness, fraud or obstruction of the course of justice. None of this was alleged. Action was accelerated upon the assumption of office of MMD government in 1991, we are therefore persuaded that the deportations were politically motivated. This provision of the

Charter reflects the fact that freedom of expression is a fundamental human right, essential to an individual personal development, political consciousness and participation in the public affairs of his country. The Commission has to determine whether the "deportations", being politically, motivated violate the provisions of Article 9(2) of the African Charter as the two victims were denied the right to freedom of conscience as stipulated in Article 8 of the Charter.

(47) Article 8 of the African Chater states:

> "Freedom of conscience, the profession and free practice of religion shall be guaranteed.No one may, subject to law and order, be submitted to measures restricting the exercise of these freedoms".

(48) Article 10 of the Charter states;

> "Every individual shall have the right to the free association provided that he abides by the law".

(49) In deporting the two men, the government of Zambia has denied them the exercise of their right to freedom of association. This is so since they have been prevented from associating with their colleagues in the United National Independence Party and participating in their activities.

(50) As the African Commission ruled in the case of John K. Modise/Botswana, by forcing Banda and Chinula to live as stateless persons under degrading conditions, the government of Zambia has deprived them of their family and is depriving their families of the men's support, and this constitutes a violation of the dignity of a human being. Thereby violating Article 5 of the Charter, which guarantees the right to: "the respect of the dignity inherent in a human being and to the recognition of his legal status".

(51) The forcible expulsion of Banda and Chinula by the Zambian government has forcibly broken up the family unit which is the core of society thereby failing in its duties to protect and assist the family as stipulated in Article 18(1) and 18(2) of the Charter;

> (1) "The family shall be the natural unit and basic of society. It shall be protected by the State . . .
>
> (2) The State shall have the duty to assist the family which is the custodian of morals and traditional values recognised by the community."

(52) Article 7(1)(a) states that:

> "Every individual shall have the right to have his cause heard.
>
> . . .
>
> (a) the right to an appeal to competent national organs against acts of violating his fundamental rights as recognised and guaranteed . . ."

(53) The Zambia government by denying Mr. Chinula the opportunity to appeal his deportation order has deprived him of a right to fair hearing which contravenes all Zambian domestic laws and international human rights laws.

For these reasons, the Commission:
holds a violation of Article 2;
holds a violation of Article 7(1)(a);
holds a violation of Article 8;
holds a violation of Article 9(2);
holds a violation of Article 10;
holds a violation of Article 18(1) and (2);

6. 221/98 – Alfred B. Cudjoe v. Ghana

Rapporteur:
24th session – Commissioner B. Pityana
25th session – Commissioner B. Pityana

Facts:

(1) The complainant is a Ghanaian citizen, formerly employed at the Embassy of Ghana in Conakry, Guinea.

(2) He alleges that his contract as translator/bilingual secretary at the said Embassy was wrongly terminated, by letter dated 24 June 1994.

(3) He claims that his dismissal was based on a report produced by the Guinean authorities, describing him as the brains behind an attack against the Ghanaian Chancery and the Ghana Airways offices in Conakry, perpetrated by furious Ghanaian residents.

(4) The complainant states that he did not have the opportunity of seizing any appellate authority before being dismissed for the above-mentioned reasons.

(5) The complainant presented a decision handed down by the Commission on Human Rights and Administrative Justice of Ghana, dated 18 May 1997, to the effect that the complainant's dismissal without benefits was null and void and that Mr. Alfred Cudjoe was entitled to some compensation.

(6) He further states that the Ministry of Foreign Affairs refused to comply with this decision.

(7) He sent a copy of the said decision to the Commission.

Substance of Grievance:

(8) The complainant alleges violation of articles 7, 4 and 15 of the African Charter on Human and Peoples' Rights.

Procedure before the Commission:

(9) At the 24th ordinary session held in Banjul, The Gambia, from 22–31 October 1998, the Commission decided to be seized of the communication and requested the complainant to provide it with more information as regards the exhaustion of all internal remedies.

(10) On 26 November 1998, letters were dispatched to both parties to inform them of the Commission's decision.

(11) At the 25th session, held in Bujumbura, Burundi, from 26 April to 5 May 1999, the Commission deliberated on the admissibility of the communication.

Law:

Admissibility:

(12) In terms of the provisions of Article 56, 5 of the African Charter on Human and Peoples' Rights:

> "communications . . . relating to Human and Peoples' Rights received by the Commission, shall be examined if they . . . are sent after exhausting local remedies, if any, unless it is obvious that this procedure is unduly prolonged."

(13) The African Commission observes that while the complainant has attached to his dossier the decision granted in his favour by the Ghanaian Human Rights Commission, he does not give any indication (despite the request made to him in this regard following deliberations at the 24th session) as to the procedure he has followed before the courts. For, it should be clearly stated, the internal remedy to which Article 56, 5 refers entails remedy sought from courts of a judicial nature, which the Ghanaian Human Rights Commission is clearly not. From the African Commission's point of view, seizing the said Commission can taken as preliminary amicable settlement and should, in principle, considering the employer's failure to react, be followed by an action before the law courts.

For these reasons, the Commission:

(14) In conformity with the above-mentioned provisions of the Charter, declares the communication inadmissible due to non-exhaustion of internal remedies.

Final Communiqué of the Twenty-fourth Ordinary Session of the African Commission on Human and Peoples' Rights

Banjul, 22–31 October 1998

1. The 24th Ordinary Session of the African Commission on Human and Peoples' Rights was held from 22–31 October 1998 in Banjul, The Gambia.

2. The opening ceremony took place on 22 October 1998 under the Chairmanship of Mr. Youssoupha Ndiaye, Chairman of the Commission..

3. The Session was declared opened by the Honourable Justice F. M. Chomba, the President of the Court of Appeal of the Gambia.

4. Speeches were also delivered by Mr. Harry Octavianus Olympio, Minister for the Promotion of Democracy and the Rule of Law, of the Republic of Togo on behalf of State Parties to the Charter and Ms. Sy Aissata Satigui of the Mauritania Association for Human Rights as a representative of the NGOs with observer status with the Commission.

5. The Chairman of the Commission informed delegates and participants at the Session of the tragic and untimely death of Commissioner Alioune Blondin Beye, who died in a plane crash near Abidjan, Côte d'Ivoire on 20 June 1998. A minute's silence was observed in honour of the departed Commissioner.

In his memory, the 24th Ordinary Session of the Commission was termed "Alioune Blondin Beye Session", and at the fourth sitting of the Session, his surviving colleagues paid tribute to him. Commissioners recalled his dedicated service to the African Commission as well as his zeal in the promotion and protection of human rights in Africa. The Commission decided to institute a human rights award named "the Alioune Blondin Beye Award" in his honour.

6. State delegates from Angola, Ethiopia, Zambia, Benin, Mauritania, Burkina Faso, Nigeria, Rwanda, Cameroon and Sudan addressed the Commission.

7. With respect to the human rights situation in Africa, various NGOs representatives expressed their concerns about the deteriorating human rights situation in the Great Lakes Region (Burundi, Rwanda and the Democratic Republic of Congo) and in other parts of Africa.

The representatives of the Governments of Mauritania, Burkina Faso, Zambia and Nigeria also responded to the statements of the NGOs concerning the human rights situation in their respective countries.

8. The Commission was briefed on the disturbing humanitarian situation in Burundi due to the embargo imposed on this country by States of this region. It therefore decided to take up the matter with the current Chairman of the OAU with a view to asking him to intercede with his colleagues who imposed the said sanctions against

Burundi for them to consider the possibility of lifting them, in accordance with the spirit of the decisions of the Assembly of Heads of State and Government of the OAU held in Ouagadougou, Burkina Faso, in June 1998.

9. The relationship between the Commission and NGOs was discussed with contributions from States delegates and NGOs observers.

10. The Commission has decided to use the existing revised and simplified guidelines for the preparation of States reports. The Commission resolved to organise a seminar for African Ambassadors in Addis Ababa on the issue of submission of States reports to the Commission. The Secretary was directed to write to States Parties attaching the said revised guidelines together with an explanatory note on procedures and timetable for the consideration of outstanding States reports.

11. Angola presented its initial State report in accordance with Article 62 of the Charter. Consideration of the initial reports of South Africa, Seychelles and Chad was postponed to the 25th Ordinary Session. The Commission expressed strong displeasure at the absence of these States to present their reports to the Commission.

12. The Commission took note of the bombing of a pharmaceutical plant in Khartoum and deplored the harmful consequences on human rights.

13. The Commission decided to send Commissioner Ben Salem to Sierra Leone to meet President Ahmed Tejan Kabbah so as to ask him not to proceed with further execution of those sentenced to death.

14. The representatives of the Governments of Senegal and Mauritania addressed the Commission on issues arising from the missions undertaken to their countries on 1–7 and 19–27 June 1996 respectively.

15. The Commission welcomed the holding of talks between the parties to the Guinea Bissau conflict and expressed its support for the ongoing peace process, paying particular tribute to the Head of State of The Gambia Col (Rtd) Yahya J. J. Jammeh. A resolution to this effect was adopted by the Commission.

16. In commemoration of the 50th Anniversary of the Universal Declaration of Human Rights, the Commission decided to issue a statement, which would be circulated to all States parties to the Charter.

17. During the private sessions, the Commission considered a total number of 66 communications and made the necessary recommendations

18. The Commission adopted six resolutions.

19. The African Commission on Human and Peoples' Rights expresses its profound gratitude to the Government of the Republic of the Gambia for its efforts in making the session a success.

20. The session was declared closed on 31 October, 1998 by Hon. Justice G. Gelaga-King of the Gambia Court of Appeal.

21. The Chairman of the Commission held a press conference after the closing ceremony.

Done in Banjul on 31 October 1998

Reflection on the Establishment of an Early Intervention Mechanism in Cases of Massive Human Rights Violations

Twenty-fourth Ordinary Session
Banjul, 22–31 October 1998
DOC/OS/52 (XXIV)

MECHANISMS FOR URGENT RESPONSE TO HUMAN RIGHTS EMERGENCIES UNDER ARTICLE 58 OF THE AFRICAN CHARTER ON HUMAN AND PEOPLES' RIGHTS

1. The Commission or its bureau should act promptly in cases of massive violations of human rights or emergency situations.

2. The Commission should conduct on-site visits, make diplomatic approaches and contact national and international organisations concerned with human rights.

3. If a State is uncooperative, the Commission should organise meetings near the State or at its headquarters.

4. The Commission can also authorise a member of a working group to compile an appropriate report for the Commission on the situation.

5. The Commission should exercise its competence under Article 45(i) to report on and make public its views on an emergency given that Article 59 on confidentiality relates to Chapter 3 of the Charter.

6. The Commission should organise focal points, in collaboration with member states and NGOs, linked to the Commission and collect information and give warning of emergency.

7. The Commission should include in its agenda an item "Emergency Situations" to cover the immediate past and present situations and these should be discussed in open sessions. Aspects of the same agenda may be discussed in private.

8. The Commission should report emergency situations to the Assembly or the Chairman as specified in Article 58. It should, more especially, give publicity to the outbreak of emergencies and to its findings after investigations. The impact of such publicity on public opinion is a weapon that cannot be underestimated in the protection of human rights.

9. The Commission should render interim reports to half-yearly ministerial conferences on emergency situations.

Non-Compliance of State Parties to Adopted Recommendations of the African Commission: A Legal Approach

Twenty-fourth Ordinary Session
Banjul, 22–31 October 1998
DOC/OS/50b (XXIV)

1. During its 22nd Ordinary Session, held in Banjul, The Gambia, from 2–11 November 1997, the African Commission on Human and Peoples' Rights was seized by its Secretary of the issue of Non-Compliance of State Parties to adopted recommendations of the Commission on the communications submitted before it in accordance with the relevant provisions of the African Charter (Agenda Item 11-b).[1]

2. It was particularly stated that the non-compliance of concerned state parties to the recommendations constituted one of the major factors of the erosion of the Commission's credibility.

3. After a lengthy discussion, it was decided that:

(a) A study should be conducted on the various aspects of the matter; and
(b) Recommendations made by the Commission on communications submitted before it, should be included in its Annual Report forwarded to the OAU Assembly of Heads of States and Governments for adoption.

4. The issue discussed here is that of ensuring the compliance of State parties to the recommendations of the Commission and thereby meeting the expectations of complainants that have entrusted the Commission with their complaints.

5. The aim of this study is to propose series of solutions for the Commission's consideration whilst highlighting the difficulties in which the Commission found itself in the course of the past years vis-à-vis the attitude of State Parties which with the exception of Cameroon[2] has been to generally ignore its recommendations.

6. The past practice of the Commission has been to consistently make use of literal interpretation of the provisions of Article 59(1) which stipulates the following: "All measures taken within the provisions of the present Charter shall remain confidential until such a time as the Assembly of Heads of State and Government shall otherwise decide". And indeed every annual report of the Commission contains all the decisions and recommendations adopted on the communications and the Assembly of Heads of

[1] *Cf.* DOC/OS/20 (XXII), Add. 2.

[2] *Cf.* Communication No. 39/90, Annette Pagnoulle (on behalf of Abdoulaye Mazou) v. Cameroon.

State and Government has always adopted the Commission's reports without debate. Moreover the States concerned by the recommendations so adopted have never raised any objection against the reports nor made any reservations; be it against the conclusions of communications brought against them, or against reports of missions undertaken in their territories brought against them, or against reports of missions undertaken in their territories by the Commission. In spite of all this, state Parties in their large majority have never given the expected outcome to the recommendations. With the sovereignty of the Assembly of heads of State and Government and the Charter's non-provision of alternative methods of compensation for victims of Human Rights violations, the said victims find themselves without any remedy after the aforementioned process followed by the Commission. This frustrating situation suggests that the Commission should interpret and apply the provisions of the Charter in a more dynamic way.

7. Coming back to Article 59(1) mentioned above, note could be taken of the fact that comparatively the terms are quite similar to the text of Article 5(3) and (4) of the Optional Protocol (1) to the International Covenant on Civil and Political Rights, adopted by the General Assembly of the United Nations in its Resolution 2200 A (XXI) of 16 December 1966. However, the United Nations and most particularly the General Assembly has evolved in its perception of Human Rights issues. It thus decided to convene in 1989, a world conference with the aim of examining progress achieved so far in the domain of human rights since the inception in 1948 of the Universal Declaration of Human Rights, identifying obstacles to the full realisation and finding the means to overcome them, with the aim of bringing human rights closer to its natural subject, the HUMAN BEING. This process led to the Conference and to the Vienna Declaration adopted on 25 June 1993 by one hundred and seventy one (171) countries, the goal being to achieve a concrete implementation of human rights norms.

8. The African Commission is a conventional organ precisely entrusted *inter alia* with the mission of helping in the development of the culture of respect of fundamental rights of the human being, throughout the continent. To enable it aid in the advancement of human rights issues and justify its existence, it would be judicious for the Commission to explore other efficient ways and methods towards the State Parties.

9. In this regard, the Commission could by reviewing the number of recommendations it had made on the communications where it had found that there had been violations of human rights, make the ratio with the number of concerned states, and then assign some of its members with explanatory and consultative mission to the said states. The aim being to have a frank and critical dialogue with the States and help them to comply with the said recommendations. This initiative could be limited in time and should involve both interested National and International NGOs.

10. The other axis of intervention could be the systematic incorporation of all cases of human rights violations that were found by the Commission into the agenda of the Committee of Ambassadors and other plenipotentiaries accredited to the Organisation of African Unity (OAU) and to the agenda of the OAU Council of Ministers. The idea here being to "heckle" states accused of human rights violations and therefore to get rid of the process of confidentiality which has shown its limits and insufficiencies.[3]

11. Furthermore, Rule 108 of the Rules of procedure stipulates that: "The Commission may issue through the Secretary and for the attention of the media and the public, releases on the activities of the Commission in its private session". By making use of this provision, the African Commission could get itself closer to the procedure adopted by the UN in its Resolution II (XXXV of 1979) concerning cases of forced disappearances in Chile. The said resolution was adopted by the UN Commission for Human Rights and it appointed for the first time a special rapporteur to deal with a situation of violations of Human Rights brought before it. The raison d'être of this approach was to get rid of the straitjacket of confidentiality which as aforementioned does not allow any progress since the state can at any time turn a blind eye.

12. The Member(s) thus appointed could *inter alia* be mandated to assist States Parties concerned, in close collaboration with the Secretariat, in preventive activities and to sort out human rights problems being faced by the States. The experience has shown that in most cases, violations of human rights suffered by individuals are as a result of the ignorance of state agents directly concerned with such matters in their daily activities.

13. Moreover, this would enhance dialogue with States parties, ameliorate their perception of the Commission and in so doing contribute to the edification and enhancement of the Rule of Law on the Continent; the rule of law being a situation where through the institution of a State, the rights of all would be recognised, respected without discrimination, and where public authorities submit themselves to the law in all their endeavours.

DRAFT RESOLUTION ON THE IMPLEMENTATION OF THE RECOMMENDATIONS OF THE AFRICAN COMMISSION ON HUMAN AND PEOPLES' RIGHTS (ACHPR)

The African Commission on Human and Peoples' Rights, meeting at its 24th Ordinary Session in Banjul, The Gambia, from 22–31 October 1998,

Considering that the mission of promotion and protection of human and peoples' rights entrusted to it by the African Charter on Human and Peoples' Rights implies *inter alia* elaboration and promotion of principles intended to help state parties solve legal problems related to the enjoyment of human and peoples' rights and fundamental freedoms,

Considering that in the process of achievement of the above-mentioned mandate deriving from the provisions of Article 45(1)(b) and (2) of the African Charter on Human and Peoples' Rights, the Commission makes recommendations on the basis of

[3] See annexed draft resolution.

communications brought before it by individuals, groups of individuals and state parties alleging violations of human and peoples' rights,

Noting that state parties in ratifying without any reservation, the African Charter on Human and peoples' Rights have thus agreed to accept the authority and the essential role of the Commission in the promotion and protection of Human and Peoples' Rights throughout Africa,

Noting further that the member states of the Organisation of African Unity (OAU) have solemnly reaffirmed their adherence to the principles enunciated by the Universal Declaration of Human Rights as well as to the African Charter on Human and Peoples' Rights that the latter adherence was renewed through Article 3(g) of the treaty instituting the African Economic Community,

Noting in addition that the procedure followed by the African Commission on Human and Peoples' Rights is similar to the one instituted in Article 41(1)(a) of the International Covenant on Civil and Political Rights adopted by the General Assembly of the United Nations in its Resolution 2200 A (XXI) of 16 December 1966, and complemented by those of Articles 1, 2, 3 and 4(1) and also by Article 5 of the optional Protocol (1) of the above-mentioned Covenant, which entered into force on 23 March 1976,

Recalling that the Vienna Declaration of 25 June 1993 and its programme of action, the elaboration of which OAU member states actively participated in and adhere to, calls upon the African Community to proceed in carrying human rights closer to their prime subject: the human being, and that the said process is the one followed by the African Commission on Human and Peoples' Rights,

Convinced that compliance of state parties to its recommendations will contribute to the enhancement of the work of the Commission as well as to the improvement of the conditions of the population under their jurisdiction and also contribute to the promotion and enhancement of the rule of law in Africa,

Recalling further that the Commission would not properly achieve its mission of promotion and protection of human and peoples' rights without the co-operation of state parties,

1. CONGRATULATES those state parties who have complied with its recommendations and encourage them to continue in the same way;
2. CALLS UPON all state parties to the African Charter on Human and Peoples' Rights to respect without delay the recommendations related to the communications seized by the Commission;
3. DECIDES (without prejudice to the provisions of Articles 58 and 59 of the Charter) to submit at every session of the Council of Ministers a report on the situation of human rights in Africa and on the compliance with its recommendations by the State Parties;
4. REQUESTS all state parties to the African Charter on Human and Peoples' Rights to endeavour to comply with the said recommendations to implement them within a maximum period of ninety (90) days starting from the date of notification of the recommendation (by the Commission) and to indicate the measures taken for their execution.

Inter-Session Activities

Twenty-fourth Ordinary Session
Banjul, 22–31 October 1998
DOC/OSA/53(b) (XXIV)

Between the 23rd and 24th Session of our Commission the main activities that I undertook can be summarized as follows:

- 27–20 April 1998. Participation in the first Mediterranean Meeting of National Institutions for the protection and promotion of Human Rights organized by the Moroccan Advisory Council on Human Rights at Marrakech (Morocco).
- 18–22 May 1998. Participation in the Conference on the establishment and strengthening of National Human Rights Institutions organized through the initiative of the Ethiopia Parliament in Addis Ababa.
- 24 May 1998. Participation in activities marking Africa day organized in Algiers by the Algerian Ministry of Foreign Affairs.
- 1 June 1998. Organization of "Children's Parliament" day on the occasion of World Children's Day. On this occasion 380 children had a session in the parliament (National Peoples' Assembly and Senate). In taking the floor, I indicated that this event was being held within the framework of the Fiftieth Anniversary of the Universal Declaration of Human Rights.
- 12–16 June 1998. At the request of the Chairman Mr. Ndiaye, I represented our Commission at the Seminar organized for the celebration of the 10th Anniversary of the Great Green Human Rights Charter in Tripoli (Libya). In my statement at the opening ceremony in the presence of Colonel Geddafi, I underscored the importance of the role of the African Commission on the promotion of Human and Peoples' Rights.
- 1–6 July 1998. Participation in the 2nd meeting of African National Institution for Human Rights protection and promotion organized in Durban (South Africa) at the invitation of the South African Human Rights Commission.
- 9 July 1998. During my visit to Sudan, I had a working session at the Interights headquarters with Mr. Ibrahima Kane (Interights) and Mr. Tahar Boumedra (African Society) to evaluate progress registered in the proposed convening of the seminar on the right to a fair trial.
- 18 August 1998. During the 54th Session of the Human Rights Sub-committee in Geneva, I had a meeting with the Coordinating Committee of African NGOs based in this country (Mr. Maluza and Mrs. Bineta Diop).
- 27 September 1998. Working session in Algiers with Mr. Benrom Dhane, President Elect of the Executive Committee of Amnesty International on the occasion of the General Assembly of the Algerian Section of Amnesty International.

- 4 October 1998. Working session with UNDP Resident Representative in Algiers for the organization of the celebration of the Fiftieth Anniversary of the Universal Declaration of Human Rights.

M. K. Rezag-Bara
Member of the African Commission
on Human and Peoples' Rights

Activity Reports of Commissioners

Twenty-fourth Ordinary Session
Banjul, 22–31 October 1998
DOC/OSA/53(a) (XXIV)

1. At the 23rd Ordinary Session of the Commission held in Banjul, The Gambia, 20–29 April 1998, I was given responsibility for promotional activities in the following countries: Botswana, Lesotho, Malawi, Namibia, Nigeria, South Africa, Swaziland, Zambia and Zimbabwe. This is my second activity report since becoming a member of the Commission in June 1997.

2. As I understand it, my responsibilities entail monitoring the state of and developments in human rights in the countries of responsibility, engage with other partners in promotional activities as well as maintaining liaison with the governments and NGOs on human rights issues especially the role of the African Commission.

3. As in the last report, I shall divide my report into three sections: Status of Human Rights, Activities and Future Programmes.

STATUS OF HUMAN RIGHTS

4. There has been much to cause concern about human rights in our region during the period under review. Of particular concern has been the irruption of the civil war in the Democratic Republic of the Congo in August. There has been an uprising led from the eastern part of the Congo ostensibly with the support of the armed forces of Rwanda and Uganda. The Tutsi-led rebels seek to overthrow the government of Laurent Kabila and to establish a government, as they say, that is based on human rights and that is inclusive of all the democratic forces in the Congo. On the side of the armed forces of the DRC has joined the armies of Angola, Namibia, Zimbabwe and lately, Chad and, if the reports are true, The Sudan. There was division within SADC about the appropriate mechanism for intervening in the Congo conflict. The states that have joined to support President Laurent Kabila led by Zimbabwe insisted that it was the duty of SADC states to come in defence of a legitimate government in the face of an armed uprising. Others led by South Africa desire to negotiate a peaceful settlement. In the end, the principle of intervention was accepted by SADC. This, however, has meant that a peaceful resolution of the conflict was remote especially as the government of Kabila refuses to negotiate directly with the rebel movement. The war is intensifying.

5. Closer home, a similar conflict raged in Lesotho in September. For over a month opposition demonstrators had rendered Lesotho ungovernable by maintaining a round-the-clock picket on the Royal Palace grounds. later junior officers ousted the

leadership of the military, there was sporadic violence and government was effectively paralysed. The cause of this unrest was the refusal by the opposition parties to accept the results of the General Elections held in May. They argued that the results were fraudulent. The governing Lesotho Congress for Democracy was returned with all but one of the seats. The elections were declared free and fair by the international observers.

6. In the face of the persistent civil unrest, the SADC appointed a commission of inquiry led by Justice Pius Langa, Deputy President of the Constitutional Court of South Africa. The Commission found that there was no "conclusive proof that the announced results and the actual results (were) correct or rigged". The Commission recommended, however, that the government establish an Independent Electoral Commission that enjoys the confidence of the people. The Commission also indicated that Lesotho might wish to consider a different electoral system than the Westminster model which excluded other parties in a first-past-the-post system.

7. Subsequent to the publication of the report and in the face of a virtual coup d'état, SADC dispatched armed forced represented by the South African and Botswana armies at the request of the government of Lesotho which had become paralysed and unable to govern. This was by all accounts a controversial move. The government of South Africa justified its military intervention on the basis of SADC agreements to resist coups d'état in the region by all means.

8. The cases of the Congo and Lesotho raise some difficult questions about the management of peace and conflict resolution mechanisms in Africa. It is noticeable that the OAU has taken the backseat in this conflict and certainly failed to establish its authority as a custodian of peace and democratic government in Africa. Even less has there been any reference to the Commission. It is interesting that the government of the DRC has not considered resort to Article 47 to lodge a complaint against Rwanda and Uganda. It suggests either ignorance or lack of confidence in the mechanisms provided by the Charter. No government appears to have thought to use the good offices of the Commission to address the conflict situation prevailing in the countries. Finally, this circumstance points to a need for the Commission to pay more attention to the organisation and management of elections in a manner that is independent and enjoys the confidence of the electorate.

9. In South Africa, the focus of human rights development during this year has been the programme towards the adoption of a National Action Plan for Human Rights. The process is now complete and the plan is being drafted and will be presented to Cabinet for approval before the end of October. At the same time South Africa has prepared and submitted its initial report in terms of Article 62 of the Charter. South Africa acceded to the Charter in July 1996. A workshop on the African Charter was held in September as part of the NAP and country report process.

10. On the more negative side, there has been outrage about incidents of xenophobia in the country. In September three asylum seekers from Senegal and Mozambique were murdered by a mob of unemployed South Africans. The brutality of this deed has spurred many of us into action. It must be stated that there have been reports of hostility towards foreigners from Africa in our country but this latest incident has shocked many of us by its callousness, brutality and inhumanity. As a result, the South African Human Rights Commission convened a conference on Xenophobia and Human Rights on 15 October. The conference, attended by government, NGOs and ourselves adopted a programme of public awareness and education, called for a coherent government policy on immigration and urged South Africans to exercise hospitality and to be welcoming to foreigners and called upon government to step up job-creation programmes and ensure a more effective criminal justice system. The Commission will oversee the implementation of this programme.

11. The border dispute between Botswana and Namibia continues to cause concern. It is hoped that the proposed international mediation will bring this matter to a peaceful resolution. There has been strong criticism of the SWAPO government of Namibia for seeking to amend the constitution in order to allow President Sam Nujoma to serve a third term of office. It is feared that the use of the parliamentary majority to change the constitution on a matter that goes to the heart of democracy bodes ill for Namibia's democracy. Questions are being asked as to whether the people of Namibia can trust that SWAPO will not use its majority to vote in a President for Life or even a one-party state? Namibia's High Commissioner to London resigned in protest.

12. Swaziland held its general elections on 16 October. There was strong opposition to the elections which are considered undemocratic because the Swazi king rules as an absolute monarch and the will of the people does not prevail. Parliament under the tinkundla or traditional system has no real power. The government argues that the system reflects the will of the majority of the people of Swaziland. There are warning signs that the political system in Swaziland will remain unstable as a result.

13. Zambia and Zimbabwe pose a different set of problems. In both countries there has been vociferous outcries against gay and lesbian people. The official rhetoric lends itself to hostility to people who espouse a different sexual preference. The attempted coup in Zambia resulted in widespread repression and hounding of the opposition personalities. There were reports that those detained were tortured and the trials cannot be fair. Even within the ruling party there are reports of a vendetta against dissent. The democratic institutions like the electoral system need to be revisited if a latent explosion is not to erupt. There are reports that the government of Zambia is using the citizenship laws recently enacted and the threat of deportation against government critics within opposition parties or elsewhere. In both countries questions about the freedom of the press remain. The government of Zimbabwe has had to deal with critical opposition to its economic policies. The combination of high taxation, rising food prices and increasing salaries and allowances of government resulting in expensive and unaffordable government has resulted in several demonstrations against government policies. The land redistribution programme seems to have stalled or is being reversed in the face of the government's inability to afford the cost of acquisition of land.

14. Remarkably, the only ray of hope in this otherwise dismal picture is Nigeria. The death of military dictator Sani Abacha and the accession to power of General Abdulsalami Abubakar raised hopes that the era of military governments is drawing to an end. General Abubakar has already instituted some reforms and promises a return to democracy. He has released many detainees from the democratic opposition and Wole Soyinka made a much-publicised return from exile on 15 October. I believe that the situation in Nigeria, though encouraging, needs both support and close monitoring.

15. It is clear that a critical lesson to peace and social stability in Africa are democratic systems that have the support of the people, an effective and independent election managing body, an electoral system that is inclusive of a wider political opinion in the country as well as independent institutions to promote democracy. I recommend that the Commission sends representatives to observe elections so as to be able to identify areas which might cause problems for democracy in the future.

ACTIVITIES

16. In May I attended the British Council International Seminar on National Systems for the Improvement of Human Rights. The seminar was valuable in that it had participants from national institutions and from countries developing national human rights systems. It also provided an opportunity to look at development in Ireland following the signing of the Good Friday Agreement which, it was hoped, would bring an end to sectarian violence. At the time preparations were afoot for the first elections under the system that would give effect to the Good Friday Agreement.

17. Immediately after Belfast, I attended the international conference in Addis Ababa on the proposal to establish a national human rights institution and the office of the ombudsman in Ethiopia. Once again the conference was widely representative and provided opportunities to share perspectives on the human rights systems nationally and regionally. I prepared a paper on National Institutions at Work for both conferences.

18. On 1–3 July 1998, the South African Human Rights Commission hosted the 2nd Conference of African national institutions in Durban. We were privileged to have the Chairman of the Commission as one of the keynote speakers at the conference. The conference adopted the Durban Declaration which, we hope will be presented to the Commission for consideration. The full report of the conference is not yet available but should be distributed by the end of November. I hope to have available for distribution a short version of the report and the Declaration during this session.

19. On 20–24 July I attended the ICJ Triennial Meeting in Cape Town, 20–24 July 1998 on the Rule of Law in a Changing World. The meeting gathered together some eminent jurists and discussed some of the critical challenges for the rule of law in the world today.

20. In June I invited ambassadors from the countries I have promotional oversight over to a briefing meeting. The meeting only took place on 10 September. It was attended by about six of the nine embassies even though all had indicated interest. The ambassadors welcomed my initiative. We agreed that I would endeavour to have a briefing session at least once a year. I also undertook to supply them with a report on each session of the Commission which they would transmit to their governments.

21. I wrote to all the NGOs with observer status in the Commission from the countries I have promotional responsibility for. I shared with them the Communiqué of the last session and indicated ways in which we could strengthen contact. As a result of my approach, I am beginning to receive invitations from several states to address meetings. I approached the Secretariat to make the arrangements for my visit to Nigeria in the light of the changes in that country. I understand that the Secretariat has been in touch by diplomatic means with the Nigerian authorities. I hope that the visit can take place early in the new year.

22. In September, I held a briefing meeting with South African NGOs with observer status in the Commission. We looked at the Agenda for this session, examined how we could raise awareness for the Charter and the Commission in our country and we agreed to finalise plans for a Workshop in Southern Africa. It was agreed that:

- A Workshop of all NGOs affiliated to the Commission from SADC countries be held early 1999.
- The issue of impartiality of the Commission be raised at the coming Commission meeting.

23. I am proud to be a member of the International Human Rights Policy Council. This is a human rights policy think tank that identifies critical areas for applied research. The secretariat of this new international NGO is in Geneva. The last meeting was held in Lima, Peru, 2–4 October. A variety of research projects were discussed: Universality, The Responsibility of Non State Actors; Conflict Resolution, The Role of the Media, Performance and Legitimacy of National Institutions and the International Financial Crisis.

24. In october I visited Zambia at the invitation of the Permanent Human Rights Commission of Zambia. I was keynote speaker at the national human rights conference. Accompanied by the Chairperson of the Zambian Commission, Judge Lombe Chibesakunda, I had the privilege of meeting the Minister of Home Affairs with whom I raised the matter of William Banda who was deported to Malawi. I pointed out that the Commission had not received a reply to its communication following the decision to be seized of this matter last April. The minister assured me that a reply was being prepared in time for the October meeting of the Commission. The minister assured me that the government of Zambia was trying to abide by the Charter and to establish a culture of human rights in the country. He believed that the government deserved the support of the African Commission in its endeavours.

FORTHCOMING ACTIVITIES

17–19 November Keynote Speaker, Botswana National Conference on Human Rights

4–5 December	Workshop of National Institutions, Paris, France
7–8 December	Keynote Speaker, World Council of Churches Assembly, Harare, Zimbabwe
10 December	International Human Rights Day activities in South Africa
January 1999	African Conference on Indigenous Peoples, Arusha, Tanzania
March 1999	NGO Conference

N. Barney Pityana
Johannesburg, 16 October 1998

Second Meeting of the Working Group on the Additional Protocol to the African Charter on Women's Rights in Africa

Dakar, 14–15 June 1999

REPORT OF THE FIRST MEETING OF THE WORKING GROUP ON THE ADDITIONAL PROTOCOL TO THE AFRICAN CHARTER ON WOMEN'S RIGHTS

Banjul, 26–28 January 1998

1. The first meeting of the working group on women's rights was held in Banjul, The Gambia from 26–28 January 1998. The meeting was presided over by Mr. Youssoupha Ndiaye, Chairman of the African Commission.

2. The meeting was attended by the following members of the group:

(i)	Mr. Youssoupha Ndiaye	Chairman
(ii)	Prof. E. V. O. Dankwa	Co-ordinator
(iii)	Mrs. Julienne Ondziel-Gnelenga	Member of the Commission
(iv)	Mrs. Zoe Tembo	ACDHRS
(v)	Mrs. Tokunbo Ige	ICJ
(vi)	Mme. Aissata De	WILDAF
(vii)	Mr. Germain Baricako	Secretary to the Commission

3. Mrs. Vera Duarte-Martins, the vice-chairperson of the African Commission was absent from the meeting.

4. The meeting was declared open by the Chairman of the Commission, Mr. Youssoupha Ndiaye, at the Conference hall of the host organisation, the African Centre for Democracy and Human Rights Studies.

Item I: Adoption of Agenda

5. Professor Dankwa, the Co-ordinator of the working group, read out the proposed Agenda and it was adopted as presented.

(i) Introductory remarks were made by Professor E. V. O. Dankwa;
(ii) An overview of the existing instruments relating to women;
(iii) Consideration of the Draft Protocol on the rights of women;
(iv) Discussion on the terms of reference and the appointment of a special rapporteur on the rights of women;
(v) Adoption of the report of the meeting.

Item II: Adoption of a Working Method for the Group

6. Professor Dankwa proposed a working method which was adopted as follows:

(i) Decide on additions to the Nouakchott Document;
(ii) Decide on items to take out of the document;
(iii) Decide on the elimination of repetitive provisions in the protocol;
(iv) Draft an instrument that can be presented to the Commission;
(v) Circulate the draft instrument for comments;
(vi) Have another meeting to review the comments received.

Item III: Appointment of a Special Rapporteur for Women

7. The Co-ordinator pointed out that in appointing a Rapporteur for the rights of women, the terms of reference of the Special Rapporteur on Extra-judicial Executions in Africa and also those of the Special Rapporteur on Prisons in Africa should be borne in mind since it would be beneficial in formulating the terms of reference for the former.

8. After a long discussion, the secretary to the Commission outlined the procedure for the adoption of such instruments within the OAU.

9. A number of bodies including experts and Ministers will consider the draft instrument before it is submitted to the Assembly of Heads of State and Government for adoption.

Item IV: Consideration of the Draft Protocol on the Rights of Women

The following amendments were made to the Draft Protocol.

10. The Preamble
The title of the instrument should read “on the rights of women in Africa”.

11. Paragraph 2
On the second line, “forms of” is to be inserted just before “discrimination”.

12. Paragraph 3
Add:

(a) “CEDAW and all other international conventions and international instruments relating to the rights of women”;
(b) “universal” between “inalienable” and “independent”.

Delete: “now” from the last line.

13. Paragraph 6
In the French version, on the first line, the word “considèrent” should be replaced by “reconnaissent”.

14. Paragraph 7

To read:

"CONCERNED with the fact that discrimination against women in Africa continues, despite the ratification of the African Charter on Human and Peoples' Rights and other international human rights instruments by a majority of African States and their solemn commitment to eliminate all forms of discrimination against women."

15. Paragraph 8

Delete from the last line, "peace . . . in Africa" and replace with "all spheres of life".

16. Article 1

Add: "in all spheres of life" to the end of the article.

17. Article 2

(a) Add: "dignity" to the last line between "equality" and "justice".
(b) The expression "cultural values" should be replaced with "positive African traditions".
(c) It was also noted that this Article contains a Right and a Duty and it is better to separate the two.

18. Article 3

(a) Delete: "and" after "legislation" on the last line.
(b) Add: "and all spheres of life" at the end of the Article.

19. Article 4

(a) On the second line, "Shall" is to remain.
(b) The second paragraph should be replaced with article 5(a) CEDAW.

20. Article 5

(a) On the provision that prohibits the medical and scientific experiments on women, "without their consent" is to be added to the end of the sentence.
(b) Insert "and/or morally" between "physically" and "harmful" on the first line of the last subsection.

21. Article 6

(a) Two proposals have been made for the amendment of this provision:

  (i) Polygamy shall be prohibited except otherwise consented to by both parties;
  (ii) Polygamy shall be prohibited, and in any country where it exists, the law shall strive to work towards its gradual elimination.

(b) It was observed on the issue of registration of marriages that, to require registration for the legal validity of every marriage may render many marriages invalid and work to the detriment of women, but it was also observed that in some jurisdictions, registration is a pre-requisite for the legal validity of a marriage; and this works to the advantage of the woman.

(c) The minimum age for marriage should be fixed to safeguard the health and dignity of the girl.

(d) It was also noted that the age of majority is not necessarily the same as the legal age for marriage.

22. Article 7

(a) The provision dealing with the rights of a surviving spouse to reside in the former matrimonial home, is to read as follows:

> "The surviving spouse shall have the right to continue to live in the matrimonial residence as long as need be and if the general interest of the family has been taken into consideration."[1]

(b) It was noted also that the property might not belong to the family; therefore the right cannot be exercised by the surviving spouse.

23. Article 8

This provision is to be deleted since it is being provided for in other international instruments and municipal law.

24. Article 9

(a) The French text is to read "States Parties should commit themselves to take appropriate measures".

(b) On the English text, the last word on the first line of the provision should be "services and aid".

(c) The two subsections (a) and (b) of this provision have been merged.

25. Article 10

Adopted.

26. Article 11

Adopted but the last line "against rape and other sexual assault" should be moved to Article 5 which deals with violence against women.

27. Article 12

The following changes have been made:

(a) Delete:

(i) all brackets but the contents remain.

(ii) "Sexual harassment . . . etc." and end the sentence.

(b) State parties to this protocol commit themselves to take all appropriate measures to.

[1] Family in this context refers to the surviving spouse and the children.

Add: to the English text

(i) Identify the cause of violence against women and take pleasures to eliminate such violence.
(ii) Punish perpetrators of such violence committed against women.
(iii) Provide for the rehabilitation and reparation for victims of such violence.

28. Article 13
The provision on the education of the girl child should now read: "Promote the education of girls by providing free education through grants and bursary".

29. Article 14

(a) Add: "Ensure transparency in employment and dismissal relating to women" as the second subsection.
(b) Delete: "the introduction . . . work, etc.".

30. Article 15
Adopted but paragraph 17 of the Beijing Declaration should be added.

31. Article 16
Adopted.

32. Article 17
Add: "Adequate" on the first line just before "housing".

33. Article 18
Delete: "their life" from the first line.
Add: "intolerance" after "fundamentalism".

34. Article 19
Adopted, but add: "satisfactory" between "healthy" and "environment".

35. Article 20
The provision dealing with the adverse effects of SAP is to be rewritten.

36. Article 21
The first line is to include "State parties to the Charter".

37. Article 22
Adopted.

38. This working group after discussions, taking into account her experience and commitment in the field, has proposed Madame Julienne Ondziel to be the Special Rapporteur on the rights of women in Africa because of her experience.

39. The working group has considered and adopted terms of reference for the Special Rapporteur on the rights of women in Africa, which is Annex II of this report.[2]

[2] Annex I is the Draft Protocol as amended.

DRAFT ON PROTOCOL TO THE AFRICAN CHARTER ON HUMAN AND PEOPLES' RIGHTS ON THE RIGHTS OF WOMEN

The states parties to this protocol:

Considering that Article 66 of the African Charter on Human and Peoples' Rights provides for special protocols or agreements if necessary to supplement the provisions of the African Charter and that the OAU Assembly of Heads of State and Government has in June 1995, endorsed the decision of the African Commission on Human and Peoples' Rights to elaborate a draft protocol on the Rights of Women;

Considering that Article 2 of the African Charter on Human and Peoples' Rights enshrines the principle of non-discrimination on the grounds of race, ethnic group, colour, sex, language, religion, political or any other opinion, national and social origin, fortune, birth or other status;

Considering also that Article 18 of the African Charter on Human and Peoples' Rights calls on all African states to eliminate all discrimination against women and to ensure the protection of the rights of women as stipulated in international declarations and conventions;

Recalling that women's rights have been recognised and guaranteed in all international human rights instruments, notably the Universal Declaration of Human Rights, the International Covenant on Civil and Political Rights and the International Covenant on Economic, Social and Cultural Rights, CEDAW and all other international conventions and covenants relating to the rights of women are now recognised as being inalienable, interdependent and indivisible human rights;

Noting that women's rights and women's essential role in development have been reaffirmed in the United Nations Plans of Action on the Environment and Development in 1992, on Human Rights in 1993, on Population and Development in 1994 and on Social Development in 1995;

Considering also that the plans of action adopted in Dakar in November 1994 and in Beijing in September 1995 call on all Member States of the United Nations to take concrete steps to give greater attention to the human rights of women in order to eliminate all forms of discrimination and of gender-based violence against women;

Noting that Articles 60 and 61 of the African Charter on Human and Peoples' Rights recognise regional and international norms on human and peoples' rights as being important reference points for the application and interpretation of the Charter;

Concerned that despite the ratification of the African Charter on Human and Peoples' Rights and other international human rights instruments by a majority of African States and their solemn commitment to eliminate all forms of discrimination against women, discrimination against women in Africa continues;

Noting that many people in Africa continue to perceive human and peoples' rights as being the exclusive preserve of men despite the fact that women play a fundamental role in all spheres;

HAVE AGREED UPON THE FOLLOWING:

Article 1
For the purposes of this present Additional Protocol, and in conformity with Articles 2 and 18 of the African Charter on Human and Peoples' Rights discrimination against women means any distinction, exclusion or restriction based on sex whose effects compromise or destroy the recognition, enjoyment or the exercise by women – regardless of their matrimonial status – on an equal basis with men, of human rights and fundamental freedoms in all respects.

Article 2
Women shall enjoy on the basis of equality with men, the same rights and respect for their dignity and contribute to the preservation of those African cultural values that are positive and are based on the principles of equality, dignity, justice and democracy.

Article 3
In order to eliminate effectively all forms of discrimination against women, State Parties to this Protocol shall take all necessary measures to integrate a gender perspective in their policy decisions, legislation, development plans and all spheres of life.

Article 4
In order to attain equality between the sexes, State Parties to this Protocol shall:

(a) take specific positive action in those areas where discrimination against women in law and in fact continues to exist;
(b) modify the social and cultural patterns of conduct of men and women, with a view to achieving the elimination of prejudices and customary and all other practices which are based on the idea of the inferiority or the superiority of either of the sexes or on stereotyped roles for men and women.

Article 5
In conformity with Articles 4 and 5 of the African Charter on Human and people's Rights, States Parties to this Protocol shall:

(a) never sentence pregnant women to death;
(b) prohibit all forms of trafficking;
(c) prohibit the commercial exploitation of prostitutes;
(d) prohibit medical or scientific experiments on women without their consent;
(e) prohibit all traditional and cultural practices which are physically and/or morally harmful to women and girls and which are against recognised international norms (including force-feeding, genital mutilation, infibulation, etc.);
(f) protect women against rape and other sexual assaults as war crimes and punish them as such.

Article 6
(1) No marriage shall take place without the free and full consent of both parties.

(2) The minimum age of marriage for men and women shall be the same and shall not be less than the age of majority:

(a) Polygamy shall be prohibited except otherwise consented by both parties; and in any country where polygamy exists, the law shall strive to work towards its elimination;
(b) Women shall have the same rights as men in marriage.

(3) In order to be legally recognised, every marriage shall be recorded in writing and immediately registered, in the presence of the husband and wife, with the competent authorities;
(4) The husband and wife shall be mutual agreement choose their place of residence;
(5) A married woman shall have the right to keep her maiden name, to use it as she pleases – jointly or separately with her husband's surname – and to give her maiden name to her husband and children;
(6) A married woman shall have the right to retain or change her nationality or to confer it on her husband and children;
(7) A man and a woman shall have the same rights and responsibilities towards their children;
(8) During her marriage, the wife shall have the right to acquire her own property and to administer and manage it freely; and in cases of joint ownership of property the husband and wife shall have the same rights.

Article 7

(1) Divorce or annulment of a marriage shall be effectuated only by judicial order. Women shall have the same rights as men to seek divorce or annulment of a marriage and, after divorce or annulment, with respect to the children and property of the marriage.
(2) It shall be prohibited to subject widows to inhuman, humiliating and degrading treatment.
(3) In the case of death of one spouse, nobody shall have the right – whatever the matrimonial regime – to deprive the surviving spouse of the right to live in the former matrimonial home. The surviving spouse shall have the right to continue to live in the matrimonial residence as long as need be and if the general interest of the family has been taken into consideration.
(4) After the death of the husband, the widow shall be by law the guardian of the children and she shall have the right to remarry if she wishes.
(5) A widow shall have the right to inherit her husband's property.

Article 8

With reference to Articles 7 and 25 of the African Charter on Human and Peoples' Rights, States Parties to this Protocol shall:

(a) Take all appropriate measures to facilitate the access of women to legal services;
(b) Put in place adequate structures to inform women and make them aware of their rights.

Article 9
In conformity with Article 13 of the African Charter on Human and Peoples' Rights, States Parties to this Protocol commit themselves to:

(a) take specific action to promote the equal participation of women in the political life of their countries, ensuring that:

  (i) women can participate without any discrimination in all elections;
  (ii) women are represented equally with men in all electoral and candidate lists;
  (iii) include women equally with men at all levels of the development and execution of state policy.

Article 10
(1) In conformity with Article 23 of the African Charter on Human and Peoples' Rights, women shall have the same rights as men to promote and maintain peace and to live in peace.
2) State Parties to this Protocol commit themselves to take all appropriate measures to involve women, on an equal basis:

  (a) in programmes of education for peace and a culture of peace;
  (b) in the structures for conflict prevention, management and resolution at local, national, regional and international levels, in particular within the mechanisms of the OAU;
  (c) in the local, national, regional and international structures for the establishment and management of camps for refugees and displaced persons and for the distribution of food.

(3) State Parties additionally commit themselves to reduce military expenditure significantly in favour of spending on social development, while guaranteeing the effective participation of women in the distribution of these resources.

Article 11
(1) On the basis of Article 4 of the African charter on Human and Peoples' Rights, in this Protocol violence against women shall mean all acts directed against women as women which cause or could cause them physical, sexual, or psychological harm or suffering, including the threat of such acts; or the imposition of arbitrary restrictions on or deprivation of fundamental freedoms in private or public life.
(2) State Parties to this Protocol commit themselves to take all appropriate measures to:

  (a) prohibit all forms of violence against women – physical, mental, verbal or sexual, domestic and family – whether they take place in the private sphere or in society and public life including sexual harassment, sexual abuse or exploitation, rape, etc.;
  (b) identify the cause of violence against women and take measures to eliminate such violence;

(c) punish perpetrators of such violence committed against women;
(d) provide for the rehabilitation and reparation for victims of such violence.

Article 12

(1) In conformity with Article 17 of the African Charter on Human and Peoples' Rights, women shall have equal education opportunities with men.
(2) State Parties shall take all appropriate measures to:

(a) eliminate all discrimination towards women in education;
(b) eliminate all references in text books and syllabuses to the stereotypes which perpetrate such discrimination.

(3) State Parties shall take specific positive action to

(a) promote an increased literacy rate among their citizens and in particular among women;
(b) ensure that primary education is free and compulsory for all and that secondary education is free and compulsory for girls;
(c) promote the education of girls by providing free education through grants and bursary.

Article 13

With reference to article 15 of the African Charter on Human and Peoples' Rights, States Parties to this Protocol shall guarantee women equal opportunities to work. In this respect, they commit themselves to:

(a) promote equality in the terms of remuneration and conditions of work for women;
(b) ensure transparency in employment and dismissal relating to women;
(c) allow women freedom to choose their own job, with decent conditions of work, and to protect them from exploitation by their employers;
(d) regulate the occupations and economic activities dominated by women, in particular the informal sector of the economy;
(e) put in place a system of protection and national insurance for women working in the informal and formal sectors of the economy;
(f) introduce a minimum age of work and prohibit children from working below that age, and to prohibit the sexual exploitation of children;
(g) recognise the value of and to protect the work of women in the home;
(h) guarantee adequate pre- and post-natal maternity leave;
(i) recognise motherhood and the upbringing of children as a social function for which both parents must take responsibility, as well as the State and employers.

Article 14

(1) With reference to article 16 of the African Charter on Human and Peoples' Rights, women shall have the same right to health as men. As part of this right, they shall have the right to control their fertility, including the right to decide whether to have children, how to space their children, to choose any method of contraception and to protect themselves against sexually transmitted diseases.

(2) State Parties to this Protocol shall take appropriate measures to:

(a) ensure that adequate and if necessary free health services are available to women especially those in rural areas;
(b) establish pre- and post-natal health and nutritional services for women during pregnancy and while they are breastfeeding.

Article 15

(1) Every woman, like every man, shall have the right to adequate supplies of wholesome food.
(2) State Parties to this Protocol shall take appropriate measures to:

(a) guarantee to women access to clean drinking water, to sources of domestic fuel, to land, and to the means of producing food;
(b) establish adequate systems of supply and storage to ensure food security.

Article 16

Every woman, like every man, shall have the right to housing and to acceptable living conditions in a healthy environment. To ensure this right, State Parties to this Protocol commit themselves to grant to women, whatever their marital status, access to state provided/social housing sufficient for their needs.

Article 17

(1) Women shall have the right to live their life in a positive cultural environment and to participate at all levels in the determination of cultural policies.
(2) State Parties to this Protocol shall take all appropriate measures to protect women and society from the harmful effects of all forms of fundamentalism and from any other cultural or religious practices contrary to this right.

Article 18

(1) In conformity with Article 24 of the African Charter on Human and Peoples' Rights, women shall have the right to live in a healthy environment.
(2) State Parties shall take all appropriate measures to:

(a) involve women in the management of the environment at all levels;
(b) promote research into renewable energy sources;
(c) regulate the management, processing and storage of domestic waste;
(d) ensure that the proper standards are followed for the storage, transport and destruction of toxic waste.

Article 19

(1) With reference to Articles 21, 22 and 24 of the African Charter on Human and Peoples' Rights, women shall have the right to fully enjoy their right to development.
(2) State Parties to this Protocol shall take all appropriate measures to:

(a) ensure that women can participate fully at all levels in the development and execution of development policies;

(b) ensure that women have access to credit and to financial, economic and natural resources;
(c) take into account indicators of human development specifically relating to women in the working out of development policies;
(d) ensure that in the implementation of trade and economic policies such as structural adjustment programmes, the negative effects of such measures do not affect women.

Article 20

(1) This Protocol shall be open for signature, ratification and accession by the State Parties.
(2) Instruments of ratification or accession to this Protocol shall be deposited with the Secretary General of the OAU.
(3) This Protocol shall come into force one month after the deposit of fifteen instruments of ratification or accession.
(4) For each of the States Parties that ratify or accede to this Protocol after its coming into force, the Protocol shall come into force at the date of deposit of the instrument of ratification or accession.
(5) The Secretary General of the OAU shall inform the Member States of the OAU of the coming into force of this Protocol.

Article 21

This Protocol may be amended if a State Party makes a written request to that effect to the Secretary General of the OAU. The Assembly of Heads of State and Government adopts the draft amendment after all the States Parties have been duly informed of it and the Commission has given its opinion. The amendment shall be approved by a simple majority of the State Parties. The Commission may also, through the Secretary General of the OAU, propose amendments to this Protocol. The amendment shall come into force for each State Party which has accepted it one month after the Secretary General of the OAU has received notice of the acceptance.

DRAFT TERMS OF REFERENCE FOR THE SPECIAL RAPPORTEUR ON THE RIGHTS OF WOMEN IN AFRICA

The decision relating to the appointment of a Special Rapporteur on the rights of women in Africa was adopted at the 19th session of the Commission in Ouagadougou in March 1996 (see Report). This appointment was postponed to this session to define the terms of reference and the profile of the Rapporteur.

I. Justification

In the implementation of the African Charter on Human and Peoples' Rights, the Commission has always put forward diverse concerns concerning the specificity of the situation of the rights of women in Africa.

The Commission has noted that the provisions of the Charter do not ensure an effective protection of the fundamental rights of women.

It is worth noting that the Vienna Conference of 1993 has reaffirmed that the rights of women form an integral part of human rights, and that the pertinent recommendations of this Conference have been the foundation of the conclusions of the Dakar and Beijing Conferences of 1994 and 1995 respectively.

Taking into account the aforesaid, and in order to assist the Commission in the effective implementation of its mandate with regard to women, in conformity with Article 45 of the Charter, it is necessary to appoint a Special Rapporteur on the rights of Women in Africa.

1. Mandate

(a) To carry out a study on the situation of the human rights of women in Africa.

(b) To draw up guidelines on the drafting and examination of States parties' reports on the rights of women in Africa.

(c) Ensure or make a follow up on the implementation of the Charter by States parties. In this vein, the Special Rapporteur will prepare a report on the situation of violations of women's rights and propose recommendations to the Commission.

(d) The Special Rapporteur will assist African governments in the development and implementation of their policies of promotion and protection of women's rights in Africa.

(e) He or she will encourage and work with NGOs in the field of promotion and protection of women's rights.

(f) He or she will serve as a link between the Commission and inter-governmental and non-governmental organisations at regional and international levels in order to harmonise the initiatives on the rights of women.

(g) In this regard, the Special Rapporteur will collaborate with Special rapporteurs from the UN and other regional systems.

2. Duration of the Mandate

The initial duration of the mandate of the Special Rapporteur will run up to the year 2002. However, he or she will have a period of two years to submit his/her interim report and proposals for the future.

3. Area of Investigation

All OAU member States parties to the African Charter. Any other State hosting any organ likely to have information on women's rights in Africa.

4. Report

The Special Rapporteur shall inform the Commission at each session about the progress of his or her work and the difficulties encountered.

He or she will prepare an annual report which shall be annexed to the Commission's Report to the Assembly of Heads of State and Government of the OAU.

NB: The elaboration of the financial provisions for the fulfilment of the Special Rapporteur's mandate for 1998–2000 remains to be done.

II. Criteria for Appointment of Special Rapporteur

(a) Must be a citizen of a State party to the Charter.
(b) Must have a high consideration and competence in matters of women's rights, particular consideration will be given to a person with legal experience.
(c) Must accept and be committed to execute, within the time allowed, the duty as defined in the terms of reference and is wholly responsible to the Commission.

III. Appointment Procedure

The working group was mandated to propose a candidate for the position to the Commission.

NB: At its last meeting held in January 1998 in Banjul, the Gambia, the working group has decided to propose Mrs. Julienne Ondziel-Gnelenga for the position of Special Rapporteur on the Rights of Women in Africa.

Final Communiqué of the Twenty-fifth Ordinary Session of the African Commission on Human and Peoples' Rights

Bujumbura, 26 April to 5 May 1999

1. At the invitation of the Government of the Republic of Burundi, the 25th Ordinary Session of the African Commission on Human and Peoples' Rights was held from 26 April to 5 May 1999 in Bujumbura, Burundi.

2. The opening ceremony took place on 26 April 1999, under the chairmanship of Mr. Youssoupha Ndiaye, Chairman of the African Commission.

3. The Session was opened by the 1st Vice President of the Republic of Burundi, His Excellency, Mr. Frédéric Bamvuginyumvira.

4. Speeches were also made by:

- Dr. Manto Tshabalala-Msimang, Deputy Minister of Justice of the Republic of South Africa, in her capacity as Representative of the Delegates present at the Session; and
- Mr. Mohammed Monieb of the Arab Organisation for Human Rights, on behalf of the Non-Governmental Organisations.

5. The Secretary General of the Organisation of African (OAU) addressed the African Commission on 27 April 1999, in the presence of States delegates, National Human Rights Institutions, and Human Rights Non-Governmental Organisations. In his speech, Dr. Salim Ahmed Salim congratulated the Government of Burundi for its efforts in hosting this Session. These efforts are an indication of the country's firm desire to commit itself to the path of democratisation and respect for human rights. He also recalled the African States' undertaking, in the Grand Baie Declaration and Plan of Action, adopted in Mauritius on 16 April 1999, at the 1st Ministerial Conference on Human Rights in Africa, to promote and protect human rights. He also called on African States to ensure quick ratification of the additional protocol creating the African Court on Human and Peoples' Rights, and the African Charter on the Rights and Welfare of the Child. Finally, Dr. Salim Ahmed Salim reiterated the need to evaluate the structure and functioning of the Secretariat of the African Commission on Human and Peoples' Rights, to strengthen this organ and enable it fulfil its mission in a satisfactory manner.

6. The African Commission deliberated on the state of its relations with Non-Governmental Human Rights Organisations. It deplored the lack of co-operation on the part of some of them: indeed, of the 231 NGOs with observer status, only 25 regularly submit their biennial activity reports to the Secretariat of the Commission. The Commission adopted new criteria for the granting of and enjoying observer status.

7. Burkina Faso, Chad, Mali, and South Africa presented their initial reports, in accordance with Article 62 of the Charter. The examination of Seychelles' initial report was deferred to the 26th Ordinary Session. The Commission deplored the fact that this State did not send any delegates to present its initial report. Mali submitted its initial report.

8. The States delegates made presentations to the Commission on the human rights situation in their respective countries.

9. Various NGOs expressed their concern regarding the deterioration of the human rights situation in certain parts of the continent. These violations include extra-judicial, summary and arbitrary executions, arbitrary arrests and detentions, inhuman conditions of imprisonment and detention, restrictions to the freedoms of expression, movement and association, military coups d'état, forced disappearances, violations against women and children in countries engaged in armed conflict. The NGOs also condemned the coups d'état which took place in Niger and Comoros.

10. All the members of the Commission presented reports on their activities during the inter-session period. The Special Rapporteur on the Rights of Women in Africa, the Special Rapporteur on Extra-judicial, Summary and Arbitrary Executions, and the Special Rapporteur on Prisons and Conditions of Detention in Africa also presented their reports.

11. The Chairman of the Commission informed all participants that two States, Senegal and Burkina Faso, had ratified the Additional Protocol to the African Charter on Human and Peoples' Rights on the creation of the African Court on Human and Peoples' Rights. Consequently, the Commission decided to take appropriate measures with a view to the expeditious ratification of the said Protocol.

12. The working group on the draft Protocol on Women's Rights presented its report to the Commission, which took due note of it.

13. As part of its promotion activities, the Commission decided to organise a series of seminars and conferences.

14. During its closed sessions, the Commission was seized of 81 communications, about 60 of which were examined.

15. The Commission adopted seven resolutions.

16. The Commission visited a displaced persons' camp in Carama.

17. The African Commission on Human and Peoples' Rights expresses its appreciation for the ongoing efforts for peace and national reconstruction in Burundi. The Commission thanks the Burundian Government and People for the warm welcome and fraternal hospitality extended to it, which contributed to the success of its proceedings.

18. The Session was declared closed on 5 May 1999 by the First Vice President of the Republic of Burundi, His Excellency, Mr. Frédéric Bamvuginyumvira.

19. The Chairman of the Commission held a press conference following the closing ceremony.

Issued in Bujumbura, Burundi, May 5, 1999

Annotated Agenda of Twenty-fifth Session

Twenty-fifth Ordinary Session
Bujumbura, Burundi, 26 April to 5 May 1999
DOC/OS (XXV)/81

Item 1: Opening Ceremony (Public Session)

The programme of the opening ceremony will be prepared in due course.

Item 2: Adoption of the Agenda (Private Session)

Pursuant to Article 8 of the Rules of Procedure of the Commission, "At the beginning of each session, the Commission shall, if necessary, after the election of officers in conformity with Rule 17, adopt the agenda of the Session on the basis of the Provisional Agenda referred to in Rule 6.

Item 3: Organisation

Under this item, the Commission shall in particular:

(a) appoint the Rapporteur of the Session;
(b) set the working hours of the session; and
(c) establish a working programme for each day.

Item 4: Introductory Note of the Secretary on the Activities of the Commission (Public Session)

The Secretary to the Commission will present an overview on the activities of the Commission performed during the intersession and major questions which will be discussed during the present Session.

Item 5: Observers (Public Session)

The Commission will hear statements from the delegates of States and other observers and examine questions on the relations between the African Commission on Human and Peoples' Rights and the NGOs, and the cooperation between the Commission and the National Human Rights Institutions.

Item 6: Periodic Reports (Public Session)

The Commission shall also examine the initial reports of Chad, Seychelles, South Africa and Burkina Faso.

Item 7: Reflexion on the Establishment of an Early Intervention Mechanism in Cases of Massive Human Rights Violations (Public Session)

The Commission had already started the examination of this issue during its last two sessions. It shall thus continue its consideration on this matter.

Item 8: Promotional Activities (Public Session)

Along with questions of promotion in general, it is expected that the Commission would examine the following:

(a) Activity Reports of Commissioners;
(b) The Report of the Special Rapporteur on extrajudicial, summary or arbitrary executions;
(c) The Special Rapporteur on prisons and conditions of detention in Africa;
(d) The report of the Special Rapporteur on the rights of women in Africa;
(e) The Draft Protocol to the African Charter on the Rights of Women;
(f) The strategy for a quick ratification of the Additional Protocol to the African Charter on Human and Peoples' Rights on the establishment of an African Court on Human and Peoples' Rights;
(g) Situation of people with disability;
(h) Organisation of Seminars and Conferences;
(i) Human Rights Situation in Africa.

Item 9: Review of Some Provisions of the African Charter in the Light of the Protocol on the Establishment of an African Court on Human and Peoples' Rights and Mainly the Issue of Incompatibility of the Membership of the Commission

The Commission will have to reflect on the review of the Charter in the light of the provisions of the Protocol on the establishment of an African Court on Human and Peoples' Rights

The Commission started its consideration of this matter during its 24th session and had decided to conduct an in-depth examination during the subsequent session when, because of lack of time, the issue was postponed to the present session. A member of the Commission was entrusted with the elaboration of a paper on this subject. The Commission will therefore continue to examine this matter.

Item 10: Review and Newsletter of the African Commission on Human and Peoples' Rights (Public Session)

The Commission will have to think about the measures to put in place to ensure a good quality and a regular publication of the Review and the Newsletter.

Item 11: Protective Activities

(a) *Examination of mission reports (public session)*: The Commission will examine the report on the mission undertaken in Nigeria.
(b) *Examination of communications (private session)*: The Commission will examine 75 communications for which the files have been prepared.

Item 12: Administrative and Financial Matters (Private Session)

(a) *Report of the Chairman of the Commission*: The Chairman will present his activity report for the past intersession period.
(b) *Financial and administrative situation of the Secretariat*: The Secretary to the Commission would have also to present a Report on this matter.
(c) *Question concerning the Headquarters*: When it offered to host the Commission in 1988, The Gambia promised to build a permanent headquarters for the Commission. The Commission will examine the progress of the preparatory work relating to the construction of the headquarters by the host country.
(d) *Participation of the Commission in certain activities of the OAU*: The Commission will continue to reflect on the possibilities of participating more significantly in certain activities of the OAU (prevention, management and resolution of conflicts; question of refugees and displaced persons; supervising the democratic process, in particular the monitoring of elections; the establishment of the African Economic Community, etc.).

Item 13: Methods of Work

The Commission will continue to reflect on the improvement of its methods of work.

Item 14: Evaluation of the Implementation of the Mauritius Plan of Action (Private Session)

The Commission will have to examine the evaluation of the implementation of the Mauritius Plan of action.

Item 15: Logo of the Commission (Private Session)

The Commission will have to examine different proposals initiated on this matter.

Item 16: Dates, Venue and Draft Agenda of the 26th Session (Private Session)

The Commission will confirm the dates, venue of its next session. It will also establish the draft agenda.

Item 17: Any Other Business (Private Session)

Non-substantive questions which were not included in the agenda may be raised and treated under this item.

Item 18: Preparation of the Report of the Session, the Twelfth Annual Activity Report of the Commission and the Final Communiqué of the Session

The Commission will prepare the Report of the Session, the Twelfth Annual Activity Report of the Commission and Final Communiqué of the Session.

Item 19: Adoption of the Report of the Session, the Twelfth Annual Activity Report of the Commission and the Final Communiqué (Private Session)

The Commission will examine and adopt the Report of the Session, the Twelfth Annual Activity Report of the Commission and the Final Communiqué before concluding the Session.

Item 20: Reading of the Final Communiqué and Closing Ceremony (Public Session)

The Final Communiqué will be read and followed by the closing ceremony of the Session.

The programme of this ceremony will be distributed in due course.

Item 21: Press Conference (Public Session)

After the closing ceremony, the Chairman will give a Press Conference.

Status of Submission of NGOs' Activity Reports (as at 31 March 1999)

Twenty-fifth Ordinary Session
Bujumbura, 26 April to 5 May 1999

The African Commission on Human and Peoples' Rights during its 11th Ordinary Session held in Tunis, Tunisia, in March 1992, had decided that the Non-Governmental Organisations (NGOs) to which it had granted Observer Status must submit to its Secretariat, once every two years, a report on their activities. Here below is a status of submission of these reports.

**The overdue reports are highlighted*

Name of NGO	Ref No.	Date on which OS was granted	Date on which reports were/are due	Report submitted and date on which it was submitted
1. Amnesty International	1	Apr 1988 3rd Session	1st report Apr 1994 2nd report Apr 1996 3rd report Apr 1998 4th report Apr 2000	1st report Apr 1994 2nd report Apr 1996 3rd report Apr 1998
2. Commission Internationale des Juristes	2	Apr 1988 3rd Session	1st report Apr 1994 2nd report Apr 1994 3rd report Apr 1998 4th report Apr 2000	1st report Apr 1994 1st report Apr 1994 3rd report Apr 1998
3. Association Africaine de Droit International	3	Apr 1988	**1st report Apr 1994** **2nd report Apr 1996** **2nd report Apr 1996** 4th report Apr 2000	
4. Centre International de Formation à l'Enseignement des Droits de l'Homme et de la Paix	4	Oct 1988 4th Session	1st Report Oct 1994 **2nd report Oct 1996** **3rd report Oct 1996** 4th report Oct 2000	1st report Oct 1994
5. Union des Avocats Arabes	5	Oct 1988 4th Session	1st report Oct 1994 **2nd report Oct 1996** **3rd report Oct 1996** 4th report Oct 2000	1st report Oct 1994
6. Egyptian United Nations Association	6	Oct 1988 4th Session	**1st report Oct 1994** **2nd report Oct 1996** 3rd report Oct 1998 4th report Oct 2000	

Name of NGO	Ref No.	Date on which OS was granted	Date on which reports were/are due	Report submitted and date on which it was submitted
7. Union des Journalistes Africains	7	Oct 1988 4th Session	**1st report Oct 1994** **2nd report Oct 1996** **3rd report Oct 1996** 4th report Oct 2000	
8. La société Africaine	8	Oct 1988 4th session	**1st report Oct 1994** **2nd report Oct 1996** **3rd report Oct 1998** 4th report Oct 2000	
9. Association Sénégalaise d'Etudes et de Recherches Juridiques	9	Apr 1989 5th Session	**1st report Oct 1994** **2nd report Oct 1996** **3rd report Oct 1998** 4th report Apr 2000	
10. Association des Consultants Internationaux en Droits de l'Homme	10	Apr 1989 5th Session	1st report Apr 1994 **2nd report Oct 1996** **3rd report Oct 1998** 4th report Apr 2000	1st report Apr 1994
11. Human Rights Internet	11	Nov 1989 6th Session	1st report Nov 1994 **2nd report Oct 1996** **3rd report Oct 1998** 4th report Nov 2000	1st report Nov 1994
12. Le Mouvement Burkinabé des Droits de d'Homme et des Peuples	12	Nov 1989 6th Session	1st report Nov 1994 **2nd report Oct 1996** 3rd report Nov 1998 4th report Nov 2000	1st report Nov 1994 2nd report Nov 1998
13. Le Comité des Juristes pour les Droits de l'Homme	13	Nov 1989 6th Session	**1st report Nov 1994** **2nd report Nov 1996** **3rd report Nov 1998** 4th report Nov 2000	
14. African Centre for Democracy and	14	Nov 1989 6th Session	1st report Nov 1994 2nd report Nov 1996 **3rd report Nov 1998** 4th report Nov 2000	1st report Nov 1994 2nd report Nov 1996 3rd report Nov 1998
15. Arab Organization for Human Rights	15	Nov 1989 6th Session	1st report Nov 1994 2nd report Nov 1996 **3rd report Nov 1998** 4th report Nov 2000	1st report Nov 1994 2nd report Nov 1996 3rd report Nov 1997
16. Observatoire de l'Information	16	Nov 1989	**1st report Nov 1994** **2nd report Nov 1996** **3rd report Nov 1998** 4th report Nov 2000	
17. Human Rights Watch	17	Nov 1989 6th Session	1st report Nov 1994 2nd report Nov 1996	1st report Nov 1994 2nd report Nov 1996

Name of NGO	Ref No.	Date on which OS was granted	Date on which reports were/are due	Report submitted and date on which it was submitted
			3rd report Nov 1998 4th report Nov 2000	
18. La Commission Catholique pour la Justice et la Paux au Zimbabwe	18	Apr 1990 7th Session	1st report Apr 1994 2nd report Apr 1996 3rd report Apr 1998 4th report Apr 2000	1st report Apr 1996 2nd report Apr 1997 3rd report Apr 1998
19. Organisation Internationale pour l'élimination de Toutes les Formes de Discrimination Raciale	19	Apr 1990 5th Session	**3rd report Apr 1994** **2nd report Apr 1996** **3rd report Apr 1998** 4th report Apr 2000	
20. Association Internationale des Jeunes Avocats	20	Oct 1990 8th Session	**1st report Oct 1994** **2nd report Oct 1996** **3rd report Oct 1998** 4th report Oct 2000	
21. La Société Africaine de Droit Internationale et Comparé	21	Oct 1990 8th Session	1st report Oct 1994 2nd report Oct 1996 3rd report Oct 1998 4th report Oct 2000	1st report Oct 1994 2nd report Oct 1996 3rd report Mar 1999
22. Fédération Internationale des Droits de l'Homme	22	Oct 1990 8th Session	**1st report Oct 1994** **2nd report Oct 1996** **3rd report Oct 1998** 4th report Oct 2000	
23. Secretariat du Commonwealth	23	Oct 1990 8th Session	**1st report Oct 1994** **2nd report Oct 1996** **3rd report Oct 1998** 4th report Oct 2000	
24. Le Fonds pour la Paux	24	Oct 1990 8th Session	**1st report Oct 1994** **2nd report Oct 1996** **3rd report Oct 1996** 4th report Oct 2000	
25. Organisation pour les Libertés Civiles	25	Oct 1990 8th Session	**1st report Oct 1994** **2nd report Oct 1996** **3rd report Oct 1998** 4th report Oct 2000	
26. Interights	26	Oct 1990 8th Session	1st report Oct 1994 2nd report Oct 1996 3rd report Oct 1998 4th report Oct 2000	1st report Oct 1994 2nd report Oct 1996 3rd report Mar 1999

Name of NGO	Ref No.	Date on which OS was granted	Date on which reports were/are due	Report submitted and date on which it was submitted
27. Institut International des Droits de l'Homme	27	Oct 1990 8th Session	**1st report Oct 1994** 2nd report Oct 1996 **3rd report Oct 1998** 4th report Oct 2000	1st report Oct 1996
28. Union Interafricaine des Avocats	28	Oct 1990 8th Session	**1st report Oct 1994** **2nd report Oct 1996** **3rd report Oct 1998** 4th report Oct 2000	
29. Institut Arabe des Droits de l'Homme	29	Oct 1990 8th Session	1st report Oct 1994 2nd report Oct 1996 **3rd report Oct 1998** 4th report Oct 2000	1st report Oct 1996
30. Ligue Burkinabé des Droits de l'Homme et des Peuples	30	Mar 1991 9th Session	1st report Mar 1994 2nd report Mar 1996 **3rd report Mar 1998** 4th report Mar 2000	1st report Mar 1994 2nd report Mar 1996
31. Commission Africaine des Promoteurs de la Santé et des Droits de l'Homme	31	Mar 1991 9th Session	1st report Mar 1994 2nd report Mar 1996 **3rd report Oct 1998** 4th report 2000	1st report Mar 1994 2nd report Mar 1996
32. Human Rights Africa	32	Mar 1991 9th Session	1st report Mar 1994 2nd report Mar 1996 **3rd report Mar 1998** 4th report Mar 2000	1st report Mar 1994 2nd report Mar 1996
33. Lawyers Committee for Civil Rights Under Law	33	Mar 1991 9th Session	**1st report Mar 1994** **3rd report Mar 1996** **3rd report Mar 1998** 4th report Mar 2000	
34. International Human Rights Association of American Minorities	34	Mar 1991 9th Session	**1st report Mar 1994** 2nd report Mar 1996 **3rd report Mar 1998** 4th report Mar 2000	1st report Mar 1996 2nd report Mar 1997
35. Constitutional Rights Project	35		**1st report Mar 1994** **2nd report Oct 1996** **3rd report Oct 1998** 4th report Mar 2000	
36. Ligue Tunisienne pour la Défense des Droits de l'Homme	36	Mar 1991 9th Session	**1st report Mar 1994** **2nd report Mar 1996** **3rd report Mar 1998** 4th report Mar 2000	

Name of NGO	Ref No.	Date on which OS was granted	Date on which reports were/are due	Report submitted and date on which it was submitted
37. Comité pour la Défense des Droits de l'Homme	37	Mar 1991 9th Session	1st report Mar 1994 2nd report Mar 1996 3rd report Mar 1998 4th report Mar 2000	
38. International Human Rights Law Group	38	Oct 1991 10th Session	1st report Oct 1994 2nd report Oct 1996 3rd report Oct 1998 4th report Oct 2000	
39. Minnesota Advocates for Human Rights	39	Oct 1991 10th Session	1st report Oct 1994 2nd report Oct 1996 3rd report Oct 1998 4th report Oct 2000	
40. Fédération Internationale de l'Action des Chrétiens pour l'Abolition de la Torture	40	Oct 1991 10th Session	1st report Oct 1994 2nd report Oct 1996 3rd report Oct 1998 4th report Oct 2000	1st report Oct 1994 2nd report Oct 1996 3rd report Oct 1997
41. Union Interafricaine des Avocats	41	Oct 1991 10th Session	1st report Oct 1994 2nd report Oct 1996 3rd report Oct 1998 4th report Oct 2000	
42. Groupe d'Etudes et de Recherches sur la Démocratie et le Développement Economique et Social en Afrique	42	Oct 1991 10th Session	1st report Oct 1994 2nd report Oct 1996 3rd report Oct 1998 4th report Oct 2000	
43. Anti-Slavery International for the Protection of Human Rights	43	Oct 1991 10th Session	1st report Oct 1994 2nd report Oct 1996 3rd report Oct 1998 4th report Oct 2000.	1st report Oct 1996 2nd report Oct 1998
44. Congressional Human Rights Foundation	44	Oct 1991 10th Session	1st report Oct 1994 2nd report Oct 1996 3rd report Oct 1998 4th report Oct 2000	
45. L'Association des Juristes Africains	45	Oct 1991 10th Session	1st report Oct 1994 2nd report Oct 1996 3rd report Oct 1998 4th report Oct 2000	
46. Ligue Ivoirienne des Droits de l'Homme	46	Oct 199 10th Session	1st report Oct 1994 2nd report Oct 1996 3rd report Oct 1998 4th report Oct 2000	

Name of NGO	Ref No.	Date on which OS was granted	Date on which reports were/are due	Report submitted and date on which it was submitted
47. Association pour la Promotion de l'Etat de Droit	47	Oct 1991 10th Session	**1st report Oct 1994** **2nd report Oct 1996** **3rd report Oct 1998** 4th report Oct 2000	
48. Recontre Africaine pour la Défense des Droits de l'Homme	48	Oct 1994 10th Session	1st report Oct 1994 2nd report Oct 1996 3rd report Oct 1998 4th report Oct 2000	1st report Oct 1994 2nd report Oct 1996 3rd report Oct 1998
49. The Decade of Human Rights Education	49	Oct 1991 10th Session	**1st report Oct 1994** **2nd report Oct 1996** **3rd report Oct 1998** 4th report Oct 2000	
50. Marangopoulos Foundation for Human Rights	50	Oct 1991 10th Session	**1st report Oct 1994** **2nd report Oct 1996** **3rd report Oct 1998** 4th report Oct 2000	
51. Legal Research and Resource Development Centre	51	Oct 1991 10th Session	1st report Oct 1994 **2nd report Oct 1996** **3rd report Oct 1998** 4th report Oct 2000	1st report Oct 1994
52. Organisation Mondiale Contre la Torture	52	Oct 1991 10th Session	1st report Oct 1994 2nd report Oct 1996 **3rd report Oct 1998** 4th report Oct 2000	1st report Oct 1994 2nd report Oct 1996
53. International Services for Human Rights	53	Oct 1991 10th Session	**1st report Oct 1994** 2nd report Oct 1996 **3rd report Oct 1998** 4th report Oct 2000	1st report Oct 1996
54. Ligue Internationale Des Droits de l'Homme	54	Oct 1991 10th Session	**1st report Oct 1994** **2nd report Oct 1996** **3rd report Oct 1998** 4th report Oct 2000	
55. Association Nationale des Droits de l'Homme	55	Oct 1991 10th Session	**3rd report Oct 1994** **2nd report Oct 1996** **3rd report Oct 1998** 4th report Oct 2000	
56. African Bar Association	56	Oct 1991 10th Session	**1st report Oct 1994** **2nd report Oct 1996** **3rd report Oct 1998** 4th report Oct 2000	
57. Ligue Centrafricaine des Droits de l'Homme	56	Oct 1991 10th Session	**1st report Oct 1994** 2nd report Oct 1996 **3rd report Oct 1998** 4th report Oct 2000	1st report Oct 1997

Name of NGO	Ref No.	Date on which OS was granted	Date on which reports were/are due	Report submitted and date on which it was submitted
58. Egyptian Organization for Human Rights	58	Oct 1991 10th Session	1st report Oct 1994 2nd report Oct 1996 **3rd report Oct 1998** 4th report Oct 2000	1st report Oct 1994 2nd report Oct 1996
59. Institut des Droits de l'Homme de l'Université Catholique de Lyon	59	Mar 1992 11th Session	**1st report Mar 1994** **2nd report Mar 1996** **3rd report Mar 1998** 4th report Mar 2000	
60. Ligue Bissau-Guinénne des Droits de l'Homme	60	Mar 1992 11th Session	**1st report Mar 1994** **2nd report Mar 1996** **3rd report Mar 1998** 4th report Mar 2000	
61. Société Internationale pour les Droits de l'Homme	61	Mar 1992 11th Session	**1st report Mar 1994** **2nd report Mar 1996** **3rd report Mar 1998** 4th report 2000	
62. Syndicat National de Presse Marocaine	62	Mar 1992	**1st report Mar 1994** **2nd report Mar 1996** **3rd report Mar 1998** 4th report Mar 2000	
63. Juristes pour les Droits de l'Homme	63	Mar 1992 11th Session	1st report Mar 1994 2nd report Mar 1996 **3rd report Mar 1998** 4th report Mar 2000	1st report Mar 1994 2nd report Mar 1996
64. Observatoire Panafricain de la Démocratie	64	Mar 1992 11th Session	**1st report Mar 1994** **2nd report Mar 1996** **3rd report Mar 1998** 4th report Mar 2000	
65. Comité International de	65	Mar 1992 11th Session	1st report Mar 1994 2nd report Mar 1996 **3rd report Mar 1998** 4th report Mar 2000	1st report Mar 1994 1nd report Mar 1996
66. "Article 19" International Centre Against Press Censorship	66	Mar 1992 11th Session	1st report Mar 1994 2nd report Mar 1996 **3rd report Mar 1998** 4th report Mar 2000	1st report Mar 1994 2nd report Mar 1996
67. Comité National des Droits de l'Homme	67	Mar 1992 11th Session	**1st report Mar 1994** **2rd report Mar 1996** **3rd report Mar 1998** 4th report Mar 2000	
68. Commission Béninoise des Droits de l'Homme	68	Mar 1992 11th Session	**1st report Mar 1994** **2nd report Mar 1996** **3rd report Mar 1998** 4th report Mar 2000	

Name of NGO	Ref No.	Date on which OS was granted	Date on which reports were/are due	Report submitted and date on which it was submitted
69. Arab Libyan Commission for Human Rights	69	Mar 1992 11th Session	**1st report Mar 1994** **2nd report Mar 1996** **3rd report Mar 1998** 4th report Mar 2000	
70. Fénération des Juristes Africaines	70	Mar 1992 11th Session	**1st report Mar 1994** **2nd report Mar 1996** **3rd report Mar 1998** 4th report Mar 2000	
71. International Centre for Human Rights and Democratic Development	71	Mar 1992 11th Session	1st report Mar 1994 2nd report Mar 1996 3rd report Mar 1998 4th report Mar 2000	1st report Mar 1994 2nd report Mar 1996 3rd report Mar 1998
72. Fédération Nationale des Unions de Jeunes Avocats	72	Oct 1992 12th Session	1st report Oct 1994 2nd report Oct 1996 **3rd report Oct 1998** 4th report Oct 2000	2st report Oct 1994 2nd report Oct 1996
73. Association Tchadienne pour la Promotion et la Défense des Droits de l'Homme	73	Oct 1992 12th Session	1st report Oct 1994 2nd report Oct 1996 3rd report Oct 1998 4th report Oct 2000	1st report Oct 1994 2nd report Oct 1996 3rd report Mar 1999
74. Union Interafricaine des Droits de l'Homme	74	Oct 1992 12th Session	1st report Oct 1994 2nd report Oct 1996 **3rd report Oct 1998** 4th report Oct 2000	1st report Oct 1994 2nd report Oct 1996
75. Swaziland Association of Human Rights	75	Oct 1992 12th Session	**1st report Oct 1994** **3rd report Oct 1996** **3rd report Oct 1998** 4th report Oct 2000	
76. Women in Law and Development in Africa	76	Oct 1992 12th Session	1st report Oct 1994 2nd report Oct 1996 **3rd report Oct 1998** 4th report Oct 2000	1st report Oct 1994 2nd report Oct 1996
77. Southern African Research and Development	77	Oct 1992 12th Session	**1st report Oct 1994** **2nd report Oct 1996** **3rd report Oct 1998** 4th report Oct 2000	
78. Network of Activists and Researchers on Integrated Human Rights In Africa	78	Oct 1992 12th Session	**1st report Oct 1994** **2nd report Oct 1996** **3rd report Oct 1998** 4th report Oct 2000	

Name of NGO	Ref No.	Date on which OS was granted	Date on which reports were/are due	Report submitted and date on which it was submitted
79. African Studies Association	79	Oct 1992 12th Session	**1st report Oct 1994** **2nd report Oct 1996** **3rd report Oct 1998** 4th report Oct 2000	
80. Association Malienne des Droits de l'Homme	80	Oct 1992 12th Session	1st report Oct 1994 2nd report Oct 1996 **3rd report Oct 1998** 4th report Oct 2000	1st report Oct 1994 2nd report Oct 1996
81. Sudan Human Rights	81	Oct 1992 12th Session	1st report Oct 1994 2nd report Oct. 1996 **3rd report Oct 1998** 4th report Oct 2000	1st report Oct 1994 2nd report Oct 1996
82. Zimbabwe Human Rights Association	82	Oct 1992 12th Session	1st report Oct 1994 2nd report Oct 1996 **3rd report Oct 1998** 4th report Oct 2000	1st report Oct 1994 2nd report Oct. 1996
83. Association pour le Développement des Initiatives Villageoises	83	Oct 1992 12th Session	1st report Oct 1994 2nd report Oct 1996 **3rd report Oct 1998** 4th report Oct 2000	1st report Oct 1994 2nd report Oct 1996
84. International Pen	84	Oct 1992 12th Session	1st report Oct 1994 2nd report Oct 1996 **3rd report Oct 1998** 4th report Oct 2000	1st report Oct 1994 2nd report Oct 1996
85. World University Service	85	Oct 1992 12th Session	1st report Oct 1994 **2nd report Oct 1996** **3rd report Oct 1998** 4th report Oct 2000	1st report Oct 1994
86. Ligue Burundaise pour la Défense des Libertés Fondamentales et du Pluralisme			**1st report Oct 1994** **2nd report Oct 1996** **3rd report Oct 1998** 4th report Oct 2000	
87. Ligue Camerounaise des Droits de l'Homme pour la Défense des Libertés Fondamentales et du Pluralisme	86	Oct 1992 12th Session	**1st report Oct 1994** **2nd report Oct 1996** **3rd report Oct 1998** 4th report Oct 2000	
88. Organisation Marocaine des Droits de l'Homme	88	Oct 1992 12th Session	**1st report Oct 1994** **2nd report Oct 1996** **3rd report Oct 1998** 4th report Oct 2000	

Name of NGO	Ref No.	Date on which OS was granted	Date on which reports were/are due	Report submitted and date on which it was submitted
89. Muleide – Women, Law and Development	89	Oct 1992 12th Session	**1st report Oct 1994** **2nd report Oct 1996** **3rd report Oct 1998** 4th report Oct 2000	
90. Ghana Committee on Human and Peoples' Rights	90	Oct 1992 12th Session	**1st report Oct 1994** 2nd report Oct 1996 **3rd report Oct 1998** 4th report Oct 2000	1st report Oct 1997
91. Organisation Guinéenne des Droits de l'Homme et du Citoyen	91	Oct 1992 12th Session	1st report Oct 1994 2nd report Oct 1996 **3rd report Oct 1998** 4th report Oct 2000	1st report Oct 1994 2nd report Oct 1996
92. Association des Journalistes Tunisiens	92	Oct 1992 12th Session	1st report Oct 1994 **2nd report Oct 1996** **3rd report Oct 1998** 4th report Oct 2000	1st report Oct 1994
93. The Danish Centre for Human Rights	93	Oct 1992 12th Session	1st report Oct 1994 2nd report Oct 1996 **3rd report Oct 1998** 4th report Oct 2000	1st report Oct 1994 2nd report Oct 1996
94. African Human Rights and Justice Protection Network	94	Oct 1992 12th Session	**1st report Oct 1994** **2nd report Oct 1996** **3rd report Oct 1998** 4th report Oct 2000	
95. Agir Ensemble pour les Droits de l'Homme	95	Oct 1992 12th Session	**1st report Oct 1994** 2nd report Oct 1996 **3rd report Oct 1998** 4th report Oct 2000	1st report Oct 1996
96. Association Rwandaise pour la Défense des Droits de la Personne et des Libertés Publiques	96	Oct 1992 12th Session	**1st report Oct 1994** **2nd report Oct 1996** **3rd report Oct 1998** 4th report Oct 2000	
97. Centre Béninois pour le Développement des Initiatives à la Base	97	Mar 1993 13th Session	1st report Mar 1995 2nd report Mar 1997 **3rd report Mar 1999** 4th report Mar 2001	1st report Mar 1995 2nd report Mar 1997
98. CUSO West Africa Office	98	Mar 1993 13th Session	1st report Mar 1995 2nd report Mar 1997 **3rd report Mar 1999** 4th report Mar 2001	1st report Mar 1995 2nd report Mar 1997

Name of NGO	Ref No.	Date on which OS was granted	Date on which reports were/are due	Report submitted and date on which it was submitted
99. National Society for Human Rights of Namibia	99	Mar 1993 13th Session	**1st report Mar 1995** **2nd report Mar 1997** 3rd report Mar 1999 4th report Mar 2001	
100. Association Chrétienne pour l'Abolition des Tortures et pour le Respect des Droits de l'Homme	100	Mar 1993 13th Session	**1st report Mar 1995** **2nd report Mar 1997** **3rd report Mar 1999** 4th report Mar 2001	
101. The African Institute for Human Rights and Peace Research	101	Mar 1993 13th Session	**1st report Mar 1995** **2nd report Mar 1997** **3rd report Mar 1999** 4th report Mar 2001	
102. International Association of Lawyers for Human Rights	102	Mar 1993 13th Session	**1st report Mar 1995** **2nd report Mar 1997** **3rd report Mar 1999** 4th report Mar 2001	
103. Universal Defenders of Democracy	103	Mar 1993 13th Session	**1st report Mar 1995** **2nd report Mar 1997** **3rd report Mar 1999** 4th report Mar 2001	
104. Women Concerned	104	Mar 1993 13th Session	**1st report Mar 1995** **2nd report Mar 1997** **3rd report Mar 1999** 4th report Mar 2001	
105. Association Egyptienne des Supporters des Droits de l'Homme	105	Mar 1993 13th Session	**1st report Mar 1995** **2nd report Mar 1997** **3rd report Mar 1999** 4th report Mar 2001	
106. Comité International pour le Respect et l'Application de la Charte Africaine	106	Mar 1993 13th Session	**1st report Mar 1995** **2nd report Mar 1997** **3rd report Mar 1999** 4th report Mar 2001	
107. Centre de Promotion des Droits de l'Homme	107	Mar 1993 13th Session	1st report Mar 1995 2nd report Mar 1997 **3rd report Mar 1999** 4th report Mar 2001	1st report Mar 1995 2nd report Mar 1997
108. Ligue Cap Verdienne des Droits de l'Homme et des Peuples	108	Mar 1993 13th Session	1st report Mar 1995 2nd report Mar 1997 **3rd report Mar 1999** 4th report Mar 2001	1st report Mar 1995 2nd report Mar 1997

Name of NGO	Ref No.	Date on which OS was granted	Date on which reports were/are due	Report submitted and date on which it was submitted
109. Legal Research and Resource Centre for Human Rights	109	Mar 1993 13th Session	1st report Mar 1995 2nd report Mar 1997 **3rd report Mar 1999** 4th report Mar 2001	1st report Mar 1995 2nd report Mar 1997
110. Ligue Tchadienne des Droits de l'Homme	110	Mar 1993 13th Session	1st report Mar 1995 2nd report Mar 1997 **3rd report Mar 1999** 4th report Mar 2001	1st report Mar 1995 2nd report Mar 1998
111. International Federation of Women Lawyers	111	Mar 1993 13th Session	1st report Mar 1995 **2nd report Mar 1997** **3rd report Mar 1999** 4th report Mar 2001	1st report Mar 1996
112. Organisation Nationale des Droits de l'Homme du Sénégal	112	Dec 1993 14th Session	**1st report Dec 1995** **2nd report Dec 1997** 3rd report Dec 1999 4th report Dec 2001	
113. National Justice and Peace Commission, Catholic Mission	113	Dec 1993 14th Session	**1st report Dec 1995** **2nd report Dec 1997** 3rd report Dec 1999 4th report Dec 2001	
114. Collectif des Ligues et Associations de Défense des Droits de l'Homme au Rwanda	114	Dec 1993 14th Session	**1st report Dec 1995** **2nd report Dec 1997** 3rd report Dec 1999 4th report Dec 2001	
115. International Network for Indigenous Affairs	115	Dec 1993 14th Session	**1st report Dec 1995** **2nd report Dec 1997** 3rd report Dec 1999 4th report Dec 2001	
116. The Centre for Human Rights	116	Dec 1993 14th Session	1st report Dec 1995 2nd report Dec 1997 3rd report Dec 1999 4th report Dec 2001	1st report Dec 1995 2nd report Dec 1997
117. Ligue des Droits de la Personne dans la Région des Grands Lacs	117	Dec 1993 14th Session	**1st report Dec 1995** **2nd report Dec 1997** 3rd report Dec 1999 4th report Dec 2001	
118. International Commission or Jurists (Kenya Section)	118	Dec 1993 14th Session	**1st report Dec 1995** 2nd report Dec 1997 3rd report Dec 1991 4th report Dec 2001	1st report Dec 1997

Name of NGO	Ref No.	Date on which OS was granted	Date on which reports were/are due	Report submitted and date on which it was submitted
119. Foundation for Human Rights Initiative	119	Dec 1993 14th Session	1st report Dec 1995 2nd report Dec 1997 3rd report Dec 1999 4th report Dec 2001	1st report Dec 1995 2nd report Dec 1997
120. Media Rights Agenda	120	Dec 1993 14th Session	**1st report Dec 1995** **2nd report Dec 1997** 3rd report Dec 1999 4th report Dec 2001	
121. Inter African Network for Human Rights and Development (AFRONET)	121	Dec 1993 14th Session	**1st report Dec 1995** **2nd report Dec 1997** 3rd report Dec 1999 4th report Dec 2001	
122. International Alert	122	Dec 1993 14th Session	1st report Dec 1995 2nd report Dec 1997 3rd report Dec 1999 4th report Dec 2001	1st report Dec 1995 2nd report Dec 1997
123. University of Namibia	123	Dec 1993 14th Session	**1st report Dec 1995** **2nd report Dec 1997** 3rd report Dec 1999 4th report Dec 2001	
124. Ligue Camerounaise des Droits de l'Homme	124	Dec 1993 14th Session	**1st report Dec 1995** **2nd report Dec 1997** 3rd report Dec 1999 4th report Dec 2001	
125. Ethiopian Human Rights Council	125	Dec 1993 14th Session	**1st report Dec 1995** **2nd report Dec 1997** 3rd report Dec 1999 4th report Dec 2001	
126. Association pour la Défense des Droits de l'Homme et des Libertés	126	Dec 1993 14th Session	1st report Dec 1995 2nd report Dec 1997 3rd report Dec 1999 4th report Dec 2001	1st report Dec 1995 1nd report Dec 1997
127. Penal Reform International	127	Dec 1993 14th Session	1st report Dec 1995 2nd report Dec 1997 3rd report Dec 1999 4th report Dec 2001	1st report Dec 1995 2nd report Dec 1997
128. Association Zaïroise de Défense des Droits de l'Homme	128	Dec 1993 14th Session	**1st report Dec 1995** **2nd report Dec 1997** 3rd report Dec 1999 4th report Dec 2001	

Name of NGO	Ref No.	Date on which OS was granted	Date on which reports were/are due	Report submitted and date on which it was submitted
129. Association des Journalistes du Cap Vert	129	Dec 1993 14th Session	**1st report Dec 1995** **2nd report Dec 1997** 3rd report 1999 4th report Dec 2001	
130. Community Legal Resource and Advice Center	130	Apr 1994 15th Session	1st report Apr 1996 2nd report Apr 1998 3rd report Apr 2000 4th report Apr 2002	1st report Apr 1996 2nd report Apr 1998
131. The Botswana Centre for Human Rights	131	Apr 1994 15th Session	2st report Apr 1996 **2nd report Apr 1998** 3rd report Apr 2000 4th report Apr 2001	1st report Apr 1996
132. African Network for the Prevention and Protection Against Child Abuse and Neglect	132	Oct 1994 16th Session	**1st report Oct 1996** **2nd report Oct 1998** 3rd report Oct 2000 4th report Oct 2002	
133. Centre for Applied Legal Studies	133	Oct 1994 16th Session	1st report Oct 1996 **2nd report Oct 1998** 3rd report Oct 2000 4th report Oct 2000	1st report Oct 1996
134. Mouvement de Protestation Civique	134	Oct 1994 16th Session	1st report Oct 1996 **2nd report Oct 1998** 3rd report Oct 2000 4th report Oct 2002	1st report Oct 1996
135. International Society for Human Rights	135	Oct 1994 16th Session	**1st report Oct 1996** **2nd report Oct 1998** 3rd report Oct 2000 4th report Oct 2002	
136. Organisation Sénégalaise d'Appui au Développement et au Droits de l'Homme	136	Oct 1994 16th Session	**1st report Oct 1996** **2nd report Oct 1998** 3rd report Oct 2000 4th report Oct 2002	Repport (1995–1996–1997)
137. All African Conference of Churches	137	Oct 1994 16th Session	1st report Oct 1996 **2nd report Oct 1998** 3rd report Oct 2000 4th report Oct 2002	1st report Oct 1996
138. Centre for Justice and International Law	138	Oct 1994 16th Session	**1st report Oct 1996** 2nd report Oct 1998 3rd report Oct 2000 4th report Oct 2002	2nd report Oct 1998

Name of NGO	Ref No.	Date on which OS was granted	Date on which reports were/are due	Report submitted and date on which it was submitted
139. The English International Association of Lund	139	Oct 1994 16th Session	1st report Oct 1996 **2nd report Oct 1998** 3rd report Oct 2000 4th report Oct 2002	1st report Oct 1996 2nd report Oct 1997
140. Swedish NGO Foundation for Human Rights	140	Oct 1994 16th Session	1st report Oct 1996 **2nd report Oct 1998** 3rd report Oct 2000 4th report Oct 2000	1st report Oct 1995 2nd report Oct 1996 3rd report Oct 1997
141. Association Angolaise des Droits de l'Homme	141	Mar 1995 17th Session	**1st report Mar 1997** **2nd report Mar 1999** 3rd report Mar 2001 4th report Mar 2003	
142. Human Rights Information and Documentation System	142	Mar 1995 17th Session	1st report Mar 1997 **2nd report Mar 1999** 3rd report Mar 2001 4th report Mar 2003	1st report Mar 1997
143. Women Justice Programme	143	Mar 1995 17th Session	1st report Mar 1997 **2nd report Mar 1999** 3rd report Mar 2001 4th report Mar 2003	1st report Mar 1998
144. Association Mondiale pour les Orphelins et Enfants Abandonnés	144	Mar 1995 17th Session	**1st report Mar 1997** **2nd report Mar 1999** 3rd report Mar 2001 4th report Mar 2003	
145. Comité Africain pour le Droit et le Développement	145	Mar 1995 17th Session	**1st report Mar 1997** **2nd report Mar 1999** 3rd report Mar 2001 4th report Mar 2003	
146. Association Mauritanienne des Droits de l'Homme	146	Mar 1995 17th Session	**1st report Mar 1997** **2nd report Mar 1999** 3rd report Mar 2001 4th report Mar 2003	
147. Mouvement des Réfugiés Mauritaniens au Sénégal pour la Défense des Droits de l'Homme	147	Mar 1995 17th Session	1st report Mar 1997 2nd report Mar 1999 3rd report Mar 2001 4th report Mar 2003	1st report Mar 1997 2nd report Mar 1998
148. S.O.S. Esclaves (Mauritanie)	148	Mar 1995 17th Session	1st report Mar 1997 **2nd report Mar 1999** 3rd report Mar 2001 4th report Mar 2003	1st report Mar 1997

Name of NGO	Ref No.	Date on which OS was granted	Date on which reports were/are due	Report submitted and date on which it was submitted
149. Groupe d'Etudes et de Recherches sur la Démocratie Economique et Sociale en Mauritanie	149	Mar 1995 17th Session	**1st report Mar 1995** **2nd report Mar 1999** 3rd report Mar 2001 4th report Mar 2003	
150. Tchad non-violence	150	Mar 1995 17th Session	1st report Mar 1997 **2nd report Mar 1999** 3rd report Mar 2001 4th report Mar 2003	1st report Mar 1997
151. Human Rights Society of the Gambia	151	Mar 1995 17th Session	**1st report Mar 1997** **2nd report Mar 1999** 3rd report Mar 2001 4th report Mar 2003	
152. The Ugandan Association of Women Lawyers	152	Mar 1995 17th Session	**2nd report Mar 1999** **2nd report Mar 1999** 3rd report Mar 2001 4th report Mar 2003	
153. Liberia Human Rights Chapter	153	Mar 1995 17th Session	1st report Mar 1997 2nd report Mar 1999 3rd report Mar 2001 4th report Mar 2003	1st report Mar 1997 2nd report Mar 1998
154. Institut Africain pour la Démocratie	154	Mar 1995 17th Session	1st report Mar 1997 **2nd report Mar 1999** 3rd report Mar 2001 4th report Mar 2003	1st report Mar 1997
155. Comité Algériuen des Droits de l'Homme	155	Oct 1995 18th Session	**1st report Oct 1997** 2nd report Oct 1999 3rd report Oct 2001 4th report Oct 2003	
156. Observatoire International des Prisons	156	Oct 1995 18th Session	1st report Oct 1997 2nd report Oct 1999 3rd report Oct 2001 4th report Oct 2003	1st report Oct 1997
157. Association Nationale pour l'Alphabétisation et la Formation des Adultes	157	Oct 1995 18th Session	**1st report Oct 1997** 2nd report Oct 1999 3rd report Oct 2001 4th report 2003	
158. Association pour le Progrès de la Femme et de l'Enfant	158	Oct 1995 18th Session	1st report Oct 1997 2nd report Oct 1999 3rd report Oct 2001 4th report Oct 2003	1st report Oct 1997

Name of NGO	Ref No.	Date on which OS was granted	Date on which reports were/are due	Report submitted and date on which it was submitted
159. Liberia Watch for Human Rights	159	Oct 1995 18th Session	**1st report Oct 1997** 2nd report Oct 1999 3rd report Oct 2001 4th report Oct 2003	
160. Ligue Togolaise des Droits de la Femme	160	Oct 1995 18th Session	**1st report Oct 1997** 2nd report Oct 1999 3rd report Oct 2001 4th report Oct 2003	
161. Foundation for Research on Women's Health, Productivity and the Environment	161	Oct 1995 18th Session	1st report Oct 1997 2nd report Oct 1999 3rd report Oct 2001 4th report Oct 2003	1st report Oct 1997
162. Synergies Africa	162	Oct 1995 18th Session	1st report Oct 1997 2nd report Oct 1999 3rd report Oct 2001 4th report Oct 2003	1st report Oct 1997
163. Association des Réfugiés Mauritaniens au Sénégal	163	Oct 1995 18th Session	1st report Oct 1997 2nd report Oct 1999 3rd report Oct 2001 4th report 2003	1st report Oct 1997
164. Centre Nord–Sud	164	Oct 1995 18th Session	1st report Oct 1997 2nd report Oct 1999 3rd report Oct 2001 4th report Oct 2003	1st report Oct 1997
165. Association pour la Préservation de la Torture	165	Oct 1995 18th Session	**1st report Oct 1997** 2nd report Oct 1999 3rd report Oct 2001 4th report Oct 2003	
166. Association of Female Lawyers of Liberia	166	Oct 1995 18th Session	**1st report Oct 1997** 2nd report Oct 1999 3rd report Oct 2001 4th report Oct 2003	
167. Association Internationale pour la Démocratie en Afrique	167	Oct 1995 18th Session	1st report Oct 1997 2nd report Oct 1999 3rd report Oct 2001 4th report Oct 2003	1st report Oct 1997
168. Liga Moçambica dos Dereitos Humanos (LDH)	168	Mar 1996 19th Session	**1st report Mar 1998** 2nd report Mar 2000 3rd report Mar 2002 4th report Mar 2004	

Name of NGO	Ref No.	Date on which OS was granted	Date on which reports were/are due	Report submitted and date on which it was submitted
169. Forum das ONG dos Dereitos do Homen e da Crianca dos Palop	169	Mar 1996 19th Session	**1st report Mar 1998** 2nd report Mar 2000 3rd report Mar 2002 4th report Mar 2004	
170. Association des Juristes Maliennes	170	Mar 1996 19th Session	**1st report Mar 1998** 2nd report Mar 2000 3rd report Mar 2002 4th report Mar 2004	
171. Pan African Movement	171	Mar 1996 19th Session	**1st report Mar 1998** 2nd report Mar 2000 3rd report Mar 2002 4th report Mar 2004	
172. Conseil pour le Développement de la Recherche Economique et Sociale en Afrique	172	Mar 1996 19th Session	**1st report Mar 1998** 2nd report Mar 2000 3rd report Mar 2002 4th report Mar 2004	
173. Shelter Rights Initiative	173	Mar 1996 19th Session	**1st report Mar 1998** 2nd report Mar 2000 3rd report Mar 2002 4th report Mar 2004	
174. Movement International pour le Développement en Afrique	174	Mar 1996 19th Session	**1st report Mar 1998** 2nd report Mar 2000 3rd report Mar 2002 4th Mar 2004	
175. Association Tchadienne des Juristes	175	Mar 1996 19th Session	**1st report Mar 1998** 2nd report Mar 2000 3rd report Mar 2002 4th report Mar 2004	
176. Foundation Idole "Foni"	176	Mar 1996 19th Session	**1st report Mar 1998** 2nd report Mar 2000 3rd report Mar 2002 4th report Mar 2004	
177. SOS Orphelins	177	Mar 1996 19th Session	**1st report Mar 1998** 2nd report Mar 2000 3rd report Mar 2002 4th report Mar 2004	
178. African Centre for Democracy, Human Rights and the Protection of Prisoners	178	Mar 1996 19th Session	**1st report Mar 1998** 2nd report Mar 2000 3rd report Mar 2002 4th report Mar 2004	

Name of NGO	Ref No.	Date on which OS was granted	Date on which reports were/are due	Report submitted and date on which it was submitted
179. Avoicats Sans Frontières	179	Mar 1996 19th Session	1st report Mar 1998 2nd report Mar 2000 3rd report Mar 2002 4th report Mar 2004	1st report Mar 1997 2nd report Mar 1998
180. Rassemblement Democratique des Femmes du Niger	180	Mar 1996 19th Session	**1st report Mar 1998** 2nd report Mar 2000 3rd report Mar 2002 4th report Mar 2004	
181. Association de Sauvetage de l'Enfance en Danger	181	Mar 1996 19th Session	**1st report Mar 1998** 2nd report Mar 2000 3rd report Mar 2002 4th report Mar 2004	
182. Association Ivoirienne pour la Promotion des Droits de l'Homme	182	Mar 1996 19th Session	**1st report Mar 1998** 2nd report Mar 2000 3rd report Mar 2002 4th report Mar 2004	
183. Center for Economic and Social Rights	183	Oct 1996 20th Session	**1st report Oct 1998** 2nd report Oct 2000 3rd report Oct 2002 4th report Oct 2004	
184. Human Rights Committee of South Africa	184	Oct 1996 20th Session	**1st report Oct 1998** 2nd report Oct 2000 3rd report Oct 2002 4th report Oct 2004	
185. Agence pour la Diffusion du Droit Internationale en Afrique Centrale	185	Oct 1996 20th Session	**1st report Oct 1998** 2nd report Oct 2000 3rd report Oct 2002 4th report Oct 2004	
186. Groupe de Réflexion et d'Action Femme Démocratie et Développement	186	Oct 1996 20th Session	**1st report Oct 1998** 2nd report Oct 2000 3rd report Oct 2002 4th report Oct 2004	
187. National Institute for Public Law and Research	187	Oct 1996 20th Session	**1st report Oct 1998** 2nd report Oct 2000 3rd report Oct 2002 4th report Oct 2004	
188. Centre Africain pour l'Education aux Droits Humains	188	Oct 1996 20th Session	**1st report Oct 1998** 2nd report Oct 2000 3rd report Oct 2002 4th report Oct 2004	

Name of NGO	Ref No.	Date on which OS was granted	Date on which reports were/are due	Report submitted and date on which it was submitted
189. Legal Resources Foundation	189	Oct 1996 20th Session	**1st report Oct 1998** 2nd report Oct 2000 3rd report Oct 2002 4th report Oct 2004	
190. Institut de l'Océan Indien pour les Droits de l'Homme et la Démocratie	190	Oct 1996 20th Session	**1st report Oct 1998** 2nd report Oct 2000 3rd report Oct 2002 4th report Oct 2004	
191. Kenya Human Rights Commission	191	Oct 1996 20th Session	**1st report Oct 1998** 2nd report Oct 2000 3rd report Oct 2002 4th report Oct 2004	
192. Center for Civil and Human Rights	192	Oct 1996 20th Session	**1st report Oct 1998** 2nd report Oct 2000 3rd report Oct 2002 4th report Oct 2004	
193. Nord–Sud XXI	193	Oct 1996 20th Session	**1st report Oct 1998** 2nd report Oct 2000 3rd report Oct 2002 4th report Oct 2004	
194. Agence de Coopération Culturelle et Technique	194	Oct 1996 20th Session	**1st report Oct 1998** 2nd report Oct 2000 3rd report Oct 2002 4th report Oct 2004	
195. Association pour le Progrès et la Défense des Droits des Femmes Maliennes	195	Oct 1996 20th Session	**1st report Oct 1998** 2nd report Oct 2000 3rd report Oct 2002 4th report Oct 2004	
196. Association Camerounaise des droits de l'Enfant	196	Oct 1996 20th Session	**1st report Oct 1998** 2nd report Oct 2000 3rd report Oct 2002 4th report Oct 2004	
197. Observatoire Congolais des Droits de l'Homme	197	Oct 1996 20th Session	**1st report Oct 1998** 2nd report Oct 2000 3rd report Oct 2002 4th report Oct 2004	
198. Fondation Ndadaye M. pour les Droits de l'Homme, la Démocratie et le Développement	198	Apr 1997 21st Session	1st report Apr 1999 2nd report Apr 2001 3rd report Apr 2003 4th report Apr 2005	

Name of NGO	Ref No.	Date on which OS was granted	Date on which reports were/are due	Report submitted and date on which it was submitted
199. Ligue Mauritanienn et les Droits de 'Homme	199	Apr 1997 21st Session	1st report Apr 1999 2nd report Apr 2001 3rd report Apr 2003 4th report Apr 2005	
200. International Human Rights Organisation for the Rights to Feed Oneself	200	Apr 1997 21st Session	1st report Apr 1999 2nd report Apr 2001 3rd report Apr 2003 4th report Apr 2005	1st report Apr 1997
201. Femmes-Africa-Solidarité	201	Apr 1997 21st Session	1st report Apr 1999 2nd report Apr 2001 3rd report Apr 2003 4th report Apr 2005	1st report Apr 1998
202. Comité de Solidarité avec les Victimes de la Répression en Mauritanie	202	Apr 1997 21st Session	1st report Apr 1999 2nd report Apr 2001 3rd report Apr 2003 4th report Apr 2005	
203. Collectif des Rescapés, Anciens Détenus Politiques, Civils Torturés (CRADPOCIT)	203	Apr 1997 21st Session	1st report Apr 1999 2nd report Apr 2001 3rd report Apr 2003 4th report Apr 2005	
204. Women, Law, and Development Centre	204	Apr 1997 21st Session	1st report Apr 1999 2nd report Apr 2001 3rd report Apr 2003 4th report Apr 2005	
205. Association de Familles des Prisonniere et Disparus Sahraouis	205	Apr 1997 21st Session	1st report Apr 1999 2nd report Apr 2001 3rd report Apr 2003 4th report Apr 2005	
206. Association of Episcopal Conference of Anglophone West Africa	206	Apr 1997 21st Session	1st report Apr 1999 2nd report Apr 2001 3rd report Apr 2003 4th report Apr 2005	
207. Government Servants Association (GSA)	207	Nov. 1997 22nd Session	1st report Nov 1999 2nd report Nov 2001 3rd report Nov 2003 4th report Nov 2005	
208. Human Rights Defence Group	208	Nov. 1997 22nd Session	1st report Nov 1999 2nd report Nov 2001 3rd report Nov 2003 4th report Nov 2005	

Name of NGO	Ref No.	Date on which OS was granted	Date on which reports were/are due	Report submitted and date on which it was submitted
209. Zambia Independent Monitoring Team (ZIMT)	209	Nov. 1997 22nd Session	1st report Nov 1999 2nd report Nov 2001 3rd report Nov 2003 4th report Nov 2005	
210. Afro-Asian People Solidarity Organisation	210	Nov. 1997 22nd Session	1st report Nov 1999 2nd report Nov 2001 3rd report Nov 2003 4th report Nov 2005	
211. Syndicats des Avocats de Mauritania	211	Nov. 1997 22nd Session	1st report Nov 1999 2nd report Nov 2001 3rd report Nov 2003 4th report Nov 2005	
212. Comité National pour l'Eradication des Sequelles de l'Esclavage en Mauritanie (CONALESEM)	212	Nov. 1997 22nd Session	1st report Nov 1999 2nd report Nov 2001 3rd report Nov 2003 4th report Nov 2005	
213. El Hanane (Tendresse)	213	Nov. 1997 22nd Session	1st report Nov 1999 2nd report Nov 2001 3rd report Nov 2003 4th report Nov 2005	
214. Association d'Appui et d'Eveil "PUGSADA"	214	Nov. 1997 22nd Session	1st report Nov 1999 2nd report Nov 2001 3rd report Nov 2003 4th report Nov 2005	
215. Catholic Commission for Justice and Peace (CCJP)	215	Nov. 1997 22nd Session	1st report Nov 1999 2nd report Nov 2001 3rd report Nov 2003 4th report Nov 2005	
216. Islamic Relief Association (ISRA)	216	Nov. 1997 22nd Session	1st report Nov 1999 2nd report Nov 2001 3rd report Nov 2003 4th report Nov 2005	
217. Cairo Institute for Human Rights Studies (CIHRS)	217	Nov. 1997 22nd Session	1st report Nov 1999 2nd report Nov 2001 3rd report Nov 2003 4th report Nov 2005	
218. Prisoners' Rehabilitation and Welfare Action (PRAWA)	218	Nov. 1997 22nd Session	1st report Nov 1999 2nd report Nov 2001 3rd report Nov 2003 4th report Nov 2005	

Name of NGO	Ref No.	Date on which OS was granted	Date on which reports were/are due	Report submitted and date on which it was submitted
219. Ligue Mauritanienne pour la Défense des Droits de la Femme	219	Nov. 1997 22nd Session	1st report Nov 1999 2nd report Nov 2001 3rd report Nov 2003 4th report Nov 2005	
220. Ligue Africaine des Droits de l'Homme et des Peuples (Section de Madagascar)	220	Nov. 1997 22nd Session	1st report Nov 1999 2nd report Nov 2001 3rd report Nov 2003 4th report Nov 2005	
221. Sudanese Jurists Union	221	Nov. 1997 22nd Session	1st report Nov 1999 2nd report Nov 2001 3rd report Nov 2003 4th report Nov 2005	
222. Ligue Algérienne des Droits de l'Homme (LADH)	222	Nov. 1997 22nd Session	1st report Nov 1999 2nd report Nov 2001 3rd report Nov 2003 4th report Nov 2005	
223. Direitos Humanose Desenvolvimento	223	Nov. 1997 22nd Session	1st report Nov 1999 2nd report Nov 2001 3rd report Nov 2003 4th report Nov 2005	
224. Association Mauritanienne pour la Protection des Droits de la Femme	224	Nov. 1997 22nd Session	1st report Nov 1999 2nd report Nov 2001 3rd report Nov 2003 4th report Nov 2005	
225. Zambia Reconstruction Organisation (ZAMRO)	225	Apr 1998 23rd Session	1st report Apr 1999 2nd report Apr 2001 3rd report Apr 2003 4th report Apr 2005	
226. Legal Defence Centre	226	Apr 1998 23rd Session	1st report Apr 1999 2nd report Apr 2001 3rd report Apr 2003 4th report Apr 2005	
227. Medical Rehabilitation Centre for Trauma Victims	227	Apr 1998 23rd Session	1st report Apr 1999 2nd report Apr 2001 3rd report Apr 2003 4th report Apr 2005	
228. Centre for Human Rights and Rehabilitation	228	Apr 1998 23rd Session	1st report Apr 1999 2nd report Apr 2001 3rd report Apr 2003 4th report Apr 2005	

Name of NGO	Ref No.	Date on which OS was granted	Date on which reports were/are due	Report submitted and date on which it was submitted
229. National Institute for Public Interest, Law and Research Trust	229	Apr 1998 23rd Session	1st report Apr 1999 2nd report Apr 2001 3rd report Apr 2003 4th report Apr 2005	
230. Ligue Africaine des Droits de l'Homme	230	Apr 1998 23rd Session	1st report Apr 1999 2nd report Apr 2001 3rd report Apr 2003 4th report Apr 2005	
231. Friendship Foundation International	231	Apr 1998 23rd Session	1st report Apr 1999 2nd report Apr 2001 3rd report Apr 2003 4th report Apr 2005	

Some statistics:

(1) NGOs granted observer status with the African Commission: **231**
(2) African NGOs granted observer status with the African Commission: **119**
(3) NGOs who have submitted all their due reports: **25**
(4) NGOs who have submitted some of their due reports: **61**
(5) NGOs who have not submitted any reports: **115**
(6) NGOs whose first report is awaited during 1999: **32**

The Human Rights Situation in Africa

Twenty-fifth Ordinary Session
Bujumbura, 26 April to 5 May 1999
DOC/OS(XXV)/96

At the 24th Ordinary Session of the African Commission on Human and Peoples' Rights, participants in the debate on the situation of human rights in africa (Item 8g of the agenda), in their great majority, deplored the erosion of human rights on the Continent. In particular, many Non-Governmental Organisations (NGOs) expressed their concern about the prevailing situation in the Great Lakes region, Algeria, Cameroon, Mauritania, Lesotho, Sierra Leone, Uganda, Guinea-Bissau, etc. Among other things, they condemned extra-judicial executions, arbitrary arrests and detentions, the bad treatment inflicted upon refugees and displaced persons, slavery, and the negation of the primacy of law in Africa.

Indeed, since the end of the Cold War and with the wind of democratisation that has blown through almost all African countries in the early and late 90s, the Continent has been beset with a cycle of crises that are economic, social and political in nature.

It is on record that even in those countries that are not in a state of internal conflict or of war with their neighbours, there have been serious violations of human rights. however, the situations of conflict are the terrain for the most massive and serious violations of human rights on the Continent.

While the economic impact of these crises has an indeniably heavy impact on the daily lives of the people, their political dimensions have an even greater impact, considering the devastating effects that they have.

Practically no part of the continent has been spared the tensions, which vary from inter-state conflicts to intra-state conflicts, with increasingly worrying humanitarian consequences, affecting millions of persons, especially children, women and the aged. To the extent that the few advances as regards human rights on the Continent, when there are any, seem so negligible, even if they do not deserve to be completely ignored. Such situations should not, under any circumstances, leave an institution like the African Commission on Human and Peoples' Rights unmoved. It is, after all, the foremost mechanism for the protection and promotion of Human Rights at the continental level.

I. INTER-STATE CONFLICTS

For various reasons, the principle of "*Uti possidetis juris*" which enshrined the inviolability of the frontiers inherited from colonisations, has been repudiated by some African States. This has resulted in hostilities between such states and one or many of their neighbours, bringing in their wake the serious of disasters and human rights violations that such a situation could not but cause for the civil populace: disruption of tranquility, peace and the social fabric, summary and arbitrary executions, dispossession of material belongings, rape, massive exodus, and other exactions.

Such was the case with the military clashes between Cameroon and Nigeria over the Bakassi peninsula, over which both States are claiming sovereignty. It should be acknowledged, to their credit, that both States eventually accepted to take the dispute before the International Court of Justice, which provides an opportunity for a judicial settlement of the dispute.

The war between Ethiopia and its neighbour Eritrea also falls within this category of inter-state conflicts. Unfortunately, despite the offers of good offices and mediation from certain States and international organisations, including the Organisation of African Unity (OAU), this conflict has continued till today. It would be desirable to see peaceful methods of settlement taking the place of the use of arms in this dispute, a development which would help to heal the deep wounds that have been created by the breach of peace in that part of the Continent.

II. INTRA-STATE CONFLICTS

These types of conflicts are currently the most widespread in Africa. The brutal expression of discontent, the forceful conquest of power, ethnic cleavages sometimes exacerbated by economic rigors or the limited availability of planting and grazing land, the rejection of elections suspected to have been rigged, and many other such causes, give rise to internal conflicts with dramatic consequences.

The particularities of the war in the Democratic Republic of Congo undoubtedly deserve to be highlighted, in the sense that the conflict is an internal war but also has strong inter-state implications. Indeed, several States, near or far from the country, have acknowledged the presence of their troops on Congolese territory. Some are there to support the internal rebellion, others to uphold the incumbent regime. This makes the situation so much more delicate, reduces the chances for a resolution of the conflict, prolongs it and adds to the suffering of the people.

As for the situation in Angola, it is all the more disturbing considering that the internal conflict in that country has lasted for decades, is gulping substantial resources and has resisted all the international community's efforts to find a solution. Many Angolans have been born into war and know no other culture than that, which is perilous to the future of the society.

III. HUMANITARIAN REPERCUSSIONS OF CONFLICTS

Whether they are internal or they involve several States at once, the armed conflicts confronting the African Continent have very worrying humanitarian consequences. Massive exoduses of people, summary executions, rape, looting, forced conscription of children and other combatants in the armed forces have become commonplace. The consequences of these conflicts also include famines, the propagation of diseases, the rise in criminality, the degradation, often irreversible, of the environment, etc.

In Sierra Leone, for example, the images of massacres as well as atrocities committed against the civilian populace, in the form of horrible mutilations of their limbs, have been seen all around the world, relayed by the media.

In Zimbabwe, press freedom is coming under increasing pressure, regardless of the provisions of the African Charter, which proclaim it. Workers' rights are also being increasingly threatened. The situation deserves to be monitored closely.

In Burkina Faso, the assassination of the journalist Norbert Zongo, and three of his compatriots, is equally regrettable. A commission of enquiry has been set up to clarify the case – a high level of tension has prevailed since the incident took place.

In Mauritania, the environmental concerns of a citizen allegedly led to his being taken to court. There is a need to follow up the case very closely, in view of the appeals that have already been made to the Commission.

In Guinea Bissau, Angola, Ethiopia, Eritrea, Congo Brazzaville, Algeria, Nigeria, Chad, and Sudan, it is usually the civilian population that bear the heaviest burden of the crises.

IV. A FEW REASONS FOR HOPE

Though they have been minimal, some advances have been recorded in the field of human rights, and are worthy of mention.

Among these advances, one must note, among others, the generally favourable in the area of democratisation and of the principle of the rule of law in some African countries.

There is also a growing interest on the part of States in the activities of the Commission; this has manifested itself in the remarkable progress achieved in some States where it recently undertook missions. Furthermore, one notes a more favourable reaction as regards the fulfilment of the obligations emanating from Charter provisions: submission of periodic reports by the States to the Commission, establishment of National Commissions for Human Rights, etc.

Also on the credit side one must certainly count the adoption of an important human rights instrument like the Additional Protocol to the Charter on the establishment of an African Court of Human and Peoples' Rights. But much remains to be done for the ratification of this protocol, to achieve its entry into force, and ultimately the actual establishment of the above-mentioned Court.

Nevertheless, these advances pale into insignificance beside the gravity of the threats and violations of human rights on the ground. There lies, in all its entire dimension, the immense task of the Commission.

V. WHAT SHOULD THE AFRICAN COMMISSION ON HUMAN AND PEOPLES' RIGHTS DO?

The African Commission on Human and Peoples' Rights should express a clear position on this situation and take the necessary measures, in line with its mandate as prescribed in the African Charter on Human and Peoples' Rights.

By adopting such an attitude, the Commission would not only be doing its duty but, will, moreover, give hope to the helpless people who have, very often lost all they had and do not know who to turn to. Besides, it will by so doing recover its credibility, to the extent that it would be playing the vanguard role that is expected of it and which is currently being played by non-African organisations, without any consultation with the Commission.

To this effect it could issue an appeal:

- to the States, for a greater awareness of the need to ensure enhanced fulfilment of the provisions of the African Charter on Human and Peoples' Rights which they are expected to comply with. This implies, as a matter of priority, providing the Commission itself with resources commensurate with its mission of promoting and protecting human rights on the Continent, as well as expediting the ratification of the Protocol on the establishment of the African Court of Human and Peoples' Rights;
- to the OAU and the international community with a view to supporting the efforts for the re-establishment of peace where such are already ongoing, such as in Burundi, Democratic Republic of Congo, Guinea-Bissau, Sierra Leone, Sudan, Ethiopia and Eritrea, especially, and for peace efforts to be resumed wherever they seem to have stalled, such as Angola and Congo Brazzaville;
- to warring groups, for them to become aware that they are also expected to respect human rights and that the Commission is prepared to help them in this regard, with a view to preparing for a return to peace;
- to national, regional and international organisations for the defence of human rights, as well as civil society, for them to intensify their work in areas of information, human rights education, and to consolidate their cooperation with the Commission for the restoration of peace, the strengthening of the rule of law and the flourishing of human and peoples' rights in Africa.

INDEX